WRITER AND PUBLIC
IN FRANCE

WRITER AND PUBLIC IN FRANCE

From the Middle Ages to the Present Day

by

JOHN LOUGH

Professor of French in the
University of Durham

CLARENDON PRESS · OXFORD

Oxford University Press, Walton Street, Oxford OX2 6DP

OXFORD LONDON GLASGOW
NEW YORK TORONTO MELBOURNE WELLINGTON
IBADAN NAIROBI DAR ES SALAAM LUSAKA CAPE TOWN
KUALA LUMPUR SINGAPORE JAKARTA HONG KONG TOKYO
DELHI BOMBAY CALCUTTA MADRAS KARACHI

British Library Cataloguing in Publication Data
Lough, John
    Writer and public in France.
    1. French literature – History and criticism
    2. Literature and society
    I. Title
    840'.9   PQ142   77–30365

    ISBN 0–19–815749–5

*Printed in Great Britain by
Cox & Wyman Ltd
London, Fakenham and Reading*

Preface

MY first debt in the writing of this book is to the Council of the University of Durham which granted me leave for the academic year 1973-4 and to the Leverhulme Trustees who awarded me a research fellowship for this period. A whole year's release from routine duties enabled me to sort out material which had been collected over the years, to fill in many gaps, and to write the greater part of this book.

I owe a considerable debt to a number of French people who have provided me with information and documents about present-day conditions in France and who have often given up a good deal of their time to answering my questions, in particular to MM. Philippe Dumaine and Jean Rousselot, successive secretaries-general of the Société des gens de lettres; M. Nicolas Rouart, Chef du service juridique de la Société des auteurs et compositeurs dramatiques; M. Roger Pierrot, Conservateur en chef du Département des imprimés, Bibliothèque nationale; M. Jean-Loup Bourget, Cultural Attaché at the French Embassy in London, and Mlle Marie Troubnikoff of the Syndicat national de l'édition.

Various colleagues in the Department of French of this university have provided me with pieces of information and suggestions or further reading, especially in the field of the Middle Ages and Renaissance, in particular Mr. Robert Anderson, Dr. Jennifer Britnell, Mr. Geoffrey Bromiley, Dr. Richard Maber, and Dr. Dudley Wilson. Amongst colleagues in other universities who have provided prompt and very helpful information I should like to mention especially Mrs. Elizabeth Armstrong of Somerville College, Oxford, and Dr. A. J. Holden of the University of Edinburgh. I owe a particular debt to Professor Brian Woledge of University College, London, for his patience in commenting on two successive draft chapters on the Middle Ages and for offering from his expert knowledge of the period suggestions which enabled me to fill in a number of gaps.

How much this book owes to many hundreds of books and articles will be obvious to any informed reader, but I should like to mention here a number of works to which I owe a great deal: the *Histoire de la langue française* of Ferdinand Brunot; the *Histoire générale de la presse française* by C. Bellanger, J. Godechot, P. Guiral, and F.

Terrou; *L'Apparition du livre* by Lucien Febvre and H. J. Martin; *Livre, pouvoirs et société à Paris au XVIIe siècle* by H. J. Martin; *La Statistique bibliographique de la France sous la monarchie au XVIIIe siècle* by R. Estivals; and *Le Livre français. Hier, aujourd'hui, demain*, produced under the direction of Julian Cain, R. Escarpit, and H. J. Martin.

I am grateful to Professor Édouard Gaede of the University of Nice for permission to quote a number of passages from *L'Écrivain et la sociètè* (Nice, 1972).

Above all, I am indebted to my wife who has read through the manuscript and, as usual, has offered many valuable suggestions which have simplified and clarified the text.

Finally, I am grateful to Mrs. Margaret Jackson for transforming successive versions of a somewhat untidy manuscript into printable typescript.

Durham   J.L.
February 1977

Contents

Contents

Introduction

W H E N told of the full title of this book, colleagues on both sides of the Channel have been known to blink. That the main part of it is devoted to the period from 1600 onwards will be seen from a glance at the table of contents. The material for these chapters has been collected over a period of some thirty years, and a simplified and provisional interpretation of it was offered in two earlier books dealing with the seventeenth and eighteenth centuries[1] and more recently in one on the nineteenth century.[2] A book on Paris theatre audiences in the seventeenth and eighteenth centuries[3] also has some bearing on the subject treated here. In writing these chapters account has naturally been taken of recent work by a considerable number of scholars and of new material which has come to light over the years.

It might well be held that the period from 1600 to the present day is too long for a single person to cope with. Clearly, there is plenty of room for detailed studies of relations between writer and public in each of the centuries in question. On the other hand, there is also a case for a broad treatment of the theme since concentration on any one period is apt to prevent one from seeing the wood for the trees; that it can occasionally lead to a certain lack of perspective is indeed demonstrated by the relevant chapters in my earlier books.

To go further back into the sixteenth century was not an altogether inviting prospect, but to start the story of relations between writer and public in 1600 soon appeared unsatisfactory since it is a completely arbitrary date, devoid of any real significance. Clearly, what gradually transformed this relationship was the invention of printing and its arrival in France in 1470; this involved going back another century and more into the past. If the result is a relatively brief chapter, this is due not only to thinner knowledge in the present writer, but also to the shortage of relevant material compared with what is available for later centuries.

Having decided to attempt to deal with the impact of printing, one is

[1] *An Introduction to Seventeenth Century France*, London (Longman), 1954 and *An Introduction to Eighteenth Century France*, London (Longman), 1960.

[2] *An Introduction to Nineteenth Century France*, London (Longman). 1978 (in collaboration with M. Lough).

[3] *Paris Theatre Audiences in the Seventeenth and Eighteenth Centuries*, London, 1957.

inevitably driven still further back into the past; in order to give some idea of the revolution produced by this new invention, it seemed essential to offer at least a sketch of relations between writer and public in the Middle Ages. The scanty material available for such an inquiry is mainly responsible for the brevity of this opening chapter; none the less it is hoped that it will serve its purpose, namely to set the scene for later developments down to our own day. The first two chapters are thus frankly introductory and rely heavily on the work of others. The rest offer a synthesis of my own researches and of those of scholars of the last hundred years.

In the nature of things the sketch offered in these pages can only be highly provisional. However, even a rough sketch of the evolution of the relations between writer and public through the ages seemed to provide a subject for a useful book, even if its main value were to consist in raising all manner of problems and indicating a large number of fields which might profitably be investigated, or indeed in encouraging a completely different approach to these problems.

Although the words 'writer' and 'public' are all that could be got into a reasonable short title, the relations between them obviously imply, at different periods, the existence of such intermediaries as patrons, publishers (of periodicals and newspapers as well as books), actors (professional and amateur), the cinema, radio, and television, and these all figure more or less prominently in the pages which follow. The gradual emergence of a standard French language and its diffusion over the whole country as well as the slow spread of literacy must form the background to the story related here.

The long period of gestation which this book has gone through has made only too evident the difficulties involved in treating this subject. There is the initial problem of defining what is meant by a 'writer'. In its broadest sense it clearly includes the author of a school textbook or of a learned tome in any branch of knowledge or even of instructions for erecting a prefabricated garage. It is, however, often taken in the narrower sense indicated by the definition given in the *Shorter Oxford English Dictionary*: 'One who writes, compiles, or produces a literary composition'. For the present purpose a writer is taken to be a person who produces a work or works which fall within the various literary genres which have come into existence through the centuries, though the frontiers have been left deliberately vague, partly to accommodate the very different forms which the occupation has taken between the jongleur and the writer of television plays. There is too an obvious difference between the man or woman for whom writing is a full-time occupation and those for whom it is not; it goes without saying that spare-time writers play a prominent part in this study as so many of the greatest names in French literature come into this category.

The next difficulty is the very variable amount of material bearing on these relations which we possess for different periods in the past. Despite all the efforts of scholars in the last two hundred years the medieval period remains comparatively shadowy as so little information about its literary history has survived. Many of the greatest of its works of literature have no known author. Learned specialists, when dealing with the topics discussed in this book, frequently contradict one another, no doubt for the simple reason that the evidence on which to base a firm opinion is lacking. With the sixteenth century we enter an age of which rather more is known, though compared with the details of the literary life of the next two centuries which have come down to us the data on which to base a study of this kind are often lacking or, if still available in various odd corners, have not yet been investigated.

With the seventeenth and eighteenth centuries we are on firmer ground, and although our curiosity concerning all sorts of questions such as the number of books produced by French writers (published outside as well as inside France) remains unsatisfied and although we could wish that far more publishers' agreements had come down to us, it is possible to form a fairly clear picture of the relationship between the writer and his public in this period.

Paradoxically, although for the nineteenth century we suffer from an excess of material, vast quantities of this remain unexplored. Publishers' agreements of such writers as Hugo, Balzac, George Sand, and Flaubert have been brought to light, but, although no doubt many have been destroyed, great numbers must still be hidden away in publishers' offices along with their accounts. Again it is an odd fact that, thanks to the labours of Carrington Lancaster, we know far more about the day-to-day history of the Comédie-Française from 1680 down to 1774 than for the nineteenth century. Few Paris theatres of this period (and their number had greatly increased after 1789) have been the subject of serious study, even though most of the material, starting with that in the Comédie-Française, must still be available.

For the twentieth century the plethora of material is no doubt even more frightening, but in the nature of things a great deal of it is inaccessible. There would be little point in approaching a French publisher or theatre manager and asking to see his accounts; a similar approach to a contemporary writer would be equally certain to be repulsed. A great deal of information about the period from 1914 onwards will no doubt gradually become available over the next fifty to a hundred years, but it cannot be made use of now. On the other hand, as for the previous period, there are no doubt masses of relevant material to be culled from newspapers, periodicals, memoirs, and correspondences. The published material alone is enormous, and little of it has so far been investigated from the point of view which concerns us here. All that a single individual can do is to go to the obvious sources and follow up any hints he may find about some others which are less obvious; he is only too conscious that he is merely scratching the surface.

For the last century and a half there is available a variety of statistics on all sorts of topics touched on in this book, such as the population of France, the decline of illiteracy, the numbers of people receiving various forms of education, and the number of book titles produced. Even here there are gaps in the statistics, and almost always they need to be interpreted with considerable caution. The further one goes back into the past, the less such rough guides are available. Though all sorts of efforts have been made by quantitative historians to fill in the gaps in our statistical knowledge of the past, the results are seldom satisfactory. They will often argue that, inadequate as their data are, they are 'better than nothing', but a sceptical reader can scarcely be expected to agree; if mechanically interpreted, they may well be worse than nothing. These methods have been applied to book production in the seventeenth and eighteenth centuries, though the results of the investigations unfortunately do not carry conviction. It is no doubt sad that we can form only the roughest notions of conditions in a whole series of important fields touched on in this study; but there is no point in deceiving ourselves into thinking that solutions to these problems have been found when it is clear that they have not.

It will be seen that a certain, if fragmentary amount of information about the income derived by writers from such sources as patrons, publishers, and theatres has come down to us, even from quite early periods. This has naturally been made use of in successive chapters of this book, but we are here faced with an insoluble problem. The value of money has continually changed through the ages, sometimes slowly, sometimes very rapidly, as we know to our cost. It is quite common when writing about the past to attempt to translate sums of money into their modern equivalents.[1] The exercise has always seemed to me to be pointless; not only is the value of money in our time constantly changing, but people's way of living and expectations have varied so greatly from age to age. In this book the raw figures of the original documents are reproduced; very occasionally, for the benefit of readers on this side of the Channel, an equivalent in English money *of the time* is given in order to try to offer some notion of the kind of sum involved.

Many pages could be given up to discussing the innumerable problems encountered in writing a book of this type, but since its wide sweep obviously demands a considerable amount of space, as much of this as possible needs to be devoted to the task of tracing through the ages the history of the relations between writer and public.

[1] This was done by G. d'Avenel in *Les Revenus d'un intellectuel de 1200 à 1913. Les Riches depuis sept cents ans.* 2nd ed., Paris, 1922.

I The Middle Ages

IF we go back roughly a thousand years to begin our study of the relations between writer and public in France, we immediately come up against the awkward fact that at that date, although in the geographical sense what it is now fashionable to call 'l'Hexagone' undoubtedly existed, anything resembling the map of France as we know it today was only slowly to emerge through the centuries. The territory which is nowadays under the control of the Fifth Republic is both larger and different in shape from the collection of separate domains, large and small, which owed a somewhat nominal allegiance to their diminutive overlord, the King of France. Even five centuries later, despite an enormous increase in their power, its rulers did not yet exercise complete sovereignty over the whole of their kingdom; and this was significantly smaller as well as much less populous than the France of our day.

What little writing was done in the tenth century was very rarely in the vernacular; it was in Latin, and though this was still a living language to those who knew it, such knowledge was confined to a tiny minority among the population, to those connected in some way with the Church. Until at least the sixteenth century the great majority of learned works were to continue to be written in Latin, and with the Rennaissance Latin verse was to enjoy a renewed popularity which lasted well into the seventeenth century.

As early as the ninth century the existence of a vernacular distinct from Latin was clearly recognized as, for instance, when in 813 the Council of Tours decreed that preaching should be in what it called *lingua romana rustica.* Yet it was centuries before a unified French language emerged to challenge the supremacy of Latin. Even leaving aside the various other languages which flourished in the territory that is now France—Breton and Flemish in the north, German in the east, Basque and Catalan in the south-west, Italian in Corsica—we have to remember that for centuries the main part of the country was divided linguistically between the dialects of the north (*langue d'oïl*) and those of the south (*langue d'oc*, otherwise known as Provençal or by specialists as Occitan). The gap between these two groups of dialects was so considerable that as late as 1442 we find an educated southerner, a future bishop of Montauban, when in negotiations with the English, apologizing for having to write in Latin as he had difficulty in doing so in French.[1] It was not until the fifteenth century that French gradually began to supersede both Latin and the local dialects in the southern half of the kingdom and then only as the written language; the gulf between the language spoken in northern and southern France continued for very much longer.

There were naturally considerable differences between the dialects of both the *langue d'oc* and the *langue d'oïl*. In the south the Gascon dialect stood very much apart from the rest, and in the north there were even more groups of dialects. Yet these dialects seem to have been comprehensible among members of the same language group, as is shown in the well-known verse from one of the chansons of Conon de Béthune in which he complains of the way the Queen, the mother of the young Philippe Auguste, had laughed at his Picard dialect when, around 1180, he appeared at the French King's court:

> La Roïne n'a pas fait ke cortoise,
> Ki me reprist, ele et ses fieus, li Rois,
> Encoir ne soit ma parole franchoise,
> Si la puet on bien entendre en franchois;
> Ne chil ne sont bien apris ne cortois,
> S'il m'ont repris se j'ai dit mos d'Artois,
> Car je ne fui pas norris a Pontoise.[2]

It was only very gradually that, thanks to the emergence of Paris as the seat of government of the French kings, the dialect of the Île-de-France triumphed over its rivals, especially that of Picardy, to become the standard language, first in the north and later, but only very slowly, in the south. Some dialects of the *langue d'oïl* extended beyond the frontiers of what is modern France, particularly in the north-east where the Picard and Walloon dialects stretched into what is now Belgium. It is true that for centuries in the Middle Ages large areas of France, from Normandy down to the Pyrenees, were at various times in English hands, but notoriously this did not mean that English was spoken or written by the inhabitants of these regions; the very opposite had happened, since the Normans had imposed their brand of the *langue d'oïl* on this side of the Channel. Anglo-Norman long continued to be used at court and competed with Latin as the official and legal language; a considerable literature developed in it, while during the twelfth

---

[1] A. Brun, 'La Pénétration du français dans les provinces du Midi du XVᵉ au XIXᵉ siècle', *Le Français moderne*, 1935, p. 149.

[2] *Chansons*, ed. A. Wallensköld, Paris, *CFMA*, 1921, p. 5.

century the court of the English kings offered a certain amount of patronage to writers from France.

From the twelfth to the fourteenth centuries the languages of France and their literature exercised an influence on Europe comparable to that enjoyed by French language and literature in the age of Voltaire and Rousseau. Provençal literature was particularly influential in the twelfth and thirteenth centuries; the troubadours were active not only in the southern half of France, but also in northern Spain and in Italy. If Latin continued to reign as the international language, the *langue d'oïl* soon came to enjoy a wide popularity abroad, in places as far apart as England after the Norman Conquest and the Near East to which it had been transported by the Crusades. The prestige of its literature carried it to Italy as well as to Germany and the Low Countries. A number of Italians wrote in French. There is, for instance, the well-known explanation of this anomaly offered by one of them, Brunetto Latini, writing in the thirteenth century: 'Et se aucuns demandoit pour quoi cis livres est escriz en roumanç, selonc le raison de France, puis ke nous somes italien, je diroie que c'est pour .ii. raisons, l'une ke nous somes en France, l'autre por çou que la parleure est plus delitable et plus commune à tous langages.'[1]

However delectable the vernacular dialects spoken in northern and southern France may have been considered outside the area which had produced them, none of them was held to be worthy of study in any of the various educational institutions which came into existence in medieval France. This continued to be true even when, among the various dialects of the *langue d'oïl*, that of the Île-de-France had emerged as the standard literary language. Latin, which continued to be spoken as well as written, was for centuries to enjoy an unrivalled prestige. In the Middle Ages a limited amount of schooling seems to have been sometimes available even for children from the most modest homes; a considerable number of *petites écoles* existed at varying periods at parish level, particularly in the towns, though there is some evidence that they were also to be found in rural districts. Paris even had some schoolmistresses as well as schoolmasters, so presumably the education of girls was not totally neglected. But even where such *petites écoles* existed and were regularly attended, they were essentially religious foundations with extremely limited educational aims, and reading was taught from the Psalter, which meant in Latin. What the language of instruction was in such schools we have no means of telling.

[1] *Li Livres dou Tresor*, ed. F. J. Carmody, Berkeley and Los Angeles, 1948, p. 18.

A more advanced form of education, covering the *trivium* (grammar, rhetoric, and logic) and sometimes also the *quadrivium* (arithmetic, geometry, astronomy, and music), was offered in the schools established by monasteries and especially by cathedral chapters. It was out of these that universities like that of Paris, the most famous of them all, developed towards the end of the twelfth century. The University of Paris gradually came into official existence between 1200 and 1260, and in the same century others were established at Orleans, Montpellier, and Toulouse. These and the numerous others which were founded down to the end of the Middle Ages generally had three higher faculties—those of theology, law, and medicine, but by far the largest was the faculty of arts which, until the abolition of universities in the Revolution, offered the sort of general education provided in more recent times by *lycées* and *collèges*. It goes without saying that in the three specialist faculties Latin was the medium of instruction, but the same was also true of the earlier stages of education in the faculty of arts. Centuries were to pass before the French language and its literature entered the curriculum of French schools.

If even a hundred years ago in countries like England and France illiteracy was still widespread, more particularly among women, it can well be imagined that in the Middle Ages the ability to read was restricted to a tiny proportion of the population. This state of affairs inevitably influenced the literature of the period, especially down to the thirteenth century. A great deal of the literature in the dialects of the two vernacular languages was composed, not to be read silently, but to be recited (often with a musical accompaniment) or read aloud. After centuries of the predominance of the printed word the coming of radio and television has in some respects made us once more familiar with such a situation.

Another striking characteristic of the medieval literature which has come down to us is the predominance of works in verse, whether it be in the epic or the romance or in drama. Indeed, surprising as it may appear, before roughly 1200 there is no record of any literary work in French written in prose.[1] In the present age when, with very rare exceptions, the poet cannot easily secure a publisher, it is difficult to imagine a state of affairs in which writing in prose was unknown; it is perhaps almost as difficult to visualize how, even after the emergence of a literature in prose, largely based at first on the adaptation of older

[1] See B. Woledge and H. P. Clive, *Répertoire des plus anciens textes en prose française depuis 842 jusqu'aux premières années du XIIIᵉ siècle*, Geneva, 1964.

epics and verse romances, poetry still enjoyed tremendous prestige. Indeed, that prestige was to endure far beyond the end of the Middle Ages and, as we shall see, was even to produce a handsome livelihood for those poets who were fortunate enough to obtain the support of powerful patrons.

Among the various forms of entertainment offered by the *joglar* in the south and the jongleur in the north was the recitation of such works as lives of saints, *chansons de geste*, fabliaux, lays, and verse romances, sometimes before popular audiences in such places as shrines and churches on routes followed by pilgrims, sometimes in baronial halls before a more select company. A vivid account (no doubt made more vivid to most readers by being available in a modern French translation) of the kind of entertainment offered by jongleurs is to be found in an anonymous thirteenth-century Provençal romance, *Flamenca*, which describes the festivities at a wedding at which the King of France was present in person:

Puis on enleva les nappes et devant chacun on apporta de beaux coussins avec de grands éventails; chaque convive eut le sien et put s'arranger à sa guise. Ensuite se levèrent les jongleurs, tous voulant se faire écouter. Alors vous eussiez entendu retentir des cordes d'instruments montées à tous les tons. Quiconque savait un nouvel air de viole, une chanson, un descort, un lai, faisait de son mieux pour se pousser en avant. L'un vielle le lai du chèvrefeuille, l'autre celui de Tintagel; l'un a chanté le lai des parfaits amants, l'autre celui que composa Ivain. L'un joue de la harpe, l'autre de la viole; l'un de la flûte, l'autre du fifre; l'un de la gigue, l'autre de la rote; l'un dit les paroles, l'autre les accompagne, l'un joue de la cornemuse, l'autre du frestel; l'un de la musette, l'autre du chalumeau; l'un de la mandore, l'autre accorde le psaltérion avec le monocorde; l'un fait jouer des marionnettes, l'autre a jonglé avec des couteaux; l'un rampe à terre et l'autre fait des cabrioles; un autre a dansé avec sa coupe (pleine à la main); l'un a passé à travers un cerceau, l'autre saute; aucun ne manque à son métier.

Ceux qui eurent envie d'entendre divers récits de rois, de marquis ou de comtes, purent en écouter autant qu'ils voulurent. Aucune oreille n'y chôma, car l'un conta de Priam, l'autre de Pyrame, l'un conta de la belle Hélène, comment Pâris la séduisit et l'enleva; d'autres contaient d'Ulysse, d'Hector et d'Achille; d'autres, d'Énée et de Didon, et comment à cause de lui celle-ci resta dolente et malheureuse . . .

and so the list of works recited by the jongleurs continues for another seventy lines.[1]

[1] *Les Troubadours. 'Jaufré', 'Flamenca', 'Barlaam et Josaphat'*, ed. and trans. R. Lavaud and R. Nelli, Paris, 1960, pp. 674–83.

In theory there was a clear distinction between the *joglar*/jongleur who merely recited the works of others and the troubadour/*trouvère*, sometimes of high birth, who had the more creative function of composing them. Certainly a *trouvère* like Chrétien de Troyes, writing in the second half of the twelfth century, felt himself to be a cut above the jongleurs of whom he wrote contemptuously in the opening lines of his romance, *Erec et Enide*:

> D'Erec, le fil Lac, est li contes,
> que devant rois et devant contes
> depecier et corrompre suelent
> cil qui de conter vivre vuelent.

Already, four centuries before Ronsard, he goes on to speak of his art as destined to enjoy eternal fame:

> Des or comancerai l'estoire
> qui toz jorz mes iert an mimoire
> tant con durra crestïantez;
> de ce s'est Crestiens vantez.[1]

Similarly, his contemporary, Wace, makes the claim that only the writer can confer immortality:

> Bien entend e cunuis e sai
> que tuit murrunt e clerc e lai,
> e que mult ad curte duree
> anprés la mort lur renumee,
> si par clerc nen est mis en livre;
> ne poet par el durer ne vivre.[2]

In practice, however, the distinction between the two often breaks down as the troubadour/*trouvère* might sometimes recite or sing his own compositions, while the *joglar*/jongleur—for instance, the thirteenth-century poet, Rutebeuf—might sometimes perform his own works.[3] Occasionally, a jongleur would manage to find a more or less permanent post as an entertainer in the household of some prince or great nobleman and thus acquired the status of a *ménestrel*. Such was the career of the thirteenth-century poet, Adenet le Roi, who in *Les Enfances Ogier* stresses the debt which both he and the jongleurs owed to his patron, Guy, comte de Flandre:

---

[1] *Erec et Enide*, ed. M. Roques, Paris, *CFMA*, 1952, p. 1, lines 19–26.
[2] *Le Roman de Rou*, ed. A. J. Holden, 3 vols., Paris, *SATF*, 1970–3, i. 166, ll. 137–42.
[3] See E. Faral, *Les Jongleurs en France au Moyen Age*, 2nd edn., Paris, 1964, pp. 73–9.

Li jougleour deveront bien plourer
Quant il morra, car moult porront aler
Ainz que tel pere puissent mais recouvrer;
    Or le nous vueille Dieus longuement sauver.[1]

Yet while the importance of oral transmission in the diffusion of much of medieval literature is rightly stressed, long before the invention of printing reached France in 1470, works were not only being written down, but copies of them were also in circulation.

By the thirteenth century, with the gradual spread of literacy, a public for books written in the vernacular had emerged; there was now a demand for manuscript copies of a type not supplied by the monastic scriptoria which in any case generally worked only for their own libraries. If the copyists established outside the monasteries were 'clerks', they did not confine themselves to producing copies of works in Latin for use in the universities which regulated strictly this side of their business (the Paris printers and booksellers were long to remain 'suppôts de l'Université'); they also turned out copies of works in the vernacular, though it is far from clear how this side of the business of the stationers and booksellers was organized.

A certain number of what are taken to be jongleurs' copies of medieval works—small and somewhat battered volumes—have come down to us, but many of the *chansons de geste*, romances, fabliaux, and other works of literature have survived in handsome volumes containing a large collection of separate works which were perhaps copied specially for their owner. Thus one thirteenth-century manuscript[2] contains, in addition to two other works, no fewer than five romances by Chrétien de Troyes as well as Wace's *Roman de Brut* and Benoît de Sainte-Maure's *Roman de Troie*. What is more, at the end of one of the works the scribe puts in a little advertisement for himself (the church in question was at Provins where big fairs were held):

Explycyt li chevaliers au lyeon.
Cil qui l'escrist Guioz a non;
Devant nostre Dame del val
Est ses ostex tot a estal.

Certainly by the fourteenth century, well before the coming of printing, the production and distribution of manuscripts, sometimes

[1] *Œuvres*, ed. A. Henry, 5 vols., Bruges and Brussels, 1951–71, iii. 60, ll. 32–5.
[2] Bibliothèque nationale, MS. fr. 794.

elaborately illuminated, had become an organized trade. The part which the writer himself now played in the publication of his work remains none the less very obscure. Some manuscripts, of course, were specially prepared by the author for presentation to his patron, but beyond this his part in the diffusion of his work has not been clearly established.

It is unfortunately the case that we know singularly little about the lot of the medieval writer who lacked either private means or some paid occupation which left him leisure to pursue his craft. It is clear that, in the absence of the varied sources of income derived from the publication and performance of his works which began to emerge with the invention of printing, the writer had to depend on the generosity of patrons.[1] The humble relationship in which a writer in this position stood to his patron is symbolized in a conventional illustration which is often to be found in the richly illuminated and handsomely bound copy of his work which was prepared for presentation: there the writer is shown kneeling at the feet of the King or Queen or other high personage to whom the work is offered. There is, for instance, the example of the poet Eustache Deschamps, offering a volume to Charles VI,[2] or that of the poetess, Christine de Pisan, kneeling at the feet of his queen, Isabeau de Bavière, and presenting a copy of her works.[3]

Patronage, however, can take a variety of forms, and information about medieval writers is so scanty that it is almost impossible to form a clear idea of relations between writer and patron even during the later part of the period. To begin with, we do not even know the name of the authors of large numbers of works, including some of the most famous. The *Chanson de Roland*, like almost all the *chansons de geste*, is an anonymous work, as are *La Châtelaine de Vergi*, *Aucassin et Nicolette*, *Maître Pierre Pathelin*, and the Provençal romance, *Flamenca*. Indeed, in some cases not only is the author of a medieval work unknown, but even the dialect in which it was first composed is uncertain. The copies of works written before the fourteenth century which have

---

[1] Some useful information about patronage in medieval France is to be found in the general study of K. J. Holzknecht, *Literary Patronage in the Middle Ages*, Philadelphia, 1923; reprinted London, 1966. See also M. D. Stanger, 'Literary Patronage at the Medieval Court of Flanders', *French Studies*, 1957, pp. 214–19.

[2] Bibliothèque nationale MS. fr. 20020, reproduced in *Œuvres complètes*, ed. de Queux de Saint-Hilaire and G. Raynaud, 11 vols., Paris, *SATF*, 1878–1903, ii, frontispiece.

[3] British Library, Harleian MS. 4431, reproduced in *Œuvres poétiques*, ed. M. Roy, 3 vols., Paris, SATF, 1886–96, iii, frontispiece.

come down to us were not made during the author's lifetime. What is more, even when it is possible to attach a name to a work, it often tells us little or nothing. All that can be deduced about the authors of the two well-known poems on Tristan is that Thomas was an Anglo-Norman and Béroul probably a Norman. Virtually all that is known about Marie de France is contained in her own statement: 'Marie ai num, si sui de France'; in other words, she came from somewhere on the other side of the Channel and probably spent a long period at the court of Henry II. Even so outstanding an author as Chrétien de Troyes remains a very shadowy figure; all that is really known about his life is that his career as a writer fell in the period roughly 1160–90 and that he found patrons in Marie, comtesse de Champagne, and Philippe d'Alsace, comte de Flandre. *Le Chevalier de la Charrete*, for instance, opens with the lines:

> Puis que ma dame de Chanpaigne
> vialt que roman a feire anpraigne,
> je l'anprendrai molt volontiers
> come cil qui est suens antiers . . .[1]

Similarly, near the beginning of *Le Conte du Graal* Chrétien tells us of this romance

> qu'il le fet por le plus prodome
> qui soit an l'empire de Rome:
> c'est li cuens Phelipes de Flandres,
> qui mialx valt ne fist Alixandres . . .[2]

However, we have no idea what form or forms that patronage took. The *Roman de la Rose* is one of the most celebrated works produced in medieval France, but although they wrote in the following century we still know nothing of the life and career of either Guillaume de Lorris who began the poem or of Jean de Meung who finished it. It is true that rather more is known about writers of the fourteenth and fifteenth centuries such as Guillaume de Machaut, Eustache Deschamps, Christine de Pisan, or François Villon; even so our knowledge is very fragmentary when compared with what scholars have been able to assemble for sixteenth-century writers like Ronsard or Montaigne.

In the Middle Ages the lot of the writer was undoubtedly even more varied than in modern times. Not only was a good deal of the literature

---

[1] *Le Chevalier de la Charrete*, ed. M. Roques, Paris, *CFMA*, 1958, p. 1.
[2] *Le Conte du Graal*, ed. F. Lecoy, Paris, *CFMA*, 1972, i. 5, ll. 11–14.

of the period the work of priests, monks, and nuns whose livelihood was assured, but at one extreme one finds persons of the very highest rank who did not disdain to write poetry. The first known troubadour was Guillaume IX (1071–1127), duc d'Aquitaine and comte de Poitou, a much more powerful ruler than his nominal overlord, the King of France. His great-grandson, Richard I of England, who was also duc d'Aquitaine, was not only on friendly terms with many troubadours, but also capable of composing poems himself in both *langue d'oc* and *langue d'oïl*. In northern France a powerful baron like Thibaut (1201–53), comte de Champagne and later King of Navarre, wrote poems of courtly love in the same tradition, while in the fifteenth century Charles d'Orléans, who stood very close to the throne of France (his son was to become king as Louis XII), kept up the tradition. The troubadours also included among their number several amateurs of noble birth such as Jaufré Rudel and Rainbaut d'Orange, while among the *trouvères* of northern France there were aristocratic poets like Conon de Béthune, the Châtelain de Coucy, and Gace Brulé.

At the other extreme came the jongleurs, for the most part men of humble birth who depended for their living on the proceeds of their performances, either in the open before more or less plebeian audiences (probably not very generous), or from their appearances in baronial halls. Apparently, these could prove quite lucrative and could produce very handsome gifts such as clothes and horses from the lords and ladies present, but obviously it was also an uncertain source of income. This is made clear in the famous chanson of the thirteenth-century jongleur, Colin Muset, which opens with the lines:

> Sire cuens, j'ai vielé
> Devant vous en vostre ostel,
> Si ne m'avez riens doné
> Ne mes gages aquité:
> C'est vilanie![1]

In contrast to this light-hearted poem there is the gloomy lament of another jongleur of the period, Rutebeuf, in the begging verses which he addressed to Philippe III—'C'est de la Povertei Rutebeuf'. This begins:

> Je ne sai par ou je coumance
> Tant ai de matyere abondance
> Por parleir de ma povretei.

[1] *Chansons*, ed. J. Bédier, 2nd edn., Paris, *CFMA*, 1938, p. 9.

Por Dieu vos pri, frans rois de France,
que me doneiz queilque chevance,
si fereiz trop grant charitei.[1]

Such scanty evidence as there is would seem to show that Rutebeuf's
complaints about his poverty were justified, though right through the
centuries when the impecunious writer was compelled to rely on
patronage, one must treat with caution lamentations of this kind.

Some jongleurs, we have seen, succeeded in finding a place in a
princely or noble household and became in other words *ménestrels*. So
long as their patron lived and they retained his favour, they could at
least count on a modestly comfortable existence among the minor
officials attached to him. This relationship is reflected in the dedication
to his lord, Robert d'Artois, with which Adenet le Roi rounded off his
Cléomadès:

A noble conte preu et sage
d'Artois, qui a mis son usage
en Dieu honnorer et servir,
envoi mon livre por oÿr
comment il est fais et dités.
Or vueille Dieus que il soit tes
que li quens le reçoive en gré
et li doinst par sa grant bonté
honnour d'armes et d'amour joie.
Si m'aït Dieus, je le vorroie.
ainsi soit il que je l'ai dit!
Amen, amen, et explicit.[2]

Sometimes, however, the relationship between poet and patron could
end on a sour note. Half-way through *Le Roman de Rou* the Jersey
poet, Wace, offers fulsome thanks to Henry II of England who had
made him a canon of Bayeux:

Par Dieu aïe e par le rei
—altre fors Deu servir ne dei—
m'en fu donnée, Deus il rende,
a Baieues une provende.
Del rei Henri segont vos di,
nevo Henri, pere Henri.

---

[1] *Œuvres complètes*, ed. E. Faral and J. Bastin, 2 vols., Paris, 1959–60, i. 570–1.
[2] *Œuvres*, v (1), p. 552, ll. 18688–98.

Yet in the end he abandoned the poem out of pique at the favour shown by the King to a rival, Benoît de Sainte-Maure. In the closing lines Henry II appears in a distinctly less favourable light when Wace writes:

> Li reis jadis maint bien me fist,
> mult me dona, plus me pramist,
> e se il tot doné m'eüst
> ço qu'il me pramist, mielz me fust;
> nel poi aveir, ne plout al rei,
> mais n'est mie remés en mei.

And he rounds off the poem with the disgruntled couplet:

> Ci faut le livre Maistre Wace;
> quin velt avant faire sin face.[1]

There is a well-known passage in Gautier d'Arras's *Eracle* in which he speaks first of powerful people who will not listen to poets:

> il tienent ordre et ont tel riule
> que il ne prisent une tiule
> cançon ne son ne rotruenge,
> car Covoitise les calenge;
> il n'a el monde canteour,
> maistre estrument ne conteour
> qui un seul mot lor ost tentir,
> car ne s'i voelent assentir
> a oïr fable ne cançon,
> car aver sont li eschançon
> et cil qui donent a laver
> et il meïme sont aver:
> s'on i velt joie entremeller,
> lors commencent d'el a parler.

Such miserable behaviour is contrasted with the open-handed generosity of Thibaut, comte de Blois:

> Molt est li quens Tibaus preudon,
> bien a ataint dusques en son.
> Il vient sovent u gens s'assemble,
> mais cuidiés vous que il s'en emble?
> A l'endemain del parlement
> s'en fuient tout communalment

[1] ii, ll. 5313–18, 11425–30, 11439–40.

a l'ajornee, je vous di,
mais il atent jusc'a midi
con s'il estoit lor cambrelens.
Lors fait aporter ses berlens
et les eskiekiers por nombrer
l'avoir dont se velt descombrer.[1]

Like their successors in later centuries medieval writers had inevitably
to lay it on thick when dedicating their works to a patron. Thus
Charles VI, whose reign was one of the most calamitous in the whole of
French history, is praised by Christine de Pisan in extravagant terms:

Tres excellent Majesté redoubtee,
Illustre honneur en dignité montee,
Par la grace de Dieu royauté digne,
Puissant valeur, ou tout le monde encline,
Tres digne lis haut et magnifié,
Pur et devot, de Dieu saintifié,
Cil glorieux de qui vient toute grace
Vous tiengne en pris et croisse vostre attrace.
A vous, bon roy de France redoutable,
Le VIe Charles du nom notable,
Que Dieux maintiengne en joie et en santé
Mon petit dit soit premier presenté.[2]

Other patrons besides the kings and queens of France were available
for medieval writers. The professional troubadours were able to count
on finding support not only in southern France, but also in Spain and
Italy, and sometimes even further afield. Wace was not by any means
the only French writer to whom Henry II showed favour. In the prologue to her *Lais* Marie de France addresses him in the usual flattering
terms:

En l'honur de vus, nobles reis,
Ki tant estes prus e curteis,
A ki tute joie s'encline,
E en ki quoer tuz biens racine,
M'entremis des lais assembler,
Par rime faire e reconter,
En mun quoer pensoe e diseie,

---

[1] *Eracle*, ed. G. Raynaud de Lage, Paris, *CFMA*, 1976, pp. 2–3, ll. 33–46, 61–72.
[2] *Le Livre du Chemin de Long Estude*, ed. R. Püschel, Berlin and Paris, 1887, p. 1, ll. 1–12.

Sire, kes vus presentereie.
Si vos les plaist a receveir,
Mult me ferez grant joie aveir,
A tuz jurz mais en serrai liee.
Ne me tenez à surquidiee
Si vos os faire icest present,
Ore oëz le commencement![1]

Eleanor of Aquitaine's interest in literature, composed both in *langue d'oc* and *langue d'oïl*, is well known. On the strength of a statement by Layamon, the English translator of Wace's *Roman de Brut*, it is generally accepted that the French work was presented to her,[2] while she is also taken to be the 'riche dame de riche rei' to whom Benoît de Sainte-Maure's *Roman de Troie* is dedicated in a passage in which the poet contrasts this paragon of all the virtues with other members of her sex:

De cest, veir, criem g'estre blasmez
De cele que tant a bontez
Que hautece a, pris e valor,
Honesté e sen e honor,
Bien e mesure e saintée,
E noble largece e beauté;
En cui mesfait de dames maint
Sont par le bien de li esteint;
En cui tote science abonde,
A la cui n'est nule seconde
Que el mont seit de nule lei.
Riche dame de riche rei,
Senz mal, senz ire, senz tristece,
Poissiez aveir toz jorz leece![3]

It should be added that some sceptics who cannot see such a eulogy fitting Eleanor of Aquitaine have tried to find another dedicatee more worthy of it. However, it is generally accepted that these lines were addressed to her during the period when, after the dissolution of her marriage to Louis VII, she was Henry's queen.

In France itself there were other members of the royal family besides

[1] *Les Lais*, ed. J. Rychner, Paris, *CFMA*, 1966, pp. 2–3, ll. 43–56. It should be added that such is the uncertainty surrounding much of medieval literary patronage that some scholars consider that it is to Henry's son that the *Lais* are dedicated, while others prefer to suspend judgement.

[2] *Le Roman de Brut*, ed. I. Arnold, 2 vols., Paris, *SATF*, 1938–40, l, p. lxxviii.

[3] *Le Roman de Troie*, ed. L. Constans, 6 vols., Paris, *SATF*, 1904–12, ii. 302, ll. 13457–70. (See also vi. 188–9.)

the King and Queen to whom writers could offer their works. Thus in 1401 Christine de Pisan addressed the opening lines of *Le Débat de deux amants* to Louis d'Orléans, the father of the poet, who was soon to be assassinated at the orders of the duc de Bourgogne, Jean Sans Peur:

> Prince royal, renommé de sagece,
> Hault en valeur, poissant, de grant noblece,
> Duit et apris en honneur et largece,
> Trés agreable
> Duc d'Orliens, seigneur digne et valable,
> Filz de Charles, le bon roy charitable,
> De qui l'ame soit ou ciel permanable,
> Mon redoubté
> Seigneur vaillant, par votre grant bonté
> Mon petit dit soit de vous escouté,
> Ne par desdaing ne soit en sus bouté
> Par pou de pris.[1]

In the middle of the same century we find that, for all his criminal record and wild life, Villon had some relations with the poet prince, Charles d'Orléans, and his court at Blois, and among his poems is one addressed to Jean II, duc de Bourbon, in which he asks for a loan, no doubt a polite way of seeking a gift of money. The 'Requête à Mons. de Bourbon' opens with a verse which combines flattery with touches of humour in a manner later to be followed by Clément Marot:

> Li mien seigneur et prince redoubté,
> Fleuron de lys, royalle geniture,
> Françoys Villon, que Travail a dompté
> A coups orbes, par force de bature,
> Vous supplie par ceste humble escripture
> Que lui faciez quelque gracieux prest,
> De s'obliger en toutes cours est prest,
> Si ne doubtez que bien ne vous contente:
> Sans y avoir dommaige n'interest,
> Vous n'y perdrez seulement que l'attente.[2]

Dedications of medieval romances when they were turned into prose, particularly in the fifteenth century, can be just as fulsome as those produced by poets, as, for instance, in this passage from Gerbert

---

[1] *Œuvres poétiques*, ii. 49, ll. 1–12.
[2] *Œuvres*, ed. A. Longnon, 2nd edn., Paris, *CFMA*, 1914, p. 90.

de Montreuil's prologue to the *Roman de la violette*, addressed to
Charles de Nevers:

Tres hault et puissant prince et mon tres redoubté seigneur monseigneur
Charles, conte de Nevers et de Retel, baron de Donzy, moy, qui tous les
temps de ma vye, des le commenchement de vostre plus flourye jonesse, ay
esté et suis vostre tres humble et obeïssant serviteur, pour la tres singulyere,
vraye et naturelle amour que j'ay tous jours eu et ay et voel avoir toutte ma
vye, comme tenu suis de vous servir, complaire et obeïr en toutes choses,
meismement en celles que je sentiroie vous estre plaisantes et agreables, come
ung serviteur est tenu et obligyé de faire a son seigneur et maiste, et aussy
pour ce que je vous sens estre enclin a prendre plaisir et vous esleesier a voir
et oÿr lire les plaisantes et gracieuses histoires des fais des nobles et vaillans
princes jadis vos predecesseurs, et meismement de tous aultres nobles hommes
qui par cy devant, par leurs proeces et vaillances, au confort et a l'ayde de
leur noble chevalerye ont fait leurs conquestes dont puis ils sont possessé
et tenu leurs terres et seignouryes et par ce acquis honneur, gloire et grant
recommandation de proece, et tant que leurs fais ont esté et sont encores pris
pour bonne exemple, miroir et fondacion aux nobles et vaillans homes qui
depuis eulx ont rengné et rengnent encores sur terre, et dont la memoire des
homes vivans seroit estainte et faillye se n'estoit que leurs dis et fais feuissent
mys et redigés par escript en aourné et plaisant langaige selonc le petit en-
tendement de ceulx qui ad ce faire labeurent.[1]

The humble relationship in which a writer stood to his patron in
medieval times is clearly illustrated here.

The reception accorded to these works when they were handed over
to their patron is nowhere clearly described. When Eustache
Deschamps wrote a ballade to tell Guillaume de Machaut of the favourable way in which Louis de Male, comte de Flandre, had received the
handsomely bound copy of his *Voir Dit*, he does not go beyond polite
banalities when he writes:

> Les grans seigneurs, Guillaume, vous ont chier.
> En vos choses prannent esbatement.
> Bien y parut a Bruges devant hier
> A Monseigneur de Flandres proprement
> Qui par sa main reçut benignement
> Votre Voir Dit sellé dessus la range,
> Lire le fist; mais n'est nul vraiement
> Qui en die fors qu'a vostre louenge.[2]

---

[1] Quoted in G. Doutrepont, *Les Mises en prose des épopées et des romans chevaleresques
du XIVe au XVIe siècle*, Brussels, 1939, pp. 354–5.
[2] *Œuvres complètes*, i. 249.

What sort of rewards medieval writers expected to receive in return for dedicating their works to a patron is much less clear than in later centuries. The favours which the professional *trouvère*, Gautier d'Arras, was seeking from Baudouin V, comte de Hainaut, to whom he dedicated his romance, *Eracle*, in return for producing another work for him cannot be deduced from the lines which round off the poem:

> Quens Bauduin, a vos l'otroi;
> ains que passent cinc ans u troi,
> metrai aillors, espoir, m'entente.
> Sire, je sui de bone atente,
> mais gardés que n'i ait engan:
> se me premesse n'est auan,
> dont gardés qu'ele soit en tens;
> vos savés assés que je pens.
> Dius me doinst gré de mon signor
> de ce et d'el adiés grignor.[1]

It is true that on one occasion we do find very precise details about the rewards which a medieval writer could obtain. In an epilogue to *La Vie de Saint Thomas Becket* the poet, Guernes de Pont-Sainte-Maxence, speaks with delight of the welcome he received when he came over to England shortly after the murder of the saint in 1170 and produced a revised version of his poem in Canterbury. In this addition to the *Vie* he speaks of Becket's sister, the Abbess of Barking, who 'M'at doné palefrei e dras; n'i faillent nis li esperun.' Nor were these the only gifts he received for producing this work; he speaks also of 'Or, argent, robes en mes sas, chevals, autre possessiun.'[2] Unfortunately, interesting as such detail is, the subject of this work and the special circumstances under which it was written make the information of very limited value.

Hard cash was occasionally received in return for dedications, at any rate by the fifteenth century. We know, for instance, that the duc de Bourgogne, Philippe le Hardi, who was Charles VI's uncle, commissioned Christine de Pisan to write *Le Livre des fais et bonnes meurs*, and although he died before she handed over the work, in 1406 his successor, Jean Sans Peur, paid her 100 écus for it. He followed this up with further payments of 50 francs d'or in 1407, 100 in 1408, and 50 in 1412, though we do not know exactly what these later sums were

---

[1] *Eracle*, p. 202, ll. 6559–68.
[2] *La Vie de Saint Thomas Becket*, ed. E. Walberg, Paris, *CFMA*, 1936, p. 192.

for.[1] Nor is it known why Christine was given 200 livres in 1411 by order of Charles VI.[2] Earlier Guillaume de Machaut had received a money gift of 300 écus from Amédée VI, comte de Savoie, in return for a poem which he had dedicated to him.[3] In the fifteenth century we even learn of playwrights receiving money payments for the performance of their works. Thus in 1452 the municipal authorities of Abbeville paid Arnoul Greban ten écus d'or for a copy of his *Mystère de la Passion*,[4] and when, twenty years later, a chapter of the order of the Golden Fleece was held at Valenciennes, it was recorded that 'maistres Jean Molinet fit une belle comedie, pour laquelle eult x ecus'.[5] No doubt these sums of money were welcome to both men, but neither was seeking to make a living by writing plays; Molinet was soon to become *indiciaire* (historiographer) to the dukes of Burgundy, while Greban was organist and choirmaster at Notre-Dame and later became a canon at Le Mans.

Presumably a *ménestrel* like Adenet le Roi at the court of the Count of Flanders received a modest salary and occasional gifts, possibly in addition to his keep, but he was more a practising musician than a writer and probably recited other people's works such as *chansons de geste*, lives of saints, and romances. But what the precise relationship was between a rather earlier writer like Chrétien de Troyes and his successive patrons, Marie de Champagne and Philippe de Flandre, we have no means of telling.

One form of literary patronage which was to endure throughout the *ancien régime* may be traced back to the Middle Ages. Many medieval writers were tonsured 'clerks' and therefore in a position to hold livings in the Church without necessarily being ordained priests. Thus the Catholic Church became willy-nilly a patron of secular literature. No doubt some of the authors of anonymous works came into this category as well as certain of those who are little more than names to us; it has been suggested, for instance, that Chrétien was perhaps a canon at Troyes. However, we have definite information about a number of medieval writers who were rewarded for their literary efforts with livings in the Church. Wace, we have seen, acknowledged in *Le*

[1] G. Doutrepont, *La Littérature française à la cour des ducs de Bourgogne*, Paris, 1909, p. 277.

[2] M. J. Pinet, *Christine de Pisan 1364–1430. Étude biographique et littéraire*, Paris, 1927, pp. 110, 145.

[3] *Œuvres*, ed. E. Hoepffner, 3 vols., Paris, *SATF*, 1908–21, i, p. xxvii.

[4] P. Champion, *Histoire poétique du quinzième siècle*, 2 vols., Paris, 1923, ii. 151–2.

[5] Doutrepont, *La Littérature française à la cour des ducs de Bourgogne*, p. 365.

Roman de Rou that he had been appointed to a canonry at Bayeux by Henry II. Some two centuries later Guillaume de Machaut's musical and poetic talents brought him a number of patrons; one of these, Jean de Luxembourg, the King of Bohemia, secured for him appointment to a canonry at Rheims, while the poet and historian, Froissart, became a *curé* and later chaplain to one of his patrons. In the fifteenth century there is the example of Jean Molinet who, in addition to succeeding Georges Chastellain as historiographer to the dukes of Burgundy, was also made a canon at Valenciennes after he had become a widower.

In the Middle Ages as in later periods down to our own day there were no doubt writers who, without holding the high rank of royal, princely, or aristocratic poets, none the less occupied a position in society which enabled them to write in their spare time without any thought of trying to earn a living by their pen. The civil servants of the nineteenth and twentieth centuries who have also been, writers had their medieval ancestors. One thinks, for instance, of a high civil servant like the poet, Alain Chartier, who held a post of secretary to Charles VI and later to Charles VII as well as a canonry in Paris, and who was sent on a variety of diplomatic missions to such countries as Italy and Scotland. A prolific writer like Eustache Deschamps had begun by studying law and then succeeded in attaching himself to the powerful duke, Louis d'Orléans, under whom he held various administrative posts, including one of *bailli* at Senlis, while the Arras poet, Jean Bretel, belonged to a wealthy middle-class family and succeeded his father and grandfather in the post of *sergent héréditaire* of a rich abbey.

Seeing that it was only long after the invention of printing that a writer even began to enjoy at least the possibility of making a living out of what he could earn from such sources as publishers and the theatre, one would imagine that the medieval writer who lacked means or a job which left him leisure to write must have been wholly dependent on such support as he could secure from a patron or patrons. It is therefore puzzling to encounter the claim that already as early as the beginning of the fifteenth century Christine de Pisan was 'un véritable homme de lettres'.[1] It is argued that Christine acted as her own publisher in the sense that she had copies of her works made not only for members of the royal family, but also for cultured members of the Paris middle classes; it is then implied that the income she received from these copies of her works was adequate to support her as a widow with children to bring up. There seems insufficient evidence for

[1] Pinet, *Christine de Pisan*, p. 452.

such a view; the few payments which she is known to have received from Charles VI and especially Jean Sans Peur would not have been enough, if she lacked all private means, to enable her to make ends meet. Although her father had been a physician to Charles V and her husband a high civil servant, her position does not appear to have been very different from that of other medieval writers who received occasional money gifts from patrons to whom they presented their works. The professional writer, able to dispense with both private means and patronage, did not begin to emerge in France until the eighteenth century at the earliest.

Even when we come closer to modern times it is extremely hard to define with any sort of precision the kind of public which a writer has in mind when he puts pen to paper; no doubt in all ages it has depended very much on the type of writing in which he was engaged. Where the Middle Ages are concerned, it is difficult to get beyond a few tentative generalizations. Medieval society is remote from our experience, and in any case it underwent considerable changes in the course of several centuries. Moreover, much of its literature was transmitted to the public not through the written word, but orally. This is an area in which, owing to our fragmentary knowledge of the conditions under which works of literature were diffused, the experts disagree more than usual. Indeed, they may often be found arguing with themselves, putting first one possible interpretation of the scanty facts at their disposal, then the opposite one, and are finally reduced by sheer lack of evidence to sitting rather uncomfortably on the fence.

It is, for instance, generally agreed that the jongleurs recited their *chansons de geste* to a variety of audiences. It can be argued that, in an age when illiteracy extended very high up the social scale and even to many members of the upper classes, the works which they performed were equally acceptable to popular audiences out in the open and to the more aristocratic inmates of feudal castles. Even the latter formed of course, a fairly mixed audience since it might contain not only lords, but also their attendants and menials. In their opening lines *chansons de geste* often appear at first sight to be given out as addressed to an aristocratic audience, as in *Le Charroi de Nîmes*:

> Oiez, seignor, Deus vos croisse bonté
> Li glorieus, li rois de majesté!
> Bone chançon plest vous a escouter
> Del meillor home qui ainz creust en Dé?[1]

[1] Ed. J. L. Perrier, Paris, *CFMA*, 1931, p. 1, ll. 1–4.

The same kind of opening is found to another twelfth-century *chanson de geste*, *Le Couronnement de Louis*:

> Oiez, seignor, que Deus vos soit aidanz!
> Plaist vos oïr d'une estoire vaillant
> Bone chançon corteise et avenant?[1]

La Prise d'Orange which dates from the end of the same century begins with the same formula:

> Oëz, seignor, que Deus vos beneïe,
> Li glorieus, li fils sainte Marie,
> Bone chançon que je vos vorrai dire![2]

It has indeed been calculated that 40 per cent of all *chansons de geste* have such an opening.[3] Yet it has been pointed out that though the jongleurs may have liked to give the impression that they were performing for lords and ladies in baronial halls, the way in which they sometimes go to the length of explaining the simplest points to make them clear to the dimmest intelligence would seem to suggest that they also had in mind the needs of a somewhat slow-witted rural audience brought together by a fair or some religious festival. Indeed, it has been argued that the use of the term *seigneurs* in these and in other works such as lives of saints does not have any precise social significance.

In contrast, the lyric poetry which originated in the south with the troubadours and spread to the north in the second half of the twelfth century with the emergence of the *trouvères* was profoundly aristocratic, at least in origin. Indeed, as we have seen, many of these poets were themselves members of the aristocracy, though in both north and south there were also professionals, often of quite humble extraction. Yet for all its aristocratic origins, this sophisticated *poésie courtoise* gradually reached a bourgeois public, particularly in north-east France in such prosperous commercial centres as Arras. There from the end of the twelfth century onwards writers were brought together with wealthy members of the middle class in the Confrérie des ardents and also in the more select literary society known as le Puy; and it was there that such writers as Jean Bodel and Adam de la Halle flourished.

---

[1] Ed. E. Langlois, 2nd edn., Paris, *CFMA*, 1925, p. 1, ll. 1–3.
[2] Ed. C. Régnier, Paris, 1967, p. 95.
[3] P. Gallais, 'Recherches sur la mentalité des romanciers français du Moyen Age' *Cahiers de civilisation médiévale*, 1970, p. 333.

On the other hand, the so-called *romans courtois*—the *romans d'aventure* as well as the *romans d'antiquité* and the *romans bretons*—were undoubtedly written primarily for an aristocratic audience in which the influence of women was preponderant. Such works were composed, not to be recited like the *chansons de geste*, but to be read aloud in a small group. One thinks here, for instance, of the audience for which Chrétien de Troyes wrote his romances—that around his first patron, Marie de Champagne. However, it has been argued that the slightly later romances of Jean Renart, though written for princely patrons, betray more bourgeois influences in their greater realism.

What sort of a public fabliaux were meant for is a question which has given rise to sharp differences of opinion. At one time it was held that just as the *romans courtois* were directed primarily at an aristocratic audience, so the fabliaux were meant for the entertainment of a bourgeois, even plebeian public. In reaction against this view it has even been argued that the fabliau was an exclusively aristocratic genre, but it is clear that such poems were part of the repertoire of the jongleurs and must therefore have reached a wide public. It has been pointed out that the butt of the fabliaux is almost always a bourgeois, peasant, or cleric, which would indicate that, despite the popular origins of many of the fabliaux, they were by no means destined for the exclusive entertainment of the lower orders in feudal society.

From the thirteenth century onwards the gradual spread of literacy led to an expansion of the reading public. There is no way of measuring this growth in literacy, but it is generally accepted that it occurred mainly among the newly emerged middle classes of lawyers, civil servants, and merchants and, of course, their womenfolk. It was not that the public for literature in the fourteenth and fifteenth centuries had ceased to include a considerable aristocratic element. What was beginning to develop in this new context of a literature made to be read was the restricted audience which was to persist throughout the *ancien régime*—one which took in educated persons, even of quite modest origins, as well as all the upper classes of society right up to the throne.

The development of drama in the Middle Ages naturally presents a somewhat different picture; though for the same reason as with other forms of literature—lack of solid knowledge—it is a somewhat blurred one. Notoriously medieval drama, even in its comic forms, had religious origins. Plays began by being performed inside churches and then on the church steps. However, it is not easy to decide exactly what sort of an audience was attracted to performances of such early plays as Bodel's *Jeu de Saint Nicolas*, Rutebeuf's *Miracle de Théophile*, or Adam de la Halle's *Jeu de la feuillée* and *Jeu de Robin et Marion*, but it has been suggested that they required a fairly sophisticated public and can scarcely have attracted plebeian spectators.

By the fifteenth century, however, dramatic performances were becoming much more common, both in Paris and in provincial towns. Though most of the actors were amateurs, there were apparently a few professionals, possibly drawn from the ranks of the jongleurs. In Paris, although the Confrérie de la Passion was not given letters patent by Charles VI until 1402, it had certainly existed earlier than that and had performed both mystery and miracle plays before the King. Less serious forms of drama such as morality plays, farces, and *sotties* were performed by other groups of amateurs, La Basoche and Les Enfants sans souci; occasionally, all three groups would combine to offer the public a wide variety of serious and comic plays. Groups of this kind existed not only in Paris but in many provincial towns; it is quite clear that the spectators at such performances, especially those of mystery plays such as Arnoul Greban's *Mystère de la Passion*, were not only numerous, but were drawn from a wide variety of social classes from the nobility down to the plebs. The sixteenth century was to see at least the beginnings of a narrowing of the sections of society from which spectators at dramatic performances were drawn, a process which was to continue in the seventeenth century, especially in Paris, where theatre-goers tended more and more to be drawn only from the upper and middle classes of society. The drama of the fifteenth century inevitably included a variety of ingredients to suit the tastes of these very mixed audiences.

This preliminary chapter ends when, early in the sixteenth century, printing began to exercise a significant influence on the production and diffusion of contemporary literature in the vernacular. Of the *incunabula* produced in France from 1470 onwards an enormous proportion were in Latin, medieval as well as classical; something like half the books printed were religious works. A certain number of older books in the vernacular such as the *Roman de la Rose* and particularly prose romances were put through the press, and some fifteenth-century writings such as those of Christine de Pisan and Villon also secured the wider diffusion which the printing-press made possible. However, it was not until after 1500 that the full impact of this invention began to revolutionize the relations between the writer and his public by making available to him a wider audience than ever before. Its effect on his economic position was to be even more gradual as, if he tried to make a living by his pen, he was long to continue to be dependent on various forms of patronage.

II   The Impact of Printing

PRINTING began in France in 1470 when, six years before Caxton
introduced the new invention to Westminster, three German printers
were brought to Paris and installed in the Sorbonne. Soon more
printing-shops were set up in the capital, and they rapidly spread to a
great many provincial centres. Lyons, which for almost a century was
to prove a serious rival to Paris, acquired its first printer in 1473;
between 1500 and 1599 15,000 books were printed in Lyons against
25,000 in Paris.[1]

Even so the impact of the new art on literature written in French was
to be only very gradual. As late as 1538 we find Clément Marot presenting his patron, Anne de Montmorency, with a handsomely executed
manuscript copy of his 'dernières Œuvres . . . non imprimées'.[2] What
is more, even a hundred years after the invention of printing—one
thinks here, for instance, of the poetry of Desportes—works of literature continued to find a wide diffusion in manuscript form long before
they reached print. Nor must one forget that, as in later centuries,
religious works, ranging from missals and psalters to devotional works
and controversial writings, were far and away those most frequently
printed. If, as we have seen, a high proportion of the books printed
down to 1500 were in Latin, classical or medieval, the opening decades
of the sixteenth century, in France as elsewhere in Europe, saw a vast
outpouring of editions of Latin, Greek, and Hebrew texts from the
ancient world, while throughout the century translations from Italian
and Spanish as well as from Latin and Greek formed a considerable
part of the book production of the age. It would be wrong to suggest
that in the early decades after the invention of printing contemporary
literature in French was entirely neglected, but it was not until roughly
the middle of the sixteenth century that books in French began to form
the majority of those printed in Paris and that literary works in French
represented a really significant proportion of the output of the printing-
presses of the country.

Even at the end of the sixteenth century the territory under the
control of the French kings was much smaller than that of the Fifth

[1] L. Febvre and H. J. Martin, *L'Apparition du livre*, Paris, 1958, p. 271.
[2] C. A. Mayer, *Clément Marot*, Paris, 1972, pp. 402–20.

Republic. At this stage in her history France had yet to acquire such provinces as Alsace, Lorraine, Franche-Comté, Savoy, Nice, and Roussillon as well as a considerable area on her north-eastern frontier. Though by the standards of the time she had a large population, this smaller territory contained far fewer inhabitants than it does today; estimates of the population of France in this period can be little more than guesswork, but it was probably no more than a third of what it is in the 1970s. What is more, the country was much less centralized and controlled from Paris than it was to be from the time of Richelieu and Louis XIV onwards. The court was not yet finally established in the Paris region; although considerable additions were made to such palaces as the Louvre, the kings of France and their court often led a nomadic existence which took them far from the capital, most often to the châteaux of the Loire Valley.

Although Paris was already pre-eminent in the cultural life of the country, it did not by any means enjoy the near monopoly which was to be its in later centuries when almost all writers were drawn to the capital and such activities as printing, publishing, and drama were mainly concentrated there. In the sixteenth century many works continued to be written all over the provinces and to find a printer or bookseller in some local centre. Although from time to time Montaigne came to Paris on business, most of his life was spent in and around Bordeaux, and the first two editions of his *Essais* were printed there and not in Paris. In the first half of the century the prosperous city of Lyons with its flourishing trade, banking, and fairs, had its circles of humanists and poets. Its printers and booksellers brought out not only works of such native writers as Maurice Scève, Pernette du Guillet, and Louise Labé, but also those of all manner of other authors such as the first book of the *Illustrations de Gaule* of Lemaire de Belges, Rabelais's *Pantagruel* and *Gargantua*, and the 1538 edition of Clément Marot's collected works.

In this period the French language, that of Paris and the court of the French kings, was still very far from being universally spoken or even understood throughout the length and breadth of the kingdom. Even leaving aside the areas in which such completely separate languages as Breton or Basque were spoken, dialects both of French and, south of the Loire, of *langue d'oc* continued to be widely used and, in the absence of generally accepted standards, often made their appearance in works of literature. It is true that a standard language was gradually emerging, as Palsgrave pointed out as early as 1530:

In all this worke I moost folowe the Parisyens and the countreys that be con-
teygned bytwene the ryver of Seyne and the ryver of Loyre which the
Romayns called somtyme Gallya Celtica; for within that space is contayned
the herte of Fraunce where the tongue is at this day most parfyte and hath of
moost auncyente so contynued . . . There is no man of what parte of Fraunce
so ever he be borne, if he desire that his writynges shulde by had in any
estymation, but he writeth in suche language as they speke within the
boundes that I have before rehersed.[1]

Like Du Bellay, Ronsard repeatedly urged that one way of enriching
the French language so as to make it the rival of the ancient tongues
was to make copious use of words drawn from all manner of dialects.
None the less he had reluctantly to concede that, since France was now
united under one monarch,

> sommes contraincts, si nous voulons parvenir à quelque honneur,
> parler son langage courtizan, autrement notre labeur tant docte qu'il soit,
> seroit estimé peu de chose, ou (peult estre) totallement mesprisé. Et pour-ce
> que les biens et les honneurs viennent de tel endroit, il faut bien souvent
> ployer sous le jugement d'une damoyselle ou d'un jeune courtizan, encores
> qu'ils se connoissent d'autant moins en la bonne & vraye Poësie qu'ils font
> exercice des armes et autres plus honorables mestiers.[1]

His final view in matters of language is summed up in the posthumously
published preface to *La Franciade*: 'Je te conseille d'user indifferem-
ment de tous dialectes, comme j'ay desja dict: entre lesquels le
Courtisan est toujours le plus beau, à cause de la Majesté du Prince;
mais il ne peut estre parfaict sans l'aide des autres . . .'[2]

Although by the middle of the sixteenth century French had made
considerable inroads into the regions where once the *langue d'oc* had
reigned supreme, it was generally only the upper and middle classes of
society which had been won over, and often their brand of French was
still sharply differentiated from that spoken to the north of the Loire.
In a well-known passage in the *Essais* Montaigne comments on his
own situation as a writer born in Périgord, in the region of the *langue
d'oc*, and thus on the different kinds of language spoken in the France
of his day:

Mon langage françois est alteré, et en la prononciation et ailleurs, par la
barbarie de mon creu: je ne vis jamais homme des contrées de deçà qui ne
sentit bien evidemment son ramage et qui ne blessast les oreilles pures

---

[1] *Eclaircissement de la langue francoyse*, London, 1530, bk. I, Ch. xli.
[2] *Œuvres complètes*, ed. P. Laumonier, Paris, 1914– , xiv. 12.
[3] Ibid. xvi. 350.

françoises. Si n'est-ce pas pour estre fort entendu en mon Perigordin, car je n'en ay pas plus d'usage que de l'Alemand; et ne m'en chaut guere. C'est un langage, comme sont autour de moy, d'une bande ou d'autre, le Poitevin, Xaintongeois, Angoumoisin, Lymosin, Auvergnat: brode, trainant, esfoiré. Il y a bien au dessus de nous, vers les montaignes, un Gascon que je treuve singulierement beau, sec, bref, signifiant, et à la verité un langage masle et militaire plus qu'autre que j'entende; autant nerveux, puissant et pertinant, comme le François est gratieux, delicat et abondant.[1]

His ambiguous linguistic situation is summed up in the famous sentence: 'C'est aux paroles à servir et à suyvre, et que le Gascon y arrive, si le François n'y peut aller.'[2] However, in practice this meant no more than that the text of the *Essais* has a sprinkling of *gasconismes*.

The spread of French as a written language in the southern half of the kingdom was undoubtedly speeded up by the promulgation, in 1539, of the Ordonnance de Villers-Cotterêts.[3] Article 111 laid it down that in order to avoid the ambiguity caused by the use of Latin in the judgements of courts 'nous voulons que doresnavant tous arrestz ensemble toutes aultres procedures soient de nos cours souveraines ou aultres subalternes & inferieures, soient de registres, enquestes, contractz, commissions, sentences, testamens & aultres quelzconques actes & exploit[s] de justice, ou qui en dependent soient prononcez, enregistrez & delivrez aux parties en langage maternel francois, & non aultrement'.[4] Although principally directed against the use of Latin, this ordinance represented a distinct change in government policy towards dialects as ordinances published in 1490, 1510, and even as late as 1535 had allowed their use in legal proceedings. Now the words 'en langage maternel francois, & non aultrement' had an influence in the southern part of the kingdom which went far beyond the legal world; French quickly became the written language of the whole of southern France, a process which was obviously speeded up by both the coming of printing and the rise of Protestantism.

Yet if the educated classes in the south of France became at least bilingual, they formed only a very small proportion of the population, and the great majority of the inhabitants of town and country no doubt continued in their illiteracy or semi-literacy to speak their native

---

[1] *Essais*, ed. P. Villey, 3 vols., Paris, 1930–1, i. 613–14.

[2] Ibid. i. 329.

[3] See. A. Brun, *Recherches historiques sur l'introduction du français dans les provinces du Midi*, Paris, 1923.

[4] See the facsimile in P. Rickard, *La Langue française au seizième siècle*, London, 1968, p. 23.

dialect. Even in the second half of the seventeenth century a northerner
like Racine was to encounter considerable linguistic problems when he
went so far south as Uzès in Languedoc.

If in this period standard French had to struggle against the dialects
of both north and south, it remained a vulgar tongue in face of Latin
which still occupied its traditional place in most forms of education.
Large numbers of new books produced by Frenchmen continued to be
written in Latin. As late as the 1580s we find Montaigne—no doubt
with affected modesty—declaring that if he had thought his essays
deserved to endure, he would have written them in Latin and not in
such an unstable language as French: 'J'escris mon livre à peu
d'hommes et à peu d'années. Si ç'eust esté une matiere de durée, il
l'eust fallu commettre à un langage plus ferme. Selon la variation
continuelle qui a suivy le nostre jusques à cette heure, qui peut esperer
que sa forme presente soit en usage, d'icy à cinquante ans ?'[1] It was not
only learned and scientific works which were written in Latin; an
enormous amount of poetry was turned out in the same language.
Though nowadays this neo-Latin poetry is left to the specialists, it
undoubtedly played an important part in the literature of the French
Renaissance. Moreover, it could even on occasion attract sufficient
court patronage to ensure a livelihood to the writer; the now forgotten
poet, Salmon Macrin (1490–1557), dedicated a volume of his neo-
Latin verse to Francis I and was duly rewarded with a post of *valet de
chambre du roi*, which he managed to keep when Henry II came to the
throne.[2]

Though this neo-Latin poetry retained its importance well into the
following century, as a literary language French made great strides in
this period. The Ordonnance de Villers-Cotterêts had an indirect
influence on its development as a literary language in that it led to an
increased interest in it in legal circles which formed a considerable part
of the educated public of the age. When, ten years later, in 1549, the
young Du Bellay published his famous *Deffence et illustration de la
langue francoyse*, it contained nothing about the role of the French
language which had not been said earlier by such writers as the printer,
Geoffroy Tory, who in 1529 in his *Champfleury* had advanced claims
for its use in both literary and learned works. Indeed, despite his eulogy
of French, Du Bellay, like Ronsard, was to publish neo-Latin verses.

[1] *Essais*, iii. 397.
[2] See I. D. McFarlane, 'Jean Salmon Macrin (1490–1557)', *Bibliothèque d'Humanisme et Renaissance*, 1959, pp. 55–84, 311–49; 1960, pp. 73–89.

Yet the success enjoyed by the French poetry which they and other members of the Pléiade produced undoubtedly strengthened the position of French as a literary language and in the long run contributed to the gradual elimination of Latin from this field.

Other factors helped the progress of French. Paradoxically, in the long run the humanists' passion for Classical purity had the effect of killing Latin as a living language since their scorn for the corrupt and barbarous form which it had taken on in medieval times meant denying it all possibility of adapting itself to the needs of a world very different from that of ancient Rome. What is more, the spread of printing also worked in favour of French. Latin was known either imperfectly or not at all by a great many of those who were able to read, and in order to reach the largest possible public, as the economics of publishing require, both translations into French and new works in French were put on the market in ever-increasing numbers in the course of the century.

Even the public capable of reading books in French must inevitably have been extremely restricted in size, given the degree of illiteracy which still prevailed, at times quite high up the social scale, even among members of the *noblesse d'épée*. Henri de Montmorency (1534–1614) who was appointed *connétable de France* by Henry IV in 1593 could not even sign his name. We have no means, however crude, of measuring the degree of illiteracy in this period over the whole of France; no doubt, as in later centuries, there were considerable variations between men and women, between region and region, and also between town and country. There was, for instance, a striking contrast in the degree of literacy between the urban and rural populations of Languedoc.[1] In the period 1574–6 72 per cent of the peasants who sought loans in the office of a Montpellier *notaire* were unable either to sign their name or write their initials; whereas amongst the artisans 63 per cent could write their names and another 11 per cent their initials. Likewise in the period 1575–93 in the archives of the chapters of Béziers and Narbonne 90 per cent of the agricultural labourers and some 65 per cent of peasant farmers were unable to produce more than their mark, in contrast to the artisans of this region in the period 1575–89 34 per cent of whom could sign their name and 33 per cent write their initials, while 98 per cent of what are described as 'bourgeois et marchands' could sign their names.

The history of primary education in sixteenth-century France

[1] See E. Le Roy Ladurie, *Les Paysans de Languedoc*, 2 vols., Paris, 1966, i. 344–8.

remains remarkably obscure. It is sometimes maintained that, after declining in the fifteenth century, it experienced a distinct revival in the following period. This is attributed partly to the Reformation, in two rather different respects: on the one hand, the Protestants, given the importance they attached to the study of the Bible, encouraged the establishment of *petites écoles*, while on the other, from the Council of Trent onwards, the Counter-Reformation urged the necessity of providing more of such education to save children from the menace of Huguenot heresies. How far such aims were translated into actual schools remains obscure; in the second half of the century when the claims of primary education were being advanced from these very different quarters, France was torn by a civil war which clearly cannot have had other than a crippling effect on existing schools and must have made the creation of new ones difficult. Real progress could only come after the Edict of Nantes had brought religious peace to France in 1598. *Petites écoles*, occasionally for girls as well as boys, undoubtedly existed in the sixteenth century, but it is impossible to provide an over-all picture of the state of this form of education in that period.

Rather more solid information is available about secondary education. By this period *collèges* had ceased to be largely confined to the training of young clerks; they now took in large numbers of boys of all classes—those of modest origins as well as those from noble and bourgeois families—who were destined for secular careers. Here again the Reformation had an impact on education, as did Humanism. From the 1520s onwards many town councils set up *collèges*, starting with Lyons in 1527, followed by Dijon and Bordeaux among others. These new schools, imbued with Humanism, often became centres of heresy, and with the Counter-Reformation came the Catholic riposte in the form of the schools set up by the newly founded Society of Jesus. Its schools were to be the backbone of French secondary education down to their closure in 1762.[1] From modest beginnings at Billom in Auvergne in 1558, they gradually spread to a considerable number of towns and cities, including Paris, though their main development did not occur until the seventeenth century. Part of their success was due to the fact that day-pupils paid no fees. The Huguenots too were anxious to found their own *collèges*, though this only became possible, and even then on a limited scale, at the end of the century. In the

[1] They were also closed after an attempt on the life of Henry IV in 1594, but were allowed to reopen in 1603.

meantime the *collèges* in the faculties of arts in the established universities were relatively in a state of decline.

In all these *collèges* the acquisition of a knowledge of Latin was almost the sole object of the education offered. A tiny place might be allowed to French in the teaching of small boys at the beginning of their school career, but once that was finished with, it was compulsory to speak Latin inside and outside the class-room. Characteristically, the contract of a sixteenth-century headmaster of a *collège* imposed on him the obligation to see that this rule was observed: 'Il constraindra les escoliers de parler latin en tous temps et lieu. Ils auront charge chascun de faire noter a son normateur les escoliers de sa classe quant parleront françoys, en quelque lieu et temps que ce soyt pour en estre punis le samedi.'[1] While it seems clear that secondary education expanded considerably in this period and took in boys from a very wide variety of social classes from the nobility downwards, there was as yet no similar provision for girls; and clearly the contribution of these *collèges* to the advancement of the French language and its literature was negligible.

It goes almost without saying that this was even more true of the three higher faculties of theology, law, and medicine, all of which remained attached to Latin as a means of instruction and discussion. On the whole, the universities may be said to have been in decline; this applies to the most illustrious of all, the University of Paris. The new Humanism found a home in Paris not in the University but in what was to become in 1610 the Collège Royal with its own building and to survive the Revolution under the new name of Collège de France. It was founded by Francis I in 1530 when he established chairs of Greek, Hebrew, and mathematics, held by *lecteurs royaux*. Paradoxically, in the second half of the century some professors of this citadel of Humanism—they included Ramus—were bold enough to insist on lecturing in French, but this was altogether exceptional in this period.

For the first hundred years or so after printing came to France it was only very gradually that some order was brought into the book trade. Any printer or bookseller was at first free to bring out a new edition of a work already printed if he saw the prospect of making a profit; at this stage there was no legal impediment to so doing. In the early sixteenth century a printer or bookseller (rarely an author) would seek from the authorities a *privilège* for a work which he was about to

---

[1] Quoted in A. Brun, *Recherches historiques sur l'introduction du français dans les provinces du Midi*, Paris, 1923, p. 442.

publish, i.e. a ban on other printings of the same work for a period of years long enough to give him some chance of disposing of the edition. From 1508 onwards Louis XII issued such *privilèges* in the form of royal letters patent which forbade unauthorized reprints of the work for a definite period, generally two or three years, on French territory (centuries were to pass before an international copyright convention at last emerged). However, as these *privilèges* were expensive and required contacts at court, recourse was often had to other authorities such as the *prévôt de Paris*.[1] The Paris Parlement was also an important source of *privilèges*; the first one recorded was granted in 1508, but as the *arrêt* contains the phrase, 'Vu aussi les anciens arrêts de la dite Cour en pareil cas', it may be assumed that the practice went back earlier than that.[2]

Although later a *privilège* was to become also a licence to print since it could only be granted after a manuscript had been examined and approved by a censor, originally its purpose was a purely economic one, to safeguard the interests of printer, bookseller, or author. Obtaining a licence to print was a quite separate matter, and at first the control exercised by the authorities over the entirely new phenomenon of printed books was somewhat haphazard and confused. Traditionally, censorship of books had been exercised by the University of Paris, particularly its faculty of theology. The first royal edict on the subject of censorship appeared in 1521; it entrusted the preliminary examination of theological works to the University. The Paris Parlement also had its say in such matters and would frequently refer works to the faculty of theology. Moreover, in 1526, after clashes between Francis I and the faculty of theology over its excesses of zeal in this field, letters patent, confirmed in 1537, gave the Parlement jurisdiction over work written by members of the faculty. For some time both the University and the Parlement continued to exercise jointly a power of censorship over theological works, while permissions to print were given by the Parlement for works in other fields.

In the course of the century, however, the Crown gradually took over control of the printing and publication of books. In 1537 Francis I instituted the *dépôt légal* when he issued a declaration requiring one copy of every printed book to be sent to the library of the château at

---

[1] See e.g. E. Armstrong, 'Notes on the Works of Guillaume Michel, dit de Tours', *Bibliothèque d'Humanisme et Renaissance*, 1969, pp. 257–81, for interesting details on the subject of *privilèges*.

[2] N. Herrmann-Mascard, *La Censure de livres à Paris à la fin de l'Ancien Régime (1750–1789)*, Paris, 1968, p. 7.

Blois. It was not until 1566 that the Crown finally took out of the hands of the Parlement the preliminary censorship of books and transferred it to the Chancellor. Article 78 of the Ordonnance de Moulins reads:

Défendons aussi à toutes personnes que ce soit, d'imprimer ou faire imprimer aucuns livres ou traitez sans notre congé et permission, et lettres de privilége expédiées sous nostre grand scel: auquel cas enjoignons à l'imprimeur d'y mettre et insérer son nom, et le lieu de sa demeurance, ensemble ledit congé et privilége, et ce sur peine de perdition de biens et punition corporelle.[1]

Thanks to its power of granting a monopoly to a particular printer or bookseller through a *privilège* the monarchy was on paper in a position to enforce its control over the book trade since permission to print and a *privilège* were now given in the same document. In practice, the censorship still had many loopholes; several of these were not closed until the following century, and then with the result that henceforth many books written in France were published abroad right down to the end of the *ancien régime*.

Although the control over the production of books was decidedly unsystematic, printers, booksellers, and writers were all engaged in what could be extremely hazardous occupations. An examination of Renouard's *Répertoire*[2] shows that in the sixteenth century, an age of bitter religious strife, printers and booksellers who gave offence to the authorities were liable to be arrested and often brutally punished—imprisoned, banished, flogged, sent to the galleys, hanged, or burnt at the stake. The most famous example of such treatment was that of the writer and printer, Étienne Dolet, who was brought to Paris from Lyons, found guilty of 'blasphème, sédition, exposition de livres prohibés et damnés', and in 1546 hanged and burnt in the place Maubert. Writers too could incur savage penalties; in 1529 the humanist, Louis de Berquin, was burnt at the stake for heresy, and in 1572 Godefroi Vallée was hanged for having published a deistic pamphlet, *La Béatitude des Chrestiens, ou le Fléo de la foy*.

Writers like Marot and Rabelais led a somewhat dangerous existence. In 1526 Marot spent two or three months in prison for having failed to observe Lent, and in 1534, after 'l'affaire des placards', he had to flee from Paris and seek refuge first at the court of Marguerite de Navarre at

[1] F. A. Isambert (ed.), *Recueil général des anciennes lois françaises depuis l'an 420 jusqu'à la Révolution de 1789*, 29 vols., Paris, 1821–32, xiv. 210–11.
[2] P. Renouard, *Répertoire des imprimeurs parisiens, libraires, fondeurs de caractères et correcteurs d'imprimerie depuis l'introduction de l'imprimerie à Paris (1470) jusqu'à la fin du seizième siècle*, Paris, 1965.

Nérac and then at that of Ferrara. It was only after two years of exile that he was allowed to return to France and the court, and then he was required to make a humiliating retractation of his errors. Six years later he had to flee again, to Savoy, Geneva, and finally Turin where he died in exile in 1544.

Rabelais had several brushes with authority. *Pantagruel* was condemned by the Sorbonne, and in later editions of the first two parts of his novel he had to replace words like *théologiens* and *Sorbonicoles* by *sophistes*; this did not prevent the two works from being condemned by the Sorbonne. When the *Tiers Livre* appeared in 1546, it too was condemned and Rabelais thought it expedient to seek refuge in Metz for a period. The appearance of the *Quart Livre* in 1552 led to a similar censure by the Sorbonne which referred the matter to the Paris Parlement. At this point Rabelais fades out of our ken. These examples make it abundantly clear that, whatever were the loopholes in the official control over the press, no such thing as freedom existed.

Even after the great expansion of theatrical activity in Paris in the seventeenth century, it was not until the early years of the eighteenth century that the government set up a regular theatre censorship in the capital. In the sixteenth century the Parlement as well as the Crown played a prominent role in deciding what was put on the stage. This power had been exercised by the Parlement at least as early as 1442 when it had imprisoned some Basochiens who had defied a ban and given a public performance; it had also ordered them not to perform any plays in future without special permission.[1] There were frequent clashes between the Parlement and the Basoché down to 1561 when the judges took the final step of making sure that nothing was added to the censored text which these actors were to perform by decreeing that 'sera à cette fin ledit jeu paraphé et biffé au bout de chaque article, et la copie laissé [*sic*] au greffe pour y avoir recours s'il y echet'.[2] This put an end to the satirical performances of the Basochiens.

It was to the Parlement that the Confrères de la Passion turned in 1548 to seek a renewal of their privileges when they moved into their new theatre at the Hôtel de Bourgogne; this request produced the famous judgement which severely restricted their activities:

La Cour a inhibé & deffendu, inhibe & deffend auxdits Supplians, de joüer le Mystere de la Passion de Notre Sauveur, ne autres Mysteres sacrez, sous peine d'amande arbitraire, leur permettant néantmoins de pouvoir joüer

[1] H. G. Harvey, *The Theatre of the Basoche*, Cambridge, Mass., 1941, p. 225.
[2] Ibid., p. 231.

autres Mysteres prophanes, honnestes, & licites, sans offenser ou injurier autres personnes . . .[1]

On occasion Crown and Parlement clashed over theatrical matters. On 19 May 1577 the Italian company known as I Gelosi, which had been invited by Henry III to come to France to play before the court, began a highly successful series of public performances in Paris at the Hôtel de Bourbon. On 26 June the Parlement ordered the Italian actors to stop performing on the grounds that 'toutes ces comœdies n'enseignoient que paillardises et adultères, et ne servoient que d'escole de desbauche à la jeunesse de tout sexe de la ville de Paris'. Although a month later the Parlement haughtily rejected the letters patent from the King presented by the Italian actors, L'Estoile noted in his journal that at the beginning of the following September 'ils recommencèrent à jouer leurs comœdies en l'Hostel de Bourbon, comme auparavant, par la permission et jussion expresses du Roy'.[2] It was once more the Parlement which, presumably on political grounds, intervened in 1594 to ban the performance in a *collège* of a lost play, Louis Léger's *Chilpéric, roi de France, second du nom,* and ordered that the author 'sera presentement mené et conduit à la Conciergerie du Palais, pour être ouï et interrogé sur le contenu dudit cahier, répondre à telles conclusions que ledit procureur général du roy pourra prendre, et être contre lui procédé ainsi que de raison.[3] Thus although there was as yet no systematic control over the theatre, neither playwrights nor actors were at liberty to put what they liked on the stage.

It is often stated that in the sixteenth century the advent of printing brought no improvement whatsoever in the financial position of the writer who lacked other resources and who depended for a living on what he could earn through patronage, since printers and booksellers paid him nothing for his labours. This may well have been true in the opening decades of the century so far as works of literature were concerned. Volumes of Clément Marot's poetry seem to have sold extremely well, but in the preface to the 1538 edition of his works we find him criticizing very bitterly the printers and booksellers who had brought out the earlier volumes: 'Certes j'ose dire sans mentir (toutesfoys sans

---

[1] C. and F. Parfaict, *Histoire du théâtre français depuis son origine jusqu'à présent,* 15 vols., Amsterdam and Paris, 1735–49, ii. 3.

[2] *Mémoires-Journaux,* ed. G. Brunet *et al.,* 12 vols., Paris, 1875–96, i. 189, 192, 201, 202.

[3] L. E. Dabney, *French Dramatic Literature in the Reign of Henri IV,* Austin, 1952, p. 317.

reproche) que de tous ces miens labeurs le proffit leur en retourne. J'ay planté les Arbres, ils en cueillent les fruictz. J'ay trayné la Charrue, ilz en serrent la moisson, et à moy n'en revient qu'un peu d'estime entre les hommes, lequel encor ilz me veulent estaindre, m'attribuant œuvres sottes & scandaleuses.'[1] In 1545 we find another writer, Jean Bouchet, addressing the printers who had brought out his works:

> Et ces livretz qui sont en prose & rime
> Avez passez soubz vostre forme et lime
> Et imprimez, ou aulcuns ont eu gaing,
> Et non pas moy, car mon labeur fut vain.[2]

On the other hand, if by the first half of the seventeenth century writers of literary works such as poetry and plays were receiving at least modest amounts of hard cash from printers and booksellers in return for their labours, it is a fair assumption that this process must have had at least its beginnings in the sixteenth century. Sometimes the hints that this was the case are tantalizingly vague as in the sentence in the 1588 (Paris) edition of the *Essais* in which Montaigne writes: 'J'achette les imprimeurs en Guiene, ailleurs ils m'achettent.'[3] This would seem to imply that although he derived no financial advantage from the first two editions which were produced in Bordeaux, he received some cash payment for those published later in Paris. More explicit is the verse in an indignant sonnet which Agrippa d'Aubigné penned in 1574 in his 'Vers funèbres sur la mort d'Étienne Jodelle Parisien Prince des Tragiques'. In this poem he speaks of the mystery of what had happened to Jodelle's manuscripts:

> L'un tient un lopin dont il bave sans cesse,
> L'autre en tient un cayer enfermé dans l'estuy.
> Un autre à qui l'argent ne feroit tant d'ennuy
> Le vent à beaux testons pour mettre sur la presse.[4]

The last two lines make it clear that at this date money payments could be expected from, the publication of poetry.

We are not, however, reduced to mere speculation on this point. At least three contracts between booksellers and poets are extant for the second half of the sixteenth century. The first of these to come to light was the text of an agreement signed on 24 July 1585 between Du

---

[1] Mayer, *Clément Marot*, pp. 423–4.
[2] *Epistres morales et familieres du traverseur*, Poitiers, 1545, fo. 47v.
[3] *Essais*, iii. 48.
[4] E. Jodelle, *Œuvres complètes*, ed. E. Balmas, 2 vols., Paris, 1965–8, ii. 370.

Bartas and the Paris booksellers, Timothée Jouan and Abel L'Angelier.[1] This was for a new edition of 'les premieres œuvres dudit sieur du Bartas, revues, corrigees et augmentees'. The agreement was for eight years (the booksellers were to take out a *privilège* for that period) and the poet was to receive 'la somme de cent trente trois escu sol. un tiers' within ten months of the signing of the agreement. Although the projected edition seems never to have been published,[2] this agreement shows not only that a poet could at this date obtain a cash payment for his works, but also that such payments were not limited to the first edition of his writings.

A little more is known about Ronsard's relations with printers and booksellers. There is first of all the famous letter addressed to his old friend, Jean Galland, which is summarized by Guillaume Colletet as follows:

Par une de ses lettres, datée de sa maison de Croix-Val, le 9e jour de septembre 1584,[3] j'apprends que jusques alors il n'avoit reçu aucun advantage de tous les libraires qui avoient tant de fois imprimé ses escrits, mais que pour cette édition qu'il preparoit & qu'il avoit exactement revue, il entendoit que Buon, son libraire, luy donnast soixante bons ecus, pour avoir du bois, pour s'aller chauffer cet hyver avec son amy Gallandius, & s'il ne le veut faire, dist-il, il exhorte son amy d'en parler aux libraires du Palais qui en donneront sans doubte davantage, s'il tient bonne mine & qu'il sçache comme il faut faire valoir le privilege perpetuel de ses œuvres: . . . & ensuitte il lance plusieurs traits de raillerie contre l'avarice de certains libraires qui veulent proffiter de tout, recevoir tousjours & ne donner jamais rien.[4]

If this outburst against the avarice of publishers was to be repeated over and over again by many French writers down the ages, the letter is none the less misleading. While, like Du Bartas's contract, it proves that in the 1580s sums of money could be obtained from the publication of poetry, it gives a wrong impression about the state of affairs before the closing decades of the century. Some thirty years earlier, on 9 May 1553 to be precise, Ronsard had signed an agreement for a new edition of his *Amours* for which he was paid, as was his friend Muret for his commentary on the poems. The following abridged version of the agreement was published by the scholar who unearthed it:

[1] Duc de Fezensac, 'Saluste du Bartas et ses éditeurs parisiens', *Bulletin du bibliophile* 1900, pp. 232–4.

[2] See G. Du Bartas, *Works*, ed. U. T. Holmes *et al.*, 3 vols., Chapel Hill, 1935–40, i. 204–5.

[3] If the date is correctly given, the letter refers to the posthumous, 1587 edition, but it should perhaps read '1583' and would thus refer to the 1584 edition.

[4] *Œuvres complètes*, xviii. 501.

Pierre de Ronssart et Marc Anthoine de Muret, led. de Ronssart sr de Sarceau et led. Muret bachellier en droict civil, demourans à Paris, confessent avoir . . . receu de . . . Katherine Lhéritier, vefve de feu . . . Maurice Delaporte, . . . libraire . . . , par les mains de Ambroys Delaporte, son filz, facteur et négociateur . . . , trente escus d'or soleil . . . , vallans ensemble soixante neuf livres tournois, c'est assavoir led. de Ronssart, vingt trois livres tournois pour l'augmentation par led. de Ronssart faicte en son livre qu'il a composé des *Amours*, par cy devant imprimé par lad. vefve, et led. Muret quarente six livres tournois pour avoir commenté led. livre d'*Amours* . . , et en ce faisant a promis . . . led. Delaporte, tant pour luy que pour sad. mère, de n'imprimer ou faire imprimer doresenavant led. livre sans l'exprès consentement dud. de Ronssart.[1]

It will be noticed that even this earlier agreement shows that payments to a writer were not, as is often stated, limited to what he could extract from a printer or bookseller for the first edition of his work.

Before and especially after this date Ronsard must have signed many more agreements with printers and booksellers for authorized editions of his voluminous works. So far only one other has been discovered. It was signed less than a year later, on 28 April 1554, and was again with Katherine de la Porte. Its contents are summarized as follows by Professor Lebègue:

. . . Le poète vendait à la libraire, au prix de trente-quatre écus d'or soleil, 'les Quatre premiers livres des Odes de Pierre de Ronssart, reveuz et augmentez de nouvel, dedyés au Roy, et le Bocage de Pierre de Ronssart, dedié à Pierre Paschal du bas pais de Languedoc', à charge de les faire imprimer 'jusques à telle quantité que bon luy semblera durant et pendant le temps de six ans'. Et il transférait à la veuve et au fils de Maurice de la Porte le privilège royal de six années que d'Avanson avait signé le 4 janvier 1554 (n. st.)[2]

Clearly, Ronsard's oft quoted letter of 1584 cannot be taken at its face value.

Since the appearance of Mademoiselle Annie Parent's *Les Métiers du livre à Paris au XVIᵉ siècle* (*1535–1560*)[3] added a great many more to the meagre number of sixteenth-century agreements which were previously known, we are relatively well informed about the relations of the writers of the time with printers and booksellers. It can well be

[1] E. Coyecque, 'Simples notes sur Ronsard et sur son livre des *Amours*' (1552–1553), *Revue des livres anciens*, 1916, p. 222.

[2] *Œuvres complètes*, 2nd edn., Paris, 1965, vi. 275.

[3] Geneva and Paris, 1974.

imagined that these agreements took all sorts of forms.[1] The twenty agreements, published in full in appendices,[2] range in date from 1533 to 1559 and cover all manner of works, some in Latin, though most of them in French (these include quite a number of translations). At one extreme there is the type of contract between an author who deals directly with the printer of his work, supplies the paper, pays for the printing, and receives all the copies.[3] At the other extreme there is the agreement between Nicolas de Herberay and two booksellers for his translation of the *Amadis de Gaule*; in 1540 in return for the transfer of his *privilège* for the first four books he was to receive 80 écus and twelve unbound copies.[4]

Interesting as these documents are, unfortunately they do not add to our information about what authors of literary works could receive in the way of payment from printers and booksellers. And although at any rate from, the 1550s onwards poets like Ronsard and Du Bartas could expect to receive some financial reward for their labours, it still remains a fact that the sixteenth-century writer who lacked private means or a well-paid post which left him leisure to write depended for a livelihood on patronage.

As in earlier centuries, writers came from a wide variety of backgrounds. If one is asked to name some sixteenth-century French writers, one of the first that comes to mind is a royal personage, Francis I's sister, Marguerite de Navarre, well known as a patron of innumerable men of letters besides Clément Marot and Rabelais.[5] Francis I himself did not disdain to write poetry, though there is some uncertainty as to which of the poems attributed to him were really his own unaided work. His grandson, Charles IX, was likewise both a patron of men of letters and a practising poet. To him are attributed the famous lines addressed to Ronsard:

> L'art de faire des vers, dût-on s'en indigner,
> Doit être à plus haut prix que celui de régner:

[1] Even in the last third of the twentieth century writers of highly specialized academic works do not aspire to an agreement offering royalties or even a lump sum in return for their labours. The most favourable contract which they can hope for is one whereby the publisher agrees to produce the work at his own expense and offers merely the usual number of free copies. Often they have to bear part of the cost of printing and binding in exchange for a share in the profits (if any) or even to meet the entire cost of printing and binding and entrust the sale of the work to a publisher on a commission basis.

[2] Les *Métiers du livre, pp. 286–311*.

[3] Ibid. pp. 286–8.　　　　[4] Ibid. pp. 300–1.

[5] P. Jourda, 'Le Mécénat de Marguerite de Navarre', *Revue du seizième siècle*, 1931, pp. 253–71.

Tous deux également nous portons des couronnes,
Mais, roi, je les reçus; poète, tu les donnes.

Although Michel d'Eyquem, seigneur de Montaigne, apparently did not disdain to accept money for an edition of his *Essais* when it was offered, he was obviously not in need either of receiving such payment or of patronage; he had inherited a comfortable social situation from his father, and after holding the post of *conseiller* in the Bordeaux Parlement he later acted as mayor of that city. A great many of the prominent writers of the period held posts at various levels in the legal world. After a brilliant career as an *avocat* Étienne Pasquier was appointed *avocat général* at the Cour des comptes while Pibrac, the author of the famous quatrains, ended up as a *président à mortier* in the Paris Parlement. Another poet, Nicolas Rapin, beginning as an *avocat*, rose through various legal posts to be *lieutenant criminel* of Paris. Robert Garnier found sufficient leisure to write his plays while acting as a judge at Le Mans and later holding the post of *lieutenant criminel* of Maine; he ended by purchasing a post of *conseiller* in the Grand Conseil. Earlier in the century Jean Bouchet had been a very successful *procureur* at Poitiers.

Among writers of independent means there was, for instance, Pontus de Tyard who inherited a château and considerable wealth from his mother and was later appointed bishop of Chalon. Other Lyons poets stood aside from the struggle for the various forms of patronage which were available to writers of the age. Although Maurice Scève's father had been a wealthy man who held the posts of *échevin* and *juge-mage* of Lyons, he himself does not seem to have been well off, but it is clear that he did not seek the conventional forms of patronage. Of the two famous women of the group, Pernette du Guillet and Louise Labé, the first was of noble birth and married a nobleman, while the second was the daughter and wife of wealthy ropemakers.

The minor nobility contributed some writers, such as Jean de La Taille, Agrippa d'Aubigné, and Du Bartas. Remy Belleau was also of noble birth, though he was attached to the household of the marquis d'Elbeuf to whose son he acted as tutor. Jacques Peletier held a variety of teaching posts, including a chair of mathematics, while Jean de Sponde, after abjuring Protestantism like his master, Henry IV, ended up as a *maître des requêtes*. Jacques Grévin qualified as a doctor and practised in a variety of countries. Although Rabelais also became a physician, it is a little difficult to classify a man who had such a varied career.

None the less the sixteenth century numbered many writers who owed the greater part of their livelihood to what they could obtain in the way of patronage by attracting attention to themselves through their skill as writers. Throughout the whole of the period patronage played such an important part in the literary life of France that a considerable volume could be devoted to a study of the various forms which it took, as the information available, though far from complete, is much fuller than for the Middle Ages.

The rat race of the life at court, which was the centre of literary patronage, is vividly described by the poets of the time as, for instance, in the disillusioned lines of Olivier de Magny:

> Celluy qui suyt la court, s'il n'est heuré des cieux
> D'y pouvoir demeurer librement & sans peine,
> Sent dedans chacun nerf & dans chacune veine
> Couler de iour en iour ung traict ambitieux.
>
> Il a tousjours l'esprit veillant & soucieux,
> Et comme vif argent se tourmente & demeine,
> Il bastit en resvant cent chasteaux sur l'arene,
> Et n'arreste jamais ny les piés ny les yeux.[1]

In a remarkably frank passage in the 'Complainte contre Fortune' which Ronsard addressed to a potential patron, Cardinal de Châtillon, he confesses how completely he was carried away by ambition when he came into contact with the court:

> Adonc l'ambition s'alluma dans mon cueur,
> Credule je conceu la Royale grandeur,
> Je conceu Eveschez, Prieurez, Abayes,
> Soudain abandonnant les Muses, esbahyes
> De me voir transformer d'un escolier contant
> En nouveau courtizan, demandeur inconstant.
> O que mal aisement l'ambition se couvre!
> Lors j'apris le chemin d'aller souvent au Louvre . . .
> Je brulay du desir d'amasser & d'avoir:
> J'apris à desguiser le nayf de ma face,
> Espier, escouter, aller de place en place,
> Cherchant la mort d'autruy: miserable moyen,
> Quand par la mort d'autruy on augmente son bien.[2]

The disappointments which lay in wait for many poets in their search if not for wealth, at least for a modest security, are described again and

---

[1] *Les Souspirs*, ed. E. Courbet, Paris, 1874, pp. 90–1.
[2] *Œuvres complètes*, x. 22–3.

again in their writings. There are, for instance, the bitter lines of Antoine de Baïf in which he regrets not having chosen a humbler, but more secure calling:

> O que j'eusse été coquetier!
> Deux fois me trouvant la semaine
> Au marché, j'usse de ma peine
> Le loyer par un gain present:
> Là où la nuit & la journee
> Travaillant du long de l'annee,
> Je n'ay pas un chetif present.
> Et ma teste ademy pelee
> Grisonne: et ma barbe meslee
> Montre des toufets de poil blanc.
> De dents ma bouche est degarnie:
> La goutte desja me manie:
> Et n'ay de rente un rouge blanc.[1]

Such lamentations are not, of course, to be taken at their face value, but they do reveal how poets in this dependent position felt in their gloomier moments. One can compare with this the melancholy sonnet in *Les Regrets* which Du Bellay addressed to Baïf advising him to give up poetry for the more lucrative profession of *avocat*:

> Si tu m'en crois (Baïf), tu changeras Parnasse
> Au palais de Paris, Helicon au parquet,
> Ton laurier en un sac, & ta lyre au caquet
> De ceulx qui, pour serrer, la main n'ont jamais lasse.
> C'est à ce mestier là que les biens on amasse,
> Non à celuy des vers, où moins y a d'acquêt
> Qu'au mestier d'un boufon ou celuy d'un naquet.
> Fy du plaisir (Baïf) qui sans profit se passe.
> Laissons donc, je te pry, ces babillardes sœurs,
> Ce causeur Apollon, & ces vaines doulceurs,
> Qui pour tout leur tresor n'ont que des lauriers verds.
> Aux choses de profit, ou celles qui font rire,
> Les grands ont aujourdhuy les oreilles de cire,
> Mais ils les ont de fer, pour escouter les vers.[2]

Yet a sixteenth-century poet never gave up hope of receiving favours from the mighty; characteristically, Du Bellay inserted among the last sonnets of *Les Regrets* a whole series of poems offering fulsome praise

---

[1] *Euvres en rime*, ed. C. Marty-Laveaux, 5 vols., Paris, 1881, ii. 450–1.
[2] *Les Regrets* CLIV.

of potential patrons—Michel de l'Hospital, the future Chancellor (CLXVII), Charles de Guise, Cardinal de Lorraine (CLXVIII), Odet de Coligny, Cardinal de Châtillon (CLXIX), Mary Stuart, the fiancée of the Dauphin, the future Francis II (CLXX), the Queen, Catherine de Médicis (CLXXI), the Dauphin (CLXXII), Jeanne d'Albret, the daughter of Marguerite de Navarre (CLXXIII), the King's sister, Marguerite de France (CLXXIV–CLXXIX), and finally, in the very last poem of the collection (CXCI), Henry II himself. This reads:

> Sire, celuy qui est a formé toute essence
>   De ce qui n'estoit rien. C'est l'œuvre du Seigneur.
>   Aussi tout honneur doit flechir à son honneur,
>   Et tout autre pouvoir ceder à sa puissance.
> On void beaucoup de rois, qui sont grands d'apparence.
>   Mais nul, tant soit il grand, n'aura jamais tant d'heur
>   De pouvoir à la vostre egaler sa grandeur,
>   Car rien n'est apres Dieu si grand qu'un roy de France.
> Puis donc que Dieu peult tout, & ne se trouve lieu
>   Lequel ne soit enclos sous le pouvoir de Dieu,
>   Vous, de qui la grandeur de Dieu seul est enclose,
> Elargissez encor sur moy vostre pouvoir,
>   Sur moy, qui ne suis rien, à fin de faire voir
>   Que de rien un grand roy peult faire quelque chose.

The tone in which the poet addresses the King, the source of so many different forms of literary patronage, is abject enough, but it could easily be paralleled in the fulsome eulogies of potential patrons penned by innumerable other writers of the age.

Many sixteenth-century literary works appeared, of course, without any sort of dedication. Montaigne's *Essais* were published without one, and of the four books of Rabelais's novel which appeared during his lifetime only the *Tiers Livre* and the *Quart Livre* bear a dedication. Again quite often the writer was obviously seeking no material reward from his dedication and merely offered his book to a friend, as Ronsard did when he addressed his *Folastries* to a certain Janot who is generally taken to be Baïf.

Dedications could take various forms. When Ronsard published his *Quatre premiers livres des Odes*, he addressed the first poem in the collection to Henry II. A longer work like the first four books of *La Franciade* opens with an invocation to the Muse of epic poetry which is followed immediately by four lines to Charles IX to whom the work is dedicated:

CHARLES MON PRINCE, enflez moy le courage,
En vostre honneur j'entrepren cet ouvrage,
Soyez mon guide, & gardez d'abismer
Ma nef qui flotte en si profonde mer.

Lines of this kind addressed to a dedicatee can sometimes appear rather grotesque. Du Bartas's poem, *La Judit*, had originally been commissioned by Jeanne d'Albret, the extremely puritanical Queen of Navarre, but she was dead by the time it was published in 1574, and the poem was dedicated to her daughter-in-law, Marguerite de Valois, whose amorous career was to furnish material for the *chronique scandaleuse* for the next forty years. After four lines in which he sets forth the subject of his poem Du Bartas goes on to offer it to Marguerite:

Fille du grand HENRY, et compagne pudique
D'un autre grand HENRY, o MARGUERITE unique,
Qui decores la France, oy ce vers qui ne dit
Rien, si non ton beau los sous le nom de Judit.

Sometimes, as one might expect, a prose work contains a dedicatory epistle in prose, as with the three books of Lemaire de Belges's *Illustrations de Gaule*, offered to Marguerite d'Autriche, Claude de France, and Anne de Bretagne respectively, or the *Defence et Illustration de la langue francoyse* which Du Bellay presented to his cousin, the powerful cardinal, or the *Quart Livre* which Rabelais dedicated to Cardinal de Châtillon. The epistle might, however, be in verse as with the ten-line poem, 'François Rabelais à l'esprit de la Royne de Navarre', with which the *Tiers Livre* opens. Most collections of verse which contain a dedicatory epistle have it in verse, but occasionally they are in prose as with the *Recueil de poésie* which Du Bellay presented in 1549 to Henry II's sister, Madame Marguerite, or Ronsard's *Elegies, Mascarades et Bergerie* which was dedicated to Elizabeth I in 1565. Here Ronsard seizes the opportunity to flatter two patrons at one and the same time as he links together the Regent, Catherine de Médicis, and the Queen of England. 'C'est pourquoy,' he writes, 'il m'a semblé que je serois envieux de l'aise & repos de ce present siecle, si participant en la generalle & particuliere allegresse en laquelle je voy pacifiquement le peuple detenu, je ne rendoy un tesmoignage de ceste prudente Gynecocratie, sous laquelle l'estat publique est vertueusement policé ...' Plays generally have epistles in prose, for instance Grévin's *Théâtre* which was offered to the fourteen-year-old duchesse de Lorraine, and Garnier's *Théâtre*, dedicated to Henry III. When Garnier published

Les Juifves in 1583, he offered it to one of the King's favourites, the duc de Joyeuse, who in addition to being a well-known patron of men of letters was also governor of the province in which the playwright held the post of *lieutenant criminel*. It is interesting to see that the possession of this post did not prevent Garnier from hinting pretty broadly that he was open to accept some sort of reward for his dedication. After saying that he would get into trouble with the Muses if he did not join in the chorus of praise for the Duke's generosity to men of letters, he goes on:

Car combien que, ou par l'infelicité du siècle, ou par defaut de merites ou par un malheur particulier, les peines que j'ai prises à les caresser, m'ayent esté autant infructueuses jusques icy, que les assidus et desagreables labeurs de ma vacation; si veux-je, Monseigneur, vous regracier des bienfaits que les lettres reçoivent journellememt de vous, comme si j'estois du nombre des mieux fortunez, et vous en demeurer autant redevable que l'un d'iceux.

It was apparently not until well into the seventeenth century that writers began to satirize the excessive eulogies which were inevitably part and parcel of most dedicatory epistles.

We have much more precise information about the persons who dispensed patronage and about the forms which this took than we have for the Middle Ages, but there are inevitably gaps in our knowledge. Though one could easily fill a large volume with lists of individual poems or other works which sing the praises of all manner of individuals from members of the royal family down to relatively humble personages who might be able to use their influence with potential patrons, in the great majority of cases we do not know what result (if any) was achieved by the writer. In addition to dedicating their works to great noblemen and powerful clerics, poets made a point of praising high civil servants many of whom had some influence on the payment of royal gifts and pensions. As the author of a work on Baïf amusingly puts it: 'On pourrait établir une liste très complète de ces fonctionnaires royaux sous les derniers Valois avec les seules dédicaces de Baïf.'[1] This could no doubt equally well apply to other writers at this and other periods in the sixteenth century.

In practice, almost all the information we have about *effective* patronage of writers of this period relates to royal or princely personages. Writers did not necessarily confine their attentions to the French royal family. If we do not know what results followed from Baïf's attempts to secure the patronage of Philip II of Spain and the Emperor

[1] M. Augé-Chiquet, *La Vie, les idées et l'œuvre de Jean-Antoine de Baïf*, Paris, 1909, p. 139.

Maximilian,[1] according to a near-contemporary source in 1540 Clément Marot presented a manuscript of his translation of the Psalms to the Emperor Charles V in Paris and received from him a gift of 200 doubloons.[2] In 1565, when shortly after a peace treaty had been signed between England and France, Ronsard dedicated his *Elegies, Mascarades et Bergerie*, to Queen Elizabeth I, according to his biographer, Claude Binet, he received in return 'un diamant d'excellente valeur', while, if we may rely on the same source, Mary Queen of Scots had so great an admiration for his poetry that from her prison in 1583 she had him sent a present of 'un buffet de deux mille escus'.[3]

The patronage extended to writers by successive dukes of Burgundy in the fifteenth century was prolonged into the sixteenth century by the regent of the Netherlands, Marguerite d'Autriche; after Jean Lemaire de Belges had entered her service while she was duchesse de Savoie, he accompanied her to the Netherlands in 1507. There he was made a canon at Valenciennes and succeeded Jean Molinet as *indiciaire* (historiographer). A few years later, however, he abandoned Marguerite and sought a new patron in the French Queen, Anne de Bretagne, to whom he had already dedicated various works; she gave him the post of *indiciaire* in 1512 and he was sent off to Brittany to collect material for a history of the province. But patronage was always a chancy business; Anne de Bretagne died at the beginning of 1514, and after that all trace of Lemaire is lost.

Although their interest in literature varied considerably, all the Valois kings from Louis XII to Henry III were generous in their patronage of men of letters; in this respect they formed a striking contrast with the first two Bourbon monarchs, in particular with Henry IV whose parsimony was a source of constant lamentations among the writers of his reign. At the court of Louis XII and his queen, Anne de Bretagne, *rhétoriqueur* poets like Jean Marot and Guillaume Crétin enjoyed considerable favour; this was earned by such propaganda writings as Jean Marot's *Voyage de Gênes* which relates in verse the King's expedition into Italy.

Francis I carried patronage of both literature and learning much further. In addition to founding what was to become the Collège de France, he encouraged Amyot to produce his famous translation of Plutarch. His sister, Marguerite de Navarre, was also important as a patron during his reign; it was with her that Clément Marot found his

---

[1] Ibid. pp. 142–3. [2] Mayer, *Clément Marot*, p. 463.
[3] *La Vie de P. de Ronsard*, ed. P. Laumonier, Paris, 1909, p. 28.

first post (he describes himself on several occasions as 'secretaire de la reine de Navarre') before succeeding his father in a post in the King's household; Bonaventure des Périers was later to become secretary and *valet de chambre* to Marguerite. Claude Chappuys and Mellin de Saint-Gelais were court poets who won particular favour with Francis I.

Henry II was less interested in literature than his father, but none the less he was bombarded with eulogies by the poets of the time, including those of the Pléiade. His sister, Marguerite, was a great admirer of these younger poets who tried to use her as go-between in seeking royal favours. Ronsard in particular sought feverishly to secure the King's support, courting the two powerful cardinals, Lorraine and Châtillon, in the hope that they would use their influence to help him to secure it. Despite his constant offering of the bait of the great epic poem, *La Franciade*, he received relatively little in the way of royal patronage during this reign; this was largely reserved for established poets like Lancelot de Carles and Mellin de Saint-Gelais.

After Henry II's accidental death and the accession of Charles IX, the regent, Catherine de Médicis', acted as patron to a number of writers, Italian as well as French. The King himself proved to be most generous in his encouragement of writers. At long last Ronsard received his reward for the countless eulogies of royal personages which he had penned from the very beginning of his career as a poet; even Baïf also secured some modest pickings in exchange for all his pleas for assistance, and the young Desportes was enabled to make a start on his career as a court poet.

Although Henry III lacked his brother's keen interest in literature, he continued the Valois tradition of generous patronage to men of letters. Ronsard turned out large quantities of court verse during his reign, but he was never in great favour with the new king; yet even Baïf secured some reward for his long efforts, and Desportes did particularly well. In contrast to her husband, Henry of Navarre, Marguerite de Valois was also renowned for her generosity to men of letters; she carried the dynasty's traditional interest in literature into the opening decades of the seventeenth century.

The forms which this royal patronage could take in the sixteenth century were extremely varied. Kings could make money gifts, sometimes substantial, to writers whose works gave them pleasure. According to Brantôme, after attending a performance of his play Henry II 'donna à Jodelle, pour la tragedie qu'il fit de Cleopatre cinq cens escus à son espargne, et outre lui fit tout plein d'autres graces, d'autant que c'estoit chose nouvelle et très belle et rare, certes'.[1] Although Jodelle died in poverty, he did receive various money gifts from Charles IX; in 1572, for instance, he was given 500 livres 'en considération des services qu'il luy a ci-devant et de long tems faictz' and also in order to 'se faire penser et guarir d'une maladie de laquelle il est à présent détenu', while in his will, drawn up in the following year, he speaks of 'deux cens escus a luy donnez par le roy' as being still due to him.[2] Money gifts could be received for all sorts of reasons; one thinks, for instance, of the 'cent écus d'or soleil' which Clément Marot received from Francis I in answer to his pleas in the famous *épître* 'Au Roy, pour avoir été desrobé'.[3] Another of Marot's poems addressed to Francis I, the 'Eglogue soubs les noms de Pan & Robin', returns thanks for a rather more unusual gift, that of 'une maison, grange et jardin, le tout enclos de murailles, et scitué et assis ès fauxbourg Saint-Germain des Prez de Paris, en la rue du Cloz-Bruneau'.[4] Presumably Marot was able to take possession of this house, but it must be said that the grant of a gift of money was no guarantee that the cash would actually be received, as an entry in L'Estoile's journal for 1585 makes clear:

En ce temps, Henri Estienne estant venu de Genève à Paris, et le Roy lui aiant donné mil escus pour le livre qu'il avoit fait *De la préexcellence du langage françois*, il y eust un trésorier, qui, en voiant son brevet expédié, lui en voulust donner six cens escus tout comptant, lesquels il refusa, lui en offrant cinquante escus. De quoi ledit trésorier se moquant, lui dit qu'il voioit bien qu'il ne sçavoit ce que c'estoit que finances, et le laissa là, après lui avoir dit qu'il reviendroit encores à l'offre qu'on lui avoit faite, mais qu'il ne la retrouveroit pas.

In the end Henri Estienne had to go back to Geneva without receiving a single sou.[5]

What was, on paper at least, more valuable to a writer than occasional money gifts was a royal pension. On the whole these would appear to have been less frequently granted to writers than in the later centuries of the *ancien régime*, though Antoine de Baïf, for instance, claimed that he had been 'pensionnere/Des trois Freres & de la Mere', that is of Francis II, Charles IX, Henry III, and Catherine de Médicis.[6] Unfortunately, the royal treasury, particularly in the troubled years of the

[1] *Œuvres complètes*, ed. P. Mérimée and L. Lacour, 13 vols., Paris, 1858–93, iv. 125.
[2] *Œuvres complètes*, i. 50, 52.   [3] Mayer, *Clément Marot*, p. 179 n.
[4] Ibid. pp. 448–9.
[5] L'Estoile, *Mémoires-Journaux*, ii. 203–4.
[6] *Euvres en rime*, v. 190.

Wars of Religion, seldom paid punctually, and being on the list of recipients was in practice no guarantee that the money would actually be forthcoming. Again a writer might be given a post in the royal household. In the first half of the century poets like Jean and Clément Marot were given the title of *valet de chambre du roi* and drew a modest salary for what appears to have been a sinecure. Sometimes, as in the case of Claude Chappuys, for instance, this post was held together with that of librarian; or the latter post, as with Mellin de Saint-Gelais, could be combined with other occupations at court. Another title which could be conferred on writers was that of *lecteur du roi*. In the second half of the century it was customary to appoint writers to posts of *secrétaire de la chambre du roi*; these were probably also sinecures, though poets like Baïf and Desportes who held the title were not necessarily paid for what they did or did not do. Another post in the royal household which could be offered to writers was that of *aumônier du roi*; this was one of the posts held by Mellin de Saint-Gellais, and on his death Ronsard succeeded him, one of the rare pieces of patronage which he managed to extract from Henry II.

It is, however, notorious that the sixteenth century was the age in which the kings of France exercised their patronage of literature largely at the expense of the Catholic Church. Many of the writers of the time were tonsured clerks and, remaining unmarried, were eligible to hold livings in the Church even if they were rarely ordained priests. The more modest appointments such as those to *cures* were, of course, made by all manner of patrons, from the Pope to mere laymen; they were none the less sought after and obtained by a great many writers in the sixteenth century, from Rabelais to Ronsard and Baïf. Canonries were held by a procession of writers from Lemaire de Belges to Desportes; thanks to the influence of his powerful cousin, Cardinal Du Bellay, the poet of *Les Regrets* held for a time among other Church livings a canonry at Notre-Dame de Paris, and he was indeed buried there as a former canon. Quite a number of sixteenth-century writers ended up as bishops—Antoine Héroët, Lancelot de Carles, Pontus de Tyard, and, of course, Amyot who had acted as tutor to Charles IX and Henry III.

Ronsard, for instance, made it clear that he would have been quite happy to accept a bishopric. In his scornful retort to Protestant attacks on his *Discours des Misères de ce temps* he wrote:

> Or sus, mon frere en Christ, tu dis que je suis Prestre:
> J'ateste l'Eternel que je le voudrois estre

Et avoir tout le chef & le dos empesché
Desoubs la pesanteur d'une bonne Evesché.[1]

However, what he and many other writers before and after his time really had their eye on was the secure income to be derived from holding *in commendam* one or more abbeys or priories. Such posts could be held by almost anyone, including even laymen, and as they entitled the *abbé* or *prieur en commende* to draw at least a third and sometimes more of the income of the religious house in question, they were naturally much sought after, and by no means only by writers, as this was a means which the King could employ to reward all kinds of services.

The competition to secure them was therefore very severe, as the example of Ronsard shows. All his efforts during the reign of Henry II to secure this mark of royal favour were in vain; between 1553 and 1557 he got himself appointed to a number of *cures*, but he had to content himself with these and with the fairly modest post of *aumônier du roi* to which he succeeded in 1558. It was not until six years later, during the reign of Charles IX, that he secured his first success in the long struggle for an abbey or priory. Finally, in 1565 he installed himself in the priory of Saint-Cosme-les-Tours where he was to spend a good deal of his time in his later years and where he was buried. Although he held other priories, it is notorious that he was nowhere near as successful in this hunt for a secure form of income as his younger rival, Desportes, who gradually managed to build up a degree of affluence on which seventeenth-century writers looked back with a mixture of envy and admiration.

Like Ronsard, Desportes had been tonsured at an early age. Although he would appear to have received some royal patronage during the reign of Charles IX (in the *privilège* of the 1573 edition of his works he is described as *secrétaire de la chambre du roi*), it was only under Henry III that he began to acquire a substantial income by holding abbeys *in commendam*. In 1582 he was appointed to two abbeys, took minor orders, and gave up writing the love-poetry on which his reputation had been established. The real plum came only in 1594 when he was appointed to the abbey of Bonport by Henry IV; this was, however, as a reward for his political services which shortly afterwards secured for him the title of *conseiller du roi*. Besides his abbeys Desportes had other sources of income such as a canonry at the Sainte

---

[1] *Œuvres complètes*, xi. 120.

Chapelle; altogether he was able to spend the last ten years of his life (he died in 1606) in what were for a poet unusually affluent circumstances.

Although even royal hands did not disdain to hold a pen and to turn out both verse and in the case of Marguerite de Navarre other writings too, and although such persons as highly placed dignitaries concerned with the administration of justice devoted their leisure to literary pursuits, the social status of the writer who sought to make his way in the world by means of his talents alone was undoubtedly a lowly one in sixteenth-century France. It is true that there were considerable differences in the social origins of such writers. Often these remain uncertain, particularly with writers of the early part of the period such as Jean Marot or Lemaire de Belges, but it is fairly clear that these men were of humble birth. Others belonged to fairly well-off middle-class families; Desportes, for instance, seems to have been born into a prosperous family of this type at Chartres, while both Ronsard and Du Bellay belonged to the minor nobility. Ronsard's father had been a soldier and had held a post at court; the future poet was no doubt intended to follow in his footsteps when he was sent to court as a page and then became a *valet d'écurie* until for medical reasons he had to give up all notion of following a career in the army and was tonsured. Du Bellay belonged to the elder and also less distinguished branch of a noble family; his cousins Guillaume, a famous general, and Jean, the cardinal, whom he accompanied to Rome, were both patrons of Rabelais. Yet both these poets were clearly conscious of the fact that in the aristocratic society of the day their calling was regarded as inferior to that of *the* aristocratic career, the army; Ronsard, it will be remembered, compares his calling with that of the noblemen who 'font exercice des armes et autres plus honorables mestiers'.[1] Moreover, as we have seen, the financial position of such writers was highly precarious, and while some managed in the end to obtain sufficient patronage to ensure a reasonably comfortable existence, others—Jodelle, for example—ended up in poverty, and many others who lacked independent means or a secure occupation must often have been uncertain as to where the next meal was to come from.

It is obvious that what was mainly responsible for the poor financial position of those sixteenth-century writers who sought to earn a living by their pen was the extreme smallness of the reading public in a society the great bulk of whose members were completely illiterate.

[1] *Œuvres complètes*, xiv. 12.

One can, it is true, trace back to this period the emergence of what is known as the *littérature de colportage*, the chapbooks hawked around the country by pedlars. These undoubtedly had a considerable influence on the spread of Protestantism in France, and besides religious tracts they included almanachs, textbooks, lives of saints, and, towards the end of the century, romances of chivalry which were to remain extremely popular throughout the *ancien régime* with this more or less plebeian public. Yet clearly these little chapbooks did nothing to provide an audience for contemporary writers who had their eye on the very restricted public furnished by the court and, more generally, the still very narrow circle of educated people.

Given what must have been an extremely small reading public, it is surprising how large a number of editions was reached by certain works of the period. Marot's *L'Adolescence Clémentine*, for instance, went through no fewer than twenty-two editions between 1532 and 1538, and between 1538 and 1544 there were at least seventeen editions of a new volume of his works. One could add that between 1539 and the end of the century more than five hundred editions of his translation of the Psalms appeared, but this last example was obviously altogether exceptional and was due to the success of his translation in Protestant circles. Rabelais's writings also secured a striking success; in the course of the sixteenth century there were altogether over fifty editions of the five books of his novel, from *Pantagruel* to the *Cinquième Livre*, and some thirty editions of his collected works appeared between 1553 and 1600. Marguerite de Navarre's *Heptaméron*, published posthumously in 1559, had a rather more modest success, but by 1598 it had gone through at least nine editions. Ronsard's long and prolific career as a poet produced in total a very considerable number of editions of single works as well as no fewer than nine editions of his bulky collected works down to 1597. The much shorter career of Du Bellay inevitably meant a smaller number of editions of separate works, yet between 1561 and 1597 a collection of his French verse went through at least eight editions.

Some of these figures are certainly impressive, but as we have no means of telling how large were the individual printings of these editions they do not tell us very much; one is inclined to assume that almost all these editions were very small by twentieth-century standards, but this is obviously not susceptible of proof.

In recent years valiant attempts have been made to tackle the problem of the size of the reading public from the other end, by studying the sixteenth-century inventories preserved in notarial or public archives.[1] While these works make fascinating reading, one cannot help wondering whether they have produced results which adequately reward their authors for the immense labour involved in wrestling with these ancient documents. To begin with, there are all sorts of uncertainties. Where no books are mentioned in the inventories it is far from certain that the person concerned had none. Again, very often large numbers of books are simply lumped together without any effort being made to reproduce individual titles as in 'XLIX livres tant de loix que de droit canon avec IIII XX XIII petits livres de diverses grandeurs, le tout prisé par Fremyn Wassespasse, libraire, à la somme de XXI L. X S'.[2] Again the lawyers who drew up these inventories and the clerks who wrote them down were not concerned with bibliographical niceties; it is thus often impossible to decide whether a work was manuscript or printed, what language it was written in, and above all what was its correct title. Interesting as these studies may be, they do not tell us more than what we could already guess, namely that book ownership was mainly restricted to members of the upper and fairly prosperous middle classes of the period, particularly those whose profession called for the possession of manuscript and printed works.

Inevitably, a great deal of sixteenth-century literature in the vernacular, particularly poetry which still remained the writer's chief passport to fame, was addressed in the first instance to court circles. One thinks here particularly of poets like Marot or, later in the century, Desportes. It is interesting to find Marot writing in the preface to the edition of the works of Villon which he published in 1533: '... & ne fay doubte qu'il n'eust emporté le chapeau de laurier devant tous les poetes de son temps, s'il eust esté nourry en la court des Roys, & des Princes, là ou les jugemens se amendent, & les langaiges se pollissent'.[3] On the other hand, the attitude of the Pléiade poets towards the court was ambiguous. Their high idea of the poet's calling (they saw in him the guide and prophet of humanity, alone able to confer immortality on mere mortals such as kings) made them despise the taste of the court. In his *Deffence et Illustration* Du Bellay not only urges 'celuy qui aspire à une

---

[1] A. H. Schutz, *Vernacular Books in Parisian Private Libraries of the Sixteenth Century according to the Notarial Inventories*, Chapel Hill, 1955; R. Doucet, *Les Bibliothèques parisiennes au XVIᵉ siècle*, Paris, 1956; and A. Labarre, *Le Livre dans la vie amiénoise du seizième siècle. L'Enseignement des inventaires après décès 1503–1576*, Paris and Louvain, 1971.

[2] Labarre, *Le Livre dans la vie amiénoise*, p. 152.

[3] Mayer, *Clément Marot*, p. 237.

gloyre non vulgaire' to 'fuyr ce peuple ignorant, peuple ennemy de tout rare & antique sçavoir';[1] his scorn also falls on the courts which welcome ignorant rhymesters whom he addresses in contemptuous terms: 'Je suis d'opinion que vous retiriés au bagaige avecques les pages et laquais, ou bien (car j'ay pitié de vous) soubs les fraiz umbraiges, aux sumptueux palais des grands seigneurs & cours magnifiques des princes, entre les dames & damoizelles, ou votz beaux & mignons ecriz, non de plus longue durée que vostre vie, seront receuz, admirés & adorés.'[2]

In the preface to the first edition of his *Odes* which appeared in the following year Ronsard expresses a similar contempt for the taste of courtiers when he writes: 'Je ne fai point de doute que ma Poësie tant varie ne semble facheuse aus oreilles de nos rimeurs, & principalement des courtizans qui n'admirent qu'un petit sonnet petrarquizé, ou quelque mignardise d'amour qui continue tousjours en son propos.'[3] The contrast between the Pléiade's ideal of poetry filled with what Ronsard called 'rare et antique érudition' and that of the court poet is vividly brought out by the highly satirical poem, 'Le Poete courtisan', which Du Bellay published in 1559, towards the end of his short career:

> Je veux en premier lieu que sans suivre la trace
> (Comme font quelques uns) d'un Pindare & Horace,
> Et sans vouloir comme eux voler si haultement,
> Ton simple naturel tu suives seulement.
> Ce proces tant mené, & qui encore dure,
> Lequel des deux vault mieulx, ou l'art, ou la Nature,
> En matiere de vers, à la court est vuidé:
> Car il suffit icy que tu soyes guidé
> Par le seul naturel, sans art & sans doctrine,
> Fors cest art qui apprend a faire bonne mine.
> Car un petit sonnet qui n'ha rien que le son,
> Un dixain a propos, ou bien une chanson,
> Un rondeau bien troussé, avec' une ballade,
> (Du temps qu'elle couroit) vault mieux qu'une *Iliade*.
> Laisse moy doncques là ces Latins & Gregeoys,
> Qui ne servent de rien au poëte François,
> Et soit la seule court ton Virgile & Homere,
> Puis qu'elle est (comme on dit) des bons esprits la mere.

---

[1] *La Deffence et Illustration de la langue francoyse*, ed.Chamard, H. Paris, 1948, pp. 180–1.
[2] Ibid. p. 173.   [3] *Œuvres complètes*, i. 47.

La court te fournira d'argumens suffisants
Et seras estimé entre les mieulx disants.
Non comme ces resveurs, qui rougissent de honte
Fors entre les sçavants, desquels on ne fait compte.[1]

Yet despite this haughty attitude towards what they regarded as the ignorance and bad taste of the court, despite their devotion to Classical models and their high idea of a learned poetry written in French, from the very beginning Ronsard and Du Bellay sought favour with the court and turned out the kind of verse which was likely to find favour there, not disdaining any more than other poets of the age to write love-poems on behalf of their royal or aristocratic patrons.

At the other extreme Maurice Scève who wrote for an élite far removed from the 'Peuple au vil gain intentif' and who produced in his collection of love-poems, *Délie, object de plus haulte vertu*, a work of prodigious obscurity which has only quite recently come into fashion again, neither sought nor obtained during his lifetime a wide circle of readers. A contemporary like Étienne Pasquier speaks of Scève's 'sens si tenebreux & obscur, que le lisant, je disois estre trés-content de ne l'entendre, puis qu'il ne vouloit estre entendu':[2] while Peletier du Mans penned lines which might well be addressed to many poets of more recent times:

Tes vers obscurs donnent a maintz espritz
En les lisant, fascherie & torment:
Pource qu'on croit que tu les as escriz
Pour parapres y faire le comment,
Ou bien affin, & je ne say s'on ment,
Qu'en eux ne soit ta pensée choisie:
Or s'il y a fruit en ta Poesie,
On le deust lire a clair sans commentaire:
Mais si tu veux cacher ta fantaisie,
Il ne faudroit seulement que te taire.[3]

But then Scève could please himself as to how and what he wrote; he was obviously not seeking to attract royal or noble patronage. His *Délie*, first published in Lyons in 1544, was reprinted in Paris in 1564, but it had to wait nearly three hundred years for a third edition, until 1862.

The history of the theatre in the sixteenth century remains somewhat

[1] *Œuvres poétiques*, ed. H. Chamard, 6 vols., Paris, 1908–31, vi. 152–3.
[2] *Œuvres*, 2 vols., Amsterdam, 1723, i. 702.
[3] *Œuvres poétiques*, ed. M. Françon, Rochecorbon, 1958, p. 277.

confused, partly for lack of documentary evidence. Although many plays which were written in this period remained unpublished and have frequently been lost, a great number are preserved in print and some went through a substantial number of editions, those of Robert Garnier, for instance. Particularly in the first half of the century medieval forms of drama—mysteries, moralities, miracles, and farces—continued to flourish not only in Paris, but in a considerable number of provincial centres, large and small. The Paris Parlement's ban on the performance of 'Mysteres sacrez' in 1548 may have prevented their continued performance in the capital, but neither it nor subsequently the Parlements of Bordeaux and Rennes stopped the continued performance of this type of medieval drama over the length and breadth of France, in places well into the seventeenth century.

Two important changes in the theatrical world did, however, occur in the course of this century. The first was the emergence, from the 1540s onwards, of companies of professional actors. It is true that to begin with these appear to have consisted of a mere handful of members and to have lacked actresses, but by the end of the century companies of strolling players were to be found in a great many French provinces, and they also carried French plays to the Low Countries and Germany even if, despite the ending of the Wars of Religion, none was yet able to secure a permanent foothold in Paris. There in 1548 the Confrérie de la Passion had moved into a specially constructed theatre at the Hôtel de Bourgogne, and although the Parlement had imposed restrictions on the kind of plays which it might perform there, it had confirmed its monopoly of theatrical performances in Paris: 'Et deffend ladicte Cour à tous autres de joüer ou representer doresnavant aucuns Jeux ou Mysteres, tant en la ville, Faubourgs que Banlieue de Paris, sinon sous le nom de ladicte Confrairie, & au profit d'icelle . . .'[1] It was not until 1597 that these decidedly crude amateur actors finally abandoned all idea of offering performances themselves and decided that in future they would simply let out their theatre to companies of professional actors. Before that date only one such company is definitely known to have performed there, that of Agnan Sarat and Pierre Dubuc who in 1578 signed an agreement 'par lequel iceux compagnons comédiens promettent de représenter comédies moyennant le prix mentionné au dit marché'.[2] It is certain, however, that in these years theatrical

---

[1] C. and F. Parfaict, *Histoire du théâtre français* ii. 3–4.
[2] S. W. Deierkauf-Holsboer, *Le Théâtre de l'Hôtel de Bourgogne*, 2 vols., Paris, 1968–70, i. 25.

performances by professional companies were given elsewhere in Paris. We know of this because the Confrérie made vigorous efforts to enforce its monopoly; in 1584 a company which performed at the Hôtel de Cluny was compelled by the Parlement to leave Paris. The Confrérie tended to be less successful in dealing with infractions of their monopoly by other professional actors—the companies of Italian actors who made frequent visits to Paris in the second half of the century—because they had the support of the court which had invited them to come to France.[1] The first recorded visits of Italian actors to the court and to Paris took place towards the end of the reign of Charles IX in 1571 and 1572, and others were to follow under Henry III in 1577, 1583, and 1584; they were to be continued during the reign of Henry IV.[2]

In addition to the gradual emergence of a professional theatre which was to develop more fully in the following period, the sixteenth century also saw an attempt to make a complete break with medieval traditions in drama and to create two new genres, those of tragedy and comedy, based on Classical models. This development was forecast by Du Bellay in rather casual terms when he wrote in his *Deffence et Illustration*: 'Quand aux comedies & tragedies, si les roys & les republiques les vouloint restituer en leur ancienne dignité, qu'ont usurpée les farces & moralitez, je seroy' bien d'opinion que tu t'y employasses, & si tu le veux faire pour l'ornement de ta Langue, tu scais ou tu en doibs trouver les archetypes.'[3] It was the young Jodelle who in the winter of 1552–3 first endeavoured to create this new drama with the production of his tragedy, *Cléopâtre captive*, and his comedy, *Eugène*. These were not performed at the Hôtel de Bourgogne, but were simply given two amateur performances on improvised stages, the first at the Hôtel de Reims at which Henry II was present, and the second at the Collège de Boncourt where, according to Pasquier, 'toutes les fenêtres estoient tapissées d'une infinité de personnages d'honneur, & la Cour si pleine d'escoliers que les portes du College en regorgeoient. . . . Et les entreparleurs estoient tous hommes de nom: Car mesme Remy Belleau, & Jean de La Peruse, jouoient les principaux roullets'.[4] From the first, in contrast to the traditional forms of drama, comedy and tragedy based on Classical models were intended for an audience

---

[1] Ibid. i. 25–7.

[2] A. Baschet, *Les Comédiens italiens à la cour de France sous Charles IX, Henri III, Henri IV et Louis XIII*, Paris, 1882.

[3] pp. 125–6. 　　　　　[4] *Œuvres*, i. 704.

restricted to a relatively small section of the community, from the king and court down to the tiny minority of the population which had received a classical education. Between *Cléopâtre captive* and the end of the century a considerable number of tragedies were printed, though only Robert Garnier with eight plays (one of them a tragicomedy) can be said to have made a really substantial contribution to the new genre. Comedies were fewer in number; only one writer, Pierre Larivey published any considerable quantity, and his nine plays, published between 1579 and 1611, were merely adaptations from the Italian. The professional playwright—and then at first only in the form of a *poète à gages*, the hired poet of a company of actors—was not to emerge until the end of the century with Alexandre Hardy.

Performances of comedies in French at court were not unknown in the second half of the century, but, when the disorders of the time allowed of such entertainments, its taste ran more to ballet and to the *commedia dell'arte*; tragedy, on the other hand, despite Henry II's enthusiasm for Jodelle's *Cléopâtre*, never really secured a foothold there, largely it is said because of Catherine de Médicis's aversion to this form of drama. If performances of these plays were often first given by amateurs such as students or the author's friends, there seems no doubt that they were eventually taken up by the professional touring companies. For instance, in 1594 when the actor, Adrien Talmy, petitioned the authorities at Arras to allow his company to perform there, he placed at the head of the list of the plays which it was proposed to produce 'Premierement *les Juifves*, aultrement dict *Captivité de Sedicie soubs Nabuchodonosor* ainsy qu'elles sont redigez par Robert Garnier en ses tragedies; ensemble *la Troade, les Amours de Phedre à Hipolite*, comme contenu dans ledict Garnier . . .'[1]

What complicates the history of this new genre in the last half of the sixteenth century is that the use of the word 'tragédie' on the title-page of a play can be misleading. On the one hand, this designation is frequently given to plays which remained in the medieval tradition of drama. More important is its use in a type of play which emerged in the last quarter of the century and which it is nowadays fashionable to call 'baroque'—a tragedy which ignored such conventions as the unities and the ban on physical action on the stage underlying the new form of drama based on that of the Ancients. In contact with audiences up and down the country and at the hands of that prolific writer, Alexandre

[1] R. Lebègue, 'Le Répertoire d'une troupe française à la fin du XVIe siècle', *Revue d'histoire du théâtre*, 1948, pp. 15–16.

Hardy, tragedy became something very different from,what the theorists of the Pléiade had imagined it was going to be.

Traditionally, the various forms of medieval drama from mysteries to farces contained elements which might appeal to a very wide range of spectators from kings to the plebs, from the learned to the wholly illiterate. Although when the Confrères de la passion petitioned the Parlement for a renewal of their privileges, they declared that hitherto 'il leur étoit loisible faire joüer & representer par personnages plusieurs beaux Mysteres à l'édification & joye du commun populaire',[1] Francis I did not disdain to attend performances of mysteries; we know that in 1539, along with his sons and courtiers, he was present at a performance of one given by the Confrérie. All over France groups of amateurs continued to perform plays of the older type right to the end of the century and beyond. What sort of audiences these attracted it is difficult to say, but in Paris as long as the Confrérie de la Passion continued to give performances at the Hôtel de Bourgogne, they appear to have been largely plebeian. In 1588 a certain Rolland du Plessis in his *Remonstrances très humbles au Roy de France* denounced

les ieux et spectacles publics qui se font lesdits iours de festes et Dimanches, tant par les estrangers Italiens que par des François, et par dessus tous ceux qui se font en une Cloaque & maison de Sathan, nommee l'hostel de Bourgongne par ceux qui abusivement se disent Confraires de la Passion de Jesus-Christ.

En ce lieu se donnent mille assignations scandaleuses au preiudice de l'honnesteté & pudicité des femmes & à la ruine des familles des pauvres artisans, desquels la salle basse est toute plaine, & lesquels plus de deux heures avant le jeu, passent leur temps en devis impudiques, en ieux de cartes & de dez, en gourmandise & yvrongnerie tout publiquement, d'où viennent plusieurs querelles & batteries . . .

Par ce moyen Dieu est grandement offensé tant en laditte transgression des festes, que par les susdits blasphemes, ieux & impudicitez qui s'y commettent. D'avantage Dieu y est courroucé en l'abus et prophanation des choses sainctes, dont ils le servent. Et le public interessé par la desbauche et ieux des artisans. . . .

Ceux qui deffendent telles choses disent une seule raison d'apparance, assavoir que tels ieux & spectacles sont bons pour le menu peuple, afin de le destourner des berlans & autres desbauches qu'il fait lesdits iours de festes, & qu'apres avoir travaillé toute la sepmaine en peine & tristesse, cela luy sert de resioüyssance & plaisir, & le retire de vices plus grands.[1]

[1] C. and F. Parfaict, *Histoire du théâtre français* ii. 3.
[2] pp. 182–7.

If one cannot take at its face value this puritanical denunciation of the contemporary theatre, it makes it clear that such audiences were at least extremely mixed and that the lower orders still participated in such theatrical performances as were available in the capital.

The new forms of drama established in the second half of the century by the Pléiade and its followers were aimed, as we have seen, at a much more select group of spectators. In so far as the tragedies and comedies composed in this period were actually performed by amateurs or professional actors in Paris or at various places in the provinces, they too must in practice have been seen for the most part by fairly mixed audiences. The court, partly owing to the disorders from which France suffered for some forty years in the second half of the century, did not exercise the influence on drama which it was to have in the seventeenth century. Yet the advent of Renaissance drama with its deliberate appeal to a relatively restricted section of the community did at least fore-shadow the narrowing of theatre audiences which was to occur in the following century.

So far as relations between writer and public are concerned, the sixteenth century marks a decided movement away from medieval times towards a state of affairs more familiar to the modern reader. If literacy was still too thinly spread for the invention of printing to have anything like its full impact, it had already produced what, compared with conditions in the age of manuscripts, was a massive diffusion of books in general and of works written in French in particular. Although most writers were still heavily dependent on patronage, by at least the second half of the century they were beginning to receive modest sums for their works from printers and booksellers, and this process was to continue in the next century even though it was not until much later that writers in France could make themselves independent of patron-age. Although the professional playwright had not yet appeared, he was soon to do so thanks to the emergence of a professional theatre; earnings from writing for the stage were eventually to make an import-ant contribution to the gradual emancipation of the writer from patronage, though in the process the audience for which plays were written became a much narrower one than it had been in earlier centuries.

III The Seventeenth Century

ONE striking feature of the literature of seventeenth-century France compared with that of the previous age is the way in which it was firmly concentrated in Paris where the court and government were now established at the centre of an increasingly centralized country. Not only were practically all new books printed and published there, but it was in Paris that the relatively narrow public known in the language of the time as 'la cour et la ville' had its tastes catered for by writers who flocked to the capital from all corners of France. There were, of course, very large numbers of Parisians among them, starting with Molière and Boileau, and others like Racine and La Fontaine came from relatively near to the capital. Pierre Corneille, like any other writer from the provinces, hastened to seek a reputation in Paris, but only deserted Rouen and settled in the capital when he was fifty-six; but this was exceptional. Throughout this period writers from all over France came to Paris and the court and settled there as soon as they could. Malherbe came from Caen (he was already fifty by the time he managed to secure a foothold at court) and Théophile de Viau from near Agen, in the south-west. Guez de Balzac belonged to the region rather further north, around Angoulême, and d'Urfé to the Forez on the eastern side of the Massif Central. Voiture was from Amiens, but Cyrano de Bergerac, despite his name, came from Paris. In this period there was no provincial centre famed for its writers, printers, and book-sellers as Lyons had been in the sixteenth century: literature was produced in Paris and in the first instance at least catered for the tastes of the court and polite society there.

This concentration of literature in the capital inevitably restricted its audience. With the expansion of the kingdom under Louis XIV fresh foreign tongues were added to those already spoken—Flemish, Catalan, and the German of Alsace—while in the south Occitan was only slowly losing ground. A contemporary writer makes a clear distinction between the languages spoken in the regions north and south of the Loire: 'Aujourd'hui chaque province a sa façon de parler et ses dialectes. Toutefois l'on y reconnaît en gros une différence de langage entre les provinces qui sont deçà Loire et celles qui sont delà. Les uns parlent français et les autres gascon, prenant ce terme-là comme on le prend communément à Paris pour ceux du Languedoc et du Dauphiné, de la Provence et de la Guyenne prise en ses plus larges limites.'[1]

A letter of Racine to La Fontaine gives a well-known, though no doubt somewhat highly coloured account of the tribulations of a Frenchman from the north when he crossed the linguistic frontier. Racine's troubles began long before he reached his journey's end at Uzès in Languedoc:

J'avais commencé dès Lyon à ne plus guère entendre le langage du pays, et à n'être plus intelligible moi-même. Ce malheur s'accrut à Valence, et Dieu voulut qu'ayant demandé à une servante un pot de chambre, elle mit un réchaud sous mon lit. Vous pouvez vous imaginer les suites de cette maudite aventure, et ce qui peut arriver à un homme endormi qui se sert d'un réchaud dans ses nécessités de nuit. Mais c'est encore bien pis en ce pays. Je vous jure que j'ai autant besoin d'un interprète, qu'un Moscovite en aurait besoin dans Paris. Néanmoins je commence à m'apercevoir que c'est un langage mêlé d'espagnol et d'italien: et comme j'entends assez bien ces deux langues, j'y ai quelquefois recours pour entendre les autres, et pour me faire entendre. Mais il arrive souvent que j'y perds toutes mes mesures, comme il arriva hier, qu'ayant besoin de petits clous à broquette pour ajuster ma chambre, j'envoyai le valet de mon oncle en ville, et lui dis de m'acheter deux ou trois cents de broquettes: il m'apporta incontinent trois bottes d'allumettes. Jugez s'il y a sujet d'enrager en de semblables malentendus. Cela irait à l'infini si je voulais vous dire tous les inconvénients qui arrivent aux nouveaux venus en ce pays comme moi.[2]

In such regions of France both preaching and elementary teaching (where it was available) were no doubt given in the local dialect.

For instance, the bishop who succeeded Antoine Godeau, one of the poets who had adorned the *salon* of Mme de Rambouillet and who had been given the sees of Grasse and Vence by Richelieu, said of him: 'Vous l'avez vu souvent, au milieu des enfants et des paysans, leur enseigner la doctrine en leur idiome vulgaire; vous l'avez admiré dans les visites de ce diocèse, s'efforçant de faire des sermons en proven-çal avec un abaissement extrême et une charité inconcevable.'[3] At Uzès Racine found it singularly embarrassing not to be able to speak with the *curés* and schoolmasters whom he encountered there:

[1] C. de Varennes, *Le Voyage de France*, Paris, 1643, pp. 16–17.
[2] *Œuvres complètes*, ed. R. Picard, 2 vols., Paris, 1950–2, ii. 401–2.
[3] A. Cognet, *Antoine Godeau, évêque de Grasse et de Vence*, Paris 1900, p. 358.

On me fait ici force caresses à cause de mon oncle. Il n'y a pas un curé ni un maître d'école qui ne m'ait fait le compliment gaillard, auquel je ne saurais répondre que par des révérences, car je n'entends pas le français de ce pays, et on n'entend pas le mien: ainsi je tire le pied fort humblement; et je dis, quand tout est fait: *Adiousias.* Je suis marri de ne les point entendre pourtant, car si je continue davantage à ne leur pouvoir répondre, j'aurai bientôt la réputation d'un incivil ou d'un homme non lettré.[1]

Alongside such evidence one must, of course, set such facts as that in the years which they spent in the provinces from 1645 to 1658 Molière and his company appear to have performed mainly in the southern half of France and to have found audiences to support them. Yet obviously there is a considerable difference between being able to understand a language and being able to speak and write it fluently and correctly. There is no question that the number of people capable of appreciating literature written in the language of Paris and the court was severely restricted at this period.

On the other hand, by the second half of the seventeenth century French books had begun to acquire an international market as the language attained a new popularity in other European countries. It was steadily replacing Latin as the language of the world of learning and becoming the second language of cultured people everywhere. Writing in 1684 from his exile in Holland, Bayle could declare:

Tout le monde veut savoir parler français, on regarde cela comme une preuve de bonne éducation; on s'étonne de l'entêtement qu'on a pour cette langue, et cependant on n'en revient point; il y a telle ville où pour une école latine, on en peut bien compter dix ou douze de françaises; on traduit partout les ouvrages des anciens, et les savants commencent à craindre que le latin ne soit chassé de son ancienne possession.[2]

A number of French periodicals were published outside France, and, the market for French books being vast, they were printed in Holland and half a dozen other European countries. While this provided possibilities of publication for French writers who harboured thoughts judged dangerous by the authorities at home, the pirating of almost any book published in France which made its mark meant that its author was deprived of part of his legitimate earnings since such works could often be bought inside the national frontiers.

It is obvious that inside France the number of people able to read,

---

[1] *Œuvres complètes*, ii. 405.
[2] *Nouvelles de la République des Lettres*, 7 vols., Amsterdam, 1684–7, ii. 618–19, Aug. 1684.

let alone write, was still extremely small. It is true that the movement stimulated by the Reformation, for the Protestant minority, and by the Counter-Reformation, for the overwhelmingly Catholic majority, led in the seventeenth century to a considerable, though extremely patchy development of elementary education. Indeed, in 1698 there issued forth from Versailles a solemn royal declaration which laid down the principle of compulsory primary education; but its real object was only to secure that the children 'dont les pères et les mères ont fait profession de la religion prétendue réformée' should be instructed in the Catholic faith. It is merely as a kind of afterthought that it adds the words 'comme aussi pour apprendre à lire et même à écrire à ceux qui pourront en avoir besoin'. Needless to say, such Protestant schools as had existed had been closed long before this declaration appeared.

There was undoubtedly considerable interest in elementary education, particularly in the Catholic Church which down to the Revolution was to keep it under strict control. Religious orders such as the Ursulines were founded for the education of girls, and at the end of the century Jean Baptiste de la Salle set up the Frères de la doctrine chrétienne who did a great deal for elementary education in the towns. Elementary schools existed all over France, but in very varying quantities. Naturally, the towns were generally better provided than most of the country though in some regions most parishes had schools. There were the so-called *petites écoles* which, in addition to offering religious instruction, taught reading, writing, and elementary arithmetic. These were fee-paying, but there were also charity schools. In addition, in the towns there were guilds of scriveners (*maîtres écrivains*) who, among other activities, taught their art and such things as elementary mathematics and accounts; they took their pupils from a very wide age group and even taught some girls.

However, the great bulk of elementary education was under the direct control of the Catholic Church. One bizarre consequence of this was that boys and girls continued for the most part to learn to read in Latin, not because Latin was a more phonetic language than French, but because the first task of their mentors was to familiarize them with the service of the Catholic Church. Only after they had learned to read in Latin were they taught to read in French. The progressive theorists of the time protested against this practice, but in vain. It goes without saying that even where there were *petites écoles* or other forms of elementary education the pupils did not get anywhere near an initiation into French literature.

There are no statistics whatever to tell us how many children at any period in the seventeenth century received an education of this kind. Even when it was available (and theoretically there ought to have been two schools in every parish as the Church insisted on keeping boys and girls apart), attendance was no doubt very sporadic except possibly in winter. How far education at this level penetrated we have no better means of telling than the results of the inquiry published in 1880 by a retired *recteur*, Louis Maggiolo, into the number of men and women who on marriage could sign their name in the register at various dates in the past, starting with the period 1686–90.[1] This inquiry had its weaknesses; it could not include Paris (its parish registers had gone up in smoke in the Commune) and the *instituteurs* who were responsible for carrying it out did so with varying degrees of zeal. Above all, the ability to write one's name, elegantly or clumsily, tells one very little about an individual's educational attainments and in particular about his ability to read. However, these are the only figures we have. According to them 21 per cent of the men and women in the period 1686–90 were able to sign their names in the parish register when they married. Two things stand out clearly from this inquiry. The proportion of men able to sign their names was double that of women—29 per cent against 14; the education of girls was to remain much neglected until the second half of the nineteenth century. In this period as in the later ones investigated by Maggiolo two Frances emerge: one to the north of a line drawn from Mont-Saint-Michel to Geneva, relatively well provided for, the other to the south of this line, in a much more backward state. It should be added that the hundred years between 1686–90 and 1786–90 saw a substantial improvement; the number of women able to sign their names very nearly doubled, and there was also a very considerable rise in the number of men able to do so.

We are somewhat better informed about the development of higher and secondary education in this period, although statistical detail is mostly lacking. Here Latin continued to be almost exclusively the medium of instruction, certainly in the faculties of theology, law, and medicine which alone corresponded to our universities, and it was very nearly so in the colleges run by the universities and by such religious

---

[1] The results of this inquiry are conveniently summarized and critically examined in M. Fleury and P. Valmary, 'Les Progrès de l'instruction élémentaire de Louis XIV à Napoléon III d'après l'enquête de Louis Maggiolo (1877–1879)', *Population*, 1957, pp. 71–92.

orders as the Jesuits and the Oratorians which corresponded to our secondary schools. The boys who frequented them were generally thrown straight into their Latin grammar composed in Latin verse. The Oratorian Malebranche protested against this practice in *La Recherche de la vérité*:

N'est-il pas évident qu'il faut se servir de ce qu'on sait pour apprendre ce qu'on ne sait pas, et que ce serait se moquer d'un Français que de lui donner une grammaire en vers allemands pour lui apprendre l'allemand ? Cependant on met entre les mains des enfants les vers latins de Despautère pour leur apprendre le latin, des vers obscurs en toutes manières à des enfants qui ont même de la difficulté à apprendre les choses les plus faciles.[1]

It was only gradually, in the second half of the century, that some progress was made towards teaching the French language, but this did not occur by any means in all schools and, where instruction in it was given, this was confined to the lower forms. French literature was naturally not taught in any way; Latin verse continued to exercise an enormous attraction for the more learned writers of the time, at any rate down to the 1660s: Father Rapin's famous poem, *Hortorum libri IV*, was published in 1665. Yet although theological, legal, scientific, and other works continued to be written in Latin, their production was definitely declining. In 1665 we find Chapelain writing sadly to a scholar in Strasbourg about the unwillingness of Paris publishers to take on learned works in Latin:

Nous éprouvons la même supinité en nos libraires de deçà pour les grandes et solides entreprises. L'esprit des Avences, des Étiennes, des Turnèbes et des Vascosans n'anime plus la presse, et lorsqu'il s'agit de mettre au jour quelque ouvrage des Anciens ou en langue ancienne, aucun d'eux n'y veut mordre, et ils ne prêtent l'oreille qu'à des traductions en langue vulgaire, à des comédies ou à des romans, parce que notre cour est ignorante et qu'elle n'achète que de ces bagatelles-là.[2]

There was, as we shall see, a considerable gulf between the taste of the learned and that of the court and those under its influence.

We have no means of telling how many students frequented the French faculties of theology, law, and medicine in the seventeenth century, but by present-day standards their numbers must have been tiny. We are somewhat better informed about the secondary colleges,

---

[1] *Œuvres complètes*, ed. H. Gouhier, 20 vols., Paris, 1958–68, iii. 8.
[2] *Lettres*, ed. T. de Larroque, 2 vols., Paris, 1880–3, ii. 376.

thanks largely to the patient researches of Father François de Dainville.[1] Although there remain all sorts of gaps in our knowledge, two things in particular stand out. Firstly, these colleges (those of the Jesuits were free) drew in boys from a wide variety of social groups; their pupils were by no means confined to the more aristocratic and wealthy sections of the community. Sons of artisans and peasants formed quite a sizeable minority. Secondly, in addition to the larger colleges, many of which took those of their pupils who cared to stay on as far as the final years of philosophy, there were scattered over the country a great many smaller schools which fed the larger ones. This relatively generous provision of some form of secondary education was far from meeting with universal approval. Richelieu was only one among many who denounced this state of affairs when he wrote in his *Testament politique*:

Comme la connaissance des lettres est tout à fait nécessaire à une république, il est certain qu'elles ne doivent pas être indifféremment enseignées à tout le monde.

Ainsi qu'un corps, qui aurait des yeux en toutes ses parties, serait monstrueux, de même un État le serait-il, si tous les sujets étaient savants. On y verrait aussi peu d'obéissance que l'orgueil et la présomption y seraient ordinaires; le commerce des lettres bannirait absolument celui de la marchandise, qui comble les États de richesses; il ruinerait l'agriculture, vraie mère nourrice des peuples, et il déserterait en peu de temps la pépinière des soldats, qui s'élèvent plutôt dans la rudesse de l'ignorance que dans la politesse des sciences; il remplirait enfin la France de chicaneurs plus propres à ruiner les familles et troubler le repos public qu'à procurer aucun bien aux États.[2]

His remedy is simple and brutal—'réduire tous les collèges des villes, qui ne sont pas métropolitaines, à 3 ou 4 classes suffisantes pour tirer la jeunesse d'une ignorance grossière'.[3] Twice during the reign of Louis XIV, in 1667 and 1685, the government ordered its *intendants* to conduct a census of the schools of this type in their *généralités* with the plain object of reducing their numbers. However, no action was ever taken and what appears to have reduced numbers in schools much more in the closing part of the reign was the economic depression which France went through. Far from seeing a decline in the importance of

---

[1] See his 'Effectifs des collèges et scolarité aux XVIIe et XVIIIe siècles dans le Nord-Est de la France', *Population*, 1955, pp. 455–88, and 'Collèges et fréquentation scolaire au XVIIe siècle', ibid., 1957, pp. 467–94.

[2] *Testament politique*, ed. L. André, Paris, 1947, p. 204.

[3] Ibid. p. 206.

such schools, the eighteenth century was to witness their further growth, which produced a renewal of hostility to them in some quarters.

Not only was the audience of the seventeenth-century writer severely restricted, but he was by no means free to communicate directly with it. Here it is a curious fact that the government took much more decisive action against dangerous thoughts expressed in print than against those expressed on the stage. It is true that in 1619 the *lieutenant civil* of Paris decreed that before performing any plays or farces the actors must submit them first to the *procureur du roi*,[1] but this seems to have remained a dead letter. We hear occasionally of plays being taken off suddenly after one or more performances; but there was no question of a playwright having to submit his work for examination before it could be performed. It appears that Cyrano de Bergerac's *La Mort d'Agrippine* had to be taken off hastily; it is notorious that Molière, after giving a first performance of *Tartufe* at Versailles, had to battle for five years to secure the right to perform it in public, while after giving fifteen lucrative performances of his *Dom Juan* down to Easter 1665, he did not continue with it after the usual break, presumably because the authorities had given him a pretty broad hint not to do so. Later in the century, in 1687, Campistron's tragedy, *Phraate*, had to be withdrawn after only three performances, and in 1697 the Italian actors were expelled from France after they had put on a play called *La Fausse Prude* which appears to have reflected adversely on Mme de Maintenon.

No doubt authors in this period generally exercised considerable caution over what they put into their plays, and the actors too over what they performed; but the fact remains that it was not until 1701, perhaps even 1706, that manuscripts of plays had to be submitted to an official censor and given his approval before they could be put on the stage.[2]

Very different was the position in the book trade which hitherto had been partly free, partly regulated by the government. In 1618 letters patent established a guild for the printers, booksellers, and binders of Paris, and from this date down to the Revolution government control over the book trade became more and more rigorous. These letters patent laid it down that 'pour éviter aux abus, désordres et confusion qui arrivent journellement par l'impression d'infinis livres scandaleux, libelles diffamatoires sans noms d'auteurs, ni du lieu où ils sont

---

[1] N. de Lamare, *Traité de la police*, 4 vols., Paris, 1705–38, i. 440.
[2] P. Mélèse, *Le Théâtre et le public à Paris sous Louis XIV (1659–1715)*, Paris, 1934, pp. 79–80.

imprimés' which it blamed on the excessive numbers of printers, book-sellers, and binders in Paris, in future only one of each of these was to be admitted each year so as to reduce their numbers.[1] They also ordered the *syndic* of the guild and his deputies to examine all books brought into Paris and to confiscate all 'livres ou libelles diffamatoires contre l'honneur de Dieu, bien et repos de l'État, imprimés sans nom d'auteur et le nom du libraire où ils auraient été imprimés ou contrefaits sur ceux qui auraient été imprimés par aucuns des libraires de cette ville de Paris.[2] The same letters patent also regulated the status of the *colporteurs* who had emerged during the Wars of Religion:

Les colporteurs ne pourront tenir apprentis, magasin, ni boutique, ni imprimer, ni faire imprimer en leurs noms; mais porteront au col, dans une balle, pour vendre les almanachs, édits et petits livres, qui ne passeront point huit feuilles, brochés ou reliés à la corde, et imprimés par un libraire ou maître imprimeur de cette ville de Paris, auquel sera son nom, sa marque et sa permission; le tout à peine de confiscation et de dix écus d'amende.[3]

The Crown was determined that it should no longer share the task of censoring books either with the Parlement or the Faculty of Theology at the Sorbonne. The Ordonnance de Moulins had forbidden the publication of 'aucuns livres ou traités sans notre congé et permission, et lettres de privilége expédiées sous notre grand scel'.[4] A *privilège* was not, of course, granted unless the Chancellor was satisfied that the work had been approved by a censor, but until the 1620s religious works were often examined by members of the Faculty of Theology who had not been appointed by him. This situation was finally brought to an end in 1629 by the Code Michaux which made it clear that a *privilège* could not be granted unless 'il n'ait été présenté une copie du livre manuscrit à nos chancelier ou garde des sceaux, sur laquelle ils commettront telles personnes qu'ils verront être à faire selon le sujet et matière du livre, pour le voir et examiner'.[5] In other words, henceforth all manuscripts were to be examined by a censor appointed by the Chancellor. By the 1630s the system seems to have been working pretty thoroughly if we may judge by a letter of Mersenne to Descartes, written in 1637, after the foundation of the Académie française: 'Jamais on ne fut plus exact qu'à présent pour l'examen des livres, car Monsieur le Chancelier a des agents affidés pour juger ce qui est pour la

---

[1] Isambert, *Recueil général des anciennes lois françaises* xvi. 121.
[2] Ibid. xvi. 122.   [3] Ibid. 123.   [4] Ibid. xiv. 210.
[5] Ibid. xvi. 238–9.

théologie, d'autres pour la politique, l'Académie de Paris pour les pièces tant en vers qu'en prose, et des mathématiciens pour le reste.'[1]

As can well be imagined, control over the whole book trade was greatly strengthened at the high point of absolutism, under Colbert and his successors. In 1666 an *arrêt du Conseil* forbade the admission of any new printers to the Paris guild and shortly afterwards twelve printers were ordered to close down. Until 1683 only two new printers and five booksellers could (with royal permission) be admitted to the guild. Although the government ordered a census of all printers and booksellers throughout France, its restrictive measures do not seem to have had much effect outside the capital. Even in Paris, while there was certainly a reduction in the number of printers and printing-works, this was not as drastic as might have been expected. An *arrêt du Conseil* of 1683 laid it down that the number of Paris printing-works should not exceed thirty-six and that no more master printers should be admitted to the guild until they had been reduced to the same number. Yet when a fresh census was taken in 1701, there were still fifty-one printing-works in Paris. It was mainly the smaller ones which had gone; this undoubtedly contributed to a certain concentration in the industry.

What happened in Paris was now of fundamental importance. Gone were the days when provincial centres like Rouen or even more Lyons had vied with the capital in the production of new books. Not only was this now virtually monopolized by the Paris printers and booksellers, but the fact that in the second half of the century they could count on securing the renewal of their *privilèges* meant that little was left for the provincial printers and booksellers to do in the way of book production except for turning out surreptitiously pirated editions. The appointment of La Reynie as *lieutenant de police* in 1667 meant more energetic steps to prevent the printing of 'mauvais livres' on clandestine presses in the capital. Printing-works were closely inspected and steps were taken to control the transfer of presses and type-cases. La Reynie also endeavoured to see that the books which arrived from the provinces and abroad were closely examined by the *syndic* of the guild and his deputies.[2]

The appointment of a new Chancellor, Pontchartrain, in 1697, led to a reinforcement of government control. He put at the head of the newly

---

[1] *Correspondance*, ed. C. de Waard and B. Rochot, Paris, 1932—, vi. 188.

[2] The results of their handiwork can be seen in Anne Sauvy, *Livres saisis à Paris entre 1678 et 1701*, The Hague, 1972.

created Bureau de la librairie his nephew, abbé Jean Paul Bignon. The latter proceeded to order a census of printers, booksellers, and binders for the whole of France. This took place in 1701 and three years later an *arrêt du Conseil* fixed (in a downward sense naturally) the number of printers who might be established in each town. The census had revealed the following number of printing-works in the principal centres:

Paris 51	Troyes 11
Lyons 29	Toulouse 11
Rouen 29	Rennes 8
Bordeaux 12	Strasbourg 8[1]
Caen 12	

Only a minority of these actually printed books. All these numbers were to be gradually reduced in the course of the eighteenth century. The central government was increasingly hostile to provincial printers who were less easy to control than those in Paris. It is characteristic of this attitude that Pontchartrain should have written to the *Intendant* of Rouen in 1701 that 'l'impression des mauvais livres se fait à Rouen avec plus de liberté que jamais'.[2]

This period also saw a more restrictive attitude to the granting of permissions to publish. In 1701 letters patent differentiated clearly between (1) a *privilège* valid for the whole of France, (2) a local *privilège*, and (3) a *permission* which conferred no sort of monopoly either general or local and did not prevent another printer from issuing or reissuing the same work. At the same time, the preliminary censorship was tightened up. By this date there were already a large number of official censors (fifty-six for the period 1699–1704): these were, incidentally, men of high standing in their particular speciality. They included, for instance, Fontenelle as well as distinguished doctors, scholars, and scientists. The censor gave his opinion, favourable or otherwise, but the final decision for or against a work lay with the Chancellor. One result of the ever more repressive policies of Louis XIV was to increase the prosperity of foreign publishers and printers, particularly the Dutch. In order to try to stem the flood of French books published abroad and smuggled into France, in 1710 it was laid down that all books coming from outside France must be examined

---

[3] C. Lanette-Claverie, 'La Librairie française en 1700', *Revue française d'histoire du livre*, 1972, p. 11.

[2] Quoted by J. Quéniart, *L'Imprimerie et la librairie à Rouen au XVIIIe siècle*, Paris, 1969, pp. 22–3.

either in Paris or in a selected number of provincial towns—Rouen,
Nantes, Bordeaux, Marseilles, Lyons, Strasbourg, Metz, Rheims, and
Amiens (Lille was soon added to the list), but these efforts were in vain.

The fate meted out to printers, booksellers, and writers when they
came into contact with the repressive machine of an absolute monarchy
could be extremely brutal. If the opening decades of the century were a
period of relative freedom, they also saw bouts of savage repression of
dangerous thoughts. In 1618 the poet, Étienne Durand, was executed in
Paris for composing a satire directed against Louis XIII and the duc de
Luynes, and in the following year the Italian philosopher, Vanini, was
burnt at the stake at Toulouse. Four years later Théophile de Viau was
condemned in his absence to the same fate, a sentence finally reduced to
one of banishment when he was arrested, but his health never recovered
from his imprisonment while awaiting trial, and he died shortly after
his release. In 1662 Claude Le Petit was sent to the stake for his *Bordel
des Muses*. At various periods in the century printers who had infringed the law where whipped, imprisoned, banished, or put to death.

As we have seen, the relations of printers and booksellers with the
state were governed by the issue of *privilèges* by the Chancellor. This
institution which had its origin in the sixteenth century involved both
permission to publish a work and the guarantee of a monopoly of its
publication for a stated term of years. Such *privilèges* were granted not
only for new works, but also on occasion for older ones; moreover,
they could be extended after the first period of years had expired. As
most books in our period were first published in Paris, this gave the
printers and booksellers of the capital a marked advantage over their
provincial competitors who were debarred from reprinting a work if its
original *privilège* was prolonged. Government policy in this matter
underwent considerable fluctuations. In 1618 letters patent severely
restricted such extensions as they forbade Paris printers and booksellers to 'obtenir aucune prolongation des privilèges ... s'il n'y a
augmentation des livres desquels les privilèges sont expirés'.[1] However,
some thirty years later, in 1649, fresh letters patent were issued which
permitted the granting of *privilèges* for older books and allowed the
extension of those which had expired. Although the Paris Parlement
never registered this clause, the legislation brought forward by
Colbert in the 1660s confirmed it, much to the dismay of the provincial
printers and booksellers who were thus deprived of the legal right to
reprint books whose *privilèges* had expired. For the next hundred years

[1] Isambert, xvi. 124.

or so, until the *arrêt du Conseil* of 1777, Paris printers and booksellers, like their counterparts in this country down to a famous judgement by the House of Lords in 1774, enjoyed in practice perpetual copyright in the works which they acquired. Inevitably, their provincial rivals were much aggrieved at this virtual monopoly though they did their best to get their own back by a certain amount of pirate publishing. In 1697 the *Intendant* of Lyons, once the most prosperous provincial centre of of the book trade, after mentioning the decline in its exports to Spain, went on:

Pour ce qui est des livres de France, il ne s'en imprime guère de nouveaux à Lyon parce que les auteurs sont payés bien plus grassement par les libraires de Paris. Il ne saurait non plus s'en imprimer d'anciens à cause des continuations de privilèges, et par là les imprimeurs et libraires de Lyon sont dans une espèce de nécessité de contrefaire les livres de Paris et de pratiquer les contraventions qu'on leur reproche et sans lesquelles ils mourraient de faim.[1]

One would like to compare, both with the sixteenth century and later periods, the scale of the seventeenth-century book trade in Paris and the provinces, but although much statistical material has survived, its incompleteness presents insuperable difficulties of interpretation.

The register of requests for *privilèges* was begun only in 1696, while those for the registration of the *privilèges* granted by the Chancellor run only from 1654 to September 1700 and from 1703 onwards, and those for *permissions* only from 1635 to 1651 and from 1653 to 1664. The obligation to deposit copies of works as they were published led to the production of a series of registers, but anyone interested in book production in this period can derive little from them. Those for the Bibliothèque du roi start only in 1684, and while the registers maintained by the Chambre syndicale cover the period from 1626 to 1704, they were kept so irregularly as to be quite useless to the historian of the book trade.

Graphs based on such unreliable figures tell us little. The number of *privilèges* asked for between 1700 and 1715 is given in figures ranging from 256 to 741 which contrast strangely with the 6, 7, and 60 given for 1697, 1698, and 1699, especially as the numbers of *privilèges* granted for these same three years appear in the registers of the Chambre syndicale as 158, 189, and 134. The statistics for the *dépôt légal* kept by the Chambre syndicale from 1626 to 1704 are quite useless; according to them the number of books deposited ranged from 1,200 in 1676 to none

---

[1] Quoted in Jacqueline Roubert, 'La Situation de l'imprimerie lyonnaise à la fin du XVIIe siècle' in *Cinq études lyonnaises*, Geneva and Paris, 1966, p. 98.

in 1634, 1641, 1647, 1648, 1658, 1660, 1671–4, and 1696. Even in the period after 1715 there are, as we shall see, considerable difficulties in interpreting the fuller figures which are available in these and similar registers.[1]

In any case, one has to remember that in this period an increasing number of French books, many but by no means all reprints, were turned out surreptitiously in the provinces of France and in countries like Holland. From the 1630s onwards the Elzevirs of Leyden produced innumerable pirated editions of successful works; they reprinted *Le Cid* three times between 1638 and 1643. Or to take a later example of a highly successful work, Lesage's *Le Diable boiteux*, a recent detailed examination of the different editions shows that the original bookseller, the Veuve Barbin, brought out four in 1707 and that between that date and 1711 a Lyons bookseller, by agreement with Mme Barbin, brought out another, while three more appeared in Amsterdam as well as four more pirated editions, two of them bearing the name of the original publisher and two no publisher's name but merely a probably bogus place of publication, 'Amsterdam'.[2]

What is more, increasing numbers of French books made their first appearance from foreign printing-presses—not only works like the *Histoire amoureuse des Gaules* or the writings of the *Libertins* or the products of the Huguenot *Refuge*, but even several of the works of Father Malebranche of the Oratory. Even if they could be satisfactorily established, any statistics which took into account only what was officially published in France in this period would be bound to give a false impression of the literary and intellectual life of the country.

Professor Martin has recently endeavoured to approach the problem from a different angle.[3] In order to measure the fluctuations in the production of books in Paris in this period he began by extracting from the first 189 volumes of the *Catalogue général* of printed books in the Bibliothèque nationale some 17,500 volumes published there between 1601 and 1700, ignoring works of less than 48 pages. The

---

[1] Whatever one may think of the results achieved, anyone interested in the history of the French book trade must owe a tremendous debt to the scholarly investigation of sources carried out by Robert Estivals in *Le Dépôt légal sous l'ancien régime de 1537 à 1791*, Paris, 1961, and particularly *La Statistique bibliographique de la France sous la monarchie au XVIIIe siècle*, Paris, 1965.

[2] Lesage, *Le Diable boiteux*, ed. R. Laufer, Paris, 1970, pp. 22–38.

[3] In *Livre, pouvoirs et société au XVIIe siècle (1598–1701)*, 2 vols., Geneva, 1969, a work which covers an enormous amount of ground and to which this chapter is obviously indebted.

drawbacks of this approach are frankly discussed. It is probable, for instance, that the *dépôt légal* worked better at the end of the century than at the beginning and took in reprints as well as original editions; so that the later years are over-represented in the catalogue. Moreover, as the stock of seventeenth-century books printed in Paris has been augmented by gift and purchase down to the present day, it is essentially a haphazard collection in which various periods could be under- or over-represented. What is more, it is pretty certain that its stock of books from this period is overweighted in the direction of the learned; it is, for instance, well known that the Bibliothèque de l'Arsenal is better supplied with editions of seventeenth-century plays than the Bibliothèque nationale.

However, despite these drawbacks Professor Martin goes merrily ahead with his graphs. These are certainly interesting, yet it must be said that where they carry conviction it is simply where they convey the obvious—for example, Graph III. 1 which shows the steady decline in the number of books published in Latin or III. 2 which shows a similar decline in folios and a steep rise in smaller formats. But the really essential graph—'I. Bibliothèque Nationale. Production annuelle conservée (Catalogue auteurs, t.I–CLXXXIX)'—does not tell us, year by year, how many books were printed and published in Paris, but merely what numbers from each year have been preserved in this particular library. It is impossible to draw from it firm deductions about the prosperity or otherwise of the Paris book trade at any given period of the century. Nor do we feel greatly enlightened when we are faced with the graphs which deal with the fortunes of the various literary genres. It is difficult, for instance, to see what is the point of Graph XVI which gives the holdings of the Bibliothèque nationale in editions of comedies, pastoral plays, tragedies, and tragicomedies; it is far less valuable than the graph provided by Professor Scherer in *La Dramaturgie classique en France*[1] which does actually enable the reader, within certain limits carefully defined by the author, to follow through the century the fortunes of the different dramatic genres. Despite all the labour expended on these statistics, this cannot be said to be the most successful part of *Livre, pouvoirs et société*, invaluable as the work undoubtedly is in all sorts of other ways.

Even though it could be wished that far more information were available, it is clear that the financial relations between publishers and writers were still very different from what they are today. The periodi-

[1] Paris, 1950, p. 459.

cal press which in later centuries was to provide writers with both a vehicle for the publication of their works and a source of income was only at its very beginnings in the seventeenth century. The *Gazette*, founded by Théophraste Renaudot in 1631, was merely a news-sheet, and the *Journal des savants*, which dates from 1665, concentrated on new publications and discoveries in the fields of science and learning. Despite its political content with its abject flattery of Louis XIV which secured for it heavy royal subsidies, the *Mercure galant*, founded by Donneau de Visé in 1672 and, after a gap for 1675–6, re-established in 1677, was rather closer to a literary review; but although it enriched its editor (for some years he shared the profits with his partner, Thomas Corneille), it did not provide an outlet for the writings of other authors.

One thing is clear: it was still quite impossible for an author who devoted all his time to writing to make a living by his pen. It is generally held that where the seventeenth-century bookseller made a money payment to an author, this was calculated on the basis of the first printing since, even if there were subsequent editions, the shortness of the period for which *privileges* were granted, meant that once this period had come to an end, any other bookseller was free to reprint the work. In any case, if it was a success, it was certain to be pirated either in the provinces or abroad.

There is, however, some evidence that occasionally contracts did contain a stipulation that the author should obtain an additional payment if his book was reprinted. Moreover, the length of time for which *privilèges* were granted by the Chancellor varied enormously in the course of the century. While it is roughly true to say that they generally expired after five to ten years, there were surprising variations. Corneille's long career furnishes some extraordinary contrasts, particularly in the years down to 1651. In this period the *privilèges* for his plays were mostly given for five, six, seven, or ten years, but a term of twenty years was fixed in 1637 for *La Galerie du Palais*, *La Place royale*, *La Suivante*, and *Le Cid* and again in 1651 for *Pertharite*. In contrast, for the plays of the period 1659–74 *privilèges* were granted for much shorter periods—five, seven, nine, or ten years. By this time the renewal of *privilèges* was becoming almost automatic, and it could hardly be said that with a successful work the bookseller's profit was likely to be limited to what he could get out of the first edition. Thus while La Bruyère's bookseller obtained a ten-year *privilège* for *Les Caractères* in 1687, in 1693 he had no difficulty in securing an extension for a further period of ten years after its expiration. It is true that this did not protect him against pirated versions, but nine editions put out between 1688 and 1696 by the original bookseller made quite a good start for the work.

Whether La Bruyère shared in any way in the profits to be derived from his book is far from clear. It is customary to trot out the passage in which Maupertuis (born in 1698) is made to relate the well-known story:

M. de La Bruyère venait presque journellement s'asseoir chez un libraire nommé Michallet, où il feuilletait les nouveautés et s'amusait avec un enfant fort gentil, fille du libraire, qu'il avait pris en amitié. Un jour, il tira un manuscrit de sa poche, et dit à Michallet: 'Voulez-vous imprimer ceci (c'étaient les *Caractères*)? Je ne sais si vous y trouverez votre compte; mais, en cas de succès, le produit sera la dot de ma petite amie.'[1]

Certainly the name of the bookseller is correct; but it is difficult to see how Mademoiselle Michallet, the daughter of an extremely prosperous printer and bookseller, could have been promised much of a dowry from the sales of the very slim volume which the first edition of *Les Caractères* made.

Many writers of the time seem to have been content to accept from their bookseller a number of free copies of a work (as many as fifty or a hundred) in exchange for the transfer of the *privilège*. We know from the contract which Descartes signed with a Leyden bookseller for the publication of his *Discours de la méthode* that he was due to receive 200 copies of the first two editions, totalling 3,000 copies altogether, covered by the agreement.[2] A cash payment, generally a modest one, seems to have been commoner, though there are also examples of profit-sharing as with Saint-Amant's epic, *Moïse sauvé*, and his *Dernier recueil*.[3] Unfortunately, our information as to the amounts of money involved is extremely scrappy, and writers on the subject find themselves repeating the same few examples. It must be remembered that the payments received were based on relatively small printings, probably of the order of 1,000 to 1,500 copies. We know, for instance, from a lawsuit in 1658 that Corneille's three plays, *Nicomède*, *Androm-ède*, and *Pertharite*, were printed in editions of 1,200 to 1,250 copies,

[1] J. H. S. Formey, *Mémoires de l'Académie des sciences et belles-lettres de Berlin*, Berlin, 1792, pp. 24–5, quoted in La Bruyère, *Œuvres*, ed. G. Servois, 5 vols., Paris, 1882–1922, i, p. cxviii.

[2] G. Cohen, *Écrivains français en Hollande dans la première motié du XVIIe siècle*, Paris, 1920, pp. 503–4.

[3] J. Lagny, *Bibliographie des éditions anciennes des œuvres de Saint-Amant*, Paris, 1961, pp. 56–8, 130–1.

while shortly afterwards the size of the edition of Brébeuf's epic, *Pharsale*, was 1,200.[1]

Some of our information comes from lawsuits concerning pirated editions. For instance, in 1660 1,250 copies of Molière's *Sganarelle ou le cocu imaginaire* were printed for an unauthorized edition,[2] while in the following year 1,500 copies of a pirated edition of various works of Cyrano de Bergerac were confiscated in Paris.[3] At the end of the century we find the Chancellor, Pontchartrain, complaining to the *Intendant* in Rouen about the printing there of two editions of Fénelon's *Télémaque*; these were each said to consist of 1,000 copies.[4]

Examples of the scattered information to be found about payments to authors may well begin with a passage from the 1626 edition of Sorel's *Francion* where the poet Musidore is made to defend writers who receive payment for their work:

Mais quoi, trouvez-vous indécent de se faire donner une récompense par les libraires pour notre labeur? Y sommes-nous pas aussi bien fondés que les avocats à se faire payer pour leurs écritures? Apprenez que s'il y a eu autrefois de la honte à ceci, elle est maintenant toute levée, puisqu'il y a des marquis qui nous en ont frayé le chemin, et quoiqu'ils fissent donner l'argent à leurs valets de chambre comme pour récompense de les avoir servis, cela tournait toujours à leur profit, et les exemptait de payer les gages de leurs serviteurs.[5]

This is undoubtedly a reference to the fact which had come out in a lawsuit that, in addition to receiving for himself sixty copies of the work, d'Urfé made the bookseller pay 1,000 livres to his 'homme de chambre' for the third part of *L'Astrée*, published in 1619.[6] By the standards of the first half of the century this seems to have been a fairly generous payment, though such rare documents as have come down to us are not always easy to interpret. For instance, in 1644 Georges de Scudéry signed an agreement for the publication of his *Discours politiques des des rois* by which he was to receive 800 livres for each of the two parts of the work together with thirty copies; he acknowledged the receipt of 1,000 livres, the remaining 600 livres to be paid when the manuscript of the second part was handed over. In practice, the first

---

[1] Martin, *Livre, pouvoirs et sociéte*, p. 377.
[2] E. Campardon, *Documents inédits sur J. B. Poquelin Molière*, Paris, 1871, p. 5.
[3] Cyrano de Bergerac, *L'Autre Monde*, ed. F. Lachèvre, Paris, 1932, p. lvii.
[4] *Correspondance administrative sous le règne de Louis XIV*, ed. G. B. Depping, 4 vols., Paris, 1850–5, ii. 618–19.
[5] *Francion*, ed. E. Roy, 4 vols., Paris, 1924–31, ii. 91.
[6] Martin, *Livre, pouvoirs et société*, pp. 429, 450.

part of the work did not appear until 1648 and the second part was never published.[1] In the same year Tristan L'Hermite received only 600 livres for three works: 400 livres for *Les Amours* and 100 livres each for his *Œuvres chrétiennes* and *Vers héroïques*.[2] But while the last two works did not appear until 1646 and 1648 respectively, *Les Amours* had been published in 1638; presumably this was payment for a new edition.

Novelists certainly seem to have done fairly well out of booksellers by the middle of the century. At least La Calprenède received 3,000 livres for the second and third parts of his *Cléopâtre* in 1646.[3] In 1654 Scarron was paid the more modest sum of 1,000 livres for the second part of his *Roman comique* which appeared three years later, but one has some difficulty in believing that in 1648 he signed an agreement which gave him 11,000 livres for eleven books of his *Virgile travesti*. Indeed, the scholar who unearthed this agreement added a footnote to this extraordinary figure: 'Vérification faite, il n'y a point d'erreur de lecture.'[4] In the end only seven cantos of the poem appeared, presumably because, having drawn the money, Scarron had no incentive to finish it. He was certainly in the habit of living on booksellers' advances, as in 1653 he handed over a revised edition of his poetry in return for a discharge from debts of this kind. We have unfortunately no precise information about what Mademoiselle de Scudéry earned from her novels, although Tallemant informs us that 'les livres de cette fille se vendent fort bien. Elle en tirait beaucoup; mais son frère s'amusait à acheter des tulipes.'[5]

If the same writer is to be believed, Chapelain did fairly well out of his bookseller when the first part of *La Pucelle* at last appeared in 1656:

Il a dit qu'il lui coûtait quatre mille livres pour les figures qui, par parenthèse, ne valent rien; cependant il est constant qu'outre cent exemplaires que Courbé lui a fournis, dont il y en a plusieurs qui, à cause du grand papier et de la reliure, reviennent à dix écus et davantage, et cinquante qu'il lui a fallu donner encore et qu'il n'a point payés, il est constant que le libraire lui a donné deux mille livres et, depuis, mille livres, quand, pour empêcher la

---

[1] E. Angot, 'Les *Discours politiques des rois* de Georges de Scudéry', *Revue d'histoire littéraire*, 1924, pp. 101–2. If a second edition was called for, he was to receive another 200 livres for each part.

[2] Martin, *Livre, pouvoirs et société*, pp. 426–7.

[3] Ibid. 426–7. Tallemant has a rather confused account of La Calprenède's dealings with the booksellers (*Historiettes*, ed. G. Mongrédien, Paris, 8 vols., 1932–4, vi. 266).

[4] A. de Boislisle, 'Paul Scarron et Françoise d'Aubigné', *Revue des questions historiques*, 1893, pp. 438–9.

[5] *Historiettes*, vii. 43.

vente de l'édition de Hollande, il en fallut faire ici une en petit; parce que dans le traité il y a deux mille livres pour la première édition et mille pour la seconde.[1]

Of course, Tallemant's word is not the equivalent of a document from the archives, any more than are de Visé's statements, in the controversy over *Sertorius*, that abbé d'Aubignac who had accused Corneille of money-grubbing had received 200 écus (600 livres) for his *Pratique du théâtre* and 12 pistoles (120 livres) for his *Royaume de la coquetterie*.[2] We are also indebted to a not wholly reliable source—Guéret's *La Promenade de Saint-Cloud*—for the information that La Fontaine received 1,500 livres for *Les Amours de Psyché et de Cupidon*: 'Sa *Psyché* n'a pas eu le succès qu'il s'en promettait, et Barbin commence à regretter les cinq cents écus qu'il en a donnés.'[3]

To return to the solid ground of authors' contracts we may note in passing one which is of interest, not for the work in question, a *Nouvelle vie des saints tirée des auteurs ecclésiastiques*, but for the fact that it stipulates payments not only for a second edition, but even for a third. It was made in 1675 between the actor, Rosimond, and a Rouen bookseller named Lucas; the relevant part of the agreement runs as follows:

. . . Ledit sr. Jean Lucas promet et s'oblige aussi envers led. sr. de Rozimont aud. nom de payer la somme de six cents livres en cette ville de Paris, francs et deniers, quatre mois après la première édition qui aura été faite dud. livre. Et en cas d'une seconde, il s'oblige de payer pareille somme de six cents livres quatre autres mois après; et en cas de la troisième, la somme de trois cents livres quatre mois aussi après.

The author was also to receive thirty copies of each edition, 'reliés et couverts en veau'.[4] That payments for editions beyond the first were not altogether uncommon is proved by an amusing passage in Lesage's *Diable boiteux*:

Dans la maison qui joint celle du marchand, loge un fameux libraire. Il a imprimé depuis peu un livre qui a beaucoup de succès. En le mettant au jour, il promit de donner cinquante pistoles à l'auteur, s'il réimprimait son ouvrage. Il rêve en ce moment qu'il en fait une seconde édition sans l'en avertir.

[1] Ibid. iii. 168.
[2] *Défense du 'Sertorius' de M. de Corneille*, Paris, 1663, pp. 65, 109.
[3] Reprinted in F. Bruys, *Mémoires historiques, critiques et littéraires*, 2 vols., Paris, 1751, ii. 204.
[4] G. Monval, '*La Fameuse Comédienne* et la *Vie des saints*', *Le Moliériste*, vii, pp. 343-4.

—Oh pour ce songe-là, dit don Cléofas, je suis persuadé qu'il aura son plein et entier effet. Je connais messieurs les libraires. Ils ne se font pas un scrupule de tromper les auteurs.[1]

It will be seen that the amount of hard information which we possess about what writers earned from booksellers in this period is extremely small, though we are better informed about the earnings of playwrights from this source. Such information as we possess about the payments they received would seem to show that, if they improved somewhat in the course of the century, they were never large.

In 1625, for instance, Alexandre Hardy made an agreement for the publication of twelve of his plays for which he received the paltry sum of 180 livres.[2] Five years later André Mareschal fared rather better since he received 125 livres for the two *journées* of his tragicomedy, *La Généreuse Allemande*.[3] In 1636 Benserade was paid 150 livres for his tragedy, *Cléopâtre*,[4] and La Calprenède 200 for his *Mithridate*.[5] In the same year Rotrou sold four plays for the sum of 750 livres and in the next he sold ten to the same publishers for 1,500.[6] Unfortunately, we have no information about what Corneille earned from the publication of his plays, and what we know about the earnings of Molière and Racine from this source is very meagre. The first edition of *Tartufe* was published, so the title-page tells us, 'aux dépens de l'auteur'; it was quickly followed by a second edition for which, according to a contemporary source, the publisher paid 2,000 livres.[7] The same writer maintains that sales even of successful plays were often not large: 'Une pièce peut être bonne pour les comédiens, et ne valoir rien pour les libraires. Quand elle sort du théâtre, pour aller au Palais, elle est presque tout usée, et la curiosité n'y fait plus courir.'[8] This was certainly a larger sum than Molière's widow received for seven unpublished plays— *Dom Garcie de Navarre*, *L'Impromptu de Versailles*, *Dom Juan*, *Mélicerte*, *Les Amants magnifiques*, *La Comtesse d'Escarbagnas*, and *Le Malade imaginaire*— which appeared in the collected edition of his works published in 1682. According to contemporary sources the

---

[1] Ed. Laufer, p. 208.

[2] S. W. Deierkauf-Holsboer, *Vie d'Alexandre Hardy, poète du roi 1572–1632*, 2nd edn., Paris, 1972, pp. 210–11.

[3] G. Monval, 'André Mareschal', *Le Moliériste*, ix, pp. 20–9.

[4] A. Jal, *Dictionnaire critique de biographie et d'histoire*, 2nd edn., Paris, 1872, p. 194.

[5] Martin, *Livre, pouvoirs et société*, p. 426.

[6] Jal, *Dictionnaire*, p. 1087.

[7] Guéret, *La Promenade de Saint-Cloud*, in Bruys, *Mémoires* ii. 204.

[8] Ibid. 205.

bookseller paid her 1,500 livres.[1] Information about what Racine earned from the publication of his plays is extremely difficult to come by. It is often said that he received 200 livres for *Andromaque*, but no reputable source is given for this statement. All that Louis Racine has to say about what his father earned from publishing his plays is that 'le profit qu'il en retira fut fort modique'. He adds: 'et il donna dans la suite *Esther* et *Athalie* au libraire, de la manière dont Boileau avait donné tous ses ouvrages'.

Taking money from booksellers was regarded in many quarters, even quite late in the century, as degrading for the writer. Boileau's attitude is well known. Speaking of the *Satires*, Louis Racine writes:

Il ne voulut recevoir aucun profit du libraire. Il donna, en 1674, avec la même générosité ses *Épîtres*, son *Art poétique*, le *Lutrin* et le *Traité du Sublime*. Quoique fort économe de son revenu, il était plein de noblesse dans les senti-ments; il m'a assuré que jamais libraire ne lui avait payé un seul de ses ouv-rages, ce qui l'avait rendu hardi à railler dans son *Art poétique*, Chant IV, les auteurs qui 'mettent leur Apollon aux gages d'un libraire', et qu'il n'avait fait les deux vers qui précèdent:

> Je sais qu'un noble esprit peut sans honte et sans crime
> Tirer de son travail un tribut légitime

que pour consoler mon père, qui avait retiré quelque profit de l'impression de ses tragédies.[2]

The mercenary nature of writers of the time had earlier been attacked by Guéret in *La Promenade de Saint-Cloud* where we find the following dialogue:

Vous ne sauriez croire, dit Cléante, combien ce commerce qui se fait avec les libraires et les comédiens, gâte tous les jours de bonnes plumes. On ne voit quasi plus personne qui travaille purement pour sa propre gloire, et l'argent fait faire la plupart des livres que vous voyez. Pourquoi pensez-vous que Baudoin nous a donné tant de traductions; que Saumaise a tant gâté de papier, et que Boursault a déjà fait tant de nouvelles? C'est que ses messieurs-là ont eu besoin de ce trafic; et j'en connais tels qui assignent leurs créanciers sur leurs libraires, et qui les remettent au premier ouvrage.

C'est de là, dis-je alors, que nous vient cette grande multitude, de livres nouveaux. Car enfin, si ceux qui se mêlent d'écrire, n'avaient soin que de leur

---

[1] De Tralage, Recueil, Bibliothèque de l'Arsenal, MS. 6544, vol. iv. 240 v. L. Bordelon, in his *Diversités curieuses pour servir de récréation à l'esprit*, 5 vols., Amsterdam, 1699, i. 104, gives the same figure and adds the comment: 'Si cela est vrai, il y a longtemps qu'ila retiré son argent; il y gagnera encore de quoi bâtir un appartement des plus magnifiques dans le Ch. T., si l'envie lui en prend. Les auteurs n'en vont pas jusque-là; les libraires leur taillent des morceaux trop petits; mais pour les consoler, ils leur promettent de la gloire.'

[2] J. Racine, *Œuvres complètes*, i. 41.

réputation, il ne sortirait pas tant de volumes de leur cabinet, et ils employer-
aient plutôt toute leur vie à polir une seule pièce.[1]

At the end of the century one finds a satirical passage on the way large
numbers of authors set about writing books simply in order to get
money out of booksellers:

Ils commencent d'abord par imaginer le titre d'un livre. N'ayant encore que
le titre qu'ils ont imaginé, ils vont offrir l'ouvrage au premier libraire qui
voudra leur en donner de l'argent. Comme ils ont soin que le titre qu'ils ont
imaginé soit spécieux, le libraire est gagné par la beauté du titre et entre
aussitôt en composition. On règle le prix sur la grosseur du volume. Trente
pistoles pour un in-douze qui se vendra trente sols, et qui aura un beau titre,
ce n'est pas trop. Voilà le marché conclu. Le libraire avance quelque petite
chose ou du moins la promet par un billet. L'auteur se retire et va dépêcher le
livre dont il a déjà vendu le titre, et que l'acheteur attend avec autant d'impatience que le vendeur en a pour le livrer. En quinze jours ou trois semaines
voilà le livre fait. On gagne un réviseur, et on obtient un privilège, et un
homme qui n'avait pas de pain, a trente pistoles et est devenu auteur.[2]

That authors should attempt to make a living from what they could
earn from the publication of their works seemed to one Paris bookseller, writing in the 1680s, a new and scandalous abuse. Looking back
on the good old days when writers would be prepared to contribute
towards the cost of producing their books or at least ask nothing for
them, a bookseller declared with some indignation that 'l'art de
composer est pour ainsi dire devenu un métier pour gagner sa vie'.[3]

There is, however, no evidence that even at the end of the reign of
Louis XIV it had become possible for a writer to make a modest living
out of what he received from the booksellers, though at first sight the
earnings of playwrights from the performance of their works would
seem to have improved enormously in the course of this period.
Although plays appear to have brought in only modest amounts on
publication, the establishment of a professional theatre in Paris
undoubtedly offered playwrights the possibility, given a successful
play, of earning in a short space of time relatively large sums of money.
This was, of course, a gradual development. During the first quarter of
the seventeenth century a motley succession of companies followed one

---

[1] Bruys, *Mémoires* ii. 223–4.
[2] P. de Villiers, *Entretiens sur les contes de fées*, Paris, 1699, pp. 12–13.
[3] *Mémoires sur la contestation qui est entre les libraires de Paris et ceux de Lyon* (quoted in Martin, *Livre, pouvoirs et société*, p. 915).

another in the capital's only theatre, the Hôtel de Bourgogne. While performances were sometimes given elsewhere, the Hôtel de Bourgogne was often empty for long periods. It was not until 1629 that one company was permanently established there, and in the same year a troupe of actors which was later to install itself at the Théâtre du Marais also arrived in Paris and set up a second theatre which owed much of its success to the early plays of Pierre Corneille.

Down to that date the position of the playwright who lacked the support of a patron had been a very humble one. He was a mere *poète à gages*, that is he was hired by the company of actors to write so many plays a year. The classic case of the *poète à gages* at the beginning of the seventeenth century is that of Alexandre Hardy, though the poet, Théophile de Viau, appears to have performed that function for a period, and this was certainly the case with Corneille's contemporary, Rotrou, at the beginning of his career.

A great many documents concerning Hardy and his relations with the actors have been brought to light in recent decades.[1] Yet so many pieces of the jigsaw puzzle are missing that he still remains a very shadowy figure. Was he an actor as well as a playwright? All we can glean from the archival documents which actually bear his signature is that in 1611 he is listed second, immediately after Valleran Le Conte, the leader of the company, then in Paris, among the 'comédiens du roi'.[2] Nine years later at Marseilles 'Sr Alexandre Hardy, parisien, poète ordinaire de Sa Majesté' signed an agreement with a company of actors headed by Pierre le Messier (Bellerose) to produce twelve plays in the space of two years in return for one share in the net receipts of the company. It is to be noted that Hardy was not necessarily to accompany the actors on their travels as the agreement provides that in his absence his share 'lui sera fidèlement gardée, conservée de mois en mois ou autrement pour lui faire tenir le plus diligemment possible'. In addition he sold the actors the original of a pastoral play for 75 livres and five copies of plays for 100 livres.[3] Five years later, in Paris, he signed a receipt for the sum of 50 livres, the first instalment of the 100 livres to be paid by the same company for his comedy, *Le Jaloux*.[4] A week later he signed a second agreement giving him permission to publish five of his plays 'nonobstant que par le contrat entre eux fait en l'année mil six cent vingt en la ville de Marseille il ne soit permis aud. Sr Hardy de faire imprimer les pièces contenues aud. contrat'.[5] How-

---

[1] By Deierkauf-Holsboer in her *Vie d'Alexandre Hardy, poète du roi*.
[2] Ibid. p. 204.   [3] Ibid. pp. 214–16.   [4] Ibid. p. 211.   [5] Ibid. p. 212.

ever, some fifteen months after this, in January 1627, obviously having broken with Bellerose, he signed an agreement with another company; this document is in very poor condition, but we can glean from it that from 15 November 1626 Hardy undertook to produce six plays a year for a period of six years in return for a share in the net receipts, to be paid to him 'par chacun mois en sa maison en cette ville de Paris'.[1]

Exciting as these documents are, they still leave many gaps in our knowledge of Hardy's career as a playwright (and actor?). In 1628, near the end of his career, he declared in the 'Au lecteur' of the fifth volume of his *Théâtre* that he had written six hundred plays. Far from seeking to suggest, as some contemporaries and later writers have done, that he wrote even more plays than that, one wonders whether this is not a considerably inflated figure; after all, the only two agreements which have come down to us speak of six plays a year, a fairly formidable number, and Hardy's long career in the theatre certainly did not extend over a hundred years. What is, however, clear is that the thirty-four plays which he published in the 1620s represent only a very small part of his output. The documents in question show that such was Hardy's state of dependence on the actors that he could not publish the plays he wrote for them without their permission and that such permission was only given very sparingly.

The young Rotrou appears to have begun his career under similar conditions. In a letter of 1632 Chapelain speaks regretfully of 'la servitude honteuse' in which the playwright found himself,[2] and the fourteen plays which he sold to publishers in 1636 and 1637 when, thanks no doubt to patronage, he had escaped from this bondage, must have gone back to the period when, like Hardy, he was not free to publish them. However, by the 1630s playwrights of Rotrou's generation were less dependent on the actors and were beginning to earn much larger sums than the 100 livres which Hardy had obtained for a comedy in 1625. It is true that our information on this subject is extremely slight until in 1659 La Grange began to keep his famous register of the doings of Molière's company, but we do know from the inventory drawn up after the death of Charles Le Noir, the founder of the Marais theatre, that in 1637 his widow claimed that the company owed 'à la communauté du dit défunt et d'elle la somme de quinze cents livres sur

---

[1] Ibid. pp. 213–14.
[2] *Lettres,* i. 6.

lesquelles elle a en ses mains deux pièces de théâtre valant six cents livres chacune'.[1]

That by this date there was money to be earned by writing plays is made clear by the frequent attacks on the alleged graspingness of Pierre Corneille. In the violent controversy which followed the production of *Le Cid* his rival, Mairet, penned the well-known lines:

Vos caravanes de Rouen à Paris me font souvenir de ces premiers marchands qui passèrent dans les Indes; d'où par le bonheur des temps autant que par la simplicité de quelques peuples ils apportèrent de l'or, des pierreries et d'autres solides richesses, pour des sonnettes, des miroirs et de la quincaille qu'ils y laissèrent. Vous nous avez autrefois apporté la *Mélite*, la *Veuve*, la *Suivante*, la *Galerie du Palais* et de fraîche mémoire le *Cid*, qui d'abord vous a valu l'argent et la noblesse, qui vous en restent avec ce grand tintamarre de réputation qui vous bruirait encore aux oreilles, sans vos vanités et le malheur de l'impression.[2]

In 1643, at the beginning of the reign of Louis XIV, Corneille even went so far as to attempt to strengthen his bargaining position as a playwright by obtaining letters patent which would have given him the right to control for an unspecified period of years the performance of his plays both in Paris and the provinces, whereas the custom of the time allowed them to be performed by any company once they had been published. However, the document bears in the margin the words: 'Privilège Corneille refusé.'[3] Unfortunately, we have no information about what Corneille actually earned from the performance of his plays in the first half of his career, and all we know about the proceeds from the plays of the last part is that Molière, in 1667 and 1670, paid him 2,000 livres for *Attila* and *Tite et Bérénice*.[4]

For a good part of the century payment of a lump sum of this kind seems to have been common. There are a few other instances of this method being used in Molière's theatre. We also know that La Calprenède received from Molière an advance of 800 livres[5] for a play he never wrote and that when the Marais theatre was merged with his company in 1673 it owed Boursault 1,300 livres for his tragedy,

---

[1] S. W. Deierkauf-Holsboer, *Le Théâtre du Marais*, 2 vols., Paris, 1954–8, i. 168.
[2] 'Épître familière' in A. Gasté (ed.), *La Querelle du Cid*, Paris, 1898, p. 290.
[3] *Œuvres complètes*, ed. C. Marty-Laveaux, 12 vols., Paris, 1862–8, i, pp. lxxiv–lxxv.
[4] La Grange, *Registre (1659–1683)*, ed. B. E. and G. P. Young, 2 vols., Paris, 1947, i. 88, 118.
[5] Ibid. i. 54.

Germanicus.[1] However, such payments gradually gave way to a different system whereby the author received a fixed share of the receipts from the performances of his play. With this method of payment playwrights from the 1660s onwards could receive what must have appeared large sums of money. Unfortunately, we have no information about the amount of money which Racine's plays from *Andromaque* to *Phèdre* brought in as none of the registers of the Hôtel de Bourgogne has been preserved. They were, of course, not uniformly successful, but *Andromaque* seems to have had a very good first run and for *Bérénice* he could claim that 'la trentième représentation a été aussi suivie que la première', while according to Bayle *Iphigénie* was 'applaudie ... à l'Hôtel de Bourgogne pendant 40 représentations consécutives',[2] by the standards of the time a quite exceptional success. To form some idea of what he must have received from the actors we can only look at what successful authors of tragedies received at the Comédie-Française from its foundation in 1680 onwards. The most successful tragedies of the period down to 1715 were Campistron's *Alcibiade* which brought its author 2,839 livres in 1685–6 and Crébillon's *Rhadamiste et Zénobie* from the performances of which he drew 2,918 livres in 1711.

These were substantial sums of money, and yet the example of Racine's contemporaries shows that even with successes of this kind writing plays did not offer in the long run a satisfactory career. Payments for performances were strictly limited to a play's first run; after that the original company or any other troupe of actors in Paris or the provinces was free to put on the play without paying the author a penny. Between 1683 and 1693 Campistron had performed the same number of plays as Racine—nine tragedies and one comedy. If *Alcibiade* proved highly lucrative by the standards of the time, the rest of his plays were less successful, and the total sum which he received from the Comédie-Française was in the neighbourhood of 11,500 livres, not much more than 1,000 livres a year.

Other types of play could earn even larger sums, the record being held by the 'pièce à machines', *La Devineresse*, for which the two authors, Thomas Corneille and Donneau de Visé, received 5,651 livres in 1679–80. As they shared this amount between them they were not made as rich as Boursault who ten years later drew 3,291 livres from the first run of his comedy, *Les Fables d'Ésope*. Yet striking as this play's success was, it has to be considered along with the other four plays of

[1] G. Monval, 'L'Affaire Auzillon', *Le Moliériste*, viii, p. 84.
[2] *Nouvelles lettres*, 2 vols., The Hague, 1739, i. 208.

Boursault which were put on at the Comédie-Française between 1683
and 1694; they brought in altogether just over 5,000 livres. A letter
written by Boursault towards the end of the highly successful first run
of *Les Fables d'Ésope* contains the very significant remark: 'Qui serait
assuré de faire deux pièces par an avec le même succès, n'aurait guère
besoin d'autre emploi'.[1] But this was an obvious impossibility.

Writing for the stage in this period had its advantages. Not only
could the author of a really successful play earn a substantial sum of
money in a short period; now that a professional theatre had been
established, a successful play had become what it was long to remain,
the quickest way for a young writer to get himself known, as Charles
Sorel pointed out in the 1660s:

Comme la plupart des gens du siècle ne pensent qu'à leur plaisir, ce leur est
une chose fort agréable de s'entretenir des comédies qu'on représente: aussi
aucun auteur n'acquiert de la réputation en si peu de temps que ceux qui ont
travaillé pour le théâtre; en cinq ou six représentations de leur pièce il se
trouve que quatre ou cinq mille personnes y ont assisté, et en font encore le
rapport à quantité d'autres.[2]

Yet even in the second part of our period, playwriting, though supported by a fair amount of patronage, did not offer what one could call
a career. The example set by Racine in abandoning the theatre for a
lucrative position at court was not by any means unique.

The contrast between the affluence of the actor from the middle of
the century onwards and the more modest financial rewards of the
playwright was noted by several contemporaries. 'Le comédien, couché
dans son carrosse, jette de la boue au visage de CORNEILLE, qui est à
pied' wrote La Bruyère in 1688.[3] The contrast was implied again when
Lesage, soon to abandon the Comédie-Française for good out of
disgust at the haughty attitude of its actors, wrote in *Le Diable
boiteux*: 'Ici gît un comédien que le déplaisir d'aller à pied, pendant
qu'il voyait la plupart de ses camarades en équipage, a consumé peu à
peu.'[4] The average earnings of an actor at the Comédie-Française with
a full share in the receipts came to roughly 4,900 livres in the period
1680–1701, plus possibly another 1,000 livres from the royal subsidy,
not to mention the pension of 1,000 livres on which he could count

[1] *Lettres nouvelles*, 4th edn., 3 vols., Paris, 1722, i. 258.
[2] *La Bibliothèque française*, 2nd edn., Paris, 1667, p. 211.
[3] *Les Caractères*, ed. R. Garapon, Paris, 1962, 'Des jugements', 17.
[4] Ed. Laufer, p. 156.

when he retired. With this we may compare the lot of a prolific play-wright like Campistron whose ten plays in ten years produced an average yearly income of just over 1,000 livres. Or putting it another way, we find that the total amount paid out each year to *all* authors of new plays works out at a little over 5,300 livres—less than *each* full-share actor earned in an average year when he had received his share of the royal subsidy.

What is more, the actors themselves drew a considerable proportion of the money paid out for new plays. It is fairly certain that the man who made the most money out of writing plays in seventeenth-century France was Molière who in the space of only fifteen years earned some 50,000 livres with his pen, plus a royal pension of 1,000 livres from 1663 onwards. This was in addition to his earnings as an actor. La Grange who joined his company at Easter 1659 wrote in his register: 'Total de ce que j'ai reçu depuis que je suis comédien à Paris, 25 avril 1659, jusqu'à la mort de M. de Molière, 17 fevrier 1673 et reste de la d.année 51,670 1. 14 s.'[1]—an average of over 3,500 livres a year. After the foundation of the Comédie-Française actors like Baron, Champ-meslé, and especially Dancourt also earned substantial sums of money by writing plays. Between 1683 when he joined the company and 1700 Dancourt had over thirty plays performed at the Comédie-Française and from these he drew, over and above his earnings as an actor, some 20,000 livres.[2]

Thus if, as in Shakespeare's England, the professional theatre led the way in providing relatively large financial rewards for writers, none the less playwriting did not offer a real career in the way it was to do in the nineteenth century, at any rate for the writer who was able to turn out a series of successes. The playwright, like other writers of the time, was driven to depend to a large extent on various forms of patronage, if he did not possess a private income or some occupation which allowed him sufficient leisure to write. There is unfortunately no detailed history of literary patronage in this period, but its main features are reasonably clear.[3]

In this period and indeed down to 1789 we continue to witness the paradox that the Catholic Church played willy-nilly a leading role as a

[1] *Registre* i. 145.
[2] For further details on earnings from the theatre see my article, 'The Earnings of Play-wrights in Seventeenth-Century France', *Modern Language Review*, 1947, pp. 321–36.
[3] Although its subject is dedications, Wolfgang Leiner's *Der Widmungsbrief in der französischen Literatur (1580–1715)*, Heidelberg, 1965, offers a great deal of material for a history of literary patronage.

patron of literature in the narrow sense of the term, that is of poetry, drama, and the novel as distinct from devotional and didactic works. The Catholic Church provided a haven for young men with scholarly, intellectual, and literary interests regardless of whether they had a vocation or not. There were many *abbés* going around in ecclesiastical costume whose connection with the Church was extremely tenuous, as La Bruyère noted in a famous passage in *Les Caractères*.[1]

Since the Concordat of 1516 the Crown had had at its disposal a good deal of the Church's wealth through its right to appoint to almost all high ecclesiastical posts. Poets continued to be rewarded with appointments to bishoprics. In his *Satire II*, written early in the century, Régnier makes fun of the ambitious poet:

> Un autre, ambitieux, pour les vers qu'il compose
> Quelque bon bénéfice en l'esprit se propose,
> Et, dessus un cheval comme un singe attaché,
> Méditant un sonnet, médite un évêché.[2]

In 1606 Jean Bertaut, who had earlier figured as a poet at the court of Henry III, was appointed bishop of Sées by Henry IV, and thirty years later Antoine Godeau, who, because of his small height, was nicknamed 'le nain de Julie' at the Hôtel de Rambouillet, was elevated by Richelieu to the remote diocese of Grasse and Vence where he distinguished himself by his apostolic zeal.[3]

Much more common among the writers of the time was a readiness to draw an income from livings in the Church without any obligations as to residence or work in return for the money. Régnier himself held a canonry at Chartres, while Boisrobert, a notorious *libertin* in both senses of the word, managed to ingratiate himself with Richelieu and among various other livings in the Church held a canonry at Rouen. Laymen could be rewarded by the Crown for their literary efforts by being given pensions on bishoprics or abbeys; Malherbe kept on receiving promises of just such a reward from Henry IV. Benserade, famous above all for his ballets, drew later in the century pensions from one bishopric and two abbeys.

A further way in which the Crown could reward writers (and others) was by making them abbots or priors *in commendam*. Boisrobert held two such lucrative sinecures, and Chapelain was another writer of the time whose wealth was mainly derived from such appointments.

[1] 'De quelques usages', 16.
[2] *Œuvres complètes*, ed. J. Plattard, Paris, 1930, p. 22.
[3] See above, p. 69.

Writers whose names have worn better than these also drew an income, if only a modest one, from such posts. Tonsured at the age of eleven, Boileau drew money from holding the post of prior, though he is said to have later repaid it. Again, after Racine had failed to secure a living through his uncle at Uzès and until he found some better way of augmenting his earnings as a playwright, he held for several years the title of prior of two or more houses.

The seventeenth century inherited from the previous age the belief that the king had an important role to play as a patron of literature. This notion was, however, to be severely shaken during the reigns of Henry IV and Louis XIII, neither of whom lived up to what was expected of them. During their reigns there were constant laments for the loss of the patronage which the Valois kings had bestowed on men of letters, as, for instance, in Maynard's epigram:

> Apollon, que ton cœur s'ouvre
> A des regrets infinis:
> Ceux qui t'appelaient au Louvre
> Sont poussière à Saint-Denis.
>
> Ma lyre a peu de pareilles;
> Mais le Prince que je sers,
> Éloigne de ses oreilles
> Les charmes de mes concerts.
>
> Adieu, Cour; adieu, Fortune,
> Puisqu'un Orphée importune
> Le plus auguste des rois.
>
> Cet accident me convie
> A pleurer toute ma vie
> Sur la tombe des Valois.[1]

Henry IV heard of the existence of Malherbe, but was afraid to send for him to come to court as that would have meant offering him a pension. In 1605 the poet was presented to the King for whom he wrote the famous ode on the expedition to put down the rebels in Limousin. His disciple, Racan, relates the royal reaction: 'Le roi trouva ces vers si admirables qu'il désira de le retenir à son service, et commanda à M. de Bellegarde de le garder jusqu'à ce qu'il l'eût mis sur l'état de ses pensionnaires. M. de Bellegarde lui donna sa table, et l'entretint d'un homme et d'un cheval, et mille livres d'appointements.'[2] This appar-

---

[1] *Poésies*, ed. F. Gohin, Paris, 1927, p. 80.
[2] *Mémoires pour la vie de M. de Malherbe* in *Malherbe, Poésies*, ed. M. Allem and P. Martino, Paris, 1937, p. 261.

ently meant that the duc de Bellegarde, the *grand écuyer*, gave Malherbe a post under him which was paid out of Treasury funds, but down to Henry's assassination in 1610 Malherbe was constantly on the look-out for a pension of one sort or another. In 1608, for instance, he wrote to a friend: 'Sa Majesté me fit cet honneur lundi au soir, de me renouveler la promesse de la pension sur la première abbaye, évêché ou archevêché. Je ne sais quand j'en verrai l'effet; jusque-là il se faut contenter de sa bonne volonté.'[1] All that Malherbe ever extracted from Henry was fine promises; it was only when power passed into the hands of the Regent, Marie de Médicis, that he at last received the pension for which he had waited so long.

Both as queen and as queen mother Marie de Médicis was the recipient of numerous dedications, including one from D'Urfé for his pastoral play, *Sylvanire*. She was alleged to have inspired this work, and we know that she gave a pension to Boisrobert so that he could produce a translation of Guarini's *Pastor fido*.[2] She gave a substantial pension to the poet Gombaud, according to Tallemant, because of his resemblance to a former flame of hers in Florence.[3] However, like many other pensions under the *ancien régime*, it was neither paid in full nor very regularly. The Regent proved a much more generous patron to Malherbe than her husband; she gave him a pension of 1,200 livres, later increased to 1,500, though he clearly had some difficulty in extracting the money from the Treasury. In 1617 his hopes of receiving a pension on the archbishopric of Rouen were dashed, but he did succeed in obtaining a concession of building plots for twenty-two houses at the port of Toulon, which promised a considerable income, though it appears that in the end he derived no profit from his speculation.

It was not apparently entirely unknown for Louis XIII to act as a patron of men of letters. The poet, Gombaud, Tallemant assures us, after receiving for a time a pension from the Regent, 'eut huit cents écus du feu roi, mais quand la guerre fut déclarée, on ne paya plus de pensions poétiques' and all that his friends could do was to get half of it restored.[4] In 1624 Malherbe was rewarded with a gift of 1,500 livres for a sonnet, and two years later he was given the post of *trésorier de France* in Provence.[5] Even Théophile received royal patronage for a time; at his trial he complained that the *Procureur général* had not

[1] *Œuvres*, ed. A. Adam, Paris, 1971, p. 398.
[2] É. Magne, *Le plaisant abbé de Boisrobert*, Paris, 1909, p. 51.
[3] *Historiettes*, iii. 141–2.   [4] Ibid. iii. 142–3.
[5] See *Œuvres*, p. 205, and R. Lebègue, 'La Fin de Malherbe', *XVIIᵉ siècle*, 1965, p. 72.

produced the patent for the pension conferred on him by the King.[1] Yet Louis can be said to have shown little interest in literature and men of letters. Tallemant even goes so far as to state: 'Il raya après la mort du Cardinal toutes les pensions des gens de lettres, en disant: "Nous n'avons plus affaire de cela.".. He goes on to relate the famous anecdote about the King's attitude to *Polyeucte*:

Depuis la mort du Cardinal, M. de Schomberg lui dit que Corneille voulait lui dédier la tragédie de *Polyeucte*. Cela lui fit bien peur, parce que Montauron avait donné deux cents pistoles à Corneille pour *Cinna*. 'Il n'est pas nécessaire, dit-il.—Ah! Sire, reprit M. de Schomberg, ce n'est point par intérêt.—Bien donc, dit-il, il me fera plaisir.' Ce fut à la reine qu'on le dédia, car le roi mourut entre deux.[2]

Like his father Louis XIII left literary patronage largely to others. *Polyeucte*, however, was by no means the only play dedicated to his widow, Anne of Austria, when she assumed her powers as regent in 1643. Other works too were offered to her, including the first canto of Scarron's *Virgile travesti*. Until he misbehaved in the Fronde by producing a *mazarinade*, he drew 1,500 livres a year from the Regent from 1643 onwards.[3]

In the troubled days which stretched from Louis XIII's minority to that of his son, the period down to and including the Fronde, the princes of the blood and great noblemen played a considerable part in the literary life of France. Some of their patronage was undoubtedly disinterested. One thinks, for instance, of the comte de Belin and the encouragement which he gave to various playwrights such as Mairet in the 1630s. Often, however, their motives in offering board and lodging and/or pensions to writers were decidedly non-literary. Poets would be expected to write verses to their patron's latest mistress or to the woman destined for that part. This was a function which Mathurin Régnier was not prepared to accept:

> De porter un poulet je n'ai la suffisance,
> Je ne suis point adroit, je n'ai point d'éloquence
> Pour colorer un fait ou détourner la foi,
> Prouver qu'un grand amour n'est sujet à la loi,
> Suborner par discours une femme coquette,
> Lui conter des chansons de Jeanne et de Paquette,
> Débaucher une fille . . .

[1] F. Lachuère, *Le Procès du poète Theophile de Viau*, 2 vols., Paris, 1909, i. 434–5.
[2] *Historiettes*, iii. 159–60.
[3] A. de Boislisle, 'Scarron et Françoise d'Aubigné', p. 115.

. . . Il est vrai que ceux-là qui n'ont pas tant d'esprit
Peuvent mettre en papier leur dire par écrit,
Et rendre par leurs vers leur muse maquerelle,
Mais, pour dire le vrai, je n'en ai la cervelle.[1]

Another function of the writer in these turbulent times before the authority of the monarchy was firmly established, was to act as publicity manager for his patron, to avenge any insults to him by other writers and to attack his enemies.

This was the period of the century in which dedications were most freely lavished on great noblemen and their womenfolk. The duc de Montmorency who ended his career on a scaffold at Toulouse after the failure of his rebellion in 1632 was much courted by writers of the time such as Hardy, who dedicated a volume of his plays to him, and Mairet and Scudéry, both of whom offered him their first play. Along with other great noblemen such as the comte de Candale he was also a patron of Théophile de Viau. Among those to whom Corneille dedicated his early plays were the comte and comtesse de Liancourt and the duc de Longueville, the governor of Normandy. The Duke certainly earned the dedication of Chapelain's epic, *La Pucelle*, when it at last appeared in 1656; he had been paying for it at the rate of 2,000 livres a year since 1633. According to Tallemant this is how the relationship started: the Duke, a descendant of the comte de Dunois who had played an important part in driving the English out of France, had been shown the first two books of the poem by a third party:

M. de Longueville vit les deux livres, en fut charmé, et dit à M. d'Andilly qu'il mourait d'envie d'arrêter M. Chapelain . . . M. de Longueville fait que M. Lemaître, l'avocat, lui mène M. Chapelain et après avoir causé quelque temps ensemble, M. de Longueville entre dans son cabinet avec M. Lemaître, tire d'une cassette un parchemin, demande le nom de baptême de M. Chapelain, et en remplit le vide . . . M. Chapelain le prend, et, arrivé chez lui, trouve que c'était un brevet de deux mille livres de pension sur tous les biens de M. de Longueville, sans obliger M. Chapelain à quoi que ce soit.[2]

The amount is confirmed by a contract of 1645 by which the Duke ensured that the pension should last as long as Chapelain lived.[3] It is even said that when the poem at last appeared, he increased the amount of his gift.

[1] *Satire III* (*Œuvres complètes*, pp. 29–30).
[2] *Historiettes*, iii. 159–60.
[3] Jal, *Dictionnaire*, p. 361.

One could reel off long lists of great noblemen and their womenfolk to whom all manner of works were dedicated in the period down to about 1660; they range from the Condés, father and son, to much less illustrious figures. But it was not only such high-born aristocrats who attracted the attention of writers. Though those who laboriously composed dedications were not necessarily offering thanks for money favours already received or anticipated, a great many were. And in this period *financiers* often had more ready cash available than patrons with blue blood. Yet even contemporaries were shocked by the dedication to a *nouveau riche* named Montauron which Corneille affixed to his *Cinna*; it is true that he was by no means the first writer to flatter this man (Tristan L'Hermite, for instance, had got in earlier with a dedication of a volume of poetry), but people were taken aback by his comparison between Montauron and the Emperor Augustus and in particular by the directness of such lines as 'cette générosité, à l'exemple de ce grand empereur, prend plaisir à s'étendre sur les gens de lettres, en un temps où beaucoup pensent avoir trop récompensé leurs travaux quand ils les ont honorés d'une louange stérile'. If it is true, as Tallemant alleges, that Corneille received 2,000 livres in return for this dedication,[1] at this stage in the century this was probably more than he earned for his tragedy from the actors and the bookseller combined.

Although in the period before 1660 official patronage from the Crown was on a very modest scale and that from great noblemen and other private individuals was very important, an extremely prominent part was played by certain of the King's ministers, by Richelieu above all, but also by the Chancellor, Séguier, and later by Mazarin, and, towards the end of this part of the century, by Foucquet. No doubt Richelieu's gifts to writers went in part to men who acted as propagandists for his policies, but he did have a genuine interest in poetry and the drama and proved a generous patron of those writers who won his favour. It is true that his likes and dislikes were somewhat unpredictable. The poet, Maynard, for instance, never succeeded in ingratiating himself with him; he got a friend to read to the Cardinal a poem addressed to him in which the poet is made to encounter that great patron, Francis I, in the underworld and which ends with the pointed verse:

> Mais s'il demande à quel emploi
> Tu m'as occupé dans le monde

[1] *Historiettes*, ii. 160.

> Et quels biens j'ai reçus de toi,
> Que veux-tu que je lui répondes.[1]

Back came Richelieu's brutal answer: 'Rien.'

According to Segrais the Cardinal gave a large part of his income to men of letters: 'Le cardinal de Richelieu n'avait que quatre cent mille livres de rente, et il en donnait quarante mille écus aux gens de lettres par les pensions qu'il leur faisait. Il mettait là l'argent qu'il aurait mis à sa table, qu'il ne pouvait pas tenir à cause qu'il était valétudinaire.'[2] His strong interest in drama helped to stimulate the production of plays in the 1630s down to his death in 1642; the output of new plays in these years was greater than in any corresponding period in the century. The financial support which he gave to playwrights made up for the still modest payments which they received from the actors and booksellers. 'N'était que Monseigneur le Cardinal se délasse parfois en l'honnête divertissement de la comédie et que Son Éminence me fait l'honneur de me gratifier de ses bienfaits,' wrote Tristan in 1639 in the preface to his *Panthée*, 'j'appliquerais peu mon loisir sur les ouvrages de théâtre.' All that even a successful play brought its author was, he declared, 'du bruit et de la fumée'.

It can well be imagined that Richelieu was overwhelmed with dedications by writers anxious to join in the gold-rush or dutifully offering thanks for favours received. All manner of works—serious and light, in prose and in verse—were dedicated to him, but plays were particularly prominent. In 1641, for instance, Corneille presented his humble duty to Monseigneur le Cardinal duc de Richelieu in the diedication of *Horace* in which he begins by declaring that 'après tant de bienfaits que j'ai reçus d'elle, le silence où mon respect m'a retenu jusqu'à présent passerait pour ingratitude', and continues to the end in this grovelling tone. Earlier, he had dedicated *Le Cid* to the Cardinal's favourite niece, Mme de Combalet, later duchesse d'Aiguillon; she was also the recipient of many dedications as long as her uncle lived, but when he had vanished from the scene, she no longer served as an intermediary between the impecunious writers and her uncle's favour, so that she quickly dropped out of dedicatory epistles.

Richelieu's death was undoubtedly a severe blow to the writers of the time, particularly the playwrights. They above all people must have

---

[1] *Poésies*, p. 112.

[2] *Œuvres diverses*, 2 vols., Amsterdam, 1723, i. 170. A. Aubery in his *Histoire du Cardinal duc de Richelieu*, Paris, 1660, pp. 610–11, names twenty-six writers from a list of those whom he supported financially.

echoed the sentiments expressed so irreverently in Benserade's famous epigram:

> Ci-gît, oui gît par la morbleu,
> Le Cardinal de Richelieu,
> Et ce qui cause mon ennui,
> Ma pension avecque lui.'[1]

The considerable decline in the number of new plays produced in the years after his death was no doubt due in the main to the failure of any new patron to take quite the same interest in drama. It is true that Mairet and Benserade had given up writing for the theatre before Richelieu's death; but other dramatists of Pierre Corneille's generation ceased writing for the stage between 1642 and the outbreak of the Fronde in 1648. In 1643 Scudéry announced his retirement in the preface to his *Arminius*, and after the publication of his *Herménegilde* in the same year La Calprenède turned to the novel. La Serre and Desmaretz de Saint-Sorlin, both in varying degrees favourites of Richelieu, also abandoned the career of playwright about the same time. It is significant that another author, Du Ryer, although he did not entirely cease writing plays, should have found that the badly paid hack-work of translation offered a more solid livelihood.

Scarron's *Épître chagrine*, written in 1652, vividly portrays the havoc created in the literary world by Richelieu's death:

> Les pauvres courtisans des Muses
> Sont aujourd'hui traités de buses,
> Qu'autrefois défunt Richelieu,
> Qu'ils ont traité de demi-dieu,
> Traitait de la façon qu'Auguste,
> Prince aussi généreux que juste,
> A traité les hommes savants,
> Dont les vers sont encore vivants . . .
> Les beaux vers et la belle prose
> Valent aujourd'hui peu de chose:
> Se voir en auteur érigé
> Est un sinistre préjugé
> Pour la fortune d'un pauvre homme.[2]

---

[1] *Œuvres*, 2 vols., Paris, 1697, i. p. x.

[2] *Poésies diverses*, ed. M. Cauchie, 2 vols., Paris, 1947–61, ii. 57–8. There is another well-known passage on this subject in Furetière's *Nouvelle allégorique*, Amsterdam, 1658, p. 100.

He does, however, admit the existence of at least one patron in high office, Pierre de Séguier, who was Chancellor from 1635 to 1672 and succeeded Richelieu as patron of the Académie française. Somewhat cynically Tallemant wrote of his favours to men of letters: 'Pour être loué, il donnait sur le sceau, et à proprement parler, c'était le public qui payait ces beaux esprits.'[1] Séguier's patronage of men of letters went as far back as 1633 when he became *garde des sceaux*; his interest in writers was greeted with enthusiasm in a letter of Chapelain's of that year.[2] Séguier duly received his quota of dedicatory epistles; as well as getting one from Scarron, he found himself addressed by Corneille in the dedication to *Héraclius* (1647) in the usual flowery terms: '... Les nouvelles faveurs que j'ai reçues de vous m'ont donné une juste impatience de les publier ... On sait par toute l'Europe l'accueil favorable que Votre Grandeur fait aux gens de lettres ... Votre bonté ne dédaigne pas de répandre sur moi votre bienveillance et vos grâces.' Scarron, however, in this poem of lamentations does leave out a literary patron of some importance, Richelieu's successor, Cardinal Mazarin.

No doubt Mazarin was not so exceptionally generous towards men of letters as Richelieu had been, and Scarron had had an unfortunate experience with the Cardinal. In 1644 he had dedicated to him his burlesque poem, *Le Typhon ou la Gigantomachie*, but without receiving the anticipated reward. His rage overflowed into the famous sonnet:

> Après que, d'un style bouffon
> Pur et net de pédanteries,
> J'eus bâti mon pauvre *Typhon*
> De cent mille coyonneries.
>
> Avide d'or comme un griffon
> (D'or, d'argent ou de pierreries)
> Je le couvris non d'un chiffon,
> Mais de chiffres et d'armoiries.
>
> Mon livre étant ainsi paré
> Et richement élaboré,
> J'en régalai le mauvais riche.
>
> Mais (ô malheureux Scarronnet!)
> Il n'en fut jamais un si chiche:
> Déchire ton chien de sonnet.[3]

Mazarin's unpopularity during the Fronde led to frequent attacks on his failure to assist men of letters. This called forth a very pointed

[1] *Historiettes*, iii. 231.   [2] *Lettres*, i. 53.   [3] *Poésies diverses*, i. 507–8.

retort from his librarian, Gabriel Naudé, in which he named a whole list of writers who had not only received pensions and gifts from Mazarin, but had heaped eulogies upon him.[1]

Among the names given are those of Guez de Balzac, Corneille, Chapelain, Maynard, Colletet, and Gomberville, and he goes on to quote, for instance, the poem in which Corneille offered thanks for the pension of 2,000 livres which Mazarin had given him in return for the dedication of his *Pompée*:

> C'est toi, grand cardinal, âme au-dessus de l'homme,
> Rare don qu'à la France ont fait le ciel et Rome . . .[2]

After the collapse of the Fronde dedicatory epistles once more rained down on Mazarin, both from the playwrights (including Quinault and Thomas Corneille) and from a variety of authors. He continued to offer pensions and other gifts to quite a number of writers; what is more, as his first biographer points out,[3] in his will, made in March 1661, he took care to ensure that these pensions were paid during the lifetime of the recipients and did not die with him.

None the less, it is clear that in his last years Mazarin was eclipsed as a patron by another member of the government, Nicolas Foucquet, the *Surintendant des finances*.[4] In the eight years in which he held that office, until his downfall in 1661, Foucquet gradually built up a considerable clientèle among writers as well as among the nobility. Sometimes his patronage consisted of making sure that royal pensions continued to be paid with reasonable promptness (this was always a difficult point), but in addition he offered gifts and pensions to quite a crowd of writers, under the guidance of his secretary, Pellisson. The young Boursault, who confesses to having been 'surpris d'une générosité si grande', was given 30 louis (330 livres) for a sonnet.[5]

Naturally, this new source of patronage quickly became known and the inevitable dedications followed—from Scarron (a play for Monsieur

---

[1] *Jugement de tout ce qui a été imprimé contre le Cardinal Mazarin depuis le sixième janvier jusqu'à la Déclaration du premier avril mil six cent quarante-neuf*, n.p., n.d. [Paris, 1649], pp. 236–9.

[2] *Œuvres complètes*, x. 95.

[3] A. Aubrey, *Histoire du Cardinal Mazarin*, 2 vols., Paris, 1695, ii. 591. This statement can be confirmed by reference to his will (Bibliothèque nationale, Mélanges Colbert, vol. 74, fos. 1–39).

[4] A great deal of information about this side of Foucquet's activities is to be found in U. V. Chatelain, *Le Surintendant Foucquet protecteur des lettres, des arts et des sciences*, Paris, 1905.

[5] *Lettres nouvelles*, ii. 7.

and the second part of the *Roman comique* for Madame), from Quinault, and from both Pierre and Thomas Corneille (it was to be the last time Pierre penned a dedication). Scarron was always appealing to Foucquet's generosity; for instance, in his 'Épître à M. Pellisson' he gives thanks for the sum of 3,000 livres which had temporarily got rid of his creditors.[1] A number of poets drew pensions from the *Surintendant*, among them La Fontaine who indeed was partly involved in his patron's downfall. It was Foucquet who persuaded Pierre Corneille to return to the theatre with his *Œdipe*, for which he was duly rewarded, though whether the 2,000 livres he received was simply a once-for-all gift or a pension remains obscure.[2] Thomas Corneille among other playwrights also received some reward, as in the dedication of his tragedy, *La Mort de Commode*, he speaks of the 'bienfaits' which he had received from his patron. Mlle de Scudéry also appears to have received money from the *Surintendant*.

Foucquet's fame as a patron was soon to be eclipsed by that of the young Louis XIV, now that he had taken over the reins of power on Mazarin's death. Apparently, the idea of making use of the royal bounty to men of letters in order to boost the prestige of the monarchy goes back to 1657 when Colbert, acting on the advice of Costar and Ménage, had drawn up a list of writers who were to be encouraged.[3] It was not until 1663 that, acting this time on the advice of Chapelain, Colbert persuaded Louis XIV to make a great splash with the announcement of this large-scale patronage of men of letters, scholars, and scientists, foreign as well as French. On 9 June 1663 Jean Loret broke the news of this great event to the world in his *Muse historique*:

> Le bruit est venu jusqu'à moi
> Que par un ordre exprès du Roi,
> Monsieur Colbert, qui du royaume
> Est réputé grand économe,
> A pris dans le royal trésor
> Quantité de bons louis d'or,
> Pour donner, non pas à des rustres,
> Mais à tout plein de gens illustres,
> Qui sont courtisans des neuf sœurs
> Et des lettres hauts professeurs;
> Et, ce que j'y vois d'importance,
> Non seulement à ceux de France,

---

[1] *Poésies diverses*, ii. 319.   [2] Chatelain, *Foucquet*, p. 169.
[3] His *Mémoire des gens de lettres célèbres de France* is to be found in P. N. Desmolets, *Continuation des mémoires de M. de Salengre*, 2 vols., Paris, 1726, ii. 317–45.

Mais aux étrangers et aux forains
Dépendant d'autres souverains;
Tels présents rendent témoignage
Que le Roi généreux et sage,
Du grand Auguste imitateur,
Des sciences est amateur;
Et c'est en ce jeune monarque
Une excellent et belle marque,
Que sous son règne on doit encor
Voir refleurir le siècle d'or.[1]

The reign of Louis XIV was a golden age in the history of French literature, but it is difficult to give the credit for this to his patronage. The King certainly came to know most of the great writers of the age. Molière, both as actor and playwright, was prominent in court entertainments and was also rewarded with a pension as a man of letters. Racine was not on the first list of recipients, understandably, as he was a mere novice, but he was quick to put his name forward. On 22 June Chapelain wrote in a letter to Colbert: 'J'aurai dans peu de jours une ode française d'un jeune homme appelé Racine, qu'il m'a apportée et qu'il repolit sur mes avis. La matière en est la guérison de Sa Majesté'.[2] A year later Racine got his reward with a modest pension the amount of which rose steadily as his fame as a playwright grew. Boileau was much slower in being introduced to the court, and although he was offered a royal pension in 1674, he does not appear to have actually received it until 1676. However, in the following year Racine and he were made *historiographes du roi*.

Too much has been made of Louis's interest in literature. The terms in which Voltaire and subsequent historians have spoken of his munificence seem somewhat exaggerated when we look at the cold facts. The maximum amount paid to all recipients of the gifts doled out from 1663 onwards—to writers, scholars, and scientists, foreign as well as French—came to just over 100,000 livres (this was in 1669), about half what a single journey of the court to Versailles cost at this date. It was no doubt inevitable that in offering these sums of money to the men of letters of the time Louis and his minister, Colbert, should have failed to discriminate between the really great writers of the reign and the second-rate and those who are now totally forgotten; any scheme of patronage—even when it is run by a committee of the

---

[1] *La Muse historique*, ed. C. Livet, 4 vols., Paris, 1857–78, iv. 61–2.
[2] *Lettres*, ii. 313.

Arts Council in our day—must run that risk. Thus we seek in vain for the name of La Fontaine among the recipients of the royal bounty, while in the 1660s men like Molière and Racine received pensions which in no way distinguished them from third-rate writers. Down to his death in 1674 Chapelain drew regularly 3,000 livres a year; neither Corneille nor Racine ever received more than 2,000, while Molière had to be content with 1,000, decidedly less than either Ménage or Cotin whom he was to make fun of in *Les Femmes savantes*.

Moreover, the aim of Louis and Colbert in giving these pensions was far from disinterested. At any rate to begin with the money was doled out simply to encourage the production of propaganda writings which would boost the name of 'Louis le Grand' at home and abroad. On 9 June 1663 Chapelain wrote to Colbert: 'J'ai vu ceux de ma connaissance qui vous doivent les gratifications qu'ils ont reçues de Sa Majesté et les ai portés, mais sans peine, à célébrer sa convalescence.'[1] He goes on to say that he soon hopes to have their contributions, in both French and Latin, and in the meantime he offers his own sonnet. He also recommends various people for a royal gift, among them abbé Cotin, 'un de nos plus fameux académiciens', who has composed 'un madrigal très joli' on the subject set. In his letters to the foreign recipients Chapelain makes it abundantly clear that the continuation of these favours depends entirely on the furnishing of suitable eulogies of Louis XIV which would serve to advance his fame. It was also made clear to recipients at home and abroad that in distributing these gifts Louis and Colbert

ne s'obligent à personne et veulent être toujours libres de les départir ou non, selon que le procédé des gratifiés les y conviendra sans qu'on ait droit de l'exiger d'eux ni de se plaindre quand ils ne le feraient pas, comme d'une chose à laquelle ils ne se sont point engagés ni soumis par leurs promesses. C'est pourquoi personne n'en a de brevets ni de patentes. J'ai été bien aise de vous expliquer cela afin que vous vissiez combien judicieusement ils se comportent en cela comme en toutes autres choses, et que c'était le meilleur expédient qu'ils pussent prendre pour tenir les esprits en haleine et empêcher qu'on ne prît leurs libéralités pour des revenus réglés et que sur cette assurance on ne s'endormît et demeurât les bras croisés contre la principale intention.[1]

In practice, the famous pensions to men of letters were to have a relatively short life.

The cost of Louis's wars and the heavy expenditure on buildings

---

[1] Ibid. ii. 306.   [2] Ibid. ii. 495.

like Versailles soon drastically reduced the amount of money available for this purpose. Charles Perrault, himself the recipient of a substantial pension, explains in amusing fashion how, from the time of the outbreak of the war with Spain in 1667, this source of income began to show signs of drying up:

Tout ce qui se trouva d'hommes distingués pour l'éloquence, la poésie, les mécaniques et les autres sciences, tant dans le royaume que dans les pays étrangers, reçurent des gratifications, les uns de 1,000 écus, les autres de 2,000 livres, les autres de 500 écus, d'autres de 1,200 livres, quelques-uns de 1,000 livres, et les moindres de 600 livres. Il alla de ces pensions en Italie, en Allemagne, en Danemark, en Suède, et aux dernières extrémités du Nord; elles y allaient par lettres de change, et à l'égard de celles qui se distribuaient à Paris, elles se portèrent la première année chez tous les gratifiés par le commis du trésorier des bâtiments,[1] dans des bourses de soie et d'or les plus propres du monde; la seconde année dans des bourses de cuir, et comme toutes choses ne peuvent pas demeurer au même état et vont naturellement en diminuant, les années suivantes il fallut les aller recevoir soi-même chez le trésorier en monnaie ordinaire, et les années commencèrent à avoir quinze ou seize mois. Quand on déclara la guerre à l'Espagne, une grande partie de ces pensions s'amortirent.[2]

The expenditure on these gifts revived after the end of this short war and indeed reached its peak in 1669; but the outbreak of the war with Holland in 1672 had much more serious consequences.

In the following year—the tenth anniversary of the inauguration of these royal gifts—Chapelain wrote to a foreign scholar of

le trouble que le gouffre de Bellone a mis aux sources des bienfaits, absorbant toutes choses pour nourrir ce monstre dévorant qui les a fait tarir, non seulement pour les étrangers, mais pour les naturels et pour ceux qui semblaient à couvert de tout ce retranchement sur notre Parnasse, sur moi-même qui m'en prévalais fort utilement et fort honorablement.[3]

This was somewhat of an exaggeration as Chapelain's heirs received in due course his usual 3,000 livres when he died in the following year; but from this point onwards only a handful of writers were still receiving gifts. Among the favoured few were Racine and Quinault, who was now producing the libretti for Lulli's operas; Boileau joined the select band in 1676, but after 1673 Corneille received nothing for

---

[1] The money was paid out by one of the departments run by Colbert, the Surintendance des bâtiments.

[2] *Mémoires de ma vie*, ed. P. Bonnefon, Paris, 1909, pp. 48–9. The effect of the war with Spain on these gifts is confirmed by Chapelain, *Lettres*, ii. 527.

[3] *Lettres*, ii. 813 n.

nine years, until shortly before his death in 1684. Even before that, like many other people, he had suffered delays in the payment of these royal gifts, a situation which produced the following lines which are generally attributed to him:

Au Roi, sur le retardement du paiement de sa pension.

Grand Roi, dont nous voyons la générosité
Montrer pour le Parnasse un excès de bonté
    Que n'ont jamais eu tous les autres,
Puissiez-vous dans cent ans donner encore des lois,
Et puissent tous vos ans être de quinze mois
    Comme vos commis font les nôtres![1]

Though the chaotic state of the accounting makes it difficult to know exactly when these much publicized gifts to men of letters faded out, they do not seem, even on this restricted scale, to have lasted beyond 1690.

It is true that the King's patronage of writers could take other forms which are not recorded in the accounts of the Surintendance des bâtiments. For instance, in 1683 Madeleine de Scudéry, now well into her seventies, was informed by Mme de Maintenon that she had been granted a royal pension of 2,000 livres.[2] Two days later Mme de Sévigné wrote to friends in the provinces to pass on the news:

Vous savez comme le Roi a donné deux mille livres de pension à Mlle de Scudéry; c'est par un billet de Mme de Maintenon qu'elle apprit cette bonne nouvelle. Elle fut remercier Sa Majesté un jour d'appartement; elle fut reçue en toute perfection; c'était une affaire que de recevoir cette merveilleuse Muse. Le Roi lui parla et l'embrassa pour l'empêcher d'embrasser ses genoux. Toute cette petite conversation fut d'une justesse admirable; Mme de Maintenon était l'interprète. Tout le Parnasse est en émotion pour remercier et le hèros et l'héroïne.[3]

Again, Boileau and especially Racine drew substantial sums, which were quite distinct from their pensions as men of letters, from their posts of *historiographes du roi*, though these too were reduced in the financial stringency caused by the Nine Years War. Moreover, Racine, even before he had abandoned writing for the public theatre, had received a handsome gift from Louis XIV; the post of *trésorier de*

---

[1] *Œuvres complètes*, x. 185.
[2] *Lettres*, ed. M. Langlois, 4 vols., Paris, 1935–9, ii. 480.
[3] *Lettres*, ed. E. Gérard-Gailly, 3 vols., Paris, 1955–7, ii. 929.

France, which was a complete sinecure and brought in an income of 2,400 livres, was simply conferred on him by the King in 1674 without his having to lay out a penny for its purchase. What is more, in 1690 at the height of his favour with Louis XIV and Mme de Maintenon, Racine was not only allowed to purchase a post of *gentilhomme de la chambre*, but he was enabled to buy it on the cheap, at less than a fifth of its market value.

Despite all this it would be as well not to exaggerate the role of Louis XIV as a patron of literature. In his later years piety made him avoid the theatrical performances for which he had shown such enthusiasm in the early part of his reign; and the increasing disorder in the royal finances as a result of the economic depression and the long years of war would seem to have made the period from the 1690s onwards one in which writers could draw little support from the royal Treasury. Indeed we shall see that in the reigns of Louis XV and Louis XVI the Crown did more for men of letters than was ever attempted by Louis XIV during his long reign.

In these years from 1661 to 1715 the King was not by any means the only source of literary patronage. It is true that the proportion of books bearing fulsome dedications tends to fall from the beginning of Louis XIV's personal reign,[1] but at its end writers were still hard at it seeking for generous patrons to flatter in a fashion which is amusingly described by Lesage in *Le Diable boiteux* in his portrait of a playwright who has just composed a new tragedy:

Il a dessein de la dédier, et il y a six heures qu'il travaille à l'épître dédicatoire; il en est à la dernière phrase en ce moment. On peut dire que c'est un chef-d'œuvre que cette dédicace: toutes les vertus morales et politiques, toutes les louanges que l'on peut donner à un homme illustre par ses ancêtres et par lui-même, n'y sont point épargnées; jamais auteur n'a tant prodigué l'encens.—A qui prétend-il adresser cet éloge? reprit l'écolier.—Il n'en sait rien encore, répliqua le diable; il a laissé le nom en blanc. Il cherche quelque riche seigneur qui soit plus libéral que ceux à qui il a déjà dédié d'autres livres; mais les gens qui payent les épîtres dédicatoires sont bien rares aujourd'hui.[2]

Such cynical remarks on the subject of patronage were by no means new. As far back as 1647 Scarron had published a volume of his *Œuvres burlesques* with a dedication 'A très honnête et très divertis-

---

[1] See Leiner, *Der Widmungsbrief in der französischen Literatur*, p. 27.
[2] Ed. Laufer, p. 96.

sante chienne Dame Guillemette, petite levrette de ma sœur'. In the course of this he has many highly satirical things to say about the practice of dedicating works with mercenary intentions, but this did not prevent him from offering nearly all his later writings to a great variety of patrons—to Louis XIV, la Grande Mademoiselle, Séguier, Foucquet and his wife, Retz, and a whole crowd of noblemen and their wives.

Furetière, comfortably off thanks to his livings in the Church, was a more consistent critic of the practice. In his satire, *Les Poètes*, published in 1655, he makes fun of the needy writer's hopes not only of making money out of the actors for a play, but also of extracting some from a bookseller and especially a patron:

> Il espérait tirer cent écus du libraire,
> Et vendre cent louis l'épître liminaire,
> N'ayant qu'à dédier l'œuvre au premier faquin
> Qui payerait chèrement l'or et le maroquin.[1]

In the following decade, in *Le Roman bourgeois*, he carried his satire of patronage and dedications much further. Towards the end of the novel the inventory of the possessions of a recently deceased poet called Mythophilacte is introduced. To his best friend he had bequeathed his 'grand Agenda ou Almanach des dîners': 'Cet almanach de dîners est fait en forme de table divisée par colonnes et contient une liste de tous les gens qui tiennent table à Paris, ou des autres connaissances du défunt à qui il allait demander à dîner. Cela est distribué par mois, par semaines et par jours, tout de même qu'un calendrier.' This reliance on other people for his main meal of the day is defended by one of the characters on the simple grounds: 'Car comment pourrait vivre autrement un auteur qui n'a point de patrimoine? Il aurait beau travailler nuit et jour, dès qu'il est à la merci des libraires, il ne peut gagner avec eux de l'eau pour boire.'[2] Among the manuscripts listed in this inventory is one which attracts the attention of the persons to whom it is being read out; it is entitled *Somme dédicatoire, ou examen général de toutes les questions qui se peuvent faire touchant la dédicace des livres, divisée en quatre volumes*. Ten pages of the novel are then devoted to an analysis, chapter by chapter, of the four volumes. This is followed by a list of the sums of money which a patron could be expected to offer in

---

[1] *Le Roman bourgeois, suivi de Satyres et de Nouvelle allégorique*, ed. G. Mongrédien, Paris, 1955, p. 264.
[2] pp. 209–11.

return for the dedications of a poem; these range from a pension of
2,000 livres for an epic (a hit at Chapelain?) downwards.[1] Finally
comes the *pièce de résistance*, a violent satire of dedicatory epistles
which quite outdoes Scarron's earlier effort since here a dog is replaced
by the hangman: 'Épître dédicatoire du premier livre que je ferai. A
très haut et très redouté seigneur Jean Guillaume, dit S. Aubin, maître
des hautes œuvres de la ville, prévôté et vicomté de Paris.'[2]

Despite satirical attacks on dedications and on patronage writers
continued to seek support from persons of high rank, from members of
the royal family downwards, and also from men whose wealth made up
for their lack of blue blood. Louis XIV's cousin, la Grande Mademoiselle, was a frequent recipient of dedications, and until they fell out in
1672, she employed the writer, Segrais, as her secretary with the title of
gentilhomme ordinaire. One of the advantages of having such a patron
was that her influence could be used to gain further advantages. In 1665
Mademoiselle wrote to Colbert in the following terms about the
absence of her protégé's name from the previous year's list of writers
who received gifts from the King:

M. de Segrais qui est de l'academie et qui a beaucoup travalié pour la gloire
du roy et pour le public aïant esté oublié lannée passée dans les gratifications
que le roy a faict aux baus esprits, m'a prié de vous faire souvenir de luy c'est
un certin homme de mérite et qui est à moy il y a long temps j'espère que cela
ne nuira pas à vous obliger à avoir de la considération pour luy c'est ce que je
vous demande et demeurerai monsieur Colbert votre afectionée amie Ch.
Marie-Louise d'Orleans.[3]

Louis XIV's two sisters-in-law—Henriette d'Angleterre and then
Charlotte Élisabeth—were also the recipients of dedications; the
former had presented to her Molière's *L'École des femmes* and Racine's
Andromaque though it is noticeable that both men gave up adding
dedications to their plays once they had attained a certain degree of
success in the theatre. The Dauphine (Marie-Anne-Christine de
Bavière) who took a considerable part in the running of the Comédie-
Française was much courted by writers, particularly playwrights, in the
1680s. Her husband received even more dedications, but seems to have
taken less interest in literature than his son, the duc de Bourgogne, to
whom La Fontaine dedicated the last book of his fables in 1693. His
reward came quickly; when he fell seriously ill in that year and was

---

[1] p. 227.   [2] p. 228.
[3] Depping, *Correspondance administrative* iv. 557.

persuaded to renounce the proceeds from a new and revised edition of his *Contes*, the young Duke sent him a present of 50 louis.[1]

The princes of the blood also continued to act as patrons, starting with the Grand Condé to whom Corneille dedicated his *Rodogune* and Molière, two decades later, his *Amphitryon*. We catch a glimpse of the way minor writers sought money from such a patron in *L'Europe vivante* of Samuel Chappuzeau; he relates how he went to Chantilly to present the first volume of this work to Condé and his son, Monsieur le duc, and spent two days there. 'Après avoir reçu de belles marques de la générosité de ces deux princes,' he continues, 'je montai à cheval vers le minuit pour prendre la route de Calais.'[2] Condé's brother, Conti, and after him the wives of later holders of the title figure prominently among the list of dedicatees, while towards the end of Louis XIV's reign the duchesse du Maine, a granddaughter of Condé, became well known as a patron of writers.

A study of La Fontaine's career after the downfall of Foucquet shows the varied sources from which patronage could come in the period from 1661 onwards. We have seen how at the end of his life he received financial assistance from the young duc de Bourgogne; thirty years earlier he had entered the household of the dowager duchesse d'Orléans, Louis XIV's aunt, as one of her *gentilshommes*. Mazarin's niece, the duchesse de Bouillon, was an enthusiastic patron of the poet. After the death of the duchesse d'Orléans La Fontaine lived for some twenty years in the household of Mme de la Sablière, and when she died in 1693, he spent the last two years of his life in the house of D'Hervart, a wealthy judge. But he had other high-born patrons in the latter part of his life. In a letter in verse written in 1689 to the duc de Vendôme the poet relates how abbé de Chaulieu who managed the affairs of the duke and his brother has promised him some money:

> Sur cet espoir j'ai par avance
> Quelques louis au vent jetés
> Dont je rends grâce à vos bontés...
> Le reste ira, ne vous déplaise,
> En vins, en joie, *et caetera*,
> Ce mot-ci s'interprétera
> Des Jeannetons, car les Clymènes
> Aux vieilles gens sont inhumaines.[3]

---

[1] La Fontaine, *Œuvres complètes*, ed. H. Régnier, 11 vols., Paris, 1883–92, i, pp. clxxxviii–clxxxix.

[2] *L'Europe vivante*, 2 vols., Geneva, 1667–71, ii. 102–3.

[3] *Œuvres complètes*, ix. 447.

Three years later we find him singing the praises of Monsieur le duc who in 1709 was to succeed to the title of prince de Condé; from him the poet had received a gift of 100 louis.[1]

Throughout the personal reign of Louis XIV writers continued to find patrons among the aristocracy. When Corneille at last moved permanently from Rouen to Paris in 1662, he seems for some years to have been accommodated with his wife and family at the Hôtel de Guise. Abbé d'Aubignac in the course of attacks on his recent plays speaks of the duc de Guise providing him with 'le couvert et la table'.[2] One particularly prominent patron, over a period extending from the 1640s to the 1680s, was the comte, later duc, de Saint-Aignan, *de l'Académie française*. 'Quels sont les poètes de son temps', asks abbé d'Olivet, 'qui n'ont pas laissé des témoignages publics de ce qu'ils croyaient devoir, ou à ses lumières, ou à ses bienfaits?'[3] Racine dedicated his first play to him, and the writers who offered their works to him ranged from Tristan in 1645 to Boursault in 1683. Boursault was one of those who was rewarded in hard cash, as he himself relates: 'Par reconnaissance de la protection qu'il m'avait donnée, je lui dédiai *Marie Stuart*, une tragédie que j'avais faite. Il la reçut de la manière la plus obligeante . . . et me pria de ne pas trouver mauvais que pour s'acquitter faiblement de l'obligation qu'il m'avait, il me fit un présent de cent louis.'

As Boursault hesitated to accept such a large sum, '"Je vois bien, ajouta-t-il, que vous ne me croyez pas assez riche pour vous donner cent louis tout d'un coup. Eh bien, puisque vous voulez avoir la complaisance de vous accommoder à ma fortune, souffrez au moins que je vous en donne vingt présentement, et que je continue de mois en mois jusqu'à ce que je sois quitte."' Boursault assures the reader that the instalments were promptly paid.[4]

Another frequent recipient of dedications in this period was the marquis, later duc, de Montausier, also an academician, the son-in-law of Mme de Rambouillet, who was put in charge of the education of the Dauphin and was made governor of Normandy. It is interesting to see the advice about how to write a dedication given by Chapelain to the author of a collection of Latin verse who, for the sake of variety, wished to offer it to the Duke's daughter:

[1] Ibid. 467.   [2] *Quatrième dissertation*, Paris, 1663, p. 117.
[3] P. Pellisson and P. J. T. d'Olivet, *Histoire de l'Académie française*, ed. C. Livet, 2 vols., Paris, 1858, ii. 249.
[4] *Lettres nouvelles*, i. 129.

Quant à la dédicace,[1] puisque, pour ne pas sortir de la maison de Montausier, vous regardez Madame la comtesse de Crussol, il n'y a aucune sorte de bien que vous n'en puissiez dire: naissance, éducation, vertu, esprit, taille, grâce, douceur, civilité. Par occasion vous pourrez parler du père et de la mère et de la grand-mère du côté maternel, comme vous savez trop bien qu'il se doit. Sa modestie ne souffre pas que vous appuyez sur l'article de la beauté. Avec tout cela ne l'entreprenez pas sans la participation de M. le duc de Montausier qui, allant faire le tour de la Normandie par l'ordre du Roi, passera à Caen et vous donnera moyen de lui en dire deux paroles.[2]

A striking example of patronage towards the end of this period is furnished by the duc de Vendôme's bounty to Racine's successor in tragedy, Campistron. We have seen how the ten plays which he had performed at the Comédie-Française between 1683 and 1693 did not bring him in all that much money. In 1691 he wrote the libretto of an opera for performance at a fête held at the Duke's château at Anet. According to the Frères Parfaict[3] the Duke was so pleased with it that he sent the author 100 louis. However, his friends assured him that 'la somme n'était pas assez pour M. de Vendôme et qu'il pouvait en espérer une récompense plus considérable'. Campistron was only with difficulty persuaded to refuse the money, but found in the end that he had done well to follow their advice. The Duke took him into his household and made him *secrétaire de ses commandements* and in 1694 secured for him the post of *secrétaire général des galères* which carried with it a salary of 3,000 livres.[4]

We may conclude that although by the second half of the century payments by publishers were improving and those to be received from playwriting had risen steeply, patronage was to remain a necessity until well into the following century if a writer was to survive.

In this country in the second half of the twentieth century the air is filled with lamentations over the financial plight of writers.[5] It can well be imagined that, under the considerably less favourable circumstances of seventeenth-century France, their bitter complaints would fill whole volumes. From one end of the century to the other references to

---

[1] Writing to another correspondent, Chapelain gives this interesting piece of information: 'Comme l'épître dédicatoire est la dernière feuille qui s'imprime, vous aurez du temps pour y penser et pour l'exécuter' (Lettres, ii. 551).

[2] Ibid. 417.

[3] *Histoire du théâtre français* xiii. 231.   [4] Jal, *Dictionnaire*, p. 309.

[5] See R. Findlater, *The Book Writers: Who are they?*, London, 1966, and *Public Lending Right. A Matter of Justice*, ed. R. Findlater, London, 1971, etc.

the poverty of writers abound. Shortly after 1600 Mathurin Régnier composed his *Satire II* in which he describes in vivid terms the poverty of the poet:

> Aussi, lorsque l'on voit un homme par la rue
> Dont le rabat est sale et la chausse rompue,
> Ses grègues aux genoux, au coude son pourpoint,
> Qui soit de pauvre mine et qui soit mal en point,
> Sans demander son nom, on le peut reconnaître;
> Car si ce n'est un Poète, au moins il le veut être.[1]

The following lines are attributed by Boursault to Maynard (incidentally, the latter could scarcely be considered to have been on the breadline himself as he could afford to purchase a judicial post in the provinces):

> Malherbe a souvent dans les crottes
> Laissé la semelle des bottes
> Qu'il portait faute de souliers:
>
> Moi, pour payer ce que je mange,
> Mes fourchettes et mes cuillers
> Retournent sur le Pont-au-Change.[2]

In his *Excuse à Ariste*, published in the year of *Le Cid*, Corneille takes up the theme of the lack of rewards for the writer:

> Le Parnasse autrefois dans la France adoré
> Faisait pour ses mignons un autre âge doré,
> Notre fortune enflait du prix de nos caprices,
> Et c'était une blanque à de bons bénéfices;
> Mais elle est épuisée, et les vers à présent
> Aux meilleurs du métier n'apportent que du vent.[3]

Writers of the period do not confine themselves to generalities. A long list of poverty-stricken writers is given at the end of the century by Vigneul-Marville who describes in the following terms the very modest circumstances to which Pierre Du Ryer, one of Corneille's rivals, was reduced in the latter part of his career as a writer:

M. Du Ryer traduisait les auteurs à la hâte pour tirer promptement du libraire Sommaville une médiocre récompense, qui l'aidait à subsister avec sa pauvre famille dans un petit village auprès de Paris. Un beau jour d'été nous allâmes plusieurs ensemble lui rendre visite. Il nous reçut avec joie, nous

---

[1] *Œuvres complètes*, p. 18.   [2] *Lettres nouvelles*, ii. 185.
[3] *Œuvres complètes*, x. 75–6.

parla de ses desseins, et nous fit voir ses ouvrages; mais, ce qui nous toucha, c'est que, ne craignant pas de nous laisser voir sa pauvreté, il voulut nous donner la collation. Nous nous rangeâmes dessous un arbre, on étendit une nappe sur l'herbe, sa femme apporta du lait, et lui des cerises, de l'eau fraîche et du pain bis. Quoique ce repas nous semblât très bon, nous ne pûmes dire adieu à cet excellent homme sans pleurer de le voir si maltraité de la fortune, surtout dans sa vieillesse et accablé d'infirmités.[1]

Obviously neither writing plays nor turning out translations had brought wealth to Du Ryer.

Round about the time of Du Ryer's death in 1658 another lament on the sad state of poverty to which the writer was subjected came from the pen of the *libertin* poet, Claude Le Petit, who was shortly after to be burnt at the stake:

> Quand vous verrez un homme avecque gravité,
> En chapeau de clabaud promener la savate,
> Et le col étranglé d'une sale cravate,
> Marcher arrogamment dessus la chrétienté.
>
> Barbu comme un sauvage, et jusqu'au cul crotté,
> D'un haut de chausse noir, sans ceinture et sans patte,
> Et de quelques lambeaux d'une vieille buratte,
> En tout temps constamment couvrir sa nudité;
>
> Envisager chacun d'un œil hagard et louche,
> Et, mâchant dans ses dents quelque terme farouche,
> Se ronger jusqu'au sang la corne de ses doigts;
>
> Quand, dis-je, avec ces traits vous trouverez un homme,
> Dites assurément: c'est un poète françois!
> Si quelqu'un vous dément, je l'irai dire à Rome.[2]

The earliest version of Boileau's first satire appears to belong to the same period; its message is made clear in the opening lines:

> Cet auteur si fameux dont la muse fertile
> A charmé tant de fois et la Cour et la Ville,
> Mais qui n'étant vêtu que d'un simple bureau,
> Passe l'été sans linge, et l'hiver sans manteau;
> Et dont le corps tout sec et la mine affamée
> N'en sont pas mieux refaits pour tant de renommée;
> Las de perdre en rimant et sa peine et son bien.

---

[1] Vigneul-Marveille [Noël Bonaventure d'Argonne], *Mélanges d'histoire et de littérature*, 3 vols., Paris, 1700–1, i. 193–4.
[2] F. Lachèvre, *Le Libertinage au XVIIᵉ siècle*, 14 vols., Paris, 1909–24, v. pp. xlii–xliii.

> D'emprunter en tous lieux et de ne gagner rien,
> Sans habit, sans argent, ne sachant plus que faire,
> Sort de Paris chargé de sa seule misère . . .[1]

According to his Boswell, Brossette, the writer whom Boileau originally had in mind in penning these lines was Tristan L'Hermite who had died in poverty in 1655.

Among the many clauses of the will of the writer, Mythophilacte, in Furetière's *Roman bourgeois* which bear on the state of the profession in this period is the following:

> *Item*, à chacun des pauvres auteurs qui se trouvent à mon enterrement, je donne et lègue un exemplaire d'un livre par moi composé, intitulé: *L'Exercice iournalier du poète*, dont la délivrance leur sera faite sitôt que ledit livre sera achevé d'imprimer, dans lequel ils trouveront un bel exemple de constance pour supporter la faim et la pauvreté, avec une oraison très ardente que j'ai faite en leur faveur, afin que les riches aient plus de compassion d'eux qu'ils n'ont eue de moi.[2]

Furetière's tone in discussing the position of writers is always satirical. Very different are the eloquent protests of La Bruyère in *Les Caractères*; like the poet in Boileau's satire, La Bruyère's writer is so disgusted by his failure to make a living by his pen that he is ready to give up:

> . . . Je renonce à tout ce qui a été, qui est et qui sera livre. *Bérylle* tombe en syncope à la vue d'un chat, et moi à la vue d'un livre. Suis-je mieux nourri et plus lourdement vêtu, suis-je dans me chambre à l'abri du nord, ai-je un lit de plumes, après vingt ans entiers qu'on me débite dans la place? J'ai un grand nom, dites-vous, et beaucoup de gloire: dites que j'ai beaucoup de vent qui ne sert à rien. Ai-je un grain de ce métal qui procure toutes choses?

After a review of various professions—reputable and otherwise—La Bruyère makes his writer continue: 'Et sans parler que des gains licites, on paie au tuilier sa tuile, et à l'ouvrier son temps et son ouvrage; paye-t-on à un auteur ce qu'il pense et ce qu'il écrit? Et s'il pense très bien, le paye-t-on très largement? Se meuble-t-il, s'anoblit-il à force de penser et d'écrire juste?'

These are obviously rhetorical questions. The only solution which the author sees is to secure a good, well-paid job which allows one leisure to write:

> Folie, simplicité, imbécillité, continue *Antisthène*, de mettre l'enseigne d'auteur ou de philosophe! Avoir, s'il se peut, un *office lucratif* qui fasse prêter à

---

[1] *Œuvres complètes*, ed. A. Adam, Paris, 1966, pp. 866–7.
[2] p. 207.

ses amis, et donner à ceux qui ne peuvent rendre; écrire alors par jeu, par oisiveté, et comme *Tityre* siffle ou joue de la flûte; cela ou rien; j'écris à ces conditions, et je cède ainsi à la violence de ceux qui me prennent à la gorge et me disent: 'Vous écrirez'.[1]

La Bruyère would certainly have made an excellent propagandist for the Société des gens de lettres.

The poverty of the writer and his inability to make a living without the help of a patron continue to be stressed just as heavily at the end of the period as at the beginning. In 1700 we find the obscure satirist, Pierre Henry, echoing Mathurin Régnier at the beginning of the century:

> Malheur! trois fois malheur à celui qui, pour vivre,
> Ne sait pour tout métier que composer un livre!
> Sans un bon Mécénas qui lui donne du pain,
> A la honte du siècle il crèvera de faim.[2]

The poverty and squalor of a writer's existence are again stressed by Lesage seven years later in *Le Diable boiteux*:

Portez la vue au-delà sur la droite, continua le diable, et tâchez de démêler dans un grenier un homme qui se promène en chemise à la sombre clarté d'une lampe. J'y suis, s'écria l'écolier, à telles enseignes que je découvre dans ce galetas un grabat, un placet, une table et des murs tout barbouillés de noir. —Le personnage qui loge si haut est un poète, reprit Asmodée; et ce qui vous paraît noir, ce sont des vers tragiques de sa façon dont il a tapissé sa chambre; car il est obligé, faute de papier, d'écrire ses poèmes sur le mur.[3]

Though one could scarcely be expected to take literally this description of the writer's lot, clearly Lesage is far from suggesting that it was a happy one.

On the other hand, Corneille acquired with his contemporaries from quite early on in his career—'Corneille est excellent, mais il vend ses ouvrages'[4] as a poet put it in 1634—a reputation for being solely concerned with making money and, what is more, for succeeding in doing so. Tallemant, for instance, declared: 'En vérité, il a plus d'avarice que d'ambition, et pourvu qu'il en tire de l'argent, il ne se tourmente guère

---

[1] 'Des jugements', 21. Cf. 17 which contains the bitter words: 'Il n'y a point d'art si mécanique ni de si vile condition, où les avantages ne soient plus sûrs plus prompts et plus solides.'

[2] F. Fleuret and L. Perceau (eds.), *Les Satires françaises du XVIIe siècle*, 2 vols., Paris, 1923, ii. 289.

[3] Ed. Laufer, p. 15.   [4] A. Gaillard, *Œuvres*, Paris, 1634, p. 33.

du reste.[1] On the other hand, writing some years after the death of both men, La Bruyère could say fairly accurately of Chapelain and Corneille: 'C. P. était fort riche, et C. N. ne l'était pas: la *Pucelle* et *Rodogune* méritaient chacune un autre sort.'[2] That Corneille died in utter poverty was for a long time a widely accepted view, but one which is no longer held; doubtless in his later years he exaggerated his financial problems (he had a large family to provide for and his royal pension was paid only very irregularly). However, he was certainly less well off than Chapelain with his comfortable income from the patronage of the duc de Longueville and later Louis XIV, as well as from several quite valuable Church livings. Chapelain undoubtedly died a rich man though his contemporaries disagree about the precise amount of his wealth; Segrais, who puts it higher than anyone else, speaks of an estate of 400,000 livres of which 240,000 were in cash, and an income, presumably in his later years, of 15,000 livres.[3] Very little of this money can have come to him through the sale of his works to publishers.

Among other writers who were roughly contemporaries of Corneille, Voiture was even wealthier, yet this was certainly not due to his writings which only appeared posthumously; he was the son of a wealthy wine-merchant and owed most of his prosperity to the posts which he held at court and in the administration. The novelist, Gomberville, was also a wealthy man (according to Tallemant[4] he had an income of 15,000 livres), but he was a nobleman who inherited a fair amount of property from his father.

It is interesting to find Charles Sorel in 1672 attempting to refute the commonly held view that it was wrong to write for money and that the introduction of monetary rewards for writers had simply led to the production of a great many bad books. He argues that it has also produced good books which would not otherwise have been written since poverty is the mother of invention:

Ceux qui écrivent pour le gain doivent être fort exaltés par des considérations si puissantes. On les voit souvent meilleurs écrivains que les riches, parce qu'on suppose que s'ils se sont adonnés à écrire plutôt qu'a une autre profession, c'est qu'ils ont la capacité requise, et que de plus ils emploient une extrême diligence pour obtenir les choses dont ils ne se peuvent passer, au lieu

---

[1] *Historiettes*, vii. 181. See also e.g. d'Aubignac, *Deux dissertations . . .*, Paris, 1663, p. 96; *Troisième dissertation*, Paris, 1663, p. 7; *Quatrième dissertation*, pp. 118–19, 121–2; and *Carpenteriana*, Paris, 1724, p. 110.

[2] 'Des jugements', 14.   [3] *Œuvres diverses*, i. 225–6.

[4] *Historiettes*, vi. 48.

que les riches, n'ayant besoin de rien, travaillent avec moins de soin et moins d'attachement.[1]

Here we see emerging the concept of the professional writer, but it is clear that, like other writers who lacked private resources, in his later years Sorel himself had extreme difficulty in making a living by his pen.

It is not, however, sufficient to confine our attention to the economic position of the writer in this period; we must also take into account his social status. In a society still dominated by blue blood this was undoubtedly a lowly one, especially if he strove to make a living out of his earnings from booksellers and actors and from such scraps as he could pick up in the way of patronage.

Even the nobleman who took to writing and actually making his works public felt it necessary to offer an apology for doing such a thing. In 1628 in his preface to *Tyr et Sidon*, a tragicomedy by Jean de Schélandre, a nobleman who seven years later was to be mortally wounded in the Thirty Years War, Ogier felt compelled to offer the reader some explanation of the author's involvement in writing:

Faisant profession des lettres et des armes, comme il fait, il sait les employer chacune en leur saison; de sorte qu'il ne serait pas homme pour entretenir le théâtre de combats en peinture, tandis que les autres se battent à bon escient, si des considérations importantes, qu'il n'est pas besoin que tu saches, ne lui donnaient malgré lui le loisir de solliciter des procès et de faire des livres.[2]

Playwrights of Corneille's generation included two noblemen— Georges de Scudéry and La Calprenède—who justify in most truculent terms their excursions into literature, making it clear that as officers and gentlemen they are in a very different class from other writers of the time. In 1631, for instance, in the preface to his tragicomedy, *Ligdamon et Lidias*, Scudéry offered this retort to those who held that writing was 'un métier indigne d'un gentilhomme': 'La poésie me tient lieu de divertissement agréable, et non pas d'occupation sérieuse. Si je rime, c'est qu'alors que je ne sais que faire, et n'ai pour but en ce travail que le seul désir de me contenter, car, bien loin d'être mercenaire, l'imprimeur et les comédiens témoigneront que je ne leur ai pas vendu ce qu'ils ne me pouvaient payer.' Yet such was the discredit in which playwriting was held that when Mme de Rambouillet used her influence to get Scudéry appointed governor of the fortress of Notre-Dame de la Garde at Marseilles, according to Tallemant the

---

[1] *De la connaissance des bons livres*, Amsterdam, 1672, pp. 40–1.
[2] *Ancien théâtre français*, ed. E. L. N. Viollet-le-Duc, 10 vols., Paris, 1854–7, viii. 22–3.

Secretary of State concerned expressed his doubts at the wisdom of the appointment, since he held 'qu'il était de dangereuse conséquence de donner ce gouvernement à un poète, qui avait fait des poésies pour l'Hôtel de Bourgogne et qui y avait mis son nom'.[1] La Calprenède in the preface to his tragedy, *La Mort de Mithridate*, published in 1637, declared: 'La profession que je fais ne me peut permettre, sans quelque espèce de honte, de me faire connaître par des vers, et tirer de quelque méchante rime une réputation que je dois seulement espérer d'une épée que j'ai l'honneur de porter.' He adds that he is only publishing his play because manuscript copies of it are in circulation and because 'un valet de chambre, plus soigneux de quelque petit gain que de votre satisfaction', may publish a very incorrect version of it.[2]

The swashbuckling poet and novelist, Vital d'Audiguier, told Théophile de Viau, if we are to believe Tallemant, 'qu'il ne taillait sa plume qu'avec son épée'. "Je ne m'étonne donc pas, dit Théophile, que vous écriviez si mal"'.[3] Even in the second half of the century, when the aristocratic prejudice against a nobleman who demeaned himself by writing was growing weaker, we still find writers of noble rank testifying to its continued existence. In the last volume of *Le Grand Cyrus*, published in 1653, we find Madeleine de Scudéry complaining (she puts the words into the mouth of Sapho herself):

Car enfin je pose pour fondement que dès qu'on se tire de la multitude par les lumières de son esprit, et qu'on acquiert la réputation d'en avoir plus qu'un autre, et d'écrire assez bien en vers ou en prose, pour pouvoir faire des livres on perd la moitié de sa noblesse, si l'on en a; et on n'est point ce qu'est un autre de la même maison et du même sang, qui ne se mêlera point d'écrire.[4]

As late as 1678 we find the Italian Primi Visconti declaring in his notes on his stay at the court of Louis XIV:

En France, en effet, on n'estime que les titres de guerre; ceux des lettres et de toute autre profession, sont méprisés et l'on considère comme vil l'homme de qualité qui sait écrire; je sais que les seigneurs d'Urfé ont honte que leur aïeul Honoré d'Urfé ait écrit le poème de l'*Astrée*.[5]

Though by this period in the century the aristocratic prejudice against writing was dying out, in these circles there was still felt to be a

---

[1] *Historiettes*, vii. 37.
[2] See also the preface to his *Comte d'Essex* (1639) and the dedication of his tragicomedy, *Édouard* (1640).
[3] *Historiettes*, viii. 7.
[4] *Artamène ou le Grand Cyrus*, 10 vols., Paris, 1649–53, x. 328–9.
[5] *Mémoires sur la cour de Louis XIV*, trans. J. Lemoine, Paris, 1908, pp. 225–6.

gulf between the nobleman who wrote for pleasure and the bourgeois professional writer. When asked for her opinion of the *Maximes* of the duc de La Rochefoucauld before they appeared in print, the duchesse de Schomberg (as Mlle de Hautefort she had received the amorous attentions of Louis XIII) commented on various points of style in them and added: 'Ces modes-là de parler me plaisent parce que cela distingue bien un honnête homme, qui écrit pour son plaisir et comme il parle, d'avec les gens qui en font métier.'[1] When one of the characters in *Le Grand Cyrus* assures Sapho that 'tous les hommes de la cour caressent fort tous ceux qui se mêlent d'écrire', he gets a crushing answer: 'Je vous assure, répliqua Sapho, qu'ils les caressent d'une étrange manière; car enfin presque tous les jeunes gens de la cour traitent ceux qui se mêlent d'écrire, comme ils traitent des artisans.'[2]

Apparently, the situation had not changed all that much since 1632 when Chapelain had declared that at the court 'poète, chantre, baladin, caimand, bouffon et parasite, pour ne rien dire de plus, y sont synonymes et ne passent que pour un'.[3] That a nobleman did not like to be confused with an author is vividly brought out in an episode in a work of an obscure writer named Préchac, *Le Voyage de Fontainebleau*, published in 1678. He describes how he accompanied an Englishman to the court and found himself suddenly revealed for what he was, an author, in other words 'un excrément du Parnasse'!

Nous étions en conversation sur une galerie en attendant qu'on nous apportât à manger, lorsqu'un homme de la cour m'ayant aperçu, m'appela par mon nom et me demanda si je ne voulais pas lui faire voir comment j'avais fini l'*Héroïne Mousquetaire*.[4] Ce compliment me fit rougir, et jugeant par les regards de l'Anglais que j'étais découvert pour auteur, je répondis à ce courtisan qu'il me faisait plus de tort qu'il ne pensait, puisque j'étais avec des personnes qui me regardaient comme un cavalier fort important, et non pas comme un excrément du Parnasse.[5]

Racine undoubtedly came up against this prejudice when he found himself suddenly translated from the world of the theatre to the court of Louis XIV. Primi Visconti records a significant conversation with a great nobleman on this topic in 1679: '... Comme dans ses vers il faisait parler Alexandre avec des sentiments de plébéien, le maréchal d'Estrades me dit qu'il craignait qu'il n'en fît autant dans l'histoire de

[1] La Rochefoucauld, *Maximes*, ed. J. Truchet, Paris, 1967, p. 566 n.
[2] x. 329.   [3] *Lettres*, i. 18.   [4] Published in 1677.
[5] *Le Voyage de Fontainebleau*, Paris, 1678, pp. 21–2.

Louis, étant donné que l'auteur était un homme du peuple.'[1] However, Racine was undoubtedly a skilful courtier and he gradually succeeded in adapting himself. We catch occasional glimpses of the two new historiographers in the letters of Mme de Sévigné in which aristocratic prejudice is blended with the marquise's feeling that her exiled cousin, Bussy Rabutin, would have been a much better choice for the post. In November 1677 she passes on to him an anecdote concerning the King and the two writers:

Le Roi leur dit, il y a quatre jours: 'Je suis fâché que vous ne soyez venus à cette dernière campagne; vous auriez vu la guerre, et votre voyage n'eût pas été long.' Racine lui répondit: 'Sire, nous sommes deux bourgeois qui n'avons que des habits de ville; nous en commandâmes de campagne; mais les places que vous attaquiez furent plus tôt prises que nos habits ne furent faits.' Cela fut reçu agréablement. Ah! que je connais un homme de qualité à qui j'aurais bien plutôt fait écrire mon histoire qu'à ces bourgeois-là, si j'étais son maître! C'est cela qui serait digne de la postérité![2]

Racine's skill in adapting himself to the atmosphere of Versailles is reflected in the way he warned his elder son that it was not his plays which brought him the flattering attentions of various princes of the blood and great noblemen:

. . . Sans fatiguer les gens du monde du récit de mes ouvrages, dont je ne leur parle jamais, je me contente de leur tenir des propos amusants, et de les entretenir de choses qui leur plaisent. Mon talent avec eux n'est pas de leur faire sentir que j'ai de l'esprit, mais de leur apprendre qu'ils en ont. Ainsi quand vous voyez M. le Duc passer souvent des heures entières avec moi, vous seriez étonné si vous étiez présent, de voir que souvent il en sort sans que j'aie dit quatre paroles; mais peu à peu je le mets en humeur de causer, et il sort de chez moi encore plus satisfait de lui que de moi.[3]

Such were the methods which Racine used to obliterate gradually the memory of his bourgeois status as a writer. Both his success in this endeavour and the aristocratic disdain for the writer are admirably reflected in the duc de Saint-Simon's verdict on him: 'Rien du poète dans son commerce, et tout de l'honnête homme'.[4]

Where the gulf between nobleman and bourgeois writer was

---

[1] *Mémoires su la cour de Louis XIV*, p. 244.

[2] *Lettres*, ii. 386–7. See also her sarcastic account of the presence of Racine and Boileau at the siege of Ghent in the following year (ibid. 395).

[3] Louis Racine, *Mémoire sur la vie et les ouvrages de Jean Racine*, in *Œuvres complètes*, i. 81–2.

[4] *Mémoires*, ed. A. de Boislisle, 43 vols., Paris, 1879–1930, vi. 170.

revealed most clearly in the seventeenth century—not only in France, but also in England as the treatment received by Dryden at the hands of the Earl of Rochester shows—was the beating-up by a gang of hired thugs inflicted on an author who gave offence to his betters. 'Les poètes ne se vengent qu'à coups de plumes et qu'avec des pointes d'épigrammes,' an anonymous writer warned Boileau in a counter-attack on his satires. 'Les ducs et pairs et les marquis le font à coups d'étrivières, et les bâtonnades ne leur coûtent qu'à commander. On a vu depuis peu couper des nez; on pourrait bien voir dans peu des oreilles coupées.'[1] The reference to noses is to an episode during the Fronde; a nobleman, the marquis de Vardes, who had been insulted by an obscure pamphleteer, had the offender seized by his servants who,

> Ayant pris l'auteur par les basques,
> Coupèrent à coups de ciseau
> Son très infortuné naseau,
> Ce qui fait qu'après cet outrage
> On peut dire de son ouvrage:
> 'Ce sont des discours mal tournés
> D'un auteur qui n'a point de nez.'[2]

Even a cultured nobleman, a member of the Académie française, like the comte de Bussy-Rabutin lost all sense of proportion when he imagined that a mere bourgeois writer like Boileau was on the point of forgetting the distance in rank which separated them. His fury is conveyed in this passage from a letter written to Father Rapin from his exile in Burgundy:

Il a passé en ce pays un ami de Despréaux, qui a dit à une personne de qui je l'ai su, que Despréaux avait appris que je parlais avec mépris de son 'Épître au Roi' sur la campagne de Hollande, et qu'il était résolu de s'en venger dans une pièce qu'il faisait. J'ai de la peine à croire qu'un homme comme lui soit assez fou pour perdre le respect qu'il me doit et pour s'exposer aux suites d'une pareille affaire. Cependant, comme il peut être enflé du succès de ses satires impunies, qu'il pourrait bien ne pas savoir la différence qu'il y a de moi aux gens dont il a parlé, ou croire que mon absence donne lieu de tout entrprendre, j'ai cru qu'il était de la prudence d'un homme sage d'essayer à détourner les choses qui lui pourraient donner du chagrin et le porter à des extrémités.

Je vous avouerai donc, mon révérend père, que vous me ferez plaisir de

[1] É. Magne, *Bibliographie générale des œuvres de Nicolas Boileau-Despréaux*, 2 vols., Paris, 1929, ii. 144.
[2] Loret, *La Muse historique*, i. 139.

m'épargner la peine des violences, à quoi pareille insolence me pousserait infailliblement. J'ai toujours estimé l'action de Vardes, qui sachant qu'un homme comme Despréaux avait écrit quelque chose contre lui, lui fit couper le nez. Je suis aussi fin que Vardes, et ma disgrâce m'a rendu plus sensible que je ne serais si j'étais à la tête de la cavalerie légère de France.[1]

Such phrases as 'le respect qu'il me doit' and 'la différence qu'il y a de moi aux gens dont il a parlé' (the writers whom Boileau had satirized) bring out vividly the social gulf which separated nobleman and writer in this period.

Four years after this incident, which was finally smoothed over, both Boileau and Racine were involved in a much more dangerous situation arising out of the controversy provoked by *Phèdre*. The two men were accused of being responsible for a sonnet, 'Dans un palais doré, Damon, jaloux et blême . . .', which was highly insulting to the patrons of Racine's rival, Pradon. Bussy naturally considered that there was only one remedy for such unheard of insolence on the part of mere writers:

Jamais il n'y eut rien de si insolent que ce sonnet; deux auteurs reprochent à un officier de la couronne qu'il est ni courtisan, ni guerrier, ni chrétien; que sa sœur, la duchesse de Mazarin, est une coureuse et qu'il a de l'amour pour elle quoiqu'il soit Italien. Et bien que ces injures fussent des vérités, elles devaient attirer mille coups d'étrivières à des gens comme ceux-là; cependant l'affaire fut accommodée.[2]

It seems that before this happened Racine and Boileau were for a while in serious danger of being beaten up and had to take refuge in the Hôtel de Condé. Some contemporaries even alleged that Boileau did suffer this fate. A poem of the time begins:

> Dans un coin de Paris, Boileau, tremblant et blême,
> Fut hier bien frotté, quoiqu'il n'en dise rien . . .[3]

No doubt this was merely what the author of these lines would have liked to happen, but undoubtedly a satirist like Boileau was in some danger of incurring the punishment which awaited writers who forgot the distance which separated them from their betters.

A less dramatic example of the disrepute in which the calling of writer was held is furnished by Quinault. After producing some fifteen plays in as many years and securing election to the Académie française, he made a wealthy marriage, and although he continued to produce

---

[1] *Correspondance*, ed. L. Lalanne, 6 vols., Paris, 1858–9, ii. 210–11.
[2] Ibid. iii. 208.   [3] Magne, *Bibliographie*, ii. 212.

libretti for Lulli's operas, he gave up writing plays and sought the social standing conferred by an official post. According to the author of 'La Vie de P. Quinault' in the collected edition of his works which appeared in 1715,

Quinault, se voyant bel esprit titré, voulut acquérir une charge qui lui donnât un rang dans le monde. C'est ce qu'il fit en achetant celle d'auditeur des comptes. Lorsqu'il croyait s'en mettre en possession, on fit quelque difficulté de le recevoir. Messieurs de la Chambre des Comptes disaient qu'il n'était pas de l'honneur d'une compagnie aussi grave que la leur de recevoir dans leur corps un homme qui avait paru pendant plusieurs années sur les théâtres pour y faire représenter ses tragédies et ses comédies.[1]

However, the resistance of the members of the court was of short duration and Quinault was admitted in the end. Then there is the curious story of the lawsuit in which the young librettist and playwright, Danchet, found himself involved. He had been engaged as tutor to two boys by their widowed mother, and when she fell ill, she made him promise not to abandon her sons and by her will left him a life annuity. After the success of his first libretto, *Hésione*, in 1700, the boys' relatives, to quote a near-contemporary account of the matter, 'voulurent exiger de lui la promesse de ne plus travailler pour le théâtre. Il refusa de prendre un engagement qu'il se sentait incapable de tenir. Sur son refus, on ne se contenta pas de lui ôter ses élèves; on prétendit même le priver de sa pension viagère.' When the case was tried, Danchet was allowed to keep the annuity, but lost his post as tutor.[2]

In considering the attitude to their art of writers who sought to make a living with their pen from the uncertain proceeds of patronage and what they could earn from booksellers and (in the case of playwrights) from the theatre, we have to bear in mind not only the inadequacy of the financial rewards offered by writing, but also the low repute in which the profession of man of letters was held in the aristocratic, semi-feudal society of the day. Writing plays did become decidedly more lucrative from the 1630s onwards: it also offered a quick route to fame for the successful dramatist. But it did not offer a career. Not only were the proceeds of patronage uncertain and the income from publication small, but, although a really successful play could quickly

[1] *Théâtre*, 5 vols., Paris, 1715, i. 19.
[2] J. Dubu, 'La Condition sociale de l'écrivain de théâtre au XVIIe siècle', *XVIIe siècle*, 1958, pp. 178–9.

produce a substantial sum of money, this income dried up after a few weeks. The example of the two Corneille brothers, both of whom had a long and prolific career as playwrights, shows clearly that writing for the theatre was far from leading to affluence.

In practice, the theatre drew writers to it only to repel them, not only when their plays were a failure, but even when they were quite successful, simply because writing for the public stage brought neither wealth nor social standing. Quinault was not the only playwright of the time who gave up writing for the public theatres; there is the far more striking case of Racine who at the age of thirty-seven and at the very height of his powers, as *Phèdre* had just shown, threw it all up and wasted his talents in the function, shared with Boileau, of historiographer royal. Studied in the context of the uncertain economic rewards of the dramatist's profession and the low social prestige enjoyed by its practitioners, Racine's abandonment of the public theatre appears less mysterious than it once did. The interpretation of this sudden step—one which can be traced back to Louis Racine—which attributes it to a sudden religious crisis can no longer be accepted. The great majority of Racine's contemporaries whose opinion of his action has come down to us were in no doubt as to the reason for it. It is true that there may have been other, more intimate reasons into which, at this distance in time, we cannot hope to probe, but it seems reasonably clear that it was not religious scruples, but the prospects of worldly advancement through a career at court which led Racine to forsake the drama for the post of historiographer with its greater social prestige and its higher and more permanent emoluments.

In the preface to the 1683 edition of his works his colleague, Boileau, speaks of his post of historiographer as 'le glorieux emploi qui m'a tiré du métier de la poésie',[1] and a similar phrase is applied to Racine himself by Longepierre, another dramatist, in his *Parallèle de M. Corneille et de M. Racine*. Although he declares that everyone deplores the loss sustained by the theatre because of Racine's new role as panegyrist of Louis XIV, he exclaims: 'Heureux de pouvoir jouir lui-même des regrets du public (bonheur qui n'est pas fait pour les vivants) et de devoir à l'emploi glorieux qui l'a tiré du théâtre ce premier gage d'immortalité.'[2] What is more, after Quinault and Racine, Campistron also abandoned writing for the stage and ended up in the

---

[1] *Œuvres complètes*, p. 857.

[2] In A. Baillet, *Jugements des savants sur les principaux ouvrages des auteurs*, 8 vols. Amsterdam, 1725, iv. 383.

comfortable sinecure of *secrétaire général des galères* which his aristo-cratic patron secured for him.

Paradoxically, the position of the writer in what is one of the greatest ages of French literature was decidedly precarious. Unless he had private means or a comfortable job, he seldom rose above hardship or even poverty. Some writers were fortunate enough to be able to use the reputation which they had acquired with their pen to rise in the social scale, but, as with Racine, this could bring about the virtual abandon-ment of their career as men of letters. Socially the writer was despised; even when admitted to 'le monde', to the world of the Paris *salons*, he was looked upon as an inferior being who was expected to show appropriate deference to those superior to him in rank or wealth. He could still be subjected to brutal ill-treatment if he forgot his place. And although in the last decades before the Revolution both his economic and social standing were to be greatly improved, this was to be a very slow and gradual process.

The humble position of the writer in seventeenth-century France was obviously due in considerable measure to the fact that owing to the smallness of the reading and theatre-going public it was not yet possible for the writer to make himself independent of patronage. Illiteracy was still widespread; well over half the population lay outside the potential market of publishers through inability to read or even ignorance of French, not to mention the impossibility of having access to books for economic reasons. There were, it is true, the extremely cheap chapbooks (*livres de colportage*) on which a great deal of attention has recently been concentrated.[1] These little books, crudely printed on cheap paper and often with blue covers which gave to them the name of *Bibliothèque bleue*, appear to have originated in Troyes and to have found imitators in other publishing centres, mainly in northern France, such as Rouen and naturally Paris. Relatively few of them, at any rate in the seventeenth century, can be said to have had a literary content, even taking the word in a wide sense; the volumes offered for sale by pedlars at markets and fairs or hawked from door-to-door all over the countryside included almanachs and books of prophecies, and works

[1] The largest work on the subject still remains C. Nisard, *Histoire des livres populaires*, 2nd edn., 2 vols., Paris, 1864, but more recent works include P. Brochon, *Le Livre de colportage en France depuis le XVIᵉ siècle*, Paris, 1954; R. Mandrou, *De la culture populaire aux XVIIᵉ et XVIIIᵉ siècles: la Bibliothèque bleue de Troyes*, Paris, 1964; G. Bollème, *La Bibliothèque bleue. La Littérature populaire en France du XVIᵉ au XIXᵉ siècle*, Paris, 1971, and *La Bible bleue, anthologie d'une littérature 'populaire'*, Paris, 1975; and A. Morin, *Catalogue descriptif de la Bibliothèque bleue de Troyes*, Geneva and Paris, 1974.

on a wide variety of subjects—religious (including lives of saints), educational, medical, recreational, and comic (for example, on the subject of women). One enormously popular work was *Le Bonhomme Misère*, a bizarre tale which is not, as one might imagine, a vehicle for social protest. Where they border on literature is in keeping alive the legends and even the romances of the Middle Ages; one encounters, for instance, versions of the legend of the Wandering Jew and such works as *Les Conquêtes du Grand Charlemagne, Huon de Bordeaux,* and *Les quatre fils Aymon.*

There are many unsolved mysteries about this sub-literature which remained extremely popular until the middle of the nineteenth century before it was gradually wiped out by the coming of the cheap, popular newspaper. Who read these works in the seventeenth century when illiteracy was so widespread and when French was not spoken in large parts of the country? Part of the answer might be that these chapbooks were used for reading aloud in the famous *veillées* of the country people and thus enjoyed a much wider audience than might at first be imagined. On the other hand, there are scraps of evidence to show that chapbooks were not always entirely directed at a popular audience nor read only by the plebs. Some of the books on technical subjects such as cookery or letter-writing were obviously aimed at readers of some education, and in practice chapbooks seem to have fallen into all sorts of hands. If one of the peasants in a Troyes chapbook, *Agréables conférences de deux paysans de Saint-Ouen et de Montmorency sur les affaires du temps,* published during the Fronde, claims to have read three extremely popular works of the kind—Aesop's fables, *Till Eulenspiegel,* and *Jean de Paris.*[1]—the second of these works was also familiar to one of the Paris bourgeoises in *Les Caquets de li'accouchée,* 'qui avait lu les romans'.[2]

Although French chapbooks appear to have originated in the provinces, at Troyes, there is some evidence that even in the first half of the seventeenth century they had penetrated to the capital. An inventory of 1698 shows that a Paris printer held considerable stocks of the products of a colleague in Troyes, while a member of the Oudot family, famous for its introduction of chapbooks at that centre, was established as a bookseller in the capital and was succeeded there by his widow. Sometimes printed in the capital, but more often imported from Troyes, the little volumes of the *Bibliothèque bleue* must have found readers not

---

[1] *Agréables conférences* . . . , ed. F. Deloffre, Paris, 1961, p. 94.
[2] Ed. E. Fournier, Paris, 1855, pp. 226–7. (The original edition dates from 1622.)

only in the small towns and among the country people, but in Paris itself.[1] A curious anecdote of Tallemant which, though often quoted, is by no means clear in its meaning illustrates the difficulty of deciding what sort of readers these chapbooks catered for. The story concerns the princesse de Conti, the daughter of the duc de Guise murdered at Blois, whose amorous affairs brought her notoriety during the reigns of Henry IV and Louis XIII (she died in 1631): 'Lorsque le cardinal de Richelieu l'envoya en exil dans le comté d'Eu, elle logea chez un gentilhomme nommé M. de Jonquières, vers Compiègne, parce que son carrosse rompit ... Le soir qu'elle y arriva, pour passer son chagrin, elle demanda quelque livre et lut avec plaisir un vieux *Jean de Paris* tout gras qui se trouva dans la cuisine.'[2] It would be unreasonable to try to extract from this one sentence more evidence as to reading habits in France at this time than it can furnish, but it would at least seem to suggest three things: first, that a provincial nobleman did not have any books to offer his unexpected guest; second, that the copy of a famous chapbook brought out from the kitchen was read by the menials there; third, that such a chapbook could be enjoyed (*faute de mieux?*) by a princess of the blood. It should be noted that according to Tallemant the princess 'avait beaucoup d'esprit', was a patron of men of letters, and had herself composed a *roman à clef*.

There is, of course, some evidence that while in the first instance most works of literature were conceived and written in Paris—now with the court and government established there the unchallenged centre for the publication of new books—and produced for the relatively narrow social group known as 'la Cour et la Ville', they could also reach a much wider circle of readers. Though the appearance of circulating libraries on both sides of the Channel is generally considered to be an eighteenth-century phenomenon, it seems clear that booksellers both in Paris and the provinces were already lending out books for a small fee. One of the minor characters in Furetière's *Roman bourgeois*, a pedantic young woman whose great ambition it is to produce a book, declares that she would have no difficulty in getting one published 'car j'ai un libraire qui me loue des romans'.[3] A recent study of a Grenoble bookseller's business in the period 1648–65 has shown that he was in the habit of hiring out novels to his customers,[4]

---

[1] See Martin, *Livre, pouvoirs et société*, pp. 706–7, 955–8.
[2] *Historiettes*, i. 56. [3] p. 82.
[4] H. J. Martin, 'Les Registres du libraire Nicolas; étude sur la pénétration du livre à Grenoble au milieu du XVIIe siècle', in *Centre méridionel de rencontres sur le XVIIe siècle. Deuxième colloque de Marseille*, Marseilles, 1973, pp. 89–90.

while during his stay at Poitiers in the 1660s as a law student Sir John Lauder recorded in his diary dealings of this kind with one of the book-sellers of the town: 'I have payed 18 souse for the lean of Romances from Mr. Courtois, as Clelie and the sundry parts of Almahide, penned by Scuderie.'[1] In any case it was no doubt possible then as it is today to beg, borrow, or steal a book, so that the economic barrier was not insurmountable.

One has, of course, to beware of taking literally the term *le peuple* when it is applied by writers of the time to the reading public or to theatre audiences; it does not necessarily have the exclusively plebeian meaning which it was later to acquire. It is sometimes used merely to mean 'public', though what adds to the confusion is that one can find the two words used together in the same sentence as in Chapelain's preface to the second part of *La Pucelle*: 'Il n'est pas sans doute facile d'en faire accroire au public; et par le public j'entends le sénat, les chevaliers, et ce qu'il y a d'honnêtes gens parmi le peuple.'[2] While in the same preface he does exclude from the public for whom he is writing what he calls 'cette populace grossière qui n'a ni raison ni savoir', he does definitely include in it 'le bourgeois aussi bien que le courtisan, les femmes ordinaires aussi bien que celles de la plus haute condition'.[3]

Peuple is in fact frequently used by writers of the time to cover those of their readers who, while standing outside the relatively restricted circle of 'la cour et la ville', in other words the upper classes of the capital, were none the less capable of taking an intelligent interest in literature. In commenting on the popularity enjoyed by the novel, Sorel declares that those who are most addicted to it are 'les femmes et les filles, et les hommes de la cour et du monde, soit qu'ils soient gens d'épée, ou que leur oisiveté les fasse plaire aux vanités du siècle'. The popularity of the novel with women he attributes to the fact that there they find themselves placed on a pedestal. Girls like novels, he declares, because 'l'on y trouve quelquefois des princes humiliés devant une petite bergère'. 'Quelle espérance', he adds significantly, 'cela ne donne-t-il point aux filles de bas lieu ou de médiocre?'.[4] This certainly implies that at any rate the novel, whoever it may have been written for in the first instance, reached quite a large public.

Although Boileau repeatedly emphasizes that his aim is to please the

---

[1] Sir John Lauder, Lord Fountainhall, *Journals, with his Observations on Public Affairs and other Memoranda 1665–1676*, ed. E. D. Crawford, Edinburgh, 1900, pp. 157–8.

[2] *Opuscules critiques*, ed. A. C. Hunter, Paris, 1936, p. 285.

[3] ibid., pp. 293–4.

[4] *De la connaissance des bons livres*, pp. 150–2.

King and various distinguished members of the aristocracy, he also claims for his poetry a broad public, provincial as well as Parisian, one drawn from a wider circle than that of the court, when he writes, for instance:

> Sais-tu pourquoi mes vers sont lus dans les provinces,
> Sont recherchés du peuple, et reçus chez les princes ?[1]

This is confirmed as regards the *Satires* by Baillet when he speaks of them having won the approval 'des personnes qualifiées à la cour, à la ville et dans les provinces, celle des personnes d'esprit et des honnêtes gens, et celle même de la populace qui a coutume de se divertir de la folie la plus grave et la plus sérieuse des poètes'.[2] Again in the preface to *Les Caractères* La Bruyère, perhaps rather surprisingly, does not exclude what he calls '[le] simple peuple' from the circle of readers whom he and other writers should have in mind since he declares that it is a section of society 'qu'il n'est pas permis de négliger'.[3]

None the less it remains a fact that a great deal of seventeenth-century French literature was expressly directed at the king and court and more generally at the upper classes of the day. Yet it is also true that the poets, playwrights, and novelists of this period did not, like Ronsard and other members of the Pléiade, address themselves to a narrow, intellectual, learned élite. There are some interesting remarks on this point in the account which Racan left behind of the life of his master, Malherbe. Defending his translations and paraphrases, Malherbe declared 'qu'il n'apprêtait pas les viandes pour les cuisiniers', which Racan interprets as meaning that 'il se souciait fort peu d'être loué des gens de lettres qui entendaient les livres qu'il avait traduits, pourvu qu'il le fût des gens de la cour'. What is more, Racan (he writes in the third person) declares that he defended his own poems against Malherbe's criticisms on the grounds that the faults in them were known only to three or four people of his circle and that 'il faisait des vers pour être lus dans le cabinet du roi et dans les ruelles des dames, plutôt que dans sa chambre ou dans celles des autres savants en poésie'.[4]

It is interesting to see that in the 1660s, in *Le Parnasse réformé*. Guéret should have made this point explicit when he has Malherbe in the underworld rebuke Ronsard for his abuse of classical learning and his failure to appeal to those readers who really mattered:

Epitre IX (Œuvres complètes, p. 134).
[2] *Jugements des savants iv. 372.*   [3] *Les Caractères, p. 62.*
[4] *Mémoires pour la vie de M. de Malherbe, p. 274.*

Vous ne devriez pas tant vous infatuer d'Homère ni de Pindare; il valait mieux songer à plaire à la cour, et considérer que les dames, qui sont la plus belle moitié du monde, et le sujet le plus ordinaire de la poésie, ne savent ni latin, ni grec. Combien trouverez-vous, je ne dis pas de courtisans, mais de gens doctes, qui puissent entendre ce sonnet:

> Ha! qu'à bon droit les Charites d'Hommere
> Un fait soudain comparent au penser,
> Qui parmy l'air peut de loin devancer
> Le Chevalier qui tua la chimere.
>
> Si tôt du vent une Nef passagere
> Poussée en mer ne pourroit s'elancer,
> Ny par les champs ne le sauroit lasser
> Du faux & vray la prompte messagere.
>
> Le Vent Borée ignorant le repos,
> Conceut le mien de nature dispos
> Qui par la Mer & par le Ciel encore,
>
> Et sur les champs animé de Vigueur
> Comme un Zetés s'envole apres mon cœur
> Qu'une Harpye en se jouant devore.

Avouez-le franchement, a jouta-t-il, vous aviez grand besoin de Muret pour attraper votre pensée. Votre sonnet, quoique rempli d'un beau sens, était bien mal sans son commentaire, et vos *Charites d'Homere*, votre *Chevalier tueur de chimere*, votre *prompte Messagere du faux & vray*, en un mot votre *Zetés* auraient embarrassé bien des lecteurs, sans compter toutes vos lectrices.[1]

It was not, of course, absolutely impossible in seventeenth-century France for a woman to learn Latin or even Greek, as the case of Anne Lefebvre, the daughter of a famous classical scholar and the wife of another, was soon to show when she won fame as Mme Dacier; but it was extremely rare. It is not even certain that some of the women of the time, such as Mme de Sévigné, who are said to have had a reading knowledge of Latin did actually possess it.

A fairly considerable number of men did have the opportunity to acquire a pretty good knowledge of Latin, though Greek was neglected; Racine had an exceptional opportunity of learning it at Port-Royal. In the more widely frequented schools such as those of the Jesuits even the instruction was in Latin. While it is true that boys of noble families were not kept at home to work under private tutors, but were sent to a school, their sojourn there was often fairly brief as they

---

[1] *Le Parnasse réformé*, nouvelle édition, Paris, 1674, pp. 69–71. (Ronsard's sonnet is *Les Amours*, xv.)

embarked on a military career very young, and often put in a period at an *académie* before going into the army. A smattering of mathematics which would be useful for a military career, together with fencing, riding, and dancing, were the accomplishments which a young noble-man was expected to pick up there before embarking on his career as a soldier at sixteen or seventeen.

There were, of course, some learned noblemen, but especially in the first part of the century there is plenty of evidence that many were extremely ignorant. In the 1650s, for instance, we find Racan—le marquis de Racan—writing to Chapelain:

J'ai vu des Gascons qui ne pouvaient comprendre que la politesse des lettres pût compatir avec les qualités éminentes d'un homme de guerre, et quand on leur disait que quelqu'un de leur pays et de leur connaissance écrivait bien en prose et en vers, ils ne manquaient jamais de répartir qu'il était fort homme d'honneur.

Il y a céans un gentilhomme qui me touche de fort près, qui, après avoir été sept ans au collège, s'est défait de son latin comme d'un habit indécent à un cavalier, et a cru que c'était assez imiter la valeur, la bonne conduite et la gentillesse des maréchaux de Toiras, d'Effiat et de feu Chantal que d'imiter leur mauvaise orthographe. Pour moi, je ne passe point si à coup d'une extrémité à l'autre, et crois pouvoir être soldat sans être tout à fait brutal.[1]

The strength of many noblemen's prejudice against education is seen in the amusing account given by Saint-Évremond of an argument on this subject. One nobleman praises learning, and in support of his case quotes the example of the Grand Condé, but he is suddenly interrupted by a nobleman of the old school who puts the other side of the question with a brutality which is highly comic:

A commencer par Monsieur le Prince, il alla jusqu'à César, de César au grand Alexandre, et l'affaire eût été plus loin si le commandeur ne l'eût interrompu avec tant d'impétuosité qu'il fut contraint de se taire. 'Vous nous en contez bien, dit-il, avec votre César et votre Alexandre. Je ne sais s'ils étaient savants ou ignorants; il ne m'importe guère; mais je sais que de mon temps on ne faisait étudier les gentilshommes que pour être d'Église; encore se conten-taient-ils le plus souvent du latin de leur bréviaire. Ceux qu'on destinait à la cour ou à l'armée, allaient honnêtement à l'académie. Ils apprenaient à monter à cheval, à danser, à faire des armes, à jouer du luth, à voltiger, un peu de mathématiques, et c'était tout. Vous aviez en France mille beaux gens-d'armes, galants hommes. C'est ainsi que se formaient les Thermes et les Bellegardes. Du latin! De mon temps du latin! Un gentilhomme en eût

---

[1] *Œuvres complètes*, ed. T. de Latour, 2 vols., Paris, 1857, i. 341.

été déshonoré. Je connais les grandes qualités de Monsieur le Prince, et suis son serviteur; mais je vous dirai que le dernier connétable de Montmorency a su maintenir son crédit dans les provinces et sa considération à la cour, sans savoir lire'.[1]

It should be added that there is something caricatural in the way this defence of ignorance in noblemen is put forward, and that Bellegarde died in 1646 and Thermes and Montmorency in 1614.

Even in the 1660s we find writers commenting on the hostility of the court to any form of learning. In 1662 Chapelain twice complains to Nicolas Heinsius of this. 'A peine connaît–elle les [lettres] françaises,' he wrote, 'depuis que la danse, la chasse et les carrousels occupent tous les cœurs et tous les esprits.'[2] Two months later he again declared that the great majority of courtiers were 'apedeftes ensevelis dans la matière, ou dissipés en jeux, en danses, en chasses, sans soupçonner qu'il y ait autre chose que cela de considérable dans la vie'.[3] Shortly afterwards, in his *Satire IV*, Boileau makes a similar attack on aristocratic ignorance and contempt for learning of any kind. After a brief satirical portrait of the pedant come these lines:

> D'autre part un galant de qui tout le métier
> Est de courir le jour de quartier en quartier,
> Et d'aller à l'abri d'une perruque blonde,
> De ses froides douceurs fatiguer le beau monde,
> Condamne la science, et blâmant tout écrit,
> Croit qu'en lui l'ignorance est un titre d'esprit;
> Que c'est des gens de cour le plus beau privilège,
> Et renvoie un savant dans le fond d'un collège.[4]

It was in this period, in 1665 to be precise, that Bussy-Rabutin was elected to the Académie française; looking back on this event in his memoirs, he speaks of the change in attitude which was gradually occurring among the nobility:

Jusqu'ici la plupart des sots de qualité, qui ont été en grand nombre, auraient bien voulu persuader, s'ils avaient pu, que c'était déroger à la noblesse que d'avoir de l'esprit; mais la mode de l'ignorance à la cour s'en va tantôt passer; et le cas que fait le Roi des habiles gens achèvera de polir toute la noblesse du royaume.[5]

---

[1] *Œuvres*, 9 vols., n.p., 1751, ii. 81.   [2] *Lettres*, ii. 215 n.
[3] Ibid. 232 n. *Apedeftes* = 'ignorant, illiterate people' (cf. Rabelais, bk. V. Ch. 16. 'Comment Pantagruel arriva en l'Isle des Apedeftes').
[4] *Œuvres complètes*, p. 26.
[5] *Mémoires*, ed. L. Lalanne, 2 vols., Paris, 1857, ii. 217.

It is in fact amusing to see how far Bussy carried his enthusiasm for recruiting aristocratic members to the Académie. In a letter of 1677 he actually writes: 'Il est vrai que l'Académie se remplit fort de gens de qualité; il faut pourtant y laisser toujours un nombre de gens de lettres, quand ce ne serait que pour achever le Dictionnaire et pour l'assiduité, que des gens comme nous ne sauraient avoir en ce lieu-là.'[1] Noblemen were, of course, to play an important role in the Académie down to the Revolution and well beyond; yet they had not been among the members of that body when it was founded by Richelieu. Their introduction began somewhat oddly when in 1652 one of its members, the Chancellor, Séguier, persuaded it to elect his grandson, the seventeen-year-old marquis de Coislin, who remained a member for half a century, down to his death in 1702.[2]

Even during the personal reign of Louis XIV it cannot be said that the education of the average nobleman was carried all that far as we can see from a widely read book published in 1661 by a nobleman, Jacques de Callières, *La Fortune des gens de qualité et des gentilshommes particuliers, enseignant l'art de vivre à la cour, suivant les maximes de la politique et de la morale*. The author strives to attain a happy mean between ignorance and too much learning. An excess of learning, he argues, would hinder rather than help a nobleman in his career: 'A le bien prendre, à quoi sert cette grande science à un homme de guerre qu'à le rendre pauvre, en l'empêchant de s'appliquer à sa fortune? Quelle utilité tirera-t-il de la philosophie d'Aristote et de Platon, ou de la *Rhétorique* de Quintilien?'[3] Yet the other extreme of ignorance is also to be avoided:

Ce n'est pas que je sois du sentiment d'un de nos ducs et pairs, qui croyait qu'un gentilhomme offensait sa noblesse quand il parlait latin. J'approuve non seulement qu'il [le] sache, mais de plus j'estime qu'il est très difficile qu'il puisse prétendre à la qualité d'un fort honnête homme s'il n'a aucune connaissance des bonnes lettres.[4]

Hence, so far as his military training permits, the nobleman should acquire a modest stock of knowledge:

J'approuve fort qu'il étudie jusqu'à l'âge de seize ou dix-sept ans; aussi bien jusque-là n'est-il encore propre à rien; mais quand il aura tiré du collège ce qu'un bon écolier en peut apprendre, qu'il partage son temps et qu'il en soit

---

[1] *Correspondance*, iii. 202.
[2] G. Boissier, *L'Académie française sous l'Ancien Régime*, Paris, 1909, pp. 18–19.
[3] p. 215.   [4] Ibid. p. 223.

bon méanger en le donnant aux exercices qui lui sont propres et aux sciences qui lui sont nécessaires; qu'il apprenne à se servir de ses armes et de son cheval qu'il sache la géométrie, les fortifications, la géographie, l'histoire latine et française, qu'il apprenne le dessin et, s'il se peut, qu'il ajoute à la langue latine l'allemande, l'italienne et l'espagnole.[1]

This was no doubt the ideal. In practice, the accomplishments which the author demands of the nobleman are not very great. What he requires above all is a stock of general knowledge sufficient to equip him for an ordinary conversation among men of his class on such subjects as war, hunting, and horses. This minimum should be sufficient to prevent him from making gross blunders: 'Ne serait-il pas ridicule de mettre Nuremberg en Italie et Florence en Allemagne, de dire que le bucentaure est le doge de Venise, que Jules-César et Charlemagne ont été bons amis, et qu'Alexandre le Grand fut bien malheureux de mourir sans confession?'[2]

None the less it is significant that he does require of a nobleman an interest in literature: 'Je voudrais aussi qu'il eût appris les poètes anciens et modernes, qu'il sût faire des vers en notre langue, pourvu que cette étude fît son divertissement et non pas sa passion'.[3] That interest was undoubtedly shared by the women of the upper classes of society who gravitated round the court or at least lived in Paris. The memoirs of Pierre Lenet offer a vivid picture of the literary occupations of the people assembled at Chantilly around the dowager princesse de Condé in the spring of 1650 at a critical point in the Fronde, just after the arrest of Condé, Conti, and their brother-in-law, the duc de Longueville:

Tout cela[4] nous attirait des couplets de chansons, des sonnets et des élégies qui ne divertissaient pas moins les indifférents que les intéressés. On faisait là des bouts-rimés et des énigmes qui occupaient le temps aux heures perdues. On voyait les unes et les autres se promener sur le bord des étangs, dans les allées des jardins ou du parc, sur la terrasse ou sur la pelouse; seules ou en troupes, suivant l'humeur où elles étaient; pendant que d'autres chantaient un air et récitaient des vers, ou lisaient des romans sur un balcon en se promenant, ou couchées sur l'herbe.[5]

The interest in certain forms of literature shown by both men and women of the upper classes is well illustrated by the vogue of *L'Astrée.*

[1] Ibid. p. 216.	[2] Ibid. p. 224.	[3] Ibid. p. 225.
[4] Various love intrigues.
[5] *Mémoires*, in *Nouvelle collection des mémoires sur l'histoire de France*, ed. J. P. Michaud and J. J. Poujoulat, 31 vols., Paris, 1836–9, 3rd Ser. ii. 230–1.

In his account of Cardinal de Retz Tallemant tells how party games were based on this novel:

> Dans la société de la famille, Mme de Guéméné en était, on se divertissait, entre autres choses, à s'écrire des questions sur l'*Astrée*, et qui ne répondait pas bien, payait pour chaque faute une paire de gants de frangipane. On envoyait sur un papier deux ou trois questions à une personne, comme, par exemple, à quelle main était Bonlieu, au sortir du pont de la Bouteresse, et autres choses semblables, soit pour l'histoire, soit pour la géographie; c'était le moyen de savoir bien son *Astrée*.[1]

Retz himself gives an even more striking illustration of the interest shown by the nobility in this novel when he describes the scene during the first stage of the Fronde, at the return from an expedition, in January 1649, of Noirmoutier, all armed and accompanied by other armed men, to the apartment of the duchesse de Longueville:

> Ce mélange d'écharpes bleues, de dames, de cuirasses, de violons qui étaient dans la salle, de trompettes qui étaient dans la place, donnait un spectacle qui se voit plus souvent dans les romans qu'ailleurs. Noirmoutier, qui était grand amateur de l'*Astrée*, me dit: 'Je m'imagine que nous sommes assiégés dans Marcilly.'—'Vous avez raison, lui répondis-je, Mme de Longueville est aussi belle que Galatée, mais Marsillac (M. de La Rochefoucauld le père n'était pas encore mort), n'est pas si honnête homme que Lindamor.'[2]

The concept of the 'honnête homme', like the interest of the upper classes in literature, was fostered by the development of social life in the *salons* of seventeenth-century Paris.

Though these did not suddenly spring up in 1601, they undoubtedly underwent a great development in this period and exercised a considerable influence on the French language as well as on literature. Now that the court as well as the administrative machine were permanently established in the Paris region, there was available in the capital a large leisured class whose interest in literature was stimulated by its contact with men of letters in the *salons* which grew up in the course of the century. Thus began the domination which the high society of Paris ('le monde') was to exercise over French literature down to the Revolution. The concept of the 'honnête homme' which developed in this milieu was a thoroughly aristocratic ideal. In the literature of the time—Furerière's *Roman bourgeois* is a good example—the nobleman,

---

[1] *Historiettes*, v. 124.
[2] *Œuvres*, ed. A. Feillet, 10 vols., Paris, 1870–96, ii. 171–2.

polished and refined by the *salons* through contact with the fair sex, is contrasted with the clumsy and dull bourgeois. In this process of refinement conversation played an important part; and though, as we can tell from Tallemant's *Historiettes*, gossip and scandal, news and rumour furnished a good deal of the material for conversation in a famous *salon* like that of the marquise de Rambouillet, some place was also found for a discussion of literary matters in which writers could join with men and women of the upper classes. Poems and plays were read; occasionally plays were even performed, and all forms of literature gave rise to discussions which were both light and intelligent. In 1638, contrasting Mme de Rambouillet's *salon* with the inferior one held by a rival, Chapelain wrote to Balzac: 'Vous ne sauriez avoir de curiosité pour aucune chose qui le mérite davantage que l'hôtel de Rambouillet. On n'y parle point savamment, mais on y parle raisonnablement, et il n'y a lieu au monde où il y ait plus de bon sens et moins de pédanterie.'[1]

The influence of the *salons* on literature derived in part from the way in which women were placed on a pedestal there. The importance of pleasing women is constantly stressed by writers in this period. Somaize attributes Voiture's success to his ability to do so:

C'est une chose qui ne reçoit point de doute que c'est aux femmes que les auteurs veulent plaire, et que c'est pour acquérir la gloire, dont les précieuses sont maîtresses, qu'ils travaillent; et c'est cette sorte de gloire que Valère [Voiture] s'était acquise au plus haut point qu'elle puisse monter, puisqu'il n'était pas moins l'agrément des ruelles que les plus belles d'entre les dames qu'il fréquentait.[2]

The vogue of the novel is also attributed by various critics of the time, often somewhat sourly, to the influence of women. France's supremacy in this genre in the seventeenth century is put down by Huet to the greater freedom enjoyed by French women compared with those of Spain and Italy; this produces what he calls 'la politesse de notre galanterie':

C'est cet art qui distingue les romans français des autres romans et qui en a rendu la lecture si délicieuse qu'elle a fait négliger des lectures plus utiles. Les dames ont été les premières prises à cet appât: elles ont fait toute leur étude des romans et ont tellement méprisé celle de l'ancienne fable et de l'histoire qu'elles n'ont plus entendu des ouvrages qui tiraient de là autrefois leur plus grand ornement.

[1] *Lettres*, i. 215.
[2] *Le Dictionnaire des précieuses*, ed. C. Livet, 2 vols., Paris, 1856, i. 242.

Their example has been followed by men with the result that both poets and novelists, seeing that a knowledge of classical antiquity was no longer of any use to them, have ceased to study what they dared not introduce into their writings. 'Ainsi,' he concludes, 'une bonne cause a produit un très mauvais effet, et la beauté de nos romans a attiré le mépris des belles-lettres, et comme l'ignorance les avait fait naître, ils ont aussi fait renaître l'ignorance.'[1] However, he does not condemn the novel for that reason or for its immorality. Indeed the future bishop even argues that, at any rate with 'les jeunes personnes du monde', the picture of love presented in such works should not have bad effects, but should rather offer a warning of its dangers.

It is noticeable how often the influence of women on both poetry and the novel is linked with that of the courtier, both lacking that familiarity with classical culture which in the eyes of the critics of the age was indispensable to a truly educated man. For instance, Chapelain, in offering advice to Georges de Scudéry on the second part of his novel, *Almahide*, warns him that he must bear in mind that this is a genre which is destined for 'les courtisans et les dames' and that the style should take into account the fact that 'les lecteurs des romans ne sont ni philosophes ni gens d'État, mais sont gens de cour ou femmes délicates'.[2] Likewise Sorel's account of what forms of literature were fashionable around 1670 stresses the importance of the court and of women: 'En général les ouvrages qu'on voit ordinairement entre les mains de la jeunesse et des personnes de la cour sont les poésies, les romans, les lettres, les harangues et quelques discours galants que ceux qu'on met au rang des beaux esprits ont faits par une espèce de vanité pour acquérir l'estime des grands ou l'approbation des dames.'[3] There is a well-known passage in Huet's *De l'origine des romans* in which he stresses the educational influence which novels can have on youths fresh from school, though only on those who are 'destinés à vivre dans le commerce du grand monde':

... Rien ne dérouille tant un esprit nouveau venu des universités, ne sert tant à le façonner et le rendre propre au monde que la lecture des bons romans. Ce sont des précepteurs muets qui succèdent à ceux du collège et qui apprennent aux jeunes gens, d'une méthode bien plus instructive et bien pus persuasive, à parler et à vivre, et qui achèvent d'abattre la poussière de l'école dont ils sont encore couverts. Je parle seulement des jeunes gens qui sont

---

[1] *Lettre-traité sur l'origine des romans*, ed. F. Gégou, Paris, 1971, pp. 139–40.
[2] *Opuscules critiques*, pp. 441–2.
[3] *De la connaissance des bons livres*, p. 54.

destinés à vivre dans le commerce du grand monde où ils sont obligés de n'être pas ridicules, et où ils le seraient souvent s'ils n'entendaient rien au langage de la galanterie; car pour ceux qui sont appelés aux emplois d'une vie obscure et retirée, la connaissance de l'amour et de ses intrigues leur est fort inutile.[1]

In the novel as in poetry the members of the upper classes of society were clearly regarded as a very important category of potential readers.

In the 'Au lecteur' of his *Églogues*, Segrais confesses that while in these poems he would have preferred to have gone in for 'une entière imitation des choses antiques, comme à la règle la plus juste que l'on puisse choisir', he has been compelled to make certain concessions to the taste of his contemporaries 'après avoir remarqué que le goût de mon siècle s'y portait et qu'elles plaisaient davantage de cette sorte aux dames et aux gens de la cour'.[2] Similarly, Father Rapin stresses the influence of this section of the reading public on the development of poetry in the first half of the century, away from bombast to the opposite excess of 'un discours pur et châtié', without metaphors and figures of speech, a style made popular by writers like Voiture and Sarasin: 'Le goût du siècle qui aimait la pureté, les femmes qui sont naturellement modestes, la cour qui n'avait alors presque aucun commerce avec les savants de l'antiquité, par son antipathie ordinaire pour la doctrine et l'ignorance universelle des gens de qualité, donnèrent de la réputation à cette manière.'[3] When he began his *Nouvelles de la République des Lettres* it was made clear to Bayle that he must not produce his journal 'uniquement pour les savants', and that 'il faut tenir un milieu entre les nouvelles de gazettes et les nouvelles de pure science, afin que les cavaliers et les dames, et en général mille personnes qui lisent, et qui ont de l'esprit sans être savants, se divertissent . . .; il faut égayer un peu les choses, y mêler de petites particularités, quelques petites railleries, des nouvelles de romans et de comédies, et diversifier le plus possible'.[4] While it is clear that he looks beyond this narrow social category of readers, he is also aware of how important they are.

How the seventeenth-century writer, whether he liked it or not, was compelled to direct his works not to a learned, but to a social élite is strikingly illustrated in the words of abbé de Villiers: 'C'est la moindre chose que de plaire aux savants. Il faut plaire à la cour. Il faut être du

---

[1] p. 142.   [2] *Œuvres diverses*, ii. 60.
[3] *Réflexions sur la Poétique de ce temps*, ed. E. T. Dubois, Geneva and Paris, 1970, p. 54.
[4] *Œuvres diverses*, 4 vols., The Hague, 1737, iv. 610–11.

goût des dames pour réussir.'[1] Although La Bruyère uses the phrase in a context where he is attacking the vogue of *turlupinades* among young courtiers, he is clearly firm in his belief that the court is 'le centre du bon goût et de la politesse'.[2] Mme de Sévigné was shocked by Furetière's attack on La Fontaine and Benserade in the controversy aroused by his dictionary and his exclusion from the Académie française. She wrote indignantly to Bussy-Rabutin: 'Je trouve que l'auteur fait voir clairement qu'il n'est ni du monde, ni de la cour, et que son goût est d'une pédanterie qu'on ne peut même espérer de corriger.' She was especially shocked that a man should dare to condemn 'le beau feu et les vers de Benserade, dont le Roi et toute la cour a fait ses délices'.[3]

Mme de Sévigné does not actually apply to Furetière the contemptuous term 'bourgeois' which was frequently used to dismiss a writer's claims in this aristocrat-dominated society, but Pradon, for instance, in his counter-attack on Boileau writes contemptuously of his *Satire III*: 'On voit dans cette satire comme dans les autres qu'il se tue à chercher des images ridicules; mais quoiqu'il s'efforce d'être plaisant et qu'il se donne toujours un air goguenard, on ne reconnaît que trop que c'est un bourgeois qui gausse.'[4] La Bruyère applies the term 'bourgeoisie' in a highly pejorative sense to readers of this class when, for instance, he speaks scathingly of the vogue for 'questions d'amour' and by implication of the novels of Madeleine de Scudéry in which they were prominent: 'La lecture de quelques romans les avait introduites parmi les plus honnêtes gens de la ville et de la cour; ils s'en sont défaits, et la bourgeoisie les a reçues avec les pointes et les équivoques.'[5] As the climax of his devastating portrait of Cydias-Fontenelle La Bruyère links the term with that of the despised provinces; this 'composé du pédant et du précieux' is 'fait pour être admiré de la bourgeoisie et de la province'.[6]

When one comes down to considering whether individual works of literature or particular genres were primarily intended for an aristotratic audience or for readers drawn from a lower section of society, there are considerable difficulties. It could well be held that novels of writers like La Calprenède with their royal or princely characters involved in warlike and amorous adventures reflect the tastes of their

---

[1] *Entretiens sur les tragédies de ce temps*, Paris, 1675, p. 59.
[2] 'De la société et de la conversation', 71.
[3] *Lettres*, iii. 126.
[4] *Le Triomphe de Pradon sur les satires du sieur D****, The Hague, 1686, pp. 43–4.
[5] 'De la société et de la conversation', 68.
[6] Ibid. 75.

aristocratic readers; but what of a novel like Scarron's *Roman comique*? On the one hand, we find Segrais rebuking the author for his choice of characters: 'Le *Roman comique* de Scarron n'a pas un objet relevé; je le lui ai dit à lui-même. Il s'amuse à critiquer les actions de quelques comédiens; cela est trop bas.'[1] On the other hand, the modern reader is somewhat taken aback when he sees the academician Costar, writing, it is true, to Scarron, finding amusing even the crudest episodes of the novel: 'Un galant homme, nourri à la cour et qui entend la belle, la fine et la délicate raillerie, peut rire, sans se faire tort, des aventures de Ragotin, de celles du marchand du Bas-Maine et de cent autres semblables.'[2] Certainly, both Mme de Sévigné and her daughter were familiar with Scarron's novel.[3]

Again, one finds the most contradictory views expressed on the vogue for the burlesque which raged from the 1640s onwards. Boileau's attack on 'le Burlesque effronté' is almost too well known to be quoted yet again:

> Cette contagion infecta les provinces,
> Du clerc et du bourgeois passa jusques aux princes.
> Le plus mauvais plaisant eut des approbateurs;
> Et jusqu'à d'Assoucy tout trouva des lecteurs.
> Mais de ce style enfin la cour désabusée
> Dédaigna de ces vers l'extravagance aisée,
> Distingua le naïf du plat et du bouffon
> Et laissa la province admirer le *Typhon*.[4]

In other words, for Boileau the fashion for burlesque passed from the despised lower orders to the court and then moved away again to the despised provinces. One cannot attach much significance to d'Assoucy's retort to Boileau that the court had never ceased to admire those examples of burlesque verse which were worthy of 'une cour si fine et si éclairée', especially as he adds: 'Et si l'on me demande pourquoi ce burlesque qui a tant de parties excellentes et de détours agréables, après avoir si longtemps diverti la France, a cessé de divertir notre cour, c'est que Scarron a cessé de vivre et que j'ai cessé d'écrire.'[5] It is interesting to see that the first canto of Scarron's *Virgile travesti* was dedicated to the Regent, Anne of Austria, another to the Chancellor,

---

[1] *Œuvres diverses*, i. 194.   [2] *Lettres*, 2 vols., Paris, 1658–9, i. 799.
[3] *Correspondance*, ed. R. Duchêne, Paris, 1972—, i. 537.
[4] *Œuvres complètes*, p. 159.
[5] *Aventures burlesques*, ed. E. Colombey, Paris, 1858, p. 290.

Séguier, two of them to presidents of the Paris Parlement, and others to great noblemen and their wives. Even allowing for Scarron's constant efforts to secure lucrative patronage, it is clear that burlesque verse, though popular in tone, was directed at the court and the upper classes of society. Balzac declared that if this fashion continued, 'A la fin il se trouverait des esprits si amateurs des vilaines nouveautés qu'ils voudraient introduire à la cour la langue des gueux et celle des bohêmes.'[1] The wide social spectrum covered by this fashion is stressed by both Pellisson and Sorel. 'Chacun s'en croyait capable,' writes Pellisson, 'depuis les dames et les seigneurs de la cour jusqu'aux femmes de chambre et aux valets.'[2] According to Sorel this disease affected the whole of France:

Quantité de gens sans étude, et de toutes conditions, et même des femmes et des filles, s'entr'écrivent des lettres en vers, quoique jusques à ce temps-ci plusieurs n'eussent osé mettre la main à la plume. On trouve aussi des hommes qui a peine savent lire, lesquels ont la hardiesse de faire imprimer des livres en vers de cette nature, et c'est bien ce qui en montre la facilité.[3]

At the end of the century, in Perrault's *Parallèle des anciens et des modernes* an *abbé* defends the type of burlesque found in *Virgile travesti* and declares that Scarron 'a toujours senti le galant homme et a toujours eu l'air de la cour et du beau monde', while a *président* will only accept the kind of burlesque verse found in Boileau's *Lutrin*, 'un burlesque fait pour divertir les honnêtes gens, pendant que l'autre, bas et rampant, ne réjouit que le menu peuple et la canaille'.[4]

That the taste of the court and of the upper classes of Paris was not in practice excessively refined, particularly in the first half of the century, is pretty obvious when we consider the drama of the period. It is true that we know virtually nothing of the spectators whom the numerous touring companies who travelled in the provinces drew to their performances; even as far as Paris is concerned (and it was undoubtedly the centre of theatrical activity, at any rate from the 1620s onwards) we have extraordinarily little hard information about the sort of spectators who attended theatrical performances in the opening decades of the century. However, from the period round about 1630 onwards, when the theatre undoubtedly became a flourishing industry in the capital, there is enough evidence for us to form a fairly clear picture of the

---

[1] *Œuvres*, 2 vols., Paris, 1665, ii. 687.
[2] *Histoire de l'Académie française*, i. 79–80.
[3] *De la connaissance des bons livres*, p. 251.
[4] *Parallèle des anciens et des modernes*, 4 vols., Paris, 1688–97, iii. 291–5.

audiences which had the privilege of seeing the plays of Corneille, Molière, and Racine put on for the first time.

It is unfortunate that the history of the French theatre in the opening decades of the century should be so obscure despite all the efforts of modern scholars to ferret out the relevant documents.[1] At a time when England had produced Shakespeare and his contemporaires and in Spain Lope de Vega was at the height of his powers, not a single masterpiece was performed on the French stage. What is more, while London had as many as five theatres, Paris had officially only one, the Hôtel de Bourgogne, though performances were sometimes given at other places; and it was not until 1629 that any company was able to establish itself permanently in this theatre. Until then it was hired by a whole series of companies—mostly French, but occasionally also Italian, or even English at the very beginning of the century; none of these managed to secure enough support from audiences to enable it to last out longer than a short period.

The striking thing about the plays of the opening part of the century —be they comedies, tragedies, tragicomedies, or pastoral plays—is their aesthetic and moral crudity. From this it is only too easy to conclude that the audience which frequented the Hôtel de Bourgogne or various improvised theatres in the capital was a plebeian one, lacking the refining influence of the upper classes of society and especially that of respectable women. Attractive as this conclusion may be, it is not altogether borne out by the facts. The theatre was undoubtedly a much less fashionable entertainment than it was to become by about 1630; the plays produced were of little literary worth and were often extremely crude, even obscene, in their subject-matter and language. Yet though the theatre seems to have been a relatively cheap form of entertainment at the beginning of the century, there are fragments of evidence which suggest that audiences were much more mixed than is often suggested.

There is, for instance, some evidence that not only some young bloods of the aristocracy, but even solid bourgeois attended the theatre in these decades. What is more, the documents on which historians of the theatre rely in order to exclude respectable women from audiences of the time are no more conclusive than those produced by scholars who attempt to do the same for the London theatres of Shakespeare's day. Thus the apparently categorical statement of abbé

---

[1] By far the most successful in the present century has been Mme S. W. Deierkauf-Holsboer; see her three works, *Vie d'Alexandre Hardy*, *Le Théâtre du Marais*, and *Le Théâtre de l'Hôtel de Bourgogne*.

d'Aubignac, writing in the 1660s, that 'il y a cinquante ans qu'une honnête femme n'osait aller au théâtre' is considerably modified by the rest of the sentence: 'ou bien il fallait qu'elle fût voilée et tout à fait invisible, et ce plaisir était comme réservé aux débauchées qui se donnaient la liberté de regarder à visage découvert'.[1] In other words, d'Aubignac does admit that some 'honnêtes femmes' did go to the theatre in the opening decades of the century, even if they went veiled. Charles Sorel, writing a few years later, is even further from denying that respectable women were present in the theatre earlier in the century. 'Autrefois,' he declares, 'toutes les femmes se retiraient quand on allait jouer la farce.'[2] What is even more explicit is one of the rare pieces of contemporary evidence, that provided by the Basle doctor, Thomas Platter. In 1599 after taking his doctor's degree in Montpellier, he spent some time in Paris and attended performances given at the Hôtel de Bourgogne by Valleran le Conte and his company. There is certainly a reference to the presence of women in the galleries in his description of performances given by Valleran:

Er sampt seinem volck spilen auf einer erhöhten brüge, mitt tapissereyen umbhenget, in einem sehr grossen saal, in welchem die gemeinen leüt, so nur den halben theil bezahlen, stehen miessen; welche aber dopplet gelt geben, die lasset man auf ettliche gäng hinauf, da sie sitzen, stehen oder auf den gängen mitt den armen ligen unndt alles zum besten sehen können, dahin sich auch dass frauwenzimmer zeverfügen pfleget.[3]

Even if information about the composition of theatre audiences at the beginning of this period is extremely hard to come by, it would certainly seem rash to conclude that neither men of the upper classes nor respectable women frequented the theatre in these years.

It is clear that the attitude of the court of Henry IV and of the young Louis XIII cannot have been as negative as has often been imagined. Meagre as our information undoubtedly is, it suffices to prove that in these years the court did not regard theatrical performances as entirely beneath contempt, as an entertainment suited only for the plebs, for a horde of ruffians and dissolute women. Although its interest in drama was certainly not as great as it was to be at the high point of the reign of Louis XIV, it certainly did not turn its back on this form of entertainment.

[1] *Dissertation sur la condemnation des théâtres*, Paris, 1666, pp. 243–4.
[2] *De la connaissance des bon livres*, p. 166.
[3] *Beschreibung der Reisen durch Frankreich, Spanien, England und die Niederlande*, ed. R. Keiser, 2 vols., Basle and Stuttgart, 1968, ii. 586.

We know, for instance, that on at least one occasion the court of Henry IV—the King and great noblemen, the Queen and ladies—transported itself to the Hôtel de Bourgogne to be present at the sort of performance which, we are asked to believe, no respectable woman could possibly have gone near. In January 1607 L'Estoile wrote in his journal: 'Le vendredi 26ᵉ de ce mois fut jouée, à l'Hôtel de Bourgogne, à Paris, une plaisante farce, à laquelle assistèrent le roi, la reine, et la plupart des princes, seigneurs et dames de la cour.'[1]

A great deal of valuable information about the interest taken by the court in drama in the first two decades of the century is hidden away in the journal kept by Jean Héroard, the physician attached to the Dauphin, the future Louis XIII. Substantial extracts from the journal were published in 1868,[2] but further references to theatrical performances attended by Louis in the early part of his reign can be tracked down in the manuscript preserved in the Bibliothèque nationale.[3] Marie de Médicis and Henry IV himself were keenly interested in the visits of Italian actors, and several companies visited Paris and the court before the end of the reign. Curiously enough, the first theatrical performance attended by the Dauphin, at the age of three, was one given at Fontainebleau by an English company.[4] In addition to taking part in juvenile amateur dramatics at court and attending there performances by French and Italian actors, on three occasions in 1609 the boy was taken to see plays given at that place of perdition, the Hôtel de Bourgogne.[5]

Performances at the court of Henry IV were brought to an abrupt end by his assassination in 1610, but by the middle of the following year Héroard records the young King's attendance at performances given by a company of French actors at Fontainebleau,[6] and later in the year he went no fewer than five times in a month to the Hôtel de Bourgogne to see the same actors.[7] For most of 1612 there appears to have been little theatrical activity at court, but in November of that year a new phase began which lasted down to February 1614. In these years of political disorder the Regent was attempting to keep the nobles occupied at court by a dizzy round of ballets and drama; it is significant that all this activity came to an end when various great noblemen, headed by the prince de Condé, left the court and set up the

[1] *Mémoires-Journaux*, viii. 271.
[2] *Journal sur l'enfance et la jeunesse de Louis XIII (1601–1628)*, ed. E. Soulié et E. de Barthélemy, 2 vols. Paris, 1868.
[3] MSS. fr. 4022–7.   [4] *Journal* i. 88.   [5] Ibid. 382–4.
[6] Ibid. ii. 67.   [7] Ibid. 78–80.

standard of revolt in the provinces, creating a crisis which led to the summoning of the États généraux.

We know from Héroard's journal that, leaving aside amateur performances, the young King was present at seventy-one performances given at court by French actors between November 1612 and September 1613. At this point another Italian company arrived on the scene, and between September and November 1613 he saw them perform forty-five times. When the Italian actors began their public performances at the Hôtel de Bourgogne, the French company returned to the court and in December Louis was present at five performances given by them. Before this phase of intense theatrical activity came to an end, in January and February 1614 the Italian company appeared another eleven times before the King. No doubt such a spate of theatrical performances at the court of the young King was exceptional, but it remains a fact that in a period of some fifteen months he was present at over 130 performances and there were no doubt others which he did not attend for one reason or another. A considerable number of the plays performed at court by these professional actors were, of course, Italian, but well over half were given by a French company or companies.

Without going any further into the details of court performances given during the regency of Marie de Médicis and the early years of Louis XIII's personal reign, we may conclude that in the opening decades of the century the French court did not by any means reject the theatre as a low and plebeian form of entertainment, utterly beneath contempt. Whether the performances in question were given at the Louvre or Fontainebleau or whether (this seems to have happened much less frequently) at the Hôtel de Bourgogne, there can be no doubt that the King and his courtiers, male and female, saw exactly the same plays—French or Italian—as were presented to the ordinary spectators in the public theatre. Clearly, we do not possess, for the opening decades of the seventeenth century, one set of crude plays written for the plebeian audiences of the Hôtel de Bourgogne and another set of refined plays written to please the more sophisticated taste of the court.

It is characteristic that the only two anecdotes in Tallemant's *Historiettes* relating to Henry IV's interest in drama concern encounters with actors who were particularly distinguished for their roles in farce—Arlequin and Gros-Guillaume.[1] His Italian queen, Marie de

[1] i. 16, 27.

Médicis, naturally took a keen interest in actors from her own country, but she seems also to have enjoyed performances by French actors, particularly in farce. After the murder of her favourite, Concini, in 1617 she endeavoured to while away the time in her exile at Blois with visits from two well-known actors of farce. The accounts of her household show that in May 1618 the sum of 90 livres was paid to 'Robert Guérin, dit la Fleur', better known as Gros-Guillaume, and in December of the same year she gave 600 livres to 'Philippe Mondor, médecin' and to 'ceux qui l'ont assisté pour jouer les comédies qu'ils ont représentées diverses fois devant nous pour notre plaisir et service'. Philippe de Mondor (his real name was Philippe Girard) was the brother of a more illustrious personage, Antoine Girard, the famous actor of farce, Tabarin, of whom Boileau was to speak with such contempt in his *Art poétique*.[1] Both brothers are mentioned in another item in these accounts, dated February 1619; Marie de Médicis orders her treasurer to pay 'Philippe de Mondor, docteur en médecine, et Antoine Girard, dit Tabarin, la somme de trois cents livres de laquelle nous leur avons fait don tant en considération de ce qu'ils ont représenté plusieurs comédies devant nous pour notre plaisir et service que pour leur faire sentir notre libéralité'.[2] It is obvious that in the opening decades of this period there was not an unbridgeable gulf between the taste of the court and that of the low-born spectators who applauded actors of farce like Gros-Guillaume and Tabarin, and that the public performances given at the Hôtel de Bourgogne and at other places in Paris did not provide an exclusively plebeian entertainment.

It is, however, probable that with the changes which took place in the theatrical world of Paris, roughly in the period 1625–35, audiences became rather less mixed than they had previously been. In these years the theatre undoubtedly became much more fashionable; there were now two companies permanently installed at the Hôtel de Bourgogne and its rival, the Théâtre du Marais, and a new generation of playwrights, among whom Corneille only gradually proved himself the most illustrious, was supported by the patronage of great noblemen and, above all, of Richelieu. For a time one continues to find references to the presence of plebeian spectators in the theatre. As late as 1663, in Molière's *Critique de l'École des femmes*, there is a famous reference to the presence of lackeys in his theatre;[3] indeed, it seems that it was not

---

[1] *Œuvres complètes*, p. 178.
[2] Bibliothèque nationale, Cinq Cents Colbert, vol. 92, fos. 187, 201, 214.
[3] Sc. 3.

until rather later that lackeys were banned by royal edict from attending the Paris theatres. It is true that the word *peuple* when applied to seventeenth-century theatre audiences can be highly ambiguous as in as in 'la cour et le peuple' it is used in a sense which obviously includes certain contexts it can mean simply 'audience, public,' and sometimes people who were far from plebeian in the modern sense of the word.

None the less in the first half of the century there are clearly some occasions when the term *peuple* applied to part of the audience has a definitely plebeian meaning. In 1639 in his *Apologie du théâtre* Georges de Scudéry makes some extremely rude remarks about plebeian spectators in the parterre such as 'cet animal à tant de têtes et à tant d'opinions qu'on appelle *peuple*', and 'cette multitude ignorante que la farce attire à la comédie'.[1] At about the same time (although not published until 1657, his *Pratique du théâtre* was written much earlier) d'Aubignac speaks scathingly of the low tastes of the plebeian section of the audience: '... La populace, élevée dans la fange et entretenue de sentiments et de discours déshonnêtes, se trouve fort disposée à recevoir pour bonnes les méchantes bouffonneries de nos farces, et prend toujours plaisir d'y voir les images de ce qu'elle a accoutumé de dire et de faire.'[2]

Then there is the often quoted passage from Sorel's *La Maison des jeux* in which he denounces the noisy *racaille* to be found among the spectators in the parterre:

Le parterre est fort incommode pour la presse qui s'y trouve de mille marauds mêlés parmi les honnêtes gens, auxquels ils veulent quelquefois faire des affronts, et ayant fait des querelles pour un rien, mettent la main à l'épée et interrompent toute la comédie. Dans leur plus parfait repos ils ne cessent aussi de parler, de siffler et de crier, et pource qu'ils n'ont rien payé à l'entrée et qu'ils ne viennent là qu'à faute d'autre occupation, ils ne se soucient guère d'entendre ce que disent les comédiens. C'est une preuve que la comédie est infâme, de ce qu'elle est fréquentée par de telles gens, et l'on montre que ceux qui ont de la puissance dans le monde en font bien peu de cas, puisqu'ils n'empêchent point que toute cette racaille y entre sans payer, pour y faire du désordre.[3]

If we are to believe such witnesses, the audience for whom Corneille and his contemporaries wrote in the 1630s still contained a noticeable plebeian element.

[1] *L'Apologie du théâtre*, Paris, 1639, p. 89.
[2] *La Pratique du théâtre*, ed. P. Martino, Paris, 1927, pp. 74–5.
[3] *La Maison des jeux*, 2 vols., Paris, 1642, ii. 424–5.

It is, however, interesting that from the middle of the seventeenth century until the closing decades of the *ancien régime* one finds scarcely any references to the presence of such spectators; it is only from the 1760s onwards that writers begin to refer, naturally with scorn, to the gradual infiltration of plebeian spectators into theatres like the Comédie-Française and the Théâtre italien. In the hundred years or so before that date it would seem as if the cheapest part of the various Paris theatres, the parterre, was largely a middle-class preserve. Among the spectators in this part of the house about whose presence we have ample evidence were budding playwrights. Naturally, when they had established themselves, they enjoyed the privilege of free admission and could choose a more comfortable way of seeing a play; we are told that Pierre Corneille sat in a box at the first performance of his younger rival's *Britannicus*,[1] but he himself refers in *La Suite du menteur* to the presence of writers in the parterre applying the famous rules to other people's plays.[2] Again one of the characters in Sorel's *Maison des jeux* replies to the criticisms of the spectators in the parterre quoted above and points out that 'la plupart de nos poètes qui sont les plus capables de juger des pièces, n'y vont point ailleurs'.[3] Towards the end of this period there are references to the presence of writers in the parterre both in Lesage's *Critique de Turcaret* and Regnard's *Critique du Légataire universel* where the Le Marquis exclaims to a disgruntled writer: 'Vous êtes là un tas de mauvais poètes cantonnés par pelotons (je ne parle pas de ceux qui sont avoués d'Apollon, dont on doit respecter les avis), vous êtes là, dis-je, comme des âmes en peine, tout prêts à donner l'alarme dans votre quartier, et à sonner le tocsin sur un mot qui ne vous plaira pas.'[4]

It may be objected that in this period there were too many poverty-stricken authors, too many 'poètes crottés' to use the language of the time, for the presence of writers in the parterre to throw much light on its social composition and in particular to prove that it contained many solid bourgeois. Yet there is plenty of evidence that this was the case, so much in fact that it would take several pages to quote it all; only a few examples can be given here. 'Le noble et le bourgeois' are frequently given in writings of the time as shorthand for the theatre audience, as when Loret speaks of a tragedy being performed at Molière's theatre 'pour le noble et pour le bourgeois'.[5] 'Le bourgeois'

---

[1] E. Boursault, *Artémise et Poliante*, Paris, 1670, p. 3.
[2] Act V, sc. 5.   [3] ii. 473.   [4] Sc. 3.
[5] *La Muse historique*, iii. 140.

is often mentioned in his own right as one of the pillars of the Paris theatres, as in Loret's reference to Molière's *Dom Juan* with its 'changements de thèâtre / Dont le bourgeois est idolâtre',[1] or in Chappuzeau's statement that, since the royal edict of 1673 has put an end to disorders there, 'le bourgeois peut venir avec plus de plaisir à la comédie'.[2] That the bourgeois mainly frequented the parterre is made clear by official documents such as that provided by d'Argenson, the *lieutenant de police*, who speaks of the greater part of the large number of spectators in the parterre of the Comédie-Française one day in 1700 when disorders broke out there, as being 'gens de collège, de palais ou de commerce'.[3] A vivid picture of the spectators on the stage contrasted with the bourgeois spectators in the parterre of the Théâtre italien towards the end of the century is to be found in the final scene of Regnard and Dufresny's comedy, *Les Chinois*:

Les Italiens donnent un champ libre sur la scène à tout le monde. L'officier vient jusques au bord du théâtre étaler impunément aux yeux du marchand la dorure qu'il lui doit encore. L'enfant de famille, sur les frontières de l'orchestre, fait la moue à l'usurier qui ne saurait lui demander ni le principal, ni les interêts. Le fils, mêlé avec les acteurs, rit de voir son père avaricieux faire le pied de grue dans le parterre pour lui laisser quinze sols de plus après sa mort.

There is also in the literature of the time[4] an extraordinary number of references to the presence in the parterre of groups of 'marchands de la rue Saint-Denis'; these were not small shopkeepers, but prosperous retailers of luxury goods.

It is interesting to note that English travellers of the time who were men of some social position found no difficulty in standing in the cheapest part of the Paris theatres which they frequented. In 1664 Edward Browne, the son of Sir Thomas Browne, the author of *Religio Medici*, who was later to become a doctor, visited Paris as part of his grand tour and stood in the parterre of Molière's theatre to see a performance of *L'École des maris*.[5] Two years later Philip Skippon, the son of Cromwell's major-general, a young Cambridge graduate who was not long afterwards to become an M.P. and a knight, attended the same theatre to see performances by the Italian actors and then by

[1] Ibid. iv. 312.
[2] *Le Théâtre français*, ed. G. Monval, Paris, 1875, p. 148.
[3] *Notes*, ed. L. Larchey and E. Mabille, Paris, 1866, p. 20.
[4] See Donneau de Visé, *Zélinde*, Paris, 1663, sc. 3; abbé d'Aubignac, *Deux dissertations . . . sur deux tragédies de M. Corneille*, pp. 28–9, and *Quatrième dissertation*, p. 184; Guéret, *Le Parnasse réformé*, p. 83; Boursault, *Artémise et Poliante*, p. 3.
[5] *A Journal of a Visit to Paris in the year 1664*, ed. G. Keynes, London, 1923, p. 16.

Molière's company, and once again he and his companions seem to have regarded it as perfectly natural to stand in the parterre.[1]

So for that matter did many a French nobleman if he went to the theatre on his own or in male company. It is true that we chiefly learn of the presence of such spectators in the parterre when they were drunk and created a disturbance, but presumably they also frequented that part of the house when they were sober. Twice during the last few months of Molière's life there were disturbances in his theatre in which 'gens d'épée' in the parterre were involved,[2] while in 1691 a performance at the Hôtel de Bourgogne was interrupted by an officer with the delightful name of Sallo, 'capitaine au régiment de Champagne', who attempted to climb on to the stage from the parterre.[3] This incident was followed by yet another royal edict expressly forbidding all persons, including officers of the troops of the royal household, to enter the theatre without paying and to create disturbances inside.[4] Needless to say, this did not put a stop to such disorders; in 1700 and 1701 d'Argenson describes various disturbances in which noblemen were involved.[5] However, the presence of officers in this part of the house was by no means always unwelcome to the actors of the different theatres; their absence was lamented when in wartime they had to return to the front with the opening of the campaigning season in spring. In Dufresny's *Départ des comédiens*, a little comedy performed at the Théâtre italien in 1694, Arlequin laments the fact that at this season of the year 'il n'est officier qui ne parte' and that spring 'dépeuple de plumets théâtres et ruelles'. He goes on:

> Qu'êtes-vous devenus, jeunes foudres de guerre,
> Qui triomphiez jadis dans ce vaste parterre?
>   Hélas! je n'y vois plus
>   Ce doux flux et reflux
>   De têtes ondoyantes,
> Qui rend en plein hiver nos moissons abondantes,
> Quand le troupeau guerrier et terrestre et marin
>   Vient piétiner notre terrain;
>   En y semant quelques paroles,
>   Nous recueillons force pistoles . . .[6]

---

[1] *An Account of a Journey through part of the Low Countries, Germany, Italy and France,* in *A Collection of Voyages and Travels,* London, 1732, vi. 731.

[2] Campardon, *Documents inédits sur Molière,* pp. 31–4, 66–9.

[3] E. Campardon, *Les Comédiens du roi de la troupe française pendant les deux derniers siècles,* Paris, 1879, pp. 290–7.

[4] Jal, *Dictionnaire,* p. 408.   [5] *Notes,* pp. 41, 54, 62.   [6] Sc. 1.

Thus if the parterre appears to have been largely the preserve of the middle classes, of merchants and professional men, including writers and aspiring writers, it also contained at least a sprinkling of noblemen, drunk or sober.

There is no question but that the all male spectators in this part of the theatre had a considerable influence. In the last year of the existence of Molière's company at 113 out of 131 performances more than half the spectators stood in the parterre.[1] It is true that both in Molière's theatre and at the Comédie-Française from 1680 onwards the doubling of prices for the parterre during the opening performances of a new play tended to reduce the number of tickets sold for that part of the house, but under ordinary conditions these spectators represented a majority among the audience whenever older plays were revived and during the first run of new plays as soon as prices for the parterre had been reduced to normal. Clearly, such spectators were extremely important from the numerical point of view, and even though the proportion of the audience which they represented generally fell during the opening performances of new plays, these were mostly well attended and on such occasions there could be at least three or four hundred spectators in the parterre. This mass of men, packed together like sardines, were obviously in a position to express their reactions in a way which had a considerable effect on the fate of the play.

At any rate from the 1660s onwards we continually find most flattering references to the good taste of the parterre. Molière's *Critique de l'École des femmes* furnishes the first example of such praise; here we see the actor-manager who knew on which side his bread was buttered and was very conscious of the fact that the spectators who bought tickets for the parterre generally represented more than half his audience. His spokesman, Dorante, makes a vigorous defence of the taste of the spectators in this part of the theatre when he rebukes the marquis for his contemptuous attitude towards them:

Apprends, Marquis, je te prie, et les autres aussi, que le bon sens n'a point de place déterminée à la comédie; que la différence du demi-louis d'or et de la pièce de quinze sols[2] ne fait rien du tout au bon goût; que debout et assis, on

---

[1] The *Registre d'Hubert* which covers the theatrical year 1672–3 has now been published in facsimile along with an *Étude critique* by S. Chevalley in the *Revue d'histoire du théâtre*, 1973, pp. 1–195.

[2] Half a louis = 5 livres 10 sous, the price of a seat on the stage or in the first row of boxes in Molière's theatre, compared with 15 sous, the ordinary price of a ticket to the parterre.

peut donner un mauvais jugement; et qu'enfin, à le prendre en général, je me fierais assez à l'approbation du parterre, par la raison qu'entre ceux qui le composent, il y en a plusieurs[1] qui sont capables de juger d'une pièce selon les règles, et que les autres en jugent par la bonne façon d'en juger, qui est de se laisser prendre aux choses, et de n'avoir ni prévention aveugle, ni complaisance affectée, ni délicatesse ridicule.[2]

What we are offered here is merely a defence of the taste of the parterre; flattery of the parterre is carried much further by Regnard in such plays as *Les Chinois* (1692)—a comedy written in collaboration with Dufresny—and in *La Critique du Légataire universel* (1708) in which one of the characters, 'le Comédien', declares: 'C'est de ce tribunal-là que nous attendons nos arrêts, et quand il a prononcé, nous n'appelons point de ses décisions.'[3]

It would be unwise to take this literally in view of the effect which such paradoxes must have had on theatre audiences drawn from the profoundly aristocratic society of the France of Louis XIV. Given the prevailing worship of rank and social position, it was inevitable that the outlook and ideals of the aristocracy should exercise a considerable influence on the drama of the age. The section of the aristocracy which gravitated around the King in Paris and later at Versailles was powerfully represented in the different theatres which served Paris in the course of the seventeenth century.

It is obvious that the more expensive seats in these theatres were occupied by persons of rank or wealth. Theatre prices rose fairly steeply in the course of the century for all sorts of reasons, including taxes; a ticket to the parterre of the Hôtel de Bourgogne which at the beginning of the century cost 5 sous, cost 18 at the end of the reign of Louis XIV. Although numerically the parterre might be extremely important, its contribution to the total receipts was much smaller than its numbers might at first suggest. This is particularly striking in Molière's theatre as there the best seats, those in the first row of boxes and on the stage, were very expensive; the result was that, to take the example of the first performance of *Le Malade imaginaire* in 1673, while 394 out of the 682 spectators stood in the parterre, tickets for that part of the theatre accounted for less than a third of the total receipts (591 livres out of 1,892), while seats on the stage and in the first row of boxes contributed more to the total—682 livres.

At the Comédie-Française the charges made for the best seats in the

---

[1] 'Beaucoup, quantitê, grand nombre' (*Dictionnaire de l'Académie française*, 1694).
[2] Sc. 5.   [3] Sc. 2.

theatre were proportionately less heavy in relation to the cost of tickets to the parterre than they had been at Molière's theatre. Even so, despite the large numbers of spectators present in the parterre on most occasions, their contribution to the total receipts of the performance fell well below 50 per cent, and could even fall to as low as a quarter. Thus even if the society of the time had not accorded the respect which it did to birth and money, the men and women of blue blood or wealth who sat in the first row of boxes or on the stage had an importance, from the financial point of view, which far outweighed their numbers. And, of course, both actors and playwrights did bestow upon the upper classes of the society of their age the respect which the prevailing social outlook demanded.

Two striking instances of this are furnished by Molière's *Critique de l'École des femmes*. First, and this example was to be followed slavishly by later writers who produced a little play of this kind in defence of their comedies, with the exception of the jealous playwright, Lysidas, all the characters who assemble in a *salon* to argue over the merits of *L'École des femmes* are drawn from the aristocracy. What is more, if Molière puts into the mouth of Dorante a defence of the taste of the parterre, the same character delivers an eloquent eulogy of the taste of the court in answer to the sneers of the bourgeois writer:

Achevez, Monsieur Lysidas. Je vois bien que vous voulez dire que la cour ne se connaît pas à ces choses; et c'est le refuge ordinaire de vous autres, Messieurs les auteurs, dans le mauvais succès de vos ouvrages, que d'accuser l'injustice du siècle et le peu de lumière des courtisans. Sachez, si vous plaît, Monsieur Lysidas, que les courtisans ont d'aussi bons yeux que d'autres; qu'on peut être habile avec un point de Venise et des plumes, aussi bien qu'avec une perruque courte et un petit rabat uni; que la grande épreuve de toutes vos comédies, c'est le jugement de la cour; que c'est son goût qu'il faut étudier pour trouver l'art de réussir; qu'il n'y a point de lieu où les décisions soient si justes; et sans mettre en ligne de compte tous les gens savants qui y sont, que, du simple bon sens naturel et du commerce de tout le beau monde, on s'y fait une manière d'esprit, qui sans comparaison juge plus finement des choses que tout le savoir enrouillé des pédants.[1]

If one is surprised to find this reference to the presence of 'gens savants' at the court, one can find other contemporary references to them such as that of abbé de Villiers who in his *Entretiens sur les tragédies de ce temps* makes one of his characters say:

[1] Sc. 6.

Si l'on plaît aux savants, on plaira bientôt à la cour, où il y a des savants aussi bien qu'ailleurs; et je puis dire que les savants de la cour valent bien les autres, puisqu'avec la science ils joignent un certain caractère d'esprit fin et délicat qui sert admirablement pour bien juger. Ce n'est plus le caprice qui distribue les louanges et les applaudissements de la cour, c'est le bon sens.[1]

This view was far from being universally accepted. In his *Épître à M. Racine* (1677) Boileau describes in vivid terms the obstacles which Molière had to overcome in his struggle for recognition and he gives a far from flattering account of the hostility shown by certain members of the nobility, both male and female, to his masterpieces:

> L'ignorance et l'erreur à ses naissantes pièces,
> En habits de marquis, en robes de comtesses,
> Venaient pour diffamer son chef-d'œuvre nouveau,
> Et secouaient la tête à l'endroit le plus beau.
> Le commandeur voulait la scène plus exacte;
> Le victomte indigné sortait au second acte;
> L'un, défenseur zélé des bigots mis en jeu,
> Pour prix de ses bons mots le condamnait au feu.
> L'autre, fougueux marquis, lui déclarant la guerre,
> Voulait venger la cour immolée au parterre.[2]

Nor is there evidence to show that Louis XIV and his courtiers showed any particular discernment in their choice of plays to be performed in the various royal palaces. During Molière's lifetime *Les Fâcheux* appears to have been the play of his most often performed at court, and there is no evidence that he ever performed *Le Misanthrope* there.

However, to conclude that in its dealings with the theatre the aristocracy did not exhibit any particular refinement of taste is not to deny that it exercised an influence on drama commensurate with its exalted place in the society of the day. The ladies and their male escorts in the more expensive boxes and the noblemen sitting or standing on the stage did play an important part in moulding the taste of the age in the theatre as in other forms of literature. Although middle-class and even for a time plebeian spectators were undoubtedly present in the audiences of the capital, given the social structure of seventeenth-century France, the upper classes, from the princes of the blood and the *grands seigneurs* and their womenfolk downwards, exercised an influence on drama which was out of proportion even to the fairly consider-

---

[1] pp. 89–90. [2] *Œuvres complètes*, p. 127.

able numbers which they furnished to the theatre audiences of the time.

Although the theorists, the real *savants* like Chapelain and Sarasin, La Mesnardière and d'Aubignac, did exercise a considerable influence on the development of French drama from 1630 onwards, it came up against decided limits. The playwrights of the time, including the very greatest of them, had to bear in mind that their audiences came to the theatre, not to see whether the famous rules laid down by the *savants* had been observed, but to be entertained. 'Notre premier but', Corneille declared in 1637 in the dedication to *La Suivante*, 'doit être de plaire à la cour et au peuple.' Nearly a generation later, in *La Critique de l'École des femmes*, Molière appeals over the heads of the *savants* to the ordinary theatre-goer when he insists that, though the rules have their place, 'je voudrais bien savoir si la grande règle de toutes les règles n'est pas de plaire, et si une pièce de théâtre qui a attrapé son but, n'a pas suivi un bon chemin'. Shortly afterwards Racine, in the preface to *Bérénice*, stressed once again that the playwright's main task was to give pleasure to the spectator: 'La principale règle est de plaire et de toucher.' And in the society of their day the spectators—male and female—drawn from the upper ranks of society formed an extremely important section of the audiences to whom writers had to attempt to give pleasure.

Mixed as those audiences undoubtedly were from the point of view of social composition, in sheer numbers they none the less represented a small élite. It is true that it is only for the last year of Molière's career in Paris that we can calculate for the first time how many spectators paid to see his company perform in the course of the theatrical year. In considering these figures, we have to bear in mind that Paris probably had a population of some half a million, one which was temporarily swollen by visitors from the provinces and from further afield, some of whom, as we know from their letters and diaries, frequented the theatres of the capital. In the theatrical year 1672–3 Molière's company performed 131 times and attracted some 52,000 spectators, an average daily attendance of 400.

Thanks to the summary of the registers of the Comédie-Française produced by the late Carrington Lancaster[1] we can work out how many spectators paid for admission to this theatre from 1680 onwards.

[1] *The Comédie Française, 1680–1701: Plays, Actors, Spectators, Finances*, Baltimore, 1941, and *The Comédie Française, 1701–1774: Players, Actors, Spectators, Finances*, Philadelphia, 1951.

Whereas Molière's company had to compete with several others, the amalgamation which produced the Comédie-Française left it to compete only with the Opéra and the Théâtre italien, and after the expulsion of the Italian actors in 1697 it was the only Paris theatre putting on straight plays. The total number of spectators fluctuated fairly violently from year to year, reaching in 1698–9 193,000, an exceptionally high figure, and falling as low as 107,000 in 1711–12. The average—nearly 140,000—looks at first sight very impressive until one does a little arithmetic. There is evidence that a small number of people went very frequently to the theatre, seeing a successful new play more than once and also being assiduous at revivals. Thus a thousand people attending the Comédie-Française fifty times in a year could account for over a third of this total, and two thousand more going twenty times a year would account for another 40,000 attendances; these three thousand people could leave only some 50,000 attendances for those spectators who went only once in the year or else only fairly infrequently.

All this is, of course, only playing with figures in an orgy of guesswork. Where we are on firmer ground in trying to assess the size of theatre audiences in the Paris of this period is by finding out how large was the number of spectators attracted by the average successful play during its first run; this gives us at least a rough idea of how many people were in the habit of attending the Comédie-Française. In the period down to 1700 Boursault's five-act comedy, *Les Fables d'Ésope*, with 43 performances attracted over 25,000 paying spectators, while one of Dancourt's one-act plays did even better, *Les Vendanges de Suresnes* having 49 performances with over 33,000 spectators paying for admission. But clearly these plays had such a vogue as to draw in people who did not normally go to the Comédie-Française. If we examine the fate of other new plays in the period 1680–1700 we find that 10,000 to 12,000 people represented the largest number of spectators who could be expected to support a new play unless it enjoyed a great vogue when the total attendance would reach from 15,000 to 17,000; or in other words, we may conclude that at the end of the seventeenth century the number of regular patrons of the Comédie-Française lay somewhere between a minimum of 10,000 and a maximum of 17,000.

The question of who frequented the Paris theatres in this period is worthy of investigation both for its own sake and for the light which it throws on the drama of the age; but it also has a wider interest. Thanks to the documents which have come down to us, with a little effort of imagination we can almost meet face to face the different social types who went to the theatre, whereas from such scrappy evidence as has survived we can form only a very hazy notion of the readers of plays and all the other forms of literature. The expression 'aristocratic audience' which is often used in connection with the drama of this age needs to be qualified; while it is true that Paris theatre audiences were a small élite in the numerical sense, they were undoubtedly more mixed in the social sense than is often imagined.[1]

Even so, the taste of the aristocratic spectators influenced in all sorts of ways what was put on the stage. Though plays, when printed, may have fallen into the hands of middle class and even more humble persons who possessed the ability and the desire to read them, they were none the less directed in the first instance to a relatively small group in the capital, to 'la Cour et la Ville', to use the phrase coined by the authors of the time to designate the social élite for whom they were writing.

[1] See my *Paris Theatre Audiences in the Seventeenth and Eighteenth Centuries*, London, 1957.

IV   The Eighteenth Century

THE years between the death of Louis XIV and the outbreak of the Revolution saw a considerable expansion of the French reading public. Not only did the population of France increase by something like a half between these two dates, but there was a sharp drop in illiteracy as measured by the only device so far discovered for this task—the proportion of married couples able to sign their names. As we have seen, this rose between 1686–90 and 1786–90 from 21 to 37 per cent. By the latter date the proportion of men able to sign their names had risen to nearly half (47 per cent) and that of women had nearly doubled, going up from 14 to 27 per cent. Even so, judged by this standard, very nearly two-thirds of new marriage partners were still illiterate when the Revolution broke out.[1]

There was indeed a curious contrast, underlined again and again by speakers in the various Revolutionary assemblies, between the extraordinary vogue which the French language enjoyed over most of Europe and its failure to cover anything like the whole population of France. Not only were large numbers of men and women illiterate, but the French language was not even spoken over considerable areas of the country. Italian (in the newly acquired island of Corsica) was now added to the foreign tongues spoken in the outlying regions where only a small minority of the inhabitants were bilingual; dialects of *langue d'oc* reigned almost supreme over France south of the Loire. In a report to the Convention on 6 June 1794 abbé Grégoire declared: 'Il n'y a qu'environ quinze départements de l'intérieur où la langue française soit exclusivement parlée', and he continued:

On peut assurer sans exagération qu'au moins six millions de Français, surtout dans les campagnes, ignorent la langue nationale; qu'un nombre égal est à peu près incapable de soutenir une conversation suivie; qu'en dernier résultat, le nombre de ceux qui la parlent purement n'excède pas trois millions et probablement le nombre de ceux qui l'écrivent correctement est encore moindre.[2]

[1] For further details see F. Furet and W. Sachs, 'La Croissance de l'alphabétisation en France. XVIIIe–XIXe siècle', *Annales. Économies, sociétés, civilisations*, 1974, vol. 29, pp. 714–37.

[2] *Le Moniteur universel. Réimpression de l'ancien Moniteur*, 31 vols., Paris, 1858–63, xx. 647. The report is also reproduced in *Lettres à Grégoire sur les patois de France, 1790–*

The contrast with the vogue enjoyed by French in the rest of Europe had already been pointed out by Talleyrand in a report to the Constituent Assembly:

Une singularité frappante de l'état dont nous sommes affranchis est sans doute que la langue nationale, qui chaque jour étendait ses conquêtes au delà des limites de la France, soit restée au milieu de nous comme inaccessible à un si grand nombre de ses habitants et que le premier lien de communication ait pu paraître pour plusieurs de nos contrées une barrière insurmontable.[1]

Although in the absence of an international copyright agreement the popularity of French books in the rest of Europe was of little financial assistance to the writers of the time, it did undoubtedly flatter their self-esteem to know that their works were read and admired abroad, and that, when they wished to express ideas unacceptable to the censorship in France, they could certainly count on finding publishers outside its frontiers. In the decades down to 1789 the French language was at the height of its popularity in Europe. It is true that, looking at the matter from an even wider angle and comparing the very different situation of French and English in the nineteenth and twentieth centuries, in this period the defeats experienced by France on land and sea, her expulsion from North America and India, deprived the French language of the possibility of becoming truly universal. Yet in Europe its supremacy was undoubted; it is notorious that many English works owed their diffusion on the Continent to being translated into French and then from French into some other tongue such as German. 'Anglais,' a French writer could exclaim in 1762, 'la France vous a fait connaître de l'Europe.'[2]

All over Europe French succeeded Latin as the international language. 'Les ouvrages français,' wrote Frederick the Great, 'se répandirent si universellement que leur langue remplaça celle des Latins, et à présent quiconque sait le français peut voyager par toute l'Europe sans avoir besoin d'un interprète.'[3] When he arrived in Berlin in 1750, Voltaire wrote to his niece: 'La langue qu'on parle le moins à la cour, c'est l'allemand; je n'en ai pas encore entendu prononcer un mot. Notre langue et nos belles-lettres ont fait plus de conquêtes que

[1] *Rapport sur l'instruction publique*, Paris, 1791, p. 94.
[2] J. B. R. Robinet, *Considérations sur l'état présent de la littérature en Europe*, London, 1762, p. 122.
[3] *Histoire de mon temps*, in *Œuvres posthumes*, 15 vols., Berlin, 1788, i. 97–8.

1794, ed. A. Gazier, Paris, 1880, and in M. de Certeau, D. Julia and J. Revel, *Une politique dela langue. La Révolution française et les patois: L'Enquête de Grégoire*, Paris, 1975.

Charlemagne.'[1] Although he became a German national hero, Frederick remained to the end entirely French both in language and culture.

Not only in Prussia, but all over Germany French was the language of the courts and the upper classes generally. 'The native language of the country,' wrote the Scottish traveller, John Moore, in the 1770s, 'is treated like a vulgar and provincial dialect, while the French is cultivated as the only proper language for people of fashion. Children of the first families are instructed in French before they acquire their mother tongue, and pains are taken to keep them ignorant of this, that it may not hurt their pronunciation of the other.'[2] Nor was this passion for French confined to Germany. Though on this side of the Channel it was somewhat restricted by a variety of factors such as a strong independent tradition in literature, it reigned over the rest of Europe, from Portugal to Russia, despite occasional efforts at resistance. Perhaps the most striking proof of the diffusion of the French language all over eighteenth-century Europe is the number of people, besides Frederick the Great, who wrote in French: at the beginning of the century, the German philosopher, Leibniz, and later Catherine the Great as well as the English historian, Gibbon, whose first work, his *Essai sur l'étude de la littérature*, was published in London in 1761. It was not the Académie française, but the Academy of Berlin (its publications, like those of the Academy of St. Petersburg, appeared in French) which in 1782 offered a prize for the best essay on the following subject:

> Qu'est-ce qui a fait de la langue française la langue universelle de l'Europe?
> Par où mérite-t-elle cette prérogative?
> Peut-on présumer qu'elle la conserve?

The prize was shared between a German professor and a Frenchman, Antoine de Rivarol, whose essay appeared in 1784 under the title, *De l'universalité de la langue française*.

The events of 1789 and the following years were to have a considerable influence on the future of the French language, abroad as well as at home. The cult which it had enjoyed in varying degrees in the rest of Europe had not been imposed by force of arms; indeed, France's

---

[1] *Correspondence and Related Documents*, ed. T. Besterman, 51 vols., Geneva, Banbury and Oxford, 1968—, x. 333.

[2] *A View of Society and Manners in France, Switzerland and Germany*, 2 vols., London, 1779, i. 427.

political and military position in Europe had sharply declined since Louis XIV had stood at the height of his power a century before the fall of the Bastille. If the events of 1789 aroused great enthusiasm in many countries outside France, the Revolutionary and Napoleonic Wars were greatly to reduce the vogue of French on the Continent; the nationalist feelings which they stirred up all over Europe led inevitably to an identification of language with nationhood and to the cult of the indigenous language or languages.

In France itself, on the other hand, the coming-together of all the varied regions under a common political system, common laws and institutions, meant a growing feeling that it was high time that the national language should be spoken and written from one end of the country to another. Indeed at moments, particularly during the Terror, this attitude was carried to excess in a most tyrannical fashion. Undoubtedly, the rush of events between 1789 and 1814 must have contributed to the spread of French inside the country, even in its more remote parts; the Revolutionary and Napoleonic armies brought together men from all the different regions, and the new laws, the proclamations, and news of victories and defeats must have been spread by word of mouth as well as by print. Yet real progress in this field could only come later with the spread of elementary education; this was not to have its full impact for boys until around the middle of the nineteenth century and even later for girls.

The state of elementary education before 1789 has been the subject of violent polemics in France for the last hundred years, and even relatively objective historians find it difficult to form a clear picture of what conditions were like over France as a whole. They undoubtedly varied very widely, and even where statistics as to the number of schools in existence in a particular region can be produced, there is no saying either how much they were really frequented or what was the quality of the teaching offered in them. There is no doubt, however, that even where there were schools, the intellectual attainments and pedagogical skill of the teachers were generally low, the buildings extremely poor, and attendance limited in number of years and largely confined to the winter months. Nor must it be forgotten that quite a number of influential people were opposed not only to any extension of education for the masses, but even to what little was available. La Chalotais (and he was congratulated by Voltaire for doing so)[1] strongly attacked the whole idea of popular education:

[1] *Correspondance* xxvi. 83.

Les Frères de la Doctrine Chrétienne, qu'on appelle *Ignorantins*, sont survenus pour achever de tout perdre; ils apprennent à lire et à écrire à des gens qui n'eussent dû apprendre qu'à dessiner et à manier le rabot et la lime, mais qui ne le veulent plus faire. . . . Le bien de la société demande que les connaissances du peuple ne s'étendent pas plus loin que ses occupations. Tout homme qui voit au delà de son triste métier, ne s'en acquittera jamais avec courage et avec patience. Parmi les gens du peuple il n'est presque nécessaire de savoir lire et écrire qu'à ceux qui vivent par ces arts, ou que ces arts aident à vivre.[1]

More important, many *Intendants* were hostile to the schools in their province; in 1782, for instance, we find an *Intendant* writing to his minister:

Non seulement le bas peuple n'en a pas besoin, mais j'ai toujours trouvé qu'il convenait qu'il n'y en eût point dans les villages. Un paysan qui sait lire et écrire quitte l'agriculture pour apprendre un métier ou pour devenir un praticien, ce qui est un très grand mal. C'est un principe que je me suis fait et je suis parvenu à empêcher bien des établissements de cette nature dans les lieux où ils tirent à conséquence.[2]

Although education was not directly financed by the state, an *Intendant* could and did prevent village communities from raising the money to set up schools.

In so far as instruction was given in French (this was obviously not the case in all regions), the main reading matter put before the pupils was the catechism and works of devotion of which the *Bibliothèque bleue* furnished quite a variety. It must be remembered that after learning the alphabet most children continued to be taught to read first in Latin. While there was undoubtedly progress in the decades before 1789, what was taught of the three Rs up and down the country scarcely equipped most pupils for more than the reading matter offered by the *Bibliothèque bleue*.

If Voltaire and even Rousseau were hostile to education for the masses, this view was not shared by a great many other writers of the time, including the Physiocrats. There was already a demand before the Revolution for a state system which would include elementary education. Many of the *Cahiers* of 1789, including some of those drawn up by the clergy and the nobility, ask for a proper system of elementary education to be set up, and the successive Revolutionary assemblies

---

[1] *Essai d'éducation nationale*, n.p., 1763, pp. 25–6.
[2] Quoted by T. Lhuillier, *Recherches historiques sur l'enseignement primaire dans la Brie*, Meaux, 1884, p. 88.

endeavoured—on paper—to meet this demand. The 1791 constitution laid down the principle of a state system, including free elementary education, though it prudently placed its realization in the somewhat remote future: 'Il sera créé et organisé une instruction publique, commune à tous les citoyens, gratuite à l'égard des parties d'enseignement indispensables pour tous les hommes, et dont les établissements seront distribués graduellement dans un rapport combiné avec la division du royaume.'[1] The Legislative Assembly took up the problem (it was for it that Condorcet produced his famous report), but while these matters were being debated, many of the elementary schools were closed as a result of the Revolution's policy on tithes and religious orders and, above all, the Civil Constitution of the Clergy. It goes without saying that in the most radical phase of the Revolution from the meeting of the Convention in September 1792 down to the fall of Robespierre in July 1794, a state system of education was frequently discussed, and indeed in October 1793 (Vendémiaire an II) a decree was passed establishing state primary schools. In practice, this did little to improve the disastrous position into which most of the schools had fallen. What is more, in the reaction which followed the fall of Robespierre a new decree was passed by the Convention which emasculated the earlier one.

Under the Directory there was no improvement in the general condition of primary education; it was no longer a state system as the state had given up paying teachers. Although Napoleon left his mark on the French educational system, he was not interested in primary schools. A law of 1802 handed back entire responsibility for them to the *communes*, and while some progress was made in certain regions, primary education remained at a very low level throughout the First Empire. The Restoration saw some improvement, but it was not until Guizot's law of 1833 that a big step forward was taken, first for boys and then later for girls.

In secondary education down to 1789 Latin continued to hold a very important place, often to the exclusion of a study either of the French language or its literature. It is true that this state of affairs was sharply criticized both by progressive teachers in the *collèges* and by the Philosophes. In his article COLLÈGE in the *Encyclopédie* d'Alembert, for instance, wrote:

Pourquoi passer six ans à apprendre, tant bien que mal, une langue morte? Je suis bien éloigné de désapprouver l'étude d'une langue dans laquelle les

---

[1] Titre premier: *Dispositions fondamentales garanties par la Constitution.*

Horaces et les Tacites ont écrit. Cette étude est absolument nécessaire pour connaître leurs admirables écrits; mais je crois qu'on devrait se borner à les entendre et que le temps qu'on emploie à composer en latin est un temps perdu. Ce temps serait bien mieux employé à apprendre par principes sa propre langue, qu'on ignore toujours au sortir du *collège* et qu'on ignore au point de la parler très mal. Une bonne grammaire française serait tout à la fois une excellente logique et une excellente métaphysique, et vaudrait bien les rapsodies qu'on lui substitue.

Among other factors working for a change in the direction of giving more attention to both French language and literature as part of a general reform of education was the closing of the Jesuit *collèges* (there were over a hundred of them scattered all over France) in 1762. Yet while there was a definite movement in favour of French, Latin still continued to have an important place in secondary education; the classes in philosophy (taken only by a minority of pupils) still continued in some *collèges* to be held in Latin, though the old custom of plunging small boys into Latin before they had learned to read in French had almost died out.

As in the seventeenth century many people were hostile to the existence of large numbers of *collèges*, often free, available to the sons of modest families. Even a writer like Louis Sébastien Mercier, despite his progressive outlook, repeatedly denounced in his *Tableau de Paris* the way in which boys were sent to *collèges* by parents anxious to see them get on in the world, and he painted a gloomy picture of the disastrous results which followed:

Aujourd'hui le petit bourgeois (qui ne sait pas lire) veut faire absolument de son fils un *latiniste*. Il dit d'un air capable à tous ses voisins auxquels il communique son sot projet: *Oh! le latin conduit à tout; mon fils saura le latin.*

C'est un très grand mal. L'enfant va au collège où il n'apprend rien. Sorti du collège, c'est un fainéant qui dédaigne tout travail manuel, qui se croit plus savant que toute sa famille et méprise l'état de son père. On l'entend décider sur tout...

Le gouvernement devrait interdire au plus tôt ces *collèges de plein exercice*,[1] où il n'y a réellement que l'apparence de l'éducation; elle semble gratuite; elle pompe les plus précieuses années de la jeunesse. Les petits bourgeois qui n'ont rien à payer précipitent en foule leurs enfants dans ces classes stériles, pour les retrouver au bout de dix ans plus sots, plus gauches et plus neufs que s'ils avaient été élevés chez un paysan, qui du moins leur aurait donné l'éducation physique et la connaissance du potager...

[1] Littré: 'Collège où les classes comprennent jusqu'à la philosophie inclusivement, avec les classes de mathématiques qui s'y joignent.'

Il faudrait qu'il fût enjoint au petit bourgeois de donner un métier à ses enfants au lieu de les envoyer sur les bancs de ces classes où tous ces vils régents volent au roi son argent et à la jeunesse le temps le plus propre à apprendre des choses utiles.[1]

None the less despite such attacks the *collèges*, whether run by the universities as their faculties of arts or by various religious orders or secular priests, continued to draw their pupils from a wide cross-section of the community, especially as quite a large number of boys did not stay for the full course either because a small *collège* did not offer it or because they chose to leave before the final philosophy course or even earlier.

Indeed, though we have no statistics for the number of boys attending *collèges* in the eighteenth century and though those for secondary education in the first half of the nineteenth century are far from reliable, it is generally accepted that it was not until the 1840s that the numbers of boys in *lycées* and *collèges* began to reach the figure which had been achieved by the 1780s; the upheaval of the Revolutionary and Napoleonic period represented a grave set-back for secondary education for boys, and it certainly did nothing to improve provision of it for girls.

The clash between the Revolution and the Catholic Church had such a serious effect on secondary education because it was so largely in clerical hands. Nearly all the *collèges* were abolished along with the universities to which some of them belonged. Partly to replace them the Convention set up *Écoles centrales*, one in the chef-lieu of each department, which offered courses in a wide variety of subjects; Stendhal attended the one in Grenoble for three years from its opening in 1796. These institutions which were a kind of cross between a secondary school and a university offered an education with a marked mathematical and scientific bias, but they had very mixed results and in any case could only reach a small minority.

The coming to power of Napoleon brought about further changes in the educational system. In 1802 the *Écoles centrales* were abolished and forty-five state *lycées* were set up in their place. Their function was summed up in the first article of the decree which established them: 'On enseignera essentiellement dans les lycées le latin et les mathématiques.' While this was not interpreted too literally to exclude French or other subjects like history and geography, the education given there was largely based on the study of Latin which had been so violently

[1] *Tableau de Paris*, 12 vols., Amsterdam, 1783–9, v. 117–19.

attacked during the Revolution. The famous law of 1808 which set up the Université covered secondary as well as higher education. On paper this law gave the state a monopoly of both forms of education, but in practice, in addition to the *lycées*, there were *collèges* run by the local authorities as well as a great many Catholic schools outside the system, though at this period these were mainly private establishments.

It is clear that when secondary education reached its peak in our period in the years before the Revolution, the number of boys able to profit from such opportunities as existed was extremely small by present-day standards. Students in universities—in the three faculties of theology, medicine, and law (the faculty of arts was part of the secondary system) —must have been tiny in numbers. In 1789 France had twenty-two universities though none was in a particularly flourishing state. Latin, it must be remembered, frequently remained the language in which the students were instructed, and in general it can be said that the universities of the eighteenth century continued in the state of decline into which they had fallen since the Renaissance. They were abolished by the Convention by a decree of September 1793, although in practice they were allowed to linger on for another couple of years. In their place were set up a number of specialist schools for advanced studies— the famous *Grandes Écoles*—such as the École normale supérieure, first established in 1794 although it did not finally get off the ground until 1808, and the École polytechnique which offered training in engineering (military as well as civil), mathematics, and the physical sciences. The Collège de France was allowed to continue its work and in addition medical schools and eventually law schools were set up before Napoleon's decree setting up the Université was issued in 1808.

Strictly speaking, this did not re-establish universities. What it did was to create a state system of education under a *grand maître*, the ancestor of the modern Minister of Education. Napoleon created not universities (they were not re-established in France until 1896), but one or more faculties of theology, law, medicine, arts, and science in each of the regions (*académies*) into which France was divided for educational purposes. The faculties of arts (facultés des lettres) and science replaced the old facultés des arts. However, the new system had scarcely begun to function when the First Empire collapsed, but we shall meet it again since, until the famous 'événements' of 1968, it dominated the whole university scene in France.

On paper at least, down to the end of the *ancien régime* the writer was no more free to communicate directly with his public than he had been under Richelieu and Louis XIV. Indeed, the censorship had become more systematic. In 1706 the theatre censorship had been entrusted to the Paris *lieutenant de police* who employed a professional writer to read the manuscript of a play and to make recommendations as to acceptance, rejection, or possible modification. While it is true that a good deal of the censor's work appears to have been concerned with cutting out personalities and minor improprieties, it is difficult to accept the view that in this period playwrights were relatively free.[1] Knowing the constraints placed upon them by the censorship, many playwrights must have watered down in advance what they would have liked to say or avoided entirely subjects which they knew would never be accepted for public performance. Quite a number of plays written and published in the second half of the century could not be performed on the public stage until the *ancien régime* had collapsed. No doubt one must not generalize from so exceptional a play as Beaumarchais's *Le Mariage de Figaro*, but with all the author's pertinacity and gift for intrigue it took him over two and a half years to bring his play from acceptance by the Comédie-française to public performance. Again, as with printed books, plays approved by the censor and the *lieutenant de police* did not necessarily have a clear run; if a play aroused the hostility of the Sorbonne or the Parlement, it could quickly be removed from the stage. Thus in 1742 Voltaire's *Mahomet* had to be suddenly taken off after only three performances.

At first the Revolution brought a reaction against this state of affairs. The censorship instituted by the monarchy gradually faded away, and it was abolished, at any rate on paper, by the famous law on the theatre of 13 January 1791. Yet, given the unsettled times, it was inevitable that it should be revived in practice and in a bewildering variety of forms, ranging from forced changes in the manuscripts of plays to a complete ban on their performance or to a demand from the authorities that they be taken off, sometimes because of the violent demonstrations and counter-demonstrations organized by rival factions among the spectators. In practice, the censorship was thus re-established and took on the most arbitrary forms; theatres which had given offence could be closed and their actors arrested, along with the author of the offending play. It can well be imagined that on taking over power in 1799 Napoleon saw to it that a rigid theatre censorship was imposed.

[1] See H. Lagrave, *Le Théâtre et le Public à Paris de 1715 à 1750*, Paris, 1972, pp. 58–71.

Gone were the turbulent days of demonstrations and counter-demonstrations which had turned many a theatre into a bear garden; from 1800 to 1814 such plays as were allowed on the stage had to pass through the hands of a committee of censors under the control of, first, the Minister of the Interior, then of the Minister of Police.[1]

The censorship of books down to 1789 continued to be regulated as under Louis XIV. The new *règlement* for the book trade, issued on 28 February 1723, which remained in force with certain modifications down to the Revolution, reiterates the old requirement:

101. Aucuns libraires, ou autres, ne pourront faire imprimer ou réimprimer, dans toute l'étendue du royaume, aucuns livres, sans en avoir préalablement obtenu la permission par lettres scellées du grand sceau, lesquelles ne pourront être demandées ni expédiées qu'après qu'il aura été remis à M. le chancelier, ou garde des sceaux de France, une copie manuscrite ou imprimée du livre pour l'impression duquel lesdites lettres seront demandées.

102. Ne pourront pareillement lesdits libraires, ou autres, faire imprimer ou réimprimer aucuns livres, ni même des feuilles volantes et fugitives, sans en avoir obtenu permission du lieutenant de police, et sans une approbation de personnes capables choisies par lui pour l'examen; et sous ledit nom de livres ne pourront être compris que les ouvrages dont l'impression n'excédera pas la valeur de deux feuilles en caractères de cicéro.[2]

The penalties for circulating books unacceptable to the authorities were set forth in an earlier paragraph:

99. Ceux qui imprimeront ou feront imprimer, vendront, exposeront, distribueront ou colporteront des livres ou libelles contre la religion, le service du roi, le bien de l'État, la pureté des mœurs, l'honneur et la réputation des familles et des particuliers, seront punis suivant la rigueur des ordonnances; et à l'égard des imprimeurs, libraires, relieurs ou colporteurs; ils seront en outre privés et déchus de leurs privilèges et immunités, et déclarés incapables d'exercer leur profession, sans pouvoir y jamais être rétablis.[3]

Successive Chancellors had at their beck and call a growing army of censors—73 in 1745, reaching 178 in 1789. In practice, control over the book trade was delegated to a series of *directeurs de la librairie*, starting with abbé Bignon in 1699 and continuing down to the Revolution.

[1] For the period 1789–1815 see H. Welschinger, *Le Théâtre de la Révolution, 1789–1799*, Paris, 1880, and *La Censure sous le Premier Empire*, Paris, 1882 (the latter work also covers the censorship of books and of the press).

[2] Isambert, *Recueil des anciennes lois françaises* xxi. 245. There is an interesting examination of 359 censors' reports for the period 1769–8 in M. Cerf, 'La Censure royale à la fin du XVIIIᵉ siècle', *Communications*, 1967, pp. 2–27.

[3] Isambert, xxi. 244.

Some of these were well-known figures such as the future Minister for War, the comte d'Argenson, who held the post from 1737 to 1740 or the *lieutenant de police*, Sartine, who combined the two posts from 1763 to 1774. The most famous of all these officials was Malesherbes who was appointed in 1750 by his father and held the post until the latter's fall from favour in 1763; he performed the tightrope act of trying to reconcile the official regulations on the book trade with a mildly liberal attitude.

Thanks to the diligent researches of Robert Estivals we now know how many *privilèges* were asked for and how many were granted in the period 1715–88 except for the years from 1716 to 1723 for which there is a gap in the records. Over a third of the applications in this period were rejected.[1] Such figures do not, however, tell us a great deal as notoriously many works in this period were not submitted to the censorship as this would have been a sheer waste of time. As Malesherbes put it on the eve of the Revolution in his posthumously published *Mémoire sur la liberté de la presse*: 'Un homme qui n'aurait jamais lu que les livres qui, dans leur origine, ont paru avec l'attache expresse du gouvernement, comme la loi le prescrit, serait en arrière de ses contemporains presque d'un siècle.'[2] It is not entirely uncharacteristic of this state of affairs that of the sixty or so volumes of the extremely modest collection of books written and published by Frenchmen between 1715 and 1789 to be found in the room in which these lines are being written (it includes works by Boulanger, Diderot, Helvétius, d'Holbach, Mably, Raynal, Robinet, and Voltaire), precisely one—Marmontel's *Bélisaire*—appeared in Paris 'avec approbation et privilège du roi'.

Undoubtedly, large numbers of books were surreptitiously produced inside France itself or else illegally imported from the printing-works of Avignon,[3] Holland, the Austrian Netherlands, Switzerland, England, and elsewhere. Despite the strict controls exercised over the Paris book trade both by the officers of the guild and state officials a good deal of clandestine printing went on inside the capital. There are a large number

---

[1] Estivals, *La Statistique bibliographique de la France*, pp. 247–8. It is a curious fact that the number registered at the Paris Chambre syndicale was much smaller than the number granted by the Chancellor (see p. 249). See also F. Furet, 'La "librairie" du royaume de France', in *Livre et société dans la France du XVIIIᵉ siècle*, i, Paris and The Hague, 1965, pp. 3–32.

[2] *Mémoires sur la librairie et sur la liberté de la presse*, Paris, 1809, p. 300.

[3] Being in papal territory, Avignon was particularly active as a printing and publishing centre in the period roughly 1740–70. See R. Moulinas, *L'Imprimerie, la librairie et la presse à Avignon au XVIIIᵉ siècle*, Grenoble, 1974.

of references to the existence of such printing in the five *Mémories sur la librairie* composed by Malesherbes during the period when he was *directeur de la librairie*.[1] A writer who was bold enough to do so, as Diderot was in his early period of rashness, could have his works clandestinely printed in the capital itself. Thanks to the bookseller, Durand, one of the four men responsible for bringing out the *Encyclopédie*, Diderot was able to have printed in Paris such works as his *Pensées philosophiques* and his *Lettre sur les aveugles*, naturally without his name on the title-page and under such disguises as 'La Haye' and 'Londres'. 'Les livres imprimés à Paris', his friend, Grimm, was later to write, 'portent sur le titre Amsterdam, Londres, Berlin, Genève; dans d'autres pays on se permet d'autres mensonges; aucun auteur un peu hardi ne veut avoir écrit dans le lieu de son séjour.'[2]

A more prudent writer would generally tend to go further afield in search of a publisher. There were publishing centres in the provinces which were less closely supervised by the authorities; some of them, notably Rouen, were well known for their production of unauthorized works. Voltaire, for instance, while he found it prudent to publish his *Lettres philosophiques* first in an English translation and then to follow it up with the French text in a London edition with a Basle imprint, also arranged for a French edition to be produced surreptitiously in Rouen, one which was immediately copied, again on the quiet, by two different Paris booksellers.

On other occasions Voltaire's works were produced in all manner of different publishing centres, in Paris itself (sometimes officially, sometimes not), in London, Amsterdam, Berlin, and most frequently of all during his later career in Geneva where he had on his doorstep the Cramer brothers who turned out innumerable works for him. Many of the best-known eighteenth-century French works first appeared in print outside France—for instance, Montesquieu's *Lettres persanes* (Amsterdam under a bogus Cologne imprint) and the *Esprit des lois* (Geneva), Prévost's *Manon Lescaut* (Amsterdam), and Rousseau's *Discours sur l'inégalité*, *La Nouvelle Heloïse*, and *Le Contrat social* (also at Amsterdam). A fairly radical writer like baron d'Holbach would publish in Paris, 'avec approbation et privilège du roi', his translations of German scientific and technological works, and send to

---

[1] See pp. 25, 44, 48, 62, 75, 82, etc. See also Herrmann-Mascard, *La Censure des livres à Paris à la fin de l'Ancien Régime*, pp. 107–9.

[2] *Correspondance littéraire, philosophique et critique*, ed. M. Tourneaux, 16 vols., Paris, 1877–82, vi. 269.

Amsterdam other works like *Le Christianisme dévoilé* or *Le Système de la nature* for which he was responsible. As he took the precaution of having the manuscripts of all these surreptitiously published works copied out in another hand before they were sent off to Amsterdam, his identity was never discovered, despite the furore which many of them created when copies began to circulate in Paris. He thus avoided any of the unpleasantness which his friend, Helvétius, experienced when he took out a *privilège* for *De l'esprit*, a much less outspoken work than, say, *Le Système de la nature*.

It was, of course, not altogether a simple matter to have many of these works, especially those which were very strictly banned, smuggled into France and especially into the capital. On paper the regulations were very stiff. The 1723 *règlement*, extended to the whole kingdom in 1744, imposed strict control over the movement of books both into France and from one part of the country to the other:

92. Défend S. M. à tous syndic et adjoints, gardes et autres officiers des communautés des libraires et imprimeurs des villes des provinces du royaume, ensemble à tous directeurs, commis, gardes, inspecteurs et autres employés dans les douanes, romaines[1] et bureaux, d'ouvrir ni visiter aucunes balles, ballots, caisses ou paquets de livres, d'estampes, ou des caractères d'imprimerie, venant des pays étrangers ou des provinces du royaume en la ville de Paris, et de les arrêter dans leur route; ains les enjoint de les laisser passer avec acquit-à-caution[2] jusqu'au lieu de leur destination; à l'effet de quoi les voituriers qui seront chargés des balles ou paquets de livres, d'estampes ou de caractères d'imprimerie, seront tenus de prendre ledit acquit-à-caution, savoir: pour les livres, estampes ou caractères venant des pays étrangers dans les premiers bureaux d'entrée du royaume, et pour ceux venant des provinces du royaume, dans le bureau du lieu d'où l'envoi sera fait, ou, s'il n'y en avait point, dans le plus prochain par où ils passeront; dans lequel bureau lesdits ballots ou paquets seront plombés par les commis des fermes de S.M., et les voituriers y feront, sur le registre des acquits-à-caution, leurs soumissions par lesquelles ils s'obligeront, ou feront pour eux obliger personnes solvables, de représenter au bureau de la douane de la ville de Paris, lesdits ballots ou paquets plombés, et de rapporter, au plus tard dans deux mois, un certificat qui sera au dos dudit acquit-à-caution, portant que lesdits ballots ou paquets ont été représentés et remis ès mains des syndic et adjoints de ladite ville, qui mettront pareillement sur lesdits acquits-à-caution leur certificat que lesdites balles, ballots ou paquets ont été portés en leur chambre syndicale. Veut que

[1] Another name for customs-houses.
[2] Littré: 'Autorisation que les employés d'une administration financière délivrent sur papier timbré, pour que telle marchandise qui n'a point encore payé les droits puisse librement circuler d'un entrepôt à un autre.'

tous les livres et livrets qui viendront des pays étrangers ne puissent entrer dans le royaume que par les villes de Paris, Rouen, Nantes, Bordeaux, Marseille, Lyon, Strasbourg, Metz, Amiens et Lille. Fait défenses à toutes sortes de personnes de les traduire, par aucunes autres villes ni par aucun autre bureau ou passage, à peine de confiscation.[1]

This strict control over the movement of books applied even to those belonging to tourists, as Smollett discovered to his disgust after landing at Boulogne in 1763. He was already annoyed to find how much duty he had to pay on such things as silver and bed- and table-linen, but worse was to come:

> What gives me more vexation, my books have been stopped at the bureau; and will be sent to Amiens at my expense, to be examined by the *chambre syndicale*; lest they should contain something prejudicial to the state, or to the religion of the country. This is a species of oppression which one would not expect to meet with in France, which piques itself on its politeness and hospitality; but the truth is, I know no country in which strangers are worse treated, with respect to their essential concerns.[2]

The inspection which took place in the Chambre syndicale of Paris and of those provincial towns which had them was theoretically a very searching one. The officers of the guild were on the look-out, not only for pirated editions of works officially published in France, but also for works which could never obtain such permission. They had to refer all works of this kind to the *Directeur de la librairie* who would decide whether they were to be destroyed, returned to the sender, or let in. In practice, the control which they exercised seems to have been fairly slack, so much so that the government gradually came to appoint its own *inspecteurs de la librairie* both in Paris and in various provincial centres; in addition to keeping an eye on printers and booksellers, they had to be present at the opening of the packets of books which arrived at the Chambre syndicale. No doubt the officers of the guild and these inspectors, not to mention customs men and police, often made their hauls of banned books, but all these precautions were frequently set at naught by the wiles employed against them.

Books could be smuggled into France by devious routes. Customs officials and others could be bribed; once the books were inside the country, there was a skilfully organized network to see that they were conveyed from the frontier to Paris and other centres. One of the main bases from which books were surreptitiously conveyed into the capital

[1] Isambert, xxi. 242–3.
[2] *Travels through France and Italy*, ed. T. Seccombe, London, 1907, p. 9.

was, improbable as it may sound, Versailles, the seat of the government (it also provided quite a good market for books of this type). The books which gave rise to this trade were not necessarily masterpieces of literature or thought; the trade term 'livres philosophiques' was used to cover pornography as well as more respectable works.[1] While there were decided risks in this illicit trade, there were also large profits to be made; the more strictly a book or pamphlet was banned, the higher rose its market value. All kinds of devices were used in this traffic. Books would be hidden in cases containing other goods. The coachmen of highly placed personages, including even ministers, could be bribed to bring consignments of such works through the gates of Paris in their carriages which, unlike those of lesser mortals, were not searched. In 1771 two young women found themselves in the Bastille for trying to smuggle banned books into Paris under their skirts; over four months passed before they were released.[2]

Even before 1750 when Malesherbes took over as *Directeur de la librairie*, at a time when the flood of unorthodox writings produced by the Philosophes and other authors was only just beginning, it was clear that the restrictive policy pursued under the Chancellor, Da guesseau, who had held the office since 1717, was far from successful, as Malesherbes pointed out:

Malgré la grande sévérité de M. le chancelier Daguesseau sur les livres, dans ses dernières années, on a vu paraître les *Pensées philosophiques*, *l'Histoire de l'âme*, les *Mœurs*[3] et mille autres. C'est ainsi que la *Gazette ecclésiastique* a existé sous l'administration de M. Hérault, qui sûrement ne protégeait pas les jansénistes.[4]

What is more, there were divided counsels in the government itself. For instance, in 1738, Daguesseau decided not to grant *privilèges* for novels and similar frivolous works;[5] but, Malesherbes explains, other ministers found this intolerable:

[1] In 1776 a bookseller from Rheims named Cazin was imprisoned in the Bastille and interrogated: 'Qu'entendez-vous, lui dit-on, par ces mots *articles philosophiques* qui se trouvent dans chacune de vos factures; il répondit que cette expression était de convention dans la librairie pour caractériser tout ce qui était prohibé.' (Charpentier, *La Bastille dévoilée*, 3 vols., Paris, 1789–90, quatrième livraison, pp. 123–4.)
[2] F. Funck-Brentano, *Les Lettres de cachet à Paris, étude suivie d'une liste des prisonniers de la Bastille (1659–1789)*, Paris, 1903, nos. 4897, 4898.
[3] By Diderot, La Mettrie, and Toussaint respectively.
[4] *Mémoires*, pp. 25–6 (Hérault was *Lieutenant de police* from 1725 to 1739; the underground Jansenist journal, *Les Nouvelles ecclésiastiques*, began publication in 1728).
[5] See G. May, *Le Dilemme du roman au XVIIIe siècle*, New Haven, 1963, pp. 75–105.

Dans les dernières années de la vie de M. Daguesseau le parti que prit ce grand magistrat de ne permettre ni romans ni brochures frivoles, engagea d'autres ministres à établir une espèce de tribunal secret de tolérance, où on assurait les auteurs et les libraires qu'ils ne seraient point poursuivis en se soumettant à un examen particulier.[1]

In fact a breach in the strict system of censorship had occurred even earlier.

Writing on the eve of the Revolution, Malesherbes traced back approximately to the time of the death of Louis XIV the institution of what were known as *permissions tacites*.[2] A manuscript or an imported book would be submitted to a censor; if he found that it could not be officially approved and given a *privilège*, it might none the less be allowed to appear, though without either a censor's approval or a *privilège*. Thirty years earlier Malesherbes had already declared: '... Depuis trente ans l'usage des permissions tacites est devenu presque aussi commun que celui des permissions publiques.'[3] He goes on to explain an amusing piece of administrative hypocrisy calculated to deceive a modern scholar working among the archives of the eighteenth-century book trade: in order not to clash with the law which forbade the printing of a book 'sans permission scellée', 'dans l'usage actuel la liste des permissions tacites, qui est déposée à la Chambre syndicale, est intitulée: *Liste des ouvrages imprimés en pays étrangers, dont le débit est permis en France.*'[4] What Malesherbes has to say on this subject is confirmed by the records. The earliest *permissions tacites* were granted in 1718, and although they were at first quite small in number, they swelled rapidly from the 1740s onwards and by the 1770s had become as numerous as those publicly conferred by the Chancellor.[5]

These were not the only breaches in the official system of control. Both the granting of *privilèges* and *permissions* and that of *permissions tacites* were officially recorded, but, as Malesherbes points out in his *Mémoire sur la liberté de la presse*, the *Lieutenant de police*, as distinct from the Chancellor and his *Directeur de la librairie*, had it in his power to tolerate works which would not qualify even for a *permission tacite*, and no official record was kept of these.[6] The circumstances under

[1] *Mémoires*, p. 1.　　　[2] Ibid. p. 311.　　　[3] Ibid. pp. 152–3.
[4] Ibid. p. 255. Or more acurately (see Bibliothèque nationale, MSS. fr. 21994, 21992) 'Registre des livres d'impression étrangère présentés à Monseigneur le Chancelier pour la permission de débiter'.
[5] Estivals, *Statistique bibliographique*, pp. 42–50 (see also the graph on p. 297).
[6] *Mémoires*, p. 317.

which certain works were unofficially tolerated Malesherbes explains as follows:

Souvent on sentait la nécessité de tolérer un livre, et cependant on ne voulait pas avouer qu'on le tolérait; ainsi on ne voulait donner aucune permission expresse . . . .

Dans ce cas . . . on prenait le parti de dire à un libraire qu'il pouvait entreprendre son édition, mais secrètement; que la police ferait semblant de l'ignorer et ne le ferait pas saisir; et comme on ne pouvait pas prévoir jusqu'à quel point le clergé et la justice s'en fâcheraient, on lui recommandait de se tenir toujours prêt à faire disparaître son édition dans le moment qu'on l'en avertirait, et on lui promettait de lui faire parvenir cet avis avant qu'il ne fût fait des recherches chez lui.

Je ne sais pas bien quel nom donner à ce genre de permission dont l'usage est devenu commun. Ce ne sont proprement que des assurances d'impunité.[1]

How many books or pamphlets benefited in this period from these *tolérances* it is impossible to say. Though, after the withdrawal of its *privilège* by the Chancellor in 1759, the last ten volumes of text of the *Encyclopédie* are sometimes said to have been published by *permission tacite*, the fact that they were surreptitiously printed in Paris and then issued, with all manner of restrictions, under the false imprint of Samuel Fauche of Neuchâtel would surely indicate that they came into the category of works which the authorities merely tolerated.[2]

It would seem that with so many possible breaches in the regulations concerning the book trade the lives of printers, booksellers, and writers must have been relatively easy, that, especially in the second half of the century, freedom of the press was almost a reality. This would, however, be an illusion. Printers and booksellers were subject to constant supervision and to the possibility of raids on their premises. It is true that none of them is known to have been punished according to the rigour of the law, to have suffered death, or to have spent long years in prison or on the galleys; unquestionably, offenders against the laws on the book trade were less savagely punished than in the previous century. Yet they remained subject to various pains and penalties for infringements of these laws, including an indeterminate sentence in royal prisons like the Bastille under a *lettre de cachet*. A printer could be deprived of his livelihood by the withdrawal of his *maîtrise* in the guild

[1] Ibid. p. 314.
[2] There is in fact no mention of the *Encyclopédie* in either of the two relevant registers of *permissions tacites* preserved in the Bibliothèque nationale—Ms. fr. 21994 for the period beginning 24 December 1750 and 21992 for the period beginning 20 March 1760 (MS. 22193 begins on 20 November 1766).

as well as suffering a spell of imprisonment or paying a heavy fine. The Rouen printer, Robert Machuel, for instance, after a spell in the Bastille lost his *maîtrise* in 1753; his shop was closed and his presses and sets of type sold up.[1] A bookseller found with banned books on his hands could also meet with severe punishment. In 1771, for example, the widow Stockdorff of Strasbourg was sent to the Bastille for having banned works smuggled into Paris, and two years later she was back again there for stocking such works as Voltaire's *Lettres philosophiques*, *Dictionnaire philosophique* and *La Pucelle* as well as d'Holbach's *Système de la nature* and *La Contagion sacrée*, not to mention a number of more or less improper works. On this occasion she was sentenced by the Châtelet to stand in the pillory and to be banished from Paris and Strasburg for nine years.[2]

In Paris colporteurs, though many of them were merely tolerated by the police and had no legal status, had greatly increased in numbers with the growing demand for books, as Malesherbes explains.[3] They were undoubtedly responsible for the distribution of a great many illicit works, both for their introduction into the capital and for their sale to customers. There were, however, risks attached to the business, as we see from the following news item:

2 October 1768.—On a exécuté ces jours-ci un arrêt du Parlement qui condamne Jean-Baptiste Jossevand, garçon épicier, Jean Lécuyer, brocanteur, et Marie Suisse, femme dudit Lécuyer, au carcan pendant trois jours consécutifs; condamne en outre ledit Jossevand à la marque et aux galères pendant neuf ans, ledit Lécuyer aussi à la marque et aux galères pendant cinq ans, et ladite Marie Suisse a être renfermée pendant cinq ans dans la maison de force de l'Hôpital Général, pour avoir vendu des livres contraires aux bonnes mœurs et à la religion. Ces livres sont: le *Christianisme dévoilé*, l'*Homme aux quarante écus*, *Éricie ou la vestale*, lesquels ont été lacérés et brûlés par l'exécuteur de la haute justice, lors de l'exécution des coupables.

On s'est récrié contre la sévérité d'un pareil arrêt, qu'on attribue à M. de Saint-Fargeau, président de la chambre des vacations, homme dur et inflexible, et dont le jansénisme rigoureux n'admet aucune tolérance.[4]

---

[1] Funck-Brentano, *Les Lettres de cachet à Paris*, no. 4215. See also Quéniart, *L'Imprimerie et la librairie à Rouen au XVIIIᵉ siècle*, p. 220.

[2] Funck-Brentano, *Les Lettres de cachet à Paris*, nos. 4906, 4952. See also J. P. Belin, *Le Commerce des livres prohibés à Paris de 1750 à 1789*, Paris, 1913, p. 103.

[3] *Mémoires*, pp. 153–4.

[4] L. P. de Bachaumont, *Mémoires secrets pour servir à l'histoire de la République des Lettres en France de 1762 jusqu'à nos jours*, 36 vols., London, 1777–89, iv. 113. The works burnt by the hangman were by d'Holbach, Voltaire, and Fontanelle respectively. Fontanelle's play was kept off the stage until after the outbreak of the Revolution.

The journalist's surprise at the severity of these sentences reflects the fact that, with occasional exceptions, the authorities' treatment of printers, booksellers, and colporteurs who offended against the strict regulations of the book trade tended to be relatively mild compared with what it had been in the seventeenth century. In a sense the same can be said of the treatment meted out to offending writers; but this generalization requires a good deal of qualification. While it is true that no French writer of the period was led to the scaffold or even languished for long years in a dark dungeon, a serious threat to their personal liberty hung over many of them whenever they put pen to paper on any subject where they might give offence to the authorities. These, it must be remembered, included not only the state and its own repressive system of *lettres de cachet*, but both the Catholic Church and the Parlements, particularly the Paris Parlement.

It is true that the Catholic Church lacked the direct power of censorship which it had once possessed, but the outcries of the faculty of theology at the Sorbonne or of highly placed clerics with the ear of the government could still bring about the banning of a work or action against the author. The possession of a *privilège* and the approval of a censor did not guarantee an author against trouble from the authorities as Helvétius found to his cost when he brought out *De l'esprit* in 1758. Though his main problem was with the Parlement, he also found himself in hot water with the Jesuits who stirred up the devout Queen and Dauphin as well as with the Sorbonne, and he was forced into making a humiliating retraction.[1] On the whole, by this period in its history the Sorbonne can be said to have been a weak body, not only unable to take any effective action against writers of unorthodox works, but also not taken very seriously by public opinion. Montesquieu ran into trouble with it over the publication of his *Esprit des lois*, but the matter dragged on for years and the censure of the offending propositions to be found in it was never published. In 1767 it only succeeded in sending up the sales of Marmontel's conte, *Bélisaire*, a harmless and dull plea for toleration which had appeared with a *privilège*, when it condemned the work. In *L'Ingénu*, which appeared in the same year, Voltaire poured ridicule on this censure by picking on one of the sentences in Marmontel's *conte* which had been condemned: 'La vérité luit de sa propre lumière, et on n'éclaire pas les esprits par les flammes des bûchers.' Presumably if this sentence is heretical, Voltaire suggests,

[1] The whole story is related in D. W. Smith, *Helvétius. A Study in Persecution*, Oxford, 1965.

then the following axiom must be orthodox: 'On n'éclaire les esprits qu'avec la flamme des bûchers, et la vérité ne saurait luire de sa propre lumière.'[1] More influential in this period was the Assemblée du clergé which, whenever it was in session in the last decades of the *ancien régime*, was constantly bringing pressure to bear on the government to take action against works of which the Church disapproved. If it had been unable to prevent the publication of the first edition of the *Encyclopédie*, it used its influence to stop it being reprinted in France; 2,000 copies of the first three volumes of a new edition were locked up in the Bastille as a result of its intervention.

The Parlement with all its panoply of legal formality and ferocious punishments was a much more serious threat to writers with unorthodox ideas. What is more, in its long struggle with the Crown it was anxious to intervene in matters concerning the book trade, although these were no longer its concern, but that of the government. While it is true that it let Helvétius off very lightly, at the same time it seized the opportunity to launch an attack on the *Encyclopédie* and in so doing far exceeded its powers when it forbade the publishers to sell any more copies until the first seven volumes had been examined by experts appointed by the court. Censorship was a matter for the Chancellor, not for the Parlement; and the government's retort to this infringement of the powers of the executive was to withdraw the *privilège* of the *Encyclopédie*, on paper putting an end to the whole enterprise.

The fate of the writer whose books fell foul of the authorities in this period can be depicted in varying lights. The Parlement frequently ordered books (though never their authors) to be burned by the hangman; this undoubtedly harmed no one and could prove a decided stimulus to sales. Similarly, if the government took action against the author by *lettre de cachet*, this could mean a free and even relatively luxurious spell in prison—generally only a matter of weeks—which added to the writer's fame and indirectly brought profits to his purse. In 1759 Marmontel was sent to the Bastille and spent a comfortable eleven days there; but his only crime was to have recited a satirical poem about a certain duke who obtained a *lettre de cachet* against him, and as he had powerful protectors in high places, his captivity was short. In the following year abbé Morellet was sent to the Bastille for having published a pamphlet against Palissot's satirical comedy, *Les*

---

[1] *L'Ingénu*, Ch. XI. On the whole controversy see J. Renwick, *Marmontel, Voltaire and the 'Bélisaire' affair'*, (*Studies on Voltaire and the Eighteenth Century* CXXI), Banbury, 1974.

Philosophes. In his memoirs he tells us that in prison he had consoling thoughts which made resignation to his fate easy:

... J'étais merveilleusement soutenu par une pensée qui rendait ma petite vertu plus facile.
Je voyais quelque gloire littéraire éclairer les murs de ma prison; persécuté, plus j'allais être connu. Les gens de lettres que j'avais vengés et la philosophie dont j'étais le martyr, commenceraient ma réputation. Les gens du monde qui aiment la satire, m'allaient accueillir mieux que jamais. La carrière s'ouvrait devant moi, et je pourrais y courir avec plus d'avantage. Ces six mois de Bastille seraient une excellente recommandation et feraient infailliblement ma fortune.[1]

In fact he spent only six weeks in the Bastille, and he had all along the knowledge that his crime (giving offence to certain highly placed lords and ladies) was regarded as a minor one.

But in an age when many writers—in contrast to the great names of the previous century—were at odds with the authorities, clashes with them did not always turn out so happily. Voltaire had two sojourns in the Bastille, one as a result of his quarrel with the chevalier de Rohan,[2] and an earlier one which lasted nearly a year for a satirical poem against the Regent. In 1734 the publication of his *Lettres philosophiques* caused a scandal; if he had been in Paris instead of Burgundy when the storm broke, he might well have joined his Rouen publisher in the Bastille. To avoid the *lettre de cachet* issued against him he had to retire for a short time over the frontier into Lorraine. In the meantime the Paris Parlement had his book burnt by the hangman as 'contraire à la religion, aux bonnes mœurs et au respect dû aux puissances'. Eleven months passed before the *lieutenant de police* allowed him to return to Paris. From 1750 when he left the capital for Potsdam down to his triumphant return twenty-eight years later, he was an enforced exile from his native city; and when he died there in 1778, full of glory, he was denied a decent burial.

In 1749 a *lettre de cachet* sent Diderot into a cell in the keep at Vincennes. Among the works on the authorship of which he was interrogated by the *lieutenant de police* in person were the *Pensées philosophiques*, burnt by the hangman three years earlier, and the *Lettre sur les aveugles* which had appeared in the previous month—both books which might well have kept him in prison for years. As it was, he

[1] *Mémoires*, 2 vols., Paris, 1821, i. 95.
[2] See below, pp. 238–9.

was released after just over three months' imprisonment, but before he was set free, he had to promise 'de ne rien faire à l'avenir qui puisse être contraire en la moindre chose à la religion et aux bonnes mœurs'.[1] Henceforth he was a marked man. No doubt this incident had a profound effect on the rest of Diderot's career as a writer and partly explains why so many of his subsequent works were not published during his lifetime.

Then there is the example of Rousseau. In 1762 he published two books, the *Contrat social* and *Émile*. Despite the tremendous influence which the former work was to have during the Revolution, its publication in Amsterdam caused him no trouble whatsoever with the French authorities. On the other hand, the appearance of *Émile* in Paris— with its author's name on the title-page and with its long and somewhat unorthodox disquisition on religion in the *Profession de foi du vicaire savoyard*—raised a storm. This time it was not the government which took action; indeed, although Malesherbes was unable to give the work either a *privilège* or an officially registered *permission tacite*, he had encouraged Rousseau to publish it in Paris. It was the Paris Parlement that acted; it condemned the work to be burnt by the hangman and ordered that 'le nommé J.-J Rousseau . . . sera pris et appréhendé au corps, et amené ès prisons de la Conciergerie du Palais'. Rousseau was compelled to flee from France and to seek refuge in Switzerland. It is true that eight years later he was allowed to return to Paris and to spend the remaining years of his life in France; but there is also no doubt that the prosecution launched by the Parlement in 1762 for the publication of a book which is not only one of the great works of eighteenth-century France, but at the same time profoundly religious, reduced Rousseau to a wandering existence and aggravated the persecution mania which for the last part of his life deprived him of happiness and peace of mind.

Other courts besides the Parlement could sometimes take it into their heads to prosecute the authors of books which they disapproved of. The Châtelet, a lower court, decided to take action against a much more harmless author, named Delisle de Sales. His *Philosophie de la nature*, first published in 1770, was condemned by this court in 1775, and in 1777 the author was sentenced to perpetual banishment from France, though in the end the sentence was quashed by the Parlement and he was merely admonished.

In 1781 the Parlement regarded it as a provocation on the part of

[1] *Correspondance*, ed. G. Roth and J. Varloot, 16 vols., Paris, 1955–70, i. 96.

abbé Raynal that he put both his name and his portrait into a new and handsome edition of his *Histoire philosophique et politique des établissements et du commerce des Européens dans les deux Indes*, a work to which Diderot among others had made a large though anonymous contribution. It condemned the work as 'impie, blasphématoire, séditieux, tendant à soulever les peuples contre l'autorité souveraine et à renverser les principes fondamentaux de l'ordre civil', and issued a warrant for the author's arrest. Raynal had to flee abroad; although he was allowed to return to France in 1784, Paris remained closed to him.

No doubt after about 1760 Voltaire, sitting safely at Ferney (though in 1766 during the tragic case of the chevalier de la Barre he was seriously threatened in his hide-out through the dragging into the case of his *Dictionnaire philosophique*) or baron d'Holbach, calmly established in his mansion in the centre of Paris, entertaining his guests, foreign as well as French, and taking the risk that the authorities might suddenly discover that he was responsible for a mass of unorthodox writings which issued from the presses of Amsterdam, no doubt such men could and did manage to say pretty well everything they wanted, however unpalatable their religious and philosophical ideas might be to the authorities. But most writers, especially those who were more or less dependent on their pen for a living, tended to be more cautious. 'La crainte des fagots,' d'Alembert once wrote, 'est très rafraîchissante.'

Writers of unorthodox views lived and worked in an atmosphere of repression, of humiliating acts of hypocrisy, and of secret denunciations. When in 1756 baron d'Holbach, the most radical of all the Philosophes in his attacks on religion in any shape or form, sought to succeed his father-in-law in the sinecure of *secrétaire du roi*, he was compelled to furnish a certificate from his *curé*. The latter duly certified that 'il connaît led. Sr. de Holbach pour homme de bonne vie et mœurs faisant profession de la Religion catholique, apostolique et romaine dont il remplit les devoirs avec édification et qu'il a une parfaite connaissance que ledit Sr. de Holbach a satisfait à son devoir pascal de l'année dernière'.[1] And this was the author of *Le Christianisme dévoilé* and the *Système de la nature*.

Zealous Catholics considered it their duty to denounce to the authorities as the worst type of miscreant men like Voltaire and Diderot for holding views on religion which are today commonplace. When Voltaire was sent to the Bastille in 1726, the *lieutenant de police* received the following anonymous letter:

[1] Archives nationales, V² 43.

Vous venez de mettre à la Bastille un homme que je souhaitais y voir il y a
plus de 15 années. Il y en a 10 à 12 qu'étant allé voir à Saint-Sulpice M.
l'abbé d'Albert, je me plaignis à lui du métier que faisait l'homme en question,
prêchant le déisme tout à découvert aux toilettes de nos jeunes seigneurs; je
voudrais être homme d'autorité pour un jour, lui dis-je, afin d'enfermer ce
poète entre quatre murailles pour toute sa vie; il ne m'a pourtant jamais fait ni
bien ni mal, n'en ayant jamais été connu; mais tout homme qui se déclare
ennemi de Jésus-Christ, notre divin maître et bon sauveur, est un impie que
nous devons poursuivre à cor et à cri.[1]

In 1747, the year after Diderot had published his *Pensées philosophiques*,
the *curé* of his parish sent in the following denunciation to the *lieutenant
de police*:

Le sieur Diderot est un jeune homme qui a passé sa première jeunesse dans le
libertinage. . . . Les propos que Diderot tient quelquefois dans la maison
montrent assez qu'il est déiste pour le moins. Il débite contre Jésus-Christ et
contre la Sainte-Vierge des blasphèmes que je n'ose mettre par écrit. On lui
demanda un jour comment il s'y prendrait avec de tels sentiments s'il se
trouvait en danger de mort. Il répondit qu'il ferait ce qu'il avait déjà fait en
pareil cas à l'âge de seize ans, qu'il appellerait un prêtre et recevrait les sacre-
ments. On se récria contre cette impiété; il ne fit qu'en rire et ajouta que pour
une pure cérémonie il ne voulait pas déshonorer sa femme et ses enfants dans
l'idée d'un public ignorant. . . . Dans un de ses entretiens, il s'est avoué
l'auteur d'un des deux ouvrages qui fut condamné par le Parlement et brûlé
il y a environ deux ans. On m'a assuré qu'il travaillait depuis plus d'un an à
un autre ouvrage encore plus dangereux contre la religion. Je tiens tous ces
faits d'une même personne qui demeure en la même maison et qui est entrée
assez avant dans sa familiarité pour savoir ce qu'il pense et ce qu'il fait. Il lui
importe comme à moi de ne point paraître dans cette affaire. . . .[2]

The *lieutenant de police*, however, did not have to rely on the unpaid
denunciations of amateurs; he had at his command a considerable body
of professional spies.

In 1762 Diderot discovered that for four years—and that largely out
of charity—he had been employing and also recommending to his
friends a copyist named Glénat who was a police spy. His eyes were
suddenly opened when a manuscript which someone else had given to
be copied ended up in the hands of the *lieutenant de police*. As it happened, Diderot had long known Sartine who was shortly to combine
this office with that of *directeur de la librairie*. This is how he relates his
interview with him to his mistress:

[1] *Correspondence* i. 291.
[2] P. Bonnefon, 'Diderot prisonnier à Vincennes', *Revue d'histoire littéraire*, 1899, p. 203.

J'avais une occasion d'aller voir le lieutenant de police, et j'y vais. Il me reçoit à merveille. Nous parlons de différentes choses. Je lui parle de celle-ci. 'Ah! oui, me dit-il. Je sais. Ce manuscrit est là. C'est un livre fort dangereux.— Cela se peut, monsieur, mais celui qui vous l'a remis est un coquin.—Non, c'est un bon garçon qui n'a pu faire autrement.—Encore une fois, monsieur, je ne sais ce que c'est que l'ouvrage. Je ne connais point celui qui l'a confié à Glénat. C'est une pratique que je lui faisais avoir de richochet; mais si l'ouvrage ne lui convenait pas, il fallait le refuser, et ne pas s'abaisser au métier vil et méprisable de délateur. Vous avez besoin de ces gens-là. Vous les employez. Vous récompensez leur service; mais il est impossible qu'ils ne soient pas de la boue à vos yeux'.

Le Sartine se mit à rire. Nous rompîmes là-dessus, et je m'en revins pensant en moi-même que c'était une chose bien odieuse que d'abuser de la bienfaisance d'un homme pour introduire un espion dans ses foyers.[1]

All that Diderot could do was to thank his lucky stars that he had not given the man anything dangerous to copy.

Some idea of the atmosphere of repression in which many of the writers of the age lived and worked is given in a passage in Mercier's *Tableau de Paris* in which he suggests that if the French must borrow such things as jockeys and whist from England, they might do well to have the equivalent of habeas corpus:

Il est onze heures du soir ou cinq heures du matin; on frappe à votre porte, votre domestique ouvre, votre chambre se remplit d'une escouade de satellites, l'ordre est précis, la résistance est superflue; on écarte de vous tout ce qui pourrait vous servir d'armes, et l'exempt, qui n'en vantera pas moins sa bravoure, prend jusqu'à votre écritoire pour un pistolet.

Le lendemain un voisin, qui a entendu du bruit dans la maison, demande ce que ce pouvait être; *Rien, c'est un homme que la police a fait enlever.—Qu'avait-il fait?—On n'en sait rien; il a peut-être assassiné ou vendu une brochure suspecte.—Mais, monsieur, il y a quelque différence entre ces deux délits.—Cela se peut, mais il est enlevé.*[2]

A new era of freedom for the writer seemed at last to have dawned in the summer of 1789 with the fall of the Bastille and the proclamation of the *Déclaration des droits de l'homme* with its article 11:

La libre communication des pensées et des opinions est un des droits les plus précieux de l'homme; tout citoyen peut donc parler, écrire, imprimer librement, sauf à répondre de l'abus de cette liberté dans les cas déterminés par la loi.

[1] *Correspondance*, iv. 158.
[2] *Tableau de Paris*, v. 159–60.

For a time all controls over the publication of books, newspapers, and periodicals seemed to have vanished; even the guild of printers and booksellers and hence all controls over the book trade were abolished with the rest by the Loi Le Chapelier in 1791.

Down to August 1792 complete freedom reigned. Newspapers and periodicals proliferated, especially in Paris; in 1790 well over three hundred were published in the capital alone. After 10 August 1792 the suppression of newspapers began; editors were arrested and some of them put to death; there was a dramatic fall in the number of newspapers and periodicals in 1793–4. During this most radical phase of the Revolution booksellers and printers had to be extremely cautious as to the works they handled. A law passed by the Convention on 29 March 1793 after the execution of Louis XVI laid it down that:

1. Quiconque sera convaincu d'avoir composé ou imprimé des écrits qui proposent le rétablissement de la royauté en France, ou la dissolution de la représentation nationale, sera traduit devant le Tribunal révolutionnaire et puni de mort.
2. Peine de mort contre ceux qui conseilleront dans des écrits le meurtre ou le pillage.
3. Les colporteurs, vendeurs ou distributeurs des écrits prohibés seront punis de trois ans de détention s'ils en découvrent les auteurs, et de deux ans de fer, s'ils ne les découvrent pas.[1]

It was only with the fall of Robespierre and the so-called 'réaction thermidorienne' that some degree of freedom of the press was restored. The Constitution of 1795 which set up the Directory contained two articles on the press. The first established the principle of freedom:

353. Nul ne peut être empêché de dire, écrire, imprimer et publier sa pensée.
—Les écrits ne peuvent être soumis à aucune censure avant leur publication.
—Nul ne peut être responsable de ce qu'il a écrit et publié, que dans les cas prévus par la loi.

Another article (355) did, however, provide for the passing of restrictive laws though it limited their operation to one year.

In practice, the press enjoyed a fair degree of freedom down to September 1797 when the threat of a royalist *coup d'état* led the majority of the members of the Directory to take preventive action in October 1797 (18 Fructidor an V) and to pass a very strict press law. This instituted most rigorous controls over newspapers which could be

---

[1] *Le Moniteur universel*, xv. 834.

suppressed and their editors deported. In order to raise artificially the price of newspapers a stamp duty (the idea was borrowed from England) was imposed; this was not to be finally abolished until 1870.

The arrival in power of Napoleon in 1799 led to an even more stringent control over books, newspapers, and periodicals. Two months later, in January 1800, a decree suppressed all but thirteen of the seventy-three newspapers published in the Département de la Seine, gagged those that were left by the threat of suppression if they deviated from policies laid down by the government, and forbade the foundation of new ones. This meant in practice that the press was back in the *ancien régime* when newspapers could only be founded with government permission. In 1805, after the renewal of war, press censorship was revived. In 1810 a decree laid it down that there should not be more than one political newspaper in each department, and it was, of course, to be strictly controlled by the *préfet*; in the following year all but four political newspapers in Paris were suppressed.

The book trade was similarly controlled. In 1805 printers were compelled to take out a *brevet* which could be revoked and to swear an oath of loyalty to the government. Books could be seized by the police without any form of legal procedure; in 1810 10,000 copies as well as the type of Mme de Staël's *De l'Allemagne* were seized by the police and destroyed (the book could not be published until three years later in London). By a decree of 5 February 1810 Napoleon set up a Direction de la librairie et de l'imprimerie to control the book trade; with it came an official censorship of books. Ninety-seven out of 157 printing-works in Paris were closed down. Booksellers (many of them were also publishers) were now compelled to apply to the *directeur de la librairie et de l'imprimerie* for a *brevet*; in order to obtain it they had to swear an oath 'de ne vendre, débiter et distribuer aucun ouvrage contraire aux devoirs des sujets envers le Souverain et à l'intérêt de l'État'. The *brevet* was to remain a requirement for both printers and booksellers down to 1870. The restrictions on the newspaper press and on the book trade were undoubtedly worse under the First Empire than they had been at the end of the *ancien régime*.

It would be extremely interesting to be able to trace in detail the growth in the production of books in this period. It is clear that a considerable increase did take place, but despite the valiant efforts of Robert Estivals it is not possible to measure it with any sort of accuracy. It is only at the very end of this period with the re-establishment of a compulsory *dépot légal* by a law of 1810 and the foundation of the

Journal de la librairie, Bibliographie de la France by a decree of 1811 that we begin to have more or less reliable figures. Even so—and this affects in particular our interpretation of the figures for the production of books for the nineteenth century as a whole—it is by no means clear as to how a book was defined in 1812. The figures for the last three years of the First Empire run thus: 1812 5,442; 1813 3,749; and 1814 (the fall is hardly surprising) 2,547. The *dépôt légal* had been abolished in 1789, and when it was re-established in 1793 it was not absolutely compulsory; the relevant decree laid it down that unless two copies of a book were deposited at the Bibliothèque nationale, action could not be taken against those who produced pirated versions of it. The figures for the years 1794–1811 are scarcely helpful since they begin with a modest 371, fall to 240 in 1796, and gradually rise to 2,872 in 1810, falling to 2,373 in 1811.[1]

It is difficult to make much of these figures since they are obviously incomplete, or to make useful comparisons between them and those available for the period down to 1789. Robert Estivals has brought together from a variety of sources figures for the period 1715–89. While theoretically the books deposited in these years in the Bibliothèque du Roi include works published both in Paris and the provinces and also those published with a *permission tacite*, they also include books of music, maps, prints, and periodicals as well as reprints. What one is to make of the figures given for titles deposited in this period[2] it is difficult to say. They start at 225 in 1715, fall as low as 111 in 1720 and 112 in 1744, do not climb as high as 302 until 1753, fall again and then rise to a new peak of 363 in 1765, jump to 397 in 1770 and to 479 in 1781. For the years 1786–9 we have figures which are quite out of line with those for the earlier years since they read: 1,615, 1,470, 1,680, 1,020.

It is difficult to see how juggling with these figures or with those which can be worked out from the records for *privilèges* and *permissions tacites* can take one very far. Undoubtedly, book production in eighteenth-century France must have been smaller than in the following century; but was it as small as figures from these sources, however skilfully put together, would suggest? Even if we were solely concerned with the number of books printed and published on French soil, they must obviously be incomplete as they take no account of books which the authorities merely tolerated or of those which were surreptitiously produced in Paris or the provinces because they were

[1] Estivals, *Statistique bibliographique*, p. 415.
[2] Ibid. p. 356.

pirated or were in some way displeasing to the authorities. In any case, we are concerned here with the total output of French writers, and if because of the international market for French books large numbers of them were pirated by printers in Avignon, Holland, the Austrian Netherlands, Geneva, and the rest, and if many French writers got round the censorship at home by sending their manuscripts abroad, there are here vast quantities of books for which we can never have any statistics, even unreliable ones.

The frequency with which works were pirated inevitably affected relations between writer and publisher in this period. No doubt the author who sent his manuscript abroad was chiefly concerned to see it in print though he would not unnaturally accept any payment that was going, as Rousseau did with Rey for several of his works; but pirated editions of his writings undoubtedly involved the average writer in a considerable loss. The situation was summed up very clearly in a sentence of a letter from Rey to Rousseau, written in 1764; 'Si vos ouvrages étaient moins recherchés, j'en vendrais davantage parce qu'on ne les contreferait pas si souvent.'[1] It was no doubt exasperating for a successful writer like Marmontel to encounter on his foreign travels a publisher who was doing very nicely out of pirated editions of his works:

A Liège, où nous avons couché, je vis entrer chez moi, le matin, un bourgeois d'assez bonne mine, et qui me dit: 'Monsieur, j'ai appris hier au soir que vous étiez ici; je vous ai de grandes obligations, et viens vous en remercier. Mon nom est Bassompierre; je suis imprimeur-libraire dans cette ville; j'imprime vos ouvrages dont j'ai un grand débit dans toute l'Allemagne. J'ai déjà fait quatre éditions copieuses de vos *Contes moraux*; je suis à la troisième édition de *Bélisaire.*—Quoi! Monsieur, lui dis-je, en l'interrompant, vous me volez le fruit de mon travail, et vous venez vous en vanter à moi!—Bon, reprit-il, vos privilèges ne s'étendent point jusqu'ici; Liège est un pays de franchise. Nous avons droit d'imprimer tout ce qu'il y a de bon; c'est là notre commerce'.[2]

Again it was an irritating experience for Bernardin de Saint-Pierre when after the publication of his *Études de la nature* in 1784 he was invited to a school speech-day:

[1] J.-J. Rousseau, *Correspondance complète*, ed. R. A. Leigh, Geneva and Banbury, 1965 – xx. 196.
[2] *Mémoires*, ed. J. Renwick, 2 vols., Clermont-Ferrand, 1972, i. 255. He adds (p. 256) that the edition of Molière with which he was presented by the publisher cost him 10,000 écus, at best a rather approximate figure.

J'ai été invité un jour à une distribution de prix présidée par un ministre qui en faisait les frais. . . . L'on m'avait réservé l'honneur d'embrasser conjointement avec lui tous les vainqueurs. Quelle fut ma surprise, lorsque j'en vis plusieurs, sortant de mes bras, emporter au bruit des applaudissements de toute l'assemblée, pour prix de morale et de vertu, mes *Études de la Nature* contre-faites.[1]

And this was after the *arrêt du Conseil* of 1777 which, as we shall see, endeavoured to strengthen the law against pirated editions produced in France.

In this period the printing centres in the provinces were almost driven into piracy in order to keep going. It is true that, as in Paris, an enforced limitation of the number of printers kept down competition; but with the concentration of literary life in the capital few manu-scripts came the way of provincial printers. They were reduced to supplying the needs of their region in religious works and educational textbooks along with a few books on local history, medicine, and law. One obvious additional source of printable matter would have been new editions of established works of literature and thought as these ceased to be copyright. Yet not only did the Paris printers and book-sellers have a virtual monopoly of new manuscripts; they claimed perpetual copyright in the works which they or their predecessors had acquired, even in the quite remote past.

Their viewpoint is clearly stated in the article DROIT DE COPIE which one of their number, the bookseller David, contributed to the *Encyclo-pédie* in 1755.[2] Once an author has transferred his work to a bookseller,

celui-ci devient aussi incontestablement propriétaire et avec la même étendue que l'était l'auteur lui-même. La propriété de l'ouvrage littéraire, c'est-à-dire, le *droit* de le réimprimer quand il manque, est alors un effet commer-çable, comme une terre, une rente et une maison; elle passe des pères aux enfants et de libraires à libraires, par héritage, vente, cession ou échange; et les *droits* du dernier propriétaire sont aussi incontestables que ceux du premier.

What is more, by its policy of renewing *privilèges* more or less automati-cally, the government had apparently conferred perpetual copyright on their owners.

By the 1760s government policy began to change, as we can see from the correspondence of Malesherbes. In 1759 he wrote to the *Intendant*

[1] M. Souriau, *Bernardin de Saint-Pierre d'après ses manuscrits*, Paris, 1905, p. 217.

[2] A more detailed statement of their views is to be found in the *Mémoire en forme de requête à M. le Garde des Sceaux rédigé par M. Louis d'Héricourt, avocat au Parlement* (1725), reprinted in E. Laboulaye and G. M. Guiffrey, *La Propriété littéraire au XVIIIe siècle. Recueil de pièces et de documents*, Paris, 1859, pp. 21–40.

of Lyons: 'Je ne suis plus d'avis que le gouvernement se lie les mains par des privilèges exclusifs si ce n'est en faveur des auteurs vivants', and shortly afterwards he showed considerable sympathy with the grievances of provincial printers and booksellers when he wrote:

Vos libraires de Lyon se sont plaints plusieurs fois, Monsieur, et avec quelque fondement, de l'avantage excessif qu'ont sur eux les libraires de Paris, tant par la facilité du débit de leurs marchandises que parce qu'ils sont plus à portée de traiter avec les auteurs. C'est effectivement de Paris que partent plus de trois quarts des ouvrages qui se composent et s'impriment dans le royaume et cette inégalité entre la librairie de la capitale et celle des provinces ne peut jamais être réparée.[1]

While this disproportion could never be entirely removed, the balance could be tilted slightly in favour of the provinces, and it was in this direction that government policy slowly moved.

It also tended to strengthen slightly the position of the writer against the bookseller. In 1761 the Paris guild of printers and booksellers received a rude shock when, despite the fact that La Fontaine had sold his *Fables* to a bookseller from whom the *privilège* had descended to a member of the guild, the government granted a *privilège* for the work to two of his impecunious female descendants. Diderot was entrusted by the guild (its *syndic* was Le Breton, the principal shareholder in the company which published the *Encyclopédie*) with the task of drawing up the draft of a memorandum in defence of the guild's claim to perpetual copyright. In this work, generally known as the *Lettre sur le commerce de la librairie*, using as his starting-point the writer's undoubted right of property in his own work, Diderot argues for perpetual copyright on the grounds that the writer has transferred his right to the bookseller or printer who holds the *privilège*:

Je le répète, l'auteur est maître de son ouvrage, ou personne dans la société n'est maître de son bien. Le libraire le possède comme il était possédé par l'auteur. Il a le droit incontestable d'en tirer tel parti qu'il lui conviendra par des éditions réitérées. Il serait aussi insensé de l'en empêcher que de condamner un agriculteur à laisser son terrain en friche, ou un propriétaire de maison à laisser ses appartements vides.[2]

Finally, when in 1777 the government issued a series of six *arrêts du Conseil* revising the regulations for the book trade, important changes

---

[1] Quoted in E. P. Shaw, *Problems and Policies of Malesherbes as 'Directeur de la Librairie' in France (1750–1763)*, New York, 1966, pp. 24, 28.

[2] See D. Diderot, *Œuvres complètes*, ed. J. Varloot, Paris, 1975—, viii. 510.

were made in the section concerning *privilèges*. The preamble to the first edict makes it clear that the aim of these changes was to improve the position of both the author and the provincial printer and bookseller; the writer, it declares, 'a sans doute un droit plus assuré à une grâce plus étendue' than the bookseller, but it also adds that in the past the law had withheld from the 'imprimeurs de province un moyen légitime d'employer leurs presses'.[1] The relevant articles of the first of the six *arrêts du Conseil* read:

2. Défend S. M. à tous libraires, imprimeurs ou autres qui auront obtenu des lettres de privilège pour imprimer un livre nouveau, de solliciter aucune continuation de ce privilège, à moins qu'il n'y ait dans le livre augmentation au moins d'un quart, sans que pour ce sujet on puisse refuser aux autres la permission d'imprimer les anciennes éditions non augmentées.

3. Les privilèges qui seront accordés à l'avenir, pour imprimer les livres nouveaux, ne pourront être d'une moindre durée que de dix années.

4. Ceux qui auront obtenu des privilèges, en jouiront non seulement pendant tout le temps qui y sera porté, mais encore pendant la vie des auteurs, en cas que ceux-ci survivent à l'expiration des privilèges.

5. Tout auteur qui obtiendra en son nom le privilège de son ouvrage, aura le droit de le vendre chez lui, sans qu'il puisse, sous aucun prétexte, vendre ou négocier d'autres livres, et jouira de son privilège, pour lui et ses hoirs, à perpétuité, pourvu qu'il ne le rétrocède à aucun libraire, auquel cas la durée du privilège sera, par le fait seul de la cession, réduite à celle de la vie de l'auteur.

6. Tous libraires et imprimeurs pourront obtenir, après l'expiration du privilège d'un ouvrage et la mort de son auteur, une permission d'en faire une édition sans que la même permission accordée à un ou plusieurs, puisse empêcher aucun autre d'en obtenir une semblable.[2]

These *arrêts du Conseil* caused a considerable stir and gave rise to a heated controversy as, on paper at least, they meant a very considerable change in the law. While the Paris printers and booksellers were furious and declared that they would be ruined,[3] writers were hardly happy with article 5; then as now selling one's own books could scarcely be regarded as a sensible way of trying to earn money from

---

[1] Isambert, xxv. 109.

[2] Ibid. 110–11.

[3] See the following documents reprinted in Laboulaye and Guiffrey: pp. 151–220, *Requête au Roi et consultations pour la librairie et l'imprimerie de Paris au sujet des deux arrêts du 30 août 1777*; pp. 265–358, abbé Pluquet, *Lettres à un ami*; pp. 367–446, *Lettre du libraire Leclerc à M. de Neville, directeur de la librairie*; pp. 447–596, *Procès-verbaux des séances du Parlement (23 avril, 10, 27 et 31 août 1779)*. (See also M. A. Merland, 'Tirage et vente des livres à la fin du XVIIIᵉ siècle: des documents chiffrés', *Revue française d'histoire du livre*, 1973, pp. 87–112.)

them. After representations by the Académie française[1] the government issued a year later a new *arrêt du Conseil* modifying this article:

L'article 5 . . . sera exécuté selon sa forme et teneur; en conséquence, tout auteur qui aura obtenu en son nom le privilège de son ouvrage, non seulement aura le droit de le faire vendre chez lui, mais il pourra encore, autant de fois qu'il le voudra, faire imprimer pour son compte son ouvrage par tel imprimeur et le faire vendre aussi pour son propre compte par tel libraire qu'il aura choisi, sans que les traités ou conventions qu'il fera pour imprimer ou débiter une édition de son ouvrage puissent être réputés cession de son privilège.[2]

This concession did something in the writer's favour, but then as now paying one's own printer and selling the work through a publisher on a commission basis was not a very satisfactory way of dealing with it, as Diderot had earlier pointed out:

J'ai écrit et j'ai plusieurs fois imprimé pour mon compte. . . . Le libraire peu scrupuleux croit que l'auteur court sur ses brisées. . . . Les correspondants de province nous pillent impunément. Le commerçant de la capitale n'est pas assez intéressé au débit de notre ouvrage, pour le pousser. Si la remise qu'on lui accorde est forte, le profit de l'auteur s'évanouit.[3]

Moreover, it is far from clear how these new laws really operated.

It was left to the Revolution to produce the first modern copyright law in France, one which safeguarded the interests of the author and his heirs in his work though that protection was limited to a period of ten years after his death. On 19 July 1793 the Convention passed the following decree:

Art. Ier Les auteurs d'écrits en tout genre, les compositeurs de musique, les peintres et dessinateurs qui feront graver des tableaux ou dessins, jouiront durant leur vie entière du droit exclusif de vendre, faire vendre, distribuer leurs ouvrages dans le territoirre de la république, et d'en céder la propriété en tout ou en partie.

II. Leurs héritiers ou cessionnaires jouiront du même droit durant l'espace de dix ans, après la mort des auteurs.

III. Les officiers de paix seront tenus de faire confisquer, à la réquisition et au profit des auteurs, compositeurs, peintres ou dessinateurs et autres, leurs héritiers ou cessionnaires, tous les exemplaires des éditions imprimées ou gravées, sans la permission formelle et par écrit des auteurs.

---

[1] Laboulaye and Guiffrey give in an appendix (pp. 623–9) *Extraits des procès-verbaux de l'Académie française* for the meetings of 7 and 23 February and 23 July 1778 at which the matter was discussed.

[2] Isambert, xxv. 371.

[3] *Œuvres complètes*, viii. 513.

IV. Tout contrefacteur sera tenu de payer au véritable propriétaire une somme équivalente au prix de trois mille exemplaires de l'édition originale.

V. Tout débitant d'édition contrefaite, s'il n'est pas reconnu contrefacteur, sera tenu de payer au véritable propriétaire une somme équivalente au prix de cinq cents exemplaires de l'édition originale.[1]

From this beginning the rights of an author and his heirs over his work were gradually to be extended, starting with Napoleon's decree of 5 February 1810 which prolonged the period for the writer's widow and children: 'Titre VI. Le droit de propriété est garanti à l'auteur et à sa veuve pendant leur vie, si les conventions matrimoniales de celle-ci lui en donnent le droit, et à leurs enfants pendant vingt ans.'[2]

As regards pirated editions produced inside France the *arrêts du Conseil* of 1777 had to deal with the awkward situation that there were in existence 'un grand nombre de livres contrefaits antérieurement au présent arrêt, et que ces livres formaient la fortune d'une grande partie des libraires de province, qui n'avaient que cette ressource pour satisfaire à leurs engagements'. It was therefore laid down that to avoid the penalties imposed for this offence (a fine of 6,000 livres on the first occasion and on the second a similar fine and loss of the *maîtrise*) the owners of such pirated copies must have them stamped within a period of two months.[3] How often the law against pirated editions was applied is not altogether clear; we do know that in 1781 a Toulouse printer who had brought out a pirated edition of Marmontel's *Contes moraux* was given the maximum fine, 2,000 livres of which went to the author.[4]

The breaking of the virtual monopoly of *privilèges* held by the Paris guild did offer openings for provincial printers and booksellers to produce editions of works which were no longer copyright. There is in existence a register of the *permissions* granted to printers in the provinces in the period from 1778 to 1789.[5] The total number granted in these years was 785 and not all of these were taken up; it is also to be noted that after reaching a peak in 1779 the number gradually declined

---

[1] *Le Moniteur universel*, xvii. 176.

[2] J. B. Duvergier, *Collection complète des lois, décrets, ordonnances, règlements depuis 1788*, 108 vols., Paris, 1824–1908, iv. 27.

[3] Isambert, xxv. 121, 123.

[4] Bauchaumont, *Mémoires secrets* xvii. 179.

[5] It has been very thoroughly studied by J. Brancolini and M. T. Bouyssy, 'La Vie provinciale du livre à la fin de l'Ancien Régime', in *Livre et société dans la France du XVIIIe siècle*, ii, Paris and The Hague, 1970, pp. 3–37.

and even a sudden upward surge in 1786 did not reach the earlier figure. For once this register provides details as to the size of the edition to be printed; it is a striking fact that nearly two-thirds of the total number of copies authorized were for religious works, whereas the category of belles-lettres was responsible for just under 20 per cent. On the whole one has the impression that the government's change of policy in 1777 did not alter matters all that much; in what was now a highly centralized country whose literary and intellectual life was concentrated in the capital publishing was unlikely to flourish in the provinces except for the production of chapbooks in centres like Troyes and Rouen.

The production of pirated editions on French territory was soon to be stamped out,[1] but in the absence of an international copyright agreement French publishers and writers were long to be plagued with those produced abroad. What made the problem especially acute in the eighteenth century was the combination of two factors—the vogue of the French language over most of Europe and the practice of French writers of sending their manuscripts to be printed abroad. The second factor, which had undoubtedly contributed to the prosperity of foreign publishers, gradually died out in post-Revolutionary France as, despite the restrictions imposed on the press by various régimes, French law was often more liberal than those of surrounding countries, and although in the 1830s and 1840s we find writers like Balzac moaning about the tremendous losses inflicted on them by pirate publishers, particularly those of Belgium, the problem was much less acute than it had been in the previous century.

With the growth of the reading public of which contemporaries were clearly conscious it is a fair assumption that the financial position of the writer was on the whole better than in the seventeenth century. It is unfortunate that as publishers' agreements were not drawn up by notaries, but were simply 'des actes passés sous seing privé', very few have come down to us and we do not have much more information about payments received by writers than the few scraps which we have for the previous age. It is interesting that French writers were envious of the much larger money payments made by publishers on this side of the Channel. Indeed, writers like Jean-Baptiste Rousseau and even Voltaire found it very advantageous to bring their works to English publishers. The exiled Rousseau came to London in 1723 and is said to have received 800 guineas (the equivalent of some 20,000 livres) for the

---

[1] Articles 425–9 of the Code pénal (1810) imposed severe penalties.

two volumes of his *Œuvres diverses*,[1] while a few years later the edition
of Voltaire's epic, *La Henriade*, which he published by subscription also
brought him a large sum of money; if we include a gift of 6,000 livres
from George I, the total came to some 30,000 livres.[2] The edition of the
Lettres philosophiques which his friend, Thiériot, brought out in London
in 1733 is alleged to have brought him 200 guineas (some 5,000 livres).[3]
The sums earned by successful English writers seemed fabulous to
French writers; in 1745 in his *Lettres d'un Français* abbé Le Blanc
speaks with bated breath of the £12,000 (and a wealthy marriage into
the bargain) which Richard Glover's epic, *Leonidas*, allegedly brought
him.[4] In 1766, when the last ten volumes of text of the *Encyclopédie* had
just appeared, Grimm penned a bitter paragraph on the meanness of
Le Breton and his partners towards the editors and contributors of the
work. 'Je ne connais guère de race plus franchement malhonnête que
celle des libraires de Paris', he declares, and he goes on to make the
inevitable comparison with conditions in this country: 'En Angleterre
l'*Encyclopédie* aurait fait la fortune des auteurs'.[5] Four years later the
news that William Robertson's *History of Charles V* had brought him
the stupendous sum of £4,000 (over 100,000 francs) caused quite a stir
in literary circles in France. We find Voltaire writing to La Harpe in
1770: 'Je voudrais que chacune de vos lignes fût payée comme aux
Robertson',[6] while another French writer declared: 'Si un libraire de
Paris en avait donné la huitième partie de cette somme, il aurait cru
faire encore à l'auteur un traitement bien généreux.'[7] This disparity
seems to have been accepted as a fact on this side of the Channel. Thus
we find David Hume giving it as one of the reasons why Rousseau
should come to England: 'Les libraires de Londres offrent aux auteurs
plus d'argent que ceux de Paris; ainsi vous pourrez sans peine y vivre
frugalement du fruit de votre propre travail.'[8]

Nevertheless, even if English writers were in a more favourable
position than their French colleagues, a similar process was at work on
both sides of the Channel. In France, at any rate in the closing decades

---

[1] C. de S. Montesquieu, *Œuvres completes*, ed. A. Masson, 3 vols., Paris, 1950–5, iii.
745.

[2] *Complete Works*, Geneva and Banbury, 1968—, ii. 75 n.

[3] Voltaire, *Correspondence* vi. 81.

[4] *Lettres d'un Français concernant le gouvernement, la politique et les mœurs des Anglais
et des Français*, 3 vols., The Hague, 1745, iii. 109. It is true that Le Blanc stresses the
humiliating side of publishing works by subscription (i. 222–4).

[5] *Correspondance littéraire* vii. 45.   [6] *Correspondence* xxxv. 441.

[7] C. G. Fenouillot de Falbaire, *Avis aux gens de lettres*, Liège, 1770, pp. 40–1.

[8] *Letters*, ed. J. Y. T. Greig, 2 vols., Oxford, 1932, i. 527.

of the *ancien régime*, it was becoming possible, as it had become earlier in England, for a writer to earn a living by his pen and thus make himself independent of patronage. Only it was a slower process in France and down to 1789 literary patronage retained an importance which it had lost before that date in England.

The old notion that there was something almost indecent in taking money for one's writings from booksellers and theatres died hard. As late as 1770 we find Fenouillot de Falbaire delivering a vehement attack on this outlook as typified by the man who asks the question: 'Est-ce qu'un auteur doit travailler pour l'argent?' The answer is given in violent terms:

Mais vous-même, monsieur, vous qui persiflez si agréablement, vous, homme riche en titre, de robe ou d'épée, qui que vous soyez, répondez-moi. La maison du souverain est entretenue avec *l'argent* de ses sujets; les ministres qui gouvernent sous ses ordres reçoivent de *l'argent* pour remplir les fonctions de leurs différents départements; la plupart des grands seigneurs passent leur vie dans les cours à ramper, à flatter, à intriguer pour obtenir des grâces qui, en dernier résultat, sont toujours de *l'argent*. L'ambassadeur chiffre, le militaire se bat, le magistrat rend la justice, l'avocat plaide, le financier calcule, le prédicateur prêche, le chanteur chante, le marchand commerce, l'artisan travaille, le paysan laboure, le médecin guérit ou tue, le curé baptise et enterre *pour de l'argent*. Tout le monde agit *pour de l'argent*, reçoit de *l'argent* pour prix de ses peines, pour salaire de ses travaux, et vous voulez que la classe des gens de lettres soit seule exceptée de cet ordre général et nécessaire. . . .[1]

Payments from booksellers appear for the most part to have consisted in a lump sum; as in this country a royalty system still lay far in the future. This seems to have been calculated by the bookseller on the returns which he could expect from the first edition. As we have seen, the prospects of further sales if the work were successful were limited by the certainty of pirated editions appearing in France or abroad, though on occasion the author might receive further payments, if only token ones.

Such payments tended to be rather low in the first half of the eighteenth century to judge from the scrappy information at our disposal. For most literary works they seem to have come within the range of 1,000 or 1,500 to 2,000 livres. We know that in 1748 Diderot received 1,200 livres for his secretly printed novel, *Les Bijoux indiscrets*,[2] but most of our information concerns the publication of plays. As so often

[1] *Avis aux gens de lettres*, pp. 32–3.
[2] A. M. Wilson, *Diderot*, New York, 1972, pp. 83–4.

happens with publishers' agreements which have come down to us from the past, these are not always easy to interpret since they frequently concern more than one work. For instance, in 1735 Destouches sold to a bookseller for 2,000 livres his *privilège* for a complete edition of his plays which would contain three new ones—*Le Tambour nocturne* (five acts), *La Fausse Agnès* (three acts), and *L'Envieux* (one act)—as well as corrections to some of his earlier works. Two years later he received only 700 livres for the publication of his tragicomedy, *L'Ambitieux et l'indiscrète.* In 1750 he received 2,400 livres for a new five-act comedy which had just had a fairly successful first run together with two other five-act plays and one in one act which was never performed.[1] These payments would appear to be rather low. In 1737 Voltaire asked for 1,200 livres for his sentimental comedy, *L'Enfant prodigue*, though he took books instead of money,[2] while in the same year La Chaussée obtained 1,600 livres for *L'École des amis* 'outre cent de livres et autres menus droits'.[3] A decade or so later prices for plays seem to have been rather higher: according to Collé[4] in 1749 Crébillon —then enjoying a fresh burst of success—received 40 louis (960 livres) from a Paris bookseller for a new edition of an old tragedy, *Xerxès*, and we know from the same bookseller's papers that he paid as much as 3,600 livres for a new one, *Catilina.*[5] In the following year Mme de Graffigny received 2,000 livres for another ephemeral success, her sentimental comedy, *Cénie.*[6]

Although we do not have as much information as we could wish about the amount of money which writers received from booksellers in the first half of the century, it is clear from these examples that the general level was still low. In comparison, at any rate in these years, writing for the theatre continued to be a relatively lucrative occupation, provided one could produce a box-office success, or, better still, a series of such plays. A successful play remained the passport to fame for a young and unknown writer. 'Tous nos beaux esprits,' wrote abbé Le Blanc in 1734, 'ne s'occupent plus que du théâtre, l'unique carrière en effet où il y ait quelque gloire à acquérir. ... Aujourd'hui un jeune

---

[1] P. Bonnefon, 'Néricault Destouches intime', *Revue d'histoire littéraire*, 1907, pp. 679–80.

[2] *Correspondence* iv. 372–3: vi. 138–9.

[3] P. Bonnefon, 'A travers les autographes', *Revue d'histoire littéraire*, 1919, p. 99.

[4] *Journal et mémoires*, ed. H. Bonhomme, 3 vols., Paris, 1868, i. 61.

[5] 'Notes du librairie Prault', *Bulletin du bibliophile*, 1850, p. 872.

[6] G. Noël, *Une 'primitive' oubliée de l'école des cœurs sensibles, Mme de Graffigny*, Paris, 1913, p. 244.

rimeur n'a pas plus tôt fait une petite épître en vers qu'il entreprend une comédie. Celui qui a fait deux odes, veut donner une tragédie.'[1] A decade later on his arrival in Paris the young Marmontel, according to his memoirs, had the following dialogue with Voltaire who had encouraged him to come to the capital:

En attendant, voyons, à quoi allez-vous travailler?—Hélas, je n'en sais rien, c'est à vous de me le dire.—Le théâtre, mon ami, le théâtre est la plus belle des carrières; c'est là qu'en un jour on obtient de la gloire et de la fortune. Il ne faut qu'un succès pour rendre un jeune homme célèbre et riche en même temps; et vous l'aurez, ce succès, en travaillant bien.[2]

Unfortunately, the playwright's career was still bestrewn with difficulties. It is true that an anonymous diatribe, *Mémoire sur les vexations qu'exercent les libraires et les imprimeurs de Paris*, published in 1725 by a certain Pierre Jacques Blondel, compares the actors' treatment of writers very favourably with what they encountered from booksellers:

Dans une profession qui passe pour proscrite, telle que celle des comédiens, il y a infiniment plus de justice et plus d'équité.

Ils font les frais de la représentation, au hasard du bon et du mauvais succès, ils se donnent mille peines, mille soins, et y mettent cent fois plus du leur, pour seconder l'auteur, que ne font les libraires.

Si la pièce tombe tout d'un coup, ils en sont pour leurs frais et pour leurs peines; si elle se soutient, ils partagent le gain avec l'auteur. Il en est toujours le maître tant qu'elle est applaudie du public; il retire chaque jour le fruit de son travail, et recueille tout à la fois de la gloire et de l'argent.

Avec les libraires, l'auteur n'a que la gloire pour partage, ils n'en sont, Dieu merci, point avides; pour l'argent, il faut qu'il leur demeure tout entier.[3]

It is clear, however, that this provides an unduly rosy picture of relations between actors and playwrights.

In Paris, right down to the Revolution, there was really only one theatre to which the young writer with serious literary ambitions could take his play. Since 1680, when Louis XIV had put an end to competition between the French companies in the capital by amalgamating

---

[1] H. Monod-Cassidy, *Un Voyageur philosophe au XVIIIᵉ siècle. L'abbé Jean-Bernard Le Blanc*, Cambridge, Mass., 1941, p. 197.

[2] *Mémoires*, i. 63.

[3] *Mémoire sur les vexations qu'exercent les libraires et les imprimeurs de Paris*, ed. L. Faucou, Paris, 1879, pp. 49–50.

them in the Comédie-Française, this theatre had enjoyed not only a monopoly of the rich repertoire of masterpieces inherited from the past, but a virtual monopoly of all new plays with literary pretentions. The Regent's recall of the Italian actors in 1716 provided a considerable amount of competition, but only in comedy. In 1769, seven years after the amalgamation of the Théatre italien with the Opéra-Comique, French plays were dropped entirely, and it was only in the last few years before the Revolution—from 1780 onwards—that it began to compete with the Comédie-Française in the field of comedy and the *drame*. Even then tragedy continued to be the monopoly of the Comédie-Française. While it is true that Marivaux had most of his plays performed at the Théâtre italien, it cannot be said that the other works produced there in the course of this period contributed much to French drama.

The virtual monopoly enjoyed by the actors of the Comédie-Française made them extremely haughty, overbearing, and oppressive to the authors who brought them new plays. Lesage who had first-hand experience of their little ways (after his *Turcaret* in 1709 he gave up writing for them and turned to the Théâtres de la foire and to the novel) inserted a blistering passage on their behaviour towards playwrights in the first volume of *Gil Blas*, published in 1715. His hero, who at one stage in the novel has entered the service of an actress named Arsénie, describes the following scene:

Notre petit laquais vint dire tout haut à ma maîtresse: Madame, un homme en linge sale, crotté jusqu'à l'échine,[1] et, qui, sauf votre respect, a tout l'air d'un poète, demande à vous parler. Qu'on le fasse monter, répondit Arsénie. Ne bougeons, messieurs, c'est un auteur. Effectivement c'en était un dont on avait accepté une tragédie, et qui apportait un rôle à ma maîtresse. Il s'appelait Pedro de Moya. Il fit en entrant cinq ou six profondes révérences à la compagnie, qui ne se leva, ni même ne le salua point. Arsénie répondit seulement par une simple inclination de tête aux civilités dont il l'accablait. Il s'avança dans la chambre d'un air tremblant et embarrassé. Il laissa tomber ses gants et son chapeau. Il les ramassa, s'approcha de ma maîtresse, et lui présenta un papier plus respectueusement qu'un plaideur ne présente un placet à son juge: 'Madame, lui dit-il, agréez de grâce le rôle que je prends la liberté de vous offrir.' Elle le reçut d'une manière froide et méprisante, et ne daigna pas même répondre au compliment.[2]

---

[1] A traditional expression to convey the poverty of the writer: see Boileau, *Satire I*: '... Tandis que Colletet, crotté jusqu'à l'échine, / S'en va chercher son pain de cuisine en cuisine...'

[2] *Gil Blas*, bk. III, Ch. xi.

Not only had the playwright to deal with haughty actors and tempera-
mental actresses before he could get his work accepted and performed;
he also had to put up with unfavourable financial conditions.

It was still the case that a writer did not receive a penny in fees for
the performance of plays given either in the provinces or abroad;
however successful his play might have been, once it was published
anyone was free to perform it anywhere without paying a fee to the
author. What is more, after its first run—long or short—a play became
the property of the actors of the Comédie-Française and the author had
no further claim on them. The *règlement* of 1697 laid it down that once
certain expenses had been met he was entitled to a fixed share in the net
proceeds from each performance—one-ninth for five-act plays and
one-eighteenth for those in three or one acts. However, these payments
ended abruptly as soon as on two successive occasions the receipts fell
below 550 livres in the winter season (1 November to Easter) and 350
livres during the rest of the year. Two years later the rule was slightly
amended to add to two successive occasions any three separate ones.
These rules remained in force until 1747 when the share of authors of
three-act plays was raised to a twelfth, but the amount of the receipts
below which a play became the property of the actors ('tombait dans
les règles', to use the jargon of the time) was raised sharply to 1,200
livres during the winter season and 800 during the rest of the year.[1] It
is notorious that the actors used all sorts of little dodges to reduce as
much as possible what they paid their authors. For instance, they
inflated their expenses so as to keep down in the books the profits from
each day's performance, and often performed a new play on days when
there was likely to be a poor audience so that receipts fell below the
prescribed minimum and it became their property. This treatment of
playwrights was to lead to a revolt in the 1770s.

Even so the author of a really successful play in the period 1715–50
could earn a fairly respectable sum of money. Though the first run of
even the most popular play did not normally exceed twenty to thirty
performances, it brought more than mere fame to an impecunious
young writer. Thus in 1748 the young Marmontel, who had taken
Voltaire's advice and sought success in the theatre, received over 3,500
livres from the Comédie-Française for his first tragedy (and no doubt
also anything up to 1,000 livres from its publication). That was the
normal amount for the average successful tragedy or comedy; Voltaire

[1] J. Bonnassies, *Les Auteurs dramatiques et la Comédie Française aux XVIIe et XVIIIe
siècles*, Paris, 1874, pp. 25–6, 28–9, 38–9.

received slightly more for *Zaïre* and *Alzire*, though sums in the neighbourhood of 4,000 livres were achieved by such highly successful plays
as Destouches's comedy, *Le Glorieux*, Crébillon's tragedy, *Catilina*,
and Mme de Graffigny's sentimental comedy, *Cénie*. Three plays of
these years stand out for their altogether exceptional first run: Voltaire
began his long career as a playwright with the striking success of his
Œdipe which brought him close on 4,500 livres, and although this was
soon to be capped by La Motte with his *Inès de Castro* and its 5,766
livres, Voltaire's *Mérope* broke all records with 6,417 livres.[1]

Inevitably, the first run of most new plays—even those which were
very far from being a failure—was much more modest, and so were the
earnings from them. Marivaux, the only playwright of this period whose
works still live on the stage today, fared very differently. During their
first run at the Théâtre italien well-known plays like *Le jeu de l'amour
et du hasard* and *Les Fausses Confidences* were seen by only relatively
small numbers of spectators. No doubt *Les Fausses Confidences*, a play
which has worn remarkably well, had an exceptionally poor start with
its first run of only five performances which attracted less than 1,700
spectators. Yet if we take one of Marivaux's more successful first runs,
that of *Le Jeu de l'amour et du hasard*, we find that, whereas the twenty-
nine performances of Voltaire's *Mérope* attracted close on 30,000
spectators to the Comédie-Française, only some 9,000 paid to see
Marivaux's comedy during its first run of fifteen performances. It has
been pointed out, it is true, that if none of Marivaux's plays met with the
immediate success of those of such contemporaries as Voltaire,
Destouches, and La Chaussée, his large output for the Théâtre italien
made a much greater impact than these figures would suggest, as his
numerous comedies were very frequently revived during the rest of the
century.[2] Indeed, it is probable that his plays were performed as often
as those of Voltaire, *the* great dramatist of the age in the eyes of his
contemporaries.

It is unfortunately impossible, owing to the gaps in the registers of
the Théâtre italien which are preserved in the Bibliothèque de l'Opéra,[3]

[1] These figures are derived from H. C. Lancaster's *The Comédie Française 1701–1774*
and from his *French Tragedy in the time of Louis XV and Voltaire*, 2 vols. Baltimore, 1950.

[2] The point is clearly established by Lagrave, *Le Théâtre et le public à Paris de 1715 à
1750*, a mine of information on the theatrical life of Paris in these years (see pp. 605–7).

[3] The invaluable summary of these registers published by C. D. Brenner in *The Théâtre
Italien. Its Repertory, 1716–1793, with a Historical Introduction*, Berkeley and Los
Angeles, 1961, gives the receipts and approximate attendances, but not unfortunately
payments to authors where these are available.

to form a precise notion of what Marivaux earned from the large number of plays which he wrote for the Théâtre italien, but as none of them appears to have had a really striking first run, his earnings can only have been modest. Even *Le Jeu de l'amour et du hasard* brought him only 1,165 livres. His two most successful plays at the Comédie-Française, *Les Serments indiscrets* and his second *Surprise de l'amour*, had a first run of only nine performances and each earned him only about 300 livres.

In fact no playwright or any other kind of writer in the first half of the eighteenth century could succeed in making a living purely from what he earned by his pen. Biographers of Lesage and Prévost sometimes claim that each of these men was the first French writer to succeed in doing so; yet this would not appear to be true of either. Each of them had to have at least some recourse to patronage. In the early part of his career (from 1697 down to 1715) Lesage received a modest annuity of 600 livres from the abbé Jules de Lyonne, the son of Louis XIV's foreign minister,[1] and we find Prévost writing a begging letter to Voltaire in which he complains that 'depuis cinq ans que je suis en France,[2] avec autant d'amis qu'il y a d'honnêtes gens à Paris, avec la protection d'un prince du sang[3] qui me loge dans son hôtel, je suis encore sans un bénéfice de cinq sous'.[4] However, in 1754 he was at last presented by the Pope with a living in the Church, a priory in the diocese of Le Mans.[5]

Both found it well-nigh impossible to live by writing alone. Lesage abandoned the Comédie-Française shortly after the semi-failure of his great comedy of manners, *Turcaret*, and devoted a considerable part of his career to turning out mere hackwork for the Théâtres de la Foire. Between 1721 and 1737 he published ten volumes of his *Théâtre de la Foire*, consisting of plays written often with one or more collaborators, and a large number still remain unpublished, making nearly a hundred altogether. A letter of J.-B. Rousseau states that Fuzelier and he received 4,000 livres a year for their services,[6] but how true this is it is impossible to say. In the novel as in drama he was compelled to produce a great many pot-boilers in order to keep the wolf from the door. In 1733 a contemporary wrote of him in terms which do not suggest that he was making a comfortable living by his pen:

[1] E. Lintilhac, *Lesage*, Paris, 1893, p. 10.
[2] i.e. since his return from exile in England and Holland.
[3] The prince de Conti.   [4] Voltaire, *Correspondence* vii. 79.
[5] H. Roddier, *L'abbé Prévost, l'homme et l'œuvre*, Paris, 1955, p. 47.
[6] J.-B. Rousseau, *Lettres sur différents sujets*, 3 vols., Geneva, 1749, ii. 67.

Lesage, auteur de *Gil Blas*, vient de donner la *Vie de M. Beauchêne, capitaine de flibustiers*. Ce livre ne saurait être mal écrit, étant de Lesage, mais il est aisé de s'apercevoir par les matières que cet auteur traite depuis quelque temps qu'il ne travaille que pour vivre et qu'il n'est pas le maître par conséquent de donner à ses ouvrages du temps et de l'application.[1]

Surprisingly little is known of the career of one of the greatest French writers of this period, but it is quite clear that even a great deal of pure hackwork did not provide him with anything approaching a reasonable living.

Nor would Prévost appear to have been any more successful. Though he lives today in one short masterpiece, *Manon Lescaut*, this is a mere fragment of the tremendous output of novels, translations, journalism, and all manner of compilations which he was driven to produce to the very end of his life. Despite the benefice which he had obtained nine years before his death, he was still working away at various projects for his publishers. The hundred octavo volumes to which his total writings are equivalent represent a career not unlike that of a Grub Street hack.

A writer like Marivaux, who was not as prolific as either Lesage or Prévost, must have fared even worse. His earnings from his plays, novels, and journalism appear to have been meagre. Although he received assistance from such patrons as Louis XV (through the good offices of Mme de Pompadour) and the Philosophe and former tax-farmer, Helvétius, and although he was a member of the Académie française, he undoubtedly led a poverty-stricken existence in the last part of his life; by then he had virtually ceased to produce new novels or plays and because of the economic conditions which then prevailed in the literary world, he could expect no income from his earlier works. The state of his finances in his last years remains obscure, but his estate produced in the end the net sum of 231 livres 19 sous, and although he left everything to his landlady, he owed her for several years' board and lodging against which all she could set was the small part of a joint annuity which had been paid out of his pocket.[2]

Voltaire certainly made no effort to earn a living by his pen. He inherited a modest competence from his father, a lawyer, but early in life he made up his mind that, if he were to attain a proper standing in the society of his day, he would have to be a rich man. Literature offered no road to wealth; being a good man of business, he used his

[1] L. Claretie, *Lesage romancier d'après de nouveaux documents*, Paris, 1890, pp. 41–2.
[2] M. J. Durry, *A propos de Marivaux*, Paris, 1960, pp. 85–90.

connections in the right places to build up for himself a comfortable income and eventually to become a wealthy man, 'M. de Voltaire, seigneur de Ferney et autres lieux.' In the early part of his career he successfully tapped such patrons as the Regent, Louis XV, and his young queen, but his aim here was less the money than the prestige which such patronage conferred. His successes in the theatre brought him in substantial sums of money; if none rose to the high figure achieved by *Mérope*, his very first tragedy, *Œdipe*, brought him the highest sum for a tragedy recorded down to this date, while *Zaïre* brought him 3,754 livres. He could also earn a certain amount of money from booksellers in the first half of his career. Yet once he had made his pile, he regarded such earnings as so much small change. When he took money from booksellers, it was often handed over at his request to struggling young writers, while his earnings from the theatre were frequently given to actors and actresses with whom he wished to remain on good terms. Voltaire was in fact an altogether exceptional figure in his age: the man of letters who was at the same time a man of substance. But he owed his wealth hardly at all to his literary work.

Another outstanding writer of the first half of the century, Montesquieu, apparently did not always disdain to accept money for his books.[1] But M. le Président de Montesquieu, a large landowner as well as a one-time judge of the Bordeaux Parlement, could scarcely be regarded as a professional writer. Though he was a member of the Académie française, he clearly regarded himself as a cut above such fellows who were driven to eke out their meagre earnings from booksellers or the theatre by accepting such forms of patronage as were available to them.

Some idea of the gradual progress of the writer towards independence can be obtained from a consideration of the careers of two other great writers of the age who began to make their mark about 1750, Rousseau and Diderot. From Rousseau's *Confessions* and correspondence we can form a fairly precise idea of his earnings as a writer, although there are certain obscurities. Why, for instance, did he receive no money payment for the four hundred or so articles on music which he contributed to the *Encyclopédie*? He was a member of the original 'société de gens de lettres' responsible for the work, and his

---

[1] There is a somewhat enigmatic reference to the financial side of the publication of *Le Temple de Gnide*, possibly brought out on a profit-sharing basis (*Œuvres complètes*, iii. 788–9).

impecunious state would certainly have justified at least the modest payment made to some of the other members of the team. Yet his statement on this point is confirmed by a study of the booksellers' accounts. Rousseau entered the field fairly late, in 1750, with his first *Discours*. This brought him no financial reward, and his second *Discours* produced probably only 600 livres from Rey. In the meantime he had done quite well out of his opera, *Le Devin du village*; in addition to obtaining 500 livres from a bookseller and 1,200 from the Opéra he received gifts of 2,400 livres and 1,200 livres from Louis XV and Mme de Pompadour for court performances, i.e. a total of over 5,000 livres. The *Lettre à d'Alembert* brought him only 720 livres, and even his novel, *La Nouvelle Héloïse*, probably *the* best seller of the whole of the eighteenth century, earned him a mere 2,160 livres from the Amsterdam bookseller, Rey, who brought out the first edition.[1] From the incredible number of pirated editions of his novel, he naturally received not a penny, except that Malesherbes insisted that the Paris bookseller who brought out the first pirated edition in France pay him 1,000 livres. For the *Contrat social* he received 1,000 livres from Rey, but he did better with *Émile*, a much longer work, as Malesherbes saw to it that his Paris bookseller paid him 6,000 livres. His polemical work, the *Lettres écrites de la montagne*, brought him 1,504 livres and his *Dictionnaire de musique*, 2,400, plus an annuity of 300 livres. Towards the end of his life he made an arrangement whereby, in return for an annuity of 1,600 livres, he was to sell the rights to an edition of his complete works (to include among other unpublished writings his *Confessions*); in the end this arrangement came to nothing, and after his death the edition of his complete works brought his heirs 24,000 livres.[2]

Given the enormous popularity of his writings, Rousseau could scarcely be said to have obtained his due, though his failure to do so was attributable not only to the parsimony of printers and booksellers, but also to the absence of an effective law of copyright. Moreover, he could scarcely be regarded as a typical man of letters of the time. He was almost savagely independent (though this did not prevent him

---

[1] He wrote to Rousseau on 7 December 1761: 'J'ai gagné sur *La Nouvelle Héloïse* 10,000 livres' (*Correspondance complète*, ix. 299). Later he provided an annuity of 300 livres for Thérèse Levasseur.

[2] For information about Rousseau's earnings see *Confessions*, in *Œuvres complètes*, ed. B. Gagnebin and M. Raymond, Paris, 1959– , i. 367, 386, 388, 511, 516, 559, 560, 561, 639; *Correspondance complète*, ii. 210, 214–16, 322 (contract); v. 79, 200; vi. 63; viii. 58, 128; ix. 371 (contract); x. 319, 320; xix. 148; xx. 204; xxii. 16, 244; and *Correspondance générale*, ed. T. Dufour, 20 vols., Paris, 1924–34, xii. 259 n.; xx. 362.

from accepting a small annuity for Thérèse Levasseur from 'Milord Maréchal', George Keith, and from half accepting a pension from George III) and for a considerable part of his life he endeavoured to eke out a living by copying music. Even his warmest admirers are compelled to admit that Jean-Jacques was an extremely odd fellow, and while it is interesting to have so much information about what he earned from his writings, his case cannot be regarded as being in any sense typical.

Nor, unfortunately, can that of Diderot. Although for the greater part of his career he struggled, unaided by any form of patronage, to make a living by his pen, a considerable proportion of his work appeared posthumously, and very often long after his death. He began his career in the 1740s by working for booksellers at such routine tasks as translating English books, and then graduated to the editorship of the *Encyclopédie*. This task was to absorb a great deal of his energy during the twenty-five years from 1747 to 1772, by which date he was nearly sixty. In 1764, when the last ten volumes of text were on the point of appearing and when it only remained to dispose of eight volumes of plates, he wrote—in a work, composed, it is true, to represent the interests of the Paris guild of printers and booksellers—of his own and other writers' earnings: 'Il y a des hommes de lettres à qui leur travail a produit dix, vingt, trente, quatre-vingt, cent mille francs. Moi qui ne jouis que d'une considération commune et qui ne suis pas âgé, je crois que le fruit de mes occupations littéraires irait bien à quarante mille écus.'[1] 120,000 livres, spread over some twenty years, was a modest, but fairly comfortable income, even if nothing like his due for his labours on the *Encyclopédie*, but, judging by his correspondence and the incomplete accounts of the enterprise, it would seem that contemporaries like Grimm and Voltaire as well as more recent writers have tended to exaggerate the parsimonious treatment which he received from Le Breton and his partners. As the work grew to ever greater proportions, his agreements with the booksellers were altered in his favour, and while his earnings bore no relation to their huge profits, undoubtedly the work did provide him with a steady, if modest income over a long period.

Yet his ability to enjoy a modestly comfortable old age and to provide his daughter with a substantial dowry was due to two factors outside his earnings as a professional writer. His share of his father's estate when the latter died in 1759 brought him a small but secure income; and if the authorities in France would not lift a finger to help a writer of such

[1] *Œuvres complètes*, viii. 531.

suspect views, he secured a generous patron in Catherine the Great who paid him, in one form or another, over 60,000 livres for his library and his manuscripts. Once again true independence with a modest affluence derived solely from his writings was not achieved by one of the greatest writers of the age.

It is rather among the second-rate writers of the last decades of the *ancien régime* that we must look for examples of men who were at least beginning to make a living by their pen. The continued growth in the reading public no doubt meant larger editions of works and more frequent reprints, and therefore better payments from booksellers. At the same time fresh sources of income were being opened up by the expanding demand for reading matter. There was, for instance, a considerable growth in the periodical press. The old-established reviews which went back into the seventeenth century—the *Gazette*, *Journal des savants* and, most important from the literary point of view, the *Mercure*—continued to flourish though their circulation was tiny by modern standards. In 1781 the *Gazette*, now the *Gazette de France*, had over 12,000 subscribers, but by 1785 competition had brought the number down to under 7,000. In 1763 the *Mercure* published a list of its subscribers, headed by the King; they numbered only 1,600—660 in Paris, 900 in the provinces, and 30–40 outside France.[1] In 1778 when the publisher Panckoucke took it over, it had only reached 1,764 subscribers, but La Harpe whom he appointed as editor declared in his *Correspondance littéraire*: 'C'est aujourd'hui le journal le plus répandu dans l'Europe; on en tire 7,000 exemplaires, ce qui est jusqu'ici sans exemple.'[2] From this post La Harpe drew a salary of 6,000 livres; it is true that he quickly quarrelled with Panckoucke and was replaced by the latter's brother-in-law, Suard. The *Mercure* which henceforth contained a much larger political element continued to prosper and is said to have had as many as 15,000 subscribers on the eve of the Revolution.

Other periodicals gradually emerged in the course of the century, for instance the *Mémoires de Trévoux*, the organ of the Jesuits, which lasted from 1701 to 1767, and the *Journal de Verdun*, founded in 1704, which kept going until 1776. Abbé Desfontaines started *Le Nouvelliste du Parnasse* in 1730, and after it was banned in 1732, he began a new periodical, his *Observations sur les écrits modernes*, which ran from 1735 to 1743: after its *privilège* was withdrawn, he published from Avignon

[1] E. Hatin, *Histoire politique et littéraire de la presse en France*, Paris, 1859–61, i. 419–20.
[2] *Correspondance littéraire*, 6 vols., Paris, 1801–7, ii. 300.

his *Jugements sur quelques ouvrages nouveaux* down to his death in 1745. His collaborator, Fréron, took up the torch and founded in the same year his *Lettres à Madame la comtesse de ****, which had a short life, being banned in January 1746. However, in 1749 Fréron founded a new periodical, his *Lettres sur quelques écrits de ce temps*, which was succeeded by the much more famous *Année littéraire*, founded in 1754; this survived Fréron's death in 1776 and lasted down to 1791. In its most prosperous period it is said to have brought him in for several years an income of over 20,000 livres.[1] Journals could also flourish out of Paris; Pierre Rousseau founded his *Journal encyclopédique* at Liège in 1756, and when its publication was banned there, he moved it to the little town of Bouillon where, despite the local and French censorship, he enjoyed a certain freedom as well as material prosperity; it ceased publication only in 1793.

A considerable number of writers could augment their income by editing and writing for these periodicals. In 1759, for instance, Jean-Jacques Rousseau was offered (and turned down) a payment of 800 livres a year for writing two reviews a month for the *Journal des savants*,[2] and twenty years later Rivarol received 150 livres a month from Panckoucke for writing reviews for the *Mercure*.[3] No doubt from the Restoration onwards periodicals were to become much more important in providing outlets for writers, and to offer them both more possibilities of publishing their work and higher remuneration, but even before the Revolution their role was by no means negligible.

Quite a number of writers found it profitable to exploit the interest of various rulers in central, northern, and eastern Europe in what was going on in the literary and intellectual circles of Paris; they sent news-sheets at regular intervals, generally fortnightly, to their paymasters. La Harpe, for instance, provided such a service for the Grand Duke of Russia, the future Paul I, from 1774 to 1791; it was later published under the title of *Correspondance littéraire*. Earlier, from 1747 to 1755, abbé Raynal had done the same for various German princes with his *Nouvelles littéraires*,[4] and in 1753 Grimm began his famous *Correspondance littéraire, philosophique et critique*, which had a fairly wide circulation as it went as far as Russia and Sweden as well as to various German courts. In 1773 he passed on the task to the Swiss, Jacques Henri

---

[1] Ibid. i. 340.   [2] *Œuvres complètes*, i. 513.

[3] A. Le Breton, *Rivarol, sa vie, ses idées, son talent d'après des documents nouveaux* Paris, 1895, p. 46.

[4] There are considerable gaps in this news-sheet.

Meister, who carried it on until 1813. Diderot was a frequent contributor and a considerable number of his works which were not printed during his lifetime were circulated as supplements to the news-sheet. It was through this means that Goethe encountered *Le Neveu de Rameau* which first appeared in print in the translation which he made of it.

In 1777 Paris acquired its first daily newspaper, *Le Journal de Paris, ou la Poste du Soir*, imitated from the *London Evening Post* which had been founded nearly three-quarters of a century earlier. With its four quarto pages this was a tiny affair compared with the voluminous newspapers to which we are accustomed nowadays, but it prospered despite one or two short periods when it was suspended by the authorities. In 1785 Suard, a mediocre academician, was appointed editor, and from his salary and his share in the profits is said to have drawn an income of 20,000 livres a year. In 1778 a second daily newspaper, the *Journal général de France*, had begun to appear in Paris, but it was one of the casualties of the Revolution, whereas the *Journal de Paris* survived until 1840.

Most of the flood of newspapers which appeared in the opening years of the Revolution had a very short life. Some, however, did survive. The *Gazette de France*, which became a daily in 1792, managed to live through the Revolutionary and Napoleonic periods and carried the royalist flag until it faded out in 1915. *Le Moniteur universel*, founded in 1789 and of great historical importance because of its reports of the debates in the Revolutionary assemblies, became the official journal under the Napoleonic régime, a position which it held until nearly the end of the Second Empire; after that it gradually withered away and finally died in 1901. Longest lived of all the newspapers founded during the Revolution was the *Journal des Débats* whose life span reached from 1789 to 1944: Napoleon treated it very harshly, changing its name to *Journal de l'Empire*, and finally, in 1811, confiscating its property. It was only with the return of the Bourbons that the owners regained possession of their newspaper.

Another source of income for writers was provided by the contemporary demand for works of popularization—for dictionaries, encyclopedias, and other works of reference. The compilation of such works could help struggling authors to pay the rent and even provide them with a comfortable income. In the 1760s an obscure *abbé* named de La Porte who in his time also edited various journals was earning a considerable annual income by helping booksellers to satisfy this demand. In the words of a contemporary: 'L'abbé de La Porte, employé par les libraires, gagne tous les ans cinq ou six mille livres à ce métier-là, et les libraires gagnent des capitaux, car le débit de toutes ces compilations est étonnant, et il ne se passe pas une semaine qu'il ne s'en publie une nouvelle.'[1]

It is true that young and unknown writers continued to receive only modest sums for their works; the first edition of *Les Liaisons dangereuses*, which is held by many people to be the greatest novel of the century, brought Laclos only 1,600 livres in 1782.[2] For his first book, his *Voyage à l' Île de France*, published in 1773, Bernardin de Saint-Pierre received only 1,000 livres, and even then he had to fight a lawsuit in order to get the whole of the money.[3] On the other hand, in Charles-Joseph Panckoucke who moved from Lille to Paris in 1760 there was at least one bookseller who was prepared to deal liberally with men of letters; he not only acquired existing periodicals like the *Mercure* and the *Journal des savants*, but he also founded new ones, and after taking a leading part in the production of the supplement to Diderot's *Encyclopédie*, in 1782 he began the publication of the enormous *Encyclopédie méthodique*. Writing in 1820, Garat speaks of his appearance on the scene in almost lyrical terms:

A lui et par lui a commencé une amélioration très remarquable dans l'existence des gens de lettres, tenus si longtemps dans la pauvreté par les gages avilissants qu'ils recevaient des imprimeurs-libraires, et par les récompenses très honorables, mais mesquines, des puissances. Ce qu'il pouvait gagner de trop sur eux, il le croyait perdu pour sa fortune personnelle. Il les enrichissait pour s'enrichir lui-même; il voulait les rendre indépendants de lui, comme de toute la terre, sûr qu'avec leur indépendance s'élèverait leur génie, se féconderaient toutes les sources des richesses de la presse et de la librairie. Il commença un jour l'exécution d'un traité avec un écrivain qu'il connaissait à peine, par lui avancer cent mille francs qui n'entraient pas dans les conditions du traité. C'était bien là les calculs d'un géomètre et d'un libraire transcendant.[4]

There is no doubt a considerable amount of exaggeration here, Panckoucke certainly did not revolutionize the position of the writer.

[1] Grimm, *Correspondance littéraire* viii. 274.
[2] The agreement is reproduced in R. Vailland, *Laclos par lui-même*, Paris, 1953, pp. 34–5. The bookseller, Durand *neveu*, who undertook to publish the work at his own expense, was to pocket all the receipts from the sale of the first 1,200 copies, and Laclos those from the sale of the remaining 800. By 7 May Laclos had received the 1,600 livres due to him and had already agreed to a second edition on the same terms.
[3] Souriau, *Bernardin de Saint-Pierre*, pp. 148–9.
[4] D. J. Garat, *Mémoires historiques sur la vie de M. Suard, sur ses écrits et sur le XVIIIe siècle*, 2 vols., Paris, 1820, i. 275–6.

though he paid his authors generously. We know that in 1769 he offered Voltaire 18,000 livres if he would contribute to the supplement to the *Encyclopédie*, an offer which Voltaire naturally turned down though he offered his services free (they were never actually given).[1] Marmontel received 4,000 livres and a copy of the supplement for contributing a hundred or so articles (not all of them new) to the work —certainly much more handsome payment than any of the contributors to Diderot's *Encyclopédie* had ever received.[2] In 1775 La Harpe signed an agreement with Panckoucke for an abridgement of Prévost's *Histoire générale des voyages* in five quarto volumes for which he was to receive 20,000 livres,[3] and in the same year Suard (the bookseller's brother-in-law) received 12,000 livres for a translation of the three quarto volumes of Hawkesworth's *Voyages*. If the work was a success, the translator was to receive another 3,000 livres, and a like sum for a one-volume abridgement.[4] Another Panckoucke agreement which has come down to us also concerns Suard; in 1779 it was agreed that, in return for some three months' work revising and, where necessary, adding to the relevant articles in the *Encyclopédie* and its supplement to make them into two quarto volumes on language and literature for the *Encyclopédie méthodique*, Suard was to receive for a total of 180 or 190 sheets 'la somme de vingt-quatre livres pour chaque feuille de copie nouvelle et ... quinze livres pour toutes les feuilles tirées du *Dictionnaire encyclopédique*, soit que ces dernières soient copiées en entier, soit qu'il y ait des retranchements ou des additions. . . . Il sera remis en outre au Sr Suard un exemplaire complet de ladite *Encyclopédie méthodique*, plus six exemplaires du *Dictionnaire de grammaire et de littérature*.'[5]

Although the Société des gens de lettres was not founded until the 1830s, already in the closing decades of the *ancien régime* writers were no longer inclined meekly to accept whatever booksellers offered them. In 1770 a vigorous attack on their grasping methods was delivered by Fenouillot de Falbaire in his *Avis aux gens de lettres*. He contrasts the rapid fortunes made by booksellers with the poverty of the majority of writers—incidentally, a very different picture from that offered by Diderot in his *Lettre sur le commerce de la librairie* six years earlier. Not only does Diderot maintain that writers, as his own example showed,

[1] *Correspondence* xxxv. 268.   [2] *Mémoires*, i. 276.

[3] *Correspondance inédite*, ed. A. Jovicevich, Paris, 1965, pp. 23–5.

[4] J. B. A. Suard, *Mémoires et correspondances historiques et littéraires*, ed. C. Nisard, Paris, 1858, pp. 71–3.

[5] A. Brulé, *La Vie au dix-huitième siècle. Les Gens de lettres*, Paris, 1928, pp. 98–100 (facsimile of the agreement).

earned fair sums of money, but he both stresses the well-known risks of publishing and argues that few members of the profession attain to wealth: 'Ah, monsieur, on a bientôt compté les libraires qui sont sortis de ce commerce avec de l'opulence; quant à ceux qu'on ne cite point, qui ont langui dans la rue Saint-Jacques ou sur le quai, qui ont vécu à l'aumône de la communauté et dont elle a payé la bière, soit dit sans offenser les auteurs, il [*sic*] est prodigieux.[1] This is not at all the picture given in the *Avis aux gens de lettres* which contrasts the profits of publishing with the poverty of the majority of writers:

Les libraires engloutissent chez nous tout le produit des livres qui s'y composent. Aussi font-ils presque tous des fortunes rapides et prodigieuses, dont on ne doit plus s'étonner. Tel qui n'avait rien en commençant ce commerce, se trouve, au bout de dix ou quinze ans, riche de sept à huit cent mille francs; et ces exemples ne sont point rares parmi eux. La plupart ont un train de maison très considérable, des ameublements chers, des campagnes charmantes, tandis qu'ordinairement l'écrivain aux ouvrages duquel ils doivent cette opulence, est relégué sous les toits, à un troisième, à un quatrième étage, où une simple lampe éclaire sa pauvreté et ses travaux.[2]

No doubt both of these accounts of the relative position of bookseller and writer contain some exaggeration; what is significant is that writers were now beginning to protest openly about the poor rewards offered by their calling and that they received some support from outside. Bachaumont speaks approvingly of the *Avis aux gens de lettres*,[3] and also takes the side of that eccentric character, Luneau de Boisjermain, in his lawsuit against the guild of printers and booksellers. In introducing the *mémoires* put out by Luneau, Bachaumont speaks thus of the relations between writers and booksellers:

On sait de quelle tyrannie usent en France les derniers avec les premiers, que le malheureux état de leurs affaires oblige ordinairement de se laisser subjuguer par ces messieurs. Cette tyrannie avait engagé plusieurs auteurs plus pécunieux et plus intelligents à faire imprimer leurs ouvrages à leurs frais, et à les faire débiter par des subalternes de confiance.[4]

What Luneau de Boisjermain had done was to have his edition of Racine printed and to sell the copies himself, thereby breaching the monopoly conferred on booksellers by government regulations. Having won his case, he then turned on the publishers of the *Encyclopédie* and demanded that they should furnish subscribers with the

---

[1] *Œuvres complètes*, viii. 515.   [2] pp. 38–9.
[3] *Mémoires secrets* v. 32.   [4] Ibid. iv. 321.

work, complete in twenty-eight volumes, at the price of 280 livres which the prospectus had announced for ten volumes.

As we have seen, the *arrêts du Conseil* of 1777 and 1778 had done something to strengthen the position of the writer as regards both copyright and pirated editions of his works; but much greater publicity surrounded the controversy which took place in these same years between playwrights and the actors, particularly those of the Comédie-Française, a controversy which is chiefly remembered today because it inevitably enters into biographies of Beaumarchais, the leading figure in it.

It was, of course, true that playwrights—provided their plays drew large audiences—could earn fairly substantial sums of money. Guimond de la Touche's tragedy, *Iphigénie en Tauride*, first performed in 1757, had a run of twenty-six performances which brought the author 5,281 livres, while two years later Lemierre pocketed 4,589 livres for his *Hypermenestre*. Unfortunately, as students of Lancaster's *The Comédie Française, 1701-1774* know all too well, not only does this work which gives day by day the author's share of the proceeds from a new play break off at the arbitrary date of Easter 1774, but after the first performance of Voltaire's *Tancrède* on 3 September 1760 no more entries under this head appear in the registers except for one quite isolated entry on 24 April 1762. It is true that reference can be made to the *dossiers* of individual authors in the archives of the Comédie-Française, but this is a time-consuming business, and in any case there is nothing of interest in those of well-known playwrights of the period such as Marmontel and Marie-Joseph Chénier and nothing at all for a writer like Saurin.

However, an examination of these documents shows that after 1760 successful plays continued to be fairly profitable. In 1765 de Belloy drew 4,587 livres from the nineteen performances (one of them given free) of his *Siège de Calais* while Sedaine's *Le Philosophe sans le savoir*, put on later that year, brought in 4,091 livres for its first twenty-eight performances. Yet neither they nor many other playwrights of the time were satisfied with the treatment they received from the Comédie-Française.

Matters were finally brought to a head when Beaumarchais entered the controversy. He was rich enough not to bother too much about what he earned from his plays, but he knew that many of his fellow playwrights were in revolt against their exploitation by the Comédie-Française. What is more, as a business man he could read accounts, and when he received those for *Le Barbier de Séville* after its highly successful first run in 1775, he refused to accept them on the grounds that they were not accurate. In the discussion which followed he showed up some of the tricks of the actors.

In reckoning the ninth of the receipts which was due to him during the first run of his play, the actors only allowed the daily sum of 300 livres for the so-called *petites loges*, boxes which the actors had let out by the year in increasing numbers since the 1750s. The average daily sum which they brought in was not 300, but 800 livres. The Comédie-Française, like other Paris theatres of the time, was compelled to contribute a proportion of its gross receipts to the upkeep of the hospitals; though known as 'le quart des pauvres', the tax paid by the Comédie-Française had been compounded for a lump sum which worked out *per diem* at about a third of the amount which it deducted from the gross receipts when presenting accounts to authors. In calculating the expenses of the theatre which were to be deducted from the gross receipts of each performance, the actors added in all sorts of items in which the author could scarcely be expected to share. Worst of all, in addition to paying him the smallest amount it dared for the first run of a new play, the actors took advantage of the regulations which laid it down that if on two successive or three separate occasions the gross receipts fell below a certain figure, the play ceased to be the property of the author. They continued to use all sorts of devices to ensure that the receipts from a play should cease to reach the necessary figure and that it should become their property as quickly as possible.[1]

The tyranny exercised by the actors over the authors who produced new plays for them was by no means entirely an economic one. Unless a writer managed to keep on the right side of the actors and actresses of the company, he could have a thin time. Although he was the author of *Le Siège de Calais* which had drawn large crowds to the theatre, de Belloy was not, unfortunately for him, on good terms with the actor, Lekain. When his tragedy, *Gaston et Bayard*, was at last put on in 1771, Collé, a fellow playwright, noted indignantly in his journal:

Il y a au moins six ans que cette tragédie est reçue et que les odieuses tractations de Le Kain ont empêché de la jouer. M. de Belloy, mourant de faim, a été forcé de la faire imprimer l'année passée, ce qui a fait tort nécessairement à la représentation. . . . Si elle n'eût pas été mise au théâtre cette année, M. de

[1] Beaumarchais, *Compte rendu de l'affaire des auteurs dramatiques*, in *Œuvres complètes*, ed. E. Fournier, Paris, 1876, pp. 585–624.

Belloy se voyait réduit à un tel excès de misère qu'il songeait à reprendre le métier de comédien qu'il a eu le malheur de faire dans sa jeunesse.

After de Belloy's death in 1775 Collé added a note: 'Il a vécu plein d'honneur et d'honneurs, et il a été réduit exactement à la mendicité qu'il cachait. Le Kain et ses confrères, en refusant de jouer ses pièces, l'ont fait mourir de misère; à la lettre, il est mort de chagrin.' He adds that Lesage's famous account of the behaviour of actors and actresses towards authors is still true: 'C'est la même chose aujourd'hui, tant cette peinture est vraie et de main de maître.'[1]

An interesting illustration of this last remark is furnished by another playwright of the time, Cailhava, in his account of his tribulations in 1763 as a young writer in getting a comedy of his performed at the Comédie-Française. The play, when presented to the theatre, gradually reached the hands of one of the actors whom the author went to see about it:

Je vole chez lui, je ne le trouve point . . .; une grosse cuisinière est assise sous la porte cochère dans son fauteuil à bras, elle épluche nonchalamment des épinards; elle me dit, en ricanant, 'N'êtes-vous pas un poète?—Hélas, oui.— Ne venez-vous pas chercher une pièce?—Hélas, oui.—Attendez.' Là-dessus elle fouille dans le tas d'herbes, en tire mon manuscrit, et me le remet.

Tout le monde se figure sans doute la mine d'un auteur secouant, le long d'une rue, les épinards dont les feuillets de son manuscrit sont décorés.

J'admirais ces ornements, bien plus modestes que les vignettes, les culs-de-lampe, dont nos plus petits almanachs sont enrichis, quand je donnai du nez dans la poitrine d'un homme aussi distingué par ses talents que par la pureté de ses mœurs. Il ne se doutait pas alors qu'un comédien dût le faire mourir de chagrin.

De Belloy, who had not yet fallen out with the actors, got his play accepted for him, but his misfortunes did not end there as he happened to cut across an actor who was engaged on one of those provincial tours in which they frequently indulged in search of extra earnings:

Mais, par malheur, un acteur essentiel gagnait alors de l'argent en province. On le pria fort indiscrètement de la part de Messieurs les Gentilshommes de la Chambre de vouloir bien se rendre à Paris. Il eut de l'humeur, promit aux comédiens qu'il quittait de les rejoindre bientôt, arriva sans savoir un mot de son rôle, le joua le lendemain d'après le souffleur, et savoura le plaisir de voir tomber une pièce qui l'avait empêché de gagner de l'argent en province.[2]

---

[1] *Journal et mémoires*, iii. 315–16.

[2] J. F. Cailhava, *Théâtre*, 3 vols., Paris, 1781–2, i. 18–21. The play in question was *La Présomption à la mode*; it certainly had only one performance.

Whether or not one accepts the literal truth of such stories (and one could quote many other clashes between playwrights and the actors in the 1760s and 1770s), there is no doubt that there was extremely bad blood between playwrights and the Comédie-Française in these years.

Although Diderot excused himself from taking part in Beaumarchais's campaign to secure better conditions for playwrights, *Le Paradoxe sur le comédien* which belongs to these years reflects the tension between the two sides. The first speaker says of the actors:

Ce despotisme que l'on exerce sur eux, ils l'exercent sur les auteurs, et je ne sais quel est le plus vil ou du comédien insolent, ou de l'auteur qui le souffre.
Le second. On veut être joué.
Le Premier. A quelque condition que ce soit. Ils sont tous las de leur métier. Donnez votre argent à la porte, et ils se lasseront de votre présence et de vos applaudissements. Suffisamment rentés par les petites loges, ils ont été sur le point de décider ou que l'auteur renoncerait à son honoraire, ou que sa pièce ne serait pas acceptée.
Le second. Mais ce projet n'allait à rien moins qu'à éteindre le genre dramatique.
Le premier. Qu'est-ce que cela leur fait ?[1]

There continued to be the same gap as in La Bruyère's day between the earnings of an actor at the Comédie-Française and those of a playwright. In 1774–5, for instance, which is described as a good year, the actor's share came to over 15,000 livres, roughly a third of which came out of the income from the *petites loges*.[2] With this one must compare the *total* sum paid out in *parts d'auteurs* for the 1770s:

1770	2416 livres
1771	8270 ,,
1772	5302 ,,
1773	8186 ,,
1774	8591 ,,
1775	7300 ,,
1777	7582 ,,
1778	13 437 ,,
1779	22 137[3] ,,

The contrast between the earnings of the individual full-share actor and *all* authors of new plays is striking, even for these last two years.

---

[1] Diderot, *Writings on the Theatre*, ed. F. C. Green, London, 1936, p. 295.

[2] D. P. J. Papillon de La Ferté, *Journal*, ed. E. Boysse, Paris, 1887, p. 381, and Archives nationales, o¹ 845, 'État général des recettes de la Comédie Française . . . pendant les années 1776 à 1777, 1777 à 1778 et 1778 à 1779'.

[3] The first six totals come from Archives nationales o¹ 845 16, and the last three from Bibliothèque nationale, MS. fr. 9228, fo. 14.

What is more, in 1774 the Théâtre italien had done something to
remove one of the grievances of playwrights—that after a certain point
they were deprived of their share in the receipts from their works even
when these were lucrative. New regulations were introduced at the
Théâtre italien which distinguished between 'représentations utiles'
which more than covered the expenses and 'représentations nulles'
which failed to do so. Authors were to share in the proceeds of the
former during the whole of their lifetime, and if they died before their
play had had fifty performances, their heirs received their share until
that number had been reached. In both cases the right of property in the
play then passed to the theatre.[1]

When in 1777 Beaumarchais invited his fellow playwrights to join in
forming a group, known rather pompously as the Bureau de législation
dramatique, to protect their interests both in Paris and the provinces,
he met with a good deal of support. What the playwrights sought from
the Comédie-Française was a fairer way of paying for new plays and
some arrangement which would allow the author to retain a play as his
own property, for himself and his heirs, so long as the actors saw fit to
perform it. There was also a considerable amount of support for a plan
to break the virtual monopoly of the Comédie-Française by setting up
a second subsidized theatre in the capital; competition, it was held,
would be a good thing, and in any case in recent years the queue of new
plays awaiting performance had caused serious hardship.

Naturally, there was not complete unanimity among the playwrights,
and in the course of his entirely disinterested efforts on behalf of the
profession Beaumarchais had to put up with a great deal of bickering.
Some writers pretended to be above these sordid money questions.
One of them, a not very distinguished playwright called Rochon de
Chabannes, wrote to him: 'Heureusement par les circonstances je me
trouve au-dessus du besoin; je ne travaille point pour de l'argent.'[2]

Negotiations with the Comédie-Française dragged on until in 1780
the government produced no fewer than three different *arrêts du
Conseil* in order to impose a settlement of the dispute. The first was
rejected by the writers and the second by the actors. The third took
back with one hand what it had given the authors with the other; it
gave them a larger share in the net receipts of each performance than
they had asked for—one-seventh for five-act plays—but raised the

[1] E. Campardon, *Les Comédiens du roi de la troupe italienne pendant les deux derniers siècles*, 2 vols., Paris, 1880, ii. 343-5.
[2] Bachaumont, *Mémoires secrets* xxvi. 90.

amount below which plays 'tombaient dans les règles' to 2,300 livres in the winter season and to 1,800 during the rest of the year.[1] This meant that while a new play might bring in more money at each of the performances during its first run, that run was almost certain to be very short.

How far this new system of payment was applied is not absolutely clear. In 1780 the Comédie-Française put on a revised version of Lemierre's *La Veuve de Malabar* which had had a poor reception in 1770 when its six performances brought the author only 645 livres. In its new version it had a run of thirty-two performances and reluctantly the actors paid out to the author the sum of 7,687 l. 17s. 2d.[2] Beaumarchais continued to receive payment for performances of *Le Barbier de Séville*, and these were based on the new system which gave the author a seventh of the net proceeds; for eight performances of his play given between September 1781 and February 1782 he received 2,018 livres, and for six more given later in this second year another 1,424 livres. The phenomenal success of *Le Mariage de Figaro* produced an extraordinarily large *part d'auteur*; on 6 July 1787 an agent for Beaumarchais received on his behalf for the first ninety-nine performances of the play (the fiftieth had been given 'au profit des mères nourrices') the unheard of sum of 59,510 l. 14s. 10d. What is more, Beaumarchais continued to draw money from later performances of the play.

Such profits from a play were utterly exceptional in this period after 1780, and playwrights were still dissatisfied with their relations with the Comédie-Française. There also remained the scandal of the refusal of provincial theatres, now very numerous, to make any payment whatsoever to writers whose plays they performed. Mercier, whose works were extremely popular in the provinces, wrote bitterly in 1778:

Voyez les pièces de théâtre représentées dans toutes nos provinces. Les citoyens s'y portent en foule et les applaudissent à plusieurs reprises. Jamais une obole n'en reviendra à l'auteur, fût-il dans l'indigence la plus extrême. On peut faire cent mille francs avec sa pièce sans qu'il en soit seulement informé. Tout le monde se partage l'argent, et il n'est jamais venu dans l'idée à personne que l'auteur pût en réclamer la moindre portion.[3]

[1] Bonnassies, *Les Auteurs dramatiques et la Comédie Française*, p. 90.

[2] The *dossier* Lemierre in the archives of the Comédie-Française from which these figures are taken also contains drafts of two bad-tempered letters written by the actors to the playwright in 1780.

[3] *De la littérature et des littérateurs* Yverdon, 1778, p. 60.

In 1784 Beaumarchais and his fellow playwrights attempted vainly to make the provincial companies pay for the performance of their plays. Once again it was the Revolutionary assemblies which made a serious attempt to clear up the whole situation. In 1790 the playwrights presented a petition to the Constituent Assembly, and on 13 January of the following year a decree was passed which not only abolished the monopoly of the privileged theatres and threw the theatrical world open to free and unrestricted competition, but also secured the rights of an author and his heirs in his work:

Art. II. Les ouvrages des auteurs morts depuis cinq ans et plus sont une propriété publique, et peuvent, nonobstant tous autres privilèges qui ont été abolis, être représentés sur tous les théâtres indistinctement.

III. Les ouvrages des auteurs vivants ne pourront être représentés, dans toute l'étendue de la France, sans le consentement formel et par écrit des auteurs, sous peine de confiscation du produit total des représentations, au profit des auteurs.

IV. La disposition de l'article III s'applique aux ouvrages déjà représentés, quels que soient les anciens règlements; néanmoins les actes qui auraient été passés entre des comédiens et des auteurs vivants, ou des auteurs morts depuis moins de cinq ans, seront exécutés.[1]

Later in the year, on 19 July, a second decree made it clear that the law covered plays which had already been performed as well as future ones:

Art. Ier. Conformément aux dispositions des articles III et . . . [*sic*] du décret du 13 janvier dernier, concernant les spectacles, les ouvrages des auteurs vivants, même ceux qui étaient représentés avant cette époque, soit qu'ils fussent ou non gravés ou imprimés, ne pourront être représentés sur aucun théâtre public dans toute l'étendue du royaume, sans le consentement formel et par écrit des auteurs ou sans celui de leurs héritiers ou cessionnaires, pour les ouvrages des auteurs morts depuis moins de cinq ans, sous peine de confiscation du produit total des représentations au profit de l'auteur ou de ses héritiers ou cessionnaires.[2]

It is true that on 30 August 1792 the Legislative Assembly passed a law less favourable to authors, but on 1 September 1793 this was repealed by the Convention which decreed that 'les lois du 13 janvier et 19 juillet 1791 seront exécutées dans toutes leurs dispositions'.[3]

It can well be imagined that to begin with after this revolution in

---

[1] *Le Moniteur universel*, vii. 118.
[2] Ibid. ix. 175.   [3] Ibid. xvii. 549.

relations between playwrights and the theatres things did not work altogether smoothly. The Comédie-Française was naturally disgusted at the loss of its monopoly and its relations with playwrights continued to be difficult. In its archives there is a letter from La Harpe who had played a leading part in securing the new law; writing on 26 February 1792, he complains that the actors had put on his tragedy, *Philoctète*, without his permission, and he points out: 'Vous avez encouru la confiscation de la recette entière de la pièce que vous avez jouée hier.' He ends his letter with a demand for a prompt answer: 'Je vous préviens que si demain à midi je n'ai pas votre réponse et un mandat pour être payé chez votre caissier sur le bordereau de la représentation, je procéderai suivant la loi.'[1]

In order to secure the payments due to them the playwrights set up a Bureau dramatique with agents in the provinces to act on their behalf in making agreements with theatres and seeing that they were observed.[2] Arrangements were gradually made with the various Paris theatres, and even the Comédie-Française, when it was re-established in 1799, came into line. However, the provincial theatres proved a harder nut to crack. In a petition to the Legislative Assembly Beaumarchais gave an amusing account of the furious resistance to the new law put up by the directors of theatres in the provinces. For instance, when he complained to the director of the Lyons theatre that he was performing *Le Mariage de Figaro* without permission, he received the blunt reply: 'Nous jouons votre *Mariage*, parce qu'il nous fournit d'excellentes recettes; et nous le jouerons malgré vous, malgré tous les décrets du monde; je ne conseille même à personne de venir nous en empêcher; il y passerait mal son temps.'[3] Yet the playwrights' agencies gradually made progress during the later years of the Revolution and during the Napoleonic period, and if the Société des auteurs et compositeurs dramatiques was not formally constituted until 1829, a considerable change for the better in the position of playwrights had already been effected.

Although in this period the writer's economic position had improved to the point where independence was just possible, patronage had not ceased to be important. Unless they had private means or held a job and

[1] He got his money. The full text of his letter and the actors' answer are given in C. Todd, 'La Harpe quarrels with the actors: unpublished correspondence', *Studies on Voltaire and the Eighteenth Century*, liii (1967), 305-7.
[2] A rival agency was set up in 1798 (see J. Bayet, *La Société des auteurs et compositeurs dramatiques*, Paris, 1908, p. 101).
[3] *Œuvres complètes*, p. 636.

only wrote in their spare time, the great majority of writers continued to look to some form of literary patronage to supplement their income or at least to tide them over difficult times. A rich man could still occasionally be found to help a struggling author. From time to time works were dedicated to patrons, though the dedication filled with nauseating flattery (Corneille's dedication of *Cinna* was the model of this type) had now gone out, as Condorcet indicated in his *Éloge de d'Alembert* in 1783. Men of letters, he declared,

ont renoncé à ces épîtres dédicatoires qui avilissaient l'auteur, même quand l'ouvrage pouvait inspirer l'estime ou le respect; ils ne permettent plus ces flatteries, toujours d'autant plus exagérées qu'ils méprisaient davantage au fond du cœur l'homme puissant dont ils mendiaient la protection; et, par une révolution heureuse, la bassesse est devenue un ridicule que très peu d'hommes de lettres ont eu le courage de braver.[1]

Yet there are numerous examples of patronage extended to writers by men in positions of wealth or power right down to the Revolution.

Rich men like Helvétius, the one-time *fermier général*, would come to the assistance of writers. In addition to helping Marivaux, Helvétius gave an annuity of 3,000 livres to the playwright, Saurin, and, when the latter married, he gave him the capital.[2] Other tax-farmers such as La Popelinière and d'Épinay were also generous patrons of men of letters,[3] while a wealthy banker like Necker, before he entered the government, had made substantial gifts to impecunious writers.[4] In 1779 a nobleman, the comte de Valbelle, left a sum bringing in an annual income of 1,200 livres for 'l'homme de lettres, qui, au jugement de l'Académie, aura le plus grand besoin de ce secours et en sera jugé le plus digne'.[5] Shortly before he was dismissed from office the duc de Choiseul gave La Harpe 3,000 livres for a play, his *drame, Mélanie*, of which he had heard a reading and which, for religious reasons (it contained an attack on the practice of dispatching unwilling girls into convents) could not be performed on the Paris stage.[6] One of the most generous patrons of men of letters was the wealthy *bourgeoise*, Mme Geoffrin; she showed a maternal solicitude for the writers, established as well as young and unknown, who frequented her

---

[1] *Œuvres complètes*, ed. A. C. O'Connor and F. Arago, 12 vols., Paris, 1847–9, iii. 69.
[2] La Harpe, *Correspondance littéraire*, i. 61. [3] Bachaumont, *Mémoires secrets* i. 22.
[4] Comte d'Angiviller, *Mémoires*, ed. L. Bobé, Copenhagen, 1933, p. 75.
[5] Meister in Grimm, *Correspondance littéraire* xii. 230.
[6] Meister in ibid. viii. 471–2. See also Bachaumont, *Mémoires secrets* v. 67. La Harpe received 4,000 livres from the publication of his play.

famous *salon*. She provided annuities for a number of them, including d'Alembert, Thomas, and Morellet, and before her death in 1777 she made provision for these to continue during their lifetime.[1] In addition, she gave all manner of presents to men of letters; Diderot, for instance, is said to have received from her various embellishments for his study.[2]

The princes of the blood also played an important part as literary patrons. The Orléans family, which stood nearest to the throne, provided all sorts of men of letters with modest pensions and sinecures. The playwright, Collé, obtained in 1760 the post of *lecteur* to the duc d'Orléans with a salary of 1,800 livres. Collé was also one of the eight *secrétaires ordinaires* of the Duke; the income from this sinecure was a modest one (only 400 livres), but it conferred some prestige and various privileges on the holder.[3] Again, in 1776, when a young writer named Lefèvre produced a successful tragedy, the Duke gave him a pension of 1,200 livres and, adds La Harpe, 'comme ce jeune auteur demandait si cette grâce l'engageait à remplir quelques fonctions auprès de Son Altesse, elle lui répondit avec une bonté très flatteuse: "Cela ne vous engage à rien qu'à travailler de plus en plus pour votre gloire".'[4] In 1787, on the eve of the Revolution, his successor, Philippe-Égalité, established pensions of 800 livres for twelve writers and scientists; four of these went to members of the Académie française and among the other writers favoured in this way was Bernardin de Saint-Pierre.[5]

Important as the patronage of private individuals continued to be, it was above all to the Crown that the writer of the time looked for encouragement and for the prestige which a royal pension conferred. We have seen how in the early part of his career even Voltaire took care to obtain pensions from the Regent, Louis XV, and his queen. In the mid-1740s he even became a courtier at Versailles and secured appointment to two posts which Racine had once held—Historiographer Royal and Gentleman of the Bedchamber. Although his departure for Potsdam in 1750 meant a breach with Versailles, he was allowed to keep his title of *gentilhomme de la chambre*, and after his pension from the King had lapsed for many years, he was delighted to find in 1762 that it had suddenly been paid again, thanks to the influence of Choiseul.[6]

[1] Meister in Grimm, *Correspondance littéraire* xi. 407: xii. 8.
[2] Wilson, *Diderot*, p. 550.   [3] Collé, *Journal et mémoires*, ii. 221 n.
[4] *Correspondance littéraire*, ii. 57.   [5] Bachaumont, *Mémoires secrets* xxxiv. 90.
[6] *Correspondence* xxiv. 220–1.

The number of gifts, pensions, posts, and sinecures which the French Government had at its disposal for men of letters was indeed considerable. 'Il y a peu de contrées en Europe', wrote Diderot in 1764, 'où les lettres soient plus honorées, plus récompensées qu'en France. Le nombre des places destinées aux gens de lettres y est très grand.' It is true that he continues ironically: 'Heureux si c'était toujours le mérite qui y conduisît! Mais si je ne craignais d'être satirique, je dirais qu'il y en a où l'on exige plus scrupuleusement un habit de velours qu'un bon livre.'[1] Obviously mediocre or bad writers, as the example of Louis XIV's pensions to men of letters had shown, have often gained encouragement from state patronage of literature. An additional reason for Diderot's cynicism is that, like many other Philosophes, he was unlikely to be favoured in any way by the government of his own country. The rift between such writers and the authorities at home combined with the tremendous vogue of French literature all over Europe to produce a considerable number of examples of patronage from foreign rulers. Catherine the Great's munificence to Diderot is merely the best-known example of this phenomenon. Frederick the Great also produced pensions for French men of letters, including d'Alembert, while the latter was offered a fabulous salary, which he declined, if only he would come to the court of Catherine to act as tutor to the Grand Duke.

No doubt it was agreeable for the Philosophes, exposed to the ill will of the government at home which, for instance, authorized the public performance at the Comédie-Française of Palissot's satirical comedy, *Les Philosophes*, to point to the favours which they received from foreign governments. Similarly in the knowledge that they were appreciated elsewhere there was some compensation for the attacks which the censor allowed Fréron to make on them in his *Année littéraire*. As Grimm put it in 1765:

Tous ces auteurs si célèbres, si admirés dans toute l'Europe sont haïs et détestés ici, et surtout généralement réputés dangereux. On entretient un homme exprès: cet homme a le privilège exclusif de leur dire des sottises deux fois par mois, et ce privilège lui vaut douze à quinze mille livres par an. . . . Je ne conçois pas cette satisfaction de la nation à entendre du mal de ceux dont les talents l'ont honorée et illustrée chez ses voisins. . . . Comment se peut-il qu'un homme à talents soit digne des bienfaits des princes étrangers, à la gloire desquels il ne peut contribuer, et indigne de la protection de son souverain, dont il illustre le règne par ses travaux?[2]

[1] *Œuvres complètes*, viii. 532.   [2] *Correspondance littéraire* vi. 309.

Or take the letter which Diderot wrote in 1770 to Sartine, the *directeur de la librairie* as well as *lieutenant de police*, when he was consulted by him about the manuscript of a satirical play (actually by his old enemy, Palissot, though he was not aware of the fact). His letter concludes:

Il ne m'appartient pas, monsieur, de vous donner des conseils; mais si vous pouvez faire en sorte qu'il ne soit pas dit qu'on ait deux fois, avec votre permission, insulté en public ceux de vos concitoyens qu'on honore dans toutes les parties de l'Europe; dont les ouvrages sont dévorés de près et au loin; que les étrangers révèrent, appellent et récompensent; qu'on citera, et qui conspireront à la gloire du nom français quand vous ne serez plus, ni eux non plus; que les voyageurs se font un devoir de visiter à présent qu'ils sont, et qu'ils se font honneur d'avoir connus lorsqu'ils sont de retour dans leur patrie, je crois, monsieur, que vous ferez sagement.[1]

Foreign patrons also had their uses when persecution threatened a writer. When Marmontel's *Bélisaire* fell foul of the Sorbonne in 1767, he tells us in his memoirs, 'les lettres des souverains de l'Europe et celles des hommes les plus éclairés et les plus sages m'arrivaient de tous les côtés, pleines d'éloges pour mon livre, qu'ils disaient être le bréviaire des rois'. Catherine the Great translated the book and dedicated her translation to an archbishop; Maria Theresa—'elle', Marmontel adds, 'qui était si sévère à l'égard des écrits qui attaquaient la religion'— ordered the work to be printed in her dominions. Marmontel made full use of such support to disarm the authorities at home; 'Je ne négligeai pas, comme vous pensez bien, de donner connaissance à la cour et au parlement de ce succès universel, et ni l'une ni l'autre n'eurent envie de partager le ridicule de la Sorbonne.'[2]

Diderot's statement about the rewards offered by the Crown to men of letters is confirmed by Necker in his *De l'administration des finances*, published only five years before the Revolution. He declares that 'les récompenses qu'on accorde en France aux savants et aux gens de lettres sont plus considérables qu'on ne pense communément'.[3] Among the items of government expenditure he lists 300,000 livres for the expenses of the various academies, including those of Science and

---

[1] *Correspondance*, x. 74–5.

[2] *Mémoires*, i. 243. Bachaumont relates the following conversation between the future Louis XVI and Charles X (then aged thirteen and ten respectively): '... Le comte d'Artois dit qu'il trouvait fort plaisant qu'un cuistre, qu'un pédant de collège, comme M. Marmontel, s'avisât de s'ériger en précepteur des rois et de leur donner des leçons; que si cela dépendait de lui, il ferait fustiger l'auteur aux quatre coins de Paris; et moi, reprit le dauphin, je le ferais pendre.' (*Mémoires secrets* iii. 160.)

[3] *De l'administration des finances de la France*, 3 vols., n.p., 1784, ii. 364.

Medicine, and for payments to writers. This is certainly a small sum compared with the 28 millions which was the total for other pensions, but encouragements to men of letters took many forms and not all of these fell directly on the Treasury. One certainly gets the impression from contemporary sources that the amount of royal patronage during the reigns of both Louis XV and Louis XVI was considerable; there is no reason to retract the heretical view that during this period of French history the Crown did far more for men of letters than it had done in the reign of Louis XIV.

Among the varied types of royal patronage were gifts to authors of successful new works. The author of a new play would normally obtain a substantial sum when it was given its first performance at court—as much as two or three thousand livres. Very often he received a pension, generally of the order of 1,000 or 1,500 livres. If mostly not very large, such pensions conferred prestige on the holder as well as making a useful contribution to his income, though it must be said that owing to the perpetual difficulties of the Treasury they were seldom regularly paid. All sorts of writers of the period—poets, playwrights, novelists—received at one time or another such pensions from the Crown, sometimes through the influence of Mme de Pompadour or even Mme Du Barry, or in the next reign that of Marie Antoinette.

In addition to such gifts and pensions the government had available all manner of posts, very often pure sinecures, with which to reward men of letters. There was, for instance, the post of *historiographe de France*; when it was vacated by Voltaire on his departure for Potsdam in 1750, it passed to Duclos and, on his death in 1772, to Marmontel; the salary was not enormous,[1] but its holder was also entitled to a free lodging and secured the *entrée* to the court. A second post of *historiographe de France* was created in 1774 for a lawyer named Moreau who had influence at court and who, though he drew no salary, was already in receipt of various pensions.[2] In addition, there were other posts of this kind which involved equally little work; there were such posts as *historiographe de la marine*, *historiographe de l'ordre du Saint-Esprit*, and so on, all of which carried a modest salary.

The Académie française had its *secrétaire perpétuel* (a post held by Duclos, d'Alembert, and Marmontel between 1750 and the Revolution) who drew a modest salary and had an equally modest flat in the Louvre.

---

[1] 3,000 livres, reduced for some years to 1,800 livres, then restored to its former level, according to Marmontel (*Mémoires*, i. 314).

[2] J. N. Moreau, *Mes Souvenirs*, ed. C. Hermelin, 2 vols., Paris, 1898–1901, ii. 23.

Sedaine, the author of *Le Philosophe sans le savoir*, was appointed secretary of the Académie royale d'architecture on similar terms, but with 'un beau logement au Louvre'.[1] In addition, there were posts of *lecteurs*, librarians, and secretaries to various members of the royal family, many of which were agreeable sinecures. Most of these posts and the salaries attached to them were relatively modest, but there were a number of real plums. Thus in 1768 abbé Barthélemy who, twenty years later was to produce *Le Jeune Anacharsis*, one of the most important works in the neo-Classical revival of the closing decades of the century, was pushed by his patron, Choiseul, into the post of *secrétaire général des Suisses* which carried with it an income of some 30,000 livres.[2]

As in earlier centuries many writers continued to bear the title of *abbé* and to owe part of their income to livings in the Church, or at least to have begun their career in it. Their situation naturally varied enormously. Though tonsured, abbé Dubos was never ordained; on the other hand, he was rewarded for his services to the Foreign Office with an abbey *in commendam*. Raynal began his career as a Jesuit, then became a secular priest, and finally dropped all ecclesiastical connections, although he continued to be known as abbé Raynal. Abbé de Bernis, before he became Foreign Minister and a cardinal, thanks to Mme de Pompadour, had begun his career as a poet, supported by a canonry and a priory bestowed on him by the Pope. Marmontel, who knew him well in the early period of his career, speaks of him as 'un poète galant, bien joufflu, bien frais, bien poupin, et qui, avec le gentil Bernard, amusait de ses jolis vers les joyeux soupers de Paris. Voltaire l'appelait la bouquetière du Parnasse, et dans le monde, plus familièrement, on l'appelait *Babet*, du nom d'une jolie bouquetière de ce temps-là.'[3] Desfontaines began his career as a Jesuit and taught for a period in Jesuit schools; he then became a curé in Normandy and finally moved to Paris where he supported himself by journalism. Abbé Pellegrin, a prolific writer, chiefly known as a librettist, was a monk in two different orders with a spell as a chaplain on a galley in between; until laid under an interdict by the Archbishop of Paris, he derived part of his income from saying masses, which gave rise to the famous couplet by an obscure poet of the time:

> Le matin catholique et le soir idolâtre,
> Il dîna de l'autel et soupa du théâtre.

---

[1] Grimm, *Correspondance littéraire* vii. 132.   [2] Bachaumont, *Mémoires secrets* iii. 285.
[3] *Mémoires*, i. 145.

Abbé Morellet does not appear to have held any benefices; he began his career as a tutor and later had a government pension, but abbé Coyer augmented the free lodging and other gifts which he derived from his former pupil, the duc de Bouillon, with livings in the Church. It was common to combine income from two sources; abbé Arnaud held an abbey *in commendam*, but he also held the post of *lecteur* and librarian to Monsieur, the future Louis XVIII, while abbé Delille combined a chair at the Collège de France with an abbey in the gift of the comte d'Artois who bestowed it on him at the request of Marie Antoinette. It is notorious that the religious vocation of writers of the period who bore the title of *abbé* was extremely variable, but it has to be borne in mind that, given the existing educational system which was largely in the hands of the Church, and the social structure of France under the *ancien régime*, it was often only by embarking on an ecclesiastical career that intelligent youths of modest origins could hope to make their way in the world. It has been pointed out, for instance, that a number of contributors to the *Encyclopédie*—men of varying religious beliefs— were *abbés*.[1]

Another important source of income for writers in the second half of the century was the pensions provided by literary journals. These pensions were at the disposal of the government, but were paid not only by journals under its direct control such as the *Gazette de France*, the *Journal des savants*, and especially the *Mercure*, but also by independent periodicals like the *Année littéraire*, the editor of which, Fréron, aroused Voltaire and the other Philosophes to fury. Periodicals of this kind were only granted a *privilège* on condition that they paid pensions to men of letters named by the government; it was apparently the weight of pensions which he had to pay which caused Fréron serious trouble in his later years.[2] When Marmontel took over the editorship of the *Mercure* in 1758, the number of pensions was substantially increased, making a total of 21,500 livres; the list then read as follows:

Cahusac	2000 livres
abbé Raynal	2000 „
Mlle de Lussan	2000 „
Bridard de La Garde	2000 „
Piron	2000 „

[1] R. Shackleton, *The 'Encyclopédie' and the Clerks*, Oxford, 1970.
[2] La Harpe, *Correspondance littéraire*, i. 342.

Séran de la Tour	1200	,,
chevalier de la Négerie	1200	,,
veuve Boissy et fils	2400	,,
Crébillon *père*	2000	,,
Saint-Foix	1500	,,
Gresset	2000	,,
Saint-Germain	1200	,,[1]

Later they amounted altogether to something of the order of 25,000 to 30,000 livres a year. The situation, as Mercier pointed out, was a rather odd one:

Le gouvernement pensionne plusieurs écrivains; mais il ne débourse pas pour cela de l'argent. Il assujettit les journaux à une taxe, et paye les gens de lettres avec les travaux des gens de lettres. Tel auteur a une pension sur une feuille satirique où il est déchiré à belles dents. Ainsi il *boit et mange son jugement et sa condamnation*, ce qui est assez plaisant.[2]

Even at the end of the *ancien régime* patronage was by no means dead. A clear idea of the various sources of income which could permit a writer who began his career in the middle of the century to reach a very comfortable standard of living is furnished by the memoirs of Marmontel. Born in 1723, he came to Paris from his very modest home in the provinces and in 1748 scored a considerable success with his first tragedy, *Denys le tyran*. He took to heart the advice given him by Mme de Tencin whose *salon* he frequented: 'Malheur, me disait-elle, à qui attend tout de sa plume; rien de plus casuel. L'homme qui fait des souliers est sûr de son salaire; l'homme qui fait un livre ou une tragédie n'est jamais sûr de rien.'[3] He gradually turned away from tragedy after he had made a name for himself in the theatre, and produced among other writings his *Contes moraux* which during his lifetime met with an extraordinary success all over Europe. If we can believe a remark of Meister's, a publisher gave him 36,000 livres for his novel or prose poem, *Les Incas*.[2] He was careful to keep in touch with the powers that be, and he used the influence of Mme de Pompadour to secure, first, a sinecure in a government office, then a pension on the *Mercure*, and finally, in 1758, its editorship. Although he soon lost this post, he retained a substantial pension (3,000 livres). By the time he finally married, in 1777, he had managed to save 130,000 livres, and in the 1780s he and his wife were leading a very comfortable existence:

[1] Marmontel, *Mémoires*, ii. 493 n. 32. [2] *Tableau de Paris*, viii. 57.
[3] *Mémoires*, i. 116. [4] Grimm, *Correspondance littéraire* xi. 544.

Sans parler du casuel assez considérable que me procuraient mes ouvrages, la place de secrétaire de l'Académie Française, jointe à celle d'historiographe des bâtiments, . . . me valaient un millier d'écus. Mon assiduité à l'Académie y doublait mon droit de présence. J'avais hérité, à la mort de Thomas, de la moitié de la pension de deux mille livres qu'il avait eue, et qui fut partagée entre Gaillard et moi, comme l'avait été celle de l'abbé Batteux. Mes logements de secrétaire au Louvre et d'historiographe de France à Versailles, que j'avais cédés volontairement, me valaient ensemble dix-huit cents livres. Je jouissais de mille écus sur le *Mercure*. . . . Je me voyais donc en état de vivre agréablement à Paris et à la campagne.[1]

In 1786 he sold an edition of his collected works for 10,000 livres.[2] Along with other members of the Académie française Marmontel benefited in 1785 from the open-handedness of the *Contrôleur-général*, Calonne; the value of the forty *jetons* distributed among the members present at each of its meetings was increased from 30 sous to 3 livres and in addition the secretary's salary was raised from 1,200 livres to 3,000. So Marmontel could write in his memoirs: 'Ainsi mon revenu d'académicien put se monter à quatre mille cinq ou six cents livres.'[3] A man of mediocre talents, he was endowed with the necessary skill to turn himself into a popular writer earning considerable sums of money; and being at the same time a successful place-hunter, he built up for himself an extremely comfortable position. Understandably, he was hostile to the Revolution from the start since he was enjoying to the full what Talleyrand once called 'la douceur de vivre' of the closing years of the *ancien régime*.

The importance of patronage on the very eve of the Revolution is brought out by Calonne's policy in 1785 of increasing pensions to men of letters.[4] This brought in no fewer than 147 applications, including well-known names, not only the inevitable Marmontel, but La Harpe, Chamfort, Saint-Lambert, Ducis, and so on. This throws considerable light both on the status of men of letters who had 'arrived' and secured official support and on the position of those who had failed to do so either because their views were unacceptable to the authorities or because they were still relatively unknown. Among the former class were men like Mercier and Delisle de Sales; among the latter were those who can be described as the denizens of Grub Street.

The latter were not a new phenomenon. They had undoubtedly

[1] *Mémoires*, i. 313.   [2] Ibid. ii. 515 n. 21.   [3] Ibid. i. 314–15.
[4] This is examined in detail by R. C. Darnton in 'The High Enlightenment and the low-life of literature in pre-Revolutionary France', *Past and Present*, 1971, pp. 81–115. The documents are to be found in the Archives nationales, F[17] 1212.

existed in much earlier periods, certainly as far back as the seventeenth century. One thinks earlier in this period of a man like Dallainval, whose little comedy, *L'École des bourgeois*, has ensured the survival of his name into the twentieth century, but who appears to have led a hand-to-mouth existence and to have been sometimes reduced to spending the night in a sedan-chair parked in the street. Again there is the famous picture of the poverty-stricken poet in his garret in Voltaire's 'Le Pauvre Diable':

> Que faisais-tu sur le Parnasse?—Hélas!
> Dans mon grenier entre deux sales draps,
> Je célébrais les faveurs de Glycère,
> De qui jamais n'approcha ma misère;
> Ma triste voix chantait d'un gosier sec
> Le vin mousseux, le Frontignan, le Grec,
> Buvant de l'eau dans un vieux pot à bière;
> Faute de bas passant le jour au lit,
> Sans couverture, ainsi que sans habit,
> Je fredonnais des vers sur la paresse,
> D'après Chaulieu je vantais la mollesse.

Or we find Diderot writing to Sophie Volland of 'l'auteur de *Zaïde*, ce petit abbé de La Mare, qui n'avait pas un sou, qui se portait mal, qui n'avait ni habit, ni pain, ni souliers:

> *Sa culotte, attachée avec une ficelle,*
> *Laissait voir par cent trous un cul plus noir qu'icelle.*[1]

It is almost superfluous to recall the crowd of impecunious writers so mercilessly caricatured as mere fawning sycophants in the pages of *Le Neveu de Rameau*. Right through the century one reads of men who are described as being 'aux gages des libraires'; a writer like Prévost spent a good deal of his life in this position and although he ultimately half emerged from it, many others must have failed to do so. Not all of them, however, ended up like Brissot in the degrading position of being a police spy.[2]

In a volume of his *Tableau de Paris* published as late as 1788 Mercier has a chapter entitled 'Misère des auteurs'. This opens with the gloomy sentence: 'La plus déplorable des conditions, c'est de cultiver les lettres sans fortune, et voilà le partage du plus grand nombre des littérateurs;

---

[1] *Correspondance*, iii. 146.
[2] See R. C. Darnton, 'The Grub Street Style of Revolution: J. B. Brissot, Police Spy', *Journal of Modern History*, 1968, pp. 301–27.

ils sont presque tous aux prises avec l'infortune.' After making the inevitable comparison between the affluence of Voltaire and the lot of the majority of writers, he goes on to draw a clear distinction between those who have been able to profit from various forms of patronage and the rest:

Ce ne sont point les académiciens qui pâtissent, ni les *historiographes*, ni M. Moreau, ni M. Désormeaux qui a écrit l'*Histoire de la Maison de Bourbon*, qu'il aime si tendrement; mais une foule de gens de mérite, modestes, studieux, et qui, trompés dans leur jeunesse par les décevantes douceurs des belles-lettres, payent cher l'attrait fatal qui les a conduits à leur culture. S'ils livrent au public le fruit de leurs travaux, le lâche contrefacteur en absorbe le profit; si c'est une pièce de théâtre, les comédiens de province s'en empareront comme d'une propriété, et feront bouillir leur marmite, tandis que l'auteur, entièrement privé de la moindre partie de la recette, languira dans un coin. Eh! n'ai-je pas vu mourir dans les horreurs de l'indigence quelques gens lettrés, timides et honnêtes? Le secours est arrivé le lendemain de leur convoi.

The chapter ends with a black picture of the writer's lot:

... Il n'y a rien de si commun que de rencontrer un homme instruit, sachant l'histoire et les langues, versé dans plusieurs connaissances politiques et morales, et d'apprendre qu'il a besoin de travailler à la feuille. Ah! loin de cette carrière, vous qui ne voulez pas connaître l'infortune et l'humiliation, ou arrangez-vous pour ne pas vieillir et mourez de bonne heure.[1]

Clearly, even at the end of the *ancien régime* there were great contrasts in the position of writers.

Inevitably, the Revolution played havoc with the finances of those who had been dependent on the royal bounty or on various wealthy and highly placed patrons for a substantial part of their income. Though the Convention abolished the Académie française, it showed solicitude for writers. In February 1793, when the sad story of the poverty-stricken old age of the Italian playwright, Goldoni, established in France since the 1760s and relying largely on royal patronage, was brought to its attention, it at once voted to restore his pension of 4,000 livres; unfortunately, he was already dead.[2] After the fall of Robespierre between October 1794 and September 1795 the Conven-

---

[1] xi. 185–7. A prolific writer, Mercier seems to have earned a fair amount of money by his pen, once he had made a name for himself. He is said to have received 6,000 livres for the last four volumes of his *Tableau de Paris* from Fauche, Favre & Cie of Neuchâtel (Charpentier, *La Bastille dévoilée*, iii. 59).

[2] M. Carlson, *The Theatre of the French Revolution*, Ithaca, 1966, pp. 151–2.

tion voted a total of some 600,000 livres for grants to writers, scholars, artists, and scientists. A considerable proportion of this money went to writers, among them Delille, Delisle de Sales, Ducis, La Harpe, Marmontel, and Palissot.[1] Under the Directory Palissot was appointed librarian of the Bibliothèque Mazarine at a salary of 3,300 livres, later raised to 5,000;[2] libraries were to be thoroughly exploited by writers in the coming century.

Although through his censorship Napoleon imposed a strait-jacket on writers, as in so many other things he continued the tradition of acting as a patron of literature. His taste was predominantly that of a soldier. 'La meilleure façon de me louer,' he once declared, 'c'est d'écrire des choses qui inspirent des sentiments héroïques à la nation, à la jeunesse, à l'armée', and he gave a large pension to the mediocre playwright, Luce de Lancival, for his tragedy, *La Mort d'Hector*, which he described as 'une pièce de quartier général'.[3] He continued the *ancien régime* practice of awarding to men of letters pensions which had to be paid by those periodicals which he allowed to appear. These seem to have ranged from 1,200 to 6,000 francs, and among those favoured in this way we find the names of Palissot (3,000), Marie Joseph Chénier (6,000), Luce de Lancival (5,000), Bernardin de Saint-Pierre (2,000), Picard (6,000), and the old poet Lebrun (1,200).[4]

By a decree issued from Aix-la-Chapelle in 1804 Napoleon established a large number of prizes for the best works of literature published in the course of the decade. He offered nine prizes of 10,000 francs and thirteen of 5,000, and later increased the number to nineteen of 10,000 francs and sixteen of 5,000. However, when in 1810 the time came to award them, none of the writers whose names were put forward was considered worthy of a prize and it was decided to prolong the period until 1819 . . . Napoleon is even said to have declared at a meeting of the Conseil d'État that his aim in establishing these prizes had been simply to 'fournir une occupation aux esprits pour les empêcher de s'occuper de choses plus sérieuses'![5]

---

[1] *Le Moniteur universel*, xxii. 181–4, 191–3; xxiii. 127–8, 130–1; xxiv. 231–2, 234–5; xxv. 669–70, 674–6.

[2] G. Saintville, 'Un Chapitre des rapports entre écrivains et libraires au XVIIIᵉ siècle: Palissot auteur', *Bulletin du bibliophile*, 1947, p. 384.

[3] Quoted in J. Charpentier, *Napoléon et les hommes de lettres de son temps*, Paris, 1935, p. 14.

[4] These figures are taken from a list drawn up in 1810 (see ibid., 177–8).

[5] Ibid. pp. 182, 201.

The status of the French writer in pre-Revolutionary society could be said to have improved more rapidly than his economic position since if the profession, though more slowly than on this side of the Channel, was moving towards independence for the successful writer, literary patronage still remained a very important source of income for him. Writing on the very eve of the Revolution, Malesherbes could argue that because of their state of dependence writers should not be asked to act as censors:

En France les gens de lettres sont une classe de citoyens très dépendante, parce que ce n'est point une profession utile par elle-même. La plupart de ceux qui l'ont embrassée, y ont été déterminés par un attrait vainqueur, ont sacrifié l'espérance de la fortune à leur satisfaction et à la gloire. Cependant comme la gloire ne fait pas vivre, c'est par des grâces de la cour ou des places auxquelles la cour nomme qu'ils ont espéré de subsister dans leur vieillesse, dans cet âge où l'aisance est devenue une nécessité.[1]

While the economic position of the writer had undoubtedly improved since 1715, perhaps even more striking advances were made in his social status.

In the profoundly aristocratic society of seventeenth-century France, although the man of letters might be tolerated so long as he 'knew his place' and behaved with the respect due to rank, he was undoubtedly looked upon as an inferior. If he was insolent (or thought to be insolent), the outraged nobleman to whom he gave offence left his punishment to a gang of toughs hired to beat him up. That, as we have seen, was the fate meted out to various writers of that age, and a punishment with which Boileau, for instance, was more than once threatened. Such an attitude towards the writer persisted among the aristocracy for several decades of the eighteenth century. The most illustrious victim of such treatment was Voltaire himself.[2] The incident, which took place in 1726, is best recounted in the words of the lawyer, Mathieu Marais:

Voltaire a eu des coups de bâton. Voici le fait. Le chevalier de Rohan le trouve à l'Opéra et lui dit: Mons de Voltaire, Mons Arouet, comment vous appelez-vous? L'autre lui dit je ne sais quoi sur le nom de Chabot.[3] Cela en resta là. Deux jours après, à la Comédie au chauffoir, le chevalier recommence; le poète lui dit qu'il avait fait sa réponse à l'Opéra. Le chevalier leva

---

[1] *Mémoires*, p. 343.

[2] He was by no means the only one (see V. Fournel, *Du rôle des coups de bâton dans les relations sociales dans l'histoire littéraire*, Paris, 1858).

[3] The chevalier's full name was Rohan-Chabot.

sa canne, ne le frappa pas et dit qu'on ne devait lui répondre qu'à coups de bâton. Mlle Le Couvreur tombe évanouie, on la secourt, la querelle cesse. Le chevalier fait dire à Voltaire, à deux ou trois jours de là, que le duc de Sully l'attendait à dîner. Voltaire y va, ne croyant point que le message vînt du chevalier. Il dîne bien, un laquais vient lui dire qu'on le demande; il descend, va à la porte et trouve trois messieurs garnis de cannes qui lui régalèrent les épaules et les bras gaillardement. On dit que le chevalier voyait ce frottement d'une boutique vis-à-vis. Mon poète crie comme un diable, met l'épée à la main, remonte chez le duc de Sully, qui trouva le fait violent et incivil, va à l'Opéra conter sa chance à Mme de Prie qui y était,[1] et de là on court à Versailles, où on attend la décision de cette affaire, qui ne ressemble pas mal à un assassinat.

It will be noticed that the lawyer who wrote these lines does not waste much sympathy on the victim of such a brutal assault. Nor did anyone else at the time, as we see from his next letter in which he again refers to Voltaire and his 'coups de bâton':

On s'est souvenu du mot du duc d'Orléans à qui il demandait *justice* sur pareils coups, et le prince lui répondit: 'On vous l'a faite.' L'évêque de Blois a dit: 'Nous serions bien malheureux si les poètes n'avaient point d'épaules.' On dit que le chevalier de Rohan était dans un fiacre *lors de l'exécution*, qu'il criait aux frappeurs: 'Ne lui donnez point sur la tête' et que le peuple d'alentour disait: 'Ah, le bon seigneur!' Le pauvre battu se montre le plus qu'il peut, à la cour, à la ville, mais personne ne le plaint, et ceux qu'il croyait ses amis lui ont tourné le dos.[2]

To crown all, the victim of the assault had to spend nine days in the Bastille and was then exiled to a distance of fifty leagues from Paris.

This episode has an interesting counterpart at the other end of the century, in an incident of 1786 which shows how times had changed. The playwright, Sedaine, gave offence to the *Intendant des menus* who was in charge of theatrical entertainments at court, a man who rejoiced in the name of Papillon de La Ferté. When Sedaine complained about the scenery and costumes provided for one of his plays which was being performed at Fontainebleau, La Ferté came rushing along, shouting ' "Où est Sedaine?" Ce poète qui l'entend, lui crie: "La Ferté, Monsieur Sedaine est ici; que lui voulez-vous?" ' The official had the further humiliation of being rebuked for his manners by Marie Antoinette herself when he complained to her about the playwright's

---

[1] The mistress of the Prime Minister, the duc de Bourbon.
[2] *Journal et mémoires*, ed. M. F. A. de Lescure, 4 vols., Paris, 1863–8, iii. 392–3.

insolence. 'Monsieur la Ferté,' she told him, 'quand le roi et moi parlons à un homme de lettres, nous l'appelons toujours *Monsieur*. Quant au fond de votre différend, il n'est pas fait pour nous intéresser.'[1]

In face of the contempt shown them in aristocratic circles, writers of the previous age blushed for their profession and did their best to rise out of it into the circles of the aristocracy and the court abandoning literature for some well-paid and honorific sinecure. The classic example of this, as we have seen, was the haste with which Racine and Boileau gave up writing plays and poetry to become *historiographes de France* and to secure the admission to court circles which this appointment carried with it.

This feeling of the social inferiority of the writer died hard in the eighteenth century. There was something challenging in the title which Voltaire, his shoulders still smarting from the blows delivered by the hired thugs of the chevalier de Rohan, gave to one of his *Lettres philosophiques* in 1734: 'De la *Considération* qu'on doit aux gens de lettres.' 'Ce qui encourage le plus les arts en Angleterre,' he wrote with clear propaganda purpose, 'c'est la considération où ils sont. Le portrait du premier ministre se trouve sur la cheminée de son cabinet; mais j'ai vu celui de M. Pope dans vingt maisons.' In a famous passage he goes on to contrast—not without a great deal of exaggeration—the happy lot of English men of letters with the lowly state of their French counterparts:

M. Addison, en France, eût été de quelque académie, et aurait pu obtenir, par le crédit de quelque femme, une pension de douze cents livres, ou plutôt on lui aurait fait des affaires, sous prétexte qu'on aurait aperçu, dans sa tragédie de *Caton*, quelques traits contre le portier d'un homme en place. En Angleterre, il a été secrétaire d'État. M. Newton était intendant des monnaies du royaume. M. Congreve avait une charge importante. M. Prior a été plénipotentiaire. Le docteur Swift est doyen d'Irlande, et y est beaucoup plus considéré que le primat. Si la religion de M. Pope ne lui permet pas d'avoir une place, elle n'empêche pas au moins que sa traduction d'Homère ne lui ait valu deux cent mille francs. J'ai vu longtemps en France l'auteur de *Rhadamiste*[2] prêt de mourir de faim; et le fils d'un des plus grands hommes que la France ait eus, et qui commençait à marcher sur les traces de son père,[3] était réduit à la misère sans M. Fagon.[4]

---

[1] Bachaumont, *Mémoires secrets* xxxiii. 199, 290.

[2] Crébillon *père*, whose tragedy, *Rhadamiste et Zénobie*, was first performed in 1711.

[3] The poet, Louis Racine; he was compelled to take a post in the provinces in the *Fermes*.

[4] Letter XXIII.

Even if the picture of the lot of English writers in this period is much overdone, it does reveal the French writer's feeling that the status of his profession was very much in need of being raised.

In the first half of the century, unless writers had private means or some occupation which left them sufficient leisure for literary pursuits, they were condemned to lead a very meagre existence. Their parents were often poor or of only modest position, and generally disapproved of their embarking on what seemed such an unpromising career, one which brought neither security nor a moderate affluence. Like Diderot, many writers led a hand-to-mouth, bohemian existence in their youth and attained a moderate affluence only in the latter part of their career. Though fêted in the *salons* of their day, they could not compete with the other guests either in rank or wealth or general polish. Moreover, their wives—generally like themselves of modest social origins— obviously could not accompany them on their expeditions into 'le monde'. Many writers of the time, at least the obscure hacks, never attained to anything as respectable as a settled home and family; they lived to the end a sordid, poverty-stricken existence.

From about the middle of the century onwards the position of writers in the polite society of Paris underwent a change. Hitherto, though they had frequented the *salons* of the capital from the time of the Hôtel de Rambouillet onwards, they had been admitted, not for their own sake, but as men of letters, that is to say, they were more or less on exhibition. By the middle of the century, however, the development of social life in Paris led to an increasing levelling of ranks, at least among those who qualified for admission to 'le monde'. People were now admitted regardless of rank, provided they had the right manners and tone. There is an interesting comment on the mingling of social classes in the polite society of Paris in the *Considérations sur les mœurs* which Duclos published in 1751: 'Les mœurs font à Paris ce que l'esprit du gouvernement fait à Londres; elles confondent et égalent dans la société les rangs qui sont distingués et subordonnés dans l'état.[1]

This levelling of ranks enabled men of letters to be admitted to 'le monde' on an equal footing with people of higher rank or greater wealth. As Duclos put it:

Le goût des lettres, des sciences et des arts a gagné insensiblement, et il est venu au point que ceux qui ne l'ont pas, l'affectent. On a donc recherché ceux

[1] C. P. Duclos, *Considérations sur les mœurs de ce siècle*, ed. F. C. Green, London, 1939, p. 15.

qui les cultivent, et ils ont été attirés dans le monde à proportion de l'agrément qu'on a trouvé dans leur commerce.

On a gagné de part et d'autre à cette liaison. Les gens du monde ont cultivé
leur esprit, formé leur goût, et acquis de nouveaux plaisirs. Les gens de lettres
n'en ont pas retiré moins d'avantages. Ils ont trouvé de la considération; ils
ont perfectionné leur goût, poli leur, esprit, adouci leurs mœurs, et acquis sur
plusieurs articles des lumières qu'ils n'auraient pas puisées dans des livres.[1]

Inevitably, this had its disadvantages. Many writers frittered away
their days in the futilities of the social round, and often had neither the
time nor the inclination to return to anything as arduous as writing a
book. In the chapter 'Sur les gens à la mode' Duclos himself wrote:
'L'homme de lettres qui, par des ouvrages travaillés, aurait pu instruire
son siècle et faire passer son nom à la postérité, néglige ses talents, et les
perd faute de les cultiver; il aurait été compté parmi les hommes illustres;
il reste un homme d'esprit de société.'[2] Other writers of the time frankly
deplored the trend. Later in the century in his *Tableau de Paris* the
satirically minded Mercier maintained that at that date in the whole of
France there were no more than thirty writers, that is men who wrote
and published regularly:

On sait que dès qu'un auteur est académicien, il pense toucher au terme de la
gloire littéraire; il ne fait plus rien que de courir les sociétés. Il est plus souvent
à table qu'à son bureau, et quand il a passé des années entières sans payer
aucun tribut au public, il appelle cela *le respecter*. A qui convient donc le
fauteuil académique? A tout homme qui ne veut plus écrire.[3]

One must not take Mercier's paradoxes literally, but there is obviously
a certain amount of truth in what he has to say about the writers of his
day, and not only the academicians.

Undoubtedly, in the closing decades of the *ancien régime* the writer,
even if he were not a man of genius, enjoyed immense prestige in the
upper-class circles of Paris. Writing after the Revolution, the comte de
Ségur contrasts the inequalities in society as a whole with the spirit of
equality which reigned in the *salons* of the capital:

Les titres littéraires avaient même, en beaucoup d'occasions, la préférence sur
les titres de noblesse, et ce n'était pas seulement aux hommes de génie qu'on
rendait des hommages qui faisaient disparaître toute trace d'infériorité, car on
voyait fréquemment, dans le monde, des hommes de lettres du second et du
troisième ordre être accueillis et traités avec des égards que n'obtenaient pas
les nobles de province.[4]

---

[1] Ibid. pp. 135–6.   [2] Ibid. p. 101.   [3] viii. 63 n.
[4] *Mémoires, souvenirs et anecdotes*, ed. F. Barrière, 2 vols., Paris, 1879, i. 53.

In case this should be taken to be a French nobleman's rosy view of life in France before 1789, it should be added that the same phenomenon was noted by English travellers in the days before the Revolution. In his travel notes for 1787 Arthur Young numbers among the advantages of life in Paris that 'the society for a man of letters, or who has any scientific pursuit, cannot be exceeded. The intercourse between such men and the great, which, if it be not upon an equal footing, ought never to exist at all, is respectable. Persons of the highest rank pay an attention to science and literature, and emulate the character they confer.'[1]

Ségur's observations are even more strikingly confirmed by what the Scottish traveller, John Moore, has to say about the position of men of letters in Paris society towards the end of the reign of Louis XV:

Many of those whose works you admire are received at the houses of the first nobility on the most liberal footing.

You can scarcely believe the influence which this body of men have in the gay and dissipated city of Paris. Their opinions not only determine the merit of works of taste and science, but they have considerable weight on the manners and sentiments of people of rank, of the public in general, and consequently are not without effect on the measures of government.

The same thing takes place in some degree in most countries of Europe, but, if I am not mistaken, more at Paris than anywhere else; because men of letters are here at once united to each other by the various academies, and diffused among private societies by the manners and general taste of the nation.

As the sentiments and conversation of men of letters influence, to a certain degree, the opinions and conduct of the fashionable world, the manners of these last have a more obvious effect upon the air, the behaviour and the conversation of the former, which in general is polite and easy; equally purified from the awkward timidity contracted in retirement, and the disgusting arrogance inspired by university honours or church dignities. At Paris the pedants of Molière are to be seen on the stage only.[2]

One reason for the new status of writers was that they had by now become a power in the land. They controlled that mysterious new force which, long before 1789, imposed severe limitations on the actions even of an absolute monarchy—public opinion. In one of the most interesting passages in his *Tableau de Paris* Mercier attempts to show that the Englishman who sees the French groaning under the

[1] *Travels in France*, ed. C. Maxwell, London, 1929, p. 91.
[2] *A View of Society and Manners in France, Switzerland and Germany*, i. 26–7.

yoke of despotism has not taken in the whole picture. The passage is all the more significant as it comes from a severe critic of the *ancien régime*:

L'Anglais aura dit: Le roi de France jouit d'une autorité presque indéfinie; il a le fer dans une main, l'or dans l'autre; il fait ployer les corps intermédiaires avec une feuille de papier; il est sûr que la noblesse sera à ses ordres quand il le voudra; la magistrature lui apporte des remontrances et se retire; le peuple n'a aucune voix, aucune force; il a livré ses biens et sa personne à son maître, qui de plus possède depuis cent ans sa fortune pécuniaire et qui d'un mot peut libérer ses immenses dettes. Il a un plus grand pouvoir encore; il défend à la pensée de paraître; il flétrit ou ridiculise les idées qui ne lui plaisent pas; et s'il n'y parvient pas pour toujours, il y parvient pour un certain temps. Il n'y a pas jusqu'à la place d'académicien qui ne soit de son choix; et Louis XIV pouvait dire à Corneille: 'Vous ne serez pas de l'Académie.'

In practice, Mercier goes on to point out, there were all sorts of limitations on the power of the monarchy and its ministers in the customs and usages of the country, reinforced by public opinion and a set of vigilant writers:

Ainsi parmi nous la liberté publique, vivante malgré de terribles atteintes, s'appuie avec plus de succès encore sur les coutumes et sur les mœurs que sur les lois écrites. L'empire des mœurs, plus absolu que les lois, parce qu'il est perpétuel, commande la modération à ceux qui seraient tentés de ne pas la connaître; car les lois ne sont respectées ou suivies qu'autant que le législateur a eu l'art de les enter sur les mœurs et les idées nationales. Enfin, la plume des écrivains, vigilante et protectrice des privilèges que la raison a créés, les maintient et défend aux souverains d'oser les attaquer.[1]

From being the humble retainers of kings and great noblemen, the mere entertainers of polite society, by the second half of the eighteenth century writers had come to exercise immense power.

This fundamental point was well brought out as early as 1751 by Duclos when he wrote in his *Considérations sur les mœurs*: 'Cependant de tous les empires, celui des gens d'esprit, sans être visible, est le plus étendu. Le puissant commande, les gens d'esprit gouvernent, parce qu'à la longue ils forment l'opinion publique, qui tôt ou tard subjugue ou renverse toute espèce de fanatisme.'[2] The most striking illustration of the new importance achieved by men of letters—now no longer merely the somewhat despised entertainers of a few thousand members

---

[1] viii. 143, 146.   [2] pp. 138–9.

of the upper classes of Paris, but the masters of public opinion over a considerable area of Europe—is to be found in Voltaire's triumphant return to Paris in 1778.

The man who fifty years before had been beaten up by the hired thugs of the chevalier de Rohan and then sent to the Bastille for daring to seek revenge, was fêted and treated with adulation at the Académie française, at the Comédie-Française, and in the streets of Paris. The novelty of this reception given to a man of letters was commented upon by a contemporary observer, Meister, when he wrote:

M. de Voltaire lui-même, toutes choses d'ailleurs égales, n'eût point joui du même triomphe sous le règne de Louis XIV, qui aimait les lettres parce qu'il aimait la louange, qui favorisait le génie et les arts, mais qui prétendait toujours leur donner la loi, et qui avait imprimé dans l'esprit de ses peuples une telle dévotion pour le trône et pour sa propre personne que l'on aurait craint de commettre un acte d'idolâtrie en prodiguant à un simple particulier des hommages dont lui-même eût été jaloux.

The apotheosis of Voltaire, he went on, was

la juste récompense, non seulement des merveilles qu'a produites son génie, mais aussi de l'heureuse révolution qu'il a su faire et dans les mœurs et dans l'esprit de son siècle, en combattant les préjugés de tous les ordres et de tous les rangs, en donnant aux lettres plus de considération et de dignité, et à l'opinion même un empire plus libre et plus indépendant de toute autre puissance que celle du génie et de la raison.[1]

To this position of influence and power which men of letters acquired in the closing decades of the *ancien régime*, the contribution of the Philosophes is obvious. Not for them the notion—summed up in the famous remark of Malherbe a hundred and fifty years earlier that 'un bon poète n'est pas plus utile à l'État qu'un bon joueur de quilles'— that the writer has no social function and that his aim is simply to entertain and give pleasure to his readers. For them the writer—over and above his other aims—has the task of enlightening his fellow men and at the same time of enlightening governments too. His power to influence public opinion is well summed up by Mercier—not, incidentally, a member of what one might call the party of the Philosophes— when he wrote in the 1780s:

De quel abîme d'erreurs et de misérables préjugés n'ont-ils pas fait sortir les administrateurs des nations? Qu'enseignent-ils, si ce n'est l'amour de l'humanité, les droits de l'homme et du citoyen? Quelle question importante

---

[1] Grimm, *Correspondance littéraire* xii. 73.

à la société n'ont-ils pas examinée, débattue, fixée? Si le despotisme s'est civilisé, si les souverains ont commencé à redouter la voix des nations, à respecter ce tribunal suprême, c'est à la plume des écrivains que l'on doit ce frein nouveau, inconnu. Quelle iniquité ministérielle ou royale pourrait se flatter aujourd'hui de passer impunément? Et la gloire des rois n'attend-elle pas la sanction du philosophe?[1]

Thus by the second half of the eighteenth century men of letters in France had overcome their old modesty and the contempt in which they had hitherto been held in an aristocratic society. They now claimed for themselves a social function of the highest importance and this claim was admitted by the general public.

When the upheaval which began in 1789 subsided ten years later, first under the Consulate and then under the Empire, a controversy began which has lasted down to our own day,[2] on the role of the man of letters in bringing about the Revolution. Counter-revolutionary writers denounced the part played by men of letters in the downfall of the *ancien régime*. In 1803 in the *Journal des Débats* Geoffroy wrote: 'Nos plus grands malheurs sont venus de l'ambition des gens de lettres, qui, pour faire les hommes d'importance, se sont jetés dans la morale et dans la politique, et se sont fait un jeu de ruiner la société et l'État pour se donner un relief de philosophie.'[3] A few days later abbé de Féletz denounced in the same newspaper a plan to encourage and support men of letters. 'D'où sont venus les maux de la Révolution?' he asked. 'N'est-ce parce que tout homme en France s'est cru un homme de lettres et que tout homme de lettres s'est cru un législateur?' The Philosophes in particular were singled out for blame: 'Des philosophes pleins de vanité et d'orgueil accréditèrent, vers le milieu du siècle dernier, cette opinion: Que de toutes les professions, la plus utile à l'État, c'était la profession des lettres; opinion fausse s'il en fut jamais.'[4]

Later Joseph de Maistre was to denounce the role of the Philosophes in his usual fiery language:

Les philosophes (ou ceux qu'on a nommés de la sorte) ont tous un certain orgueil féroce et rebelle qui ne s'accommode de rien: ils détestent sans exception toutes les distinctions dont ils ne jouissent pas; il n'y a point d'autorité qui ne leur déplaise; il n'y a rien au-dessus d'eux qu'ils ne haïssent. Laissez-les faire,

---

[1] *Tableau de Paris*, iv. 160.
[2] See e.g. the special number of *Dix-huitième siècle*, 1974, vi: 'Lumières et révolution'.
[3] *Cours de littérature dramatique*, 5 vols., Paris, 1819–20, i. 70.
[4] Abbé C. M. D. de Féletz, *Jugements historiques et littéraires*, Paris and Lyons, 1840, p. 218

ils attaqueront tout, même Dieu, parce qu'il est maître. Voyez si ce ne sont pas les mêmes hommes qui ont écrit contre les rois et contre celui qui les a établis![1]

Writers are put firmly in their place:

Il appartient aux prélats, aux nobles, aux grands officiers de l'état d'être les dépositaires et les gardiens des vérités conservatrices; d'apprendre aux nations ce qui est mal et ce qui est bien; ce qui est vrai et ce qui est faux dans l'ordre moral et spirituel: les autres n'ont pas droit de raisonner sur ces sortes de matières.[2]

Needless to say this was a view which was to be shared by very few later writers in France.

Although when seen from the angle of the twentieth century, the reading public of eighteenth-century France with probably more than half the population still illiterate seems extraordinarily small, in comparison with that of earlier ages it was undoubtedly, especially by the end of the period, relatively large. No doubt many of the new recruits to literacy had fairly primitive tastes in their reading; the wide variety of little chapbooks of the *Bibliothèque bleue* enjoyed even greater popularity and brought considerable prosperity to certain printers in towns like Troyes and Rouen who specialized in their production. Much as the government might have liked to exercise control over the sale of such works and of books in general in the provinces, Malesherbes had to admit that it was virtually impossible for it to do so:

... Dans les provinces tout est rempli de marchands vagabonds, qui étalent des livres dans les foires, les marchés, les rues des petites villes. Ils vendent sur les grands chemins; ils arrivent dans les châteaux et y étalent leurs marchandises; en un mot, leur commerce est si public qu'on a peine à croire qu'il ne soit pas autorisé.

Si on voulait remédier à cet abus en exécutant strictement la loi, il faudrait interdire tout à fait la vente des livres à ces colporteurs ou marchands forains. Or par là on gênerait beaucoup le commerce; on nuirait à la littérature et aux progrès des connaissances en ôtant le moyen d'avoir des livres à tous ceux qui habitent hors des villes.[3]

Works which could be classified as 'literature' continued to form a very small proportion of the publications of this type; as before, adaptations of medieval romances such as *Huon de Bordeaux* and *L'Histoire des*

---

[1] *Les Soirées de Saint-Pétersbourg*, 2 vols., Paris, 1929, ii. 104.
[2] Ibid. 103.   [3] *Mémoires*, pp. 154–5.

quatre fils Aymon were frequently reprinted, while *L'Histoire du bonhomme Misère* continued to be extremely popular throughout the period.

Although works of literature in this period tended for the most part to be addressed in the first instance to a relatively narrow section of the community established in the capital, they were obviously read in much wider circles. Books were undoubtedly still expensive, but they could be borrowed from one's acquaintances and increasingly on a commercial basis as *cabinets de lecture* gradually became more common in both Paris and the provinces. Unfortunately, no serious attempt at a history of such institutions, particularly in their earlier period down to the Revolution, seems yet to have been made, but it is clear that they became more numerous in the eighteenth century though it was after 1789 that they were most flourishing.

The *cabinet de lecture* offered, in return for an entrance fee, a selection of the current periodicals and new books to be read on the spot. It was also possible to pay a monthly subscription to borrow books or periodicals and take them home. Sometimes a bookseller would simply run a circulating library from his shop and lend books to be read off the premises. One of the earliest examples of this type is described by Marmontel who relates how at Clermont-Ferrand about 1740 he and his fellow schoolboys borrowed books from a circulating library kept by a bookseller in the town:

A frais communs, et à peu de frais, nous étions abonnés pour nos lectures avec un vieux libraire, et comme les bons livres sont, grâce au ciel, les plus communs, nous n'en lisions que d'excellents. Les grands orateurs, les grands poètes, les meilleurs écrivains du siècle dernier, quelques-uns du siècle présent, car le libraire en avait peu, se succédaient de main en main; et dans nos promenades chacun se rappelant ce qu'il avait recueilli, nos entretiens se passaient presque tous en conférences sur nos lectures.[1]

Although it is far from clear when *cabinets de lecture* were first established in Paris, they were certainly in existence by 1761 when *La Nouvelle Héloïse* enjoyed its sensational popularity. In the edition of Rousseau's works which he published jointly with Brizard in 1788, Mercier speaks of the success of the novel among readers of all classes:

Je me souviens que les libraires ne pouvaient suffire aux demandes de toutes classes. Ceux dont la modicité de la fortune ne pouvait atteindre au prix de l'ouvrage le louaient à tant par jour ou par heure. Tel libraire avide, j'ose

[1] *Mémoires*, i. 28.

l'assurer, exigeait dans la nouveauté douze sous par volume pour la simple lecture et n'accordait que soixante minutes pour un tome.[1]

According to the new catalogue published in 1773 by Jacques François Quillau, a bookseller in the rue Christine in the faubourg Saint-Germain, his *Magasin littéraire* which lent out books in return for a subscription of 24 livres a year, dated from 1761, the year of the publication of *La Nouvelle Héloïse*, and was the first to be established in Paris. The Bibliothèque nationale also possesses another eighteenth-century catalogue for a Paris circulating library, that of Couturier *fils* on the quai des Augustins; this bears the date of 1770.[2]

In 1762 Bachaumont had announced the opening of a *cabinet de lecture* in the capital: 'Le nommé Grangé, libraire, ouvre incessamment une salle littéraire; pour trois sous par séance on aura la liberté de lire pendant plusieurs heures de suite toutes les nouveautés.'[3] This appears to have been a relatively inexpensive establishment, at least compared with the Cabinet académique de lecture for which the bookseller, Moreau, published a prospectus in 1779, as admission was to cost 10 sous a session.[4]

In his *Tableau de Paris* Mercier has a lively chapter entitled 'Loueur de livres' though a good deal of it is given up to satirical comments on established writers like La Harpe:

Usés, sales, déchirés, ces livres en cet état attestent qu'ils sont les meilleurs de tous; et le critique hautain qui s'épuise en réflexions superflues devrait aller chez le *loueur de livres* et là voir les brochures que l'on demande, que l'on emporte et auxquelles on revient de préférence . . .

Les ouvrages qui peignent les mœurs, qui sont simples, naïfs ou touchants, qui n'ont ni apprêt, ni morgue, ni jargon académique, voilà ceux que l'on vient chercher de tous les quartiers de la ville et de tous les étages des maisons.

These last words certainly make it clear that some of the works lent out had a wide appeal and were read by sections of the community which were far from affluent.

One important part of the novel-reading public of the time is introduced, almost surreptitiously, at the end of the chapter:

[1] *Œuvres*, ed. L. S. Mercier *et al.*, 7 vols., Paris, 1788–9, iv. 458–9.

[2] Both these catalogues are to be found under the class-mark 8° Q.28 which covers a large collection of catalogues of *cabinets de lecture*, mainly nineteenth-century, from both Paris and the provinces.

[3] *Mémoires secrets* i. 195. It is said on good authority that the Bibliothèque nationale has a copy of the catalogue of this *cabinet de lecture*, but my efforts to track it down ended in failure.

[4] Ibid. xiv. 150–1.

Une mère dit à sa fille: Je ne veux point que vous lisiez. Le désir de la lecture augmente en elle. Son imagination dévore toutes les brochures qu'on lui dérobe; elle sort furtivement, entre chez un libraire, lui demande *La Nouvelle Héloïse*, dont elle a entendu prononcer le nom; le garçon sourit, elle paye et va s'enfermer dans sa chambre.[1]

More serious *cabinets de lecture* where books and periodicals had to be read on the spot were encountered by Arthur Young in his travels through the provinces. At Nantes in September 1788 he noted the existence of what would appear to have been not an institution run for private profit, but one which depended on the subscriptions of its members:

An institution common in the great commercial towns of France, but particularly flourishing in Nantes, is a *chambre de lecture*, or what we should call a book club, that does not divide its books, but forms a library. There are three rooms, one for reading, another for conversation, and the third is the library; good fires in winter are provided and wax candles.

Presumably the subscription was fairly high, whereas the institution which Arthur Young, impatient for news (the entry is dated 14 July 1789), resorted to at Metz was on a more modest scale:

They have a *cabinet littéraire* at Metz, something like that I described at Nantes, but not on so great a plan; and they admit any person to read or go in and out for a day, on paying 4 *sous*. To this I eagerly resorted, and the news from Paris, both in the public prints and by the information of a gentleman, I found to be interesting.[2]

Although our information is scanty, it is clear that by 1789 in both Paris and many provincial towns *cabinets de lecture* had become relatively common; the upheaval of the Revolution would appear to have made them more popular still and, in the years of turmoil, they often become small political clubs where people met to discuss the latest news. In 1814 Paris even acquired an English circulating library, that of Galignani, run principally for an Anglo-American clientèle. There is an amusing account of one of the numerous Paris *cabinets de lectur e* towards the end of the First Empire in *Victor Hugo raconté par un témoin de sa vie*. The poet's mother, who was an insatiable reader, paid a yearly subscription to one of these booksellers' libraries; what was no

---

[1] *Tableau de Paris*, v. 36–7.
[2] *Travels in France*, pp. 117, 174. A. Brulé (*La Vie au dix-huitième siècle*, facing p. 16) reproduces the stamp of the Société de lecture de la Fosse Nantes, 1760.

doubt less usual was the way in which she left the choice of books from it to two small boys:

Quand on aime lire, quelque livre qu'on ait commencé, on va jusqu'au bout; afin de ne pas s'engager dans une lecture trop ennuyeuse, Mme Hugo faisait essayer ses livres par ses enfants. Elle les envoyait chez son loueur, un nommé Royol, qui était un bonhomme très particulier.[1] . . . Les deux frères allaient chez ce bonhomme, fourrageaient dans sa bibliothèque et emportaient ce qu'ils voulaient. Avec ces deux pourvoyeurs qui ne manquaient jamais à sa faim de livres, Mme Hugo en consomma effroyablement et eut bientôt épuisé le rez-de-chaussée du bonhomme Royol; il avait bien encore un entresol, mais il ne se souciait guère d'y introduire des enfants. C'était là qu'il reléguait les ouvrages d'une philosophie trop hardie ou d'une moralité trop libre pour être exposés à tous les yeux. Il fit l'objection à la mère, qui lui répondit que les livres n'avaient jamais fait de mal, et les deux frères eurent la clef de l'entresol.

L'entresol était un pêle-mêle. Les rayons n'avaient pas suffi aux livres et le plancher en était couvert. Pour n'avoir pas la peine de se baisser et de se relever à tout moment, les enfants se courbaient à plat ventre et dégustaient ce qui leur tombait sous la main. Quand l'intérêt les empoignait, ils restaient quelquefois des heures entières. Tout était bon à ces jeunes appétits, prose, vers, mémoires, voyages, science. Ils lurent ainsi Rousseau, Voltaire, Diderot; ils lurent *Faublas* et d'autres romans de même nature.[2]

We see then that by the end of the First Empire *cabinets de lecture* were firmly established, though their heyday came later in the nineteenth century.

The importance of their emergence from our point of view is that they undoubtedly helped to enlarge the reading public. If they made it possible for readers who could well afford to buy books to get hold of them more cheaply, they also enabled the less well-to-do members of the community who had developed an interest in reading to lay their hands on works which they could not possibly have afforded to buy. They must have contributed to increasing the number of editions and their size in this period. It is naturally impossible here to disentangle the effect of increased interest in books inside France from the demand for French books all over Europe, but the growth in home demand must have accounted for at least a considerable part of the very large number

[1] See C. Duchet, 'Un libraire libéral sous l'Empire et la Restauration: du nouveau sur Royol', *Revue d'histoire littéraire*, 1965, pp. 485–93.

[2] A. Hugo, *Victor Hugo raconté par un témoin de sa vie*, 2 vols., Paris, n.d., i. 173–4.

of editions which the best sellers of eighteenth-century France went through. One thinks of works like *L'Esprit des lois, Candide,* and *La Nouvelle Héloïse,* but other eighteenth-century works, some of them now almost forgotten, enjoyed a more modest, but none the less surprising circulation, if we are to believe editors of the periodicals of the time. Crébillon *père*'s tragedy, *Catilina,* is said to have sold 5,000 copies in a week when it was published in 1749,[1] while, before the sales of the Paris edition of Voltaire's *L'Ingénu* were stopped, over 4,000 copies had been sold in the space of a few days,[2] and in 1782 abbé Delille's mediocre poem, *Les Jardins,* is alleged to have gone through seven editions in two months.[3] Nearly four thousand subscribers were found for the first edition of such an expensive work as the *Encyclopédie,* and while we do not know, any more than for the eight reprints produced in Italy, Geneva, and Switzerland, how many of these were French, it is a fair guess that at least half of them were.

In this period there was, of course, not just one public, but several, as critics of the time make clear. Neither Raynal nor Grimm, for instance, considered abbé Coyer to be writing for the only circles which they held to be worth writing for, the polite society of the capital. Of one of his satirical brochures Raynal wrote:

Il est rare que nos bons livres fassent beaucoup de bruit dans la bourgeoisie, aussi a-t-on soin de lui fournir, de temps en temps, une littérature telle qu'il lui faut. Un abbé Coyer vient de publier tout récemment une brochure intitulée l'*Année merveilleuse,* destinée à amuser la multitude. C'est une satire assez plaisante, quoiqu'un peu commune, de nos mœurs.[4]

In reviewing the abbé's collection of brochures published under the title of *Bagatelles morales* a few years later, Grimm also makes it clear that this was not a book for the 'best people'. After reproaching him with his 'mauvais ton', he goes on:

Cependant je ne serais pas étonné que ces bagatelles fussent regardées comme quelque chose dans la province et dans certains quartiers de Paris. Chaque quartier a ses beaux esprits; et si M. l'abbé Coyer ne réussit pas dans celui du Palais Royal ou du Faubourg Saint-Germain, il n'en est pas moins peut-être le Crébillon du Marais ou de la rue Saint-Denis.[5]

A decade or so later we find Grimm differentiating more than once between the taste of the aristocratic quarters of Paris and that of the

---

[1] Raynal, *Nouvelles littéraires,* in Grimm, *Correspondance littéraire* i. 260.
[2] Grimm, *Correspondance littéraire* vii. 418.   [3] Ibid. xiii. 178.
[4] Ibid. i. 161.   [5] Ibid, ii. 359.

more bourgeois and plebeian ones. Thus in 1766, in speaking of an anonymous *Étrennes aux dames, ou Recueil des plus nouvelles chansons* which he dismisses as 'une rapsodie', he goes on: 'L'auteur . . . nous en promet une autre beaucoup plus étendue. Je ne crois pas qu'à l'exception de quelques bourgeois de la rue Saint-Denis, cet échantillon attire beaucoup de chalands à sa boutique.'[1] In the following year he reviewed a novel of Baculard d'Arnaud's and contrasted the taste of the aristocratic quarters with that both of other parts of Paris and of the provinces:

Je suis persuadé que toutes les jeunes filles de boutique de la rue des Lombards et de la rue des Bourdonnais, qui ont du sentiment, trouvent les romans de M. Arnaud fort beaux, et que sa plume pathétique leur fait verser bien des larmes. En province cela doit paraître fort touchant aussi; mais dans le quartier du Palais Royal et dans le faubourg Saint-Germain il n'y a que moi qui sache que M. Arnaud fait des romans.[2]

Whether such estimates of the potential readership of these works were correct or not, the standpoint of both critics is clear; the only works of literature worth serious consideration were those which fitted in with the taste of the polite society of the capital.

In the previous age writers had sought to please 'la Cour et la Ville'; one striking feature of eighteenth-century French literature was the gradual eclipse of the influence of the court. The respectful and admiring attitude towards the court, summed up in La Bruyère's famous description of it as 'le centre du bon goût et de la politesse', lingers on into this period. Thus in 1729 in his continuation of Pellisson's *Histoire de l'Académie française* abbé d'Olivet could write:

Car qui doute que la cour, bien loin de nuire à un bon esprit, ne soit au contraire l'école la plus propre à le former? Et une compagnie, dont l'unique but est d'affermir le bel usage de la langue, de travailler sans cesse à la perfection du goût, n'a-t-elle pas de grands secours à espérer d'un seigneur qui vit dans le centre du goût et de la délicatesse?[3]

Another writer of this part of the century, abbé Le Blanc, argues that while men of letters are better judges of the written language, great noblemen are superior as judges of its spoken form: 'Les uns ont approfondi davantage les règles de la grammaire et l'étymologie des mots; let autres sont des témoins plus sûrs de l'usage du monde. C'est le concours des uns et des autres qui peut seul perfectionner une

---

[1] Ibid. vi. 485.   [2] Ibid. vii. 479.
[3] *Histoire de l'Académie française*, ii. 144.

langue.'[1] His next words—'La cour est le centre du goût et de la politesse'—are merely an echo of the seventeenth-century commonplace expressed by La Bruyère.

As the century wore on, there was a noticeable decline in the influence of the court at Versailles. While to the end of the *ancien régime* the Crown retained its importance as a dispenser of literary patronage, because of its isolation from Paris influence on matters of language and literature passed more and more to the polite society of the capital. In her memoirs Mme Campan sums up her first impressions of Versailles in the closing years of the reign of Louis XV: 'De lieu de réunion où l'on vît se déployer l'esprit et la grâce des Français, il n'en fallait point chercher. Le foyer de l'esprit et des lumières était à Paris.'[2] In his usual blustering way Mercier sums up this loss of influence by the court in his *Tableau de Paris:*

Le mot de *cour* n'en impose plus parmi nous comme au temps de Louis XIV. On ne reçoit plus de la cour les opinions régnantes; elle ne décide plus des réputations, en quelque genre que ce soit; on ne dit plus avec une emphase ridicule: 'La cour a prononcé ainsi'. On casse les jugements de la cour; on dit nettement, elle n'y entend rien, elle n'a point d'idées là-dessus, elle ne saurait en avoir, elle n'est pas dans le point de vue.

Du temps de Louis XIV la cour était plus formée que la ville; aujourd'hui la ville est plus formée que la cour. . . . La cour a donc perdu cet ascendant qu'elle avait sur les beaux-arts, sur les lettres, et sur tout ce qui est aujourd' hui de leur ressort. On citait dans le siècle dernier le suffrage d'un homme de la cour, d'un prince; et personne n'osait contredire. . . . C'est de la ville que part l'approbation ou l'improbation adoptée par le ʒeste du royaume.[3]

Slightly earlier John Moore had noted the same phenomenon, particularly as concerned drama:

Obedient to the court in every other particular, the French disregard the decisions pronounced at Versailles in matters of taste. It very often happens that a dramatic piece, which has been acted before the royal family and the court with the highest applause, is afterwards damned with every circumstance of ignominy at Paris. In all works of genius the Parisians lead the judgement of the courtiers and dictate to their monarch.[4]

If works of literature were disseminated more widely than ever before—both in the different classes as illiteracy declined and over the

---

[1] *Lettres d'un Français* iii. 4.
[2] *Mémoires sur la vie de Marie-Antoinette*, ed. F. Barrière, Paris, 1876, p. 48.
[3] iv. 153–4.
[4] *A View of Society and Manners in France, Switʒerland and Germany*, i. 86.

country as a whole, in remote provincial châteaux and in the towns, large and small, dotted all over France—they continued to be written for a very restricted section of the community. The great bulk of French literature was produced in the capital and, in the first instance at least, for a relatively narrow section of its inhabitants. All sorts of works—plays, poems, novels, and other books—were read aloud, discussed, and criticized in the *salons* of Paris before they were placed before a wider public through performances in the theatre or through the printing-press. A considerable number of writers established there came from the provinces like Diderot or from even further afield like Rousseau, but they produced their works in Paris and in contact with the narrow society of the capital. The concentration of the literary life of France in Paris in this period is well brought out by Mercier when he wrote of the men of letters of his day:

Si l'on compte qu'il n'y a point eu d'homme célèbre né en province qui ne soit venu à Paris pour se former, qui n'y ait vécu par choix et qui n'y soit mort, ne pouvant quitter cette grande ville, malgré l'amour de la patrie; cette race d'hommes éclairés, tous concentrés sur le même point, tandis que les autres villes du royaume offrent des landes d'une incroyable stérilité, devient un profond objet de méditation sur les causes réelles et subsistantes qui précipitent tous les gens de lettres dans la capitale et les y retiennent comme par enchantement.[1]

And in Paris the writers of the period mingled with members of the upper classes of society—with the nobility, high officials, judges of the Parlement, wealthy tax-farmers, and their womenfolk—in the different *salons* which, down to the upheaval of 1789, flourished in the capital, from those of such hostesses as the marquise de Lambert and Mme de Tencin in the first half of the century to those of Mme Geoffrin and Mme Necker in the second.

It was inevitable that the works of men of letters should reflect in all sorts of ways the tastes and outlook of this relatively narrow and select section of the community in whose company they spent a great part of their time. No doubt the works which they produced eventually reached in printed form all sections of the community which had acquired a taste for reading, and penetrated to every corner of the country; yet they were conceived in a limited circle and bore unmistakably the imprint of their origin.

One reason for the success which so many eighteenth-century

---

[1] *Tableau de Paris*, iv. 16.

French books enjoyed in the Europe of their day was that they avoided all pedantic methods of exposition and sought to appeal, even when dealing with serious and complicated subjects, to the men and women of the polite society of Paris, and beyond them to a public of 'honnêtes gens'. One thinks here, for instance, of the light form which Voltaire gave to the most serious problems in his multitude of polemical writings, from the *Contes* to the *Dictionnaire philosophique*. Montesquieu's *Esprit des lois*, though a serious historical and sociological treatise on law, is none the less adapted to the tastes of this public; side by side with the solemn, rounded periods of M. le Président we find flashes of wit and irony and a suitable admixture of spicy details to tickle the reader's palate, while this long work is made easier to read by its short sentences, short paragraphs, and the short chapters into which it is divided.

It is again characteristic that so many novels of the time reflect the influence of the polite society of Paris in their choice of characters as well as in their themes, tone, and general style. As early as 1734, when he published the second part of his unfinished novel, *La Vie de Marianne*, Marivaux spoke sarcastically of the tendency of readers to prefer characters of the highest rank:

Il y a des gens dont la vanité se mêle de tout ce qu'ils font, même de leurs lectures. Donnez-leur l'histoire du cœur humain dans les grandes conditions, ce devient là pour eux un objet important; mais ne leur parlez pas des états médiocres, ils ne veulent voir agir que des seigneurs, des princes, des rois, ou du moins des personnes qui aient fait une grande figure. Il n'y a que cela qui existe pour la noblesse de leur goût. Laissez là le reste des hommes; qu'ils vivent, mais qu'il n'en soit pas question. Ils vous diraient volontiers que la nature aurait bien pu se passer de les faire naître, et que les bourgeois la déshonorent.[1]

The same point was made in 1749 by abbé de La Porte when he reviewed the French translation of Sarah Fielding's *Adventures of David Simple*. He begins his article thus:

Nous sommes plus fastueux, nous autres Français, dans les titres que nous donnons aux livres de cette espèce. On ne voit guère en France de romans roturiers; ils sont presque tous de la première condition; il en est peu qui ne soient décorés du nom d'une terre érigée en duché, en marquisat ou en comté. *Mémoires du Duc de* ***, *Aventures du Marquis de* ***, *Confessions du Comte de* ***, c'est ainsi qu'ils s'annoncent dans le monde.

[1] *La Vie de Marianne*, ed. F. Deloffre, Paris, 1963, p. 57.

Si cependant il arrive que le héros ou l'héroïne d'un roman soit un paysan ou une paysanne, on ne fait connaître la bassesse de leur condition que pour relever davantage l'éclat de leur fortune: *Le Paysan parvenu, La Paysanne parvenue* nous annoncent quelque chose de brillant; et l'on s'attend au moins à les voir l'un et l'autre posséder en titre de marquisat les terres que leurs pères avaient labourées.[1]

The last remark is significant. Although Marivaux argued strongly in favour of a novel dealing with the affairs of ordinary people, he none the less chose as heroes of his novels characters who, despite their humble beginnings, have by the time they relate their story ended up among the upper classes of society. Jacob, the hero of *Le Paysan parvenu*, is a genuine peasant's son, but he writes his memoirs as a wealthy tax-farmer; while the heroine of *La Vie de Marianne*, although at the beginning of the novel she is depicted as an apprentice to a seamstress, ends up among the aristocracy, and although in this unfinished novel the mystery of her birth is never explained, it is hinted from the very beginning that her parents were of noble rank.

Moreover, despite the demand, voiced in various quarters, for a novel dealing with the affairs of ordinary people, critics of the time showed themselves hostile to this trend. For instance, Lesage was criticized by Marmontel on the grounds that as a satirical novel *Gil Blas* showed an inadequate acquaintance with the upper classes of society, that it lacked 'une connaissance plus familière et plus intime d'une certaine classe de la société que l'auteur de *Gil Blas* n'avait pas assez observée ou qu'il ne voyait que de loin'.[2] English novelists, especially Fielding and Smollett, were frequently criticized for concerning themselves with the lower orders, while French novels dealing with the lives of ordinary people met with a cool reception.

Thus in 1753 we find the critic, Grimm, pouring scorn on a novel which dealt with the love affairs of a young provincial who had been sent to Paris by his father to study under a *procureur*, and which consequently offers a picture of the daily life of a *procureur* and his family. The critic has nothing but disdain for such characters who are outside the narrow sphere of the polite society of the capital:

Voilà donc un roman domestique que personne cependant ne saurait lire; c'est qu'indépendamment du défaut de talent dans l'auteur, les personnages du roman sont tous des gens qui n'ont point d'existence dans la société, et dont les aventures, par conséquent, ne sauraient nous attacher. Le quartier de la

---

[1] *Observations sur la littérature moderne*, 9 vols., The Hague, 1749–52, i. 108–9.

[2] *Œuvres complètes*, 7 vols., Paris, 1819–20, iii, pt. II, p. 572.

Halle et de la place Maubert a sans doute des mœurs, et très marquées même; mais ce ne sont pas les mœurs de la nation, elles ne méritent donc pas d'être peintes.[1]

The same critic could have nothing but contempt for the famous passage in *La Vie de Marianne* in which Marivaux depicts a quarrel between two plebeian characters, a seamstress and a cabby, over the amount of a coach-fare. 'Rien n'est mieux rendu d'après nature,' he concedes, but adds scornfully, 'et d'un goût plus détestable que le tableau que je cite.'

In the same year Grimm offers a vivid picture of the narrow circle of the court and Parisian high society to which much of the literature of the age was addressed, when he writes of autumn as being generally the season

la plus stérile de l'année en nouveautés littéraires, parce que la cour étant d'un côté à Fontainebleau et presque tout le reste des habitants de Paris dispersés dans les campagnes, les auteurs et leurs hérauts les libraires sont en usage de consacrer ce temps au repos, pour avoir, dans le temps où le carnaval fait rentrer tout le monde dans le sein de Paris, les uns des succès plus brillants, les autres des ventes plus considérables.[2]

Not only would this indicate a quite different peak of the publishing year from that of today (January–February instead of the period leading up to Christmas), but the way in which the vast majority of the half a million inhabitants of Paris are obviously ignored in the phrase 'presque tout le reste des habitants de Paris' forms a delightful pendant to his earlier reference to ordinary folk as 'des gens qui n'ont point d'existence dans la société'.

Another interesting sidelight on the social tone which many critics and readers expected in the novel is provided by the way in which English novels of the time were adapted to suit French taste and their characters elevated several degrees in the social scale. Thus when Mme Riccoboni, later a prolific novelist, translated Fielding's *Amelia*, she transformed the penniless young officer with whom the heroine elopes into the scion of an aristocratic family, while the faithful Sergeant Atkinson, his one-time orderly, is elevated to the rank of lieutenant.[3]

It is, however, the drama of the age which bears perhaps most clearly the mark of the tastes, interests, and prejudices of the upper classes of the capital for whom theatre-going was such an important occupation.

---

[1] *Correspondance littéraire* ii. 269.   [2] Ibid. 293.

[3] E. A. Crosby, *Une Romancière oubliée, Mme Riccoboni: Sa vie, ses œuvres, sa place dans la littérature anglaise et française du XVIIIᵉ siècle*, Paris, 1924, pp. 122–3.

It is true that even before 1789 Paris offered a variety of theatres to suit a variety of tastes. The 'best people' frequented, in addition to the Opéra, the Comédie-Française and, from 1716 onwards, the Théâtre italien. However, already before the end of the reign of Louis XIV temporary theatres were set up for two fairs, those of Saint-Germain and Saint-Laurent, much to the disgust of the Opéra and the Comédie-Française whose monopoly these infringed. The Opéra was soon bought off, and it was left to the Comédie-Française, joined in 1716 by the Théâtre italien, to continue the struggle against these interlopers. The history of these little theatres is extremely complicated and has not yet been thoroughly studied,[1] but from them emerged the Opéra-Comique which, though officially closed from 1745 to 1752, ended up by absorbing the Théâtre italien when the two theatres were combined in 1762. Henceforth the genre of the *opéra-comique* became extremely important at the Théâtre italien; at one stage, from 1769 onwards, French plays were abandoned, then from 1780 it was the turn of Italian plays to go, and down to the Revolution the theatre performed only French plays and did offer some sort of alternative to the Comédie-Française though it was not the second theatre demanded by many playwrights in this period. From the 1760s onwards there emerged from the Théâtres de la Foire a number of small permanent theatres known as the Théâtres des Boulevards. By 1789 the fashionable promenade, the boulevard du Temple, boasted as many as six of these theatres some of which were to survive well into the nineteenth century and even beyond. The Théâtre de l'Ambigu Comique, for instance, began on this boulevard in 1769, although in 1828 it had to move after a fire to new premises in the boulevard Saint-Martin. Similarly, the Théâtre de la Gaîté, installed since 1862 as a result of the upheaval caused by Haussmann's reconstruction of Paris opposite the Conservatoire des arts et métiers, was established in 1760 on the boulevard du Temple. Audinot and Nicolet, the founders of these two theatres, were only two of the many impresarios who in the closing decades of the *ancien régime* succeeded in establishing new enterprises in Paris. The theatre occupied since 1799 by the Comédie-Française was originally built between 1786 and 1790 for one of these new enterprises, the Théâtre des Variétés Amusantes.

Though little remains alive of the large output of plays in eighteenth-century France apart from some of the works of Marivaux and Beaumarchais, it was none the less one of the great ages of the drama.

[1] The most useful book still remains M. Albert, *Les Théâtres de la Foire* (*1660–1789*), Paris, 1900.

Paris attracted the best actors and actresses as well as all the play-wrights, but it did not so completely dwarf the provinces as in the previous age. There was a great upsurge of theatrical activity there, both in garrison towns and in the great commercial centres. The authorities were anxious to see theatres established to keep officers out of mischief; thus in the 1760s the Minister for the Navy was urged by the commandant at Brest to authorize such an establishment for the following reasons: 'Le spectacle détourne du goût du jeu, de la table, des querelles, ce qui n'a que trop régné ici, et donne l'éducation et les dialogues du monde à tant de jeunes officiers qui ne sortent du départe-ment que pour aller à la mer ou à la campagne.'[1] Well over twenty provincial theatres were founded in the third quarter of the century in towns as widely scattered as Arras and Bayonne, Caen and Aix-en-Provence, and although the movement slackened off during the reign of Louis XVI, new buildings were provided for established theatres in cities like Bordeaux and Nantes. The new theatres in both these cities aroused the admiration of Arthur Young.[2]

None the less Paris still continued to play the most important part in the theatrical life of France, as was natural with the capital of a highly centralized country, drawing to itself and the neighbouring Versailles the wealthiest and most aristocratic sections of society; and down to the Revolution these unquestionably furnished a very important part of the audiences which frequented the theatres of the capital. On paper the Théâtres de la Foire and later the Théâtres des Boulevards furnished entertainment for the masses, but contemporaries make it clear that the 'best people' did not disdain to frequent them on occasion. In 1769, for instance, in speaking of the popularity of Audinot's theatre, Bachaumont declares: 'La modicité des places, dont les plus chères sont à 24 sous, met tout le monde à portée de se régaler à cette foire, en sorte que la duchesse et le savoyard s'y coudoient sans distinction.'[3] Two years later we learn from the same source that the audiences in this particular theatre were extremely mixed: 'Les filles se sont portées en foule de ce côté-là et beaucoup de libertins, d'oisifs, de freluquets avec elles. Ce monde en a attiré d'un autre genre. Les femmes de la cour, qui en cette qualité se croient au-dessus de tous les préjugés, n'ont pas dédaigné d'y paraître, et ce théâtre est la rage du jour.'[4] None the less, if

---

[1] Quoted in M. Fuchs, *La Vie théâtrale en province au XVIIIᵉ siècle*, i, Paris, 1933, p. 47.

[2] *Travels in France*, pp. 59–60, 116.   [3] *Mémoires secrets* xix. 49–50.

[4] Ibid. vi. 6–7.

some of the spectators, male and female, in these theatres were drawn from the upper classes of society, contemporary observers make it clear that the majority of their spectators were decidedly plebeian. In 1782 Bachaumont describes them as 'des gouffres où va s'engloutir le gain des artisans, des ouvriers, des manouvriers, de tout le peuple en un mot, et se perdre l'innocence des enfants des deux sexes'.[1]

That in the closing decades of the *ancien régime* there was a movement towards a mingling of spectators drawn from very different social classes is made clear by various contemporaries. Down to about 1760 audiences at the Comédie-Française remained small in numbers and were drawn from a restricted section of society, from the cultured middle classes upwards. Round about that date various contemporaries began to note a new and somewhat alarming phenomenon—the infiltration into the theatre of a number of spectators of more modest rank and education. In 1762 Grimm could still speak as if the great mass of spectators at the theatres like the Opéra, Comédie-Française, and Théâtre italien were drawn from the middle and upper ranks of society:

Ce n'est point le peuple qui fréquente chez nous les spectacles; c'est une coterie particulière de gens du monde, de gens d'art et de lettres, de personnes des deux sexes à qui leur rang ou leur fortune a permis de cultiver leur esprit: c'est l'élite de la nation à laquelle se joint un très petit nombre de gens qui tiennent au peuple par leur état ou par leur profession.[2]

Yet a dozen years later his successor, Meister, speaks contemptuously of the new spectators who in recent years had found their way into the cheapest part of the theatre—the parterre—which furnished standing room only to male spectators:

En effet, le parterre était composé, il y a quinze ans, de l'honnête bourgeoisie et des hommes de lettres, tous gens ayant fait leurs études, ayant des connaissances plus ou moins étendues, mais en ayant enfin. Le luxe les a tous fait monter aux secondes loges, qui ne jugent point, ou dont le jugement, au moins, reste sans influence; c'est le parterre seul qui décide du sort d'une pièce. Aujourd'hui cet aréopage est composé de journaliers, de garçons perruquiers, de marmitons; qu'attendre de pareils sujets? et peut-on se méprendre à la cause des disparates de leurs jugements?[3]

Meister obviously exaggerates; what this and other contemporary evidence does show is that for most of the eighteenth century the vast majority of the spectators in the cheapest part of theatres like the Comédie-Française were lawyers, schoolmasters, writers, students, in

---

[1] Ibid. xx. 252.   [2] *Correspondance littéraire* vi. 171.   [3] Ibid. x. 341.

a word 'intellectuals', members of the liberal professions, merchants, and so on—in other words what can be loosely described as 'middle class'.

Audiences at theatres like the Comédie-Française and the Théâtre italien were still remarkably small, especially when one thinks of the way in which the population of the capital's half a million inhabitants was swollen by visitors from the provinces and from abroad. The average number of spectators who paid for admission at the Comédie-Française in the period 1715–50 was actually below that for the first thirty-five years of the theatre's existence, from 1680 to 1715; it works out at roughly 117,000 (the register for 1739–40 is unfortunately missing). It is less easy to perform the same calculation for the Théâtre italien as so many registers for this period are missing; but the average for the years for which we have the necessary figures works out at the even lower figure of 80,000.[1]

From the middle of the century onwards the average figure for attendances at both theatres rose sharply. If it is only possible to make the calculation for the Comédie-Française down to Easter 1774,[2] the average down to that date rose by over 50,000 to approximately 168,000. Nor is that the whole story; in addition to selling a number of *abonnements à vie*, from the 1750s onwards the Comédie-Française derived a very considerable income from hiring out its *petites loges*, and the occupants of these, while they reduced the number of seats hitherto available for paying spectators, were obviously not recorded in the registers. At the Théâtre italien, where there were also quite a number of *petites loges*, the number of spectators paying at the door rose even more steeply, if rather unevenly, between 1750 and 1789, partly no doubt because this theatre several times changed its character. Down to its amalgamation with the Opéra-Comique in 1762, attendances were fairly large, but they swelled considerably after this change, reaching nearly 250,000 in 1763–4. After that came a decline (the French actors were dismissed in 1769), followed by a rise to 1779–80; in most of these years attendances totalled over 200,000. In 1780 it was the turn of the Italian actors to go and French actors were brought back; three years later the company moved into its new theatre, and down to 1788–9 attendances came to over 200,000.[3]

---

[1] Lagrave, *Le Théâtre et le public à Paris*, p. 185.

[2] This is the date at which H. C. Lancaster chose to end his second volume on the registers of the Comédie-Française.

[3] Figures calculated from Brenner, *The Théâtre Italien*.

None the less throughout the period from 1750 to 1789 the number of spectators who might be expected to support a new play during its first run still remained extremely small, judged by modern standards. This is puzzling in view of the steep rise in the number of spectators at the Comédie-Française after 1750. Various writers of the time stress how short this first run was. In 1765, for instance, a contemporary noted: 'Il a paru depuis quinze ans sur la scène française plus d'un ouvrage digne d'y reparaître dans tous les temps. Vingt représentations, au plus, ont épuisé le concours du public.'[1] It is a curious fact that none of the new plays which were put on at the Comédie-Française between 1750 and 1774 (the date at which Lancaster's figures break off) was seen by as many as 30,000 spectators during its first run. The most successful play in this period was the *Iphigénie en Tauride* of Guimond de La Touche which in 1757–8 reached twenty-seven performances and attracted well over 27,000 spectators to the theatre; but Sedaine's *Le Philosophe sans le savoir*, although it had twenty-eight performances attracted only 21,000 paying spectators and, its first run being interrupted by internal quarrels in the Comédie-Française, de Belloy's *Le Siège de Calais*, another of the successes of the period, attracted only 19,000 spectators during these eighteen performances.[2]

For the period between 1774 and 1789 we find similar figures for successful plays. *Le Barbier de Séville* had twenty-seven performances during its first run and drew 24,000 paying spectators to the Comédie-Française. Nine years later its success was completely dwarfed by the phenomenal first run of *Le Mariage de Figaro*—seventy-three performances in nine months (one of them given free) which attracted some 97,000 paying spectators, over three times as many as any of the previous successes of the century. How exceptional this success was in these last decades of the *ancien régime* is shown by comparison with that of *Le Barbier* or of that of other plays of the period. In 1788, for instance, Collin d'Harleville's comedy, *L'Optimiste*, had a first run of twenty-two performances and was seen by some 24,000 paying spectators. Clearly, *Le Mariage* drew to the theatre people who were not normally in the habit of frequenting the Comédie-Française. There is room for only one conclusion: that the public willing and able to support a new play was still small, not indeed perceptibly larger than it had been at the end of the seventeenth century.

[1] N.B. de La Dixmerie, *Lettres sur l'état présent de nos spectacles*, Amsterdam and Paris, 1765, p. 9.
[2] Another performance was given free.

As for the composition of these audiences, we have already seen how, in the closing decades of the *ancien régime*, a few representatives of the lower orders began to find their way to the privileged theatres. It is, however, very improbable that their small numbers exercised any real influence on the sort of plays performed at the Comédie-Française. The occupants of the cheapest part of the theatre continued, as in the previous century, to be overwhelmingly middle class. Yet although the middle classes were powerfully represented in the Paris theatres, we must not leave out of account the place occupied in them by the representatives of the upper classes of a society in which blue blood still retained an importance difficult to grasp today. French society in this period continued to be dominated by the royal family, the princes of the blood, and the countless lords and ladies who inhabited Paris and Versailles.

Little more than a dozen years before the Revolution we find Voltaire upbraiding Shakespeare for daring to introduce into a tragedy such a monstrous phrase as 'Not a mouse stirring'. In his *Lettre à MM. de l'Académie française* in which he denounced Shakespeare and his translator, Letourneur, he exclaims: 'Oui, monsieur, un soldat peut répondre ainsi dans un corps de garde; mais non pas sur le théâtre, devant les premières personnes d'une nation, qui s'expriment noblement, et devant qui il faut s'exprimer de même.'[1] The importance of the upper-class spectators in the theatres of the time is also brought out in his vivid description of a first night:

C'est un grand jour pour le beau monde oisif de Paris qu'une première représentation. Les cabales battent le tambour, on se dispute les loges, les valets de chambre vont à midi remplir le théâtre.[2] La pièce est jugée avant qu'on l'ait vue: femmes contre femmes, petits-maîtres contre petits-maîtres, sociétés contre sociétés. Les cafés sont comblés de gens qui disputent. La foule est dans la rue en attendant qu'elle soit au parterre.[3]

The ladies in the *premières loges* and the most aristocratic or wealthy male spectators on the stage were an important part of the audience, socially as well as financially. When seats on the stage were finally abolished at the Comédie-Française in 1759, Collé wrote of the change:

L'illusion théâtrale est actuellement entière; on ne voit plus César prêt à dépoudrer un fat assis sur le premier rang du théâtre, et Mithridate expirer au milieu de tous gens de notre connaissance; l'ombre de Ninus heurter et coudoyer un fermier général, et Camille tomber morte dans la coulisse sur

---

[1] *Œuvres complètes*, ed. L. Moland, 52 vols., Paris, 1877–85, xxx. 363.
[2] In order to reserve seats for their masters.   [3] *Correspondence* xii. 434 (1752).

Marivaux et Saint-Foix[1] qui s'avancent ou se reculent pour se prêter à l'assassinat de cette Romaine par la main d'Horace, son frère, qui fait rejaillir son sang sur ces deux auteurs comiques.[2]

From this same period of the century dated the very popular innovation of *petites loges*, private boxes which could be hired by the year. Women in particular loved them—and it goes without saying that these women belonged to the wealthiest and most aristocratic sections of Paris society—for reasons sarcastically described by Mercier:

Il faut donc, quand on est femme, avoir dans une *petite loge* son épagneul, son coussin, sa chaufferette, mais surtout un petit fat à lorgnette, qui vous instruit de tout ce qui entre et de tout ce qui sort, et qui vous nomme les acteurs. Cependant la dame a dans son éventail une petite ouverture, où est enchâssé un verre, de sorte qu'elle voit sans être vue.[3]

The important place occupied by the aristocratic and wealthy sections of society in Paris theatre audiences is underlined by Mme Riccoboni in the preface to her *Nouveau théâtre anglais*, published in 1769. The crudity of so much English drama, she maintains, is to be explained by a fundamental difference in the theatre audiences of London and Paris:

A Paris les grands et les riches suivent assidûment les spectacles. A Londres les personnes distinguées vont rarement à la comédie; l'emploi de leur temps et l'heure de leurs repas ne leur permettent guère d'être libres quand elle commence. C'est donc à la bourgeoisie, même au peuple, que l'on est obligé de plaire.[4]

When these lines got her into trouble with her old friend, David Garrick, she expanded her remarks and had this to say about audiences at the Opéra, Comédie-Française, and Théâtre italien:

Ici les premiers du royaume font leur séjour habituel du théâtre; les dames ont de petites loges à l'année, la comédie est le rendez-vous de la bonne compagnie. Elle ne divertit guère, mais elle occupe beaucoup. On disserte, on prône, on cabale; mille fainéants titrés n'ont d'autre ressource contre l'ennui que les chauffoirs des trois spectacles.[5]

Such a passage leaves us in no doubt as to the importance of the aristocratic section of the audience in these theatres only twenty years before the Revolution.

[1] These two playwrights enjoyed the privilege of free admission to the theatre.
[2] *Journal et mémoires*, ii. 172.   [3] *Tableau de Paris*, ii. 188.
[4] *Le Nouveau Théâtre anglais*, 2 vols., Paris, 1769, i, pp. viii–ix.
[5] D. Garrick, *Private Correspondence*, 2 vols., London, 1831–2, ii. 561.

The drama of the age certainly reflects very clearly the tastes, interests, and prejudices of the upper classes of the capital for whom theatre-going was such an important occupation. The playwrights of the period inherited from the seventeenth century the tradition that the principal characters of a tragedy must be of high birth, preferably of royal blood. Though the principle was challenged in the second half of the eighteenth century, only a small number of tragedies—including the highly successful patriotic drama, de Belloy's *Le Siège de Calais*, performed at the Comédie-Française in 1765 and portraying the famous episode of the Burghers of Calais—brought on the stage before 1789 characters of less exalted birth.

In the shocked comments on Shakespeare made by many French critics of this period one of the chief charges levelled against him is that he lacked any notion of the dignity of tragedy. Instead of confining himself to portraying characters of exalted birth he brought on to the stage a motley *canaille* of artisans, soldiers, and grave-diggers. Shakespeare also offended against other canons of the aristocratic taste of eighteenth-century France. He had no respect for the sacred rule of the proprieties (*les bienséances*) in either the themes or the language of his plays. The low manners and speech of the vulgar characters whom he introduced into his tragedies even infected those of their betters and completely destroyed the solemn, dignified tone of tragedy. Instead of rigorously excluding all comic elements and all realistic and trivial scenes, Shakespeare wallowed in them and thus completely destroyed the atmosphere of the genre.

If we look at the famous eighteenth letter of Voltaire's *Lettres philosophiques*, we see that he was horrified at some of the things that he found in plays like *Othello* and *Hamlet* even though he could not help regarding Shakespeare as a man of genius:

Vous savez que, dans la tragédie du *More de Venise*, pièce très touchante, un mari étrangle sa femme sur le théâtre, et quand la pauvre femme est étranglée, elle s'écrie qu'elle meurt très injustement. Vous n'ignorez pas que, dans *Hamlet*, des fossoyeurs creusent une fosse en buvant, en chantant des vaude-villes, et en faisant sur les têtes de mort qu'ils rencontrent des plaisanteries convenables à gens de leur métier.

He goes on to speak with equal disgust of what he had found in *Julius Caesar*—'les plaisanteries des cordonniers et des savetiers romains introduits sur la scène avec Brutus et Cassius'. Judged by the aristo-cratic standards of the age, Shakespeare's plays were bound to seem to all except a handful of French critics the very antithesis of tragedy;

despite their flashes of genius they appeared to be the outpourings of an ignorant barbarian whose only thought was to pander to the low instincts of the mob.

The influence of the polite society of Paris on the development of comedy in this period is perhaps even more striking. In his comedies Molière took in all classes of society—nobles, bourgeois, and peasants— but there was a marked tendency among eighteenth-century playwrights to confine their attention more and more exclusively to the portrayal of characters drawn from the upper classes of society. *Marquis, comtesses,* and *chevaliers,* with an occasional *président* or *conseiller* or perhaps a *fermier général* thrown in, tend to monopolize the stage. Among the numerous protests against this state of affairs which were made from the middle of the century onwards the most striking was that of Rousseau in *La Nouvelle Héloïse.* He makes Saint-Preux during his visit to Paris declare that nowadays comedy confines itself to reproducing 'les conversations d'une centaine de maisons de Paris':

Hors de cela, on n'y apprend rien des mœurs des Français. Il y a dans cette grande ville cinq ou six cent mille âmes dont il n'est jamais question sur la scène. Molière osa peindre des bourgeois et des artisans aussi bien que des marquis. . . . Mais les auteurs d'aujourd'hui qui sont des gens d'un autre air, se croiraient déshonorés s'ils savaient ce qui se passe au comptoir d'un marchand ou dans la boutique d'un ouvrier; il ne leur faut que des interlocuteurs illustres, et ils cherchent dans le rang de leurs personnages l'élévation qu'ils ne peuvent tirer de leur génie.

What is more, his hero is made to argue, that is what the theatre-going public of Paris wants:

Les spectateurs eux-mêmes sont devenus si délicats qu'ils craindraient de se compromettre à la comédie comme en visite, et ne daigneraient pas aller voir en représentation des gens de moindre condition qu'eux. Ils sont comme les seuls habitants de la terre; tout le reste n'est rien à leurs yeux. Avoir un carrosse, un suisse, un maître d'hotel, c'est être comme tout le monde. Pour être comme tout le monde il faut être comme très peu de gens. Ceux qui vont à pied ne sont pas du monde; ce sont des bourgeois, des hommes du peuple, des gens de l'autre monde, et l'on dirait qu'un carrosse n'est pas tant nécessaire pour se conduire que pour exister.

The diatribe concludes with the words: 'On n'y sait plus montrer les hommes qu'en habit doré. Vous diriez que la France n'est peuplée que de comtes et de chevaliers.'[1]

[1] *Œuvres complètes,* ii. 252.

In the same outburst Rousseau also complains that tragedy deals with characters and subjects too remote from the experience of ordinary people. This was a theme which was to be taken up by other writers of the second half of the century, by Beaumarchais, for instance, who, before he found his true vocation in comedy, wrote two *drames*, *Eugénie* and *Les Deux Amis*. In his *Essai sur le genre dramatique sérieux*, published in 1767 with the first of these plays, he roundly declares that the preference for kings and princes in tragedy is a matter of pure vanity and that the portrayal of such characters merely reduces the interest which the ordinary spectator takes in tragic heroes. 'Que me font à moi, sujet paisible d'un état monarchique du dix-huitième siècle, les révolutions d'Athènes et de Rome?' he asks. 'Quel véritable intérêt puis-je prendre à la mort d'un tyran du Péloponnèse? au sacrifice d'une jeune princesse en Aulide? Il n'y a dans tout cela rien à voir pour moi, aucune moralité qui me convienne.'[1]

The new genre of the *drame*, of which Diderot had made himself the theorist ten years earlier, aimed at portraying characters closer to the average spectator both in time and in social status than those of tragedy. The *drame* was intended by Diderot to occupy a place between the two existing genres of comedy and tragedy, and to approach more closely now to the former, now, in the form of domestic tragedy (*la tragédie bourgeoise*), to the latter. He claimed that domestic tragedy would portray characters drawn from a world close to the average spectator, and not from a more or less remote past:

Elle est plus voisine de nous. C'est le tableau des malheurs qui nous environnent. Quoi! vous ne concevez pas l'effet que produiraient sur vous une scène réelle, des habits vrais, des discours proportionnés aux actions, des actions simples, des dangers dont il est impossible que vous n'ayez tremblé pour vos parents, vos amis, pour vous-même?[2]

In a letter written to a theatre manager in Bordeaux Beaumarchais said of his second *drame* which dealt with the commercial life of Lyons and contained enthusiastic praise of the role of the merchant in society:

Elle a été jouée à Lyon, à Marseille et à Rouen avec le plus grand succès. J'aurais été bien trompé dans mes vues si le commerçant que j'ai cherché à montrer dans le plus beau jour en cet ouvrage n'était pas satisfait du rôle digne et honnête que je fais jouer à un homme de son état. . . . Je souhaite

[1] *Théâtre complet*, ed. R. d'Hermies, Paris, 1952, p. 39.
[2] *Writings on the Theatre*, p. 85.

qu'elle plaise aux négociants, cette pièce qui a été faite pour eux et en général pour honorer les gens du tiers état.[1]

Mercier, who was bold enough to argue that the theatre ought to abandon its traditional role of entertaining only the upper classes of society and should endeavour to appeal to the masses, naturally went further than either Diderot or Beaumarchais in demanding that characters of the most humble birth should be portrayed on the stage. He attacks the prevailing prejudice in the most bitter terms:

Mais voir les conditions humaines les plus basses, les plus rampantes! ajoutera-t-on encore, les mettre sur la scène! Et pourquoi pas? Homme dédaigneux, approche; que je te juge à ton tour. Qui es-tu? qui te donne le droit d'être hautain? Je vois ton habit, tes laquais, tes chevaux, ton équipage; mais toi, que fais-tu? . . . Tu souris, je t'entends; tu es homme de cour, tu consumes tes jours dans une inaction frivole, dans des intrigues puériles, dans des fatigues ambitieuses et risibles. Tu ruines tes créanciers pour paraître un homme comme il faut . . .

Verge avilie du despotisme, un tisserand, son bonnet sur la tête, me paraît plus estimable et plus utile que toi. Si je te mets sur la scène, ce sera pour la honte. Mais ces ouvriers, ces artisans peuvent y paraître avec noblesse; ce sont des hommes, que je reconnais tels à leurs mœurs, à leurs travaux. Et toi, né pour l'opprobre du genre humain, plût à Dieu que tu fusses mort à l'instant de ta naissance![2]

Yet if we look at the *drames* of Diderot, Beaumarchais, or even Mercier, we find a considerable gap between theory and practice. Diderot's *Le Père de famille* and *Le Fils naturel* portray the same world as most of the comedies of the time; their characters are drawn from the wealthy and even aristocratic sections of society. In *Les Deux Amis*, the play which Beaumarchais wrote 'pour honorer les gens du tiers état', he may transport the spectator to the despised provinces and show his main characters at grips with commercial and financial problems, but the persons he portrays belong to the nobility or are on the very fringe of it. Mercier, it is true, does sometimes depict quite plebeian characters— a peasant or a poor weaver, for instance—but the effect is destroyed by his fondness for the hackneyed device of a touching recognition-scene which suddenly transforms his characters of low or bourgeois birth into persons of rank or substance.

[1] *Théâtre complet: Lettres relatives à son théâtre*, ed. M. Allem, Paris, 1934, pp. 543–4.
[2] *Du théâtre, ou Nouvel essai sur l'art dramatique*, Amsterdam, 1773, pp. 137–8.

For all their timidity such attempts to portray bourgeois and plebeian characters on the stage had in general a hostile reception from the critics. The first reaction of Condorcet—the future revolutionary, Condorcet—to Fenouillot de Falbaire's *drame, Le Fabricant de Londres*, when it received its one and only performance at the Comédie-Française in 1771, was one of disgust at the characters portrayed in it. He wrote to Turgot: 'On a donné avant-hier, aux Français, une tragédie bourgeoise de M. de Falbaire; elle est lourdement tombée. Les mœurs insipides de la petite bourgeoisie y étaient peintes avec une vérité dégoûtante.'[1] Nor was the new genre popular with the actors of the Comédie-Française, and several authors of *drames*, especially Mercier, had difficulty in having their plays performed anywhere in Paris. It seems rather as if it was in the great commercial centres of the provinces such as Lyons, Marseilles, or Bordeaux that the new genre of the *drame* enjoyed its greatest popularity. In the preface to *Le Barbier de Séville*, published five years after *Les Deux Amis*, Beaumarchais offers ironical submission to the traditional view of the functions of tragedy and comedy: 'Présenter des hommes d'une condition moyenne accablés et dans le malheur, fi donc! On ne doit jamais les montrer que bafoués. Les citoyens ridicules et les rois malheureux, voilà tout le théâtre existant et possible, et je me le tiens pour dit; c'est fait, je ne veux plus quereller avec personne.' The resistance which was encountered by the demand for a drama which would deal with the lives and problems of ordinary people, and the very timidity of its practitioners throw interesting light on the hold of aristocratic traditions in the literary world of Paris. The situation in the theatre gives one some inkling of the influence which, partly through the *salons*, the upper classes of the capital continued to exercise on all forms of literature down to 1789.

The series of political and social upheavals which marked the years 1789–99 had considerable repercussions in the theatre. The decree of 13 January 1791 created a revolution in the Paris theatrical world. Under the *ancien régime* not only was the approval of the authorities required for the opening of a new theatre, but restrictions were imposed on the type of play which could be performed in it. The Comédie-Française, for instance, had a monopoly of all the plays which it and its antecedent bodies such as Molière's theatre and the Hôtel de Bourgogne had acquired in over a century; no other theatre in Paris could perform them or for that matter put on a tragedy. Similarly, the Théâtre italien

[1] *Correspondance inédite de Condorcet et de Turgot*, ed. C. Henry, Paris, 1883, p. 36.

had a monopoly of Paris performances of plays which it had acquired
from their authors, and it could also put on new comedies and *drames*
as well as *opéras-comiques*. The first two clauses of the decree of 13
January 1791 not only allowed any citizen to establish a theatre and
have plays performed in it, but they also removed all restrictions on the
type of plays which could be performed there:

Art.I. Tout citoyen pourra élever un théâtre public, et y faire représenter
des pièces de tous les genres, en faisant, préalablement à l'établissement de son
théâtre, sa déclaration à la municipalité du lieu.
II. Les ouvrages des auteurs morts depuis cinq ans et plus sont une propriété
publique, et peuvent, nonobstant tous anciens privilèges qui sont abolis,
être représentés sur tous les théâtres indistinctement.[1]

It is notorious that as a result of this law new theatres proliferated in
Paris; over forty were founded in the next few years under a bewildering variety of names and functioning in a confusing number of different
buildings.

The two privileged theatres, in particular the Comédie-Française,
had a chequered history in these years. The Comédie-Française
suffered from internal dissensions, and in 1791 some of its leading
actors, including Talma, set up a rival theatre; in 1793 most of the
members of the original company found their theatre closed and themselves in prison where they escaped the guillotine by an absolute miracle. After their release there were fresh splits and it was only in 1799
that the various fragments of the company could be reunited, and then
not in their old theatre, but in the building which they still occupy in
the Palais-Royal. The Théâtre italien had its troubles too; in 1793 it
changed its name to Opéra-Comique, but it was not until 1801 that the
present organization bearing that name was founded by a fusion
between it and the Troupe de Monsieur, a company founded in 1789.
From the turmoil of these years there eventually emerged another
national theatre, the Odéon. Before 1799 the Comédie-Française had
left empty its new theatre on the Left Bank, and from 1797 onwards
attempts, not very successful, were made to reopen it. Then in 1799 it
was burnt down in a disastrous fire and could not be rebuilt until 1808.
It was reoccupied in that year by a company which had been performing in another theatre, known since 1804 as the Théâtre de l'Impératrice.

Quite a number of the theatres founded during the Revolution had

[1] *Le Moniteur universel*, vii. 118.

closed their doors before Napoleon came to power. He took a considerable interest in what was going on in the theatrical world, particularly that of Paris, and especially in the state of the revived Comédie-Française. By decrees issued between June 1806 and July 1807 he can be said to have returned to the theatrical policy of the *ancien régime* since not only did he reduce to eight the number of theatres in the capital, but he also laid down what types of play they could perform. The Comédie-Française was assigned tragedy, comedy, and the *drame*, its repertoire being composed of all the plays which had been acquired by it or its antecedent bodies. It was allowed to perform comedies originally acquired by the Théâtre italien. The Théâtre de l'Impératrice, soon to be installed at the Odéon, was considered as an annex of the Comédie-Française and was restricted to comedy; its repertoire was to consist of new comedies written for it and it was to share with the Comédie-Française the right to perform plays from the Théâtre italien. The repertoire of the Opéra and Opéra-Comique was similarly carefully defined as was that of the four other theatres which were to continue to exist. The Gaîté and the Ambigu-Comique were confined to melodramas, spectacular plays, pantomimes, and farces, and the Variétés and Vaudeville to short plays interspersed with songs and to parodies. The decree of 20 July 1807 which finally regulated the number of theatres and the repertoire allotted to them required the closure of all other theatres before 15 August. One prominent victim of these measures was the Théâtre de la Porte-Saint-Martin which had been founded in 1802; however, it was to reopen in 1814 and to become one of the leading Paris theatres. As in many other spheres Napoleonic legislation was to have a long life in the theatre; it is true that the Restoration and subsequent regimes allowed a certain number of new theatres to open, but government permission continued to be required and the repertoire of theatres continued to be fixed by it. It was not until 1864 that a decree of Napoleon's nephew brought back 'la liberté des théâtres' in both senses of the word.

The events of the tumultuous years from 1789 to 1799 inevitably had considerable effects on theatre audiences; these throw light both on the sort of spectators who frequented theatres before 1789 and the audiences which were to be found in them in the following century. How much the Comédie-Française had depended on the patronage of the aristocratic and wealthy sections of the community was clearly demonstrated by the catastrophic fall which the Revolution quickly brought about in the income it derived from its *petites loges*. As early as June

1790 Meister noted: 'Sur cent mille écus de loges à l'année que retirait la Comédie Française, elle en a conservé à peine un tiers.'[1] Marie-Joseph Chénier's dossier in the archives of the Comédie-Française furnishes a document concerning the performance of his highly controversial tragedy, *Charles IX*, which contains the laconic sentence: 'Cet ouvrage a fait perdre à la Comédie 162,489 l. de petites loges par an.' On the other hand, the actors were conscious of the fact that under the new conditions they had an obligation, as their spokesman put it at the opening of a new theatrical season in April 1790, 'de procurer, à la classe des citoyens les moins aisés, la facilité d'assister à la représentation de nos chefs-d'œuvre', and he announced a plan to add to the theatre more than six hundred cheaper seats. In the end this proved financially impracticable, but in March of the following year the prices of seats in the parterre and galleries were reduced.[2]

The law of 13 January 1791 undoubtedly led to strange results by its freeing of the repertoire of the Comédie-Française and the Théâtre italien. The Théâtres des Boulevards which before the Revolution had catered mainly, though by no means exclusively, for the poorer classes of the capital, were now free to perform the masterpieces which had hitherto been the monopoly of the state theatres. The young Pixerécourt describes the result in vivid terms in a document which he composed in 1795:

Par la Révolution, ou, pour mieux dire, par le génie de la liberté, si le peuple fut appelé à la jouissance de tous les théâtres, tous les théâtres, par contrecoup, furent appelés à la jouissance de toutes les pièces; et, dans ce moment d'ébullition, Corneille étonné monte chez Nicolet,[3] et Taconnet[4] au tombeau ne désespère pas d'arriver sur les planches de Le Kain.[5]

However, we have seen that when things settled down again under Napoleon, the theatres of the capital were compelled to restrict themselves to the types of drama allotted to them. In the meantime, largely through the successes achieved by Pixerécourt himself, a new genre, that of the melodrama, had been created. Although it was called a 'drame lyrique', his first melodrama, *Victor ou l'enfant de la forêt*, was

---

[1] Grimm, *Correspondance littéraire* xvi. 27.

[2] C. G. Étienne and A. Martainville, *Histoire du Théâtre français depuis le commencement de la Révolution jusqu'à la réunion générale*, 4 vols., Paris, 1802, i. 95; ii. 48.

[3] The founder of the theatre ultimately known as the Gaîté.

[4] Actor and playwright, author of very popular playlets for Nicolet's theatre.

[5] E. Estève, 'Observations de Guilbert de Pixerécourt sur les théâtres de la Révolution', *Revue d'histoire littéraire*, 1916, pp. 551–2.

put on at the Ambigu-Comique in 1798, and the last, *Latude ou trente-cinq ans de captivité* at the Gaîté, a theatre of which he was now manager, in 1834. He was himself a cultured man and it is difficult to accept the literal truth of the words attributed to him in defence of his style: 'J'écris pour ceux qui ne savent pas lire.'[1] Indeed, it is flatly contradicted by what he says of the new genre in an essay, 'Le Mélodrame', written towards the end of his career as a playwright:

Le mélodrame a épuré le langage du peuple qui, après l'avoir vu jouer, le loue, moyennant deux sous, et le lit jusqu'à ce qu'il le sache par cœur. La poésie, ce langage des dieux, ne pouvait être comprise que par des spectateurs éclairés et instruits; la tragédie n'est point en harmonie avec l'éducation du peuple. Les grands intérêts politiques qui en font presque toujours la base, exigent, pour être appréciés, de longues études, des connaissances profondes, étendues et variées. Il a donc fallu créer un théâtre, un genre et un intérêt populaires. De là le mélodrame.[2]

Undoubtedly this type of drama was to keep its appeal well into the next period.

When Napoleon's empire collapsed in 1814 the literary and theatrical life of France had undergone considerable changes since the death of Louis XIV. The reading public had broadened with the growth of literacy; theatre audiences had expanded, though, so far as our information goes, mainly in the capital. Relations between writer and publisher and the dealings of the playwright with theatre managements were beginning to take on their modern form, while literary patronage was now clearly declining in importance. Yet these changes had been for the most part slow and gradual; many new factors were to transform the whole relationship between writer and public in the hundred years which followed down to 1914.

[1] Quoted in W. G. Hartog, *Guilbert de Pixerécourt, sa vie, son mélodrame, sa technique et son influence*, Paris, 1913, p. 191.
[2] *Paris, ou le livre des cent-et-un*, 15 vols., Paris, 1831–4, vi. 340.

V   The Nineteenth Century

THE position of French as an international language undoubtedly suffered a decline in the course of the nineteenth century. Despite the enduring prestige of French culture, in 1914 French was less important among the languages of the world than it had been a hundred years earlier.

That decline had already begun during the Revolutionary and Napoleonic period, after the tremendous vogue which French had enjoyed among the cultured classes of Europe since the age of Louis XIV. The new nationalist spirit which led to an identification of language with nationhood combined with the relatively slow growth in the population of France to reduce the importance of the French language in Europe and in the world at large. It is true that throughout this period it remained the language of diplomacy; the negotiations for the Treaty of Frankfort which sealed the victory of Germany over France in 1870 were conducted in French and the treaty was drawn up in French. Yet in the affairs of the world it was gradually giving way to English, a language which was spoken by vastly more people; by 1914 Britain and the United States alone had a population roughly three times the size of the French-speaking populations of France, Belgium, Switzerland, and Canada put together.

Although France's population was doubled by the enormous increase in her overseas possessions under the Third Republic which, starting out from the base in Algeria acquired by Charles X and subsequent rulers, extended French control over great tracts of North and Central Africa as well as Indo-China, by 1914 this had not greatly increased the number of French-speaking people. In 1899 Ferdinand Brunot wrote sorrowfully of the small impact made by the French language in the colonies, old and new:

Dans les pays de protectorat et les colonies, qui comprennent de neuf à dix millions de kilomètres carrés et de 30 à 40 millions d'habitants, nous eussions dû trouver quelques compensations aux échecs subis ailleurs. L'incurie des gouvernements en a décidé autrement. Sauf dans les anciennes colonies Saint-Pierre et Miquelon (6,000 habitants), la Guadeloupe (167,000), la Martinique (190,000), la Réunion (168,000), où du reste le français s'est transformé dans la bouche de mulâtres en un patois créole, les fonctionnaires, marins, militaires, sont à peu près seuls avec quelques rares colons à parler français. La masse indigène n'est vraiment entamée nulle part. Même en Algérie pacifiée depuis cinquante ans, le nombre des enfants qui connaissent notre langue est dérisoire. Les statistiques ne sont pas fournies—on n'oserait point—mais nous savons par ailleurs où en est la question.[1]

Clearly, the decline of French as an international language was slow and gradual; for one thing the growth in the population of other countries and the spread of education meant that, given the prestige enjoyed by French literature, there was still a considerable demand in foreign countries for the works of French writers. The position was very different during the Restoration period from what it was by, say, 1900; by that date the position of the French language in Europe and the world at large was not at all what it had been when Rivarol published *De l'universalité de la langue française* in 1784.

On the other hand, with the gradual spread of education inside the frontiers of France the language continued its advance against dialects and against the other tongues spoken in the outlying regions. The situation in Alsace was, of course, complicated by the predominance of German from 1871 down to its return to France in 1918. Improvements in communications first by better roads and then the development of a national railway network and the gradual introduction of conscription combined with the expansion of education to speed up the spread of the French language inside the country. If the dialects of French and the other languages spoken within her frontiers were far from being wiped out, they felt the impact of standard French, and even many country-dwellers who retained their native speech became more or less bilingual and could understand French and even speak it if the need arose. The growth of literacy and the emergence, from the 1860s onwards, of a cheap, popular press undoubtedly contributed a great deal to this process.

The gradual reduction in illiteracy continued through this period. The Maggiolo inquiry of 1877–9 into the number of persons who at different dates were able to sign their names in the register when they were married showed a marked improvement by 1871–5 compared with the figures for 1786–90. The percentage of men signing their names had risen from 47 to 78 and that of women from 27 to 66. There was a parallel decline in illiteracy among conscripts; this fell from over 50 per cent in the 1830s to under 20 in 1880. As in earlier periods there

[1] 'La Langue française au XIXᵉ siècle', in L. Petit de Julleville, *Histoire de la langue et de la littérature françaises*, 8 vols., Paris, 1896–9, viii. 862.

were marked differences from region to region and between town and country as well as between men and women. If the earlier gap between the performance of men and women was being gradually closed, its continued existence is explained very simply by the slower progress made in the nineteenth century in the education of girls. By 1910 the proportion of men and women on marriage and of conscripts who were illiterate had dropped to below 5 per cent.[1]

In the first part of the nineteenth century elementary education continued to be dominated by the Catholic Church. The village schoolmaster who was paid by the *commune* was the *curé*'s second in command, often acting as sexton, bell-ringer, and precentor. During the Restoration the state left it largely to local initiative to found schools, and although a considerable number were set up in these years, it was not until 1833 with the Loi Guizot that a state system was at last established. Even so France was thirty-seven years ahead of England in this respect. As one of the leaders of the so-called 'parti de la résistance' under Louis Philippe, Guizot had very narrow views as to what either the pupils in the state schools or the teachers in training should be taught. Although the law did not make primary education either compulsory or free, not only did Guizot secure the founding of large numbers of training colleges (*écoles normales*), but he effected considerable improvements in the salaries and housing of teachers who in the past had generally been miserably paid and often compelled to eke out a living by taking all manner of part-time jobs. By 1848 considerable progress had been made in the field of primary education; in his memoirs Guizot could summarize the results of the 1833 law thus:

En 1832, avant la loi du 28 juin 1833, il y avait en France 42,092 écoles primaires, communales ou privées, et dans ces écoles 1,935,624 élèves, garçons ou filles. Au 1er janvier, 1848, sous l'influence de la loi du 28 juin 1833, le nombre des écoles primaires s'était élevée à 63,028, et celui des élèves à 3,530,135. Ainsi, dans l'espace de quatorze années, l'instruction primaire avait acquis 20,936 écoles et 1,594,511 élèves de plus.[2]

Although the primary education offered was not free, provision was made for the poorer children to pay no fees. In 1837 one child in three was receiving free education, and by the 1870s this figure had risen to over half. In these forty years considerable progress was undoubtedly made though it varied a good deal from region to region; it was much

---

[1] See the graph, 'Proportion d'illettrés 1830–1914', in A. Prost, *L'Enseignement en France, 1800–1967*, Paris, 1968, p. 96.

[2] *Mémoires pour servir à l'histoire de mon temps*, 8 vols., Paris, 1858–67, viii. 613.

faster in the departments north of a line drawn from Mont-Saint-Michel to Geneva than in those to the south of it. Girls were much less favoured than boys. Often the village began with a boys' school to which a few girls were admitted; then when the village school was too small, a separate one for girls—often run by nuns—would be built. Again, there were still very few training colleges for women teachers. It was only in the period 1850–80 that rapid progress was made in the education of girls whereas with boys the big leap forward had taken place by the middle of the century.

Especially in the country attendance at school was far from satisfactory even among the boys and girls who were nominally on the register. Many of them spent only a few years at school, leaving at twelve or even ten, and there were great differences in attendance according to the season. Schools were most frequented in the depth of winter when there was nothing much to do on the land. Many peasants were unwilling or unable to see what advantages their offspring could derive from education. A gloomy account of the near illiteracy of the average peasant in 1871 is offered by Gobineau in his sombre reflections on the events of the previous year:

Lire, il ne sait pas lire, ou du moins il lit si obscurément et avec une telle peine que l'essayer lui cause beaucoup de répugnance et c'est ce qu'il fait rarement. Rien de plus simple. Il a fréquenté l'école depuis l'âge de six à sept ans jusqu' à douze, fort peu encouragé à ce faire par ses parents qui considéraient cela comme du temps perdu; les anciens du village, les hommes graves, les paysans riches, d'accord sur ce point, prononcent aujourd'hui, en 1871, qu'apprendre à lire et à écrire aux enfants des villages est un véritable malheur; du reste, pendant le temps consacré à des études si disputées, si contestées, il va sans dire que les élèves ne paraissent jamais en classe lorsqu'il y a la moisson à faire, de l'herbe à couper pour les lapins, des pommes de terre à arracher, du bois mort à ramasser, etc., etc., etc. A la fin de cinq à six années d'études aussi agitées, il n'y a rien d'extraordinaire à ce que l'enfant, désormais réclamé absolument par les travaux des champs et dont les études intellectuelles sont terminées pour jamais, ne possède au bout de ses doigts qu'une écriture aux formes fantastiques appliquées à une orthographe des plus extravagantes et un talent de lecture analogue. . . . Le paysan ne sait donc en réalité ni lire ni écrire.[1]

While this passage would appear to contain a certain amount of truth, it does not reflect adequately the undoubted progress made in previous decades. Non-attendance at elementary schools continued to cause

---

[1] *Ce qui est arrivé à la France en 1870*, ed. A. B. Duff, Paris, 1970, pp. 99–100.

problems even after the passing of the Ferry laws which were brought in as soon as the 'République des Ducs' gave way to the 'République des Républicains' in 1879.

The long struggle for the principles of 'gratuité, obligation, laïcité' in primary education was now brought to an end. In 1881 all fees in state primary schools were abolished, and in the following year attendance at school from the age of six to thirteen was made compulsory. What caused much more controversy was the secularization of state primary education; this was denounced in furious terms as 'l'école sans Dieu'. Henceforth the clergy were to exercise no control over state primary schools which were to remain completely neutral in matters of religion, though one day a week was to be left free for children to receive religious education outside the school if their parents should so desire. Primary education came more and more into the hands of the state though on the eve of the First World War about a million out of some five and a half million children were still taught in Church schools. More women teachers for the state schools were turned out by the training colleges set up in every department by a law of 1879.

In 1889 teachers in primary schools became fully fledged civil servants (*fonctionnaires*), as by a law passed in that year the local authorities ceased to be responsible for providing anything beyond the buildings and equipment of primary schools. A law of 1886 set up an *enseignement primaire supérieur* which took pupils for several years beyond the leaving age of thirteen. Entrants to the training colleges were recruited from the elementary sector of education, and it was extremely difficult for a pupil to pass from an elementary to a secondary school. In other words, elementary and secondary education were two completely separate worlds; the pejorative sense of the phrase, 'C'est un primaire', reflects the gap which existed between the two systems. None the less the hundred years between the downfall of Napoleon and the outbreak of the First World War did see a great leap forward with the virtual wiping-out of illiteracy and the creation of a vast new reading public.

In the field of secondary education the changes brought about by Napoleon's creation of the Université continued to operate. On paper the Université with the state *lycées* and the *collèges* run by the local authorities had a monopoly of secondary education, but in practice a great many Catholic schools existed outside the system, though in the first half of the century these were mainly run by private individuals and not by religious orders such as the Jesuits. The Revolution had seriously disrupted secondary education, and the number of boys receiving it, whether in *lycées, collèges,* or private schools, remained extremely small down to the middle of the century. There were only some 50,000 in 1820, and if this figure had risen to 70,000 by 1842, it is probable that secondary education was still making good the losses sustained through the Revolution.

From the 1840s onwards—the phenomenon was little more than recognized by the Loi Falloux passed in 1850 in the reaction against the Journées de juin—the Catholic Church's hold on education steadily increased, and the part played by the religious orders was now predominant. In 1863 at Toulouse Taine noted in his *Carnets de voyage*:

A Toulouse il y a soixante-dix-sept maisons religieuses sur une population de cent mille âmes; entre autres, trois énormes collèges, l'un ayant cinq cents élèves. Quand le père Léotade a été condamné,[1] beaucoup de gens l'ont déclaré martyr; l'année suivante, son collège a eu quarante élèves de plus à la rentrée.—. . . A Poitiers, à Rennes, le lycée est tombé de moitié par la concurrence . . .—A Paris, les pensionnats religieux font entrer par an, à Saint-Cyr, soixante-dix à quatre-vingts jeunes gens, qui font bande à part. Jusqu'à des bicoques comme Rethel, ils prennent tout et font tomber le petit collège municipal; tout cela depuis 1852, principalement par les Jésuites.[2]

Between 1842 and 1898 there was a very considerable expansion of secondary education for boys; the total number of pupils rose from some 70,000 to over 160,000. Yet although the numbers in the *lycées* and to some extent in the *collèges* run by local authorities rose fairly rapidly, by 1898 there were as many pupils in schools outside the public system as there were in it, and the Church secondary schools had substantially more pupils than the *lycées*. Naturally, this development was one which did not please the Republican majority in Parliament; hence the famous speech of Waldeck-Rousseau in 1900 about the 'deux jeunesses' who were growing up in France: 'Deux jeunesses . . . moins séparées encore par leur condition que par l'éducation qu'elles reçoivent grandissent sans se connaître, jusqu'au jour où elles se rencontreront, si dissemblables qu'elles risqueront de ne plus se comprendre.'

Secondary education for girls was no concern of the state until the establishment of the 'République des Républicains' in 1879. This did not mean that it did not exist, but it was given in private schools, run sometimes by lay teachers, but more often by nuns. Its scope was

---

[1] In 1847 Father Léotade, the bursar of a Catholic boarding-school in Toulouse, was sentenced to life imprisonment for the murder of a fourteen-year-old girl.

[2] *Carnets de voyage. Notes sur la province, 1863–1865,* Paris, 1897, p. 86.

somewhat restricted, as the main stress was on preparing upper- and middle-class girls to run a household that was well provided with servants. In the 1860s the Minister of Education, Victor Duruy, took the first timid step towards offering a very modest and limited form of secondary education for girls—the establishment of public lectures given by masters from the *lycées* to which girls would be brought by their mothers; this move aroused the furious hostility of the Catholic Church. However, once the Republicans were securely installed in power, they turned their attention to providing state secondary schools for girls. At first, by a law of 1880, only day schools were established, though local authorities were given powers to make provision for boarders. In the following year an École normale supérieure was set up at Sèvres to train teachers for these schools. Their numbers grew fairly rapidly; by 1883 there were 23 *lycées* and *collèges* for girls, and by 1913 this number had risen to 138. Even so at that date girls in secondary education were outnumbered by boys in the ratio of approximately 7 to 2, and the curriculum was a restricted one; it was not until 1924 that complete identity was established between the curriculum in secondary education for boys and girls.

In the hundred years since 1814 a considerable expansion in the numbers who received a secondary education had been achieved, and yet even at the end of this period only a very narrow layer of the population attained to this level. It can well be imagined that those who received a university education were a much tinier minority.

The new faculties of arts (*lettres*) and science set up by Napoleon in 1808 had for decades virtually no students in the modern sense of the term. They acted mainly as examining boards, dealing with a few candidates for the *licence* (the equivalent of our bachelor's degree) and with considerably more for the *baccalauréat* which, while it is closely akin to the Advanced Level of our General Certificate of Education, is in France a first degree and entitles the holder to enter a faculty to study for a *licence*. The relatively small numbers of pupils in secondary education is reflected in the fact that between 1816 and 1890 the numbers obtaining the *baccalauréat* ranged from some 2,000 to just under 7,000 towards the end of the period.

The professors in these two faculties gave public lectures when they felt so inclined, and while some of these, especially in Paris, drew large audiences, in the provinces they were often both ill attended and at a very low level. Taine, for instance, made the following notes in the course of a visit to Poitiers in 1864:

B . . . a vingt à soixante personnes à son cours, mais c'est le plus suivi. C . . . , professeur de philosophie, avait à peu près le même nombre d'auditeurs. La plupart sont des étudiants, ce qui empêche la bonne société d'y aller. En tout cas, selon B . . . , personne n'y prend intérêt, personne n'y travaille et n'est capable de suivre. Dans les villes comme Douai, Caen, c'est mieux: les gens du monde y amènent leurs filles; mais alors le cours devient anodin, agréable, une conversation de famille.[1]

The theatre critic, Francisque Sarcey, who as a young *lycée* master frequented the Faculté des lettres of Grenoble (he was the only student to attend the lectures of a very distinguished professor of Greek), gives a vivid account of its weaknesses:

Le professeur de philosophie était une manière de vieil aliéné, célèbre dans tout Grenoble par les excentricités de sa métaphysique. Celui de littérature française était un vieillard aimable, mais dont le cours eût peut-être été jugé un peu naïf dans un pensionnat de jeunes demoiselles. Leurs cours ne comptaient pas un seul étudiant; et, ce qui est plus extraordinaire, c'est que la ville, qui est pourtant un lieu de retraite pour les vieux éclopés de la guerre, ne leur fournissait pas un auditeur désireux de chauffer ses rhumatismes au feu ronflant du poêle et de la phrase. C'était le désert dans toute son horreur, et ces messieurs en étaient réduits à semer le bon grain de leur parole sur les bancs stériles de l'amphithéâtre.[2]

It goes without saying that at this date there were no matriculated women students; in his dictionary, published between 1863 and 1873 Littré defines *étudiante* as 'dans une espèce d'argot, grisette du quartier latin' and he goes on to give the example: 'Commis et grisettes, étudiants et étudiantes affluent dans ce bal.'

A very high proportion of French students were, of course, in Paris, but when we read of their activities—political or otherwise—in the period down to about 1880, we have to remember that they were virtually all medical or law students together with the pupils of the famous *grandes écoles,* founded during the Revolution, such as the École polytechnique or the École normale supérieure. There do not appear to be any detailed statistics available for the number of students in the different faculties before the 1880s, but the figures for graduates for the period 1876–80 (five-year average) show how small the number of students must have been, particularly in the faculties of arts and science:

[1] *Carnets de voyage,* p. 166.
[2] *Souvenirs de jeunesse,* Paris, 1885, p. 302.

Licence			Doctorat	
Lettres	*Sciences*	*Droit*	*Droit*	*Médecine*
155	165	1085	177	644[1]

The catastrophe of 1870 produced fresh thinking about higher education, and with the gradual consolidation of the Third Republic came considerable changes. Although it was not until 1896 that a law was passed setting up afresh universities in France, the faculties had already been strengthened in the 1880s. However, when the new law at last came, it was a great disappointment to many reformers as they had hoped that a small number of large universities would be set up in Paris and in a few provincial centres; instead, each of the sixteen *académies* was given its university. Many of these remained very small until after 1945.

In the closing years of the Second Empire France had some 5,000 students of law and 4,000 of medicine; by 1913 their numbers had swollen to some 16,000 and 11,000 respectively. From the 1880s onwards the number of students in the faculties of arts and science rose steadily, reaching about 6,000 in each by the eve of the First World War. The students in these two faculties were mainly absorbed into education. The total number of French students in the period 1911–13—some 40,000—reads strangely in the 1970s when it has reached almost twenty times that figure.

It is clear that while both university and secondary education underwent a considerable expansion in this period, it was a very gradual process and one which, even in the secondary field, affected only a very small minority of the population. The most significant contribution to the enormous growth in the reading public in these hundred years came from the expansion of elementary education and the virtual elimination of illiteracy.

One must not, however, overlook another important factor in that expansion. Though the population of France, especially from the middle of the century, grew much more slowly than in the previous period and in other countries such as England and Germany, the increase in the number of inhabitants was none the less considerable. Between the censuses of 1821 and 1911 the population of France, despite the loss of Alsace-Lorraine, increased by nearly a third—from some 30 millions to just under 40. Though this growth was unspectacular compared with what was happening in these years on this side

---

[1] Prost, *L'Enseignement en France*, p. 243.

of the Channel, in them France acquired nearly 10 million more potential readers.

For something like two-thirds of this period, down to the passing of the Third Republic's press law in 1881, the writer did not enjoy the freedom to communicate with his public through the printed word and the theatre which he enjoys today. Even after the downfall of Napoleon all manner of restrictions continued to hamper free communication, although under the great variety of political régimes which followed for the next sixty years control over the press was never so stringent as during the First Empire. However, two features of the pre-1814 legislation remained in force down to 1870—the stamp duty on newspapers and the *brevet* for printers and booksellers. It was only then that anyone was free to set up a printing or bookselling business.

Article 8 of the Charte constitutionnelle of 1814 proclaimed the right of Frenchmen 'de publier et de faire imprimer leurs opinions, en se conformant aux lois qui doivent réprimer les abus de cette liberté'. In practice, though with various changes in the direction of both greater freedom and greater restrictions, the Restoration imposed all sorts of limitations on the freedom of the press. Newspapers and periodicals were never free from all manner of constraints, and an offending writer could well land in prison. This was the fate of the pamphleteer, Paul Louis Courier, in 1821, and later in the same year Béranger's *chansons* earned him a spell of imprisonment. In 1828 he received a second and longer sentence together with a fine of 10,000 francs. In the repressive atmosphere of these years the Belgian book trade received considerable stimulus as it turned out reprints of books which were banned in France and published new works which could not appear there.

In the reaction against various forms of censorship practised during the Restoration article 6 of the revised Charte of 1830 proclaimed: 'Les Français ont le droit de publier et de faire imprimer leurs opinions en se conformant aux lois.—La censure ne pourra jamais être rétablie.' That does not mean, however, that the new régime proved to be particularly liberal in its attitude to the press. Indeed, the press law passed in September 1835 to put an end to the political agitation of the opening years of the reign was decidedly restrictive. The Revolution of 1848 meant the repeal of this law and the abolition of stamp duty, but in the reaction which followed the Journées de juin not only was this brought back by a law of 1850, but the caution money which newspapers had to deposit was further increased. This was only a prelude to the stringent press laws and the strict application of them which was to mark the Second Empire, particularly in its earlier years. Shortly after the *coup d'état*, in February 1852, a decree was issued which, while it did not re-establish a censorship for newspapers, maintained both caution money and stamp duty, and introduced a new system of *avertissements*. After two *avertissements* a minister could suspend a newspaper, and Louis Napoleon took powers which allowed him to suppress offending journals by decree. Some liberalization of these press laws took place in the 1860s.

Colportage was also severely restricted under the Second Empire; in this were included not only the pedlars who hawked books round the countryside, but also *cabinets de lecture* and bookstalls, including those on railway stations. Copies of books in this category had to bear the stamp of the *préfecture* of the department on which they were put on sale; and a commission was set up to compile a list of approved works. The commission rejected 556 out of 3,649 works which it examined.[1] Champfleury relates how under this regime two of his novels were banned from railway bookstalls and how he managed to get round the ban on one of them by telling the official at the Ministry of the Interior: 'Je passe condamnation sur tous mes livres qui sont incriminés en tas, n'ayant pas le temps de m'en occuper, mais il en est un qui a paru en feuilleton dans le *Moniteur*. Pouvez-vous admettre, monsieur, que le journal officiel imprime des œuvres contraires à la morale?' A new report on the book was called for and finally the ban on it was lifted.[2]

Some of the best-known writers of the Second Empire found them-selves in the dock charged with 'outrage à la morale publique et religieuse et aux bonnes mœurs'. In 1853 the Goncourt brothers were prosecuted for having quoted in a newspaper article five lines of a sixteenth-century poem; though they were acquitted, the court cen-sured them for reproducing 'des images évidemment licencieuses'. Four years later both Flaubert and Baudelaire appeared in court on the same charge. Flaubert was acquitted, though the court offered some criti-cisms of the morality of *Madame Bovary*; but Baudelaire was found guilty, fined 300 francs with costs, and ordered to remove six poems from subsequent editions of *Les Fleurs du mal*.

The proclamation of the Third Republic on 4 September 1870 was quickly followed by such measures as the abolition of stamp duty and

---

[1] P. Martino, *Le Roman réaliste sous le Second Empire*, Paris, 1913, p. 103.
[2] *Souvenirs et portraits de jeunesse*, Paris, 1872, pp. 316–17.

caution money for newspapers, but after the capitulation of Paris and the Commune the situation was gradually brought back to something like what it had been before the collapse of the Second Empire. The newspapers were very far from free, particularly during the crisis which followed the attempt at a *coup d'état* in 1877 ('le seize mai').

Writers continued to have trouble with the Commission de colportage; Hector Malot relates how, after having one of his novels banned by it during the Second Empire, another fell foul of it under the new regime, along with Daudet's *Fromont jeune et Risler aîné*.[1] Prosecutions for obscenity continued; Richepin's *La Chanson des gueux* was condemned by a Paris court in 1876. It was only when the 'République des Ducs' was replaced by the 'République des Républicains' that freedom of the press could become a reality.

'L'imprimerie et la librairie sont libres' proclaimed the first article in the law on the press passed by the Republican majority in 1881. It abolished both the necessity for official approval for the founding of newspapers and the payment of caution money; all the more serious charges such as those of obscenity had to be tried before a jury. Later laws brought some restrictions to the freedom established by this measure, but broadly speaking it continued in force for the rest of the life of the Third Republic. The judgement as to whether books should be condemned for 'outrage aux bonnes mœurs' continued to rest with the jury. Quite often writers who were prosecuted were acquitted, though this was not the case with Paul Adam's *Chair molle* which was condemned by the assize court of the Seine in 1885. There was, however, the lamentable case of a young writer, Louis Desprez, part-author of a novel of country life, *Autour d'un clocher*, which had been published in Brussels. 'C'était un pauvre être mal poussé, déjeté,' wrote Zola who tried vainly to dissuade him from assuming his own defence at his trial, 'qu'une maladie des os de la hanche avait tenu dans un lit pendant toute sa jeunesse. Il marchait péniblement avec une béquille. Il avait une de ces faces blêmes et torturées des damnés de la vie, sous une crinière de cheveux roux.'[2] In 1884 the jury found him guilty; he was fined 1,000 francs and sentenced to a month's imprisonment. This spell in prison broke him and he died shortly afterwards. While there is no official list of books condemned down to 1914,[3] it would seem

[1] *Le Roman de mes Romans*, Paris, 1896, pp. 93–9.

[2] *Œuvres complètes*, ed. H. Mitterand, 15 vols., Paris, 1966–70, xii. 641.

[3] The curious reader will find an attempt at such a list in M. Garçon, 'Les Livres contraires aux bonnes moeurs', *Mercure de France*, 15 Aug. 1931, pp. 5–39. According to this writer no books were condemned after 1914.

that, leaving aside works of pure pornography, books by serious writers were no longer prosecuted.

The history of theatre censorship follows very much the same pattern. It was fairly rigorous during the Restoration; plays about Napoleon and his exploits and even those in which the Napoleonic epic appeared more or less disguised were kept off the stage. References to such eighteenth-century writers as Voltaire and Rousseau were ruthlessly suppressed. It is true that there were occasionally periods of relative tolerance, but censorship continued to the end of the regime; in 1829 Charles X upheld the censor's ban on Hugo's *Marion Delorme* because of the unfavourable light in which his ancestor, Louis XIII, appeared in it. On paper the July Revolution meant the end of theatre censorship in France since article 7 of the constitution contained the words: 'La censure ne pourra jamais être rétablie.' The revolution was followed by a torrent of plays which had been banned under the previous regime and by new ones glorifying Napoleon, attacking the Church, and breaching the accepted standards of morality. This led to government intervention in the form of banning plays after they had been put on the stage. Hugo was filled with rage in 1832 when, after the first performance of *Le Roi s'amuse*, the government, making use of the Napoleonic decree of 1806 on censorship, banned his play on the grounds that in numerous passages 'les mœurs sont outragées'. In the preface to his play Hugo invokes the words of the 1830 constitution and then goes on: 'Or le texte ne dit pas *la censure des journaux, la censure des livres*, il dit *la censure*, la censure en général, toute censure, celle du théâtre comme celle des écrits.' All his protests were in vain and the play did not have its second performance at the Comédie-Française until fifty years later.

This was not the only play of the period to be banned by the government, but it was only after the passing of the Lois de septembre in 1835 that theatre censorship was officially brought back. The government also retained the power to ban a play after it had been put on the stage and even to close a theatre for a time. The censorship was so fairly rigorous, and even if the play got past it, it might then have to be taken off, as Balzac discovered to his cost in 1840 when his *Vautrin* was banned after its first performance.

The Revolution of 1848 meant once again a period of complete freedom in the theatre, but this did not last long. In the atmosphere of reaction which followed the Journées de juin the government used its power to ban plays, and in July 1850 theatre censorship was reestablished. Under the repressive regime of Louis Napoleon which was installed in the following year the theatre censorship was extremely vigilant and fernickety. When after the fall of the regime some of the censors' reports were published,[1] they showed how rigorous it had been, both in insisting on all sorts of alterations to plays which were eventually performed and in banning certain others completely. In 1864, for instance, a proposal to put on Musset's *drame*, *Lorenzaccio*, at the Odéon came to nothing, presumably because the censors considered the hero's murder of the tyrant duke 'un spectacle dangereux à présenter au public'. Even supporters of the regime like Augier had their difficulties over allegedly immoral characters and situations in their plays.[2]

The theatre censorship was once again abolished in 1870 with the coming of the Third Republic, but it was brought back in 1874 under the Macmahon regime and, despite many attacks on it, continued to operate until 1906. Difficulties arose chiefly over political and social questions. Thus in 1883 an adaptation of Zola's *Germinal* with its portrayal of a clash between striking miners and the armed forces was banned for a time, while a few years later Coppée's play, *Le Pater*, which dealt with an episode during the Commune, could not be performed. Plays could run into difficulties even after they had passed the censor. In 1891 there was the famous row at the Comédie-Française over Sardou's *Thermidor*; this play aroused such furious passions among spectators with conflicting views of the French Revolution that it was banned by the government after its second performance. It has to be borne in mind that even after the abolition of theatre censorship in 1906, a *maire* or, in Paris, the *préfet de police* has the power to stop the performance of plays which he considers either immoral or prejudicial to public order.

The diffusion of books, periodicals, and newspapers in this period was to be dramatically expanded by a technological revolution which at once coincided with the growth in the reading public and undoubtedly stimulated that growth. In the early part of the nineteenth century there began a revolution in the paper-making and printing industries which has continued down to our own day. This was largely concerned with the special requirements of newspaper production, but these changes affected in turn both books and periodicals. These inventions which very substantially lowered the cost of production brought about

[1] *Les Papiers secrets du Second Empire*, 13 pts., Brussels, 1870–1, pt. I, pp. 37–50.
[2] See the preface to *Les Lionnes pauvres*.

the first real transformation of the printing industry since the time of Gutenberg.

Paper had hitherto been made by hand and was very expensive. In the past the cost of setting up the type of a book had been relatively low in relation to the price of the paper on which it was printed. The accounts of a Lyons bookseller who went bankrupt in 1669 show that paper accounted for between 36 and 52·8 per cent of the cost of production of fourteen works on his list. It should also be noted that the larger the printing, the higher was the proportion absorbed by the cost of the paper.[1] Now paper could be made much more cheaply and more rapidly by machine, and the rags from which it had traditionally been made were supplemented on a massive scale by such new materials as esparto grass and particularly wood-pulp from which the newsprint for a vastly expanded newspaper industry came. As far as book production was concerned, the proportion of the cost absorbed by paper was drastically reduced, and, since the cost of typesetting was exactly the same for 10,000 as for 1,000 copies, the extra thousands of copies of a work could be produced at a very low price because paper was now cheap. It obviously paid a publisher to order as many copies as he thought he could sell of the first edition of a book and then to give as large an order as possible for any reprints which were required, as the larger the order, the smaller the cost of each individual copy.

Printing itself was revolutionized by a whole series of technical inventions, starting with 'stereotyping', i.e. setting free the type once it was composed by moulding the pages and making a duplicate printing surface in the form of a cast metal plate. Hitherto the printing-press had been made of wood; this was now replaced by iron. More important still was the application of steam-power to the printing-press; this speeded up the process enormously, while the invention of the rotary press made possible the rapid production of large numbers of copies of newspapers. The type, which had formerly been cast by hand, could also now be produced by machines. For a long time the 'copy' continued to be set by hand, but in the course of the century various machines were invented to carry out the work more rapidly; finally in the 1880s came the linotype machine, followed in the next decade by the monotype.

Thanks to the *Bibliographie de la France* we can follow through the nineteenth century the expansion of book production:[1]

[1] M. Rémillieux, 'A propos d'une faillite de libraire (Horace Boissat, 1669)', in *Nouvelles études lyonnaises*, Geneva and Paris, 1969, pp. 86–8.

Year	Books	Year	Books	Year	Books
1812	5442	1849	7378	1886	12 831
1813	3749	1850	7608	1887	12 901
1814	2547	1851	7350	1888	12 973
1815	3357	1852	7787	1889	14 849
1816	3763	1853	8060	1890	13 643
1817	4287	1854	8011	1891	14 192
1818	4827	1855	8253	1892	13 123
1819	4568	1856	12 027	1893	13 595
1820	4881	1857	12 019	1894	13 550
1821	5499	1858	13 331	1895	12 927
1822	5824	1859	11 905	1896	12 738
1823	5893	1860	11 882	1897	13 799
1824	6974	1861	12 236	1898	14 781
1825	7805	1862	11 753	1899	14 595
1826	8273	1863	12 108	1900	13 362
1827	8198	1864	12 065	1901	13 053
1828	7616	1865	11 723	1902	12 199
1829	7823	1866	13 883	1903	12 264
1830	6739	1867	11 355	1904	12 139
1831	6180	1868	11 267	1905	12 416
1832	6478	1869	12 269	1906	10 986
1833	7011	1870	8831	1907	10 785
1834	7125	1871	7245	1908	11 073
1835	6700	1872	10 559	1909	13 185
1836	6632	1873	11 530	1910	12 615
1837	6543	1874	11 917	1911	11 652
1838	6603	1875	14 195	1912	11 560
1839	6186	1876	13 642	1913	14 460
1840	6369	1877	12 764	1914	8698
1841	6300	1878	12 823		
1842	6445	1879	14 122		
1843	6176	1880	12 414		
1844	6577	1881	12 766		
1845	6521	1882	13 184		
1846	5916	1883	13 701		
1847	5530	1884	13 938		
1848	7234	1885	12 342		

If we take these figures at their face value, we see that they reflect both political events and economic trends. Expansion tended to proceed fairly slowly down to 1847 as this was a period of relatively slow economic growth, interspersed with both political and economic crises.

[1] The figures are taken from Estivals, *La Statistique bibliographique de la France*, p. 415 See also D. Bellos, 'The *Bibliographie de la France* and its sources' *The Library*, 1973, pp. 64–7.

Then came a spectacular increase in the number of books published during the Second Empire, notoriously a period of rapid economic growth. After the interruption caused by the war of 1870 and the Commune, production continued at a high level, though it could not any longer be held to reflect closely the general trends in the French economy. The highest figure for the whole of the period 1814–1914 was achieved in 1889, at the very time when, like other countries, France was experiencing a period of economic depression, and while comparable figures were to be achieved in 1898, 1899, and 1913, it cannot be said that publishing shared in the economic prosperity of 'la belle époque'. By the end of the 1890s it was clearly suffering from a crisis of over-production. Maurice Dreyfous, who had gone into partnership with Georges Charpentier in 1872 and had set up on his own in 1877, abandoned publishing and returned to writing in 1898: 'La crise qu'on a appelée le krach de la librairie sévissait avec intensité,' he explains in his memoirs. 'Des maisons d'édition, vieilles de près d'un siècle, liquidaient volontairement; d'autres, plus jeunes, finissaient de façon malencontreuse.'[1] In 1911 we find a French publisher complaining of the excessive output of books in the period 1870–1900 and congratulating himself that the situation had changed since then:

... On peut se rendre facilement compte combien il est difficile à un malheureux libraire de pouvoir, comme autrefois, causer efficacement avec ses clients de la valeur des livres dont l'inondaient les éditeurs trop généralement accueillants aux jeunes sans talent, du moins pendant cette période, car il faut le reconnaître et s'en réjouir, depuis 1900 la production va baissant chaque année. Les imprimeurs et les marchands de papier peuvent s'en plaindre, mais les éditeurs, les lecteurs et les bons auteurs surtout ont lieu de s'en montrer satisfaits.[2]

A glance at the statistics will show that while there is some exaggeration here, clearly the upward trend of the earlier period had not continued.

Unfortunately, though it is a relief to find at last for this period an absolutely complete series of statistics of book production, the cautious reader is apt to look at them with a certain scepticism. It would certainly be hazardous to try to make comparisons with other countries, including the United Kingdom, as even today each country compiles its book statistics on a basis all its own, thus ruling out any but the vaguest and

[1] *Ce qu'il me reste à dire. 1848–1900*, Paris, n.d., p. 376.
[2] M. Humblot, 'L'Édition littéraire au XIX⁰ siècle', *Bibliographie de la France*, 17 Mar. 1911, p. 9.

most general comparisons. Even if one confines oneself to France and this period of a hundred years, one cannot help wondering how consistent with each other and hence how comparable are the figures for these years. Did the criterion of what constitutes a book remain constant? Above all, how can one possibly explain the enormous leap from the 1855 figure of 8,253 books to the 1856 figure of 12,027? The average number of books produced in 1851-5 was under 8,000, and it then suddenly leaps to an average of over 12,000 in the period 1856-60. One is bound to ask whether the definition of what constitutes a book was changed between 1855 and 1856 when this extraordinary leap took place.

In 1829 Philarète Chasles published in the *Revue de Paris* an interesting article entitled 'Statistique littéraire et intellectuelle de la France pendant l'année 1828', in which he duly registers the figure of 7,616 books deposited at the Bibliothèque du Roi. He then goes on to point out that this figure is somewhat inflated:

Défalquons de cette somme (qui paraît énorme) les doubles emplois occasionnés par diverses parties des mêmes ouvrages publiés à différentes époques; par des atlas et des suppléments; par le système des souscriptions, qui fait reparaître plusieurs fois le même ouvrage sous différents numéros. Ces doubles emplois s'élèvent à 1,897; et pour résultat définitif nous trouvons un total fort raisonnable de *cinq mille sept cent dix-neuf* ouvrages, grands et petits, en un volume d'un demi-quart de feuille in-18, et en trente volumes in-folio; en français, en breton, en auvergnat, en polonais, en turc et en mandchou. . . .

This figure of 5,719 needs to be broken down further:

De ces 5,719 ouvrages, 1,992 sont des réimpressions, ou des simulacres de réimpressions. Il faut voir dans le *Catalogue de la librairie*, publié par M. Beuchot, combien ces fraudes sont fréquentes: un nouveau titre, un faux titre, un avertissement, une préface, placés à la tête de l'ouvrage, dont l'édition ancienne repose dans le magasin du libraire, déguisent son âge, et le font reparaître avec tous les honneurs de la troisième, cinquième ou septième édition. Quelquefois la seconde édition, c'est la première, c'est la seule. Assez souvent, on passe de la première à la troisième, ou même à la quatrième, en oubliant les intermédiaires. Nous avons eu la patience de suivre l'inexorable et savant bibliographe dans ses découvertes de ce genre. Quelques-unes étonneraient le lecteur; sans affliger aucune gloire vivante, contentons-nous de lui donner le total de 148 éditions anciennes, que, sans doute, comme nous, il aurait prises comme neuves.[1]

[1] pp. 195-6.

The growth in the reading public was reflected not only by the increased number of books published, but also by the increase in the number of periodicals and particularly in the enormous development of the newspaper press. Newspapers gradually extended their appeal beyond the wealthy and educated classes to take in those who, with the development of elementary education, had acquired the ability to read.

Although the Restoration could scarcely be regarded as offering freedom of the press, it was a decidedly less repressive regime than that of Napoleon and it saw a considerable development of periodicals, including many devoting themselves to literature. A considerable number of *revues* were founded (this sense of the word was imported from the English 'review'): for instance, the *Revue encyclopédique* (1819), the *Revue britannique* (1825), the *Revue française* (1828), the *Revue de Paris* and the *Revue des Deux Mondes* (1829). There were also fairly short-lived literary journals which are famous because of their connections with Romanticism such as *Le Conservateur littéraire*, founded by Hugo and one of his brothers in 1819, and *La Muse française*, established in 1823. Many of the reviews founded then and later in the century had only a brief existence (in 1840 Balzac's *Revue parisienne* lasted for exactly three numbers), but others prospered. Particularly important in the literary sphere was the *Revue des Deux Mondes* from 1831 onwards, when it was taken over by François Buloz who remained its somewhat tyrannical editor until his death in 1876. In it appeared contributions from such writers as Hugo, Vigny, Musset, Balzac, and George Sand. Among the many literary journals which flourished in the second half of the century was *La Nouvelle Revue*, founded in 1879 by Juliette Adam; in it appeared Flaubert's unfinished novel, *Bouvard et Pécuchet*, as well as works by Anatole France, Bourget, Maupassant, and Loti. Towards the end of this period one finds new reviews such as the *Mercure de France*, an old title revived in 1890 by Alfred Vallette and at first having close connections with Symbolism, or the *Nouvelle revue française*, founded in 1908 by a group of writers which included André Gide.

Important as these reviews were for the literary life of the period and for the outlets for novels, short stories, poems, and literary criticism with which they provided writers, the growth of the newspaper press was even more striking. What is more, it provided much larger sources of income for writers; indeed, it did so in a way which was not to be repeated to anything like the same extent after 1914. This was inevitably a gradual development. After Napoleon's limitation of the number of newspapers and his strict censorship there was a long way to go before, with many intervening ups and downs, freedom of the press was achieved with the Third Republic's law of 1881. From the strictly economic point of view one considerable brake on the expansion of the newspaper press down to 1870 was stamp duty. However, technological improvements in the printing of newspapers gradually made possible the production at high speed of large numbers of copies.

One tends to forget that throughout almost the whole of this period newspapers were much smaller than those we are accustomed to today; they only had four pages, the bottom of which was separated off to form what was called a *feuilleton*. It was a great event when in 1901 the leading popular newspaper, *Le Petit Parisien*, could announce, with all the fanfares of publicity then available, that henceforth it would have six pages. What is more, at the beginning of this period newspapers were uniformly expensive and by present-day standards had an astonishingly small circulation.

Down to the mid-1830s a subscription to a Paris newspaper cost 80 francs a year; this undoubtedly restricted its circulation to the fairly well-to-do. During the Restoration a number of quite prominent daily newspapers had circulations of the order of some 5,000. Anything above that figure was quite exceptional; in these years only two newspapers had circulations which at times exceeded 20,000—the *Journal des Débats* and *Le Constitutionnel*. These small circulations continued into the reign of Louis Philippe. Indeed, in 1836 these two newspapers had only 10,000 and 9,000 subscribers respectively, while the *National*, which had played a prominent part in the events leading up to the July Revolution, had barely 5,000.

1836 is an important date in the history of the French press as it was then that there appeared simultaneously two new papers, *La Presse* and *Le Siècle*, which cost 40 francs, only half the price of the existing journals. Although a paper like the *Journal des Débats* had for some time derived a fair income from advertisements, the new papers counted on being able to sell at half the usual price because of the revenue obtained from this source. Advertising revenue was to be attracted by the larger circulation produced by this lowering of the price. As Émile de Girardin, the founder of *La Presse*, put it in the first number: 'Le produit des annonces étant en raison du nombre des abonnés, il faut réduire le prix de l'abonnement à sa plus extrême limite pour élever le chiffre des abonnés à sa plus haute puissance. . . . *C'est aux annonces de payer le journal.*' In other words, the modern newspaper was born.

In order to attract custom the editors hit upon the idea of publishing novels in serial form in the *feuilleton* of their papers; this meant that novelists could derive an income from their works from two sources by publishing them first in a newspaper and then in book form. Indeed, the rivalry between these two newspapers and between them and established papers like the *Journal des Débats* led for a time, in the 1840s, to fierce competition to secure the collaboration of the outstanding novelists of the age.

Significant for the future as was the appearance of these cheaper newspapers seeking the largest possible clientèle in order to attract advertisements, their circulation still remained small by present-day standards. In 1846 the *Journal des Débats* had only some 9,000 subscribers; even *Le Siècle* had no more than 33,000, *La Presse* 22,000, and *Le Constitutionnel*, which under new management since 1844 had reduced its price too, 24,000.

Despite its repressive policies towards the press the Second Empire saw considerable developments which reflected the economic prosperity of the period and the gradual spread of education. The quality press continued to hold its own with papers like the *Journal des Débats* and a newcomer, *Le Temps* (founded in 1861), even though in 1869 they had no more than 9,000 and 11,000 subscribers respectively. There were now a number of newspapers such as *Le National, Le Siècle, Le Figaro,* and *La Liberté* with circulations between 15,000 and 65,000, but the most striking phenomenon in the history of the French press under the Second Empire was the appearance of a newspaper aiming at a mass audience in the shape of *Le Petit Journal*. Launched in 1863, it had achieved six years later a circulation of 287,000, a staggering figure at that time for a newspaper anywhere in the world. Its success was due both to its low price (5 sous) and its non-political nature; it specialized in crime reporting and in low-grade *romans-feuilletons*.

The period from 1870 to 1914 was to see a vast expansion of both the Paris and the provincial press thanks to the introduction of such innovations as the rotary press and the linotype machine. Communications were speeded up by the further development of the railway system which now penetrated into quite remote corners of France; at the same time illiteracy was gradually being reduced to very small proportions. It is estimated that in the period between 1870 and 1910 the printing of Paris newspapers rose from some one million copies to 5 million. Even though the provincial press was not yet as important as it has become in recent decades, it was also growing very fast, partly because of the appearance of low-priced newspapers in the larger cities; by the eve of the First World War it had probably reached a circulation of some 4 million.

A great deal of the increase in the circulation of the Paris newspapers came from the development of the popular press. In the period down to 1890 the *Petit Journal* continued to hold the lead in circulation, reaching one million by about that date. However, it encountered growing competition from more recently founded newspapers, and its circulation was somewhat reduced by the success of *Le Matin* and *Le Journal* which reached a million by 1913 and above all by *Le Petit Parisien* which outstripped all its rivals with nearly 1½ million by that date.

One striking feature of the Paris press in the years before 1914 was its great diversity. In addition to these four large mass-circulation newspapers it offered a wide range of choice. There was, for instance, the Catholic *La Croix*, founded in 1883, and the Socialist *L'Humanité*, founded by Jaurès in 1904; of the two *La Croix* had much the bigger circulation, as *L'Humanité* was often in considerable financial difficulties though its fortunes improved towards 1914 with the growth of the Socialist party, the S.F.I.O. The old-established quality newspapers, the *Journal des Débats* and *Le Temps*, continued to prosper; their circulation was still relatively small (some 20–25,000 copies), indeed tiny compared with that of the giants, but their influence remained considerable. In addition to a host of small papers some of which led a more or less nominal existence there were others with a fairly considerable readership such as *Le Figaro*, a daily since the Second Empire, and especially the *Écho de Paris* which, founded in 1884, had reached a circulation of 150,000 by 1913.

If writers benefited greatly from the rapid development of newspapers from the 1830s onwards, they were also gradually offered improved protection of their right of property in their work by new copyright laws. Napoleon had raised from ten to twenty years the period during which a writer's heirs enjoyed copyright for his work. Round about 1840 there was considerable agitation among writers for a much longer period; some indeed went so far as to demand a perpetual right of property. The case for it is pleaded with an extraordinarily wrong-headed eloquence in a memorandum, generally attributed to Balzac, presented in 1841 to the committee on literary property of the Chamber of Deputies. The author takes his stand paradoxically on article 5 of the *arrêt du Conseil* of 1777 and argues that the Convention and Napoleon had gone back on what had been conceded by the *ancien régime*; he speaks of 'l'exhérédation consacrée par la loi de 1793 et modifiée par le décret de Napoléon' The term of fifty years after the death of the author proposed by the Société des gens de lettres does not go far enough:

Si l'on accorde cinquante ans, pourquoi pas la perpétuité? Qui donc peut empêcher la reconnaissance de la seule propriété que l'homme crée sans la terre et la pierre, et qui est aussi durable que la terre et la pierre? Une propriété qui se trouve constituée entre la terre et le ciel, à l'aide des rebuts de la société, le noir de fumée pris à des os, et les chiffons laissés sur la voie publique.[1]

This was, of course, a forlorn hope. All that emerged from these controversies was an act of 3 August 1844 which extended the provisions of the Napoleonic decree of 1810 to the widows and children of authors of dramatic works which had hitherto been covered only by the decree of 1793.[2] However, ten years later the rights of a writer's widow and children were further extended:

Article unique. Les veuves des auteurs, des compositeurs et des artistes jouiront, pendant toute leur vie, des droits garantis par les lois des 13 janvier 1791 et 19 juillet 1793, le décret du 5 février 1810, la loi du 3 août 1844, et les autres lois et décrets sur la matière.

La durée de la jouissance accordée aux enfants par ces mêmes lois et décrets est portée à trente ans, à partir, soit du décès de l'auteur, soit de l'extinction des droits de la veuve.[3]

Finally, a law of 14 July 1866 extended the rights of the author's heirs to a period of fifty years from his death:

Art. Ier La durée des droits accordés par les lois antérieures aux héritiers, successeurs irréguliers, donataires ou légataires des auteurs, compositeurs ou artistes, est porté à cinquante ans à partir du décès de l'auteur.[4]

This term of fifty years remains the present figure in France[5] except that after both world wars it was extended to cover the period of hostilities, so that nowadays a work goes out of copyright only sixty-four years and 253 days after the author's death.[6] United Kingdom legislation remained for a long time distinctly less favourable to an author's heirs; it was only in 1911 that the term was extended to fifty years after his death.

[1] Balzac, *Œuvres diverses*, 4 vols., Paris, 1962–3, iv. 569, 571.
[2] Duvergier, *Collection complète* xliv. 404–5. [3] Ibid. liv. 176.
[4] Ibid. lxvi. 270–94. [5] See article 21 of the law of 11 Mar. 1957.
[6] H. J. Martin, 'Les Réseaux du livre', in *Le Livre français. Hier, aujourd'hui, demain*, ed. J. Cain, R. Escarpit, and H. J. Martin, Paris, 1972, p. 78.

On the other hand, for a considerable part of this period French writers were undoubtedly deprived of part of their legitimate earnings by the absence of an international copyright law. Given the fact that French continued to be an international language and that French literature enjoyed immense prestige abroad, their books both in the original and in translation could count on a wide sale in the rest of Europe as well as further afield, but that obviously made it profitable for publishers abroad to reprint their works without paying them a penny. The fact that English books were ruthlessly pirated in the United States for most of the period was no consolation; many were also reprinted in Germany—or even France![1] A number of agreements to put an end to piracy were gradually reached with other countries; for instance, in 1852 the United Kingdom Parliament ratified the Anglo-French Convention which had been signed in the previous year. This recognized the copyright of works duly registered in either country and also afforded limited protection to the writer's translation rights. Until the matter was cleared up in 1886 by the Berne Convention and subsequent international agreements French writers undoubtedly lost part of their market abroad, and many of the copies of the pirated editions found their way into France itself. Some strange things could happen; for instance, *Madame Bovary* was first published in a review, the *Revue de Paris*, but in an incomplete text; but before Flaubert's French publisher, Michel Lévy, could get the work out in book form, it had appeared, still incomplete, in Germany.[2] The same thing had happened earlier with other works; Balzac's *Le Curé de village* and Mérimée's *Colomba* made their first appearance in book form in Belgium.[3]

From 1815 onwards Belgian publishers made a particularly lucrative business not out of editions of works no longer copyright, but by undercutting French publishers with cheap editions of new books, novels being particularly vulnerable since they replaced the two or three volumes at 7.50 francs each by one volume at 3 francs or even less; the fact that they paid the author nothing helped to keep the price down. There is an interesting letter on the subject written by Nerval in 1834 from Marseilles after a journey to Italy where he had found these pirated editions everywhere:

[1] See e.g. G. Barber, 'Galignani and the Publication of English books in France', *The Library*, 1961, pp. 267–86.

[2] R. Dumesnil, *L'Époque réaliste et naturaliste*, Paris, 1945, pp. 442–3.

[3] H. Dopp, *La Contrefaçon des livres français en Belgique, 1815–1852*, Louvain, 1932, p. 115.

Pour moi, je ne rapporte dans mes poches aucune de ces jolies éditions à bon marché de Bruxelles, et crois par conséquent avoir droit à votre estime. Je suis à Marseille, où l'on vend et lit beaucoup de livres, notamment *Les Paroles d'un croyant* (édition de Bruxelles) dans les marchés, le port et les rues, sur papier gris, mais seulement chez les libraires ambulants ou étalant le long des murs.[2]

Lamennais's work was the best seller of the July Monarchy, but obviously a great many of the copies sold were not of the Paris edition.

Belgian publishers argued that they were not harming those of Paris, as they were catering for a quite different market; their point of view was stated in 1836 in the Brussels review, *L'Artiste*:

Les éditeurs de Paris raisonnent . . . comme si la contrefaçon leur enlevait leurs chalands. Mais les lecteurs des éditions de Paris et ceux de la contrefaçon composent deux classes distinctes: dans la première sont placés les riches étrangers qui veulent avoir, par goût ou par ton, tous les livres français édités à Paris; dans la seconde sont tous ceux qui lisent parce qu'ils peuvent le faire à bon marché . . . Les lecteurs de tel ouvrage paru à Bruxelles n'auraient jamais acquis celui de Paris.[2]

The Belgian output of pirated editions was at its height in the 1830s and 1840s. In his letters to Madame Hanska Balzac is continually moaning about the activities of Belgian publishers and indulging in all sorts of pipe-dreams as to how well off he would be if only such pirated editions could be stopped. In 1840 he wrote indignantly:

La Belgique a ruiné la littérature française. Quelle ingénérosité chez ceux qui nous lisent! Si chacun avait refusé l'édition belge et voulu, comme vous le faites, l'édition française; s'il s'était rencontré deux mille personnes ainsi sur le continent, nous étions sauvés; et la Belgique nous vend à vingt ou trente mille.[3]

Three years later when it was rumoured that the Belgians were about to agree to end this piracy, he dreamed of being rid of all his mountain of debts: 'Si la contrefaçon belge est supprimée, oh, je serai libéré en deux ans. Je gagnerai 100,000 fr. alors.'[4] As so often with Balzac, this was a wild exaggeration. In any case it was not until after his death that in 1852 an agreement was reached between the two governments to put an end to these pirated editions. Agreements were also negotiated with other countries until finally the Berne Convention virtually disposed of the whole problem.

[1] *Œuvres*, ed. A. Béguin and J. Richer, 2 vols., Paris, 1956, i. 763.
[2] Quoted in Dopp, *La Contrefaçon des livres français en Belgique*, p. 98.
[3] *Lettres à Madame Hanska*, ed. R. Pierrot, 4 vols., Paris, 1967–71, i. 680.
[4] Ibid. ii. 144.

It would seem that French writers of the time tended to exaggerate the ill effects of Belgian piracy. They certainly suffered much less than their predecessors in the eighteenth century from the absence of an international copyright law. The Belgian menace to French publishers and writers was fairly short lived; it began in the Restoration period and reached its peak in 1845, after which there was a rapid decline, several large firms going bankrupt through excessive competition and fierce price-cutting.[1] Moreover, already in 1838 the Paris publisher, Gervais Charpentier, had launched his collection of 3.50 fr. reprints of recent works in one volume in a small format, and his example was quickly followed by others, as Werdet, one of Balzac's numerous publishers, noted in a work published in 1860:

Lorsque Charpentier s'avisa, en 1838, de coter à 3fr. 50c. d'élégants volumes, grand in-18 sur jésus, contenant la matière d'un livre in-8° ordinaire, qui s'était vendu ou, pour mieux dire, s'était coté, de temps immémorial, de 7fr. 50c. à 9fr., il opéra une véritable révolution dans la librairie.

Et alors les moutons de Panurge de se mettre en campagne! Et les Gosselin, les Delloye, une foule d'autres éditeurs, d'adopter, à l'envi, le type Charpentier! Et des milliers de volumes d'apparaître en très peu de temps, toujours à raison de 3 fr. 50c.

. . . Depuis lors, le prix de ces volumes a continuellement baissé; il est descendu à 3 fr., à 2 fr.; il est maintenant à l fr., et il pourra fléchir encore.[2]

Competition from these cheaper editions no doubt hastened the decline of the Belgian industry.

In theory, the great changes which took place in this period should have enormously improved the lot of the writer. The progress made by elementary education and the rapid decline in illiteracy in the hundred years after 1814 gradually created a mass audience for the printed word, if only for the popular newspapers which emerged from the 1860s onwards.

It is true that even by 1900 secondary education was offered to only a very small proportion of the relevant age group, and university education only to a tiny minority; the educational scene was vastly different from what it is in the 1970s. Yet all the changes which had taken place since 1789 undoubtedly produced a much larger reading public than had existed in the age of Voltaire and Rousseau.

[1] Dopp, *La Contrefaçon des livres français en Belgique*, p. 159.

[2] E. Werdet, *De la librairie française*, Paris, 1860, pp. 139–40. There is an interesting account of reprints of works of Vigny in this series in J. Marsan, 'A. de Vigny et G. H. Charpentier (documents inédits)', *Revue d'histoire littéraire*, 1913, pp. 51–64.

In spite of this one finds repeated throughout this period the most gloomy accounts of the poverty-stricken state of the writer. Vigny was a well-known exponent of this view with his *Stello* (1831) and especially his *Chatterton* (1835) which represents the suicide by poison of the youthful English poet as the inevitable product of a materialist society which cares nothing for literature. It is true that in the preface to his play Vigny declares that he is not concerned either with the 'homme de lettres' or 'le grand écrivain' both of whom, he considers, are able to look after themselves. 'Mais,' he continues,

il est une autre sorte de nature, nature plus passionnée, plus pure et plus rare. Celui qui vient d'elle est inhabile à tout ce qui n'est pas l'œuvre divine, et vient au monde à de rares intervalles, heureusement pour lui, malheureusement pour l'espèce humaine. Il y vient pour être à charge aux autres, quand il appartient complètement à cette race exquise et puissante qui fut celle des grands hommes inspirés . . . Il a besoin de *ne rien faire*, pour faire quelque chose de son art. Il faut qu'il ne fasse rien d'utile et de journalier pour avoir le temps d'écouter les accords qui se forment lentement dans son âme, et que le bruit grossier d'un travail positif et régulier interrompt et fait infailliblement évanouir.—C'est LE POÈTE.—Celui-là est retranché dès qu'il se montre: toutes vos larmes, toute votre pitié pour lui!

As Vigny will have nothing to do with what the French call 'un second métier' for the writer, i.e. a job which will provide him with the necessary money to live on and at least some leisure to write, presumably what he is arguing for is some form of state patronage for the writer, or at any rate for an élite of writers.

This was, of course, clean contrary to the whole historical evolution in the position of the writer, away from patronage and towards making a living from what he could earn from publishers and, in the case of playwrights, from the theatre. While various forms of patronage continued to exist in the post-Napoleonic period, compared with what it had been in earlier centuries its importance was clearly in rapid decline.

During the Restoration both Louis XVIII and Charles X continued the traditions of the *ancien régime* by offering rewards to various writers, among them the young Hugo. Louis Philippe does not appear to have taken much personal interest in literature, but through various ministries the state continued to offer a modest amount of patronage to writers. Though Louis Napoleon's interest in literature was small, he did occasionally act as a patron of men of letters and under the Third Republic ministers continued to dole out some assistance to writers;

yet on the whole the nineteenth-century writer was left to wring a living out of what he could earn from publishers, theatre managers, and the editors of periodicals and newspapers. Not all writers by any means were agreed that this was an improvement. In 1834, for instance, Balzac contrasted the situation of the writer with what it had been before the collapse of the *ancien régime*: 'Nos livres ne se vendent pas aussi cher que se vendaient les livres avant la Révolution; et, avant la Révolution, sur douze écrivains, sept recevaient des pensions considérables payées ou par des souverains étrangers, ou par la Cour, ou par le gouvernement.'[1] Others wondered whether even from the point of view of the writer's dignity the change was an improvement; in practice, he had merely transferred his flattery from a minister or a king's mistress to a publisher or a newspaper proprietor. A characteristic expression of this attitude is to be found in the Goncourts' journal for 1859: 'Je lis dans la préface d'une étude sur Saint-Just le lieu commun d'usage sur la dignité apportée aux gens de lettres par la Révolution. Quoi? Parce que nous ne courtisons plus une Pompadour, un ministre? Mais nous courtisons Solar,[2] Mirès;[3] on brigue la poignée de mains de Lévy;[4] chacun caresse l'éditeur.'[5] In 1872 we find a similar disillusioned comment in a letter from Flaubert to George Sand: 'On trouve que l'écrivain, parce qu'il ne reçoit plus de pension des grands, est bien plus libre, plus noble. Toute sa noblesse sociale maintenant consiste à être l'égal d'un épicier. Quel progrès!'[6]

A very different view was put forward by the successful writers of the period. In Scribe's *Le Mariage d'argent*, performed at the Comédie-Française in 1827, one of the characters, a painter, declares:

Des protecteurs! Grâce au ciel nous ne sommes plus dans ces temps où le talent ne pouvait se produire que sous quelque riche patronage; où le génie, dans une humble dédicace, demandait à un sot la permission de passer à la postérité à l'ombre de son nom. Les artistes d'à présent pour acquérir de la considération et de la fortune n'ont pas besoin de recourir à de pareils moyens; les vrais artistes, j'entends; ils restent chez eux, ils travaillent, et le public est là qui les juge et les récompense.[7]

---

[1] *Œuvres diverses*, iii. 236.
[2] Félix Solar (1811–70), proprietor and editor of *La Presse*.
[3] Jules Isaac Mirès (1809–71), banker and newspaper proprietor.
[4] Michel Lévy (1821–75), the publisher.
[5] *Journal. Mémoires de la vie littéraire*, ed. R. Ricatte, 22 vols., Monaco, 1956–8, iii. 130.
[6] *Correspondance*, 9 vols., Paris, 1926–33, vi. 458.
[7] Act I, sc. 4.

The same view was expressed very forcibly in 1880 by Zola in an article entitled 'L'Argent et la littérature', published along with the more famous essay, 'Le Roman expérimental'. After an impecunious early career by this date Zola had begun to make money with his novels and journalism. For him the present position of the writer was infinitely preferable to the humiliating patronage of bygone days:

C'est l'argent, c'est le gain légitimement réalisé sur ses ouvrages qui l'a délivré de toute protection humiliante, qui a fait de l'ancien bateleur de cour, de l'ancien bouffon d'antichambre, un citoyen libre, un homme qui ne relève que de lui-même. Avec l'argent, il a osé tout dire, il a porté son examen partout, jusqu'au roi, jusqu'à Dieu, sans craindre de perdre son pain. L'argent a émancipé l'écrivain, l'argent a créé les lettres modernes.

He has no patience with the laments for the good old days or complaints about the failure of the state to come to the assistance of young writers:

Regretterez-vous le temps où l'on bâtonnait Voltaire, où Racine mourait d'une bouderie de Louis XIV, où toute la littérature était aux gages d'une noblesse brutale et imbécile? Comment! vous poussez l'ingratitude contre notre grande époque jusqu'à ne pas la comprendre, en l'accusant de mercantilisme, lorsqu' elle est avant tout le droit au travail et à la vie! Si vous ne pouvez vivre avec vos vers, avec vos premiers essais, faites autre chose, entrez dans une administration, attendez que le public vienne à vous. L'État ne vous doit rien. Il est peu honorable de rêver une littérature entretenue. Battez-vous, mangez des pommes de terre ou des truffes, cassez des pierres dans la journée et écrivez des chefs-d'œuvre la nuit. Seulement, dites-vous bien ceci: c'est que, si vous avez un talent, une force, vous arriverez quand même à la gloire et à la fortune.[1]

Not unnaturally, such sentiments, expressed by a very successful author, have not commanded universal approval among his fellow writers in the last hundred years or so. They scarcely fit in with the twentieth-century demand for a 'living wage' for the writer.

Many writers of the time did follow Zola's example of taking a job until they had begun to make a name for themselves and could earn a living by their pen. He had begun his career by working for the publisher, Hachette, eking out his meagre earnings with journalism. A considerable number of writers held quite minor, routine posts in the various Paris ministries. Coppée, like his father before him, was a clerk in the Ministry for War; Huysmans served for thirty years in the

---

[1] *Œuvres complètes*, x. 1277–8.

Ministry of the Interior; Maupassant held a clerical post, first in the Ministry for the Navy and then in the Ministry of Education. Although he had not drawn a salary for some years, it was only shortly before his death that he was persuaded to resign this post. No doubt some of the writers made model civil servants, but many could hardly be said to have done so. When in 1880 a publisher who had 'discovered' Maupassant sent one of his aides to seek him out at the Ministry of Education, he found him 'jouant au bilboquet dans un bureau'.[1] The way in which many writers of the time earned their salaries as civil servants is vividly described by J. H. Rosny apropos of Paul Margueritte:

> Il végétait dans un ministère et la mode était, pour les jeunes écrivains, de consacrer leurs heures, non au travail de l'État, mais au leur propre. Au demeurant, on ne leur donnait chaque jour qu'à copier quelques lettres, ce qu'un homme actif pouvait faire en une heure. Aussi est-ce au ministère que Paul Margueritte exécutait le gros de sa besogne littéraire.[2]

On the other hand, various forms of literary patronage continued throughout the whole of this period, although its importance grew progressively less. Victor Hugo's early career was undoubtedly assisted by the favours he received from Louis XVIII. The King had read to him poems from his first volume of verse, *Odes et poésies diverses*, when it appeared in 1822, and gave the poet a pension of 1,000 francs from the privy purse. 'Avec mille francs par an, on pouvait se marier', wrote his wife in *Victor Hugo raconté par un témoin de sa vie*.[3] This was soon followed by a second pension of 2,000 francs which the King directed should be paid by the Ministry of the Interior; this meant that Hugo and his wife were now well enough off, with what he was managing to earn from his writings, to leave his father-in-law's and to set up house on their own.[4] When Charles X came to the throne, he saw that both these pensions continued to be paid; indeed, when Hugo's play, *Marion de Lorme*, was banned by the censor in 1829, although the King upheld the ban, he offered Hugo an additional pension which he declined.[5] The downfall of Charles X in the following year meant that Hugo lost the pension from the privy purse, but he continued to be on the books of the Ministry of the Interior for a pension of 2,000 francs, and when he renounced the pension in 1832, the minister replied that it would continue to be paid. Apparently, Hugo never took the money,

---

[1] Humblot, 'L'Édition littéraire au XIXᵉ siècle', p. 10.
[2] J. H. Rosny (aîné), *Mémoires de la vie littéraire*, Paris, 1927, p. 32.
[3] ii. 191.   [4] Ibid. 201.
[5] E. Biré, *Victor Hugo avant 1830*, 2nd edn., Paris, 1902, p. 486.

but his attempt to get the pension transferred to 'une pauvre jeune fille poète' was a failure.[1]

Although Louis Philippe does not appear to have taken much interest in contemporary literature, as politicians of the reign like Thiers and Guizot took a keen interest in such matters, various ministries continued to pay out pensions and odd sums of money to writers. Thus in 1839 Vigny secured a pension of 1,200 francs from Villemain, the Minister for Education, for the Breton poet, Brizeux, and four years later this was doubled by another pension from the Ministry of the Interior.[2] Charles de Rémusat who was in charge of this ministry for some months in 1840 has some interesting remarks to make on the role which the state was still expected to play as patron of literature:

Le ministère de l'Intérieur était chargé des arts et des théâtres; par ce dernier point seulement, il était en rapport avec la littérature. Il y a beaucoup à critiquer dans l'intervention de l'État dans les affaires de l'esprit, et je suis loin de défendre en tout la manière dont elle était réglée et exercée. Par goût et par principe, j'aimerais mieux la liberté absolue sans protection; mais quoi qu'ils en disent, je doute que ce régime convînt beaucoup aux gens de lettres, qui sont très aises qu'il y ait pour eux des institutions, des emplois spéciaux, des encouragements comme les académies, les bibliothèques, les musées, les pensions. C'est un lieu commun de l'Histoire que l'éloge des gouvernements qui ont protégé les travaux de l'esprit; même en temps de liberté, on ne dispense pas l'État de la tâche de les seconder et de les récompenser, quoique ce ne soit pas le moyen d'en assurer l'indépendance.[3]

Despite the liberal principles which underlay much of the economic and political ideas of the period some degree of state intervention in support of men of letters was still looked for.

Louis Napoleon made some attempt to imitate his uncle's patronage of literature. The poet, Leconte de Lisle, for instance, drew a pension of 300 francs a month for a number of years,[4] in return, his enemies later alleged, for spying on the literary circles of Paris.[5] In 1858 the playwright, Ponsard, was given the substantial sum of 25,000 francs,[6] while an obscure writer named Théophile Silvestre also managed to win the Imperial favour. Indeed, from 1867 he drew a large pension—12,000

---

[1] *Victor Hugo raconté* . . . ii. 391–3.

[2] M. Pailleron, *François Buloz et ses amis*, 4 vols., Paris, 1919–23, i. 123.

[3] *Mémoires de ma vie*, ed. C. H. Pouthas, 5 vols., Paris, 1958–67, iii. 342.

[4] *Les Papiers secrets du Second Empire*, pt. V, pp. 22–5 and pt. VIII, p. 40. According to this source, the pension began in July 1864.

[5] Goncourts, *Journal*, xvi. 59.   [6] *Les Papiers secrets*, pt. V, p. 31.

francs—from the privy purse.[1] As Maxime Du Camp amusingly put it:

Ce Silvestre n'était pas bête; il avait persuadé à Napoléon III que sa misère seule l'empêchait d'être un grand écrivain. Par curiosité peut-être, et à coup sûr par bonté d'âme, l'empereur lui accorda une pension de six mille francs sur sa cassette. Silvestre empocha, ne fit rien et resta un grand écrivain à l'état latent.[2]

Again, Louis Napoleon made men of letters like Mérimée and Sainte-Beuve Senators, a post which carried with it not only prestige, but a very comfortable salary of 30,000 francs a year. Only the downfall of the Second Empire prevented two other writers, Émile Augier and Maxime Du Camp, from being similarly honoured.[3]

Occasionally the Emperor's bounty was declined. In 1861, when the Académie française failed to award George Sand a prize for which her candidature had been put forward, Louis Napoleon had soundings made to discover whether she would accept an equivalent sum (20,000 francs), but she politely refused.[4] Since 1848 Lamartine had sunk deeper and deeper into debt despite his large output of pot-boilers; the Emperor offered to come to the rescue with a 'don national' of 2 million francs, but in a letter which he made public Lamartine declined the offer, saying that he wished to remain 'l'homme qui a proclamé la République'. However, in the end he had to accept the 'récompense nationale' (an annuity of 25,000 francs) which the Corps législatif voted for him in 1867.[5]

The Emperor's cousin, princesse Mathilde, was much more interested in literature and received in her *salon* in Paris and in her country house at Saint-Gratien many of the leading men of letters of the time, such as Flaubert, the Goncourt brothers, Gautier, and Sainte-Beuve. Although Gautier already received a pension of 3,000 francs from the government, the Princess did not think it enough and appointed him her librarian, a pure sinecure which gave him an additional 6,000 francs a year. The Goncourts noted the event in 1868 in somewhat ironical terms: 'En descendant ce soir les escaliers de la Princesse, Gautier, nommé son bibliothécaire, nous demanda, en toute sincérité: "Mais au fait, dites-moi, est-ce que la Princesse a une bibliothèque?—Un

[1] *Les Papiers secrets.* pt. IX, p. 46. Du Camp, it will be noticed, gives a smaller figure.
[2] *Souvenirs littéraires*, 2 vols., Paris, 1882–3, ii. 345.
[3] *Les Papiers secrets.* pt. V, p. 31.
[4] *Correspondance 1812–1876*, 6 vols., Paris, 1882–4, iv. 251–3.
[5] F. Dumont and J. Gitan, *De quoi vivait Lamartine?*, Paris, 1952, pp. 155, 158.

conseil entre nous, Gautier; faites comme si elle n'en avait pas."[1] Indeed, they felt unable to share the accepted view of Gautier as the poverty-stricken poet driven to earn a living by the hackwork of dramatic criticism and other pieces of journalism, the view put forward by Maxime Du Camp, for instance:

Pour lui, c'est la critique dramatique qui a nourri la poésie. Or cette critique dramatique, inutile, sans autre intérêt qu'un intérêt transitoire, a pris son temps et l'a détourné d'œuvres plus sérieuses. Si, au lieu des douze ou quinze cents feuilletons qu'il a brochés dans la *Presse*, dans le *Moniteur universel*, dans le *Journal officiel*, il eût composé cinq ou six mille vers de plus, la France y eût gagné et la besogne dramatique n'y eût rien perdu.[2]

In the following month they commented on the state of relative affluence in which Gautier found himself towards the end of the Second Empire:

A voir le vrai et le fin fond des choses, ce bon Gautier est un de ces meurt-de-faim de la littérature les plus riches de ce temps-ci, avec sa place de bibliothèque, soit 6,000,—une pension sur la cassette de l'Empereur, soit 3,000,—à peu près 20,000 francs au *Moniteur* par an et le revenant-bon de ses livres. Qui est-ce qui est aussi riche que cela dans les lettres à l'heure qu'il est?[3]

Yet the frequent changes of political regime in this period could have disastrous effects on a writer's career, as Gautier explained to Edmond de Goncourt in October 1870 after the collapse of Louis Napoleon's empire:

Cette révolution, c'est ma fin, c'est mon *coup de lapin*. . . . Du reste, je suis une victime des révolutions. Sans blague! Lors de la Révolution de Juillet, mon père était très légitimiste, il a joué à la hausse, sur les Ordonnances de Juillet; vous pensez comme ça a réussi! Nous avons perdu toute notre fortune, quinze mille livres de rentes. J'étais destiné à entrer dans la vie en heureux, en homme de loisir; il a fallu gagner sa vie. . . . Enfin, après des années, j'avais assez bien arrangé mon affaire, j'avais une petite maison, une petite voiture, deux petits chevaux. Février met tout ça à bas. . . . Je retrouve l'équilibre, j'allais être nommé de l'Académie, . . . au Sénat: Sainte-Beuve mort, Mérimée prêt à mourir, il n'était pas improbable que l'Empereur voulût y mettre un homme de lettres, n'est-ce pas?[4] Je finissais par me caser. . . . Tout fout le camp avec la République.[5]

[1] *Journal* viii. 146.   [2] *Souvenirs littéraires*, ii. 378.   [3] *Journal* viii. 156.
[4] This was an illusion; Gautier's name was not on the list of persons to be created Senators on 27 July 1870 (see *Les Papiers secrets*, pt. V, p. 31).
[5] *Journal* ix. 90.

Indeed, Gautier did not long survive the disasters of 1870. None the less the Third Republic did continue down to his death in 1872 the pension of 3,000 francs which the Ministry of the Interior had paid him since 1863.[1]

Under the Second Empire various ministries continued to assist men of letters. In 1855 Baudelaire reported to his mother a conversation with the notary, Ancelle, who had been charged with the administration of the poet's affairs because of his spendthrift habits:

Je disais ce matin même à Ancelle une chose que je trouve assez raisonnable. Je lui disais: préfériez-vous que je fisse ce que font tant d'hommes de lettres, qui ont moins d'orgueil que moi, et ce que je n'ai jamais fait sous aucun ministère, sous aucun gouvernement? Demander de l'argent à un ministre me fait horreur, et cependant cela est presque un usage; il y a des fonds pour cela. Quant à moi, j'ai un orgueil et une prudence qui m'ont toujours éloigné de ces moyens-là. Jamais mon nom ne paraîtra dans les ignobles paperasses d'un gouvernement. J'aime mieux devoir à tout le monde, j'aime mieux me disputer avec vous, et tourmenter ma mère, quelque pénible que cela soit.[2]

Yet despite these proud declarations of independence two years later, on the very eve of the publication of *Les Fleurs du mal*, we find Baudelaire sending this humble letter to the Minister of Education:

Monsieur le Ministre,

Mon travail, sans suffire largement à mes besoins, m'avait permis jusqu'ici d'éviter des demandes qui m'ont toujours répugné; mais des besoins urgents me déterminent aujourd'hui à m'adresser à Votre Excellence pour solliciter un engagement sur les fonds des Sciences et des Lettres.

Si quelque considération pouvait atténuer le regret que j'éprouve de recourir à une pareille démarche, c'est la conscience que j'ai d'avoir fait tout ce qui était en moi pour l'éviter, et l'intérêt que je suis assuré de rencontrer chez Votre Excellence. Les témoignages récents de bienveillance qu'elle a données à la Société[3] dont je suis membre depuis douze ans me permettent d'espérer pour ma demande un accueil favorable.

Je prends la liberté de joindre à ma demande la liste des principaux travaux que j'ai publiés, ainsi que l'annonce de ceux qui sont en ce moment sous presse.

Je prie Votre Excellence d'agréer l'hommage de mon profond respect.[4]

[1] Maxime Du Camp, *Théophile Gautier*, Paris, 1919, p. 194.
[2] *Correspondance générale*, ed. J. Crépet and C. Pichois, 6 vols., Paris, 1947–53, i. 335–6.
[3] The Société des gens de lettres, founded in 1838 (see below p. 314). The Minister, Gustave Rouland, had recently increased the subsidy to the society (see E. Montagne, *Histoire de la Société des gens de lettres*, Paris, 1889, p. 146).
[4] *Correspondance générale*, ii. 56–7.

The result of this appeal was an award of the paltry sum of 200 francs in recognition of the poet's translation of Poe. After addressing a petition to the Empress Eugénie which secured a reduction in the fine imposed on him for publishing obscene verses in *Les Fleurs du mal*, he received from the government other small sums, ranging from 100 to 500 francs.[1]

Such modest subsidies to needy writers continued to be doled out by successive governments under the Third Republic. In 1895 that notorious cadger, Léon Bloy, wrote to Gabriel Hanotaux, an old acquaintance who had become Minister for Foreign Affairs, asking him for 500 francs to save his wife and small daughter from abject poverty. 'Ne suis-je pas éligible et, par conséquent, habile à participer aux fonds secrets dont un prévoyant Trésor inonde nos ministères?' he wrote in his diary. On this occasion his request was apparently successful as three days later we find the entry: 'Hanotaux s'est exécuté. Enfin son passage au ministère aura du moins servi à cela.' However, when in the following year he applied again, he was extremely grieved to receive only 20 francs.[2]

It is clear that by this date such financial assistance as the state continued to give was both on a very modest scale and was offered only to necessitous writers. Zola makes this point when he compares the situation in the 1880s with what it has been a century or two earlier:

D'ailleurs, les pensions ne sont plus données à titre honorifique et comme un témoignage de haute admiration; elles vont aux nécessiteux, aux écrivains dont la vieillesse n'est pas heureuse; et, le plus souvent, on les dissimule, en donnant une sinécure au pensionnaire, un emploi fictif qui met sa dignité à l'abri. En somme, les pensions se sont faites discrètes et comme honteuses; certes, elles n'entaînent aucune déchéance, mais elles sont l'indice certain d'un état de gêne qu'on aime mieux cacher.[3]

This reference to the state disguising its financial assistance to a writer by giving him some sinecure concerns particularly appointments to posts in a variety of libraries.

Zola was perhaps thinking of an illustrious example—that of Flaubert who in his last years was extremely hard up because he had helped his niece's husband in his financial difficulties. Just over a year before he died his friends endeavoured to obtain some form of state assistance for him. In March 1879 he wrote to his niece: 'J'ai tout lieu de croire qu'on

---

[1] See ibid. ii. 100, 122, 259; iii. 19 n., 198 n.; iv. 73, 178.
[2] *Journal*, 4 vols., Paris, 1963, i. 175–6.
[3] *Œuvres complètes*, x. 1274.

va *m'offrir* une pension; et je l'accepterai, bien que j'en sois *humilié* jusqu'à la moelle des os (aussi je désire là-dessus le secret le plus absolu).'[1] Shortly afterwards Jules Ferry, who had recently become Minister of Education, had Flaubert appointed to a supernumerary post at the Bibliothèque Mazarine. This was a pure sinecure, but a modest salary of 3,000 francs was attached to it.

Some insight into the persistence of state patronage of men of letters at the moment when the 'République des Républicains' was finally established is offered by a letter which Maupassant wrote to Flaubert in April 1879 when negotiations were still going on behind the scenes about coming to his assistance. While Maupassant informs Flaubert that he will be offered a pension of 5,000 francs, he warns him that there may well be some delay before the matter is finally settled:

. . . On modifie complètement tout le système des pensions pour les répartir plus équtablement. Il y a 500 hommes de lettres qui reçoivent une pension. Dans ce nombre, il y en a beaucoup qui n'en ont nullement besoin et qui gagnent ou possèdent de 8,000 à 10,000 francs par an. Il faut leur supprimer ce qu'on leur donne; mais vous comprenez que la chose est délicate et ne peut se faire en un jour. Pour vous, c'est une affaire décidée, ainsi que pour Leconte de Lisle qui avait 1,600 francs et à qui on va donner 2,000 francs.[2]

One must, of course, assume that the figure of five hundred given here is a picturesque exaggeration.

Throughout the whole of this period posts as librarians were offered to men of letters to enable them to keep the wolf from the door. Indeed, a distinguished French librarian has recently attributed to this practice part of the blame for a certain backwardness in library provision in the France of our day.[3] Most writers, if they were actually compelled to put in some hours a week in a library, did not seem to take the job very seriously. A post in a small library like the Mazarine offered all sorts of advantages, as the poet, Théodore de Banville, explains:

On n'a affaire qu'à de rares travailleurs muets et bien élevés, et on est de service une fois par semaine, avec la faculté de se faire remplacer. Au bout de quelque temps écoulé, l'Institut vous loge gratuitement dans un appartement spacieux, et souvent vous donne encore une clef de la bibliothèque pour aller prendre des livres, et un cabinet isolé de l'appartement, des bruits du ménage.[4]

---

[1] *Correspondance*, v. 508.

[2] R. Dumesnil, *Guy de Maupassant*, Paris, 1933, p. 129.

[3] R. Pierrot, 'Les Bibliothèques', in *Le Livre français. Hier, aujourd'hui, demain*, ed. J. Cain, R. Escarpit and H. J. Martin, Paris, 1972, p. 202.

[4] *Mes souvenirs*, Paris, 1882, pp. 301–2.

How the old writer, Jules Sandeau, from whom George Sand had borrowed half his name when she became tired of being merely Mme Dudevant, carried out his modest duties in this library is amusingly related by a contemporary:

Il était bibliothécaire de la Bibliothèque Mazarine et comme on n'arrivait pas à obtenir qu'il prît ses tours de service, on avait, pour sauver les apparences, fini par réduire sa tâche à une séance d'après-midi une fois par semaine. Il prenait place au fauteuil à l'heure voulue, et s'astreignait, au besoin, à la transmission des bulletins de demandes des lecteurs, mais lorsque l'un d'eux tentait d'obtenir de lui des renseignements ou un conseil comportant un effort ou un dérangement quelconque, alors il répondait, en souriant:

'Mon Dieu, Monsieur, je me permettrai de vous donner un avis utile: ne venez jamais le mercredi. C'est mon jour et je ne suis au courant de rien.'[1]

Not all writer-librarians were as lacking in conscience as this. There is even the sad case of Flaubert's friend, the poet and playwright, Louis Bouilhet, who, when he was appointed librarian at Rouen, unfortunately got so interested in the job that he tended to neglect his writing:

C'était un poste tranquille, fait pour lui. Tout en surveillant la besogne des employés et le prêt des livres, on peut rêver aux personnages du drame et chercher des rimes rares; mais la nouveauté de la fonction l'intéressa, du moins il le crut; il pensa à des classements, à des catalogues, des installations logiques, et donna à la bibliothèque un temps que la poésie réclamait. Flaubert était furieux et ne lui épargnait pas les reproches: 'On t'a mis là pour faire des vers et non pour ranger des bouquins'.[2]

No doubt Bouilhet was very much an exception.

Throughout the century all manner of writers derived from such appointments anything from a modest supplement to their income to a quite affluent position. The latter was the situation of Charles Nodier who in 1824 was appointed librarian of the Bibliothèque de l'Arsenal which was then the private property of the comte d'Artois, soon to become Charles X. It was in his *salon* at the Arsenal that the first Romantic *cénacle* met. He held this post until his death in 1844, arousing the envy of Balzac at the large income which he drew from this post, from his position as an academician, from a state pension, and in only a relatively minor way from his writings. In 1842 Balzac wrote to Mme Hanska: 'Nodier est logé dans les appartements de Sully, Nodier a une

---

[1] Dreyfous, *Ce qu'il me reste à dire*, pp. 197–8.
[2] Du Camp, *Souvenirs littéraires*, ii. 325.

place de 6,000 fr., 3,000 fr. comme académicien, 6,000 fr. comme chargé d'un travail pour le *Dictionnaire* et une pension de 2,000 fr. comme homme de lettres; en tout 17,000 fr., et il gagne bien 3,000 fr. par an.'[1] The same post of librarian at the Arsenal was occupied for some years at the beginning of this century by the poet, Heredia, who also held a literary *salon* there.

It would not seem altogether unnatural to see a scholar-critic like Sainte-Beuve in the role of librarian even though apparently he did not take his duties very seriously. In 1840, after thanking Thiers for his appointment, he wrote to his Swiss friends, the Oliviers: 'Ma Mazarine, c'est 4,000 f. par an, plus un logement dans les bâtiments de l'Institut.'[2] He did not resign this post until after the 1848 Revolution. On the other hand, Alfred de Musset, in the latter part of his life seldom sober, would seem a strange person to appoint to one of these posts except that they were mostly sinecures. Yet in 1838 he was appointed 'bibliothécaire au ministère de l'Intérieur où', Rémusat drily adds, 'il n'y avait pas de bibliothèque'.[3] After the 1848 Revolution he lost this post, but when the Second Empire came in, he was given a similar one in the Ministry of Education.[4] Poets, who generally found it hard to make a living, were often assisted in this way. Despite his secret pension from Louis Napoleon, Leconte de Lisle was rewarded in 1872 for his firm republican views and made a librarian at the Senate; and, as we have just seen, one of his disciples, Heredia, held a much more exalted post at the Arsenal some thirty years later.

With the decline in literary patronage, indeed its gradual reduction to what can only be called a charitable function, writers without private means were expected to earn a living by what they could wring out of publishers of books, periodicals, and newspapers, and, of course, if they tried their hand at drama as many did, from theatre managers.

In 1837 Vigny penned these bitter lines in his journal on the relations between writer and publisher.

LA TRAITE DES AUTEURS.—Les éditeurs sont des négriers.—Rien de difficile à un auteur qui n'a que sa plume pour vivre, comme de se dérober à eux.

L'éditeur cherche des ouvriers qui rapportent et tâche d'abord de les réduire à la plus profonde misère.

Si un ami donne secours à l'écrivain, ils critiquent l'ami jusqu'à ce qu'il

---

[1] *Lettres à Madame Hanska*, ii. 140.
[2] *Correspondance générale*, ed. J. Bonnerot, Paris, 1935– , iii. 352.
[3] Rémusat, *Mémoires de ma vie*, iii. 182.   [4] Du Camp, *Souvenirs littéraires*, ii. 249–50.

l'abandonne. Alors il travaille, on l'exploite, avec un traité on le lie pour un autre; on l'engage pour sa vie enfin, à tant par mois.

Un de ces exploiteurs est à mettre dans un roman—ou en comédie.[1]

It would not be difficult to match this diatribe with similar outbursts from contemporaries of Vigny—Balzac, for instance—or later writers such as Flaubert; yet it is clear that writers of the seventeenth or even eighteenth century would have been astounded at the wealth which gradually became available to writers of this period whose books sold in the large numbers which a greatly expanded reading public made possible.

As book publishing gradually became a specialized occupation, the old term *libraire* which could also cover retail bookselling and even printing gradually gave way in this period to the modern, though somewhat ambiguous *éditeur*, just as on this side of the Channel *bookseller* was replaced by *publisher*. Littré illustrates the gradualness of the process when he gives as the second meaning of *éditeur*: 'Particulière-ment, libraire qui publie un livre à son compte; et, adjectivement, libraire-éditeur. M. Hachette est l'éditeur de ce dictionnaire.' Indeed, it is only quite recently that publishing firms such as the Librairie Hachette and the Librairie Armand Colin have begun to drop the word *librairie* from the title-page of their books.

Publishing was still very far from being what it was for the most part to become in the second half of the twentieth century, an affair of large-scale, impersonal organizations mainly ruled by accountants. In this period relations between the writer and the owner of the one-man publishing business were intensely personal; this could lead both to friendships and to bitter quarrels. The profits to be derived from publishing did not become really large until the second half of the century with the expansion of the market for books. Under the Restoration and even the July Monarchy publishers were often small men with insufficient capital behind them and they were liable to go bankrupt, particularly in periods of economic crisis; in 1830 this was the fate that overcame Ladvocat, the leading publisher of the Restoration. It could scarcely be said that they often grew rich at the expense of their authors. Some of the most solid flourished by publishing, not new novels, plays, or poetry, but new editions of standard authors. However, some of the names familiar to us today go back to this period—Hachette (1826), Garnier (1833), and Calmann-Lévy (1836). During the Second Empire

[1] *Œuvres complètes*, ed. F. Baldensperger, 2 vols., Paris, 1948, ii. 1060–1.

other famous names emerged such as those of Larousse (1852) and Armand Colin (1870). Most of the successful firms of the period devoted a good deal of attention to educational publishing in the broad sense. We have seen how Louis Hachette was responsible for the publication of Littré's *Dictionnaire de la langue française* which appeared between 1863 and 1873, while Pierre Larousse edited and partly compiled his *Grand dictionnaire universel du XIXe siècle*, published between 1865 and 1876, a vast work which was the first of a long series of dictionaries and encyclopedias to be published by this firm.

No doubt there were many acrimonious arguments between writers and publishers in this period; quarrels were frequent and writers like Hugo or Balzac or George Sand were constantly changing their publishers. As a result of a row with Michel Lévy over the publication of a posthumous volume of his friend, Louis Bouilhet, Flaubert changed to Georges Charpentier, the son and successor of the founder of the Bibliothèque Charpentier. On the other hand, relations could be very friendly, and writers sometimes owed a great deal to the advice and even assistance which they received from publishers. For instance, Georges Charpentier and his partner, Maurice Dreyfous, came to the rescue of Zola after the 1870 war; his original publisher for the *Rougon-Macquart* had gone bankrupt and he was unable to find anyone to take on the rest of the mighty work he had planned. What he was looking for, far from hopefully, was a publisher who would provide him with a small but steady income to keep himself, his wife, and his mother while he got on with writing his novels. He offered Charpentier and Dreyfous two novels a year in return for 500 francs a month, and to his surprise the offer was accepted. Zola never managed to write more than one novel a year, but, although his publishers took a long time to get their money back, the success of *L'Assommoir* in 1877 transformed the whole relationship and Zola was offered a new and decidedly more favourable contract.[1]

In this period writers no longer remained isolated in their confrontation with publishers; but while the Société des auteurs et compositeurs dramatiques can trace its history back to its origins in the 1770s with the struggle of Beaumarchais and other playwrights to secure better terms for the profession,[2] writers in general did not form their own society—the Société des gens de lettres—until 1838.[3]

---

[1] Dreyfous, *Ce qu'il me reste à dire*, pp. 282–304.   [2] See pp. 218–25.

[3] Unfortunately, there is not yet a history of the society. The *Histoire de la Société des gens de lettres*, published in 1889 by E. Montagne, is merely a chronicle of events and anecdotes.

For several years before that date Balzac had been agitating for the founding of such a society. In 1837 a now forgotten writer named Louis Desnoyers (he was at this time editor of the newspaper *Le Siècle*) got together at his house a number of writers who agreed to form a society. In January of the following year a provisional committee with Villemain as president was set up and later in the month the society was formally established. In April the first annual general meeting was held; among those elected to the committee were Hugo, Lamennais, Dumas *père*, and Guizot. Balzac's relations with the society were, to put it mildly, somewhat eccentric. It was only in December 1838 that he applied for membership; in August of the following year, Villemain having become Minister of Education, Balzac was unanimously elected in his place for the rest of the year, being succeeded in January 1840 by Victor Hugo. After a period of intense activity on behalf of the society, in October 1841 Balzac suddenly sent in his resignation. It was refused, as was a second resignation in 1844.

The aim of the founders was to protect the interest of writers, particularly in the matter of literary property which many members, including Balzac, argued should be made perpetual. Unlike the playwrights' association which collects on behalf of its members large sums of money for the performance of their works, originally the only collecting done by the Société des gens de lettres concerned fees arising out of the reproduction in newspapers and periodicals of works of its members which had already been published. Nowadays the society also handles such things as radio and television fees. In 1846 the society received its first government subsidy—a modest 2,000 francs from the Ministry of Education—to enable it to offer financial assistance to members in need. This was later increased to 6,000 francs and the sum was doubled by a grant from the Ministry of the Interior. In 1861, thanks partly to various legacies, the society was able to establish pensions of 300 francs for those who had been members for twenty years. Early in the present century, in 1904, the society, which in 1891 had been recognized as being 'd'utilité publique', received a large sum—1,780,000 francs—from the government to make possible the payment of its pensions.

Though many distinguished French writers, including Zola, served as president of the society, in this period it did not encounter whole-hearted support from all members of the profession. Balzac was not the

1838–1938. Le Centenaire de la Société des gens de lettres de France, published in 1939 as a supplement to the Society's *Chronique*, is mainly concerned with the junketings to which the centenary gave rise.

only writer of the time to fall out with the society. George Sand resigned in 1848—on the eve of the revolution—and brought a lawsuit against it as the society had given permission to reproduce *La Mare au diable* when it was still the property of her publisher. Finally, when the case came on in 1849, baron Taylor gave the society 3,000 francs to settle the claim.[1]

Moreover, some writers of the time felt that the profession was becoming more and more concerned with vulgar questions of money. It is in the context of the foundation of the society that one must read Saint-Beuve's famous article, 'De la littérature industrielle', which appeared in the *Revue des Deux Mondes* in 1839. In it he makes fun of a letter which Balzac, as president of the society, had recently published in *La Presse*. After lamenting the poverty of many writers, Balzac had argued that it was up to the French Government to put an end to Belgian piracy of French books by subsidizing those authors whose works suffered from it:

> Pourquoi l'état ne désintéresse-t-il pas les auteurs qui sont sujets à contrefaçon et ne fait-il point passer ainsi leurs œuvres du domaine privé dans le domaine public? Aussitôt la Belgique succombe et la France a pour elle le marché européen. Après tout, que contrefait la Belgique? Les dix ou douze maréchaux de France littéraires, selon la belle expression de M. Victor Hugo, ceux qui font œuvre, collection, et qui offrent à l'exploitation une certaine commerciale.[2]

Sainte-Beuve pours ridicule on this proposal:

> Sa lettre sur la propriété littéraire . . . ne tend à rien moins qu'à proposer au Gouvernement d'acheter les œuvres des *dix ou douze maréchaux de France*, à commencer par celles de l'auteur lui-même qui s'évalue à *deux millions*, si j'ai bien compris. Vous imaginez-vous le Gouvernement désintéressant l'auteur de la *Physiologie du Mariage*, afin de la mieux répandre, et débitant les *Contes drolatiques* comme on vend du papier timbré? Des conséquences si drolatiques sont très propres à faire rentrer en lui-même le démon de la propriété littéraire, dont M. de Balzac n'a peut-être voulu, après tout, que se moquer agréablement.[3]

The article covers a lot of ground. Sainte-Beauve was particularly disturbed by the impact on literature of the cheaper newspapers like

---

[1] Montagne, *Histoire de la Société des gens de lettres*, pp. 112–14. See also G. Sand, *Correspondance*, ed. G. Lubin, Paris, 1964– , vii. 522 and viii. 303.

[2] *Correspondance*, ed. R. Pierrot, 5 vols., Paris, 1960–9, iii. 676.

[3] *Portraits contemporains*, 5 vols., Paris, 1869–76, ii. 468–9.

La Presse and *Le Siècle* which depended on advertising for a large part of their income. Independent criticism of new books was ruled out:

On eut beau vouloir séparer dans le journal ce qui restait consciencieux et libre, de ce qui devenait public et vénal; la limite du *filet* fut bientôt franchie. La *réclame* servit de pont. Comment condamner à deux doigts de distance, qualifier détestable et funeste ce qui se proclamait et s'affichait deux doigts plus bas comme la merveille de l'époque? L'attraction des majuscules croissantes de l'annonce l'emporta: ce fut une montagne d'aimant qui fit mentir la boussole. Afin d'avoir en caisse le profit de l'annonce, on eut de la complaisance pour les livres nouveaux; la critique y perdit son crédit.[1]

In his observations on the recently founded Société des gens de lettres he has a number of reservations to make. The most serious of these is one which has frequently been raised on both sides of the Channel concerning such societies:

Tout le monde peut se dire *homme de lettres*: c'est le titre de qui n'en a point. Les plus empressés à se donner pour tels ne sont pas les plus dignes. La Société songera-t-elle au mérite réel dans l'admission? peut-elle y songer? où sera l'expertise? Dans les compagnonnages des divers métiers, on ne reçoit que des ouvriers faits et sur preuves; mais, en matière littéraire, qui décidera? Voilà donc une Société qui recevra tous ceux qui s'offriront pour gens de lettres, et qui les aidera, et qui les organisera en force compacte; et dans toutes les questions, les moindres, les moins éclairés, les moins intéressés à ce qui touche vraiment les lettres, crieront le plus haut, soyez-en sûr.[2]

Nowadays when the members of the society, like those of the Society of Authors (founded much later, in 1884), are numbered by the thousand, this is a point which cannot fail to strike the outside observer.

Similar lamentations about the commercial outlook of men of letters are to be found in the Goncourts' journal. In 1874, for instance, Edmond wrote:

Les jeunes de la littérature actuelle, et les plus distingués et les plus vaillants, savent au mieux les moyens d'action sur tel ou tel éditeur, les besoins de copie de tel ou tel journal, le *dada* momentané de tel ou tel directeur de revue, enfin les chances de placement de la prose dans telle ou telle boutique, dans telle maison, dans tel papier imprimé. Ils sont à l'affût de tous les bruits,

[1] Ibid. pp. 355–6. Sainte-Beuve adds this note to 'la *réclame:*' 'Pour ceux qui l'ignorent, nous dirons que la *réclame* est la petite note glissée vers la fin, à l'*intérieur* du journal, d'ordinaire payée par le libraire, insérée le même jour que l'annonce ou le lendemain, et donnant en deux mots un petit jugement flatteur qui prépare et préjuge celui de l'article.'

[2] Ibid. p. 465.

de toutes les indiscrétions, de toutes les confidences qui se murmurent à l'oreille; ils possèdent, en vrais courtiers de lettres, tous les secrets financiers de l'industrie des lettres. C'est une connaissance de la place de Paris, qui manquait absolument à notre génération. Au fond, je crois bien que c'est le commencement de la fin de la pure littérature.[1]

A dozen years later he returned to the same theme of the growing commercialization of literature:

La littérature doit être considérée comme une carrière qui ne vous nourrit ni ne vous loge ni ne vous chauffe et où la rémunération est invraisemblable. Et c'est seulement quand on la considère ainsi, la littérature, et qu'on y entre, poussé par le diable-au-corps du sacrifice, du martyre et de l'amour du beau, qu'on peut avoir du talent. Et aujourd'hui que ce n'est plus un métier de meurt-de-faim, que les parents ne vous donnent plus leur malédiction quand vous vous faites homme de lettres, il n'y a plus, pour ainsi dire, de vraie vocation, et il se pourrait qu'avant peu de temps il n'y ait plus de talent.[2]

None the less the same writer was distinctly grieved when his own books failed to sell and bring in money; and he was extremely jealous of the big sales achieved by the novels of younger contemporaries like Daudet and Zola.

Financial dealings between writer and publisher in this period tended to be rather different from what we are accustomed to today. It is true that in the end there was evolved, as in this country, the royalty system as we know it, one under which the author receives an agreed percentage of the published price for each copy of his book which is sold. This came in, however, very gradually indeed. The outright sale of the book, especially of poetry, often for a very small sum seems to have continued, but there is no evidence that this was applied to works likely to have a considerable sale. In this country Trollope actually preferred a lump sum—often several thousand pounds—to the profit-sharing arrangement which was then customary on this side of the Channel. In France profit-sharing does not seem to have been anything like as common as in this country.

Agreements between writer and publisher in the first half of the century generally specify that the publisher is to pay the author a stated sum in return for the right to print and publish a stated number of copies of his work. This was in effect a kind of royalty system in the sense that in practice the author received for each copy printed 50 centimes or 1 franc or 2 francs. In 1833, for instance, after the success of

Indiana, George Sand signed an agreement under which she was to receive 5,000 francs from a publisher in return for the right to publish 1,600 copies of her novel *Lélia*.[1] In effect, she was getting a royalty of some 3 francs a copy, but with this important difference from a modern royalty system that she did not have to wait to receive the 5,000 francs until all the 1,600 copies were sold; it was specified in the agreement that 4,000 francs were to be paid before the day of publication and the remainder within a fortnight of that date. There was an even more striking difference compared with the normal twentieth-century publisher's agreement: George Sand did not sell her copyright to the publisher. She merely gave him a licence to print a stated number of copies *for a limited period of time*. This could be quite short—eighteen months or twelve or even less; in this case George Sand prescribed a period of only nine months from the date of publication. After that period had come to an end, the author was quite free to negotiate fresh terms for a second or subsequent editions either with the original publisher (some contracts laid it down that he should be given preference) or with another publisher or publishers. It was agreements of this sort which were signed in the 1830s and 1840s by writers like Hugo, Balzac, and George Sand.

Round about the middle of the century a different type of agreement emerges. In 1866 Baudelaire wrote to Ancelle: 'Vous aurez soin de bien vous faire expliquer ce que c'est qu'un *traité à temps* et un *traité basé sur un tirage déterminé*. Dans l'un des cas, une somme est donnée à l'auteur, en échange de l'exploitation pour un certain temps. Dans l'autre cas, on donne à l'auteur tant *par exemplaire*.'[2] This is not perhaps Baudelaire's prose at its most lucid. The second system he refers to is the one which we have just examined, but it too contained a time element. The first system he mentions was the new one; under it the author limited the period during which a publisher was allowed to sell his work, but the period was now a matter of several years; moreover, during the specified time the publisher was free to produce as many copies in as many different formats as he thought he could sell.[3] As before, the author retained his copyright, but since the agreement ran for a considerable number of years, the sum received by an established author could be quite large. A famous example is that of *Les Misérables*.

[1] *Correspondance*, ed. Lubin, ii. 219–21.

[2] *Correspondance générale*, v. 233.

[3] Both systems were sometimes used in nineteenth-century England before the gradual emergence of the royalty system. See S. H. Nowell-Smith, *International Copyright Law and the Publisher in the Reign of Queen Victoria*, Oxford, 1968, p. 51.

Hugo signed a contract to run for eight years; this secured him a lump sum of 250,000 francs (300,000 on some interpretations), leaving the publisher free to print as many copies as he liked in that period.[1]

Inevitably, there were enormous differences between what the authors of famous novels of the time received for their works. By comparison with Hugo Flaubert seems to have been extremely unfortunate over *Madame Bovary*, though clearly *Les Misérables* had a much wider appeal as it has distinct affinities with the *romans-feuilletons* of Eugène Sue. Hugo even claimed that a Paris newspaper had offered 500,000 francs for the right to publish his work as a *roman-feuilleton*, but that this was impossible owing to the lack of freedom of the press under the Second Empire.[2]

Flaubert had to content himself with publishing *Madame Bovary* in a review before it appeared in book form. In 1856 he excitedly announced to a cousin: 'Sache, ô cousin, que hier j'ai vendu un livre (terme ambitieux) moyennant la somme de deux mille francs. . . . Je paraîtrai dans la *Revue de Paris*, pendant six numéros de suite, à partir de juillet.—Après quoi, je revendrai mon affaire à un éditeur qui la mettra en volume.'[3] If this was a fair sum to receive from a review, the contract which he signed with Michel Lévy for the publication of the novel in book form seems in retrospect decidedly odd. The agreement was concluded for five years, but the sum offered—800 francs—seems a derisory amount for a first printing of 6,750 copies. Moreover, two more impressions followed in the year of publication, 1857, and then came two more in 1858 and 1862, together with a cheap edition in one volume. Altogether in the five-year period granted him by Flaubert Michel Lévy printed over 32,000 copies of *Madame Bovary* for which he paid him . . . 800 francs. It is true that he gave him an extra 500 francs in August 1857.[4] This meant that altogether Flaubert received for this masterpiece only 3,300 francs, at any rate down to 1862.

What Flaubert subsequently earned from *Madame Bovary* is unfortunately not clear since its fate was linked with that of his later works. Indeed, with the expenses of his lawsuit over the novel he claimed he was actually out of pocket: 'La littérature, jusqu'à présent, m'a coûté 200 francs.'[5] Not unnaturally, he was far from satisfied with this result.

[1] B. Leuilliot, *Victor Hugo publie Les Misérables* (*Correspondance avec Albert Lacroix, août 1861–juillet 1862*), Paris, 1970, pp. 31–2.

[2] Ibid. p. 109.

[3] *Lettres inédites à son editeur, Michel Lévy*, ed. J. Suffel, Paris, 1965, pp. 22–3.

[4] Ibid. pp. 23–6, 48 n.   [5] *Correspondance*, iv. 280.

It is true that ten years earlier he had written to Louise Colet in his usual emphatic manner: 'Quant à *gagner* de l'argent, non! non! et à en gagner avec ma plume, jamais! jamais! Je n'en fais pas le serment, parce que l'on a l'habitude de violer les serments; mais je dis suelement que cela m'étonnerait fort, vu que le métier d'homme de lettres me répugne prodigieusement.'[1] Yet in 1857 we find him writing to Jules Duplan: 'Lévy m'a écrit qu'il allait faire un second tirage: voilà 15,000 exemplaires de vendus; *aliter*: 30,000 francs qui me passent sous le nez!! . . .'[2] It should perhaps be said that Flaubert fared better than Hector Malot with the same publisher; when Malot took him his first novel, part of a trilogy, in 1859, he was told: 'Je vous donne quatre cents francs pour le droit de propriété pendant cinq ans, et vous me cédez les deux volumes qui suivront aux mêmes conditions.'[3]

In 1862, when he sold *Salammbô* to Michel Lévy for a period of ten years, *Madame Bovary* was included in the deal.[4] This time the sum he received was vastly different—10,000 francs; but it is obviously impossible to say how much of this was for *Madame Bovary*. His publisher gave out to the press that he was paying 30,000 francs for the new novel. After informing Jules Duplan of the conclusion of the contract Flaubert went on:

Maintenant, je vous prie de garder pour vous l'énoncé de ce chiffre, parce que le dit Lévy se propose de faire avec *Salammbô* un boucan infernal et de répandre dans les feuilles qu'il me l'a acheté TRENTE MILLE FRANCS, ce qui lui donne les gants d'un homme généreux.

Voilà donc, *motus*; dites seulement que j'ai vendu à des conditions avantageuses.[5]

When *L'Éducation sentimentale* appeared in 1869, Flaubert received not only the 10,000 francs stipulated in his agreement, but an additional 6,000 francs as the novel was in two volumes.[6] When he quarrelled with Michel Lévy in 1872 and went over to Georges Charpentier, as his agreement of 1862 expired on 1 January 1873, he was now free to have *Madame Bovary* reprinted by him as well as by Alphonse Lemerre, the publisher one associates with the Parnassian poets.[7] It seems doubtful whether Flaubert got much money out of these later reprints. In

[1] Ibid. ii. 39–40.   [2] Ibid. iv. 188.

[3] *Le Roman de mes romans*, p. 12.   [4] *Lettres inédites à son éditeur*, p. 61.

[5] R. Descharmes, 'Flaubert et ses éditeurs: Michel Lévy et Georges Charpentier. Lettres inédites à Georges Charpentier', *Revue d' histoire littéraire*, 1911, p. 371.

[6] *Lettres inédites à son éditeur*, pp. 143–7.

[7] Descharmes, 'Flaubert et ses éditeurs', p. 630 n.

1879, when he was distinctly hard up, we find him writing to Georges Charpentier in typically violent fashion, though one is struck by the timid tone of the closing sentences:

La *Bovary* m'embête. On me *scie* avec ce livre-là. Car tout ce que j'ai fait depuis n'existe pas. Je vous assure que si je n'étais pas besoigneux, je m'arrangerais pour qu'on n'en fît plus de tirage.—Mais la nécessité me contraint. Donc, *tirez*, mon bon. Quant à l'argent, pas besoin de me l'envoyer ici. Vous me le donnerez quand je viendrai à Paris. Une observation: vous dites mille francs pour deux mille exemplaires, ce qui remet l'exemplaire à dix sols. Il me semble que vous me donniez douze, on même treize sols par exemplaire, mais je peux me tromper.[1]

It is somewhat of a paradox that the only one of Flaubert's novels which achieved popularity during his lifetime should have brought such a small financial reward.

It was scarcely surprising if Flaubert with his dedication to Art and his contempt for the bourgeois did not make money, though in practice he was very grieved when his later works had only a modest sale. In her old age George Sand, who during her long and prolific career had made a good deal of money by her pen, pointed this out to him very bluntly apropos of his *Éducation sentimentale*:

J'ai déjà combattu ton hérésie favorite, qui est que l'on écrit pour vingt personnes intelligentes et qu'on se fiche du reste. Ce n'est pas vrai, puisque l'absence de succès t'irrite et t'affecte. D'ailleurs il n'y a pas eu vingt critiques favorables à ce livre si bien fait et si considérable. Donc, il ne faut pas plus écrire pour vingt personnes que pour trois ou pour cent mille.[2]

A few years earlier she had written to another friend:

Si vous voulez savoir ma position matérielle, elle est facile à établir. Mes comptes ne sont pas embrouillés. J'ai bien gagné un million avec mon travail; je n'ai pas mis un sou de côté; j'ai tout donné, sauf vingt mille francs, que j'ai placés, il y a deux ans, pour ne pas coûter trop de tisane à mes enfants, si je tombe malade.[3]

'Un million' sounds impressive, but one has to remember that this was roughly the equivalent of £40,000 in *English money of the time*.

According to Zola, by about 1880 this practice of selling a publisher the right to reproduce a book for a fairly long period of time was falling into disuse:

[1] *Correspondance*, viii. 207–8. [2] *Correspondance 1812–1876*, vi. 378.
[3] Ibid. v. 331.

Il n'y a pas longtemps encore, la librairie était un véritable jeu. Un éditeur achetait pour une certaine somme la propriété d'un manuscrit, pendant dix années; puis, il tâchait de rattraper son argent et de gagner le plus possible, en mettant l'œuvre à toutes les sauces. Forcément, il y avait presque toujours une dupe; ou l'ouvrage obtenait un grand succès, et l'auteur criait sur les toits qu'il était volé; ou l'ouvrage ne se vendait pas, et l'éditeur se disait ruiné par les élucubrations d'un sot.

The old system was being replaced by something approaching the present royalty system, i.e. the payment of a fixed sum for every copy printed by the publisher:

Si quelques éditeurs continuent à suivre l'ancienne mode, le plus grand nombre paye un droit fixe par exemplaire tiré; si ce droit est, par exemple, de cinquante centimes, une édition de mille exemplaires rapportera cinq cents francs à l'auteur, et il touchera autant de fois cinq cents francs que l'éditeur tirera d'éditions.[1]

While the new system related the author's earnings to the sales of his book, it was not quite the same as the royalty system to which we are nowadays accustomed, as it was based not on the number of copies actually sold, but on the number printed. A French writer expected not to have to wait until some time after the end of each accounting period to be paid for the number of copies actually sold during that period, but to receive a lump sum corresponding to the number of copies of his work printed or reprinted, without waiting for them to have been actually sold. This system seems to have been practised by some French publishers long after the end of this period; in 1929, when Paul Léautaud's *Passe-Temps* was published by the Mercure de France, the money due to him for the whole of the first edition was available on the day of publication.[2] In 1909, when the present system was coming in, we find Léon Bloy writing indignantly to a publisher complaining about the time he would have to wait—only six months, the lucky man!—before receiving any payment for his book:

L'article 2 de notre contrat que j'ai été forcé de signer et sur lequel il n'y a pas à revenir, est une clause infiniment dure en ce qu'elle me prive, *même en cas de succès*, de tout salaire pendant six mois et que, même encore, ces six mois écoulés, je ne serai payé que sur les exemplaires *vendus*. Depuis bientôt trente ans que je m'efforce de vivre de ma plume, jamais cela ne m'était arrivé. Au Mercure de France, par exemple, un livre tiré à deux mille et mis en vente le

[1] *Œuvres complètes*, x. 1270-1.
[2] *Journal littéraire*, 19 vols., Paris, 1954-66, vii. 328.

1er novembre, me vaudrait la somme de mille francs payés fort exactement à cette époque sur le chiffre du tirage.[1]

His protest availed nothing. Ultimately, however, the writer's answer was to require an advance on royalties when he signed the agreement for the publication of his book.

As in the previous century, French writers certainly considered that on this side of the Channel writing paid much better. If we turn to the autobiography of Anthony Trollope which is full of information about what he was paid for his novels (written in his spare time . . .), we find that, once he had succeeded in making a name for himself, he could command large sums of money for his writings. He soon rejected the common practice of profit-sharing since he held, as he told William Longman, that 'a lump sum down was more pleasant than a deferred annuity'.[2] At the peak of his career he could earn as much as £3,000 cash down for a long novel, and down to 1879 his novels together with a number of travel books had brought him £68,939. 17s. 5d.[3] This was the equivalent of some 1,700,000 francs in *French money of the time*.

From Balzac to Gide we find French writers looking with some astonishment at the comparative affluence of their English counterparts. In 1847 Balzac, struggling with his mountain of debt, looked with envy on the prosperity of a writer like Dickens. He wrote to Mme Hanska:

Je crois avoir le placement de 3 nouvelles, à 2 ou 3 mille chaque, et je vais essayer d'en brocher une en deux jours. Trois fois cet effort me sauveraient. C'est Laurent-Jan qui m'a donné cette idée, avec *le Cricri du foyer* de Dickens. Ce petit livre est un chef-d'œuvre sans aucun défaut. On paye cela 40,000 fr. à Dickens. On paye mieux en Angleterre qu'ici.[4]

According to the Goncourts, Gautier was similarly impressed with the comparative affluence of English men of letters when he visited London in the 1860s:

Gautier revient de Londres avec l'idée que, décidément, sa copie ne lui est pas payée trop cher en France! Il a vu la fortune d'un homme de lettres anglais, de Thackeray, qui a un hôtel et un parc à Londres. Il a dîné chez lui et il a été servi par des domestiques à bas de soie. Thackeray lui a dit qu'en faisant des

---

[1] *Journal*, iii. 117.   [2] *An Autobiography*, London, 1946, p. 108.
[3] Ibid. pp. 316–17.
[4] *Lettres à Madame Hanska*, iv. 90–1. It is unfortunately impossible to establish exactly how much Dickens actually received for this particular work, but Balzac would appear to have got hold of a somewhat inflated figure.

lectures de ses livres, il gagnait, par chaque lecture, trois ou quatre mille francs, mais que Dickens, qui était meilleur déclamateur que lui, gagnait beaucoup plus.—Est-ce qu'il n'y aurait que les aristocraties pour rétribuer les lettres?[1]

This source of income was, of course, unknown to French writers of the time, but quite apart from their readings from their works the amount of money which English writers earned from their publishers was greater than that earned in France. Fifty years later Gide was to record in his journal with some awe his meeting at Cannes with Arnold Bennett, 'installé au Californie, gagne dans les mille francs par jour; on le paie à raison d'un schilling le mot; il écrit sans s'arrêter chaque jour de six heures du matin à neuf heures, puis passe dans le cabinet de toilette, s'ablutionne et ne pense plus au travail jusqu'au lendemain matin.'[2] No doubt one obtains from such passages an exaggerated view of the affluence of English men of letters of the time; they were certainly not all rolling in money. Yet the level of financial rewards for the successful writer does appear to have been distinctly higher than in France.

It is true that, broadly speaking, the lot of the successful writer did improve in the course of this period with the expansion of the reading public and with the development of periodicals and newspapers. On the whole, the earnings of writers in the 1820s and 1830s tended to be low. Looking back on the situation in his youth round about 1830, Arsène Houssaye wrote in the 1880s:

Les journaux politiques octroyaient à peine l'hospitalité à la critique de livres et à la critique théâtrale. On n'y publiait ni romans, ni études de mœurs, ni portraits littéraires; aussi tous les jeunes esprits dévorés de l'amour des lettres se résignaient-ils à vivre de rien. Je crois que la misère n'a jamais été plus aiguë que dans ces années si fécondes. Le théâtre donnait de quoi mal vivre, le roman de quoi ne pas mourir de faim.[3]

---

[1] *Journal* v. 126–7. Thackeray had just moved into his impressive new house in Kensington, but this was only after affluence had at last come to him through the *Cornhill Magazine* which brought him in an income of £7,000 a year (see G. N. Ray, *Thackeray. The Age of Wisdom, 1847–1863*, London, 1958, p. 392).

[2] *Journal 1889–1939*, Paris, 1948, p. 378. In a letter to his agent from the Hôtel Californie dated 27 March 1912, Bennett, who had only recently begun to earn large sums of money with his novels, plays, and journalism, wrote: 'I staggered myself by a calculation yesterday which showed that my *minimum* earnings from the book and serial work which I *do* this year will be £11,000. This leaves plays out of account entirely. *Milestones* is a *real* success.' (*Letters of Arnold Bennett*, ed. J. Hepburn, i: *Letters to J. B. Pinker*, London, 1966, p. 167.)

[3] *Les Confessions. Souvenirs d'un demi-siècle, 1830–1880*, 6 vols., Paris, 1885–91, i. 191.

This was the age of 'la bohème', of poets starving in garrets, of Vigny's *Stello* and *Chatterton*. Young poets like Sainte-Beuve and Gautier met with little encouragement from publishers for their first collections of verse. Sainte-Beuve was given only 400 francs for the first edition of his *Vie, poésies et pensées de Joseph Delorme* in 1829;[1] in the following year Gautier had to publish his *Poésies* at his own expense and the volume did not sell.[2] Yet not all the poets were hard up in this period; some did succeed in getting themselves known and attracting a wide audience. Although Lamartine earned more from his prose writings (he got 250,000 francs for his eight-volume *Histoire des Girondins* which appeared in 1847), he managed to sell his poetry for fairly substantial sums. In 1823, after the earlier success of *Les Méditations*, he was given 14,000 francs for his *Nouvelles méditations*, and in 1830 he received 27,000 for his *Harmonies poétiques*.[3] The young Hugo made a very modest start with his first volume of poetry which brought him in only 750 francs;[4] But in 1827 he obtained 3,000 francs for the first complete collection of his *Odes et ballades*[5] and in 1829 the same sum for the first edition of *Les Orientales*;[6] in 1831 he received 6,000 francs for the right to publish *Les Orientales* for one year.[7] In 1835 and 1836 he pocketed 20,000 francs for reprints of his first three collections of poetry and the first edition of two new ones, *Les Chants du crépuscule* and *Les Voix intérieures*.[8] In 1839 he signed an agreement with a Société en commandite pour l'exploitation des œuvres de Victor Hugo which, on paper at least, was to bring him in 300,000 francs.[9] With his tremendous output of poetry, prose, and plays he was certainly comfortably off by the 1840s. In 1845 he could write in a letter:

Vous me croyez riche, monsieur. Voici:
Je travaille depuis vingt-huit ans, car j'ai commencé à quinze ans. Dans ces vingt-huit années j'ai gagné avec ma plume environ cinq cent cinquante mille francs.[10] Je n'ai point hérité de mon père . . .

---

[1] *Correspondance générale*, i. 111.   [2] Houssaye, *Confessions* i. 306.

[3] Dumont and Gitan, *De quoi vivait Lamartine?*, pp. 20–1 and Lamartine, *Correspondance générale de 1830 à 1848*, 2 vols., Paris, 1943–9, i. 26.

[4] A. Hugo, *Victor Hugo raconté* . . . ii. 190.

[5] P. Lacretelle, 'Victor Hugo et ses éditeurs', *Revue de France*, 15 Oct. 1923, p. 761.

[6] J. Seebacher, 'Victor Hugo et ses éditeurs avant l'exil', in *Œuvres complètes*, ed. J. Massin, 18 vols., Paris, 1967–70, vi, p. iii.

[7] A. Jullien, *Le Romantisme et l'éditeur Renduel*, Paris, 1897, p. 96.

[8] Ibid. p. 98.

[9] P. Lacretelle, 'Victor Hugo et ses éditeurs', *Revue de France*, 1 Nov. 1923, pp. 75–81; Seebacher, 'Victor Hugo et ses éditeurs avant l'exil', pp. v–xii.

[10] According to Lacretelle, *Revue de France*, 1 Nov. 1923, pp. 81–2, his earnings from publishers down to this date came to 553,000 francs.

Aujourd'hui des cinq cent cinquante mille francs, il m'en reste trois cent mille. Ces trois cent mille francs, je les ai placés. Avec le revenu, je vis, je travaille toujours, ce qui l'accroît un peu.[1]

His later volumes of poetry brought substantial sums to the exiled poet. It is true that several large editions of *Les Contemplations* and *La Légende des siècles* brought him in only 20,000 francs each.[2] None the less in 1856 he could write to Jules Janin in Paris:

La maison de Guernesey avec ses trois étages, son toit, son jardin, son perron, sa crypte, sa basse-cour, son look-out et sa plate-forme, sort tout entière des *Contemplations*. Depuis la première poutre jusqu'à la dernière tuile, les *Contemplations* payeront tout. Ce livre m'a donné un toit.[3]

By the 1860s his novels and his poetry were bringing him in large sums of money.[4] When he died in 1885, his estate was worth in round figures some four million francs.[5]

Lamartine and Hugo were obviously writers who succeeded in attracting a large audience for their poetry and so securing handsome sums from publishers. Other poets of the time were much less prosperous. In 1852 Gautier—by no means a mere beginner, but a writer at the height of his powers—probably received the princely sum of some 200 to 300 francs for his *Émaux et camées*.[6] Later poets like Leconte de Lisle could not survive without outside assistance in the form of pensions or a sinecure in a library. Things were particularly difficult for the young poet; then as now his verse was unlikely to appeal to a publisher, and if it appeared at all, it was in a very small edition and at his own expense. Coppée gives a frank account of what happened with his first two collections of poetry published towards the end of the Second Empire:

Des cinq cents exemplaires, imprimés, ai-je besoin d'en convenir? aux dépens de l'auteur, une centaine tout au plus s'écoula. Une autre centaine fut distribuée à des confrères illustres, à des critiques, à des amis, avec de flatteuses dédicaces. . . . Enfin tout se passa dans l'ordre accoutumé; la majeure partie de l'édition du *Reliquaire* et des *Intimités* resta enfouie dans les arcanes de la Librairie Lemerre, et l'on pouvait déjà prévoir le moment où, convertie en sacs et en cornets, elle envelopperait de rimes riches et de rythmes curieux le sucre de l'épicier ou le caporal du marchand de tabac.[7]

[1] *Correspondance*, Vol. I, p. 625.   [2] Lacretelle, *Revue de France*, 1 Nov. 1923, p. 83.
[3] *Correspondance*, Vol. II. p. 257.   [4] Lacretelle, *Revue de France*, 1 Nov. 1923, p. 91.
[5] Ibid. 15 Oct. 1923, p. 752.
[6] A. Boschot, *Théophile Gautier*, Paris, 1933, p. 82.
[7] *Souvenirs d'un Parisien*, Paris, 1910, pp. 148–9.

He too eked out a living by holding various posts as a librarian at the Senate and the Comédie-Française, and by doing a good deal of journalism. Indeed, in the same work he makes this confession: 'Comme la plupart de mes confrères contemporains, j'ai beaucoup écrit, beaucoup trop peut-être. Ce n'est pas de ma faute, c'est celle de mon temps, où la littérature est devenue une profession.'[1]

If a poet like Coppée who was extremely popular during his lifetime could only make a living by journalism and posts in libraries, it can well be imagined that poets like Verlaine, Rimbaud, and Mallarmé, most of whose work could only appeal to a very narrow section of the public, could not live by their pen. Verlaine and Rimbaud led, of course, extraordinarily unconventional lives, Verlaine starting out as a clerk at the Hôtel de Ville and ending up in a poverty-stricken, sordid bohemianism, Rimbaud leading a wandering existence which took him as far as Abyssinia. In contrast, Mallarmé led a much more conventional life, teaching English in various *lycées*, at first in the provinces, then in Paris. When in 1870, just before the outbreak of the Franco-Prussian War, he told another poet, Catulle Mendès, of his plans to move to Paris and earn a living by his pen, he received a very discouraging reply. Mendès explained that unless Mallarmé had a guaranteed income of 3,000 francs a year, it would be folly to make the move, and that despite half-killing himself with journalism, he himself had the utmost difficulty in making ends meet:

'Mais vouz vivez', direz-vous. Mon ami, n'essayez pas d'endurer ce que j'endure! pour faire vivre ma femme, je meurs! C'est à peine si tous les trois mois, je puis arracher à la destinée trois heures pour faire un sonnet! Ah! cette misère, la misère! un poète qui assassinerait pour avoir de quoi travailler serait-il en effet criminel? Non, je n'ose pas vous dire: partagez cet enfer. J'ai eu des jours sans pain, avec des huissiers à la porte: j'en ai eu![2]

It should be added that this gloomy picture of the life of a poet under the Second Empire is somewhat lightened by Mendès's remark that since he had obtained an annual grant of 1,500 francs from one of the ministries things were a little easier for him.

For a time Mallarmé toyed with the idea of supporting himself in Paris by translating and by running a course on French literature for a group of English girls, at the same time holding a post in one of the

---

[1] Ibid. p. 2.
[2] Mallarmé, *Correspondance, 1862–1871*, eds. H. Mondor and J. P. Richard, Paris, 1959, p. 328.

Paris libraries which would perhaps leave his mornings free for writing. In the end he kept to schoolteaching, a career into which he had drifted, as he explained in a letter to Verlaine in 1885:

Il n'y avait pas, vous le savez, pour un poète à vivre de son art, même en l'abaissant de plusieurs crans, quand je suis entré dans la vie; et je ne l'ai jamais regretté. Ayant appris l'anglais simplement pour mieux lire Poe, je suis parti à vingt ans en Angleterre, afin de fuir principalement; mais aussi pour parler la langue, et l'enseigner dans un coin, tranquille et sans autre gagne-pain obligé; je m'étais marié et cela pressait.[1]

In 1871 he moved to Paris where the famous *salon* which he held in the rue de Rome exercised a great influence on younger poets.

Among those who began to write around 1890, but reached the height of their fame only after 1914, were Claudel and Valéry, but neither of these could be said to have even attempted to live by their poetry and other writings, at any rate before the First World War. For over forty years Claudel was employed in the Foreign Service, travelling all over the world and ending his career in the 1930s as an ambassador, though even before 1914 he had made his name as a poet and playwright. Indeed, writing in 1910 to the young Jacques Rivière for whom, a few weeks later, he found a post at the Collège Stanislas, Claudel gives the gloomiest possible account of the lot of the professional writer:

Il n'y a pas de pire carrière que celle d'un écrivain qui veut vivre de sa plume. Vous voilà donc astreint à produire avec les yeux sur un patron, le public, et à lui donner non pas ce que vous aimez mais ce qu'il aime, et Dieu sait s'il a le goût élevé et délicat. Ah, je ne sais, mais plutôt que la vie d'un X,[2] il vaut mieux être sabotier. J'ai toujours dans la mémoire les figures tragiques d'un Villiers de l'Isle Adam, d'un Verlaine, avec des restes de talent sur eux comme les derniers poils d'une vieille fourrure mangée. Il n'est pas honorable d'essayer de vivre de son âme et de la vendre au peuple: de là le mépris en partie légitime que l'on a toujours eu des acteurs et des artistes.
Et vous êtes marié![3]

Valéry began publishing poetry in 1889 when he was still a law student at Montpellier, but he gave this up in 1892. Three years later, on the advice of Huysmans, he entered a competition for a post in the Ministry of War. Despite highly unfavourable reports—'esprit absolument

---

[1] *Correspondance, 1871–1885*, ed. H. Mondor and L. J. Austin, Paris, 1965, p. 301.
[2] Camille Mauclair.
[3] J. Rivière and P. Claudel, *Correspondance, 1907–1914*, Paris, 1926, pp. 195–6.

nuageux, vulgaire décadent, un Paul Verlaine dont l'administration n'a que faire'—his application was successful.[1] However, in 1900 he left this post to act as secretary to one of the directors of the Agence Havas. This occupation allowed him ample leisure, but it was only in 1912 that he returned to poetry, and down to 1922, when the death of his employer brought the relationship to an end, he continued to rely for a living on this post.

A younger writer, Georges Duhamel, who did not begin his career as a poet until well after 1900, stresses in his memoirs the small audience which poets could expect and the consequent difficulty in making a name for themselves:

La plupart des poètes ont grand-peine à se manifester, surtout s'ils doivent, ce qui est la règle pour les commencements, faire imprimer leurs ouvrages à leurs dépens, comme nous l'avions fait pour nos premiers livres. Ainsi reclus et dédaigné, le poète peut encore espérer l'hospitalité des revues, . . . les petites revues courageuses, batailleuses, anémiques, et mal sustentées. . . . Mais leur public est très faible. Les grandes revues qui consentent à parler des poètes et de la poésie sont très peu nombreuses. En 1912, on en comptait deux ou trois peut-être et le *Mercure de France* était la plus constante de celles-ci. Une place était réservée dans chaque fascicule à la critique des poètes.[2]

There is no question but that the audience for poetry had shrunk in the course of the nineteenth century.

Other forms of writing undoubtedly paid better than ever before. Writers as a whole 'had never had it so good'. For works which publishers had a reasonable expectation of selling they were willing to offer much larger sums than in earlier periods. Playwrights mainly counted on what they could wring out of theatre managers with the aid of their powerful trade union; but the publication of successful plays could bring in substantial sums. Alexandre Dumas's *Henri III et sa cour* brought him 6,000 francs in 1829 and *Christine* 12,000 in the following year,[3] while Hugo obtained 15,000 for *Hernani*.[4]

The nineteenth century was the great age of the novel, and this form of writing could produce very substantial rewards, particularly from the 1870s onwards. In the 1830s and 1840s publishers offered fairly modest sums, though it is often difficult to form any clear idea of what a particular novel brought the author owing to the system of restricting the

[1] *Œuvres*, ed. J. Hytier, 2 vols., Paris, 1957–60, i. 22.

[2] *Le Temps de la recherche*, Paris, 1947, pp. 199–200.

[3] *Mes mémoires*, ed. P. Josserand, 5 vols., Paris, 1954–68, iii. 80, 242.

[4] Sainte-Beuve, *Correspondance générale*, i. 182.

publisher to a stated number of copies for a very limited period. What the earlier editions of *Notre-Dame de Paris* brought Hugo we do not know; in February 1832 he signed an agreement with Renduel for a reprint of this and three other novels; for *Notre-Dame* the publisher was to print 1,000 copies and pay the author 1 franc each, his rights over this and the other works being limited to fifteen months. In 1835 Hugo signed a fresh agreement with the same publisher for 11,000 copies of the novel for a period of three and a half years, but though he was to receive altogether 60,000 francs, as this total covered also six volumes of his plays from *Cromwell* to *Angelo*, we cannot say how much this reprint of the novel brought him.[1]

The editors of the correspondence of Balzac and George Sand have succeeded in assembling a remarkable collection of their agreements with publishers. Unfortunately, it is not very easy to interpret these for the same reason. With Balzac there is the additional complication that in the state of financial chaos in which he lived in the 1830s and 1840s he was constantly making new agreements for works which were never written or taking advances for works which were only completed, if at all, years later.[2] George Sand's accounts were somewhat less complicated, and it is possible to give a rough idea of what she earned from at least the first printing of one of her novels in this period. It would seem to have been in the range of 2,400 to 5,000 francs, but this does not include what she received from the reviews or newspapers in which her works were first published. Again the greatest novelists of this period, Stendhal and Balzac, were not necessarily the authors who at the time commanded the widest following. The case of Stendhal is notorious: neither *Le Rouge et le Noir* nor *La Chartreuse de Parme* found many readers during Henri Beyle's lifetime. Nor did he expect them to: he ended *La Chartreuse de Parme* with the words: 'To the Happy Few' and in a letter to Balzac thanking him for his review of the work he declared: 'Je pensais n'être pas lu avant 1880.'[3] Balzac was certainly far better known during his lifetime; for one thing he published an enormous amount, but, while his financial difficulties were mainly due to his extravagance and foolish speculations, he never secured a really striking success with any of his works, and the famous collected edition of his novels under the title of *La Comédie humaine*

---

[1] Jullien, *Le Romantisme et l'éditeur Renduel*, pp. 99–100.
[2] See R. Bouvier and E. Maynial, *Les Comptes dramatiques de Balzac*, Paris, 1938 and *De quoi vivait Balzac?*, Paris, 1949.
[3] *Correspondance*, ed. H. Martineau and V. del Litto, 3 vols., Paris, 1962–8, iii. 393.

did not sell at all well during his lifetime.[1] Another writer, Champfleury, who had begun his career in the book trade, bears eloquent
testimony to this fact:

> Je vis publier divers romans nouveaux de Balzac pendant mon séjour sur le
> quai des Augustins. L'accueil qu'ils recevaient du public n'était pas encour-
> ageant.
>   Balzac se vendait médiocrement, Stendhal pas du tout.
>   Les sinistres ballots qui revenaient de province contenaient toujours des
> quantités de volumes de Balzac. . . . En 1838, personne dans le Paris lettré ne
> prononçait le nom de l'auteur de *la Chartreuse de Parme*.[2]

What complicates the task of assessing the earnings of novelists from
the 1830s onwards is the emergence of the *roman-feuilleton*. Many
novels down to 1914 made their first appearance in newspapers which
meant that the writer drew a double income from his work. Before the
foundation of *La Presse* and *Le Siècle* novels had appeared in serial
form in such reviews as the *Revue des Deux Mondes*; and they were long
to continue to do so. We have seen how *Madame Bovary* made its first
appearance in the *Revue de Paris*. The appearance of novels in serial
form in daily newspapers was a new phenomenon which arose out of
the dependence of cheaper newspapers such as *La Presse* and *Le Siècle*
on advertising and consequently on the largest possible circulation.
The situation was summed up with admirable clarity by Alfred Nettement, writing in 1845:

> Dans l'état de choses nouveau, un journal vit par l'annonce: les 40 ou 48
> francs que paient ses abonnés suffisent à peine aux frais matériels, et les frais
> de rédaction, de direction, d'administration doivent être couverts d'une autre
> manière; il faut nécessairement les demander à l'annonce. Or pour avoir
> la quantité d'annonces indispensable au paiement de ces frais il faut pouvoir
> offrir à l'industrie une publicité plus étendue que celle que peut assurer, dans
> les conditions de la presse actuelle, chacune des opinions politiques en
> particulier. Pour donner un journal à 40 ou 48 francs il fallait donc avoir
> beaucoup d'annonces; pour avoir beaucoup d'annonces, il fallait avoir beau-
> coup d'abonnés; pour avoir beaucoup d'abonnés, il fallait trouver une amorce
> qui s'adressât à toutes les opinions à la fois, et qui substituât un intérêt de
> curiosité générale à l'intérêt politique.[3]

---

[1] This state of affairs continued for a considerable time after his death. See D. Bellos,
Balzac Criticism in France, 1850–1900, Oxford, 1976, pp. 82–9, where figures for the size
of the editions of his novels, drawn from the declarations which printers were compelled
to make down to the press law of 1881, are given.

[2] *Souvenirs et portraits de jeunesse*, p. 78.

[3] *Études critiques sur le feuilleton-roman*, 2 vols., Paris, 1845, i. 2–3.

The publication of Balzac's *La Vieille Fille* which began in *La Presse* in October 1836 marks the beginning of the publication of novels in serial form in French newspapers.[1]

The competition between these two new newspapers, the old-established *Journal des Débats*, and later the *Constitutionnel* led for a while to some extremely high prices being paid to attract the popular novelists of the time. After publishing *Les Mystères de Paris* in the *Journal des Débats* in 1842–3 (he received 26,500 francs from the newspaper for it), Eugène Sue was paid the record sum of 100,000 francs for *Le Juif errant* when it appeared in *Le Constitutionnel* in 1844.[2] Dumas *père* was another writer who drew enormous sums of money from composing, with the aid of collaborators, a whole series of *romans-feuilletons* which included such well-known works as *Les Trois Mousquetaires*, first published in *Le Siècle*, and *Le Comte de Monte Cristo*, written for the *Journal des Débats*. Another prolific and highly paid novelist who cashed in on this fashion was Frédéric Soulié.

Optimistic as ever, Balzac hoped to profit from this competition which is vividly described in a letter to Mme Hanska written in 1844:

Il y a dans ce moment un combat de journaux et de feuilletons qui tombent sur nos cervelles. Véron a acheté le *Constitutionnel*, l'a mis à 48 francs,[3] et menace les 45,000 abonnés du *Siècle* avec le *Juif Errant*, acheté 100,000 fr. et un volume de G. Sand, intitulé *Jeanne*, acheté 10,000 fr., dit-on.[4] *Les Débats* ont votre serviteur,[5] qui, avec *Les Petits Bourgeois*, leur garantit leur position élevée. Voici *Le Soleil* qui va descendre dans la lice et menacer à la fois *Le Siècle* et *Le Constitutionnel*. Ceci produira une enchère folle sur les manuscrits. Alex. Dumas et Frédéric Soulié ont des traités avec *Le Siècle*; ils ne sont pas disponibles. E. Sue et G. Sand appartiennent au *Constitutionnel*. C'est un tournoi d'argent. Je suis libre et je vais tâcher d'en profiter.[6]

One hears much of the very high prices paid to novelists like Eugène Sue in this period of boom, but it will be noticed that other writers like George Sand and Balzac were paid much more modest sums for

---

[1] R. Guise, 'Balzac et le roman-feuilleton', *Année balzacienne*, 1964, p. 287 n. Strictly speaking, this was not a *roman-feuilleton* as the text of the novel was printed in the body of the newspaper.

[2] J. L. Bory, *Eugène Sue, le roi du roman populaire*, Paris, 1962, pp. 291, 296.

[3] 40 francs according to L. D. Véron in his *Mémoires d'un bourgeois de Paris*, 6 vols., Paris, 1853–5, iv. 274.

[4] The figure is correct (see George Sand, *Correspondance*, vi. 495–7, where the contract is reproduced).

[5] He had sold *Modeste Mignon* to this paper for 6,000 francs (*Lettres à Madame Hanska*, ii. 413). *Les Petits Bourgeois* was never finished.

[6] *Lettres à Madame Hanska*, ii. 417.

their works. When Balzac had earlier announced to Mme Hanska the tremendous price which Sue had been promised for *Le Juif errant*, he wrote gloomily: 'C'est ce qui ne m'arrivera jamais.'[1] What is more, for a while the extreme popularity of the *roman-feuilleton*, especially when the newspaper bound up copies to use as a bait to draw in new subscribers, meant that publishers tended to reduce what they were willing to pay novelists because they claimed that inevitably the sales of their works in book form were reduced. Thus we find George Sand writing to a newspaper editor in 1846:

... Votre grande publicité et vos primes rendent l'édition en volumes difficile et d'un maigre produit. C'est à tel point que *Le Péché de M. Antoine* n'a pas encore paru in-8°, les éditeurs n'ayant pas jugé apparemment que l'effet produit par les primes fût suffisamment épuisé. Ces retards qui se reportent sur les éditions suivantes sont des non-valeurs réelles. Les feuilletons nous font manger notre blé en herbe, mais appauvrissent tellement la librairie que nos récoltes accoutumées ne se feront peut-être plus.[2]

During the reaction which followed the 1848 Revolution *romans-feuilletons* were attacked as subversive; the vaguely socialistic novels of Eugène Sue were particularly criticized for putting wrong ideas into the heads of the masses. A law of 16 July 1850 imposed an extra stamp duty of one centime on newspapers which published novels; its clear intention was to put an end to the practice.[3] This did not mean, however, as is sometimes imagined,[4] the death of the *roman-feuilleton*.

It is true that at the time George Sand for one thought it did; on 3 August she wrote to the actor, Bocage: 'Il faut pourtant que, vous aidant, je fasse mon métier qui est de travailler pour le théâtre, car la loir sur les journaux va tuer le roman-feuilleton, et si la librairie ne se relève pas, mon état est perdu.'[5] Yet this clause was not repeated in the decree on the press issued in February 1852 after Louis Napoleon's *coup d'état*. The publication of new novels before they appeared in book form continued for many decades. The *roman-feuilleton* was exploited by a succession of low-grade writers who filled the space allotted to them with the most extraordinary and improbable adventures. The great name during the Second Empire was that of Ponson du Terrail

[1] Ibid. 342.   [2] *Correspondance*, vii. 452–3.
[3] Duvergier, *Collection complète* l. 321.
[4] Bory, *Eugène Sue, le roi du roman populaire*, p. 351: 'Le feuilleton meurt. . . . Romantisme et roman-feuilleton meurent avec cette République qu'ils ont tant contribué à créer.'
[5] *Correspondance*, ix. 647.

whose stock character, Rocambole, endowed the French language with a new adjective, *rocambolesque*, used in such phrases as 'des aventures rocambolesques'. The Goncourt brothers penned the following portrait of the author in 1861 when he was at the height of his fame and affluence:

On aperçoit, passant modestement, le profil de Ponson du Terrail, avec, à l'horizon, sur le boulevard, son dog-cart et son cocher, la seule voiture d'homme de lettres roulant sur le pavé de Paris. Le pauvre garçon, au reste, le gagne assez et par le travail et par l'humilité de sa modestie. C'est lui qui dit aux directeurs de journaux où il a un immense roman en train: 'Prévenez-moi trois feuilletons d'avance, si ça ennuie le public; et en un feuilleton je finirai.' On vend des pruneaux avec plus de fierté.[1]

Although such writings gave the *roman-feuilleton* a bad name, it must not be forgotten that down to 1914 the most reputable novelists continued to sell their works to newspapers before publishing them in book form.

It was never, of course, a universal practice. Some novelists continued to prefer publication in a review (this was the case with *Madame Bovary*, though Flaubert's *Trois contes* were later published in newspapers); but the daily press paid much better, especially when a writer had made a name for himself. Novels by writers like Edmond de Goncourt, Daudet, Zola, Anatole France, and Bourget made their first appearance in a wide variety of newspapers. Since a certain number of newspapers were willing for reasons of prestige to publish their novels, the opportunity of receiving payment twice over was one of which many writers availed themselves. In *Les Romanciers naturalistes* Zola admits that it really did not make sense for writers like himself to publish their novels in *feuilletons* when they were not designed to have each instalment break off at some exciting moment in the story with the result that they could only appear 'coupés en tranches, défigurés, n'ayant plus le balancement de lignes de leur large dessin'. Why should serious writers, he asks, publish their novels within this constricting framework? 'A cela, les directeurs m'ont toujours répondu qu'ils n'avaient, il est vrai, aucun gain, quand ils publiaient, par exemple, un roman d'Edmond de Goncourt ou d'Alphonse Daudet; seulement cette publication est honorable pour un journal, et lui donne un bon renom littéraire. Il n'y a qu'à s'incliner devant un tel argument.'[2] As late as 1909 we find even Proust, when first contemplating the writing of *A la*

[1] *Journal* iv. 213.   [2] *Œuvres complètes*, xi. 237.

recherche du temps perdu, receiving an offer from the editor of *Le Figaro* to publish his novel; he wrote in a letter to Robert Dreyfus:

Calmette, que j'ai vu ici, m'a demandé très gentiment et avec beaucoup d'insistance de publier en feuilleton dans *Le Figaro* un roman que je suis en train de faire. Je t'ajoute entre nous, que pour beaucoup de raisons, je ne crois pas que je donnerai ce roman au *Figaro* ni à aucun autre journal ou revue, et qu'il paraîtra seulement en librairie.[1]

First publication of novels in reviews continued far beyond 1914, but after that date works with literary pretensions seldom made their first appearance in newspapers.

The daily press gradually came to offer more and more openings for writers in this period. Short stories, even poems, as well a novels, appeared there, and a considerable amount of space was given up to both literature and the theatre; this was mainly filled by writers though it is at times hard to draw the line between writers and journalists. Many authors served their apprenticeship by writing for newspapers, and they continued to write for them after they had acquired standing as men of letters. Particularly with the great expansion of the industry in the opening decades of the Third Republic newspapers came to represent a very important source of income for writers.

This point is made very clearly by Zola in his essay, 'L'Argent dans la littérature':

Le journalisme surtout a apporté des ressources considérables. Un journal est une grosse affaire qui donne du pain à un grand nombre de personnes. Les jeunes écrivains, à leurs débuts, peuvent y trouver immédiatement un travail chèrement payé. De grands critiques, des romanciers célèbres, sans compter les journalistes proprement dits, dont quelques-uns ont joué des rôles importants, gagnent dans les journaux des sommes considérables.

He goes on to stress that this had not always been the case:

Ces hauts prix n'ont pas été donnés dès l'origine de la presse; très minimes d'abord, ils ont grandi peu à peu, et ils grandissent toujours. Il y a vingt ans, les hommes de lettres qui touchaient deux cents francs par mois dans un journal, devaient s'estimer très heureux; aujourd'hui les mêmes hommes de lettres touchent mille francs et davantage. La littérature tend à devenir une marchandise extraordinairement chère, dès qu'elle est signée d'un nom en vogue. Sans doute, les journaux ne peuvent s'ouvrir à tous les débutants débarqués de province, mais ils nourrissent réellement beaucoup de jeunes

---

[1] *Contre Sainte-Beuve*, ed. P. Clarac, Paris, 1971, p. 826.

gens; et la faute est à ceux-ci s'ils ne se dégagent pas un jour, pour écrire de beaux livres.[1]

Certainly, Zola was only one of the many writers of the time who made their way to literature with the help of journalism.

By the last quarter of the nineteenth century successful writers could certainly derive a large income from the publication of their works. When Zola scored his first really big success in 1877 with *L'Assommoir*, his publishers tore up the agreement whereby he was to receive merely a modest monthly salary and paid him according to the sales of the novel, which meant that he received 18,500 francs for it. From then onwards he could obtain sums of the order of 20,000 to 30,000 francs from the publication of his novels in a newspaper before they appeared in book form, and the books sold like hot cakes. In 1880 55,000 copies of *Nana* were sold by the date of publication.[2] Such success did not necessarily make Zola a happy man, as Edmond de Goncourt noted after he had listened to his sorrows:

Voici un homme qui remplit le monde de son nom, dont les livres se vendent à cent mille, qui a peut-être, de tous les auteurs, fait le plus de bruit de son vivant: eh bien, par cet état maladif, par la tendance hypocondriaque de son esprit, il est plus désolé, il est plus noir que le plus déshérité des fruits secs![3]

Zola was apparently not long in thinking of even higher sales. In 1894 Goncourt made the following note about him:

Il parle de *Lourdes*, se plaignant que la campagne catholique faite contre son livre, qui serait une bonne chose pour un volume tiré à 30,000, est très préjudiciable à un livre tiré à 120,000 parce qu'elle lui enlève les 80,000 acheteurs qui pouvaient faire monter le tirage de son livre à 200,000 exemplaires.[4]

Though his own novels were now selling much better than those which he had written down to 1870 in collaboration with his brother, Jules, Edmond de Goncourt was unable to hide his envy of Alphonse Daudet, another younger writer with whom he was on intimate terms. After the success of his novels, *Fromont jeune et Risler aîné* (1874) and *Jack* (1876). Goncourt speaks of him as 'bombardé' d'articles dans toute la presse, couronné et renté par l'Académie, *polyglotté* dans toutes les langues, gorgé d'argent par les éditions, les traductions, les reproductions, mis à l'enchère par tous les rez-de-chaussée des journaux'.[5] In

[1] *Œuvres complètes*, x. 1270.
[2] A. Lanoux, *Zola vivant*, in *Œuvres complètes*, ed. H. Mitterand, Paris, 1966–70, i. 144, 155.
[3] *Journal* xii. 94.　　　[4] Ibid. xx. 137.　　　[5] Ibid. xi. 85.

1884 Goncourt records a confession made to him by Daudet when he was writing *Tartarin sur les Alpes*: 'Il fait, sans l'avouer à personne, il fait pour une société internationale, une sorte de *Tartarin en Suisse*, une machine qu'on lui paye *deux cent soixante-quinze mille francs*! Entendez-vous, mânes de Gautier, Flaubert, Murger, etc., payées par Lévy 400 francs pour un volume et en toute propriété?[1] Five years later the same source records that Daudet was to receive 100,000 francs for the last volume of the Tartarin trilogy and that his earnings for the year would come to 200,000 francs.[2]

Whether such large earnings (tax free as France had no income tax until the First World War) continued, at any rate for the favoured few among novelists into 'la belle époque', is not clear. In 1908 Paul Léautaud recorded the following conversation with Remy de Goncourt in the offices of the *Mercure*:

Nous avons parlé du changement des conditions de publication et de vente des romans, l'époque des vraies piles aux étalages des libraires, les Zola étagés en cubes, les 120,000 francs, que gagnait par an Daudet, la publication des romans en feuilletons d'abord payés souvent 30 ou 40,000 francs. Tout cela a-t-il assez changé. Aujourd'hui, un livre qui va à 25,000, 30,000, est une rareté. Gourmont pense qu'on lit moins, ou que le public est devenu plus intelligent (cela à propos des succès de Daudet, surprenants quand on songe à ses livres, Daudet dont on ne parle plus du tout), et surtout qu'il est tourné vers des choses plus sérieuses, plus scientifiques. Que l'une ou l'autre de ces raisons soit exacte, le fait certain, je le dis à Gourmont, c'est que nous ne voyons plus aujourd'hui de succès de librairie comme les Zola ou les Daudet, pas plus que je ne crois que nous ayons des écrivains ayant aux yeux du public l'importance d'un Zola, ou d'un Daudet.[3]

This is to some extent borne out both by the stagnation in the French publishing world from the end of the nineteenth century and by what Grasset has to offer in the way of an explanation of the great upsurge of sales of books after the First World War. Writing in 1929 (he had begun his career as a publisher in 'la belle époque'), he traces it back to the success of war books like *Le Feu* of Barbusse which appeared in 1916.[4] However that may be, there is no question but that the average earnings of writers rose very considerably in the hundred years before 1914.

There seems no doubt that in nineteenth-century France the biggest

---

[1] Ibid. xiii. 116.   [2] Ibid. xvi. 141, 178.   [3] *Journal littéraire*, ii. 78.
[4] *La Chose littéraire*, Paris, 1929, p. 108.

financial rewards came from writing for the theatre. In the provinces theatres were more numerous than ever before, while in Paris, especially when, from the middle of the century onwards, the development of railways and steamships brought large numbers of tourists from the provinces and from much further afield, theatres were for the most part extremely prosperous.

When Louis XVIII returned to Paris in 1814, the capital possessed only the eight theatres which Napoleon had permitted to remain open; and for the next fifty years a new theatre continued to require a government *privilège* which normally restricted it to a particular type or types of dramatic performances. A fair number of such *privilèges* were granted during the Restoration and the July Monarchy. By 1845 the number of Paris theatres had risen to twenty-three, and in 1850 we find a writer arguing that there were now far too many:

Il n'y déjà que trop de théâtres; c'est cette production excessive, multiple, hâtive, stérile dans sa fécondité apparente, disproportionnée avec les besoins de la consommation véritable, qui paralyse les efforts de l'art sérieux, accélère la décadence littéraire et dramatique, et ruine du même coup les directeurs, les auteurs et les libraires.[1]

However, all these restrictions were swept away by a decree of 18 January 1864:

Art. Ier. Tout individu peut faire construire et exploiter un théâtre, à la charge de faire une déclaration au ministère de notre maison et des beaux-arts, et à la préfecture de police pour Paris, à la préfecture dans les départments.
4. Les ouvrages dramatiques de tous les genres, y compris les pièces entrées dans le domaine public, pourront être représentés dans tous les théâtres.[2]

Henceforth anyone could build or operate a theatre simply by declaring his intention to the authorities, and the choice of plays to be performed was restricted only by the necessity of obtaining permission for works which were still copyright. By 1905 Paris had no fewer than forty-three theatres.[3]

There were thus available a large number of theatres to suit different tastes and different purses. There were two subsidized theatres, the Comédie-Française, installed since 1799 in its present quarters in the rue de Richelieu, and the Odéon, which occupied the site opposite the

---

[1] A. de Pontmartin, 'Le Théâtre et le roman', *Revue des Deux Mondes*, 1850, v. 1128.
[2] Duvergier, *Collection complète* lxiv. 8–9.
[3] H. Lecomte, *Histoire des théâtres de Paris, 1402–1904. Notice préliminaire*, Paris, 1905, p. 59.

Luxembourg Gardens to which the Comédie-Française had moved in 1782. The affairs of the Comédie-Française continued to be regulated by a decree issued by Napoleon from Moscow in 1812, and it remained under fairly close government control. Its main task was to keep alive as many as possible of the plays in its rich repertoire going back to Corneille, Molière, and Racine; but, with varying degrees of zeal, it also performed the task of encouraging new writers. A considerable number of new plays were presented there in this period, from the neo-classical tragedies of the Restoration to the works of writers like Maurice Donnay and Henri Lavedan in 'la belle époque'.

Down to the 1850s it was far from prosperous; indeed, without the government subsidy it could scarcely have remained open. Looking back from the 1880s, the theatre critic, Francisque Sarcey, describes the poor audiences of his youth:

J'ai vu, de mes yeux vu, du temps que j'étais au collège, entre 1840 et 1848, des représentations d'œuvres classiques, jouées par un ensemble de comédiens éminents, et tels que nous ne possédons pas leurs pareils à cette heure; nous nous trouvions une cinquantaine au parterre, où les places ne coûtaient pourtant que quarante-quatre sous; les loges vides n'offraient aux yeux que de vastes trous noirs; l'orchestre seul était à peu près garni; c'était là que se rendaient les *habitués*, qui avaient presque tous leurs entrées, j'imagine.[1]

Arsène Houssaye, who took over as *administrateur* of the theatre in 1849 at a time when it still had a great attraction in the person of the famous tragic actress Rachel, explains the difficulty he had in drawing large audiences:

Paris n'était pas alors la capitale des étrangers; les chemins de fer, qui n'étaient encore que des tronçons, ne jetaient pas tous les jours ces milliers de provin-ciaux, qui aujourd'hui veulent avoir leur part de la vie parisienne; la bour-geoisie n'aimait que les théâtres à bon marché; le peuple agité ne songeait plus aux fêtes de l'intelligence. Il fallait un vrai succès pour qu'une pièce fût jouée trente fois, avec des recettes moyennes. Mlle Rachel remplissait la salle; mais dès qu'elle jouait plus de trois fois par semaine, le public manquait.[2]

There is, of course, some exaggeration here. New plays were already having longer first runs than a century earlier; quite a number ran for well beyond thirty performances in the first half of the nineteenth century. Yet the greatest successes were not those of the Romantic *drames*—Dumas's *Henri III et sa cour*, Hugo's *Hernani*, and Vigny's

---

[1] *Quarante ans de théâtre*, 8 vols., Paris, 1900–2, i. 231–2.
[2] *Confessions* iii. 37.

Chatterton—with their 43, 30, and 37 performances respectively. These were far eclipsed by the really successful plays of the period, most of them comedies. Thus Delavigne's *Don Juan d'Autriche* ran for 88 performances, while Scribe's *Bertrand et Raton* and *Le Verre d'eau* had 98 and 81 performances.

From the Second Empire onwards the Comédie-Française shared in the general prosperity of the Paris theatres. In 1859 for the first time a successful new play, Laya's *Le Duc Job*, scored a run of over a hundred performances, and a fair number of successes of this order were achieved by writers like Augier and Dumas *fils*. In 1881 Pailleron's comedy, *Le Monde où l'on s'ennuie*, had a first run of 123 performances, followed by another 80 in the next year. Even this, of course, could not compare with the successes scored in other Paris theatres by such plays as Sardou's comedy, *Madame Sans-Gêne* (1893), which had over 300 performances at the Vaudeville or Rostand's *Cyrano de Bergerac* (1897), the most successful play of the century, which ran for a year and a half at the Porte-Saint-Martin and, when published, sold over half a million copies.

The Odéon had a decidedly chequered career, especially in the first half of the century. Its second fire, in 1818, closed it down completely for over a year. It did not always have a government subsidy; at times it was operated by the Comédie-Française, and at various periods it was simply closed. It had a succession of managers some of whom quickly went bankrupt. However, it did take some part in the Romantic revolution in the theatre with such plays as Vigny's *La Maréchale d'Ancre* and Dumas's *Christine*, and later it was to put on successful new plays by writers like Ponsard, Augier, and George Sand. It undoubtedly played its part as the 'second Théâtre Français', and in certain periods gave young playwrights their chance. The famous actor-manager, Antoine, who was in charge there from 1906 to 1912 after the experiment of the Théâtre Libre, did a great deal in this direction.

In addition to these two theatres there were a considerable number of private ventures, some of which—the Ambigu, Gaîté, and Variétés—had their roots in the *ancien régime*. They did not always have a long life; some were a financial failure, others vanished to make room for Louis Napoleon's rebuilding of Paris. Under different management they might change the type of performances which they offered, especially after the decree of 1864 made this possible. Down to about the middle of the century one of the theatres founded during the Restoration in 1820, the Gymnase, specialized in the somewhat light *comédies-vaudevilles* of Scribe, and then turned to more serious comedies and *drames*, performing plays by writers like Dumas *fils*, Sardou, and Labiche, and later those of Daudet among others. By the end of the century it had become a very distinguished theatre, regarded by many as the rival of the Comédie-Française. The Vaudeville, founded in 1792, had two moves (one due to a fire) in the course of the century; despite its name (a *vaudeville* being a very light form of comedy interspersed with songs) it gradually came to perform more serious plays such as Dumas *fils*'s *La Dame aux camélias* and rivalled theatres like the Comédie-Française and the Gymnase.

Some theatres whose names have a familiar ring because well-known plays were given their first performance there had only a short life. Hugo's *Ruy Blas* had a highly successful first run when it was put on for the opening performance of a new theatre, the Théâtre de la Renaissance, in 1838; Hugo and Dumas *père* had backed the new theatre, but it had to close down after three years. Six years later Dumas obtained a *privilège* for another theatre, his Théâtre Historique, which mainly performed dramatized versions of his novels though it also put on Balzac's *La Marâtre*. However, it went bankrupt in 1851.

One of the most successful theatres in this period was the Théâtre des Variétés which mainly specialized in *vaudevilles*, including some by Scribe. During the Second Empire it enjoyed tremendous success with the operettas of Meilhac and Halévry set to the music of Offenbach. Towards the end of the century it put on a considerable number of comedies by well-known playwrights of the time. The Porte-Saint-Martin, founded in 1802, closed down by Napoleon in 1807 and re-opened in 1814, was particularly prominent down to the middle of the century. To begin with it specialized in spectacular melodramas and *féeries*, but it also put on some plays of Hugo and Dumas *père*. Two of the most famous actors of the time, Frédérick Lemaître and Marie Dorval, frequently performed there and drew large crowds.

The Porte-Saint-Martin was one of the boulevard theatres. Close by in the boulevard du Temple were the older established Théâtre de l'Ambigu and the Théâtre de la Gaîté. In the opening decades of the nineteenth century both theatres specialized in melodrama; indeed, from 1825 to 1835 the *privilège* of the Gaîté was held by Pixerécourt, the leading practitioner of this genre. These melodramas portrayed all sorts of dastardly crimes. As a satirist of the time put it:

Parricides, infanticides, vols sur les grands chemins, effractions, assassinats, rapts, faux en écriture publique et privée, séquestration de personnes, fabrication de fausse monnaie, tous les délits, tous les crimes ont été exploités par la muse du boulevard. Le Code pénal, voilà son art poétique, c'est aux annales de la Morgue, aux deux premières colonnes de l'ancien *Journal de Paris* qu'elle emprunte ses dénouements, le fer, le feu, le poison, l'échafaud, presque toutes les variantes de la mort ont été jusqu'ici présentées aux amateurs de cauchemars et d'émotions fortes.[1]

This earned for the boulevard on which these two theatres stood the nickname of 'le Boulevard du Crime'.

In the last decades of this period Paris had its *théâtres d'avant-garde* experimenting with new types of plays and new methods of production and acting. In 1887 Antoine founded his Théâtre Libre, a subscription theatre (this kept out the censor), and he proceeded to perform a mixture of Naturalist plays and very different types of drama including Ibsen's *Ghosts*. Owing to financial difficulties Antoine had to abandon this enterprise, but in 1897 he started again with the Théâtre Antoine before moving to the Odéon in 1906. In 1890 another *avant-garde* theatre was founded to produce Symbolist plays; this was the Théâtre de l'Œuvre, known at first as the Théâtre d'Art. Its manager and chief actor was Lugné-Poë who in 1912 was responsible for the staging of *L'Annonce faite à Marie*, the first of Claudel's plays to be performed. In the following year Jacques Copeau established the Théâtre du Vieux-Colombier, but for obvious reasons it was only from 1920 onwards that it really made its mark. Such experimental theatres, founded, as Copeau put it, in protest against 'l'industrialisation effrénée' of the Paris theatrical world, could obviously appeal only to a very limited audience.

Quite a number of the Paris theatres of this period went through bad patches, with financial difficulties caused by lack of public support or quite frequently because of fires; the Comédie-Française went up in flames in 1900 and it took most of the year to repair the damage. None the less, in an age before competition had arrived from the cinema, radio, and television, theatre-going was extremely popular; and it was not confined to members of the middle classes. Nor must one forget the existence of theatres in the provinces. It is true that at the beginning of this century we find a Parisian speaking, as is the wont of Parisians, in contemptuous terms of provincial taste in drama: 'Remarquons d'ailleurs que la province s'alimente surtout d'œuvres un peu grosses, vaudevilles ou mélodrames composés à son intention; joués à Paris sur une scène de troisième ordre, ces ouvrages d'exportation partent aussitôt pour les

[1] *Le Figaro*, 17 June 1828.

départements.'[1] This is undoubtedly an exaggeration as throughout this period the stars of the Paris stage would from time to time go on tour in the provinces, performing there in the same plays as in the capital.

As the profession could bring large financial rewards, there was inevitably fierce competition among playwrights and aspiring playwrights; but there was also a wider range of theatres than ever before to which their works could be offered. Moreover, the position of playwrights had been greatly strengthened since the days when Beaumarchais had taken up the cudgels for them. In 1829 the Société des auteurs et compositeurs dramatiques was formally established; eight years later, in the year before the founding of the Société des gens de lettres, it acquired legal status as a 'société civile'.

Throughout its history it has been a much tougher trade union than the Société des gens de lettres. In the interests of its members it exercised an iron control over them as well as over the managements of theatres. Once admitted to membership, a playwright was unable to withdraw from the society; he was not free to make what arrangements he liked with a theatre concerning payment for his plays. He had to adhere to the terms negotiated between the society and that particular theatre. The society collected for him the proceeds from performances of his plays in Paris, the provinces, the French colonies, French-speaking countries such as Belgium and Switzerland, and such other countries as it could make arrangements for. Exactly the same percentage of the proceeds of the performances went to the beginner as to the veteran playwright with a long series of successes behind him. The society even went so far as to extract money for the performance of plays which were no longer copyright, the proceeds going at first to the direct heirs of the author and then to the society's relief fund. The Comédie-Française was in a special position owing to its obligation to keep alive the masterpieces of the past, and in any case it paid a generous proportion of its receipts (15 per cent) to authors of copyright plays. The other leading Paris theatres paid 12 per cent, plus a large number of tickets which the author was free to sell; tickets were exacted even for plays which were no longer copyright.

Inevitably, the very success of the society produced at times some caustic comments, even from playwrights. In an essay on Scribe the poet and playwright, Théodore de Banville, wrote somewhat sarcastically:

[1] Bayet, *La Société des auteurs et compositeurs dramatiques*, p. 347.

En achevant la révolution commencée par Beaumarchais, en fondant la Société des Auteurs Dramatiques, grâce à laquelle ses confrères ne furent plus frustrés du prix de leur travail, Monsieur Scribe assit réellement la situation industrielle et financière de l'écrivain. Il est vrai que forcés de payer, les directeurs ne jouèrent plus de chefs-d'œuvre et, pour leur argent, aimèrent mieux s'approvisionner d'une marchandise courante et d'une défaite plus facile; mais ceci est un détail. C'est grâce à lui que les écrivains dramatiques, au lieu de faire rapiécer leurs souliers, comme Corneille, purent acheter des souliers neufs, contracter de riches mariages, et furent considérés dans le monde à l'égal des papetiers et des quincaillers.[1]

From time to time there were dissensions within the society, particularly as it swelled enormously in size after the decree of 1864 abolishing restrictions on the running of theatres. Younger playwrights, for instance, complained that the society's rigorous enforcement of the rule that all plays performed at a given theatre should receive the same proportion of the receipts made it difficult for young writers to get their first play accepted. Managers naturally tended to take fewer risks and to put on plays by established writers. In practice, members of the society seem to have got round the rule surreptitiously, for instance by giving part of the proceeds back to the theatre to pay for special scenery or costumes. Again the collection of performing fees in the provinces and abroad did not always work perfectly as there were obvious opportunities for fraud.

However, thanks to the society playwrights were in an extremely strong position. Theatre managers, as might be expected, were not so pleased, but though from time to time a theatre might revolt against its yoke, the society always won as it simply prevented any of its members' plays being put on by the offender.[2] There is no doubt that the successful playwrights of this period could earn large sums of money. With a bigger theatre-going public the first run of a new play could reach large figures, while once it had been abandoned by one theatre it could in due course be revived at another, in Paris or in the provinces, and continue to bring in money for the author. Scribe, who had been mainly responsible for the foundation of the society, produced a vast number of plays, either alone or in collaboration, and made a considerable fortune, estimated by one contemporary at three million francs.[3] Later in the century writers such as Dumas *fils*, Augier, Sardou, and Labiche grew

[1] *Mes souvenirs*, pp. 344–5.
[2] There is an excellent account of the history of the society down to the beginning of the present century in Bayet, *La Société des auteurs et compositeurs dramatiques*.
[3] Véron, *Mémoires d'un bourgeois de Paris*, iii. 122–3.

rich on the theatre, although others like Henri Becque, the author of *Les Corbeaux*, never shared their good fortune and died poor. Writing in 1882, the year in which this play which he had hawked round the different Paris theatres for years was at last performed, Becque spoke bitterly of the way in which established playwrights monopolized the stage:

Vingt-cinq auteurs environ, quelques-uns dans le nombre que la collaboration venait chercher, se sont partagé les théâtres. La vogue de leurs ouvrages, presque toujours légitime, excessive quelquefois, s'est chiffrée par les deux cents, trois cents et même cinq cents représentations. A un moment où ils se faisaient eux-mêmes concurrence et où ils étaient obligés souvent d'attendre le tour qui leur était garanti, comment les inconnus auraient-ils réussi à trouver le leur ? Ce n'est pas tout. Peu à peu, d'année en année, se formait un répertoire, moins grand sans doute que l'autre, mais d'un intérêt plus moderne et qui devenait pour les directeurs une mine inépuisable. Entre la pièce nouvelle et la pièce reprise, les inconnus se sont trouvés constamment étouffés. Une chance leur restait, bien petite et bien misérable chance: le bas des affiches. Mais les prétentions de nos auteurs marchaient de pair avec leur succès, et en exigeant, comme ils l'ont fait, *les droits d'auteur de la soirée*, ils out enlevé à de nouveaux venus et la possibilité d'être joués et la possibilité de vivre.[1]

Becque's last years were full of money worries; he was reduced to receiving an 'indemnité littéraire' of 1,200 francs from the Ministry of Education and a pension of 1,000 francs from the Société des auteurs et compositeurs dramatiques.[2]

There is no doubt that, as in the past, the quickest way for a writer to make a name for himself was to score a success at the Comédie-Française or the Odéon or one of the other leading theatres of the capital. What is more, success could also bring in a lot of money. Once again Zola makes this point very clearly when he compares the modest returns from a novel with what could be earned by writing for the theatre. Whereas with a novel sales of 3–4,000 ('c'est déjà une belle vente', he declares), bring in at the most 2,000 francs, earnings from a successful play are of an altogether different order:

Une pièce a cent représentations, le chiffre courant aujourd'hui pour les succès; la moyenne des recettes a été de 4,000 francs, ce qui a donc mis dans la caisse du théâtre 400,000 francs, et ce qui rapporte à l'auteur une somme de 40,000 francs, si les droits sont de 10 pour 100. Or, pour gagner la même

---

[1] *Œuvres complètes*, 7 vols., Paris, 1924–6, vi. 119–20.
[2] J. Arnaoutovitch, *Henry Becque*, 3 vols., Paris, 1927, i. 121.

somme avec un roman, il faudrait, en touchant cinquante centimes par exemple, que ce roman fût tiré à quatre-vingt mille exemplaires, tirage telle-ment exceptionnel, qu'on peut en citer quatre ou cinq exemples au plus, pendant ces cinquante dernières années. Et je ne parle pas des représentations en province, des traités à l'étranger, des reprises de la pièce.[1]

Hence the attraction which the theatre exercised on writers who had already made a name for themselves as poets or novelists. It has been argued that Romantic writers like Hugo, Musset, or Vigny were really poets and that their failure as dramatists, despite all the hubbub created by their ventures on the stage, proved that they were not born play-wrights. However that may be, it is interesting to see how again and again the great novelists of this period ended by seeking success on the stage.

This could be attempted in a variety of ways. After receiving money for his novel from, first, a newspaper and then a publisher, a writer could obtain some extra remuneration by allowing a professional to adapt his work for the stage, or else he could collaborate with such a writer in producing a stage version. It was also possible to take one's own novel and adapt it oneself; George Sand, for instance, did this very successfully with *François le Champi* which had a run of well over a hundred performances at the Odéon in the winter of 1849–50. Finally, a considerable number of novelists tried their hand at writing directly for the stage.

From 1840 onwards Balzac had several plays performed in a variety of theatres. He had long dreamed great dreams of wiping out all his debts with successful plays which would bring in large sums of money. In 1835 he had written to Mme Hanska: 'Pour me liquider, cette effroyable production de livres, qui a entraîné ces masses d'épreuves, ne suffit pas. Il faut en venir au *théâtre*, dont les revenus sont énormes comparés à ceux que nous font les livres.'[2] Three years later he reverted to the same theme: 'Cependant mon salut est au théâtre. Un succès y donne près de cent mille francs. Deux succès m'acquittent, et, deux succès, c'est une affaire d'intelligence et de travail, voilà tout.'[3] Unfor-tunately, his hopes were repeatedly dashed. In 1840 after only one performance of *Vautrin* at the Porte-Saint-Martin with Frédérick Lemaître in the leading role the play was banned by the government. Three other attempts at three different theatres never produced more

---

[1] *Œuvres complètes*, x. 1271.   [2] *Lettres à Madame Hanska*, i. 354.
[3] Ibid. 615.

than what was politely named a 'succès d'estime', and Balzac's dreams of wealth came to nothing. Ironically, in the year after his death his comedy *Mercadet*, otherwise known as *Le Faiseur*, had a most successful first run of seventy-three performances at the Gymnase when revised by an experienced playwright, and it has been frequently revived since.

It was also in 1840, this time at the Comédie-Française, that George Sand made her first attempt to augment her income by writing for the stage. The first performance of this play gave rise to an amusing description by Heine of the hostility of the prosperous professional playwrights of the time towards writers of any literary quality:

Und im Grunde kann man es den kleinen Leuten nicht verdenken, dass sie sich gegen die Invasion der Grossen so viel als möglich wehren. 'Was wollt ihr bei uns', rufen sie, 'bleibt in eurer Literatur, und drängt euch nicht zu unsern Suppentöpfen! Fur euch der Ruhm, für uns das Geld! Für euch die langen Artikel der Bewunderung, die Anerkenntnis der Geister, die höhere Kritik, die uns arme Schelme ganz ignoriert! Für euch der Lorbeer, für uns der Braten! Für euch der Rausch der Poesie, für uns der Schaum des Champagners, den wir vergnüglich schlürfen in Gesellschaft des Chefs der Klaqueurs und der anständigsten Damen. Wir essen, trinken, werden applaudiert, ausgepfiffen und vergessen, während ihr in den Revüen 'beider Welten' gefeiert werdet und der erhabensten Unsterblichkeit entgegenhungert!'

In der Tat, das Theater gewährt jenen Bühnendichtern den glänzendsten Wohlstand: die meisten von ihnen werden reich, leben in Hülle und Fülle, statt dass die grössten Schriftsteller Frankreichs, ruiniert durch den belgischen Nachdruck und den bankerotten Zustand des Buchhandels, in trostloser Armut dahindarben. Was ist natürlicher, als dass sie manchmal nach den goldenen Früchten schmachten, die hinter den Lampen der Bretterwelt reifen, und die Hand darnach ausstrecken, wie jüngst Balzac tat, dem solches Gelüst so schlecht bekam![1]

George Sand's *drame*, *Cosima*, was also a failure, and it was not until 1848 that she returned to the theatre, first with a prologue performed in the heady days after the February Revolution at the Théâtre de la République (as the Comédie-Française was temporarily called), and then in the following year with her very successful adaptation of *François de Champi* at the Odéon. Thus encouraged, she produced over the next twenty years roughly that number of plays, sometimes in collaboration, sometimes merely adapting her own novels, but mostly writing directly for the stage. All this activity led to only a very small number of successes.

[1] *Französische Zustände*, in *Sämtliche Werke*, 12 vols., Hamburg, 1885–90, X. 292–3.

The Goncourt brothers met with bitter disappointment when their play, *Henriette Maréchal*, was put on at the Comédie-Française in 1865. The performances were turned into a demonstration against the Imperial regime by a mob of students led by a young gentleman nicknamed 'Pipe-en-bois'. The brothers noted bitterly in their journal:

Ce gouvernement, si fort à ce qu'il croit et à ce qu'il fait dire, est le plus lâche des pouvoirs. Entre nous, qui ne sommes pour lui que deux hommes de lettres, et un ou plusieurs *Pipe-en-bois*, c'est-à-dire une espèce d'émeute qui a une espèce de popularité d'École il n'a pas hésité un instant. Il nous fait à peu près promettre la croix pour le 1er janvier: il ne nous la donnera pas, de peur de paraître faire une protestation contre *Pipe-en-bois*. Il a laissé *Pipe-en-bois* nous prendre à peu près un gain assuré de 50,000 francs. Il est heureux pour nous que *Pipe-en-bois* ne lui demande pas plus.[1]

The play had only six stormy performances. In 1885 it was revived with some success at the Odéon, and when Edmond produced an adaptation of their novel, *Germinie Lacerteux*, despite the hostility of the critics it had a fair run at the same theatre when it was put on at the end of 1888; but this was scarcely the success of which the two brothers had dreamed.

Flaubert too felt he had to try his hand at writing plays. He devoted a great deal of time and energy to reworking a play, *Le Sexe faible*, left behind by his friend, Louis Bouilhet, but in the end he could not get any of the Paris theatres to put it on. He had great hopes of his political comedy, *Le Candidat*, when it was performed at the Vaudeville in 1874, but it was a failure. Although in one letter to George Sand he made light of this, in the next he confessed his disappointment: 'Mais j'avoue que je regrette les "*milles*" francs que j'aurais pu gagner. Mon petit pot au lait est brisé. Je voulais renouveler le mobilier de Croisset, bernique!'[2]

Zola was also keen on securing success in the theatre as well as in the novel. His adaptation of his novel, *Thérèse Raquin*, met with a cool reception when it was first put on in 1873, and an original play, a comedy entitled *Les Héritiers Rabourdin*, fared little better in the following year. A little farce, *Le Bouton de rose*, did not reach the end of its first performance, and his *Madeleine Férat*, which had begun as a play and was then made into a novel, had to wait until Antoine put it on at the Théâtre Libre. His only successes in the theatre were at second hand when his novels were adapted by another writer. *L'Assommoir*

---

[1] *Journal* vii. 154.
[2] *Correspondance*, vii. 128.

had a triumphant success (300 performances) at the Théâtre de l'Ambigu in 1879.[1]

Alphonse Daudet stands rather apart from the novelists of the time in the sense that, quite early on in his career, in the 1860s, before he had made a name with his novels, he began writing for the stage, sometimes in collaboration, though for the most part without any real success. In 1872 he expanded one of the stories in his *Lettres de mon moulin*, 'L'Arlésienne', into a play with incidental music by Bizet; this was a failure at the time, though it was well received when it was revived in 1885. In the next twenty years he adapted several of his novels for the stage and also wrote two plays, *La Lutte pour la vie* and *L'Obstacle*, directly for it; but despite all his efforts success in the theatre always eluded him. As with Zola, it was only when his novels were adapted by other writers that they went down well with audiences.

Despite all its drawbacks—the uncertainty of success, among others—the career of man of letters came in the nineteenth century to offer at least opportunities of wealth and, perhaps more important, a status in society which raised him far above the writer of the *ancien régime* who in varying degrees had been dependent on patronage and had been looked upon as socially inferior. The changes of the previous hundred years are clearly summed up by Zola:

L'instruction se répand, des milliers de lecteurs sont créés, le journal pénètre partout, les campagnes elles-mêmes achètent des livres. En un demi-siècle, le livre, qui était un objet de luxe, devient un objet de consommation courante. Autrefois, il coûtait très cher; aujourd'hui, les bourses les plus humbles peuvent se faire une petite bibliothèque. Ce sont là des faits décisifs: dès que le peuple sait lire, et dès qu'il peut lire à bon marché, le commerce de la librairie décuple ses affaires, l'écrivain trouve largement le moyen de vivre de sa plume. Donc la protection des grands n'est plus nécessaire, le parasitisme disparaît des mœurs, un auteur est un ouvrier commun e autre, qui gagne sa vie par son travail.[2]

The use of the word 'ouvrier' has a curiously twentieth-century ring with writers' demands on both sides of the Channel for a 'living wage'; but Zola was by no means the only person to note this change in the status of the writer. At the beginning of the present century Georges d'Avenel remarked:

[1] Lanoux, *Zola vivant*, in *Œuvres complètes*, i. 166.
[2] *Œuvres complètes*, x. 1269.

Il eût été ébahi, le grand Racine qu'il était, d'entendre un de nos dramaturges contemporains traiter de haut un ministre d'aujourd'hui, dont le procédé lui avait déplu et ajouter sérieusement: 'J'ai fait sentir à cet homme toute la distance qu'il y a d'un simple ministre à un auteur dramatique comme moi!'[1]

The same writer notes, as Zola had done, the decline in the literary influence of the *salons* compared with their importance under the *ancien régime*:

... Les seuls salons dont on se souvient sont justement ceux où se rencontraient les lettrés. Si la majorité de ces derniers n'attache plus autant de prix à fusionner avec les mondains, c'est que les mondains ont perdu de leur prestige et que les lettrés en ont acquis assez pour se suffire à eux-mêmes; ils constituent un clan distinct où ils se plaisent davantage.

Members of the aristocracy, he goes on, still tend for the most part to consider themselves superior to writers:

Cette opinion, bien que soigneusement voilée, révolte, au vingtième siècle, ceux qui, au dix-huitième, ne s'en fussent point choqués. Ils entendent être conviés pour leur personne, non pour leur réputation et comme objets de parade. Un poète renommé, invité pour la première fois chez une grande dame qui lui faisait demander en même temps, s'il ne consentirait pas à dire quelques pièces de vers, après dîner, répondit narquoisement: 'Il m'arrive de réciter mes vers chez des intimes; ailleurs, c'est mille francs la strophe et je n'en dis jamais moins de trente.'[2]

French society and the position of the writer in that society had certainly changed since the days of Boileau's 'poète crotté'.

One striking feature of French life from the Restoration down to our own day has been the influence exercised by the political views of writers. A number of them—and some of the very greatest—have played a prominent role as politicians, but, even if they did not enter directly into politics, their views have been very influential. In these years, the Revolutionary period apart, for the first time in French history, political and social questions became matters of public debate, and many writers found themselves involved in the controversies and political battles of their age.

During the Restoration Chateaubriand was an outstanding figure in political life, serving three times as ambassador and holding for a period the post of Foreign Minister. When summarily dismissed from this

---

[1] *Les Français de mon temps*, Paris, n.d., p. 308.
[2] Ibid. pp. 309–10.

post in 1824, he formed around him a right-wing opposition which contributed to the fall of the Bourbons. After that he withdrew from political life. Lamartine played an important part as a critic of the July Monarchy, not only as a deputy, but also as a powerful orator at public meetings and as the author of the *Histoire des Girondins*, the revolutionary fervour of which made a deep impression when it appeared in 1847. When the February Revolution followed, he became Foreign Minister and virtual head of the provisional government. From this height he was precipitated by the Journées de juin, and his hopes of becoming the first President of the new republic came to nothing.

Hugo's political career was less impressive in the sense that he was never a member of a government, but none the less he gradually came to exercise a considerable influence. His seat in the Chambre des pairs under Louis Philippe was not of any great political importance, nor even his role as a deputy during the Second Republic from 1848 to 1851. But his resistance to Louis Napoleon's *coup d'état*, his long years of exile, his fiery attacks on the Second Empire in *Napoléon le petit* and *Les Châtiments* had made him a legendary figure for republicans when he returned at last to Paris in 1870 after the collapse of the regime. He was elected to the National Assembly in 1871 and later became a Senator; the veneration in which he was held in his last years was apparent from the enormous crowds present at his lying in state at the Arc de Triomphe and burial in the Panthéon which followed.

It is difficult to imagine that the uproar created in 1898 by the intervention of a mere writer like Zola in the Dreyfus Affair with his article 'J'accuse' could have been paralleled on this side of the Channel in the career of a novelist, however eminent. Other writers of that period were also sucked into politics, Anatole France for instance, who, improbable as it may appear to present-day readers of his works, was soon to be seen addressing socialist meetings. Naturally, other writers of the time were to be found on the opposite sides of the barricades, and both groups were busily engaged in composing and signing political manifestos of the kind which are still produced today by their successors.

The decline in illiteracy and the vast expansion of the market for literature which took place in these years naturally meant the emergence of a variety of different publics to absorb the increasing number of books which were published and the larger and more numerous editions of those works which met with some degree of popularity. It was, of course, possible for individual works to embrace, if not all these different publics from the most sophisticated to the semi-illiterate, at least a considerable area of the spectrum. At one extreme came the *livres de colportage*, the chapbooks sold at fairs and markets and hawked over the countryside by pedlars. Down to about the middle of the century these were more popular than ever before, so much so that, very early during the Second Empire, in November 1852, the Ministre de la police générale, 'frappé de l'influence désastreuse qu'avait exercée jusqu'alors sur tous les esprits cette quantité de mauvais livres que le colportage répandait presque sans obstacle dans la France entière'[1] set up a committee to examine these works and decide which should be allowed to circulate. Charles Nisard, the assistant secretary of this committee, had the idea of writing a history of these publications which still remains a standard work. Alongside the traditional works in the *Bibliothèque bleue* came a flood of novels, sometimes abridged versions of older or modern works reprinted for the purpose, sometimes merely publishers' remainders.[2] Many of the works sold in this fashion had contributed to the formation of the 'légende napoléonienne' with their glorification of the Emperor's exploits. In the closing decades of the nineteenth century, in contrast to their earlier popularity, *livres de colportage* gradually declined in importance as the market was taken away by the cheap, popular newspapers which provided a great variety of reading matter, including *romans-feuilletons*.[3]

In this period the diffusion of books was also aided by the development of libraries, even though public libraries, run by the municipal authorities, offered a very poor service compared with what gradually came to be provided in this country in the decades after the passing of the first Public Libraries Act in 1850. It is true that in France during the Revolution a great many municipal libraries had been founded as a result of the confiscation of books which had belonged to the religious houses and *émigrés* and had been declared national property. Yet this was in many ways a false start; despite these early beginnings the French public library system has continued down to our day to lag behind that provided on this side of the Channel, as French librarians are the first to admit.[4] Throughout this period municipal libraries remained for the most part badly housed and with untrained staff; the old stock of books could be very valuable to local scholars, but

[1] Nisard, *Histoire des livres populaires ou de la littérature du colportage*, i. 1.

[2] Ibid. ii. 495–518.

[3] There is an excellent account of the decline in the popularity of *livres de colportage* in J. J. Darmon, *Le Colportage de librairie en France sous le Second Empire*, Paris, 1972.

[4] See Pierrot, 'Les Bibliothèques', in *Le Livre Français. Hier, aujourd'hui, demain*, pp. 195–9.

far too little money was made available for keeping the collection of books up to date and little effort was made to draw in a wider circle of readers.

In the 1860s attempts began to be made to reach this wider public. In 1865 Paris acquired its first public library, in the XIth *arrondissement*. The aim of the mayor in setting it up was, he declared, to 'contribuer au développement de l'instruction des ouvriers et employés pour permettre à ces hommes défavorisés de s'élever dans l'échelle sociale'.[1] His example was slowly followed in other *arrondissements*, and in 1879 the *Préfet*, who had secured the foundation of ten more, brought the system under central control. A period of expansion followed down to 1902 by which time every *arrondissement* had its central library, open for a modest two or three hours a day, and branch libraries in schools, which were open for a few hours a week. By this date two million books a year were being borrowed, but that figure had been nearly halved by 1914.

Provision for libraries in provincial towns and cities continued to be extremely patchy. A recent French writer makes an interesting comparison between public libraries in Leeds and Lyons—both cities of over 400,000 inhabitants—towards the end of this period. In 1908–9 Leeds was spending more than Paris on its libraries although it had less than a sixth of the population; in addition to providing a reference library and numerous places where newspapers and periodicals could be read, its libraries lent out 1,310,000 volumes. Lyons, on the other hand, spent less than a sixth of what Leeds devoted to its library service and lent less than 70,000 books in the course of the year.[2]

For most of this period it was left mainly to private enterprise to cater for the needs of those members of the reading public who were either unable or unwilling to buy books. Just as many writers on this side of the Channel today foam at the mouth at the very mention of public libraries, so French writers of the time were extremely bitter about the way even well-to-do people preferred to get their books from a circulating library rather than buy them. In 1834 Balzac wrote angrily in the *Revue de Paris*:

[1] V. Coeytaux, 'Le Centenaire des bibliothèques municipales de Paris', *Bulletin des bibliothèques de France*, 1966, p. 64.

[2] J. Hassenforder, *Développement comparé des bibliothèques publiques en France, en Grande-Bretagne et aux Etats-Unis dans la seconde moitié du XIXᵉ siècle (1850–1914)*, Paris, 1967, pp. 74–5. This work offers a most thorough analysis of the reasons for the very slow development of public libraries in France.

En France, messieurs, dans ce beau pays où les femmes sont élégantes et gracieuses comme elles ne sont nulle part, la plus jolie femme attend patiemment, pour lire Eugène Sue, Nodier, Gozlan, Janin, V. Hugo, G. Sand, Mérimée, que la modiste ait lu le volume en compagnie le soir, dans son lit; que la femme d'un charcutier ait achevé le dénouement et l'ait graissé, que l'étudiant y ait laissé son parfum de pipe, y ait cloué ses observations lascives ou bouffonnes. . . . Il n'est pas encore admis qu'on envoie douze francs à un libraire pour lire à son aise dans un livre propre et vierge, l'œuvre nouvelle la plus intéressante qui donne quelques journées de lecture ou quelques heures de méditation, qui fait voyager dans l'histoire du pays ou dans les souvenirs de la vie!!! . . . Des femmes élégantes éternuent au milieu des *Feuilles d'automne*, par le fait d'un bourgeois qui a laissé couler du tabac en tournant un feuillet. Qui de nous n'a pas entendu dire à des millionnaires: 'Je ne puis avoir tel livre; il est toujours en lecture!'[1]

There was a vicious circle here. As circulating libraries bought a fair number of the copies of such works as novels, publishers produced them in a form which suited such important customers; novels were blown out into two or even three expensive volumes, full of blank spaces and blank pages, for each of which the libraries could charge a separate fee.[2] In the early decades of the century people naturally hesitated to pay 15 francs for a novel in two volumes when they could borrow it for a few sous.

Balzac's diatribe makes it clear that these libraries drew customers from a wide variety of social classes. In *Le Réalisme*, when discussing the poor sales of Barbey d'Aurevilly's novel, *Une Vieille Maîtresse*, Champfleury stresses the importance of the subscribers drawn from the more modest sections of the community:

M. Barbey d'Aurevilly est arrivé un peu tard avec sa *Vieille Maîtresse*, dont le défaut est d'être un peu trop distinguée pour les lecteurs habituels de cabinet de lecture. Grisettes, commis, laquais et cuisinières sont les fidèles qui contribuent à la fortune du petit temple noir, où la nourriture de l'âme se paye deux sous le volume crasseux.

'Je désirerais un ouvrage intéressant', dit une jeune femme de chambre romanesque, qui entre timidement dans ce sanctuaire dont M. Dumas est le pape.[3]

Naturally, when given *Une Vieille Maîtresse*, the girl can make nothing of it.

---

[1] *Œuvres diverses*, iii. 234–5.
[2] As with the three-decker novel in England in the same period.
[3] *Le Réalisme*, Paris, 1857, p. 287.

From fairly modest beginnings in the seventeenth century circulating libraries reached their maximum expansion in Paris about the middle of the nineteenth century. Strictly speaking, such libraries took two forms. First, there was the *cabinet de lecture*, defined in the Larousse *Grand dictionnaire universel* in the following terms:

Le *cabinet de lecture* est un établissement public dans lequel, moyennant une faible rétribution, on peut lire les journaux, les revues et autres ouvrages de littérature. C'est aussi là qu'on trouve à louer les volumes nouveaux qui paraissent et tous les livres qui forment le fonds habituel de ces sortes de bibliothèques. On peut s'abonner au *cabinet de lecture*, c'est-à-dire payer une somme par mois pour avoir la faculté d'emporter chez soi, afin de les lire, tous les livres qu'on désire, parmi ceux qui garnissent le *cabinet*.

In addition, a considerable number of bookshops also lent out books as part of their business. It is impossible to have absolutely reliable figures for the number of these two types of establishment, but a rough notion of their rapid rise and subsequent decline in nineteenth-century Paris is provided by the following figures (both types of establishment combined):

1819	23	1845	198
1820	32	1850	209
1823	83	1860	183
1837	162	1870	146
1842	207	1883	118[1]
1844	215		

These libraries varied enormously in size from the small collection of two or three thousand volumes to the 160,000 or so listed in the 1889 catalogue of the famous *cabinet de lecture* founded during the Restoration by Mme Cardinal[2] and described by Larousse as 'une véritable succursale de la Bibliothèque impériale'. Both types of library were well distributed throughout the capital, though they were thickest on the ground in the Quartier latin and the Palais-Royal region.[3] The Quartier latin had special *cabinets de lecture*, much frequented by students according to Larousse, and containing 'surtout des ouvrages traitant de la médecine ou du droit' (we have seen that these were the faculties

[1] C. Pichois, 'Les Cabinets de lecture à Paris durant la première moitié du XIXe siècle' *Annales. Économies, Sociétés, Civilisations*, 1959, p. 526.
[2] The preface (p. xiii) makes it clear that it catered for a rather limited clientèle: 'Le présent Catalogue est donc parfaitement en rapport avec les goûts et les besoins du public d'élite auquel il s'adresse.'
[3] Pichois, 'Les Cabinets de lecture', pp. 531–2.

where the great majority of students were to be found). However, although the catalogues which have come down to us show that readers were offered a very wide choice of books, there is no question but that the *cabinets de lecture* contributed to the enormous vogue of the novel in this period.

According to the *Grande encyclopédie* the number of *cabinets de lecture* in Paris fell from 118 in 1883 to 73 in 1889. Yet at that date they still retained a certain importance, as the same source points out. In addition to the *cabinet* founded by Mme Cardinal[1] the same source lists the following:

le cabinet du passage Jouffroy, fréquenté surtout par des journalistes et qui reçoit les journaux les plus importants du monde entier; le cabinet du passage de l'Opéra, également riche en journaux, mais où on lit principale- ment les revues et les romans; le cabinet des Batignolles, qui possède 40,000 volumes, celui de Delorme, rue Saint-Lazare, qui en a 30,000; enfin la *Lecture universelle*, fondée en 1870 par M. de Graët-Delalain sous le nom de *Salon littéraire national*. Ce dernier établissement où l'on ne lit pas sur place, sauf au siège central, rue des Moulins, a des succursales dans les principaux quartiers de Paris, en province et même à l'étranger. Il possède 200,000 volumes environ, dont 30,000 en langue étrangère. Les tarifs actuels sont modérés: 10 fr. par an et 2 fr. par mois en général; 5 et 10 cent. par volume et par jour.

Nor must one leave out of account the provinces. 'On trouve encore,' adds the *Grande encyclopédie*, 'beaucoup de cabinets de lecture en province où, comme à Paris, les petits libraires louent presque tous des ouvrages.'[2]

The reasons for the decline of circulating libraries from their peak in the middle of the century seem clear. Cheap editions, starting with the *Bibliothèque Charpentier* in 1838 and continuing with even cheaper ones, some issued in parts costing a few centimes, made it possible for books to be acquired by readers with the most modest purses. Competition also came from cheaper newspapers and their *romans-feuilletons*, and public libraries must have drawn away a certain number of clients.

[1] Its books were acquired by Louvain after the First World War to help to make good the losses in its University library which had been destroyed by the Germans (see Pichois, 'Les Cabinets de lecture', p. 523).

[2] Writing in 1830 Balzac had declared: 'Il est de notoriété commerciale qu'il existe en France 1,500 cabinets littéraires environ' (see R. Chollet, 'Un Épisode inconnu de l'histoire de la librairie: la Société d'abonnement général. Avec le texte inédit de Balzac', *Revue des sciences humaines*, 1971, p. 94).

However, patronized as they were by a broad cross-section of the population and scattered all over France, the *cabinets de lecture* undoubtedly made a considerable contribution to the enlargement of the reading public in this period.

No doubt many of the works which they offered their readers were of a fairly lowbrow character, appealing mainly to an unsophisticated audience. In dealing with the vogue of the novel in his article 'Statistique littéraire. De la production intellectuelle en France depuis quinze ans', published in the *Revue des Deux Mondes* in 1847, Charles Louandre wrote sarcastically:

Il faut chaque jour du nouveau pour réveiller la curiosité des abonnés des cabinets de lecture qui lisent avec l'intention de ne rien apprendre et la résolution bien arrêtée de ne jamais se fatiguer à penser, et l'on ne peut s'empêcher parfois de plaindre les écrivains qui se condamnent exclusivement à amuser les oisifs, population toujours nombreuse en France, surtout à Paris, où bien des gens, assez à l'aise pour ne rien faire, mais trop peu riches pour prendre leur part des plaisirs dispendieux, n'ont d'autre remède contre l'ennui que la promenade et les romans, quels qu'ils soient.[1]

Yet these things are always complicated; the tremendously popular *romans-feuilletons* of writers like Eugène Sue or Dumas *père* in the 1840s appear to have appealed to a wide public. Even though they were published in relatively expensive newspapers with what is by modern standards a tiny circulation, they seem to have been devoured by readers drawn from a great variety of social classes. In Reybaud's *Jérôme Paturot à la recherche d'une position sociale* there is a satirical passage in which an editor tells a budding author:

Aujourd'hui, pour réussir, il faut faire un feuilleton de ménage, passez-moi l'expression. Dégusté par le père et par la mère, le feuilleton va de droit aux enfants, qui la prêtent à la domesticité, d'ou il descend chez le portier, si celui-ci n'en a pas eu la primeur. Comprenez-vous quelles racines un feuilleton ainsi consommé a dans l'intérieur, et quelle situation cela assure sur-le-champ à un journal? Désormais ce journal fait partie intégrante de la famille.[2]

Gautier, again, stresses how wide was the appeal of such novels:

Tout le monde a dévoré les *Mystères de Paris*, même les gens qui ne savent pas lire: ceux-là se les ont fait réciter par quelque portier érudit et de bonne volonté; les êtres les plus étrangers à toute espèce de littérature connaissent la Goualeuse, le Chourineur, la Chouette, Tortillard et le Maître d'École. Toute la France s'est occupée, pendant plus d'un an, des aventures du prince

---

[1] 1847, xx. 681.   [2] New edn., Paris, 1870, p. 59.

Rodolphe, avant de s'occuper de ses propres affaires. Des malades ont attendu pour mourir la fin des *Mystères de Paris*; la magique *La suite à demain* les entraînait de jour en jour, et la mort comprenait qu'ils ne seraient pas tranquilles dans l'autre monde, s'ils ne connaissaient le dénouement de cette bizarre épopée.[1]

Writers like Lamartine, Balzac, and George Sand, politicians, well-known scholars, philanthropists, all followed the progress of the novel with rapt attention.[2]

Although it was in newspapers that many reputable novels continued to make their first appearance in print down to the end of this period, *romans-feuilletons*, specially written for serial publication and carefully ending each day at some most exciting point in the story, followed by the words 'La suite au prochain numéro', became more and more the speciality of the cheap, popular newspaper appealing to a mass readership. Again, among the increasing flood of books turned out by the speeded-up printing presses lowbrow novels and stories became increasingly prominent and found a ready market.

Needless to say, this mass of popular ephemeral literature is scarcely touched today except by specialists in search of material on the taste of the masses or insights into the social history of the time. The works of the period which are at all widely read and enjoyed in the twentieth century are only a tiny fraction of the poetry, plays, novels, and short stories which were written in the course of the century. Naturally, some nineteenth-century works which are still in print today in all manner of cheap editions, often with an extremely wide readership, were far from being among the most popular publications of their day.

Flaubert undoubtedly scored an immediate success with *Madame Bovary*, perhaps partly because of the publicity given to the book by the prosecution brought against him for obscenity, but, much to his grief, none of his later novels had anything like the same sales. *L'Éducation sentimentale* which many people today regard as his finest work did not sell particularly well. Yet, as the example of *Madame Bovary* shows, it was possible for a great work to have an immediate success; it could undoubtedly happen that works which at once won the applause of the critics and of those who regarded themselves as connoisseurs of literature made an immediate appeal to a wide public. Moreover, works which were scorned by the critics, but are today regarded as great

---

[1] *Histoire de l'art dramatique en France depuis vingt-cinq ans*, 6 vols., Leipzig, 1858-9, iii. 161-2.

[2] See N. Atkinson, *Eugène Sue et le roman-feuilleton*, Paris, 1929, pp. 63-7.

literature, could also win immediate favour with a broad spectrum of the reading public.

Poets like Lamartine and Hugo undoubtedly made an immediate appeal to a large audience, and to one which increased as their career went on and they published more and more collections of verse. It is clear that they and other Romantic poets like Vigny and Musset addressed themselves to quite a wide readership. If the somewhat difficult poetry of Nerval had to wait a century before it came into its own, a poet like Baudelaire, even though he does not appear to have found many readers during his relatively brief lifetime, certainly wrote poetry which is accessible to a fairly wide audience.

In France as in this country the novel achieved in the nineteenth century a popularity which had been foreshadowed by its growing vogue in the previous age; it has been calculated that over ten thousand novels were published in France in the course of the nineteenth century.[1] If many of the popular novelists of the age are nowadays mere names to all except specialists, some of those whose works are still read today made an obvious appeal to a very wide readership. George Sand's enormous output of novels spread over a forty-year period was deliberately designed to appeal to a wide audience, more especially in her socialistic period in the 1840s. Hugo the novelist was clearly not writing for a minority group when he composed *Notre-Dame de Paris* and especially a work like *Les Misérables* which had at once an enormous audience both in France and in many other countries. Daudet had similarly a wide appeal, not only with the Tartarin series, but with his more realistic novels. Zola eventually overcame the hostility of the critics and reached the mass audience to which his novels were obviously directed, and although his success was exceptional, other novelists towards the end of this period sought and obtained a following among a wide variety of publics.

The situation in the theatre was rather different. No doubt an extremely high proportion of French people could never have had an opportunity of going near a theatre, let alone going into one. To begin with, the population of France was still predominantly rural, and though there were theatres in the provinces, inevitably these were only to be found in towns of some size. Even in Paris, despite the popularity of theatre-going, only a minority of the adult and near-adult population can ever have seen a play actually performed, even though for a good part of this period theatres continued the *ancien régime* custom of

[1] Humblot, 'L'Édition littéraire au XIXe siècle'. p. 9.

offering free performances (*gratis*) to celebrate notable events. Though there was naturally a certain amount of movement from one type of theatre to another, many of the spectators who were accustomed to the modest prices of the cheaper seats in the more popular theatres could not afford the higher prices of the more expensive select ones or else never had the idea of going to them.

There were, of course, considerable differences in the type of audience attracted by the different theatres of Paris, situated as they were in various parts of the city. As it was situated on the Left Bank, the Odéon mostly drew much less fashionable audiences than the Comédie-Française. Students—from the faculties of law and medicine for most of this period—formed an important part of the audience. In 1843 we find Sainte-Beuve writing of the success of Ponsard's neo-classical tragedy, *Lucrèce*:

Lucrèce jouée samedi dernier a eu un vrai succès, la foule était accourue à cet Odéon désert. Les loges étaient des mieux occupées; le parterre d'étudiants intelligents et tapageurs faisait diversion et ajoutait à l'intérêt du drame. C'était évidemment un parterre instruit, car aux moindres velléités de s'étonner ou de se scandaliser, la masse semblait répondre: *mais c'est ainsi dans l'histoire, mais il faut que cela soit ainsi.* Le bachelier ès lettres était là en majorité, il était chez soi.[1]

On occasion the Odéon did, of course, attract socially more elevated spectators, as we see here. Louis Napoleon sometimes put in an appearance there as well as at the Comédie-Française. This could give rise to hostile student demonstrations as with their applause for Ponsard's satirical comedy, *L'Honneur et l'argent*, which in 1853 had attacked those who were battening on the successful establishment of the new regime. The Goncourts record a conversation with some students who had supported them in the battle over their play, *Henriette Maréchal*, when it was performed at the Comédie-Française in 1865:

En dînant ce soir avec des étudiants qui nous ont soutenus, l'un nous révélait comment les Écoles font le succès ou la chute d'une pièce. Il nous racontait comment de très bonne foi, ils avaient applaudi à tout rompre *L'Honneur et l'argent* de Ponsard, à cause d'une tirade de 'Vauriens, pieds plats . . .' que La Ferrière avait jeté, à la première, à la loge impériale.[2]

In 1864 when George Sand's adaptation of her novel, *Le Marquis de Villemer*, was put on at the Odéon, the first performance gave the republican students an opportunity to salute her as the author of a

violently anticlerical novel, *Mademoiselle La Quintinie*. At two o'clock
the following morning she wrote to her son, Maurice:

Je reviens escortée par les étudiants aux cris de 'Vive George Sand! Vive
Mademoiselle La Quintinie! A bas les cléricaux!' C'est une manifestation
enragée en même temps qu'un succès comme on n'en a jamais vu, dit-on, au
théâtre.
    Depuis dix heures du matin, les étudiants étaient sur la place de l'Odéon, et,
tout le temps de la pièce, une masse compacte qui n'avait pu entrer occupait
les rues environnantes et la rue Racine jusqu'à ma porte.[1]

If the Emperor and other members of his family were present on this
occasion, the normal audiences of the Odéon appear to have consisted
largely of students and even some manual workers. In 1889 Edmond de
Goncourt noted a conversation with an ex-student on the subject of his
adaptation of *Germinie Lacerteux* which had recently been performed at
this theatre:

Il a assisté à six ou sept représentations, a étudié le public et me donne quelques renseignements curieux. J'ai pour moi tous les étudiants de l'École de
Médecine, et pour moi encore les étudiants de l'École de Droit, qui ne sont
pas des assidus au théâtre, les étudiants pas fortunés, pas *chic*. Le monde des
petites places est également très impressionné par la pièce, et M. Marillier
me disait que les ouvriers avec lesquels il avait causé étaient enthousiasmés de
l'œuvre.[2]

In other words, like some of the other Paris theatres, the Odéon did
draw in a certain number of working-class spectators.
    They were naturally commoner in the Théâtres du Boulevard such as
the Gaîté, the Ambigu, and the Porte-Saint-Martin which attracted a
wide range of spectators as many of their seats were extremely cheap.
Some amusing glimpses of these more plebeian spectators are to be
found in *La Grande Ville. Nouveau tableau de Paris*, a series of essays
published in the 1840s. In the essay 'Les Grisettes au spectacle' there is
the following lively account of this part of the audience:

En général les grisettes affectionnent le drame, les pièces où il y a de fortes
émotions à éprouver. Et puis à l'*Ambigu*, à *la Gaîté*, aux *Folies dramatiques*,
au *Cirque*, les femmes sont admises au parterre, et la grisette voltige du
parterre à la seconde galerie; il en est quelques-unes qui montent à la troisième galerie, mais ce sont les grisettes du dernier ordre, ou plutôt ce sont de
fausses grisettes, de malheureuses ouvrières coiffées d'un fichu, qui ne comprennent pas toute la portée d'un mélodrame, et qui se mettent à casser les

---

[1] *Correspondance 1812–1876*, v. 16.   [2] *Journal* xvi. 7–8.

noix au moment le plus épineux de la pièce. Quant à l'amphithéâtre ou paradis, les grisettes qui se respectent n'y vont jamais; elles abandonnent cette place aux gamins, aux marchandes de marrons, aux vendeurs de contre-marques, aux parents des figurantes, aux gardes municipaux et aux employés aux trognons de pommes; ceux-ci sont bien obligés par leurs fonctions de se tenir au dernier amphithéâtre pour surveiller le public de l'endroit, dont un des principaux amusements est de lancer sur le parterre ou dans les loges des coquilles de noix, des noyaux de cerises dans la saison, mais surtout des trognons de pomme, car il paraît que ce fruit doit toujours donner de mauvaises pensées aux habitants du paradis.[1]

The same essay also brings in the male spectators who frequented such theatres:

Quelquefois un ouvrier en casquette, un homme du peuple assis près d'elles, leur adresse la parole et semble avoir envie de faire leur connaissance; mais elles le reçoivent fort mal, et souvent ne lui répondent pas; pour faire la conquête de ces demoiselles, il faut être artiste, ou tout au moins porter un chapeau rond et un pantalon à sous-pieds.[2]

The essay, 'Le Boulevard du Crime', by Eugène de Mirecourt also has interesting remarks to make on the subject of such plebeian audiences. Three theatres situated side by side on the boulevard du Temple and all demolished in 1862 in the reconstruction of Paris—the Funambules, Délassements-Comiques, and Lazzari—are described as 'trois théâtres exclusivement populaires, et dans lesquels il est imprudent de s'aventurer, si l'on n'a pas la blouse du titi, le tablier du maçon, la robe souillée de fange de la balayeuse ou la coiffure désordonnée de la poissarde'. After giving a description of the queue outside such theatres ('elle est exclusivement peuple'), the writer continues:

Les queues du Cirque, de l'Ambigu-Comique et de la Porte-Saint-Martin sont moins bruyantes et moins séditieuses. Le bourgeois du Marais ou de la rue Saint-Denis peut se permettre d'y introduire sa femme et sa fille, ce qu'il n'oserait jamais faire à la porte de Lazzari, des Funambules et des Délassements.

The author, however, goes on to maintain that although the audiences for the melodramas offered in certain theatres of the 'Boulevard du Crime' were not exclusively plebeian,

le véritable public des théâtres de mélodrame est le public en manches de chemise et en blouse. Celui-là seul, n'en déplaise aux avant-scènes et aux loges, prend au sérieux les fictions dramatiques; témoin ces deux hommes qui

[1] 2 vols., Paris, 1844, i. 345–6. [2] p. 354.

se placèrent un soir en embuscade à la sortie des acteurs, attendant le traître qui, pendant cinq actes, avait excité leur colère, et se promettant de l'assommer au passage.[1]

This is a prelude to an attack on the immorality of melodrama and its corrupting effect on 'le peuple'.

George Sand met with a disappointment when in 1851 she tried to attract these more modest spectators to the Théâtre de la Gaîté with her *drame, Molière*. After its brief first run she wrote rather bitterly to one of her protégés, the 'poète ouvrier', Charles Poncy, in Toulon:

Le public des I[res] représentations a très bien accueilli ce *Molière*. Mais je dois dire *entre nous*, que le public des boulevards, celui que je voudrais instruire et bien traiter, ce public à 10 sous qui doit être le peuple, et à qui j'ai sacrifié le public bien payant du Théâtre Français, ne m'a pas tenu compte de mon dévouement. Le peuple est encore ingrat ou ignorant. Il aime mieux les meurtres, les empoisonnements que la littérature de style et de cœur. Enfin, c'est encore le peuple du boulevard du crime, et on aura de la peine à l'améliorer comme goût et comme morale. La pièce délaissée par ce public-là n'a eu que 12 représentations peu suivies par lui et soutenues seulement par les lettrés et les bourgeois.[2]

There were also theatres which drew their audiences from a particular *quartier* of Paris, such as the Théâtre Montparnasse, which the Goncourts visited in 1866 out of sheer curiosity as they had heard that their play, *Henriette Maréchal*, was being put on there. They were fascinated by the unfamiliar audience and its reaction to a thirty-year-old *drame* from the Porte-Saint-Martin:

Un théâtre d'où sortent des hommes en blouse et des femmes qui remettent leurs sabots sur leurs chaussons à la porte. Dans la salle, un public mi-ouvriers, mi-portiers retirés du cordon. Nous avons d'abord vu jouer *La Chambre ardente*, où quand la Brinvilliers empoisonne, j'entends des femmes dire derrière moi: 'La garce!' Un enfant était fort curieux de savoir si on verrait Henri IV dans la pièce et le demandait à sa mère. Un public sincère, de bonne foi, mais sur lequel la pièce historique exerce une fascination.[3]

Given the French society of the day, it was inevitable that Paris theatre audiences should be predominantly middle class in composition. In 1892 Edmond de Goncourt noted in his journal:

Pour être connu en littérature, être universellement connu, on ne sait pas combien il importe d'être homme de théâtre. Car le théâtre, pensez-y bien,

---

[1] *La Grande Ville* ii. 268–9.   [2] *Correspondance*, x. 308–9.   [3] *Journal* vii. 160.

c'est toute la littérature de bien des gens, et de gens supérieurs, mais si occupés qu'ils n'ouvrent jamais un volume n'ayant pas trait à leur profession,— l'unique littérature en un mot des savants, des avocats, des médecins.[1]

It was precisely against what he regarded as the predominance of middle-class values in the theatre that Théophile Gautier protested again and again in his dramatic criticism. Writing some twenty years after the first performance of Vigny's *Chatterton*, he speaks of the hatred for everything bourgeois felt by the young writers and artists who applauded the play when it was first put on:

Le parterre devant lequel déclamait Chatterton était plein de pâles adolescents aux longs cheveux, croyant fermement qu'il n'y avait d'autre occupation acceptable sur ce globe que de faire des vers ou de la peinture—de l'art comme on disait,—et regardant les *bourgeois* avec un mépris dont celui des *renards* de Heidelberg ou d'Iéna pour les philistins approche à peine. Les bourgeois! c'était à peu près tout le monde: les banquiers, les agents de change, les notaires, les négociants, les gens de boutique et autres, quiconque ne faisait pas partie du mystérieux cénacle et gagnait prosaïquement sa vie.[2]

Again and again Gautier attacks the comedies of Scribe for the bourgeois values which contributed to their enormous success with audiences of the time. In discussing his *Oscar ou le mari qui trompe sa femme*, performed at the Comédie-Française in 1842, he lets himself go on the subject of its success:

M. Scribe est bourgeois (qu'on nous permette de nous servir ici de ce terme emprunté à l'*argot* des ateliers et qui rend notre pensée mieux que tout autre), c'est-à-dire qu'il n'entend rien à aucun art, n'a le sentiment ni de la forme ni du style, est dénué d'enthousiasme, de passion, et n'admire pas la nature.— Son mobile dramatique est l'argent; sa philosophie consiste à démontrer qu'il vaut mieux épouser un portefeuille de billets de banque qu'une femme qu'on aime, et que les intrigues d'amour offrent beaucoup d'inconvénients tels que chutes, coryzas, sauts périlleux, surprises et duels. La raison suprême, suivant M. Scribe, est un égoïsme douillet que rien ne doit faire sortir de sa chambre matelassée et de ses pantoufles de fourrure.[3]

One could go on quoting for pages from Gautier's denunciations of Scribe.

He has similar remarks to make about other playwrights of the time and the way in which they reflect the materialistic, money-grubbing

[1] Ibid. xviii. 122.
[2] *Histoire du romantisme*, Paris, 1927, pp. 153–4.
[3] *Histoire de l'art dramatique en France*. ii. 234.

society of the age. For instance, apropos of a *vaudeville*, *Le Nouveau Juif errant*, performed at the Palais-Royal theatre in 1846, he writes scornfully:

Les amours de M. Alfred et de mademoiselle Henriette ont perdu le pouvoir d'exciter la sympathie de la génération présente. Pauvre Alfred! pauvre Henriette! l'un si tendre, si délicat, si romanesque, l'autre si naïve, si chaste et si désintéressée! une page de chiffres contenant le total d'une somme de la capitalisation des intérêts, fait plus rêver les jeunes imaginations de ce siècle que la description de regards d'azur, de joues de rose et de seins de neige. Chacun vérifie le calcul, et, le trouvant juste, s'écrie: 'O grand auteur!'

Si l'on veut aujourd'hui rendre un personnage intéressant, on ne le fait plus fatal, mystérieux, byronien, ravagé par les passions, on lui constitue un ou deux millions de rentes, on décrit son hôtel et son écurie, et aussitôt don Juan, Lovelace, Oswald, Grandison, Des Grieux sont oubliés.

Les plus jeunes filles sont incapables de se prendre d'amourette pour un Roméo sans inscriptions de rentes, fût-il frais comme l'aurore et beau comme le jour. On serait mal reçu à enjamber la balustrade des balcons, si l'on n'avait pas ses poches bourrées d'actions du Nord.[1]

In penning such lines Gautier gave clear expression to the divorce which grew up in this period between the artist and the philistine, middle-class-dominated society in which he lived.

The word *bourgeois* thus acquired a new sense. Under the *ancien régime* in a society dominated by the nobility *bourgeois* used in a pejorative sense was applied by members of the aristocracy or by those of middle-class origins who adopted its attitudes to persons who did not donform in their outlook and behaviour to the standards of the cominant class. Now it came to be applied by people who were often thoroughly middle class in origins and way of life (one thinks of a *rentier* like Flaubert) to those whose outlook they considered to be closed to all notions of art.

The divorce between the artist and the society of his age goes back to the Romantic period. The exaggerations of the Romantic writers, their eccentricities, their contempt for conventional moral standards were a challenge to the whole outlook of the bourgeois whom they deliberately sought to provoke and scandalize. This tradition was carried to extremes by the younger generation of Romantics in the 1830s, the so-called Jeunes-France among whom Gautier was a leading figure; these young men, some of them later to become famous, led a

---

[1] Shares in the Compagnie des chemins de fer du Nord (*Histoire de l'art dramatique en France*, iv. 139–40).

bohemian existence and indulged in all manner of eccentricities to 'épater le bourgeois'.

This same equation of 'bourgeois' and 'philistine' was made by Flaubert. 'J'appelle bourgeois,' he told his disciple, Maupassant, 'quiconque pense bassement.' His worship of Art made it impossible for him to seek to win the favour of the multitude of his own day. In 1872 he wrote to George Sand:

J'écris (je parle d'un auteur qui se respecte) non pour le lecteur d'aujourd'hui mais pour tous les lecteurs qui pourraient se présenter, tant que la langue vivra. Ma marchandise ne peut donc être consommée maintenant, car elle n'est pas faite exclusivement pour mes contemporains. Mon service reste donc indéfini et, par conséquent, impayable.[1]

In his next letter to George Sand he explains his position more clearly:

N'allez pas croire que je compte 'sur la postérité pour me venger de l'indifférence de mes contemporains'. J'ai voulu dire seulement ceci: quand on ne s'adresse pas à la foule, il est juste que la foule ne vous paye pas. C'est de l'économie politique. Or je maintiens qu'une œuvre d'art (digne de ce nom et faite avec conscience) est inappréciable, n'a pas de valeur commerciale, ne peut pas se payer. Conclusion: si l'artiste n'a pas de rentes, il doit crever de faim![2]

For a writer like Flaubert who despised the society of his day and in particular the base, utilitarian outlook of the middle class to which he himself belonged, the only salvation lay in his art, in his pursuit of the perfect form.

Yet, as the success of *Madame Bovary* showed, a writer like Flaubert could produce work which was capable of being understood and appreciated by a fairly considerable number of his contemporaries. If he and Baudelaire could never appeal to as wide a public as Hugo or Zola, they did not, as many later *avant-garde* writers were to do, turn their back on contemporary society and write only for a tiny group of readers. Rimbaud, for instance, may have exercised a tremendous influence on later poets including Claudel, but the kind of poetry which he produced could have only a strictly limited appeal to his contemporaries. Mallarmé again was extraordinarily influential; during his lifetime he was almost idolized by the narrow group who frequented his *salon* in the rue de Rome, and Valéry was only one of the younger poets on whom he left his mark. Yet though during his lifetime he met with recognition from a small circle of readers, clearly he never sought to

[1] *Correspondance*, vi. 456.   [2] Ibid. 458.

reach anything but a tiny group among the vastly expanded reading public of his day. At the age of twenty he published an article, 'Hérésies artistiques. *L'Art pour tous*', in which he made his position perfectly plain:

Qu'un philosophe ambitionne la popularité, je l'en estime. Il ne ferme pas les mains sur la poignée de vérités radieuses qu'elles enserrent; il les répand, et cela est juste qu'elles laissent un lumineux sillage à chacun de ses doigts. Mais qu'un poète, un adorateur du beau inaccessible au vulgaire, ne se contente pas des suffrages du sanhédrin de l'art, cela m'irrite, et je ne le comprends pas.

That cheap editions of poetry, aimed at drawing in a wider audience, should be produced seemed to him incomprehensible:

On multiplie les éditions à bon marché des poètes, et cela au consentement et au contentement des poètes. Croyez-vous que vous y gagnerez de la gloire, ô rêveurs, ô lyriques ? Quand l'artiste seul avait votre livre, coûte que coûte, eût-il dû payer de son dernier liard la dernière de vos étoiles, vous aviez de vrais admirateurs. Et maintenant cette foule qui vous *achète* pour votre bon marché vous comprend-elle ?[1]

When twenty-five years later, in 1887, he collected together the poems he had so far written, they appeared in the somewhat curious form of *Les Poésies de Stéphane Mallarmé, photolithographiées du manuscrit définitif* in an edition of which only forty-seven copies were printed.

In varying degrees later writers of prose as well as poetry deliberately chose to offer their works to a similarly limited public. Claudel, for instance, cannot have expected queues to form for his *Cinq grandes odes* when they were published in 1910, while the verse dramas which he produced from 1890 onwards often appeared only in limited editions. It was not until 1912 that one of these was at last staged, and then in an *avant-garde* theatre.

We have thus the paradox that in the face of a vastly expanded reading public produced by the growth in population, the spread of education, and the reduction in the price of books, a considerable number of writers chose to confine their appeal to only a tiny fraction of that public. While it would have been impossible to appeal simultaneously to all sections of it, some writers of the age, including a number of the very greatest as well as others whose names are now almost forgotten, did aim their works at fairly wide sectors of this vast public and in many cases succeeded in attracting their interest.

[1] *Œuvres complètes*, eds. H. Mondor and G. Jean-Aubry, Paris, 1945, pp. 259–60.

For those writers who did so, there were large financial rewards; and many of those—famous or now forgotten—whose works met with only a moderate amount of success enjoyed a reasonably comfortable income, often supplemented by writing in newspapers and reviews. There is no doubt that the lot of the average writer was a very much happier one than that of his predecessors before 1789. Yet averages are notoriously deceptive; they can mask extraordinary differences. If it is true to say that in this period writers in general enjoyed in increasing measure the benefits to be derived from a more affluent society and from a greatly expanded reading public, this does not mean—any more than in earlier ages or at the present time—that the rewards to be derived from writing as a profession were equally shared. There were, as always, extremes of wealth and poverty among writers. One thinks, for instance, of the contrast between the affluence of successful writers like Zola and Daudet and the miserable existence of their contemporary, Villiers de l'Isle Adam.

Some notion of the value of the earnings of really successful writers in the decades before 1914 can be derived from a comparison with the salaries of *fonctionnaires*. In 1880, for instance, a *directeur de ministère* earned between 13,500 and 20,000 francs a year, a *conseiller d'état* 16,000, and a professor at the Collège de France 10,000[1]—roughly the equivalent of £550–800, £650, and £400 in English money of the time. On the eve of the 1914–18 War an *instititeur* earned 2,200 francs a year, a *chef de bureau* 12,000, and a university professor 15,000[2]—some £90, £480, and £600 in English money. Seen against these figures the earnings of successful writers like Zola and Daudet appear quite impressive, especially when one remembers that there was no such thing as income tax or surtax in those days. Even in comparison with quite high *fonctionnaires* they were extremely well off, at any rate once they had made a name for themselves.

A now forgotten writer stressed in the 1880s the enormous advance in the status of the profession which had taken place in the nineteenth century when he declared: 'Jamais l'homme de lettres ne se connut aussi entièrement maître de sa personne et de ses idées qu'en notre XIXᵉ siècle. Mettez en vis-à-vis son antique situation d'infériorité et sa prépondérance nouvellement conquise, l'opposition sera concluante'; or again 'Il aura fallu attendre jusqu'au XIXᵉ siècle pour assister à

---

[1] J. Fourastié, *Machinisme et bien-être. Niveau de vie et genre de vie en France de 1700 à nos jours*, Paris, 1962, pp. 28–9.

[2] P. Goulène, *Evolution des pouvoirs d'achat en France 1880–1972*, Paris, 1974.

l'émancipation notoire, incontestée, de l'écrivain. Elle a été complète, définitive.'[1] Yet the same writer then proceeds to present to the reader the reverse of the medal—a long and grisly account of the sad fate of numerous nineteenth-century French writers who had fallen by the wayside. No doubt as writing had come to offer greater financial rewards and even a certain affluence to its most successful practitioners, it attracted more and more young people, dazzled by the prospects of fame and even wealth. As the same writer puts it:

C'est un fait d'une évidence journalière, la tribu éparse des déclassés, poètes, littérateurs ou autres, se multiplie dans une progression effrayante. Chaque année, des collèges de France sortent des troupes de bacheliers ès lettres qui ne seront ni avocats, ni médecins, ni commerçants, ni fonctionnaires, qui ne veulent être ni ouvriers, ni agriculteurs, qui ne peuvent devenir ni banquiers, ni industriels, et qui, pourvus d'une ambition énorme, s'intituleront des hommes de plume.[2]

A quarter of a century later we find Rosny *aîné* declaring: 'Plus d'un écrivain doué d'un talent réel ne gagne pas dans son année la moitié de ce que gagne un balayeur municipal.'[3] Yet despite the fierce competition which the growth in the reading public engendered among writers, it can well be argued that as in this country the last decades before 1914 were the golden age of the professional writer and that in the 1970s the average writer is worse off than his predecessors two or three generations ago. What is certain is that the same inequalities remain among the members of the profession, the rewards of which can range from a lordly income to a handful of small change.

---

[1] F. Loliée, *Nos gens de lettres: leur vie intérieure, leurs rivalités, leur condition*, Paris, 1887 pp. 12, 16.

[2] Ibid. pp. 217–18.

[3] Quoted in A. Billy, *La Vie littéraire. L'Époque contemporaine (1905–1930)*, Paris, 1956, p. 146.

VI   The Twentieth Century

In the decades which have passed since the outbreak of the First World War in 1914, the population of France, after a long period of near stagnation at around 40 million, has expanded rapidly since 1945 to well over 50 million. Yet the position of the French language in the world as a whole has undoubtedly shrunk still further in relation to English which is spoken as a native language by nearly 300 million people. Even if one adds in the native speakers of French in Belgium, Switzerland, Canada, and the West Indies, the total comes to not much more than 65 million. French still remains important as a second language in the former colonial empire and has indeed produced a considerable literature in Africa as well as in Canada and the West Indies. As an international language it also retains a certain importance, though nowadays it is clear that it comes far behind English even if the French language and its literature continue to be widely studied in the schools and universities of a great many non-French-speaking countries. French writers are clearly conscious of the relatively narrow market which their books can reach, though the belief that writers in English are necessarily better off than they are, expressed in 1967 by Armand Lanoux, would seem ill founded:

Quelque chose m'a fait beaucoup réfléchir sur mon état. C'est la comparaison de l'écrivain en anglais et de l'écrivain en français. Nous sommes soumis à la loi des grands nombres, et cette loi est implacable. Il y a une équation constante entre le nombre de gens qui parlent une langue et le nombre de ses écrivains professionnels. Le français se trouve entièrement lié à la francophonie, l'anglais est lié à l'anglophonie. C'est la raison pour laquelle les Américains et les Anglais, mis dans la même situation que nous, par rapport à leur langue de support, *se trouvent dans des conditions infiniment plus confortables que les nôtres pour des raisons quantitatives.*

Notre francophonie nous met au-dessous de l'espagnol, et à peu près au niveau de l'allemand et de l'italien.[1]

There is still a world market for French books, but in recent years French publishers have had to face the disquieting fact that although exports expanded rapidly in the 1960s, imports of books increased

[1] *La Profession d'écrivain* (Université de Bordeaux, Institut de littérature et de techniques artistiques de masse), Bordeaux, 1968, p. 30.

even more rapidly, so that by 1970 they had begun to exceed sales abroad.[1]

Despite the competition of new forms of entertainment—first of the cinema which had its beginnings before 1914, then of radio from the 1920s, and finally, mainly from the 1960s, of television—a considerable expansion of the reading public has taken place. This is due to a variety of factors such as a larger population with a high proportion of young people, and the 'education explosion' of the 1950s and 1960s; another factor—not an entirely new one, as this has been a gradual process going back to at least the end of the nineteenth century—has been the growth of leisure. As in other advanced countries the number of hours spent at work each week has been drastically reduced. A large part of the population now enjoys a five-day week, a considerable number (much larger than in this country) of public holidays, and fairly long annual holidays. While not everyone in modern society is faced with the problem of what to do with such leisure, large numbers of people enjoy many free hours in the week outside the time which they spend at work and travelling to and from it. While it is true that all sorts of occupations compete for these leisure hours, some of them must go into reading—and not necessarily only of newspapers and magazines.

The development of France's cultural life since 1914 has inevitably reflected the ups and downs in her history. First came the bitter struggle, fought out largely on French soil, of the 1914–18 War; this was followed by a fairly rapid recovery, though one hampered by a period of inflation, and a certain degree of prosperity down to about 1930. Then came the economic difficulties of the 1930s followed by another war and the German occupation.

These were on the whole hard years, and as in this country a period of relative stagnation in the economic field. French losses in the First World War had a disastrous effect on an already almost stationary population in which the proportion of old people to young was exceptionally high. Even with the return of Alsace-Lorraine at the end of the war the population was smaller than it had been in 1914. On top of the low number of births during the war years came a further decline in the birth rate in the two decades which followed. It fell to a level below that of any large country, and from 1935 onwards the number of deaths regularly exceeded the number of births. If the 1939–45 War

[1] P. Laurent, 'La Diffusion du livre français à l'étranger' in *Le Livre français. Hier, aujourd'hui, demain*, pp. 248–9.

further aggravated this situation, its effects were nothing like as serious as those of the First World War. Indeed, from 1942 onwards—partly as a result of the Code de la famille, which was promulgated on the very eve of the war and greatly extended family allowances—the population trend was actually reversed.

Educational change in these years was slow. Elementary education continued to be divorced from secondary education; the gap between them was perpetuated by the existence of preparatory departments in the *lycées* and *collèges* as well as of various forms of secondary education which were merely a prolongation of the *école primaire*. It was not until 1936 that the school-leaving age was raised to fourteen by the Front populaire government. Perhaps the most significant change in French schools in these years was the series of measures passed between 1928 and 1933 to make the state system of secondary education free at all levels. Compared with what has happened in more recent decades, the expansion of university education between 1914 and 1939 appears very slow and gradual; the number of students rose from 42,000 in 1913–14 to 79,000 in 1938–9. The public library services continued to lag behind those offered by other advanced countries and little attempt was made to reach a wider public. In 1931, for instance, the Paris municipal libraries lent only some 60 per cent of the books issued in 1902.[1]

The production of books in France fluctuated violently in these years, only once reaching the highest figure attained before 1914:

1913	14 460	1930	9176
1914	8698	1931	9822
1915	4274	1932	10 603
1916	5062	1933	8204
1917	5054	1934	8389
1918	4484	1935	7964
1919	5361	1936	9319
1920	6315	1937	8080
1921	7726	1938	8124
1922	8515	1939	7505
1923	8748	1940	5549
1924	8864	1941	4007
1925	15 054	1942	7281
1926	11 095	1943	7918
1927	11 922	1944	8680
1928	11 548	1945	7291[2]
1929	10 941		

[1] Coeytaux, 'Le Centenaire des bibliothèques municipales de Paris', p. 65.
[2] Estivals, *La Statistique bibliographique de la France*, p. 415.

These figures reflect very closely the chequered history of France in this period of some thirty years. We see, first, the havoc created by the 1914–18 War and the period of rapid inflation which followed. Then came the short-lived prosperity of the late twenties which turned rapidly into the economic stagnation of the thirties. In 1935 Claude Aveline wrote gloomily of the effects of the economic depression of these years on publishing, particularly on certain new features of the 1920s such as lavish advertising and the vogue for publishers' series and *éditions de luxe*:

Depuis 1930, la plupart des collections ont cessé de paraître. L'édition de luxe est particulièrement touchée. . . . La publicité se réduit à l'annonce des titres. Les éditeurs travaillent de nouveau avec prudence. Ils n'assurent plus, dès son premier livre, la vie matérielle d'un jeune écrivain; on me parle plus de la littérature comme d'un métier. En somme, le débutant de 1935 ressemble au débutant d'avant-guerre plus qu'à son aîné d'il y a dix ans.[1]

Then came a second catastrophe, the 1939–45 War, which once again greatly reduced the number of books published.

Relations between publishers and writers underwent some changes in these years. The royalty system, based no longer on the number of copies printed, but on the number actually sold, was now firmly established for any book with a commercial sale. The writer's answer to this change was to demand an advance on royalties, a development which was not altogether agreeable to a publisher like Bernard Grasset who was extremely active in the inter-war years:

Les écrivains . . . se refusent, de nos jours, à courir avec l'éditeur la 'chance' de leur propre livre; ils trouvent plus confortable de la lui laisser courir seul. Ce grand inconnu qu'est l'avenir d'une œuvre, ils exigent de l'éditeur qu'il l'évalue. Ils lui demandent de leur assurer un minimum de gain; bien mieux, de leur verser, à la signature même de l'accord, ce gain minimum à valoir sur les droits d'auteur qui pourraient leur être dus. C'est ce qu'on appelle les *avances aux auteurs*. Et ne croyez pas qu'il s'agisse là de sommes négligeables, même pour un budget important. Des avances de vingt, trente mille francs sont fréquentes. Ces avances peuvent atteindre plusieurs centaines de mille francs, pour certains écrivains en renom.

C'est sur de pareilles sommes que joue actuellement la concurrence entre éditeurs: le plus offrant l'emporte.[2]

Even during the 1914–18 War (Barbusse's *Le Feu* was a striking example) sales of really successful works had begun to reach hitherto

---

[1] 'Le Rôle de l'éditeur dans la production littéraire', *Encyclopédie française*, 17·84–9.
[2] *La Chose littéraire*, pp. 91–3.

unknown proportions, another phenomenon noted by the same publisher:

On apprit à ne pas s'étonner de tirages élevés, atteints en quelques mois. On s'habitua à parler de soixante ou de cent mille exemplaires vendus, comme on parlait avant la guerre de dix ou douze mille, et la définition du succès s'en trouva modifiée.

Le chiffre de cent mille prit même à un certain moment, une valeur symbolique. Il s'agissait de l'atteindre ou de le dépasser. *L'ère des cent mille était ouverte.*[1]

One must, of course, beware of taking at their face value the sales figures put out by French publishers as their unreliability was a standard joke, amusingly presented in the following dialogue between publisher and author in Édouard Bourdet's comedy, *Vient de paraître*:

MOSCAT. On tirera à vingt mille pour commencer.
MARC. A vingt mille!
MOSCAT. Et puis, tu sais, ce sont des vrais mille . . . des mille de cinq cents!
MARC. Comment?
MOSCAT. Oui, parce que, chez Chamillard, par exemple, les mille sont de deux cent cinquante.[2]

In the writings of the period there are innumerable references, some of them highly amusing, to this practice of inflating sales. In 1923, for instance, Léautaud recorded in his *Journal littéraire* a conversation in the offices of the *Mercure*:

On parlait ce matin, avec Vallette et Dumur, du bluff mis à la mode par certains éditeurs pour pousser leurs auteurs. Il paraît que Gallimard lui-même n'en est pas exempt. Quand il publia *Ouvert la nuit* de Paul Morand, il annonça bientôt le 30ᵉ mille. Quand l'époque approcha, il pensa à avoir le Prix Goncourt pour ce livre. Il alla voir notamment Hennique pour tâcher de le gagner à sa cause. Hennique lui fit remarquer que Morand n'était guère dans les conditions requises pour le prix: tout de suite connu du public, son premier livre déjà tiré à 30.000, un grand succès.[3] Gallimard dut alors découvrir ses batteries et avoua à Hennique qu'il n'y avait là qu'un truc de publicité et que *Ouvert la nuit* n'avait tiré en réalité qu'à 7.000, se donnant même la peine d'apporter ses livres à Hennique pour lui prouver qu'il disait vrai.[4]

[1] Ibid. p. 109.   [2] *Vient de paraître*, Paris, 1928, p. 15.
[3] In his will Edmond de Goncourt had stipulated that the prize should be given 'à la jeunesse, à l'originalité du talent, aux tentatives nouvelles et hardies de la pensée et de la forme' (L. Deffoux, *Chronique de l'Académie Goncourt*, Paris, 1929, p. 190).
[4] *Journal littéraire*, iv. 207.

Some years later the same diarist, who was well placed through his position in a publisher's office to pick up the gossip of the book trade, related a story of how one writer got into trouble with his tax inspector over the exaggerated claims made by his publisher for the sales of one of his books:

Je lui raconte aussi l'histoire de Marcel Prévost, convoqué par son contrôleur des contributions, pour déclaration de revenu vraiment peu en rapport avec la vente affichée partout d'un roman qu'il venait de publier et obligé de lui confesser que c'étaient là artifices de libraire et que ce roman, proclamé en étant au 80ᵉ mille, en était en réalité au 30ᵉ.[1]

A famous case of a book with sales puffed up by all the modern methods of publicity has recently been examined in detail—that of *Maria Chapdelaine*, one of the best sellers of the inter-war period.[2] Curiously enough, it was not a new work which Grasset launched in 1921. It had already appeared posthumously early in 1914 as a *feuilleton* in *Le Temps* and had been published in book form in Canada two years later without making any sort of a stir. Thanks to his extremely adroit use of a whole variety of advertising devices, including the usual one of grossly exaggerating the sales of the work (as early as January 1923 he was using the figure of 600,000 copies, his 'mille' being a mere 250...), Grasset managed to sell half a million copies of his edition, and large numbers of school and other cheap editions had appeared in the same period.[3]

In addition to spending considerable sums on newspaper advertising publishers would now arrange for piles of copies of new works to be prominently displayed in bookshops together with the portrait of the author and would even arrange for him to be present to sign dedications in each copy of his book that was sold. Such devices shocked publishers of the old school like Vallette of the *Mercure*. In 1931, when the economic depression was seriously affecting the book trade and its products were selling badly, he blamed this partly on the way in which writers had accepted all these publicity devices:

Ils ont ravalé la littérature au rang d'une marchandise ordinaire. Autrefois, un écrivain n'était pas Monsieur tout le monde. Un certain prestige s'attachait à l'homme qui écrivait. D'autant plus que, généralement, on les connaissait très

---

[1] Ibid. viii. 337.
[2] See G. Boillat, 'Comment on fabrique un succès: *Maria Chapdelaine*', *Revue d'histoire littéraire*, 1974, pp. 223–53.
[3] Ibid. pp. 244–5.

peu en dehors de leurs livres. Aujourd'hui, avec cette mode des portraits, à chaque instant, ces vitrines d'auteurs avec leurs papiers, leurs pantoufles, etc., ces soirées chez un libraire pour signer des exemplaires aux premiers venus, cette exhibition perpétuelle, adieu le mystère, et le prestige. Ils se sont trop montrés. On a vu qu'ils sont des hommes comme les autres. Ils ont tout perdu, et perdu par leur faute. On gagne à rester un peu secret, un peu ignoré...[1]

A good deal of this publicity both in the daily newspapers and in the weeklies devoted to literature was provided by the *Courriers littéraires*, filled with literary gossip, and by interviews with writers. The best known of these weeklies was *Les Nouvelles littéraires*, founded in 1922 and destined for quite a long life.

It is generally agreed that daily newspapers offered fewer outlets to writers than they had done in the decades before 1914. Literary reviews, however, continued to flourish. The *Revue des Deux Mondes* went steadily on its way, remaining intensely conservative in literature as in other fields. Though past its zenith the *Mercure* still continued to publish original work in the form of novels and poetry. The *Nouvelle Revue française* was in its heyday; in 1931 Léautaud noted a conversation with Julien Benda who told him that it had 17,000 subscribers: 'Presque le double que le *Mercure*', he wrote gloomily, adding, 'Le rôle que le *Mercure* tenait autrefois.'[2]

The fashion for literary prizes which had been stimulated by the establishment of the Prix Goncourt (first awarded in 1903), quickly followed by that of the Prix Fémina–Vie heureuse (1904) and then of the Grand Prix de littérature of the Académie française, spread further in these years. A great many of them brought prestige rather than hard cash to the recipients, but a work which was awarded the Prix Goncourt was likely to bring substantial rewards to both writer and publisher, and a number of other prizes were also much sought after even if they did not normally ensure quite such large sales. It cannot be said that many of the books which received the Prix Goncourt in these years have had a long life, though there are such exceptions as Proust's *A l'ombre des jeunes filles en fleur* and Malraux's *La Condition humaine*.

The writers' societies—the Société des gens de lettres and the Société des auteurs et compositeurs dramatiques—were gradually called upon to assume fresh functions with the appearance of the cinema and radio in order to ensure that their members received the fees due to them for the reproduction of their work by these new media.

---

[1] Léautaud, *Journal littéraire*, ix. 59.   [2] Ibid. viii. 311.

The Société des auteurs et compositeurs dramatiques went through the formalities of dissolving itself in 1929, immediately recreating itself for another sixty years from that date. Paris continued to be the centre of theatrical life in France, and almost all new plays of any importance were given their first performance there. As before, the society took a tough line with theatre managements, though sometimes its members went behind its back, a fact deplored by Jean-Jacques Bernard, writing in 1935:

Aujourd'hui les auteurs ont la possibilité de se défendre sur le plan syndical. Est-ce à dire qu'ils en usent toujours bien et apportent à leur société le même appui que celle-ci leur donne? On est en droit de déplorer que l'intérêt général soit parfois sacrifié à des intérêts particuliers immédiats. Il arrive encore que les auteurs acceptent de passer sous les fourches caudines des commerçants qu'ils rendent plus forts par leur faiblesse. Il arrive qu'eux-mêmes se prêtent à des combinaisons occultes, dont la plus grave, et malheureusement la plus difficile à dépister, est la ristourne des droits.[1]

The coming of the cinema, an invention scarcely foreseen by Beaumarchais or even Scribe, was gradually, if somewhat grudgingly, recognized by the society.

The Société des gens de lettres was installed in 1930 in the Hôtel de Massa, transported stone by stone from the Champs-Élysées to a site near the Observatoire, and in 1938 it celebrated its centenary. At that date it had just over 1,000 *sociétaires* and some 3,600 *adhérents*. The notion that a writer could expect to be able to earn a reasonable living by his pen was not one which met with universal approval. It was, for instance, fiercely attacked by Bernard Grasset:

On se déclare maintenant écrivain à dix-huit ans, comme on est candidat à une grande école, ou comme l'on entre dans une maison de commerce. La littérature est un métier qui paye. Il n'exige aucun examen, aucun concours à l'origine. Il peut mener à une gloire rapide. Pourquoi ne pas le choisir de préférence à telle ou telle autre carrière difficile d'abord ou sans horizon!

Étrange conception des Lettres! Un métier, c'est quelque chose qui s'apprend. Qui donc jusqu'à maintenant eût prétendu que la littérature pût s'apprendre, que quelque chose de lentement acquis pût remplacer cette flamme intérieure, ce don sans lequel il n'est pas d'écrivain! Et comment s'étonner, dès lors, qu'abordant les Lettres sans don et avec toutes les exigences, des téméraires, tous les jours plus nombreux, finissent par constituer une véritable armée de mécontents![2]

---

[1] 'La Profession de l'auteur dramatique', *Encyclopédie française*, 17·88–2.
[2] *La Chose littéraire*, pp. 72–4.

But this was the view of a prosperous publisher... That the profession was overcrowded was certainly felt by many writers themselves, as is shown in the remark attributed to J. H. Rosny: 'Ce n'est pas une Société des Gens de Lettres qui devrait exister, mais une Société à détourner les gens des lettres.'

Quite a number of the prominent writers of this period possessed private means and were in no way dependent on what they earned by their pen. Others who were so dependent managed to write works which enjoyed a large sale and made possible a very comfortable existence, once they had made a name for themselves. A 'second métier' continued to be necessary for most writers, at least until they had established themselves in the public eye and could afford to take the risks involved in concentrating all their energies on writing. Looking back on his early life in which, in the midst of considerable hardships, he had qualified as a doctor, a successful writer like Georges Duhamel continues to offer this advice:

A tous les jeunes écrivains qui m'ont fait part de leurs angoisses, j'ai conseillé ardemment le parti du second métier, à la condition, toutefois, que le second métier n'absorbe pas la totalité de leur courage, qu'il leur fournisse, au contraire, outre des subsides, certains matériaux d'expérience humaine, de vues sur les compagnons de route, sur la société, sur le monde. S'il dispose de quelques heures par jour pour la méditation et l'écriture, un jeune écrivain peut encore être assuré du salut.[1]

It goes without saying that a great many writers of the period continued to the end to follow a quite different profession.

For the writer without private means things could be very difficult. State patronage of literature was at a very low ebb. In 1918 an agitation was started for the setting up of a Caisse nationale des lettres to subsidize writers who required such support. It was pointed out that the amount of money at the disposal of the Ministry of Education for such purposes was a mere 275,000 francs; the cry was now for 'le Million des Lettres'. Finally, on 28 June 1928 Édouard Herriot brought in a bill to create a Caisse nationale des lettres, arts et sciences to be financed by a 6 per cent royalty on works which had ceased to be copyright. This project appeared to be on the point of being realized when article 158 of the budget for 1930–1 established both a Caisse nationale des lettres and a Caisse nationale des sciences. Elaborate rules were duly drawn up for the administration of the Caisse nationale des lettres,

[1] *Le Temps de la recherche*, p. 201.

but nothing appears to have come of the project. About 1955—just before such an institution actually came into being—André Billy wrote sadly: 'En décembre 1930, la Caisse nationale fut enfin créée. Deux décrets parurent à l'*Officiel*, nommant les membres de son conseil d'administration. Il ne restait plus qu'à la remplir. Vingt-cinq ans après, elle est encore vide.'[1] He might even have added that it was virtually abolished by a decree of 25 October 1935.

The way in which the Ministry of Education's funds were distributed among needy and allegedly needy men of letters could and did give rise to controversy.[2] And the amounts of money distributed were extremely small. Léautaud, who had drawn small sums from a variety of ministries during the 1914–18 War, was not exactly thrilled when in May 1944 he received a letter from the Ministry of Education informing him that he had been awarded 'une indemnité littéraire annuelle de 8,000 francs'. His comments in his diary were somewhat caustic: 'Huit mille francs! On n'aurait pas pu aller jusqu'à la douzaine? Ce n'est pas une pension. C'est une aumône. Heureusement que je n'ai rien demandé, sollicité, qu'on n'a rien de moi: visite, démarche, lettre dans ce sens.'[3]

A certain amount of private patronage continued to exist. Valéry, driven in 1922 into the career of a full-time writer after the death of the man to whom he had acted as secretary for over twenty years, was hard put to support himself and his family. He had to have recourse to various expedients such as lectures in a large number of foreign countries as well as in France, publishing small *de luxe* editions of his writings at a high price, and selling manuscript copies of his poems. Money, even the modest payments made to an academician, was extremely important to him. A group of publishers and writers appear to have clubbed together to provide him with an annuity. Finally, the state stepped in and did things on a lavish scale: in 1933 he was appointed administrator of the Centre universitaire méditerranéen at Nice, a post which does not seem to have taken up much of his time or energies, and four years later a chair of poetics at the Collège de France was established for him. It need hardly be said that this was altogether exceptional treatment for a writer; it was only after another couple of decades had passed that the state was to embark on more systematic assistance to men of letters.

.   .   .   .   .

[1] *La Vie littéraire. L'Époque contemporaine*, p. 350.
[2] See e.g. Léautaud, *Journal littéraire*, vi. 290, 310.
[3] Ibid. xv. 341.

After 1945 France slowly emerged from the sufferings and losses of the Second World War and gradually moved towards a period of rapid economic expansion as it went through a kind of belated industrial revolution. Hundreds of thousands of its inhabitants left the countryside for the towns; these were already being swollen by the continued growth in population which increased by over ten million between the 1940s and the 1970s. This new economic climate has affected literature as well as the other arts.

The so-called 'education explosion' of recent decades—the result not only of this increase in population but also of a growing demand for this commodity—forms a sharp contrast with the earlier period when conditions in elementary, secondary, and higher education remained very much as they had been before 1914.

Elementary education was naturally the first to be affected by the higher birth rate. The total number of pupils in the state and private sectors (including those in nursery schools, since in France attendance at school is compulsory only from the age of six) rose from under 5 million in the period 1945–50 to more than 7 million in 1963–4. But it is in secondary and higher education that the increase in numbers has been most dramatic. In the same period the number of pupils in the state *lycées* trebled, and, if one adds in the *Cours complémentaires* and the *Collèges d'enseignement général*, the numbers in state secondary schools rose from 495,000 to 1,891,000. In these years the number of pupils in the private sector more or less doubled, ending up with roughly a fifth of the numbers in state secondary schools. In 1959 an ordinance was issued raising the school-leaving age from fourteen to sixteen in 1967; if, when the date came round, it proved impossible to offer full-time education to all those concerned, it would seem that now the reform has been carried through, at least in principle. In the meantime, in 1963, the government had created a new type of secondary school, the *Collège d'enseignement secondaire*, which took in pupils of a wide range of ability—in other words, a kind of comprehensive school. By 1971–2 the total number of pupils in the state and private sectors of secondary education had risen to over 4 million.

The expansion of universities since 1945 has been, if anything, even more startling. In the period 1945–50 numbers rose to 136,000 from the 1938–9 figure of 79,000; they continued to grow steadily throughout the 1950s, reaching 202,000 in 1959–60. Then came the runaway expansion of the 1960s which reflected the massive growth of secondary education; the number of university students trebled in a decade, reaching 619,000 in 1969–70, and since then the university population has continued to grow. How this shattering expansion had as one of its consequences the famous 'événements' of 1968 and the subsequent disorders in universities is too familiar a tale to relate here. The practical effects of these sweeping changes in the educational field are well brought out in the results of a recent official inquiry. Seventy-eight per cent of the age groups born in the period 1900–10 left school before the age of fifteen; for those born around 1930 the figure falls to 60 per cent, for those born around 1950 to 29 per cent, and for those born around 1958 to a mere 6 per cent. The proportion of those receiving some form of secondary education has risen from 24 per cent for the age groups born around 1935 to 55 per cent for those born around 1955. Whereas only 12 per cent of men and 5·7 per cent of women born around 1920 acquired a *baccalauréat* or some higher qualification, for those born between 1940 and 1945 the proportion has risen to 19·5 per cent and 23 per cent respectively. One interesting result of this inquiry is to establish the fact that the gap between the sexes in education has now been closed; indeed, more younger women than younger men have acquired a *baccalauréat* or some higher qualification.[1]

The effect of the enormous broadening in educational opportunities on the market for books—for works of pure literature as well as for all the rest of the varied output of French publishers—is obvious. The expansion since 1945 is revealed first in the number of titles published:

	Dépôt légal	*Syndicat national de l'édition*[2]
1945	7291	
1946	9522	
1947	14 746	
1948	16 020	
1949	12 526	
1950	11 849	
1951	11 850	
1952	11 954	
1953	11 351	
1954	11 934	
1955	11 793	
1956	11 377	
1957	11 917	
1958	11 725	11 879
1959	12 032	11 359

[1] *Brèves Nouvelles de France*, 8 Mar. 1975.
[2] This organization has put out its own figures since 1958.

Dépôt légal		*Syndicat national de l'édition*[1]
1960	11 872	11 440
1961	13 485	11 878
1962	13 282	12 622
1963	11 478	13 469
1964	13 479	13 474
1965	21 351	14 138
1966	23 823	16 242
1967	23 010	18 535
1968	18 648	18 464
1969	22 313	19 634
1970	22 935	21 571
1971	22 372	21 371
1972	24 497	22 261
1973	27 196	23 013

It is a sad fact that it would be extremely unwise to read too much into these figures. From time to time, as no doubt happened in earlier periods, all sorts of changes have been made in methods of counting the number of titles published. It has been pointed out, for instance, that if figures such as those for official publications, school textbooks, and certain theses had been added in, the total for 1964 would have come to 23,993 instead of 13,479. Again it was not until 1970 that the *dépôt légal* began to distinguish between books (over 48 pages) and brochures (6–48 pages).

The expansion in publishing in the 1960s and early 1970s is perhaps better traced in the number of copies of books produced in these years:

	Thousands
1960	167 122
1961	178 667
1962	180 033
1963	219 403
1964	204 915
1965	227 946
1966	247 492
1967	239 171
1968	224 376
1969	252 403
1970	322 489
1971	308 253
1972	336 952
1973	308 927

On close examination these figures too require a good deal of interpretation, but their general trend is clear enough. What is of course
equally clear is that since 1973 publishing, in France as in this country,
has been going through a period of crisis, and this in its turn has had
most disagreeable consequences for writers.

The 'paperback revolution' (if one may use the expression in a
French context where for obvious reasons the term 'livre de poche'
is used) came later than in this country or the United States and
Germany, but from 1953 onwards it has undoubtedly had the usual
effects, though it has sometimes been argued that it did not enlarge
the reading public, but merely offered those who were already in
the habit of buying books the opportunity of acquiring them more
cheaply.

The twentieth-century writer finds himself faced with a greatly
enlarged public and one which can be reached through an increased
variety of means. In addition to the theatre and to the printed word in
newspapers, periodicals, and books he can communicate with it
through the cinema, records, radio, and television. It is true that
daily newspapers tend to offer much fewer openings to writers than
was the case before 1914, while the weekly papers devoted purely to
literature have had a struggle to survive. The *Nouvelles littéraires* has
managed to hold out for over half a century, but the *Figaro littéraire*,
founded in 1946, has recently given up the ghost, though in recent
years both the *Quinzaine littéraire* and the monthly *Magazine littéraire*
have started to appear. While it is true that reviews with a considerable
literary content have flourished in France more than in this country,
there have been some casualties. Amongst older reviews the *Mercure*,
for instance, faded out in 1965 and the *Cahiers du Sud* in the following
year, while the *Table ronde*, founded only in 1948, disappeared in 1969.
The *Nouvelle Revue française*, which had continued to appear for some
time during the German occupation, did not resume publication until
1953. In the meantime new reviews such as *Les Temps modernes* and
Critique had emerged in 1945. *Esprit*, founded in 1932, continued to
appear, while even the *Revue des Deux Mondes*, which can trace its
history back to over a hundred years before that, began in 1972 to
modernize itself, changing its title to *La Nouvelle Revue des Deux
Mondes*. In 1960, *Tel Quel*, a new *avant-garde* periodical, appeared on
the scene.

The writer's relations with publishers have undergone some changes
in recent decades. Publishing continues as in the past to be concentrated

in Paris, and though the speeding-up of communications enables writers to live, if they wish, at some distance from the capital, the great majority tend to live if not in the capital itself, at least in the Paris region. The new copyright law passed in 1957 establishes very firmly the rights of authors in their dealings with publishers,[1] though it does not give complete satisfaction to writers in such matters as reprographics and the hiring-out of books for profit by circulating libraries. The same tendency towards concentration in publishing is visible on both sides of the Channel. In 1973 twenty French publishers were responsible for 58 per cent of the total turnover of the industry. The process had begun before 1939 with the control of Hachette over a considerable sector of the publishing world, and it has been continued by other groupings since 1945. As in this country American capital has secured a certain foothold. This concentration is not altogether welcome to the writer; publishing firms which to the uninitiated appear to be quite separate and independent bodies are often controlled by the same financial grouping, and as rejection of a book by one of the firms concerned may well mean rejection by all, the writer's chance of seeing his book in print is reduced. There is also a danger of which French writers are very much aware, that, unless publishing houses retain their identity, writers may be forced into producing books according to the sort of formula which will guarantee financial success. As one of them put it some years ago:

Autrefois, bien des maisons d'édition actuelles auraient disparu parce que c'était la loi. Mais alors que se passe-t-il ? Une puissance financière vient à leur secours, apporte des capitaux . . .
    Mais, sauvées de la faillite, les maisons qui se sont réunies sous une même garantie financière risquent de perdre leur originalité. Je crois qu'il y a une chose importante dans le domaine de l'expérimentation littéraire en France: c'est de préserver l'originalité des maisons d'édition. . . . Alors, s'il y a un danger, il n'est pas du côté du livre de poche, il est du côté de l'industrialisation hâtive et de la mainmise de la finance dans un domaine où l'individualité a vraiment une part prépondérante. S'il n'y a plus le stade artisanal, la présence humaine, le goût, le choix, l'équipe dans une maison d'édition, s'il n'y a plus que des critères économiques, si on ne publie plus que ce que veut le public, alors, là, je crois que tout est perdu.[2]

[1] Article 53, one of these dealing with the publisher's obligations, contains a sentence which might well be adopted in any future legislation in the United Kingdom: 'Il ne peut, sans autorisation écrite de l'auteur, apporter à l'œuvre aucune modification.'
[2] *La Littérature à l'heure du livre de poche* (Université de Bordeaux, Institut de littérature et de techniques artistiques de masse), Bordeaux, 1966, pp. 24–5.

Publishing like any other economic activity is being increasingly dominated by accountants.

The writer in France today tends to derive his income from several sources; this state of affairs can involve him in membership of quite a number of societies which have been set up to protect the interests of the profession. Balzac's Société des gens de lettres continues to advise writers in their relations with publishers and to collect fees for the reproduction of their works in the press; in addition it now handles the reproduction of their works on radio and television. It has a membership of some four thousand, of whom about a third are full members (*sociétaires*). A considerable number of its members also belong to the Syndicat des écrivains professionnels, now housed in the same building, the Hôtel de Massa. A more radical body, the Union des écrivains, was founded in the eventful year 1968; indeed in the heady days of May a group of its members occupied the Hôtel de Massa 'en liaison étroite avec les étudiants et les travailleurs du livre': 'Ceux qui le conduisaient, entendaient, à les en croire, "marquer leur volonté de donner à l'écrivain un statut nouveau dans une société nouvelle" alors que l'Union s'assignait assez obscurément pour objet "de se définir elle-même en définissant l'écrivain".'[1] However, the members of the Union des écrivains eventually evacuated the building; in practice, there is some overlap in membership between the two organizations.

Beaumarchais's Société des auteurs et compositeurs dramatiques is no longer concerned only with live performances in the theatre; it has added to its name the words 'Théâtre—Cinéma—Radio—Télévision', and its committee now consists of eight playwrights, three composers, two script-writers, two authors of television works, two authors of radio works, and one author or composer of works of either of these last categories. Its membership is difficult to define; in 1970 it consisted of 365 *sociétaires définitifs*, 170 *sociétaires adjoints*, 420 *stagiaires*, and a monstrous number of *adhérents* (it includes anyone who has ever produced the most insignificant play and has applied for membership of the society). They numbered something of the order of 16,000 to 18,000.[2]

As in earlier days the society continues to exercise an iron control over its members' dealings with theatre managements, requiring them

[1] J. Albert-Sorel, 'Mai-juin 1968. Tumultes et occupation', in *L'Hôtel de Massa et la Société des gens de lettres*, Paris, 1968, pp. 43–4.
[2] A. Schmidt, *Les Sociétés d'auteurs SACEM–SACD. Contrats de représentation*, Paris 1971, p. 9 n.

to conform to the agreements which it has reached as to the percentage of the receipts to be paid over to them. It has given up demanding a large number of theatre tickets which its members were free to sell, this in return for an increased percentage of the receipts (the Comédie-Française which continues to pay authors of copyright plays 15 per cent offers the best terms).[1] In the nature of things the society's dealings with the cinema, radio, and television are more complicated; indeed, in 1973 the annual general meeting gave it much fuller legal rights to act for its members in these fields than was considered necessary in the theatre. Like the Société des gens de lettres the society has long had agreements over payments to its members by the now defunct Office de la radiodiffusion et télévision françaises, but its dealings with film companies have had to be on an *ad hoc* basis. Of the two societies the Société des auteurs et compositeurs dramatiques is much the wealthier; it can afford to provide substantial pensions to its older *sociétaires* as well as offering financial assistance to members who have fallen on hard times.

There are two other societies which a writer may well find himself belonging to—the Société des auteurs, compositeurs et éditeurs de musique if he should compose songs, and the Société des droits de reproduction mécanique whose title is self-explanatory. The Société des gens de lettres and the Société des auteurs et compositeurs dramatiques both have agreements with the latter society.

The agitation for a Caisse nationale des lettres which had begun after the 1914–18 War at last led in 1946 to the passing of a law setting up such an organization under the Ministère des affaires culturelles.[2] To complicate the task of offering a brief account of its history and functions, in 1973 its name was changed to Centre national des lettres, the idea being that one day it should provide a meeting-place for writers, and in 1974 the ministry also underwent a change of name, becoming a Secrétariat d'État. The aims of the Centre (to use its new name) are defined as follows in the law of 1946:

1°) De soutenir et d'encourager l'activité littéraire des écrivains français par des bourses de travail ou des bourses d'études, des prêts d'honneur, des subventions, des acquisitions de livres ou tous autres moyens permettant de récompenser la réalisation ou de faciliter l'élaboration d'une œuvre littéraire écrite;

[1] Ibid. p. 51.
[2] Works of scholarship come mainly under the Centre national de la recherche scientifique, established in 1939 under the Ministry of Education.

2°) De favoriser par des subventions, avances de fonds ou tous autre moyens l'édition ou la réédition par les entreprises françaises d'œuvres littéraires dont il importe d'assurer la publication;

3°) D'allouer des pensions et secours à des écrivains vivants, ou aux conjoints ou aux enfants d'écrivains décédés et de contribuer au financement d'œuvres ou d'organismes de solidarité professionnelle;

4°) D'assurer le respect des œuvres littéraires quel que soit leur pays d'origine après la mort de l'auteur et même après leur chute dans le domaine public.

These were very fine sentiments, but it was not until ten years later that another law was passed defining the sources from which the income of the Centre was to come. These were:

1. Income derived from the contracts of deceased authors for a period of fifteen years after their works had ceased to be copyright.
2. A levy of 0·2 per cent on the turnover of French publishers, excluding that for school textbooks, learned and religious works.
3. A levy of 0·2 per cent on the royalties of writers, excluding those from the first 5,000 copies of a book published for the first time.
4. Gifts and legacies.
5. Subsidies from the State and other public bodies.

The functioning of the Centre at last really began after a decree of 29 November 1956 had settled the administrative details.

With the income at its disposal the Centre is now able to offer a fairly large number of modest grants to support young writers and a smaller number of more substantial *bourses* to established authors.[1] It also provides subsidies or loans to secure the publication of both new editions of literary works from earlier periods and modern works, particularly poetry, for which only small sales can be expected. It is responsible for paying the employer's contribution for certain writers under the social security scheme.

While recognizing that the creation of the Centre national des lettres is a step forward, French writers are far from satisfied with their present position. For one thing, the Centre national is only responsible for the social security contributions of those writers who draw at least 51 per cent of their income from literary work from the publication of *books*. This cuts out a large number of professional writers since

[1] Thus in May 1975 the Centre announced the award of eight of its twenty *bourses* of 2,000 francs a month to younger writers aged between twenty-four and thirty-four and four of its eight *bourses* of 5,000 francs a month to established authors aged between forty-nine and fifty-five (*Brèves Nouvelles de France*, 17 May 1975).

nowadays they often draw their income from a wide variety of other sources—newspapers, periodicals, records, lectures, the theatre, cinema, radio, and television. The Société des gens de lettres is agitating strongly for the recognition by the authorities of what it calls 'l'unicité de la profession d'écrivain'. It would also like to see the other users of the written word making the same contribution as publishers to the Centre national. In addition, writers have complicated grievances about their treatment in such matters as retirement pensions and family allowances.

They also advocate the establishment of what is called 'le domaine public payant', i.e. perpetual payments of royalties for the benefit of a literary fund in place of the fifteen-year period during which the Centre national receives such payments.[1] French writers too feel a sense of grievance about the failure of libraries to make payment for the use of their works, but it does not seem to get them into the same state of hysteria as it does some writers on this side of the Channel. Their proposals concern only the commercial circulating libraries which make a profit from lending out their works; so far no French writer has suggested that a few libraries should be burnt down in order to further the cause of Public Lending Right. Understandably, when they see the profits of many publishers, French writers would like to see some improvement in their position and in that of translators, but so far publishers have been unwilling to accept the model agreement produced by the Société des gens de lettres.

Although the secretary-general of the Centre national pointed out in 1967 that the writer's contribution represented only 1 per cent of its income, its collection of statistics does enable one to form some idea of the sort of income derived by French writers from book royalties. It need hardly be said that this reveals extraordinary contrasts. A tiny minority of writers whose works meet with large scales earn enormous sums of money, while at the base of the pyramid come vast numbers whose royalties come to quite trivial amounts (one has, of course, to bear in mind that the figures given below, as is made clear in the statement, do not take into account royalties from works of which less than 5,000 copies were sold):

Certains sont spécialisés dans les livres de lecture—et de vente—faciles et leurs droits d'auteur sont très élevés, le plus important dépassant largement 1 000 000 de francs.

[1] These can sometimes be quite substantial as when the works of Maupassant ceased to be copyright.

Nous avons fait de nombreuses études sur les auteurs d'ouvrages d'érudition; la moyenne des sommes qu'ils reçoivent est inférieure à 3 000 francs.

Nous avons noté dans nos statistiques pour la dernière année un peu plus de
13 000 écrivains pour un total dépassant légèrement 65 000 000F, soit 5 000
F pour chacun. Ces chiffres ne font pas état des éditions vendues à moins
de 5 000 exemplaires, celles-ci étant exonérées de la taxe perçue sur les droits
d'auteur au bénéfice de la C.N.L. Le nombre de 40 000 écrivains donné par
le Syndicat National des Éditeurs apparaît vraisemblable. Il s'ensuit donc qu'en
dehors du nombre de 13 000 que je viens de citer existe une poussière de
dizaines de milliers de droits d'auteur de l'ordre, sans doute, de quelques
dizaines de francs.

J'ajoute que, si l'on enlève les deux cents droits d'auteur les plus importants, la moyenne de 5 000 F que je viens d'indiquer est rabaissée à un peu
moins de 4 000 F.[1]

On this same occasion a writer, Armand Lanoux, declared that out of
the thousands engaged in this occupation 'il doit y avoir à peu près,
en tout, en France une centaine d'écrivains au maximum, qui vivent
normalement et décemment de leur profession. . . . Dans cette centaine,
nous allons peut-être en trouver une vingtaine qui vivent *uniquement du
livre*.'[2]

Of the thousands of writers in France today large numbers earn the
main part of their income from some other occupation. Journalism and
publishing continue to offer obvious ways of earning the main part of
their living as do posts in the Civil Service; vast numbers of teachers in
all manner of schools and in universities are included among the *fonctionnaires* who write books in their spare time. All manner of professions and callings—from postman to diplomat, from doctor to airline
pilot, from advertising to watch-making—number writers among their
practitioners. Many of these have no intention of abandoning their
present occupation and attempting to become full-time writers. The
solution of a 'second métier' may not appeal to some writers or would-
be writers, but there is a great deal of sense in the views put forward by
a publisher:

Reste la question du second métier. On me dit que cent écrivains seulement
vivent de leur plume. Ce sont ceux qui ont une production abondante,
régulière, dont l'œuvre correspond au goût du plus grand nombre et peut
emporter au moment où ils la publient l'adhéson du public. D'autres, au
contraire, ne peuvent, sans se renoncer, écrire que des livres réservés à deue
mille lecteurs. (Un bon nombre de chefs-d'œuvre qui ont nourri par la suite

---

[1] *La Profession d'écrivain*, pp. 18–19.   [2] Ibid. pp. 8–9.

des générations entières n'ont pas dépasse ce tirage au moment où ils ont été publiés.) Pour ceux-là, je ne vois pas le moyen de poursuivre leur œuvre sans avoir un second métier. Il leur donne l'indépendance nécessaire à toute création artistique. Ce n'est pas l'idéal, bien sûr. Mais toute autre solution n'est-elle pas utopique? Croyez-vous vraiment à l'écrivain fonctionnaire? En fait c'est souvent aux plus médiocres écrivains ou apprentis écrivains que ce second métier paraît le plus déshonorant. Julien Gracq est professeur d'histoire, et cela ne l'empêche pas d'être un de nos meilleurs romanciers. Claudel était ambassadeur et cela ne l'a pas empêché d'être un génie très fécond.[1]

Needless to say, such views are unacceptable to many writers in France.

An insight into the outlook of French writers of the present day is provided by the answers of some three hundred of them to a questionnaire sent out at the end of 1968 and the beginning of 1969 by the Centre d'études de la civilisation du 20ᵉ siècle of the University of Nice.[2] Naturally, there were some pretty gloomy and bitter replies about the poor rewards brought by writing as a profession, for instance:

C'est la profession la moins bien payée, la plus accablée de fiscalités et para-fiscalités diverses. Pas d'assistance, pas de vacances, pas de retraite. La mort à l'hôpital au bout du compte. Malraux trouve ça bien: 'Écrire est une aventure', dit-il.[3]

Or again:

La France n'a aucun respect de ses écrivains. A preuve, ce sont: la nature des contrats proposés par les éditeurs, les impôts, les allocations familiales, les cotisations à la Sécurité sociale qui écrasent l'écrivain. Tout se passe, dans ce pays, comme si on cherchait à empêcher des hommes et des femmes de s'essayer à écrire.[4]

'Travailler 10 heures par jour pour une production qui rapporte moins qu'un travail de manœuvre', moans another.[5]

There are still writers who deplore the commercialization of literature which began in the nineteenth century and who look back with longing to the golden age of patronage under the *ancien régime*, although Jean-Louis Curtis utterly rejects the whole notion, declaring: 'Je suis absolument contre toutes les formes de mécénat. Personne n'est obligé de devenir écrivain ou artiste. La société n'a pas à entretenir

[1] Ibid. p. 26.
[2] E. Gaede, *L'Écrivain et la société*, 2 vols., Nice, 1972.
[3] Jean Rousselot (i. 62).   [4] Jérôme Peignot (i. 58).   [5] Catherine Claude (i. 43).

des gens qui se situent en dehors du cycle normal de la production.'[1] There is a similar division of opinion as to the desirability of the writer having a 'second métier'. Georges Neveux declares his belief that 'les écrivains devraient avoir, chaque fois qu'ils le peuvent, un 2ème métier (un vrai: pas un métier para-littéraire) qui nourrirait leur expérience et les éloignerait du mandarinat. Ce ne fut pas mon cas. J'ai eu tort.'[2] Another established writer, Roger Caillois, takes the austere line that an author should refuse payment for his works because of the temptation to water down what he has to say so as to make more money: 'Il convient donc qu'il tire la totalité ou au moins l'essentiel de ses ressources d'un autre métier, le plus éloigné possible de celui d'écrivain. Personne ne peut faire fonds sur sa propre intégrité et capacité de résistance à la tentation.'[3] Others take the practical line that as with few exceptions present-day writers simply cannot live on what they earn with their pen, either other related activities or completely different occupations are simply a necessity. 'A part quelques exceptions rares,' writes Christian Mégret, 'les écrivains, aujourd'hui, font aussi du journalisme, donnent des conférences, s'expriment à la radio, à la télévision, ou bien encore ont un second métier, à moins que ce ne soit l'écriture leur second métier.'[4] A similar practical line is taken by Jean-Paul Clébert:

A part quelques 'élus', peu d'écrivains vivent tout à fait de leur plume. Il faut avoir un second métier ou faire de la para-littérature. Pour ma part, ne tirant pas assez de revenus de mes romans, j'écris des livres documentaires. Et suis critique de télévision. Ce travail est loin d'être déplaisant et pas du tout une corvée. J'y gagne en culture ce que j'y perds en temps.[5]

Television took on slowly in France. In 1960 less than 2 million households had a set, but by 1973, when one was to be found in 13 million households (86 per cent), saturation point had virtually been reached. Inevitably, cinema attendances fell off as television swept France, though apparently less than in this country, and since 1969 the figure of attendances has stabilized at rather less than half the figure recorded in 1957. Closures of cinemas were numerous in the 1960s, but this trend now appears to have been halted, and there is a notable increase in the number of cinemas showing films of artistic value.

The attitude of present-day writers to the cinema, radio, and television is, as might be expected, decidedly mixed. Some utterly reject

[1] i. 44.   [2] i. 196.   [3] i. 75.   [4] ii. 741.   [5] i. 287.

these forms of writing. Although prepared to make an exception for the theatre, Hubert Gonnet denounces the trend:

Cette tendance, à laquelle trop d'écrivains sacrifient sous la pression des besoins matériels, est littérairement néfaste. Le véritable écrivain doit, comme son nom l'indique, écrire, et écrire pour être lu, non parlé, chanté ou représenté. Les radio, télévision, cinéma, sont des moyens d'expression peut-être très respectables mais extra-littéraires.[1]

Others look to these new forms of writing to subsidize their more conventional works. Jean Queval, for instance, declares: 'Depuis plusieurs années, cinéma et télé me font gagner ma vie mieux que les livres. Il s'agit d'y puiser l'argent qui me permette d'écrire les prochains ouvrages. Alors j'essaie de respecter mes bienfaiteurs: en faisant de mon mieux.'[2] The same point is put more vividly still by an established writer, Albert Simonin:

Les droits d'auteur de mes romans, pour substantiels qu'en soient les tirages, et en y ajoutant des traductions en sept langues, me permettraient de mener le train de vie d'un ouvrier métallurgiste spécialisé.

Je dois donc pour m'offrir le luxe d'écrire un roman, tâcheronner au cinéma ou à la télévision, en tant que scénariste, adaptateur, ou dialoguiste.[3]

A completely different attitude—one of enthusiastic acceptance of the new media—is, however, taken up by Paul Géraldy who looks back to the beginnings of literature in the ancient world: 'La littérature tend à s'émanciper de l'écrit? Bravo. Tout bénéfice. Il faut écrire avec sa voix. Les premiers poètes: des aèdes. Le disque, la radio, c'est plus vivant, plus proche que la typographie. Bien sûr, je me suis servi d'eux.'[4]

Since 1945 a broadening of theatre audiences has been sought in two directions. In Paris, with the appointment of Jean Vilar in 1951, the Théâtre national populaire built up a considerable following among a wide public which, with the assistance of trade unions, even includes a number of workers, while the Théâtre de l'Est parisien, established in a working-class suburb, also secured a modest amount of government support. No longer is the theatrical life of France completely dominated by the capital. Whereas before 1939 virtually the only theatrical performances available in provincial cities were given by actors from Paris, from the war years onwards distinguished companies have established themselves in various parts of the country. Between 1946 and 1952 *Centres dramatiques*, supported by government subsidies, were

[1] i. 258.   [2] i. 270.   [3] i. 92.   [4] i. 257.

established at Colmar, Saint-Étienne, Toulouse, Rennes, and Aix-en-Provence,[1] and these were intended to serve not only these cities, but also the surrounding regions. Then for some years no new *Centres dramatiques* were established until in 1959 the title of *Centre dramatique national* was conferred on the Théâtre de la Cité at Villeurbanne to which Roger Planchon had moved two years earlier. In the meantime fresh provincial companies had established themselves at such centres as Caen, Lille, Grenoble, and Marseilles, and some of these were designated as *Troupes permanentes de décentralisation*, though the government support which they received was much smaller than that enjoyed by the *Centres dramatiques*. In the 1960s the situation was further complicated by the emergence of Malraux's brain-child, the *Maison de la culture*, in an increasing number of provincial centres, starting with Le Havre. Though these institutions undertake a variety of activities, they have contributed to the revival of drama in the provinces, even if they have sometimes given rise to friction with the companies already established there.

The situation in 1974 can be summed up thus: in addition to two *théâtres nationaux* at Chaillot and Villeurbanne the state also subsidized 19 *centres dramatiques nationaux*. As well as the Théâtre de l'Est the Paris region now has two other theatres in this category—those at Aubervilliers and Nanterre. Of the remaining 16, 8 (Tourcoing, Lille, Caen, Rennes, Angers, Beaune, Besançon, and Strasbourg) are in northern France, while the southern half of the country has theatres of this type in Limoges, Carcassonne, Toulouse, Marseilles, Nice, Grenoble, Saint-Étienne, and Lyons. Moreover, some measure of state support is now given to independent companies such as the Théâtre de l'Espérance in Paris and several in the *banlieue*—at Créteil, Gennevilliers, Ivry, Saint-Denis, Suresnes, and Vincennes. Subsidies are also given to a few provincial companies of this type, at La Rochelle, Metz, and Rheims as well as Bourges and Bordeaux.[2] Though a glance at a map illustrating all this theatrical activity in the provinces still reveals some curious gaps, there is no question but that live drama is now made available to those interested on a scale which would have been almost unthinkable thirty years ago.

Since the end of the last war measures have also been taken by the government to remedy the backward state of public libraries in France.

[1] D. Gontard, *La Décentralisation théâtrale en France, 1895–1952*, Paris, 1973, pp. 148–9.
[2] *Brèves Nouvelles de France*, 16 November 1974, pp. 25–7, and 23 November 1974, pp. 29–31.

A decree of 1945 set up a central organization to control and supervise French libraries—the Direction des bibliothèques de France et de la lecture publique. Its functions were to 'administrer les bibliothèques savantes, contrôler les bibliothèques municipales . . ., organiser et administrer la lecture publique'. Most towns of over 15,000 inhabitants have a municipal library, financed by the town council; about fifty of these are 'classées', that is to say the librarian and assistant librarians are civil servants paid by the state. Some of these libraries have branches in the suburbs and also mobile libraries. The state subsidizes the municipal libraries with gifts of books and especially grants towards the cost of buildings and equipment. Before 1945 nothing had been done to provide a library service for the country districts and in general the *communes* with less than 15,000 inhabitants. An ordinance of 1945 created *bibliothèques centrales de prêt* to provide for them; these are generally situated in the *chef-lieu* of the department and mobile libraries supply books which are stored in schools or the *mairie*.

All this was fine on paper, but when the committee set up by the Prime Minister, Georges Pompidou, to study 'les moyens de favoriser la lecture publique' reported in 1968, the picture of the French library system, in so far as the general public was concerned, was an extremely gloomy one. Although 17 *bibliothèques centrales de prêt* were created within a few months of the issue of the relevant ordinance, by 1966 only 41 were in existence, which meant that less than half the departments had them. Even the 13·6 million inhabitants of these favoured departments got very little out of the system:

On peut admettre que sur les 13,6 millions de Français qui devraient être touchés par ce moyen, 9,5 appartiennent à l'aire visitée par le bibliobus. En outre, tous ne sont pas des clients fidèles de la bibliothèque, en raison de la méthode même du dépôt. Le dépositaire est d'ordinaire un instituteur ou un secrétaire de mairie, non rétribué, et qui ne s'intéresse pas toujours à son fonds ni à la publicité qui pourrait lui être faite; il se borne parfois à faire profiter ses amis, ou, s'il est instituteur, ses élèves. Les statistiques, par la force des choses, sont donc très imprécises, mais on peut considérer comme un maximum l'hypothèse selon laquelle 2 à 4 % de la population adulte et 50 à 75 % de la population scolaire (soit moins de 10% de la population totale concernée) seraient clients des bibliothèques centrales de prêt.

Municipal libraries appear also in a poor light in this report:

Pour celles qui sont classées, la Direction des bibliothèques admet que les succursales et les bibliobus en service représentent environ le septième des besoins à satisfaire. Dans les autres, les collections et les bâtiments sont souvent vétustes et le personnel insuffisant: en moyenne, chaque bibliothèque emploie moins de trois personnes, dont '0,5 personne' ayant une qualification professionnelle. L'ensemble des bibliothèques municipales, qui concernent 15.400.000 personnes n'accueille ainsi que 524.000 emprunteurs, soit moins de 3 % de la population intéressée.[1]

According to the report the most optimistic statistics, if Paris is included, put the proportion of readers to the total population of France at 4·6 per cent. The comparisons with foreign countries which follow put the corresponding figure for Great Britain at 30 per cent. The report then goes on to present a table from which are extracted the figures for France and this country:

	France.	G.-B.
Nomb. de prêts ann. par habit.	0·74	9·4
Dépenses ann. par habitant (en F)	0·65	10·5

This preliminary section concludes with the following words: 'Quand donc M. Pompidou affirme que dans ce domaine *tout est à faire*, on ne saurait lui reprocher un quelconque pessimisme.'

The report makes a variety of recommendations with the aim of effecting considerable improvements to the library service.[2] Some progress is recorded in the latest statistics available, those for 1971. By then the number of readers in municipal libraries per head of the population had risen to 5·9 per cent,[3] but the only international comparison given in this document—that with England and Wales—is revealing:

	France	Angleterre et Galles	Rapport
Acquisitions annuelles de livres (en volumes) par habitant	5·504	23·130	4·2
Prêt à domicile (en volumes) par habitant	1·35	12·5	9·3[4]

For those writers on this side of the Channel to whom the public library is the enemy France must appear a veritable paradise; yet, although

[1] *La Lecture publique en France. Rapport du groupe d'études* (Notes et études documentaires, no. 3459), Paris, 1968, p. 5.

[2] The members of the committee were divided on the question of whether the service should be free. Its conclusion on this matter is: 'Il serait judicieux de ne pas fixer à ce sujet une règle impérative et, tout en conseillant la gratuité, de laisser les municipalités libres de leur choix' (p. 12).

[3] Direction des bibliothèques et de la lecture publique, *Bibliothèques municipales. Statistiques 1971*, Paris, 1974, p. 3.

[4] Ibid. p. 16.

there the public library service is relatively underdeveloped and not necessarily free, writers still have their problems.

In recent years a number of attempts have been made to investigate the reading and book-buying habits of French people. There are, of course, difficulties in accepting these as more than a very rough guide since surveys of the kind carried out are inevitably made with a very small sample. Comparisons between the results of these surveys are made difficult by the fact that they have been carried out by different organizations asking different questions of the persons approached. It is also unfortunate that any sort of comparison with the state of affairs in this country is impossible for the same reason.[1]

Two examples will show the kind of information which such surveys produce. The first of these was carried out between October 1966 and January 1967 for the Syndicat national de l'édition and the results were published under the title of *La Clientèle du livre*. The survey was based on a sample of 7,929 persons, 1,064 of whom were in the 15–19 age group. The population of France was said to fall into five groups so far as the reading and purchase of books was as concerned:

1. Non-lecteurs, non-acheteurs, ruraux: 36% de la population.
2. Non-lecteurs, non-acheteurs, urbains: 21% de la population.
3. Lecteurs, faibles acheteurs   : 18% de la population.
4. Acheteurs, faibles lecteurs   : 12% de la population.
5. Forts lecteurs, forts acheteurs   : 13% de la population.[2]

The first two categories would thus account for more than half the population over the age of fifteen. Considerable differences in book-buying were found between young and old; those over fifty (36 per cent of the population) bought only 18 per cent of the books, while the 15–19 age group were relatively heavy purchasers, partly, of course, because of their acquisition of educational works.[3] One deduction drawn from this inquiry was that television is not the enemy of the book; among those who had television there was a higher proportion of book-buyers than among those who had not.

A more wide-ranging survey was carried out at the end of 1973 on behalf of the Secrétariat d'État à la culture. The title under which the results were published a year later—*Pratiques culturelles des Français*—

[1] See e.g. the national survey the results of which are summarized in *Books and Reading Habits*, published by European Research Consultants Ltd. in 1965. There is also interesting material of a more local character in P. H. Mann, *Books and Reading*, London, 1969, and *Books, Buyers and Borrowers*, London, 1971.

[2] p. 5.   [3] Ibid. pp. 8–9.

is somewhat misleading as it covers an enormous field of leisure activities including holidays, gardening, and sport.   It has, however, an
interesting section on the ownership, reading, and acquisition of
books,[1] although it is somewhat disconcerting to discover that the
survey was based on only 1,987 interviews.[2]
On ownership of books the survey yielded the following results:

	Sur 100 Français âgés de 15 ans et plus	possesseurs de livres
	%	%
Nombre de livres passédés au foyer:		
Aucun	26·9	–
1 à 5	2·1	2·9
6 à 10	4·1	5·6
11 à 25	9·1	12·4
26 à 99	23·4	31·8
100 à 250	22·0	29·8
251 à 500	7·4	10·2
plus de 500	4·7	6·4
indéterminé	0·7	0·9

As far as reading books is concerned the report concludes that 69·7 per
cent of persons over the age of fifteen had engaged in this activity in
the course of the previous twelve months:

	Sur 100 Français âgés de 15 ans et plus
Nombre de livres lus annuellement	
Ont lu au cours des 12 derniers mois:	
	%
1 à 4 livres	14·3
5 à 9	9·3
10 à 14	13·1
15 à 24	10·3
25 à 49	8·9
50 livres et plus	12·6
nombre indéterminé	1·3
	69·7

On book-buying the survey shows that 51 per cent of the persons
questioned had spent some of their money in this way in the preceding
twelve months:

[1] i. 62–93.   [2] Ibid. ii. 144.

10·1 % une ou deux fois;
25·6% quelques fois;
15·3 % de nombreuses fois.

Finally, on the subject of libraries the survey offers the information that one person in ten goes to a library at least once a month. The following details are of some interest:

	Ensemble de la population étudiée
	%
Sont inscrits à une bibliothèque	13·2
dont:	
bibliothèque municipale	7·0
bibliothèque d'entreprise	3·0
bibliothèque privée ou paroissiale	1·7
bibliothèque itinérante (bibliobus)	1·2
bibliothèque 'tournante' ou chaîne de lecture	1·5
entièrement gratuite	6·5
où l'on paye pour chaque livre	2·2
où l'on paye un droit d'inscription périodique	5·7

Such surveys have their interest (particularly for some of the detailed information which cannot be reproduced here), but it is obviously difficult to get very far in an investigation of such a complicated problem. Clearly, French people are reading more than they did a few decades back. All these surveys stress that this is particularly true of the younger age groups, but this simply takes us back to the 'education explosion' of the last quarter of a century. That this increased demand not only for reading matter, but for all the other services which today the writer is called upon to provide, has not solved all his financial problems is scarcely surprising to anyone who has viewed the relations between writer and public in a historical context. As in the past prompt financial rewards go to only a fortunate minority.

Conclusion

WHILE it is clearly impossible to sum up in a few pages the centuries of changing relations between writer and public, a few brief concluding remarks would seem in order.

One striking feature of this long history is the way in which over the centuries fame and in some cases relative affluence have been brought by very different types of writing. Nowadays poetry notoriously cannot possibly support a writer; it is indeed one of the forms of writing which the Centre national des lettres subsidizes most frequently. Yet starting out from the monopoly position which it enjoyed among literary genres down to the twelfth century, poetry was long to remain, at any rate for the fortunate few in every age, the passport to fame and often a very comfortable existence. Even after the decline of patronage, as late as the middle of the nineteenth century, the poetry of a writer like Hugo could actually sell, even though by this date other forms of writing were even more profitable. In the intervening centuries poetry had always been one way for the young writer to make a name for himself through the circulation of his verse, often in manuscript form before it was printed, and thus to gain the patronage necessary for his subsistence.

It was only gradually, with the emergence of a professional theatre, that plays came to offer substantial rewards to writers; from the middle of the seventeenth century onwards a successful play became another way in which a young writer could make a name for himself and at the same time obtain fairly large sums of money, though it was not until the nineteenth century that the theatre began to bring in really large rewards and to offer a career, at least to the successful playwright. The novel began to become really popular only in the eighteenth century, and it was not until the following century that the professional novelist came into his own. From that time onwards the novel became the mainstay of the existence of many writers, and although in recent decades the death of the novel has repeatedly been predicted, it still remains very much alive and able to bring fame and sometimes a modest affluence to French writers of today. The position of many of them has, of course, been modified in the present century by the gradual emergence of new media such as the cinema, radio, and television.

Success with one's contemporaries has never been a guarantee of enduring fame. It is instructive to compare, for instance, the posthumous reputation of the playwrights of the last century with that of its poets. The plays of writers like Scribe, Dumas *père et fils*, Ponsard, Augier, Pailleron, Labiche, Sardou, and their successors of 'la belle époque' are now almost totally dead, whereas poets of the same age like Baudelaire, Verlaine, Rimbaud, and Mallarmé have now reached the wide audience which they never encountered or even sought during their lifetime.

A historian should not try to take on the role of a prophet, but it is part of his task to note what writers in France at the present time think lies in wait for their calling. If not entirely gloomy, the future, as they see it, appears rather different from the present state of affairs. A woman writer, Pauline Osusky, observes:

Indéniablement les Français lisent de moins en moins, le mot imprimé perd de son prestige et le public a besoin de stimulants moins exclusivement intellectuels que celui procuré par la lecture.[1]

Another, Simone Balazard, writes:

Je me demande même si l'écrivain traditionnel—qui consacre sa vie à écrire—ne va pas peu à peu disparaître pour laisser place à des écritures marginales, chacun écrivant un livre, puis passant à autre chose.

C'est que le public traditionnel—la bourgeoisie éclairée, ayant des loisirs—disparaît et que le public que nous voyons se dessiner a un visage mouvant, changeant. Il me semble qu'il sera moins qu'autrefois fidèle à un écrivain—que les 'carrières' seront de plus en plus aléatoires.[2]

In practice, as on this side of the Channel, writers in France tend to take a far from cheerful view of what the future holds in store for those who choose to pursue their calling. This sketch of the history of the relations between writer and public through the centuries does show that twentieth-century writers can communicate in far more ways than ever before with a public both much larger and much better educated than even a century ago, to go no further back into the past. Yet clearly this state of affairs cannot guarantee a comfortable living to every person who feels it in him to take up a pen or sit at a typewriter in order to compose any of the extremely varied forms of writing for which there is a demand in modern society.

[1] Gaede, *L'Écrivain et la société* i. 267.
[2] Ibid. ii. 720.

Bibliography

MANUSCRIPT SOURCES

Archives nationales. F^{17} 1212: Pensions to men of letters.
O^1 845: Maison du Roi. État général des recettes de la
Comédie Française (1776–9).
V^2 43: Secrétaires du roi.
Bibliothèque de l'Arsenal. MS. 6544: Recueil Tralage, vol. iv.
Bibliothèque de l'Opéra. Registers of Théâtre Italien.
Bibliothèque nationale. MS. fr. 794: Le Roman du St Graal, etc.
MSS. fr. 4022–7: Journal de J. Héroard.
MS. fr. 9228: Recueil de pièces relatives aux con-
testations entre les auteurs dramatiques
et la Comédie Française (1780).
MS. fr. 20020: E. Deschamps, Le livret de fragilité
d'umaine nature.
MSS. fr. 21990–4: Registers of *permissions tacites*.
Cinq Cents Colbert, vol. 92: accounts of Marie de
Médicis.
Mélanges Colbert, vol. 74: Mazarin's will.
British Library. Harleian MS. 4431: works of Christine de Pisan.
Comédie-Française. Registers and authors' files.

PRINTED SOURCES

General

AVENEL, G. D', *Les Revenus d'un intellectuel de 1200 à 1913. Les Riches depuis sept cents ans*, 2nd edn., Paris, 1922.
BELLANGER, C., GODECHOT, J., GUIRAL, P., and TERROU, F., *Histoire générale de la presse française*, 5 vols., Paris, 1969–76.
BOLLÈME, G. *La Bibliothèque bleue. La Littérature populaire en France du XVIᵉ au XIXᵉ siècle*, Paris, 1971.
—— *La Bible bleue, anthologie d'une littérature 'populaire'*, Paris, 1975.
BROCHON, P., *Le Livre de colportage en France depuis le XVIᵉ siècle. Sa littérature, ses lecteurs*, Paris, 1954.
BRUN, A., *Recherches historiques sur l'introduction du français dans les provinces du Midi*, Paris, 1923.
—— 'La Pénétration du français dans les provinces du Midi du XVᵉ au XIXᵉ siècle', *Le Français moderne*, 1935.
BRUNOT, F., *Histoire de la langue française*, 21 vols., 2nd edn., Paris, 1966–9.
Cinq études lyonnaises, Geneva and Paris, 1966.

DUVERGIER, J. B., *Collection complète des lois, décrets, ordonnances, règlements depuis 1788*, 108 vols., Paris, 1824–1908.

ESTIVALS, R., *Le Dépôt légal sous l'ancien régime, de 1537 à 1791*, Paris, 1961.

—— *La Statistique bibliographique de la France sous la monarchie au XVIIIᵉ siècle*, Paris, 1965.

FLEURY, M. and VALMARY, P., 'Les Progrès de l'instruction élémentaire de Louis XIV à Napoléon III d'après l'enquête de Louis Maggiolo (1877–1879)', *Population*, 1957.

FOURNEL, V., *Du rôle des coups de bâton dans les relation sociales dans l'histoire littéraire*, Paris, 1858.

HATIN, E., *Histoire politique et littéraire de la presse en France*, 8 vols., Paris, 1859–61.

ISAMBERT, F. A. (ed.), *Recueil général des anciennes lois françaises depuis l'an 420 jusqu'à la Révolution de 1789*, 29 vols., Paris, 1821–32.

Le Livre français. Hier, aujourd'hui, demain, ed. J. Cain, R. Escarpit, and H. J. Martin, Paris, 1972.

MANDROU, R., *De la culture populaire aux XVIIᵉ et XVIIIᵉ siècles: la Bibliothèque bleue de Troyes*, Paris, 1964.

MORIN, A., *Catalogue descriptif de la Bibliothèque bleue de Troyes*, Geneva and Paris, 1974.

NISARD, C., *Histoire des livres populaires ou de la littérature du colportage*, 2nd edn., 2 vols., Paris, 1864.

Nouvelles études lyonnaises, Geneva and Paris, 1969.

PARFAICT, C. and F., *Histoire du théâtre français depuis son origine jusqu'à présent*, 15 vols., Amsterdam and Paris, 1735–49.

I The Middle Ages

ADENET LE ROI, *Œuvres*, ed. A. Henry, 5 vols., Bruges and Brussels, 1951–71.

BENOIT DE SAINTE-MAURE, *Le Roman de Troie*, ed. L. Constans, 6 vols., Paris, *SATF*, 1904–12.

BRUNETTO LATINI, *Li Livres dou Tresor*, ed. F. J. Carmody, Berkeley and Los Angeles, 1948.

CHAMPION, P., *Histoire poétique du quinzième siècle*, 2 vols., Paris, 1923.

Le Charroi de Nîmes, ed. J. L. Perrier, Paris, *CFMA*, 1931.

CHRÉTIEN DE TROYES, *Érec et Énide*, ed. M. Roques, Paris, *CFMA*, 1952.

—— *Le Chevalier de la Charrete*, ed. M. Roques, Paris, *CFMA*, 1958.

—— *Le Conte du Graal*, ed. F. Lecoy, Paris, *CFMA*, 1972, vol. i.

CHRISTINE DE PISAN, *Œuvres poétiques*, ed. M. Roy, 3 vols., Paris, *SATF*, 1886–96.

—— *Le Livre du Chemin de Long Estude*, ed. R. Püschel, Berlin and Paris, 1887.

CONON DE BÉTHUNE, *Chansons*, ed. A. Wallensköld, Paris, *CFMA*, 1921.

Le Couronnement de Louis, ed. E. Langlois, 2nd edn., Paris, *CFMA*, 1925.

DESCHAMPS, E., *Œuvres complètes*, ed. H. de Queux de Saint-Hilaire and G. Raynaud, 11 vols. Paris, *SATF*, 1878–1903.

DOUTREPONT, G., *La Littérature française à la cour des ducs de Bourgogne*, Paris, 1909.

——— *Les Mises en prose des épopées et des romans chevaleresques du XIVe au XVIe siècle*, Brussels, 1939.

FARAL, E., *Les Jongleurs en France au Moyen Age*, 2nd edn., Paris, 1964.

GALLAIS, P., 'Recherches sur la mentalité des romanciers français du Moyen Age', *Cahiers de civilisation médiévale*, 1970.

GAUTIER D'ARRAS, *Eracle*, ed. G. Raynaud de Lage, Paris, *CFMA*, 1976.

GUERNES DE PONT-SAINTE-MAXENCE, *La Vie de Saint Thomas Becket*, ed. E. Walberg, Paris, *CFMA*, 1936.

GUILLAUME DE MACHAUT, *Œuvres*, ed. E. Hoepffner, 3 vols., Paris, *SATF*, 1908–21.

HOLZKNECHT, K. J., *Literary Patronage in the Middle Ages*, Philadelphia, 1923; reprinted London, 1966.

MARIE DE FRANCE, *Les Lais*, ed. J. Rychner, Paris, *CFMA*, 1966.

MUSET, C., *Chansons*, ed. J. Bédier, 2nd edn., Paris, *CFMA*, 1938.

PINET, M. J., *Christine de Pisan 1364–1430. Étude biographique et littéraire*, Paris, 1927.

La Prise d'Orange, ed. C. Régnier, Paris, 1967.

RUTEBEUF, *Œuvres complètes*, ed. E. Faral and J. Bastin, 2 vols., Paris, 1959–60.

STANGER, M. D., 'Literary Patronage at the Medieval Court of Flanders', *French Studies*, 1957.

Les Troubadours. 'Jaufré', 'Flamenca', 'Barlaam et Josaphat', ed. and trans. R. Lavaud and R. Nelli, Paris, 1960.

VILLON, F., *Œuvres*, ed. A. Longnon, 2nd edn., Paris, *CFMA*, 1914.

WACE, *Le Roman de Brut*, ed. I. Arnold, 2 vols., Paris, *SATF*, 1938–40.

——— *Le Roman de Rou*, ed. A. J. Holden, 3 vols., Paris, *SATF*, 1970–3.

WOLEDGE, B. and CLIVE, H. P., *Répertoire des plus anciens textes en prose française depuis 842 jusqu'aux premières années du XIIIe siècle*, Geneva, 1964.

II The Impact of Printing

ARMSTRONG, E., 'Notes on the Works of Guillaume Michel, dit de Tours', *Bibliothèque d'Humanisme et Renaissance*, 1969.

AUGÉ-CHIQUET, M., *La Vie, les idées et l'œuvre de Jean-Antoine de Baïf*, Paris, 1909.

BAÏF, J. A. DE, *Euvres en rime*, ed. C. Marty-Laveaux, 5 vols., Paris, 1881.

BASCHET, A., *Les Comédiens italiens à la cour de France sous Charles IX, Henri III, Henri IV et Louis XIII*, Paris, 1882.

BINET, C., *La Vie de P. de Ronsard*, ed. P. Laumonier, Paris, 1909.

BOUCHET, J., *Epistres morales et familières du traverseur*, Poitiers, 1545.

BRANTÔME, P. DE, *Œuvres complètes*, ed. P. Mérimée and L. Lacour, 13 vols., Paris, 1858–93.

COYECQUE, E., 'Simples notes sur Ronsard et sur son livre des *Amours* (1552–1553)', *Revue des livres anciens*, 1916.

DABNEY, L. E., *French Dramatic Literature in the Reign of Henri IV*, Austin, 1952.

DEIERKAUF-HOLSBOER, S. W., *Le Théâtre de l'Hôtel de Bourgogne*, 2 vols., Paris, 1968–70.

DOUCET, R., *Les Bibliothèques parisiennes au XVIe siècle*, Paris, 1956.

DU BARTAS, G., *Works*, ed. U. T. Holmes *et al.*, 3 vols., Chapel Hill, 1935–40.

DU BELLAY, J., *Œuvres poétiques*, ed. H. Chamard, 6 vols., Paris, 1908–31.

—— *La Deffence et Illustration de la langue francoyse*, ed. H. Chamard, Paris, 1948.

FEBVRE, L. and MARTIN, H. J., *L'Apparition du livre*, Paris, 1958.

FEZENSAC, DUC DE, 'Saluste du Bartas et ses éditeurs parisiens', *Bulletin du bibliophile*, 1900.

GARNIER, R., *Les Juifves*, Paris, 1583.

HARVEY, H. G., *The Theatre of the Basoche*, Cambridge, Mass., 1941.

HERRMANN-MASCARD, N., *La Censure des livres à la fin de l'Ancien Régime (1750–1789)*, Paris, 1968.

JODELLE, E., *Œuvres complètes*, ed. E. Balmas, 2 vols., Paris, 1965–8.

JOURDA, P., 'Le Mécénat de Marguerite de Navarre', *Revue du seizième siècle*, 1931.

LABARRE, A., *Le Livre dans la vie amiénoise du seizième siècle. L'Enseignement des inventaires après décès 1503–1576*, Paris and Louvain, 1971.

LEBÈGUE, R., 'Le Répertoire d'une troupe française à la fin du XVIe siècle', *Revue d'histoire du théâtre*, 1948.

LE ROY LADURIE, E., *Les Paysans de Languedoc*, 2 vols., Paris, 1966.

L'ESTOILE, P. T. DE, *Mémoires-Journaux*, ed. G. Brunet *et al.*, 12 vols., Paris, 1875–96.

McFARLANE, I. D., 'Jean Salmon Macrin (1490–1557)', *Bibliothèque d'Humanisme et Renaissance*, 1959–60.

MAGNY, O. DE, *Les Souspirs*, ed. E. Courbet, Paris, 1874.

MAYER, C. A., *Clément Marot*, Paris, 1972.

MONTAIGNE, M. DE, *Essais*, ed. P. Villey, 3 vols., Paris, 1930–1.

PALSGRAVE, J., *Eclaircissement de la langue francoyse*, London, 1530.

PARENT, A., *Les Métiers du livre à Paris au XVIe siècle (1535–1560)*, Geneva and Paris, 1974.

PASQUIER, E., *Œuvres*, 2 vols., Amsterdam, 1723.

PELETIER DU MANS, J., *Œuvres poétiques*, ed. M. Françon, Rochecorbon, 1958.

RENOUARD, P., *Répertoire des imprimeurs parisiens, libraires, fondeurs de caractères et correcteurs d'imprimerie depuis l'introduction de l'imprimerie à Paris (1470) jusqu'à la fin du seizième siècle*, Paris, 1965.

RICKARD, P., *La Langue française au seizième siècle*, London, 1968.

ROLLAND DU PLESSIS, N., *Remonstrances très humbles au Roy de France*, n.p., 1588.

RONSARD, P. DE, *Œuvres complètes*, ed. P. Laumonier, Paris, 1914– .

SCHUTZ, A. H., *Vernacular Books in Parisian Private Libraries of the Sixteenth Century according to the Notarial Inventories*, Chapel Hill, 1955.

III The Seventeenth Century

Agréables conférences de deux paysans de Saint-Ouen et de Montmorency sur les affaires du temps, 1649–1651, ed. F. Deloffre, Paris, 1961.

Ancien théâtre français, ed. E. L. H. Viollet-le-Duc, 10 vols., Paris, 1854–7.

ANGOT, E., 'Les Discours politiques des Rois de Georges de Scudéry', *Revue d'histoire littéraire*, 1924.

ARGENSON, M. R. DE V. D', *Notes*, ed. L. Larchey and E. Mabille, Paris, 1866.

ASSOUCY, C. D', *Aventures burlesques*, ed. E. Colombey, Paris, 1858.

AUBERY, A., *Histoire du Cardinal duc de Richelieu*, Paris, 1660.

—— *Histoire du Cardinal Mazarin*, 2 vols., Paris, 1695.

AUBIGNAC, ABBÉ F. D', *La Pratique du théâtre*, ed. P. Martino, Paris, 1927.

—— *Deux dissertations concernant le poème dramatique, en forme de remarques sur deux tragédies de M. Corneille*, Paris, 1663.

—— *Troisième dissertation concernant le poème dramatique, en forme de remarques sur la tragédie de M. Corneille, intitulée 'Œdipe'*, Paris, 1663.

—— *Quatrième dissertation servant de réponse aux calomnies de M. Corneille*, Paris, 1663.

—— *Dissertation sur la condemnation des théâtres*, Paris, 1666.

BAILLET, A., *Jugements des savants sur les principaux ouvrages des auteurs*, 8 vols., Amsterdam, 1725.

BALZAC, J. L. G. DE, *Œuvres*, 2 vols., Paris, 1665.

BAYLE, P., *Nouvelles de la République des Lettres*, 7 vols., Amsterdam, 1684–7.

—— *Nouvelles lettres*, 2 vols., The Hague, 1739.

—— *Œuvres diverses*, 4 vols., The Hague, 1737.

BENSERADE, I. DE, *Œuvres*, 2 vols., Paris, 1697.

BOILEAU, N., *Œuvres complètes*, ed. A. Adam, Paris, 1966.

BOISLISLE, A. DE, 'Paul Scarron et Françoise d'Aubigné', *Revue des questions historiques*, 1893.

BOISSIER, G., *L'Académie française sous l'Ancien Régime*, Paris, 1909.

BORDELON, L., *Diversités curieuses pour servir de récréation à l'esprit*, 5 vols., Amsterdam, 1699.

BOURSAULT, E., *Artémise et Poliante*, Paris, 1670.

—— *Lettres nouvelles*, 4th edn., 3 vols., Paris, 1722.

BROWNE, E., *A Journal of a Visit to Paris in the year 1664*, ed. G. Keynes, London, 1923.

Bussy-Rabutin, R. de, *Correspondance*, ed. L. Lalanne, 6 vols., Paris, 1858–9.

—— *Mémoires*, ed. L. Lalanne, 2 vols., Paris, 1857.

Callières J. de, *La Fortune des gens de qualité et des gentilshommes particuliers, enseignant l'art de vivre á la cour, suivant les maximes de la politique et de la morale* Paris 1661.

Campardon E., *Les Comédiens du roi de la troupe française pendant les deux derniers siècles*, Paris, 1879.

—— *Les Comédiens du roi de la troupe italienne pendant les deux derniers siècles*, 2 vols., Paris, 1880.

—— *Documents inédits sur J. B. Poquelin Molière*, Paris, 1871.

Les Caquets de l'accouchée, ed. E. Fournier, Paris, 1855.

Chapelain, J., *Lettres*, ed. T. de Larroque, 2 vols., Paris, 1880–3.

—— *Opuscules critiques*, ed. A. C. Hunter, Paris, 1936.

Chappuzeau, S., *Le Théâtre français*, ed. G. Monval, Paris, 1875.

—— *L'Europe vivante*, 2 vols., Geneva, 1667–71.

Charpentier, F., *Carpentariana*, Paris, 1724.

Chatelain, U. V., *Le Surintendant Foucquet protecteur des lettres, des arts et des sciences*, Paris, 1905.

Cognet, A., *Antoine Godeau, évêque de Grasse et de Vence*, Paris, 1900.

Cohen, G., *Écrivains français en Hollande dans la première moitié du XVIIᵉ siècle*, Paris, 1920.

Corneille, P., *Œuvres complètes*, ed. C. Marty-Laveaux, 12 vols., Paris, 1862–8.

Correspondance administrative sous le règne de Louis XIV, ed. G. B. Depping, 4 vols., Paris, 1850–5.

Costar, P., *Lettres*, 2 vols., Paris, 1658–9.

Cyrano de Bergerac, S., *L'Autre Monde*, ed. F. Lachèvre, Paris, 1932.

Dainville, F. de, 'Effectifs des collèges et scolarité aux XVIIᵉ et XVIIIᵉ siècles dans le Nord-Est de la France', *Population*, 1955.

—— 'Collèges et fréquentation scolaire au XVIIᵉ siècle', *Population*, 1957.

Deierkauf-Holsboer, S. W., *Le Théâtre du Marais*, 2 vols., Paris, 1954–8.

—— *Vie d'Alexandre Hardy, poète du roi, 1572–1632*, 2nd edn., Paris, 1972.

Desmolets, P. N., *Continuation des mémoires de M. de Salengre*, 2 vols.,. Paris, 1726.

Donneau de Visé, J., *Défense du 'Sertorius' de M. de Corneille*, Paris, 1663.

—— *Zélinde, ou la véritable Critique de l'École des femmes ou la Critique de la critique*, Paris, 1663.

Dubu, J., 'La Condition sociale de l'écrivain de théâtre au XVIIᵉ siècle', *XVIIᵉ siècle*, 1958.

Findlater, R., *The Book Writers: Who are they?*, London, 1966.

—— (ed.), *Public Lending Right. A Matter of Justice*, London, 1971.

Fleuret, F. and Perceau, L. (eds.), *Les Satires françaises du XVIIᵉ siècle*, 2 vols., Paris, 1923.

FURETIÈRE, A., *Nouvelle allégorique*, Amsterdam, 1658.
—— *Le Roman bourgeois, suivi de Satyres et de Nouvelle allégorique*, ed. G. Mongrédien, Paris, 1955.

GAILLARD, A., *Œuvres*, Paris, 1634.

GASTÉ, A. (ed.), *La Querelle du Cid*, Paris, 1898.

GUÉRET, G., *Le Parnasse réformé*, nouvelle édition, Paris, 1674.
—— *La Promenade de Saint-Cloud*, in F. Bruys, *Mémoires historiques, critiques et littéraires*, 2 vols., Paris, 1751, ii.

HÉROARD, J., *Journal sur l'enfance et la jeunesse de Louis XIII (1601–1628)*, ed. E. Soulié and E. de Barthélemy, 2 vols., Paris, 1688.

HUBERT, *Registre*, ed. S. Chevalley, *Revue d'histoire du théâtre*, 1973.

HUET, P. D., *Lettre-traité sur l'origine des romans*, ed. F. Gégou, Paris, 1971.

JAL, A., *Dictionnaire critique de biographie et d'histoire*, 2nd edn., Paris, 1872.

LA BRUYÈRE, J. DE, *Œuvres*, ed. G. Servois, 5 vols., Paris, 1882–1922.
—— *Les Caractères*, ed. R. Garapon, Paris, 1962.

LA CALPRENÈDE, G. DE C. DE, *La Mort de Mithridate*, Paris, 1637.
—— *Le Comte d'Essex*, Paris, 1639.
—— *Édouard*, Paris, 1640.

LACHÈVRE, F., *Le Libertinage au XVIIe siècle*, 14 vols., Paris, 1909–24.
—— *Le Procès du poète Théophile de Viau*, 2 vols., Paris, 1909.

LA FONTAINE, J. DE, *Œuvres complètes*, ed. H. Régnier, 11 vols., Paris, 1883–92.

LAGNY, J., *Bibliographie des éditions anciennes des œuvres de Saint-Amant*, Paris, 1961.

LA GRANGE, C. V. DE, *Registre (1659–1683)*, ed. B. E. and G. P. Young, 2 vols., Paris, 1947.

LAMARE, N. DE, *Traité de la police*, 4 vols., Paris, 1705–38.

LANCASTER, H. C., *The Comédie Française, 1680–1701: Plays, Actors, Spectators, Finances*, Baltimore, 1941.
—— *The Comédie Française, 1701–1774: Plays, Actors, Spectators, Finances*, Philadelphia, 1951.

LANETTE-CLAVERIE, C., 'La Librairie française en 1700', *Revue française d'histoire du livre*, 1972.

LA ROCHEFOUCAULD, DUC DE, *Maximes*, ed. J. Truchet, Paris, 1967.

LAUDER, SIR JOHN, *Journals, with his Observations on Public Affairs and other Memoranda 1665–1676*, ed. E. D. Crawford, Edinburgh, 1900.

LEBÈGUE, R., 'La Fin de Malherbe', *XVIIe siècle*, 1965.

LEINER, W., *Der Widmungsbrief in der französischen Literatur (1580–1715)*, Heidelberg, 1965.

LENET, P., *Mémoires*, in *Nouvelle collection des mémoires sur l'histoire de France*, ed. J. P. Michaud and J. J. Poujoulat, 31 vols., Paris, 1836–9, 3rd Ser. ii.

LESAGE, A. R., *Le Diable boiteux*, ed. R. Laufer, Paris, 1970.

LORET, J., *La Muse historique*, ed. C. Livet, 4 vols., Paris, 1857–78.

LOUGH, J., 'The Earnings of Playwrights in Seventeenth-Century France', *Modern Language Review*, 1947.

—— *An Introduction to Seventeenth Century France*, London, 1954 (rev. impression, 1969).

—— *Paris Theatre Audiences in the Seventeenth and Eighteenth Centuries*, London, 1957.

MAGNE, É., *Le plaisant abbé de Boisrobert*, Paris, 1909.

—— *Bibliographie générale des œuvres de Nicolas Boileau-Despréaux*, 2 vols., Paris, 1929.

MAINTENON, MME DE, *Lettres*, ed. M. Langlois, 4 vols., Paris, 1935–9.

MALEBRANCHE, N., *Œuvres complètes*, ed. H. Gouhier, 20 vols., Paris, 1958–68.

MALHERBE, F. DE, *Poésies*, ed. M. Allem and P. Martino, Paris, 1937.

—— *Œuvres*, ed. A. Adam, Paris, 1971.

MARTIN, H. J., *Livre, pouvoirs et société à Paris au XVIIᵉ siècle (1598–1701)*, 2 vols., Geneva, 1969.

—— 'Les Registres du libraire Nicolas: Étude sur la pénétration du livre à Grenoble au milieu du XVIIᵉ siècle', in *Centre méridional de rencontres sur le XVIIᵉ siècle. Deuxième colloque de Marseille*, Marseilles, 1973.

MAYNARD, F., *Poésies*, ed. F. Gohin, Paris, 1927.

MÉLÈSE, P., *Le Théâtre et le public à Paris sous Louis XIV (1659–1715)*, Paris, 1934.

MERSENNE, M., *Correspondance*, ed. C. de Waard and B. Rochot, Paris, 1932– .

MOLIÈRE, J. B. P., *Œuvres complètes*, ed. G. Couton, 2 vols., Paris, 1971.

MONVAL, G., '*La Fameuse Comédienne* et la *Vie des saints*', *Le Moliériste*, vii.

—— 'L'Affaire Auzillon', *Le Moliériste*, viii.

—— 'André Mareschal', *Le Moliériste*, ix.

NAUDÉ, G., *Jugement de tout ce qui a été imprimé contre le Cardinal Mazarin depuis le sixième janvier jusqu'à la Déclaration du premier avril mil six cent quarante-neuf*, n.p., n.d. [Paris, 1649].

PELLISSON, P. and OLIVET, P. J. T. D,' *Histoire de l'Académie française*, ed. C. Livet, 2 vols., Paris, 1858.

PERRAULT, C., *Mémoires de ma vie*, ed. P. Bonnefon, Paris, 1909.

—— *Parallèle des anciens et des modernes*, 4 vols., Paris, 1688–97.

PLATTER, T., *Beschreibung der Reisen durch Frankreich, Spanien, England und die Niederlande*, ed. R. Keiser, 2 vols., Basle and Stuttgart, 1968.

PRADON, N., *Le Triomphe de Pradon sur les satires du sieur D****, The Hague, 1686.

PRÉCHAC, J. DE, *Le Voyage de Fontainebleau*, Paris, 1678.

PRIMI VISCONTI, G. B., *Mémoires sur la cour de Louis XIV*, trans. J. Lemoine, Paris, 1908.

QUÉNIART, J., *L'Imprimerie et la librairie à Rouen au XVIIIᵉ siècle*, Paris, 1969.

QUINAULT, P., *Théâtre*, 5 vols., Paris, 1715.

RACAN, H. DE B., *Œuvres complètes*, ed. T. de Latour, 2 vols., Paris, 1857.

RACINE, J., *Œuvres complètes*, ed. R. Picard, 2 vols., Paris, 1950–2.

RAPIN, R., *Réflexions sur la poétique de ce temps*, ed. E. T. Dubois, Geneva and Paris, 1970.

REGNARD, J. F., *La Critique du légataire universel*, Paris, 1708.

RÉGNIER, M., *Œuvres complètes*, ed. J. Plattard, Paris, 1930.

RETZ, Cardinal de, *Œuvres*, ed. A. Feillet, 10 vols., Paris, 1870–96.

RICHELIEU, Cardinal de, *Testament politique*, ed. L. André, Paris, 1947.

ROUBERT, J., 'La Situation de l'imprimerie lyonnaise à la fin du XVIIᵉ siècle', in *Cinq études lyonnaises*, Geneva and Paris, 1966.

SAINT-ÉVREMOND, C. de S.-D., *Œuvres*, 9 vols., n.p., 1751.

SAINT-SIMON, DUC DE, *Mémoires*, ed. A. de Boislisle, 43 vols., Paris, 1879–1930.

SAUVY, A., *Livres saisis à Paris entre 1678 et 1701*, The Hague, 1972.

SCARRON, P., *Poésies diverses*, ed. M. Cauchie, 2 vols., Paris, 1947–61.

SCHERER, J., *La Dramaturgie classique en France*, Paris, 1950.

SCUDÉRY, G. DE, *L'Apologie du théâtre*, Paris, 1639.

—— *Ligdamon et Lidias*, Paris, 1631.

SCUDÉRY, M. DE, *Artamène ou le Grand Cyrus*, 10 vols., Paris, 1649–53.

SEGRAIS, J. R. DE, *Œuvres diverses*, 2 vols., Amsterdam, 1723.

SÉVIGNÉ, MME DE, *Lettres*, ed. E. Gérard-Gailly, 3 vols., Paris, 1955–7.

—— *Correspondance*, ed. R. Duchêne, Paris, 1972– .

SKIPPON, P., *An Account of a Journey through part of the Low Countries, Germany, Italy and France*, in *A Collection of Voyages and Travels*, London, 1732, vi.

SOMAIZE, A. B. DE, *Le Dictionnaire des précieuses*, ed. C. Livet, 2 vols., Paris, 1856.

SOREL, C., *Francion*, ed. E. Roy, 4 vols., Paris, 1924–31.

—— *La Maison des jeux*, 2 vols., Paris, 1642.

—— *La Bibliothèque française*, 2nd edn., Paris, 1667.

—— *De la connaissance des bons livres*, Amsterdam, 1672.

TALLEMANT DES RÉAUX, G., *Historiettes*, ed. G. Mongrédien, 8 vols., Paris, 1932–4.

VARENNES, C. DE, *Le Voyage de France*, Paris, 1643.

VIGNEUL-MARVILLE [Noël Bonaventure d'Argonne], *Melanges d'histoire et de littérature*, 3 vols., Paris, 1700–1.

VILLIERS, ABBÉ P. DE, *Entretiens sur les tragédies de ce temps*, Paris, 1675.

—— *Entretiens sur les contes de fées*, Paris, 1699.

See also under II: DEIERKAUF-HOLSBOER, L'ESTOILE, and under V: RÉMILLIEUX.

IV The Eighteenth Century

ALBERT, M., *Les Théâtres de la Foire (1660–1789)*, Paris, 1900.

ANGIVILLER, COMTE D', *Mémoires*, ed. L. Bobé, Copenhagen, 1933.

BACHAUMONT, L. P. DE, *Mémoires secrets pour servir à l'histoire de la République des Lettres en France de 1762 jusqu'à nos jours*, 36 vols., London, 1777–89.

BAYET, J., *La Société des auteurs et compositeurs dramatiques*, Paris, 1908.

BEAUMARCHAIS, P. A. C. DE, *Œuvres complètes*, ed. E. Fournier, Paris, 1876.

—— *Théâtre complet*, ed. R. d'Hermies, Paris, 1952.

—— *Théâtre complet: Lettres relatives à son théâtre*, ed. M. Allem, Paris, 1934.

BELIN, J. P., *Le Commerce des livres prohibés à Paris de 1750 à 1789*, Paris, 1913.

BLONDEL, P. J., *Mémoire sur les vexations qu'exercent les libraires et les imprimeurs de Paris*, ed. L. Faucou, Paris, 1879.

BONNASSIES, J., *Les Auteurs dramatiques et la Comédie Française aux XVIIe et XVIIIe siècles*, Paris, 1874.

BONNEFON, P., 'Diderot prisonnier à Vincennes', *Revue d'histoire littéraire*, 1899.

——'Néricault Destouches intime', *Revue d'histoire littéraire*, 1907.

—— 'A travers les autographes', *Revue d'histoire littéraire*, 1919.

BRANCOLINI, J. and BOUYSSY, M. T., 'La Vie provinciale du livre à la fin de l'Ancien Régime', in *Livre et société dans la France du XVIIIe siècle*, ii, Paris and The Hague, 1970.

BRENNER, C. D., *The Théâtre Italien. Its Repertory, 1716–1793, with a Historical Introduction*, Berkeley and Los Angeles, 1961.

BRULÉ, A., *La Vie au dix-huitième siècle. Les Gens de lettres*, Paris, 1928.

CAILHAVA, J. F., *Théâtre*, 3 vols., Paris, 1781–2.

CAMPAN, J. L., *Mémoires sur la vie de Marie-Antoinette*, ed. F. Barrière, Paris, 1876.

CARLSON, M., *The Theatre of the French Revolution*, Ithaca, 1966.

CERF, M., 'La Censure royale à la fin du XVIIIe siècle', *Communications*, 1967.

CERTEAU, M. DE, JULIA, D., and REVEL, J., *Une Politique de la langue. La Révolution française et les patois: L'Enquête de Grégoire*, Paris, 1975.

CHARPENTIER, *La Bastille dévoilée ou Recueil de pièces authentiques pour servir à son histoire*, 3 vols., Paris, 1789–90.

CHARPENTIER, J., *Napoléon et les hommes de lettres de son temps*, Paris, 1935.

CLARETIE, L., *Lesage romancier d'après de nouveaux documents*, Paris, 1890.

COLLÉ, C., *Journal et mémoires*, ed. H. Bonhomme, 3 vols., Paris, 1868.

CONDORCET, J. A. N. DE, *Œuvres complètes*, ed. A. C. O'Connor and F. Arago, 12 vols., Paris, 1847–9.

Correspondance inédite de Condorcet et de Turgot, ed. C. Henry, Paris, 1883.

CROSBY, E. A., *Une Romancière oubliée, Mme Riccoboni: Sa vie, ses œuvres, sa place dans la littérature anglaise et française du XVIIIe siècle*, Paris, 1924.

DARNTON, R. C., 'The Grub Street Style of Revolution: J. P. Brissot, Police Spy', *Journal of Modern History*, 1968.

—— 'The High Enlightenment and the low-life of Literature in pre-Revolutionary France', *Past and Present*, 1971.

DIDEROT, D., *Œuvres complètes*, ed. J. Varloot, Paris, 1975– .

—— *Writings on the Theatre*, ed. F. C. Green, London, 1936.

—— *Correspondance*, ed. G. Roth and J. Varloot, 16 vols., Paris, 1955–70.

DIDEROT, D. and ALEMBERT, J. L. D' (eds.), *Encyclopédie, ou Dictionnaire raisonné des sciences, des arts et des métiers*, 28 vols., Paris and Neuchâtel, 1751–72.

DUCHET, C., 'Un Libraire libéral sous l'Empire et la Restauration: du nouveau sur Royol', *Revue d'histoire littéraire*, 1965.

DUCLOS, C. P., *Considérations sur les mœurs de ce siècle*, ed. F. C. Green, London, 1939.

DURRY, M. J., *A propos de Marivaux*, Paris, 1960.

ESTÈVE, E., 'Observations de Guilbert de Pixerécourt sur les théâtres de la Révolution', *Revue d'histoire littéraire*, 1916.

ÉTIENNE, C. G. and MARTAINVILLE, A., *Histoire du Théâtre français depuis le commencement de la Révolution jusqu'à la réunion générale*, 4 vols., Paris, 1802.

FÉLETZ, ABBÉ C. M. D. DE, *Jugements historiques et littéraires*, Paris and Lyons, 1840.

FENOUILLOT DE FALBAIRE, C. G., *Avis aux gens de lettres*, Liège, 1770.

FREDERICK II, *Œuvres posthumes*, 15 vols., Berlin, 1788.

FUCHS, M., *La Vie théâtrale en province au XVIIIᵉ siècle*, i, Paris, 1933.

FUNCK-BRENTANO, F., *Les Lettres de cachet à Paris, étude suivie d'une liste des prisonniers de la Bastille (1659–1789)*, Paris, 1903.

FURET, F., 'La "librairie" du royaume de France au 18ᵉ siècle', in *Livre et société dans la France du XVIIIᵉ siècle*, i. Paris and The Hague, 1965.

FURET, F. and SACHS, W., 'La Croissance de l'alphabétisation en France. XVIIIᵉ –XIXᵉ siècle', *Annales. Économies, sociétés, civilisations*, 1974, vol. 29.

GARAT, D. J. *Mémoires historiques sur la vie de M. Suard, sur ses écrits et sur le XVIIIᵉ siècle*, 2 vols., Paris, 1820.

GARRICK, D., *Private Correspondence*, 2 vols., London, 1831–2.

GEOFFROY, J. L., *Cours de littérature dramatique*, 5 vols., Paris, 1819–20.

GRIMM, F. M. (ed.), *Correspondance littéraire, philosophique et critique*, ed. M. Tourneux, 16 vols., Paris, 1877–82.

HARTOG, W. G., *Guilbert de Pixerécourt, sa vie, son mélodrame, sa technique et son influence*, Paris, 1913.

HUGO, A., *Victor Hugo raconté par un témoin de sa vie*, 2 vols., Paris, n.d.

HUME, D., *Letters*, ed. J. Y. T. Greig, 2 vols., Oxford, 1932.

LABOULAYE, E. and GUIFFREY, G. M., *La Propriété littéraire au XVIIIᵉ siècle. Recueil de pièces et de documents*, Paris, 1859.

LA CHALOTAIS, L. R. DE, *Essai d'éducation nationale*, n.p., 1763.

La Dixmerie, N. B. de, *Lettres sur l'état présent de nos spectacles*, Amsterdam and Paris, 1765.

Lagrave, H., *Le Théâtre et le public à Paris de 1715 à 1750*, Paris 1972.

La Harpe, J. F. de, *Correspondance inédite*, ed. A. Jovicevich, Paris, 1965.

—— *Correspondance littéraire*, 6 vols., Paris, 1801–7.

Lancaster, H. C., *French Tragedy in the Time of Louis XV and Voltaire*, 2 vols., Baltimore, 1950.

La Porte, abbé J. de, *Observations sur la littérature moderne*, 9 vols., The Hague, 1749–52.

Le Blanc, abbé J. B., *Lettres d'un Français concernant le gouvernement, la politique et les mœurs des Anglais et des Français*, 3 vols., The Hague, 1745.

Le Breton, A., *Rivarol, sa vie, ses idées, son talent d'après des documents nouveaux*, Paris, 1895.

Lesage, A. R., *Gil Blas de Santillane*, 3 vols., Paris, 1715–35.

Lettres à Grégoire sur les patois de France, 1790–1794, ed. A. Gazier, Paris, 1880.

Lhuillier, T., *Recherches historiques sur l'enseignement primaire dans la Brie*, Meaux, 1884.

Lintilhac, E., *Lesage*, Paris, 1893.

Livre et société dans la France du XVIIIᵉ siècle, 2 vols., Paris and The Hague, 1965–70.

Lough, J., *An Introduction to Eighteenth Century France*, London, 1960 (rev. impression, 1970).

'Lumières et Révolution': special number of *Dix-huitième siècle*, 1974.

Maistre, J. de, *Les Soirées de Saint-Pétersbourg*, 2 vols., Paris, 1929.

Malesherbes, C. G. de L. de, *Mémoires sur la librairie et sur la liberté de la presse*, Paris, 1809.

Marais, M., *Journal et mémoires*, ed. M. F. A. de Lescure, 4 vols., Paris, 1863–8.

Marivaux, P. C. de C. de, *La Vie de Marianne*, ed. F. Deloffre, Paris, 1963.

Marmontel, J. F., *Œuvres complètes*, 7 vols., Paris, 1819–20.

—— *Mémoires*, ed. J. Renwick, 2 vols., Clermont-Ferrand, 1972.

May, G., *Le Dilemme du roman au XVIIIᵉ siècle*, New Haven, 1963.

Mercier, L. S., *Du théâtre, ou Nouvel essai sur l'art dramatique*, Amsterdam, 1773.

—— *De la littérature et des littérateurs*, Yverdon, 1778.

—— *Tableau de Paris*, 12 vols., Amsterdam, 1783–9.

Merland, M. A., 'Tirage et vente des livres à la fin du XVIIIᵉ siècle: des documents chiffrés', *Revue française d'histoire du livre*, 1973.

Le Moniteur universel. Réimpression de l'ancien Moniteur, 31 vols., Paris, 1858–63.

Monod-Cassidy, H., *Un Voyageur philosophe au XVIIIᵉ siècle, L'abbé Jean-Bernard Le Blanc*, Cambridge, Mass., 1941.

Montesquieu, C. de S., *Œuvres complètes*, ed. A. Masson, 3 vols., Paris, 1950–5.

Moore, J., *A View of Society and Manners in France, Switzerland and Germany*, 2 vols., London, 1779.

Moreau, J. N., *Mes souvenirs*, ed. C. Hermelin, 2 vols., Paris, 1898–1901.

Morellet, abbé A., *Mémoires*, 2 vols., Paris, 1821.

Moulinas, R., *L'Imprimerie, la librairie et la presse à Avignon au XVIIIᵉ siècle*, Grenoble, 1974.

Necker, J., *De l'administration des finances de la France*, 3 vols., n.p., 1784.

Noël, G., *Une 'primitive' oubliée de l'école des cœurs sensibles, Mme de Graffigny*, Paris, 1913.

'Notes du libraire Prault', *Bulletin du bibliophile*, 1850.

Papillon de La Ferté, D. P. J., *Journal*, ed. E. Boysse, Paris, 1887.

Pixerécourt, G. de, 'Le Mélodrame', in *Paris ou le livre des cent-et-un*, 15 vols., Paris, 1831–4, vi.

Raynal, abbé G. T. F., *Nouvelles littéraires*, in F. M. Grimm (ed.), *Correspondance littéraire*, ed. M. Tourneux, Paris, 1877–82.

Renwick, J., *Marmontel, Voltaire and the 'Bélisaire' affair (Studies on Voltaire and the Eighteenth Century CXXI)*, Banbury, 1974.

Riccoboni, M. J. (trans.), *Le Nouveau Théâtre anglais*, 2 vols., Paris, 1769.

Robinet, J. B. R., *Considérations sur l'état présent de la littérature en Europe*, London, 1762.

Roddier, H., *L'abbé Prévost, l'homme et l'œuvre*, Paris, 1955.

Rousseau, J.-B., *Lettres sur différents sujets*, 3 vols., Geneva, 1749.

Rousseau, J.-J., *Œuvres*, ed. L. S. Mercier et al., 7 vols., Paris, 1788–9.

—— *Correspondance générale*, ed. T. Dufour, 20 vols., Paris, 1924–34.

—— *Œuvres complètes*, ed. B. Gagnebin and M. Raymond, Paris, 1959– .

—— *Correspondance complète*, ed. R. A. Leigh. Geneva and Banbury, 1965– .

Saintville, G., 'Un Chapitre des rapports entre écrivains et libraires au XVIIIᵉ siècle: Palissot auteur', *Bulletin du bibliophile*, 1947.

Ségur, comte L. P. de, *Mémoires, souvenirs et anecdotes*, ed. F. Barrière, 2 vols., Paris, 1879.

Shackleton, R., *The 'Encyclopédie' and the Clerks*, Oxford, 1970.

Shaw, E. P., *Problems and Policies of Malesherbes as 'Directeur de la Librairie' in France (1750–1763)*, New York, 1966.

Smith, D. W., *Helvétius. A Study in Persecution*, Oxford, 1965.

Smollett, T., *Travels through France and Italy*, ed. T. Seccombe, London, 1907.

Souriau, M., *Bernardin de Saint-Pierre d'après ses manuscrits*, Paris, 1905.

Suard, J. B. A., *Mémoires et correspondances historiques et littéraires*, ed. C. Nisard, Paris, 1858.

Talleyrand, C. M. de, *Rapport sur l'instruction publique*, Paris, 1791.

Todd, C., 'La Harpe quarrels with the actors: unpublished correspondence', *Studies on Voltaire and the Eighteenth Century*, liii (1967).

VAILLAND, R., *Laclos par lui-même*, Paris, 1953.

VOLTAIRE, F. M. A. DE, *Œuvres complètes*, ed. L. Moland, 52 vols., Paris, 1877–85.

—— *Complete Works*, Geneva and Banbury, 1968–.

—— *Correspondence and Related Documents*, ed. T. Besterman (vols. 85–135 of *Complete Works*), Geneva, Banbury and Oxford, 1968–77.

WELSCHINGER, H., *Le Théâtre de la Révolution, 1789–1799*, Paris, 1880.

—— *La Censure sous le Premier Empire*, Paris, 1882.

WILSON, A. M., *Diderot*, New York, 1972.

YOUNG, A., *Travels in France during the years 1787, 1788 and 1789*, ed. C. Maxwell, London, 1929.

See also under II: HERRMANN-MASCARD and under III: CAMPARDON, LANCASTER, PELLISSON and D 'OLIVET, QUÉNIART.

V The Nineteenth Century

ARNAOUTOVITCH, J., *Henri Becque*, 3 vols., Paris, 1927.

ATKINSON, N., *Eugène Sue et le roman-feuilleton*, Paris, 1929.

AVENEL, G. D', *Les Français de mon temps*, Paris, n.d.

BALZAC, H. DE, *Correspondance*, ed. R. Pierrot, 5 vols., Paris, 1960–9.

—— *Œuvres diverses*, 4 vols., Paris, 1962–3.

—— *Lettres à Madame Hanska*, ed. R. Pierrot, 4 vols., Paris, 1967–71.

BANVILLE, T. DE, *Mes souvenirs*, Paris, 1882.

BARBER, G., 'Galignani and the Publication of English Books in France', *The Library*, 1961.

BAUDELAIRE, C., *Correspondance générale*, ed. J. Crépet and C. Pichois, 6 vols., Paris, 1947–53.

BECQUE, H., *Œuvres complètes*, 7 vols., Paris, 1924–6.

BELLOS, D., 'The *Bibliographie de la France* and its sources', *The Library*, 1973.

—— *Balzac Criticism in France, 1850–1900*, Oxford, 1976.

BENNETT, E. A., *Letters of Arnold Bennett*, ed. J. Hepburn, i: *Letters to J. B. Pinker*, London, 1966.

BILLY, A., *La Vie littéraire. L'Époque contemporaine (1905–1930)*, Paris, 1956.

BIRÉ, E., *Victor Hugo avant 1830*, 2nd edn., Paris, 1902.

BLOY, L., *Journal*, 4 vols., Paris, 1963.

BORY, J. L., *Eugène Sue, le roi du roman populaire*, Paris, 1962.

BOSCHOT, A., *Théophile Gautier*, Paris, 1933.

BOUVIER, R., and MAYNIAL, E., *Les Comptes dramatiques de Balzac*, Paris, 1938.

—— *De quoi vivait Balzac?*, Paris, 1949.

BRUNOT, F., 'La Langue française au XIXᵉ siècle', in L. Petit de Julleville, *Histoire de la langue et de la littérature françaises*, 8 vols., Paris, 1896–9, viii.

CHAMPFLEURY, J. F. F., *Le Réalisme*, Paris, 1857.

—— *Souvenirs et portraits de jeunesse*, Paris, 1872.

CHASLES, P., 'Statistique littéraire et intellectuelle de la France pendant l'année 1828', *Revue de Paris*, 1829.

CHOLLET, R., 'Un Épisode inconnu de l'histoire de la librairie: la Société d'abonnement général. Avec le texte inédit de Balzac', *Revue des sciences humaines*, 1971.

COEYTAUX, V., 'Le Centenaire des bibliothèques municipales de Paris', *Bulletin des bibliothèques de France*, 1966.

COPPÉE, F., *Souvenirs d'un Parisien*, Paris, 1910.

DARMON, J. J., *Le Colportage de librairie en France sous le Second Empire*, Paris, 1972.

DEFFOUX, L., *Chronique de l'Académie Goncourt*, Paris, 1929.

DESCHARMES, R., 'Flaubert et ses éditeurs: Michel Lévy et Georges Charpentier. Lettres inédites à Georges Charpentier', *Revue d'histoire littéraire*, 1911.

DOPP, H., *La Contrefaçon des livres français en Belgique, 1815–1852*, Louvain, 1932.

DREYFOUS, M., *Ce qu'il me reste à dire. 1848–1900*, Paris, n.d.

DU CAMP, M., *Souvenirs littéraires*, 2 vols., Paris, 1882–3.

—— *Théophile Gautier*, Paris, 1919.

DUHAMEL, G., *Le Temps de la recherche*, Paris, 1947.

DUMAS, A. *père*, *Mes mémoires*, ed. P. Josserand, 5 vols., Paris, 1854–68.

DUMESNIL, R., *L'Époque réaliste et naturaliste*, Paris, 1945.

—— *Guy de Maupassant*, Paris, 1933.

DUMONT, F. and GITAN, J., *De quoi vivait Lamartine?*, Paris, 1952.

FLAUBERT, G., *Correspondance*, 9 vols., Paris, 1926–33.

—— *Lettres inédites à son éditeur, Michel Lévy*, ed. J. Suffel, Paris, 1965.

FOURASTIÉ, J., *Machinisme et bien-être. Niveau de vie et genre de vie en France de 1700 à nos jours*, Paris, 1962.

GARÇON, M., 'Les Livres contraires aux bonnes mœurs', *Mercure de France*, 15 Aug. 1931.

GAUTIER, T., *Histoire de l'art dramatique en France depuis vingt-cinq ans*, 6 vols., Leipzig, 1858–9.

—— *Histoire du romantisme*, Paris, 1927.

GIDE, A., *Journal 1889–1939*, Paris, 1948.

GOBINEAU, J. A. DE, *Ce qui est arrivé à la France en 1870*, ed. A. B. Duff, Paris, 1970.

GONCOURT, E. and J. DE, *Journal. Mémoires de la vie littéraire*, ed. R. Ricatte, 22 vols., Monaco, 1956–8.

GOULÈNE, P., *Évolution des pouvoirs d'achat en France 1880–1972*, Paris, 1974.

La Grande Encyclopédie, 31 vols., Paris, 1885–1903.

GRASSET, B., *La Chose littéraire*, Paris, 1929.

GUISE, R., 'Balzac et le roman-feuilleton', *Année balzacienne*, 1964.

GUIZOT, F., *Mémoires pour servir à l'histoire de mon temps*, 8 vols., Paris, 1858–67.

HASSENFORDER, J., *Développement comparé des bibliothèques publiques en France, en Grande-Bretagne et aux États-Unis dans la seconde moitié du XIXᵉ siècle (1850–1914)*, Paris. 1967.

HEINE, H., *Sämtliche Werke*, 12 vols., Hamburg, 1885–90.

HOUSSAYE, A., *Les Confessions. Souvenirs d'un demi-siècle, 1830–1880*, 6 vols., Paris, 1885–91.

HUGO, V., *Œuvres complètes*, 45 vols., Paris, 1904–52.

HUMBLOT, M., 'L'Édition littéraire au XIXᵉ siècle', *Bibliographie de la France*, 17 Mar. 1911.

JULLIEN, A., *Le Romantisme et l'éditeur Renduel*, Paris, 1897.

KOCK, P. DE (ed.), *La Grande Ville. Nouveau Tableau de Paris*, 2 vols., Paris, 1844.

LACRETELLE, P., 'Victor Hugo et ses éditeurs', *Revue de France*, 1923.

LAMARTINE, A. DE, *Correspondance générale de 1830 à 1848*, 2 vols., Paris, 1943–9.

LANOUX, A., *Zola vivant*, in *Œuvres complètes*, ed. H. Mitterand, Paris, 1966–70, i.

LAROUSSE, P. (ed.), *Grand dictionnaire universel du XIXᵉ siècle*, 17 vols., Paris, 1865–90.

LÉAUTAUD, P., *Journal littéraire*, 19 vols., Paris, 1954–66.

LECOMTE, H., *Histoire des théâtres de Paris, 1402–1904. Notice préliminaire*, Paris, 1905.

LEUILLIOT, B., *Victor Hugo publie Les Misérables (Correspondance avec Albert Lacroix, août 1861–juillet 1862)*, Paris, 1970.

LOLIÉE, F., *Nos gens de lettres: leur vie intérieure, leurs rivalités, leur condition*, Paris, 1887.

LOUANDRE, C., 'Statistique littéraire. De la production intellectuelle en France depuis quinze ans', *Revue des Deux Mondes*, 1847.

LOUGH, J. and M., *An Introduction to Nineteenth Century France*, London, 1978.

MALLARMÉ, S., *Œuvres complètes*, ed. H. Mondor and G. Jean-Aubry, Paris, 1945.

—— *Correspondance, 1862–1871*, ed. H. Mondor and J. P. Richard, Paris, 1959.

—— *Correspondance, 1871–1885*, ed. H. Mondor and L. J. Austin, Paris, 1965.

MALOT, H., *Le Roman de mes romans*, Paris, 1896.

MARSAN, J., 'A. de Vigny et G. H. Charpentier (documents inédits)', *Revue d'histoire littéraire*, 1913.

MARTIN, H. J., 'Les Réseaux du livre', in *Le Livre français. Hier, aujourdui,'h demain*, ed. J. Cain, R. Escarpit, and H. J. Martin, Paris, 1972.

MARTINO, P., *Le Roman réaliste sous le Second Empire*, Paris, 1913.

MONTAGNE, E., *Histoire de la Société des gens de lettres*, Paris, 1889.

NERVAL, G. DE, *Œuvres*, ed. A. Béguin and J. Richer, 2 vols., Paris, 1956.

NETTEMENT, A., *Études critiques sur le feuilleton-roman*, 2 vols., Paris, 1845.

NOWELL-SMITH, S. H., *International Copyright Law and the Publisher in the Reign of Queen Victoria*, Oxford, 1968.

PAILLERON, M., *François Buloz et ses amis*, 4 vols., Paris, 1919–23.

Les Papiers secrets du Second Empire, 13 pts, Brussels, 1870–1.

PICHOIS, C., 'Les Cabinets de lecture à Paris durant la première moitié du XIXᵉ siècle', *Annales. Économies, Sociétés, Civilisations*, 1959.

PIERROT, R., 'Les Bibliothèques', in *Le Livre français. Hier, aujourd' hui, demain*, ed. J. Cain, R. Escarpit, and H. J. Martin, Paris, 1972.

PONTMARTIN, A. DE, 'Le Théâtre et le roman,' *Revue des Deux Mondes*, 1850.

PROST, A., *L'Enseignement en France, 1800–1967*, Paris, 1968.

PROUST, M., *Contre Sainte-Beuve*, ed. P. Clarac, Paris, 1971.

RAY, G. N., *Thackeray. The Age of Wisdom, 1847–1863*, London 1958.

RÉMILLIEUX, M., 'A propos d'une faillite de libraire (Horace Boissat, 1669)', in *Nouvelles études lyonnaises*, Geneva and Paris, 1969.

RÉMUSAT, C. DE, *Mémoires de ma vie*, ed. C. H. Pouthas, 5 vols., Paris, 1958–67.

REYBAUD, L., *Jérôme Paturot à la recherche d'une position sociale*, new edn., Paris, 1870.

RIVIÈRE, J. and Claudel, P., *Correspondance, 1907–1914*, Paris, 1926.

ROSNY, J. H. (aîné), *Mémoires de la vie littéraire. L'Académie Goncourt. Les Salons. Quelques éditeurs*, Paris, 1927.

SAINTE-BEUVE, C. A., 'De la littérature industrielle', in *Portraits contemporains*, 5 vols., Paris, 1869–76, ii.

—— *Correspondance générale*, ed. J. Bonnerot, Paris, 1935– .

SAND, G., *Correspondance 1812–1876*, 6 vols., Paris, 1882–4.

—— *Correspondance*, ed. G. Lubin, Paris, 1964– .

SARCEY, F., *Souvenirs de jeunesse*, Paris, 1885.

—— *Quarante ans de théâtre*, 8 vols., Paris, 1900–2.

SCRIBE, E., *Le Mariage d'argent*, Paris, 1827.

SEEBACHER, J., 'Victor Hugo et ses éditeurs avant l'exil', in *Œuvres complètes. Édition chronologique*, ed. J. Massin, 18 vols., Paris, 1967–70, vi.

SOCIÉTÉ DES GENS DE LETTRES, *1838–1938. Le Centenaire de la Société des gens de lettres de France*, Paris, 1939.

STENDHAL, *Correspondance*, ed. H. Martineau and V. del Litto, 3 vols., Paris, 1962–8.

TAINE, H., *Carnets de voyage. Notes sur la province, 1863–1865*, Paris, 1897.

TROLLOPE, A., *An Autobiography*, London, 1946.

VALÉRY, P., *Œuvres*, ed. J. Hytier, 2 vols., Paris, 1957–60.

VÉRON, L. D., *Mémoires d'un bourgeois de Paris*, 6 vols., Paris, 1853–5.

VIGNY, A. DE, *Œuvres complètes*, ed. F. Baldensperger, 2 vols., Paris, 1948.

WERDET, E., *De la librairie française*, Paris, 1860.

ZOLA, É., *Œuvres complètes*, ed. H. Mitterand, 15 vols., Paris, 1966–70.

See also under IV: BAYET, HUGO, FURET and SACHS.

VI The Twentieth Century

ALBERT-SOREL, J., 'Mai–juin 1968. Tumultes et occupation', in *L'Hôtel de Massa et la Société des gens de lettres*, Paris, 1968.

AVELINE, C., 'Le Rôle de l'éditeur dans la production littéraire', *Encyclopédie française*, xvii.

BERNARD, J.-J., 'La Profession de l'auteur dramatique', *Encyclopédie française*, xvii.

BOILLAT, G., 'Comment on fabrique un succès: *Maria Chapdelaine*', *Revue d'histoire littéraire*, 1974.

Books and Reading Habits (European Research Consultants Ltd.), London, 1965.

BOURDET, É., *Vient de paraître*, Paris, 1928.

La Clientèle du livre (Syndicat national de l'édition), Paris, 1967.

Direction des bibliothèques et de la Lecture Publique, *Bibliothèques municipales. Statistiques 1971*, Paris, 1974.

Encyclopédie française, 21 vols., Paris 1935–66.

GAEDE, E., *L'Écrivain et la société. Dossier d'une enquête réalisée sous les auspices du Centre d'études de la civilisation du 20ᵉ siècle*, 2 vols., Nice, 1972.

GONTARD, D., *La Décentralisation théâtrale en France, 1895–1952*, Paris, 1973.

LAURENT, P., 'La Diffusion du livre français à l'étranger', in *Le Livre franfrançais. Hier, aujourd'hui, demain*, ed. J. Cain, R. Escarpit, and H. J. Martin, Paris, 1972.

La Lecture publique en France. Rapport du groupe d'études (Notes et études documentaires, no. 3459), Paris, 1968.

La Littérature à l'heure du livre de poche (Université de Bordeaux, Institut de littérature et de techniques artistiques de masse), Bordeaux, 1966.

MANN, P. H., *Books and Reading*, London, 1969.

—— *Books, Buyers and Borrowers*, London, 1971.

Pratiques culturelles des Français (Secrétariat d'État à la culture), 2 vols., Paris, 1974.

La Profession d'écrivain (Université de Bordeaux, Institut de littérature et de techniques artistiques de masse), Bordeaux, 1968.

SCHMIDT, A., *Les Sociétés d'auteurs SACEM–SACD. Contrats de représentation*, Paris, 1971.

See also under V: BILLY, COEYTAUX, DEFFOUX, DUHAMEL, GRASSET, LÉAUTAUD, PIERROT.

Index